Understanding

MICROECONOMICS

FOURTH EDITION

EDWIN G. DOLAN
Ph.D. Yale University

WILLIAM DOUGHERTY
Carroll Community College

HORIZON
TEXTBOOK PUBLISHING
P.O. Box 494658 • Redding, CA 96049-4658

TEXT DESIGN AND COMPOSITION: Archetype Book Composition
COVER DESIGN: Walker Printing

ISBN: 1-60229-102-0

The views and opinions of each author do not necessarily reflect the views and opinions of the other author.

TABLE OF CONTENTS

PREFACE

As THE ECONOMY changes, teaching materials must change, too. Many such changes are incorporated in this second editions of *Understanding Macroeconomics* and *Understanding Microeconomics* from Horizon Textbook Publishing.

Many of the changes reflect the increased globalization of economic life. Years ago, international topics were confined to one or two chapters, usually tucked in at the end of textbooks, and usually skipped over in the rush to complete the semester. That approach is no longer suitable today. In the macroeconomics volume, discussion of the balance of payments, net exports, exchange rates, international financial flows, and related topics are fully integrated into the chapters where the related theory and policy issues are discussed. There is no separate international macro chapter at all. In the microeconomics volume, there is still a separate chapter at the end covering international trade and trade policy, but this is no longer the first introduction to these topics. Instead, it is a capstone chapter that pulls together individual threads of international economics that have been introduced chapter by chapter, starting in Chapter 1.

The globalization of this text is not confined to discussion of the big issues, like exchange rates or comparative advantage. It is also reflected in a wide variety of small boxed cases and examples incorporated throughout the text. These not drawn exclusively from U.S. experience, as was the case in textbooks of the past, and why should they be? Principles such as supply and demand, marginal cost, and the effects of expansionary monetary policy apply as much in Russia or Malawi as they do in Kansas or California. The inclusion of examples from many places around the world will make the presentation of economic principles more vivid both for increasingly outward-looking American students and for the large number of students from abroad who come to the United States for an education.

Other changes reflect trends in economics itself. Neoclassical models of rational choice remain the foundation of microeconomics, but they are increasingly supplemented by expanded approaches that incorporate insights of other social sciences. Users of the microeconomics volume will find these expanded approaches incorporated at many points. Similarly, recent years have seen a restoration of balance in the teaching of macroeconomics between long-run and short-run perspectives, and between the real and monetary sectors of the economy. The macroeconomics chapters of this new edition begin with an introduction to the theory of economic growth before introducing short-run business cycle considerations. Also, the chapters on money, banking, and monetary policy are moved to an earlier place in the book in keeping with their importance. The short-run "Keynesian cross" income determination model no longer receives chapter-length treatment, although it is still included in a shorter form.

As was the case with the first edition, it has been a pleasure for me to work with such an innovative publisher.

Acknowledgments

My first thanks must go to my long-time co-author, David E. Lindsey, with whom I worked on earlier editions of this text over a period of many years. During his years as Deputy Director of the Division of Monetary Affairs of the Board of Governors of the Federal Reserve System, David was able to find the ideal balance between the theory and practice of economics. Although he did not contribute to preparation of this new edition, his strong influence can still be seen in both the macroeconomic and microeconomic chapters.

Second, I thank the entire publishing and editorial staff of Horizon Textbook Publishing for introducing me to this great new concept in college publishing. I hope you, the user, benefit as much as I have.

Finally, I would like to acknowledge the support and inspiration of Jere Calmes who encouraged me to try my hand at textbook writing more than 30 years ago. Without his energy and commitment over many years, this book would never have been written.

EDWIN G. DOLAN
Lopez Island, Washington

Features of This Edition

- *State of the art pedagogy*. An abundance of case studies introduce and illustrate the subject matter of every chapter.
- *Integrated international economics.* As the world economy itself comes closer together, international economics must be more closely integrated into the principles course. Accordingly, topics in international economic theory and policy, ranging from balance of payments accounts to the foreign exchange

operations of the Fed, are introduced in the chapters in which they occur naturally, rather than presented separately in a single chapter.

Supplements

Test Bank

The accompanying Test Bank contains over 2,000 questions in a variety of formats including multiple choice, true/false, and essay questions.

Instructor's Manual

The expanded Instructor's Manual contains material which can be easily included in lectures. The manual also includes all of its traditional elements, including instructional objectives, lecture notes, and suggestions.

Study Guide

The Study Guide has hands-on applications and self-testing programs. It is available in two versions, *Macroeconomics*, and *Microeconomics*. Students can gain an advantage by reinforcing their reading and lecture notes with the following study guide features:

- *Where You're Going*. The objectives and terms for each chapter are recapped to tie concepts together.
- *Walking Tour.* The "Walking Tour" section provides a narrative summary of the chapter and incorporates questions on key points. Answers are given in the margin.
- *Hands On*. Geographical and numerical exercises clarify concepts and better prepare students for tests and quizzes.
- *Economics in the News*. A news item illustrates how concepts covered in the chapter can appear in the real world. Questions and answers reinforce the concepts.
- *Questions for Review.* These questions and answers follow the key chapter concepts, preparing students for the self-test.
- *Self-Test*. Extra test preparation increases a student's understanding and ability to succeed.
- *Careers in Economics*. Formerly an appendix in the text, this material provides students with an understanding of where the study of economics could lead them.

Economic PowerPoint Transparencies

This PowerPoint slide set combines graphics and text to further illustrate the economic principles discussed in the text.

About the Author

EDWIN G. DOLAN was born in Oklahoma and grew up in a small town in Oregon. He attended Earlham College and Indiana University, where he majored in Russian Studies and received the Certificate of Indiana University's famed Russian and East-European Institute. After earning a doctorate in economics from Yale University, he taught at Dartmouth College, the University of Chicago, George Mason University and Gettysburg College. In 1990, he began teaching in Moscow, Russia, where he and his wife founded the American Institute of Business and Economics, an independent, not-for-profit MBA program. Since retiring as President of that institution in 2001, he has taught global macroeconomics, managerial economics and public policy in Latvia, Hungary, Croatia, Bulgaria, and the Czech Republic. When not lecturing abroad, he makes his home in Washington's San Juan Islands.

PART 1

Introduction to Economics

Truth

Moral Good RIGHT	**Is it possible to KNOW truth? HOW? How can we KNOW truth?**	Immoral Evil Bad WRONG

Is truth …

Relative?
Created by the individual?

Absolute?
Unchanging and everlasting

THOMAS JEFFERSON WAS the third president of the United States, father of the University of Virginia, and author of the Declaration of Independence! We all have some idea of what Jefferson wrote from our schooling and from the holiday and celebration of this event and document every 4th of July. But do we really understand the importance and meaning of the words of the text? What precisely did Jefferson mean? Why do so many of us misunderstand what he wrote?

THE IMPORTANCE OF JEFFERSON'S WORDS …

"We Hold These Truths"?

Whose truths? Jefferson's truth? Does your personal truth agree with Jefferson's? If not, does that make your truth invalid or does it make Jefferson's truth invalid? Can truths, though diametrically opposite, still both be valid. Though your truth may not agree with mine, are our truths, nonetheless, both valid? Are the truths Jefferson referred to, the same in 1830 as they are now in 2009, or have these truths evolved and changed with the times?

"All Men Are Created Equal"?

You, and I are equally created along with every other person on the earth? You and I have the same gifts, talents, or traits as everyone else? Did Jefferson not see the differences between George Washington and the common dirt farmer from Pennsylvania? Or were these differences irrelevant to Jefferson's *truth*?

We Have a "Right to the Pursuit of Happiness"?

What did Jefferson mean by this and what was understood by the people of 1776 by this passage? So often we confuse the notion of pleasure with happiness. Did Jefferson mean we have a right to pursue *pleasure?* Some think that happiness comes from material goods. That is to say, our happiness will come from the ever more material possessions. Did Jefferson mean we have a right to pursue material luxuries and physical pleasures?

We should recognize that we may all desire pleasure all the time, but pleasure and goodness are not necessarily the same. What gives us pleasure may not necessarily be good; and what is good may not always be a source of pleasure.

Often when asked the question, "what's your goal in life?" people will respond "to be rich", "to be comfortable" and most often "I just want to be happy". Not too often do I hear the response, "I want to be *good*" or "I want to *do good.*" There is a difference between being *happy* and being *good,* or *feeling* happy and *being* good. We know that when we hear a child crying in a burning house, the good thing to do is to run into the burning house at great risk to our physical well being and lead the child out of danger. But the risk and reality of us getting burnt ourselves may not make us happy. Enjoying fast food meals 6 times a week may make us feel happy or feel good (or full), but is that behavior really good? (Watch the movie "Super Size Me".) Is feeling good equal to being good? We should all realize that the answer to this question is "NO".

We all know what makes us feel good: Christmas morning, Thanksgiving feasts, laughing at an episode of *South Park?* But does feeling good make us a good person? What is the definition of a good person? Is everyone good? Is no one *bad?* Or, perhaps, is a good person someone who performs good actions? How do we define a *bad person?* Is a bad person someone who performs bad actions or behaves badly? How are good actions defined? How are bad actions defined? Or are our actions irrelevant to the definition of *goodness* or *badness?* Are we all *good,* just some of us do *bad* things?

THE MEANING OF JEFFERSON'S WORDS

Here are some ideas on the meaning of Jefferson's words in the Declaration of Independence.

We Hold These Truths ...

We declare these truths to be true! We proclaim these truths to be unchanging and absolute. We declare these truths to not be opinions, or relative to the time in which they are contemplated or the situation of the reader. We declare these truths to not be dependent on belief, or knowledge of them.

To be Self Evident ...

To be in no need of explanation; to be undeniable; to be irrefutable; to be indisputable; to be inarguable!

That All Men Are Created Equal ...

That all people have the same privileges, prerogatives and duties before the law! And that is all. Jefferson, as asked earlier, didn't equate his class of college educated intellectuals equal in all ways to the common laborer or slaves on the southern plantations. But Jefferson did recognize human equality in the context of the law. The governor of the colony and the blacksmith were equal before the law!

That They Are Endowed by Their Creator with Certain Unalienable, Rights ...

That these rights come from a metaphysical power. President Kennedy paraphrased this concept when he said: "and yet the same revolutionary beliefs for which our forebears fought are still at issue around the globe—the belief that the rights of man come not from the generosity of the state, but from the hand of God."

Unalienable: cannot be morally taken away nor denied. It is true that one could deprive another's rights. However, this usurpation of one's human rights would be an immoral act.

Among These Life ...

We have the right not to be murdered! And that is all. Jefferson never implied that humans have a right to the physical necessities of life such as food, shelter, clothing or health care.

Liberty ...

We have the right to freedom of thought and freedom of expression (and no more).

And the Pursuit of Happiness! ...

According to the writings of Aristotle, with whom Jefferson was familiar, humans will never be happy until they are perfect. But by definition of humanity, humans will never be perfect; we are imperfect beings. Therefore, humans will never achieve total happiness. What Jefferson was implying was that we have a right to pursue perfection! Jefferson never implied that humans have a right to pleasure. In the words of John Paul II, spoken at Camden Yards, "Americans have the right to do what they ought to do, not what they want to do." Reasonable people can debate and disagree on what constitutes perfection. However, our ability to reason must cause everyone to conclude that smoking, hedonistic pleasures, or sloth are characteristics of the perfect human.

Unfortunately so often we (willingly) confuse pleasure for happiness when thinking of our rights. We do not have a right to pursue what which gives us pleasure or that which may give us a temporary sense of contentment. It is sad that after years in the American educational system so many of our fellow citizens will speak of material possessions as means to happiness in context of Jefferson's idea of rights.

Sometimes during the first class I will ask students to share with the class their goals. Usually the student will respond *"happiness"* and the second most popular response will be *"to be rich"*. Never does a student respond that their goal *"is to be good"*. There is a difference between happiness and goodness. Sometimes our happiness will result from bad behavior and sometimes *good* behavior will cause us to be *un*happy.

Concerning the difference between conservatives and liberals, the core difference is not willingness to change or unwillingness to borrow. The basic difference is the view on TRUTH. A pure conservative will view truth as an unchanging *absolute* while a pure liberal will view truth as *relative* and changing depending on the situation.

Is truth all relative? Or is truth all absolute? In the past, students have argued that truth is relative, which means that one's truth, though different than your truth is equally valid to your truth. The next step then is to defend this proposition. This usually puts the defender in an uncomfortable corner because the student is asked on the morality of slavery or the truth that the Nazis of Germany in the 1930s and 40s were not bad people. Or were the slave holders of 1830 Alabama good people since they believed slavery was not immoral? Did the slavery of 1830 become moral because of the belief of the majority of Americans in 1830 that it was moral? Or did the murder of the European Jews of 1930s and 1940s become moral because the laws of the nation require such action by the Gestapo and SS and a minority of the population believed in the morality of this genocide?

Some argue that this behavior may be judged to be bad by the standards of 2009, but then go on to question the morality or the validity of these standards. Though for us, certain things are unacceptable, but some may question if our standards are universal and then ask, "who are we to impose our values on others? What gives us the right to judge others whose standards and values are different from our own?" Students argue that since the perpetrators of slavery and genocide believed in the justice and goodness of their actions, and that the laws of the allowed and even encouraged this behavior, then they were not necessarily guilty of being wrong. So often when a student is asked if some behavior is right or wrong, the student will respond that "in their own mind, they are right, therefore, they may be different than us in 2009, but not immoral." If the question was "in the opinion of the person owning slaves; or in the opinion of the Nazi death camp guard, were these people moral?, then the answer "in their own mind" etc., would be a reasonable response. But the question is not in "their own opinion", but rather is this behavior right or wrong?

Let us think and use the ideas presented by Jefferson to answer some questions and come to some conclusions.

WHAT RIGHT DO (WE) HAVE TO MAKE JUDGMENTS ABOUT OTHER'S BEHAVIOR?

Well, if you believe Jefferson's accretion that we have the right to think, and that we have the right to express those thoughts, and that those rights come from our creator, then it is easy to explain where our right to make and express judgments come from. According to Jefferson, humans have a God-given right to judge you/me or anyone. We have a right to consider behaviors and express our conclusions. With that said however, no one has a responsibility to listen to or heed our judgments. But, we have a right to think and express those thoughts.

Have you ever watched the Jerry Springer program and listened to the people on the stage ask "what gives you the right to judge me?" Well, now you can explain to someone who asks this question what and where your right comes from.

> *"You don't know me and until you walk in my shoes, how can you judge me? Unless you have experienced what I have, you cannot make a judgment on my behavior!"*

Well, we know now why we do have a right to judge and express that judgment, but how about the experience argument? Does the argument that we can't make an accurate or valid judgement until we have had an identical or similar personal experience? Well, I hope you have never murdered a person. And I hope you have never had a close relative, or a friend murdered. And although you've not been involved in a murder, you can still make a judgment on the morality, or immorality of murder. Again, the Jerry Springer response about experiences: I have never been a high school drop-out, but I can make a valid judgment concerning the benefit or costs of high school completion.

OK—so what's the point? I want to demonstrate that there are some absolutes. I want you to start this course with the idea that all truths are not relative or situational. Some truths do not change. In response to the Nazi or slavery question, in order to accept that the slave owners were not immoral or the Nazis were not evil, you must concede the inhumanity of the African slaves or admit that Jews were something other than human. In class I once had an African American who took the relative argument of truth and when I confronted him about his own humanity he was dazed. I asked him if he became less human because someone in the class considered him less than human. I asked if his humanity was relative to the opinion of some redneck in the class who may believe that this person was not human? Then I asked rhetorically if a Jew in the class becomes less than human because a law in Germany states her so? Does her humanity depend on the relative belief or the legal statute of the nation? The African American student then had to accept the existence of his humanity an absolute The Jewish person does not become nonhuman when she crosses the border into a Nazi country and then suddenly return to a fully-human existence when she leaves that fascist country.

Finally, if you are still unconvinced, just think of RAPE. A student who was unconvinced tried to argue that even rape was situational. SHE (yes, a woman), unwilling to confront her belief that all truth was relative and situational, tried to justify rape. She tried to argue the point that even rape, in some circumstances, could be excused and considered as a moral act in some situations. Well, let me tell you now, there is no situation where RAPE is justified. So even if you still want to believe that truth is relative, please email me and explain a situation where RAPE would be justified.

CHAPTER 1

The Economic Way of Thinking

After reading this chapter, you will understand:

1. The subject matter of economics
2. The considerations underlying four fundamental economic choices:
   - What an economy will produce
   - How goods and services will be produced
   - Who will produce which goods and services
   - For whom goods will be produced
   - How to coordinate economic choices
3. How economists use theory, graphs, and evidence in their work

Scarcity

Scarcity does not mean that we don't have enough. Rather, scarcity means that in order to get one more unit of something, we must give up something else.

THE YEAR 2007 was a tough one for General Motors. In the first three months of 2008, GM lost $722 million. For all of 2007, GM lost $38.7 billion as sales of its largest SUVs plunged. Meanwhile, sales of fuel-efficient hybrids made by Toyota and Honda were booming. The cause of all this turmoil? Soaring gasoline prices and record-high world prices for the crude oil from which gasoline is refined.

Rising gasoline prices and falling SUV sales are examples of **scarcity** and the choices people make when there is not enough of something to meet everyone's wants. Though we're not running out of many resources, (pandas, whales, or whooping cranes spotted owls perhaps being the exception) a better way to view scarcity is that in order for us to get an additional unit of one commodity, we must give up something else. In this case the scarce resource is energy. For us to get more oil we must give up Alaskan tundra or the beautiful views of the Pacific Ocean off the coast of California. American consumers want to use a lot of the world's scarce energy resources to run the large cars they love so much. But consumers in rapidly growing China and India want energy to build a lifestyle based on refrigerators, air conditioners, and motor transport, too. The people of India and China just want what we have: a higher standard of living. There is not enough oil in the world to satisfy all wants at once, so choices must be made. Scarcity does not meant that we're running out of something. But scarcity means that in order to get more of a resource, we must give up something else. In order to get more crude oil, Americans will have to give up either coastal scenery along California or Arctic wilderness in Alaska. Scarcity and the way people deal with it are the central topics of **economics**, which can be defined as the social science that seeks to understand the choices people make in using scarce resources to satisfy their needs and unlimited wants.

Economics

The social science that seeks to understand the choices people make in using scarce resources to meet their wants.

Economics, as the definition makes clear, is a study not of things or money or wealth but of *people*. Economics is about people because scarcity itself is a human phenomenon. Deposits of crude oil lay undisturbed in the ground for millions of years before they became the object of human wants. Only at that point did they become *scarce* in the sense that economists understand the term. It is the focus on the human dimension of scarcity and choice that makes economics a social science rather than a branch of engineering or mathematics.

Scarcity and choice, the ideas that unify all of economics, have many different applications. The example of gasoline prices and vehicle choices are applications from **microeconomics**. The prefix *micro*, meaning "small," indicates that this branch of economics deals with the choices of small economic units such as households, firms, and government agencies. Although microeconomics studies individual behavior, its scope can be worldwide. When households, firms, and government agencies conduct worldwide trade in such goods as cars and crude oil, that trade and the policies regulating it fall within the scope of microeconomics. (Think of micro as the study of individual trees within a larger forest. Often in this course, the instructor will refer to micro as PRICE THEORY since the theme of this course is an explanation of why the price of things are what they are.) Microeconomics tries to explain individual prices. Microeconomics explains why gasoline prices rise to $4.00 a gallon or why Dereck Jeter earns $21.6 million in 2007. Sometimes, microeconomics is referred to as **price theory**.

Microeconomics

The branch of economics that studies the choices of individuals, including households, business firms, and government agencies.

Economics also has another branch, known as **macroeconomics**. The prefix *macro*, meaning "large," indicates that this branch deals with larger-scale economic phenomena. Typical problems in macroeconomics include how to maintain conditions in which people who want jobs can find them, how to protect the economy against the distortions caused by widespread price increases (inflation), and how to provide for a continued increase in living standards over time. Because of the focus of macroeconomics on employment and its attempt to explain unemployment, macroeconomics is sometimes referred to as **employment theory**. Choices studied by macroeconomics include those made by governments, for example, choices among alternative policies concerning taxes, expenditures, budget deficits, and the

Macroeconomics

The branch of economics that studies large-scale economic phenomena, particularly inflation, unemployment, and economic growth.

financial system. However, because macroeconomic phenomena, such as inflation, represent the end-result of millions of individual choices regarding the prices of particular goods and services, macroeconomics ultimately rests on a microeconomic foundation.

Whether one is dealing with microeconomics or macroeconomics, and whether with domestic or international economic relationships, all economic analysis comes down to a special way of thinking about how people choose to use scarce resources.

WHAT? HOW? WHO? FOR WHOM?

In every economy certain basic choices must be made. Among these, the most important are what goods will be produced, how they will be produced, who will do which jobs, and for whom the results of economic activity will be made available. Each of these choices is made necessary because of scarcity, and each can be used to introduce key elements of the economic way of thinking.

Factors of production

The basic inputs of labor, capital, and natural resources used in producing all goods and services.

Labor

The contributions to production made by people working with their minds and muscles.

Capital

All means of production that are created by people, including tools, industrial equipment, and structures.

Land

Anything that can be used as a productive input in its natural state, such as farmland, building sites, forests, and mineral deposits. Or simply, an economic term for natural resources.

Deciding What to Produce: Opportunity Cost

The first basic choice is that of what goods to produce. In any real economy the number of goods and services that could be produced is immense. The key features of the choice of what goods to produce, however, can be illustrated using an economy in which there are just two alternative goods, say, cars and education. For many students, going without a car (or driving an older, used car instead of a new one) is a sacrifice that must be made in order to get a college education. The same trade-off that is faced by an individual student is also faced by the economy as a whole: Not enough cars and education can be produced to satisfy everyone's wants. Somehow it must be decided how much of each good to produce.

Probably the best way our economy answers the What to Produce question is the idea of PROFIT. If a product earns a profit, it will be produced, if the product doesn't/t make a profit, it won't.

The impossibility of producing as much of everything as people want reflects a scarcity of the productive resources that are used to make all goods. Many scarce productive resources must be combined to make even the simplest of goods. For example, making a table requires lumber, nails, glue, a hammer, a saw, the work of a carpenter, and that of a painter. For convenience, productive resources are often grouped into three basic categories, called **factors of production**: labor, capital, and natural resources. **Labor** includes all of the productive contributions made by people working with their minds and muscles. **Capital** includes all the productive inputs created by people, including tools, machinery, buildings, and intangible items, such as computer programs. **Land** includes anything that can be used as a productive input in its natural state—for example, farmland, building sites, forests, and mineral deposits. Traditional economists refer to natural resources as Land.

Productive resources that are used to satisfy one want cannot be used to satisfy another at the same time. Steel, concrete, and building sites used for automobile factories cannot also be used for classrooms. People who are employed as teachers cannot spend the same time working on an automobile assembly line. Even the time students spend in class and studying for tests represents use of a factor of production that could otherwise be used as labor in an auto plant. Because production uses inputs that could be used elsewhere, the production of any good entails forgoing the opportunity to produce something else instead. In economic terms, everything has an **opportunity cost**. The opportunity cost of a good or service is its cost in terms of the forgone opportunity to pursue the best possible alternative activity with the same time or resources. Think of opportunity cost as the true cost of something. Opportunity costs are greater than the explicate costs that an accountant would present as the cost of something.

Opportunity cost

The cost of a good or service measured in terms of the forgone opportunity to pursue the best possible alternative activity with the same time or resources.

Let's go back to the example of an economy that has only two goods, cars and education. In such an economy, the opportunity cost of producing a college graduate can be stated in terms of the number of cars that could have been produced by using the same labor, capital, and natural resources. Suppose that the opportunity cost of educating a college graduate might be four Toyota Camrys. Such a ratio (graduates per car or cars per graduate) is a useful way to express opportunity cost when only two goods are involved. More typically, though, we deal with situations in which there are many goods. Having more of one means giving up a little bit of many others. (Think of the definition of scarcity above.)

In an economy with many goods, opportunity costs can be expressed in terms of a common unit of measurement, money. For example, rather than saying that a college education is worth four Camrys or that a Camry is worth one-fourth of a college education, we could say that the opportunity cost of a car is $25,000 and that of a college education is $100,000.

Useful as it is to have a common unit of measurement, great care must be taken when opportunity costs are expressed in terms of money, because not all out-of-pocket money expenditures represent the sacrifice of opportunities to do something else. At the same time, not all sacrificed opportunities take the form of money spent. *Applying Economic Ideas 1.1,* which analyzes both the out-of-pocket expenditures and the opportunity costs of a college education, shows why.

The importance of opportunity cost will be stressed again and again in this book. The habit of looking for opportunity costs is one of the distinguishing features of the economic way of thinking.

Deciding How to Produce: Efficiency and Entrepreneurship

A second basic economic choice is that of how to produce. There is more than one way to produce almost any good or service. Cars, for example, can be made in highly automated factories using a lot of capital equipment and relatively little labor, or they can be built one by one in small shops, using a lot of labor and only a few general-

APPLYING ECONOMIC IDEAS 1.1

THE OPPORTUNITY COST OF A COLLEGE EDUCATION

How much does it cost you to go to college? If you are a resident student at a typical four-year private college in the United States, you can answer this question by making up a budget like the one shown in Figure A. This can be called a budget of out-of-pocket costs, because it includes all the items—and only those items—that you or your parents must actually pay for in a year.

Your own out-of-pocket costs may be much higher or lower than these averages. Chances are, though, that these are the items that come to mind when you think about the costs of college. As you begin to think like an economist, you may find it useful to recast your college budget in terms of opportunity costs. Which of the items in Figure A represent opportunities that you have forgone in order to go to college? Are any forgone opportunities missing? To answer these questions, compare Figure A with Figure B, which shows a budget of opportunity costs.

Some items are both opportunity costs and out-of-pocket costs. The first three items in Figure A show up again in Figure B. To spend $14,000 on tuition and fees and $1,200 on books and supplies, you must give up the opportunity to buy other goods and services—to buy a car or rent a ski condo, for instance. To spend $1,100 getting to and from school, you must pass up the opportunity to travel somewhere else or to spend the money on something other than travel. Not all out-of-pocket costs are also opportunity costs, however. Consider the last two items in the out-of-pocket budget. By spending $7,000 on room, board, and personal expenses during the year, you are not really giving up the opportunity to do something else. Whether or not you were going to college, you would have to eat, live somewhere, and buy clothes. Because these are expenses that you would have in any case, they do not count as opportunity costs of going to college.

Finally, there are some items that are opportunity costs without being out-of-pocket costs. Think about what you would be doing if you were not going to college. If you were not going to college, you probably would have taken a job and started earning money soon after leaving high school. As a high-school graduate, your earnings would be about $16,000 during the nine months of the school year. (You can work during the summer even if you are attending college.) Because this potential income is something that you must forgo for the sake of college, it is an opportunity cost even though it does not involve an outlay of money.

Which budget you use depends on the kind of decision you are making. If you have already decided to go to college and are doing your financial planning, the out-of-pocket budget will tell you how much you will have to raise from savings, a job, parents' contributions, and scholarships to make ends meet. But if you are making the more basic choice between going to college and pursuing a career that does not require a college degree, the opportunity cost of college is what counts.

Figure A	**Budget of Out-of-Pocket Costs**	**Figure B**	**Budget of Opportunity Costs**
Tuition and fees	$14,000	Tuition and fees	$14,000
Books and supplies	1,200	Books and supplies	1,200
Transportation to and from home	1,100	Transportation to and from home	1,000
Room and board	7,000	Forgone income	16,000
Personal expenses	1,400		
Total out-of-pocket costs	**$24,700**	**Total opportunity costs**	**$32,200**

purpose machines. Toyota Camrys are built the first way, Ferraris and Rolls Royces the second way. The same kind of thing could be said about education. Economics can be taught in a small classroom with one teacher and a blackboard serving 20 students, or it can be taught in a large lecture hall in which the teacher uses projectors, computers, and TV monitors to serve hundreds of students.

As profit is the factor in what is produced, it plays a role in how. In this course, profit maximization is the assumed goal of the producer, and if, the goal is to maximize profits, the firm will seek out and employ the least cost method of producing. So, how do we produce the items that earn profits: the method that costs the least.

Economic efficiency

Means producing with a minimum of expense, effort, and waste.

EFFICIENCY Efficiency is a key consideration in deciding how to produce. In everyday speech, efficiency means producing with a minimum of expense, effort, and waste. Economists use a more precise definition. **Economic efficiency**, they say, refers to a state of affairs in which it is impossible to make any change that satisfies one person's wants more fully without causing some other person's wants to be satisfied less fully.[1]

Although this formal definition of economic efficiency may be unfamiliar, it is actually closely related to the everyday notion of efficiency. If there is some way to make you better off without making me worse off, it is wasteful (inefficient) to pass up the opportunity. If I have a red pen that I am not using, and you need one just for a minute, it would be wasteful for you to buy a red pen of your own. It is more efficient for me to lend you my pen; it makes you better off and me no worse off. If there is a way to make us both better off, it would be all the more wasteful not to take advantage of the opportunity. You lend me your bicycle for the afternoon and I will lend you my volleyball. If I do not ride a bicycle very often and you do not play volleyball very often, it would be inefficient for us both to own one of each item. Think of this idea as related to cars. How much would it cost to share rides to school? What is the cost of two passengers instead of one? Granted, there would be opportunity costs involved, such as time waiting for your ride, and the inconvenience of being exposed to her radio station which you may not prefer. But the American use of auto is very inefficient.

Efficiency in production

A situation in which it is not possible, given available knowledge and productive resources, to produce more of one good without forgoing the opportunity to produce some of another good.

The concept of economic efficiency has a variety of applications: one such application centers on the question of *how* to produce. **Efficiency in production** refers to a situation in which it is not possible, given available productive resources and existing knowledge, to produce more of one good without forgoing the opportunity to produce some of another good. The concept of efficiency in production, like the broader concept of economic efficiency, includes the everyday notion of *avoiding waste*. For example, a grower of apples finds that beyond some certain quantity, using more fertilizer per tree does not increase the yield of apples. To use more than that amount would be wasteful. Better to transfer the extra fertilizer to the production of, say, peaches. That way more peaches can be grown without any reduction in the apple crop.

The economist's definition also includes more subtle possibilities for improving the efficiency of production in cases where the waste of resources is less obvious. For example, it is possible to harvest crabs in Maryland. It is also possible, by building aqua tanks, to raise crabs in Vermont. Some hobbyists do have aquariums in Vermont with blue crabs in them (I think.). However, doing so on a commercial scale would be inefficient even if waterman in both states followed the most careful cultivation practices and avoided any obvious "waste." To see why, just imagine the cost of building and operating tanks large enough to produce enough crabs to satisfy the wants of the people of

Vermont. The costs and amount of resource needed to do so would be exceptionally high especially when compared to the Bay which doesn't need to be built.

HOW TO INCREASE PRODUCTION POTENTIAL Once efficiency has been achieved, more of one good can be produced only by forgoing the opportunity to produce something else, assuming that productive resources and knowledge are held constant. But over time, production potential can be expanded by accumulating more resources and finding new ways of putting them to work.

In the past, discovery of new supplies of natural resources has been an important way of increasing production potential. Population growth has always been, and still is, another source. However, as the most easily tapped supplies of natural resources are depleted and as population growth slows in the most developed countries, capital will increasingly be the factor of production that contributes most to the expansion of production potential.

Investment

The act of increasing the economy's stock of capital—that is, its supply of means of production made by people.

The act of increasing the economy's stock of capital—that is, its supply of productive inputs made by people—is known as **investment**. For our purposes, investment is not the purchase of stocks or bonds. The purchase of securities is just a transfer of ownership of assets. In this course and economics in general, investment is a trade-off of present consumption for future consumption. To build more factories, roads, and computers, we have to divert resources from the production of bread, movies, haircuts, and other things that satisfy immediate wants. In return, we put ourselves in a better position to satisfy our future wants.

Your education at Carroll is an investment. You are hoping that by forgoing other goods, your future earning potential will be enhanced. You could choose to spend your scarce income on items that would be more fun than economics class. But you are investing your scarce resources (tuition funds and TIME) and forgoing fun or other consumer items in the hope of greater future income.

From an economic point of view, investment is not buying stocks or bonds. These types of purchases are no more that a transfer of assets. Economic investment is the creation of new goods that are not used for their own sake, but rather to produce other, final goods.

Entrepreneurship

The tendency to assume RISK. The difference between management and entrepreneurship is the risk involved.

Increased availability of productive resources is not the only source of economic growth, however. Even more important are improvements in human knowledge—the invention of new technology, new forms of organization, new ways of satisfying wants. The process of looking for new possibilities—making use of new ways of doing things, being alert to new opportunities, and overcoming old limits—is called **entrepreneurship**. It is a dynamic process that breaks down the constraints imposed by existing knowledge and limited supplies of factors of production.

Entrepreneurship does not have to mean inventing something or starting a new business, although it sometimes does. It may mean finding a new market for an existing product—for example, convincing people in New England that tacos, long popular in the Southwest, make a quick and tasty lunch. It may mean taking advantage of price differences between one market and another—for example, buying hay at a low price in Pennsylvania, where growing conditions have been good in the past year, and reselling it in Virginia, where the weather has been too dry. The most important characteristic that distinguishes an entrepreneur from a manager is the penchant or propensity to assume RISK.

Households can be entrepreneurs, too. They do not simply repeat the same patterns of work and leisure every day. They seek variety—new jobs, new foods, new places to visit. Each time you try something new, you are taking a step into the unknown, which can be risky. In this sense you are an entrepreneur.

Entrepreneurship is sometimes called the fourth factor of production. However, entrepreneurship differs from the three classical factors of production in important ways. Unlike labor, capital, and natural resources, entrepreneurship is intangible and difficult to measure. Although entrepreneurs earn incomes reflecting the value that the market places on their accomplishments, we cannot speak of a price per unit of entrepreneurship; there are no such units. Also, unlike human resources (which grow old), machines (which wear out), and natural resources (which can be used up), the inventions and discoveries of entrepreneurs are not depleted as they are used. Once a new product or concept, such as gasoline-electric hybrid power for cars, text messaging on cell phones, or the limited-partnership form of business, has been invented, the required knowledge does not have to be created again (although, of course, it may be supplanted by even better ideas). All in all, it is more helpful to think of entrepreneurship as a process of learning better ways of using the three basic factors of production than as a separate factor of production in itself.

We in America are fortunate to be gifted with an abundance of all four resources. Our climate is very conducive to agriculture. We are blessed with an abundance of land (natural resources). Our labor is well nourished, well trained, highly motivated and therefore very productive. And America has enjoyed so many brilliant and innovating individuals that our standard of living is the highest in the world. It is impossible to accurately quantity the contributions of Henry Ford, Thomas Edison, Steve Jobs, and too many names to mention who have assumed risk and increased both American well being and the standard of living of the entire human race.

Deciding Who Will Do Which Work: The Division of Labor

The questions of what will be produced and how to produce it would exist even for a person living in isolation. Even the fictional castaway Robinson Crusoe had to decide whether to fish or hunt birds, and if he decided to fish, he had to decide whether to do so with a net or with a hook and line. In contrast, the economic questions of who will do which work and for whom output will be produced exist only for people living in a human society—another reason economics is considered one of the social sciences.

The question of who will do which work is a matter of organizing the social division of labor. Will everyone do everything independently—be a farmer in the morning, a tailor in the afternoon, and a poet in the evening? Or will people cooperate—work together, trade goods and services, and specialize in one particular job? Economists answer these questions by pointing out that it is more efficient to cooperate. Doing so allows a given number of people to produce more than they could if each of them worked alone. Three things make cooperation worthwhile: teamwork, learning by doing, and comparative advantage.

First consider *teamwork*. In a classic paper on this subject, Armen Alchian and Harold Demsetz use the example of workers unloading bulky crates from a truck.[2] The crates are so large that one worker alone can barely drag them along or cannot move them at all without unpacking them. Two people working independently would take hours to unload the truck. If they work as a team, however, they can easily pick up the crates and stack them on the loading dock. This example shows that even when everyone is doing the same work and little skill is involved, teamwork pays.

A second reason for cooperation applies when there are different jobs to be done and different skills to be learned. In a furniture plant, for example, some workers operate production equipment, others use office equipment, and still others buy materials. Even if all the workers start out with equal abilities, each gets better at a particular job by doing it repeatedly. *Learning by doing* thus turns workers of average productivity into specialists, thereby creating an even more productive team.

A third reason for cooperation comes into play after the process of learning by doing has developed different skills and also applies when workers start out with different talents and abilities. It is the principle of division of labor according to *comparative advantage*. **Comparative advantage** is the ability to do a job or produce a good at a relatively lower opportunity cost than someone else.

Comparative advantage

The ability to produce a good or service at a relatively lower opportunity cost than someone else.

An example will illustrate the principle of comparative advantage. Suppose two clerical workers, Bill and Jim, are assigned the job of getting out a batch of personalized letters to clients. Jim is a whiz. Using the latest office productivity software, he can prepare a letter in 5 minutes and stuff it into an envelope in 1 minute. Working alone, he can finish ten letters in an hour. Bill is clumsy. It takes him 10 minutes to prepare a letter and 5 minutes to stuff it into the envelope. Alone, he can do only four letters an hour. In summary form:

Jim: Prepare 1 letter 5 min.
Stuff 1 envelope 1 min.

Bill: Prepare 1 letter 10 min.
Stuff 1 envelope 5 min.

Without cooperation, the two workers' limit is 14 letters per hour between them. Could they do better by cooperating? It depends on who does which job. One idea might be for Jim to prepare all the letters while Bill does all the stuffing, because that way they can just keep up with each other. But at 5 minutes per letter, that kind of cooperation cuts their combined output to twelve letters per hour. It is worse than not cooperating at all.

Instead, they should divide the work according to the principle of comparative advantage. Even though Bill is slower at preparing the letters, he has a *comparative advantage* in preparation because the opportunity cost of that part of the work is lower for him: The 10 minutes he takes to prepare a letter is equal to the time he needs to stuff two envelopes. For Jim, the 5 minutes he takes to prepare a letter could be used to stuff five envelopes. For Bill, then, the opportunity cost of preparing one letter is to forgo stuffing *two* envelopes, whereas for Jim the opportunity cost of preparing one letter is to forgo stuffing *five* envelopes.

Because Bill gives up fewer stuffed envelopes per letter than Jim, the principle of comparative advantage says that Bill should spend all his time preparing letters. If he does, he can produce six letters per hour. Meanwhile Jim can spend 45 minutes of each hour preparing nine letters, and the last 15 minutes of each hour stuffing all 15 envelopes. By specializing according to comparative advantage, the two workers can increase their total output to 15 letters per hour, their highest possible joint productivity.

In this example the principle of comparative advantage points the way toward an efficient division of labor between two people working side by side. But the principle

WHO SAID IT? WHO DID IT? 1.1

DAVID RICARDO AND THE THEORY OF COMPARATIVE ADVANTAGE

(See The Worldly Philosophers, Chapter IV)

David Ricardo was born in London in 1772, the son of an immigrant who was a member of the London stock exchange. Ricardo's education was rather haphazard, and he entered his father's business at the age of 14. In 1793, he married and went into business on his own. These were years of war and financial turmoil. The young Ricardo developed a reputation for remarkable astuteness and quickly made a large fortune.

In 1799, Ricardo read Adam Smith's *The Wealth of Nations* and developed an interest in political economy (as economics was then called). In 1809, his first writings on economics appeared. These were a series of newspaper articles on "The High Price of Bullion," which appeared during the following year as a pamphlet. Several other short works added to his reputation in this area. In 1814, he retired from business to devote all his time to political economy.

Ricardo's major work was *Principles of Political Economy and Taxation*, first published in 1817. This work contains, among other things, a pioneering statement of the principle of comparative advantage as applied to international trade. Using a lucid numerical example, Ricardo showed why, as long as wool can be produced *comparatively* less expensively in England, it was to the advantage of both countries for England to export wool to Portugal and to import wine in return, even though both products could be produced with fewer labor hours in Portugal.

But international trade is only a sideline of Ricardo's *Principles*. The book covers the whole field of economics as it then existed, beginning with value theory and progressing to a theory of economic growth and evolution. Ricardo held that the economy was growing toward a future "steady state." At that point economic growth would come to a halt and the wage rate would be reduced to the subsistence level. This gloomy view and the equally pessimistic views of Ricardo's contemporary, Thomas Malthus, gave political economy a reputation as "the dismal science."

Ricardo's book was extremely influential. For more than half a century thereafter, much of the writing on economic theory published in England consisted of expansions and commentaries on Ricardo's work. Economists as different as Karl Marx, the revolutionary socialist, and John Stuart Mill, a defender of liberal capitalism, took Ricardo's theories as their starting point. Even today there are "neo-Ricardian" and "new classicist" economists who look to Ricardo's works for inspiration. (Refer to *The Worldly Philosophers* by Heilbroner (Chapter IV.)

also has broader implications. It can apply to a division of labor between individuals or business firms working far apart—even in different countries. In fact, the earliest application of the principle was to international trade (see *Who Said It? Who Did It? 1.1*). Today comparative advantage remains one of the primary motivations for mutually beneficial cooperation, whether on the scale of the workplace or on that of the world as a whole.

Whatever the context, the principle of comparative advantage is easy to apply provided one remembers that it is rooted in the concept of opportunity cost. Suppose there are two tasks, A and B, and two parties, X and Y (individuals, firms, or countries), each capable of doing both tasks, but not equally well. First ask what is the opportunity cost for X of doing a unit of task A, measured in terms of how many units of task B could be done with the same time or resources (the opportunity cost). Then ask the same question for Y. The party with the lower opportunity cost for doing a unit of task A has the comparative advantage in doing that task. To check, ask what is the opportunity cost for each party of doing a unit of task B, measured in terms how many units of task A could be done with the same time or resources. The party with the lower opportunity cost for doing a unit of task B has the comparative advantage in doing that task.

Deciding for Whom Goods will be Produced: Positive and Normative Economics

Together, the advantages of team production, learning by doing, and comparative advantage mean that people can produce more efficiently by cooperating than they could if each worked in isolation. But cooperation raises yet another issue: For whom will goods be produced? The question of the **distribution** of output among members of society has implications in terms of both efficiency and fairness.

Distribution

Who gets what and how much does each individual get.

EFFICIENCY IN DISTRIBUTION Consider first a situation in which production has already taken place and the supply of goods is fixed. Suppose, for example, that 30 students get on a bus to go to a football game. Bag lunches are handed out. Half the bags contain a ham sandwich and a root beer; the other half contain a tuna sandwich and a cola. What happens when the students open their bags? They do not just eat whatever they find—they start trading. Some swap sandwiches; others swap drinks. Maybe there is not enough of everything to give each person his or her first choice. Nevertheless, the trading makes at least some people better off than they were when they started. Moreover, no one ends up worse off. If some of the students do not want to trade, they can always eat what was given to them in the first place.

This example shows one sense in which the "for whom" question is partly about efficiency: Starting from any given quantity of goods, the allocation can be improved through trades that result in better satisfaction of some people's preferences. As long as it is possible to trade existing supplies of goods in a way that permits some people

Efficiency in distribution

A situation in which it is not possible, by redistributing existing supplies of goods, to satisfy one person's wants more fully without causing some other person's wants to be satisfied less fully.

to satisfy their wants more fully without making others worse off, **efficiency in distribution** can be improved even while the total quantity of goods remains fixed.

Efficiency in distribution and efficiency in production are two aspects of the general concept of economic efficiency. When both aspects are taken into account, the relationship between distribution and efficiency is not restricted to situations in which the total amount of goods is fixed in advance. That is so because the rules for distribution affect the patterns of production. For example, the rules for distribution affect the supply of productive resources, because most people earn their incomes by providing labor to business firms, and the amount they supply is affected by the wages they are promised. Another reason is that rules for distribution affect incentives for entrepreneurship. Some people may work hard to discover new ways of doing things even if they expect no material reward, but that is not true of everyone.

FAIRNESS IN DISTRIBUTION Efficiency is not the whole story when it comes to the question of for whom goods will be produced. One can also ask whether a given distribution is fair. Questions of fairness often dominate discussions of distribution.

One widely held view judges fairness in distribution in terms of equality. This concept of fairness is based on the idea that all people, by virtue of their shared humanity, deserve a portion of the goods and services turned out by the economy. There are many versions of this concept. Some people think that all income and wealth should be distributed equally. Others think that people have an equal right to a "safety net" level of income but that inequality in distributing any surplus beyond that level is not necessarily unfair. Still others think that certain goods, such as health care, food, and education, should be distributed equally but that it is fair for other goods to be distributed less equally.

An alternative view, which also has many adherents, judges fairness primarily in terms of the procedures through which a given distribution is carried out. In this view, fairness requires that certain rules and procedures be observed, such as respect for private property or nondiscrimination on grounds of race and gender. As long as those rules are followed, any resulting distribution of income is viewed as acceptable. In this view, equality of opportunity is emphasized more than equality of outcome.

When considering fairness in distribution, consider the concept of justice. Distribution may not be equal and may be unfair, but is this system of distribution just? For example two teachers live in the same neighborhood in similar homes. Both teachers work the normal 10-month contract for a similar step on the pay scale. But one teacher paints for hire during July and August while the other relaxes and reads. On weekends during the Fall and Spring, the painter teacher works at the golf course while the second teacher enjoys the company of his children. When the end of the year comes around, the painter teacher has more than the second teacher. This would mean that there is an unequal distribution since one teacher has more and the other teacher has less. Though it is unequal, it is just that the painter has more since she has done more and it is just that the second teacher has less since he has done less. In this case, an equal distribution would be unjust.

At this point, the student should understand that justice, equality and fairness are not necessarily identical. If every household has the same income the distribution is equal. But is equal distribution just? If some households produce more than is if just for the more productive households to have an equal share of the output than an household that produces nothing?

Positive economics

The area of economics that is concerned with facts and the relationships among them.

Normative economics

The area of economics that is devoted to judgments about whether economic policies or conditions are good or bad.

POSITIVE AND NORMATIVE ECONOMICS Many economists make a sharp distinction between the question of efficiency and that of fairness. Discussions of efficiency are seen as part of **positive economics**, the area of economics that is concerned with facts and the relationships among them. Discussions of fairness, in contrast, are seen as part of **normative economics**, the area of economics that is devoted to judgments about whether particular economic policies and conditions are good or bad.

Normative economics extends beyond the question of fairness in the distribution of output. Value judgments also arise about the fairness of the other three basic choices faced by every economy. In choosing what will be produced, is it fair to permit production of alcohol and tobacco but to outlaw production of marijuana? In choosing how to produce, is it fair to allow people to work under dangerous or unhealthy conditions, or should work under such conditions be prohibited? In choosing who does which work, is it fair to limit access to specific jobs according to age, gender, race, or union membership? As you can see, normative issues extend to every corner of economics.

Positive economics, rather than offering value judgments about outcomes, focuses on understanding the processes by which the four basic economic questions are or could be answered. It analyzes the way economies operate, or would operate if certain institutions or policies were changed. It traces relationships between facts, often looking for regularities and patterns that can be measured statistically.

Most economists consider positive economics their primary area of expertise, but normative considerations influence the conduct of positive economics in several ways. The most significant of those influences is the selection of topics to investigate. An economist who sees excessive unemployment as a glaring injustice may study that problem; one who sympathizes with victims of job discrimination may take up a different line of research. Also, normative views are likely to affect the ways in which data are collected, ideas about which facts can be considered true, and so on.

At one time it was thought that a purely positive economics could be developed, untouched by normative considerations of values and fairness. Within its framework, all disputes could be resolved by reference to objective facts. Today that notion is less widely held. Nevertheless, it remains important to be aware that most major economic controversies, especially those that have to do with government policy, have normative as well as positive components, and to be aware of the way each component shapes the way we think about those controversies.

COORDINATING ECONOMIC CHOICES

To function effectively, an economy must have some way of coordinating the choices of millions of individuals regarding what to produce, how to produce it, who will do each job, and for whom the output will be produced. This section discusses how households, businesses, and the government interact in the coordination of economic choices.

A Noneconomic Example

You, like almost everyone, have probably had the experience of shopping at a supermarket where there are several long checkout lines. In such a situation, you and other shoppers want to get through the checkout process as fast as possible. The store would like to speed your way through as well and to avoid a situation in which some lines have a long wait for service while the cashiers in other lines stand idle for lack of customers. How can this be done?

One way would be for the store to direct certain customers to certain lines. The store could use a standard rule, such as customers with names starting with A–D go to line 1, E–H go to line 2, and so on. Or the store could hire an employee to sit in a special booth and direct shoppers to one line or another.

Such a system is sometimes used to control lines. For example, the U.S. Customs service at New York's busy Kennedy International Airport has an employee on duty to direct arriving passengers to the next available agent. But supermarkets do not work that way. Instead, supermarkets leave shoppers to decide for themselves what line to join, based on information from their own observations. As you approach the checkout area, you first look to see which lines are the shortest. You then make allowance for the possibility that some shoppers may have carts that are heaped full, while others have only a few items. Using your own judgment, you head for the line you think will be fastest. (Compare the cashier lines at Burger King and McDonalds. At Burger King, there is only one line, so the risk of getting in a line with a slow cashier is eliminated. At McDonald's however, you just enter a line that you hope the person in front of you is not ordering for a 75 member marching band or that the clerk is fast and efficient.)

Hierarchy

A way of achieving coordination in which individual actions are guided by instructions from a central authority.

Spontaneous order

A way of achieving coordination in which individuals adjust their actions in response to cues from their immediate environment.

The coordination system used by the Customs Service at BWI airport is an example of coordination by **hierarchy**. Hierarchy is a way of achieving coordination in which individual actions are guided by instructions from a central authority. The approach used in supermarkets is an example of coordination by **spontaneous order**. Under this system, coordination is achieved when individuals adjust their actions in response to cues received from their immediate environment. It is *orderly* because it achieves an approximately equal waiting time in each checkout line. It is spontaneous in that coordination is achieved without central direction. Even though no shopper has the specific goal of equalizing the lines, that is the end result.

Spontaneous Order in Markets

Market

People making decisions, without coercion, as to what they want to buy, own, or what they want to sell, produce.

In economics, markets are the most important example of the coordination of decisions through spontaneous order. A **market** is any arrangement people have for trading with one another. A market is not a place. Some markets have formal rules and carry out exchanges at a single location, such as the New York Stock Exchange. Other markets are more informal, such as the word-of-mouth networks through which teenage babysitters get in touch with people who need their services. Despite the wide variety of forms that markets take, they all have one thing in common: They provide the information and incentives people need to coordinate their decisions.

Just as shoppers need information about the length of checkout lines to coordinate their efforts, participants in markets need information about the scarcity and opportunity costs of various goods and factors of production. Markets rely primarily on prices to transmit this information. If a good or factor of production becomes more scarce, its price is bid up. The increase in the price tells people it is worth more and signals producers to make greater efforts to increase supplies.

Along with transmitting information, price is the device that we use to express value. How do we know our economy values Lexis autos more than Schwinn bicycles? We can determine value by the price we are willing to pay for a Lexis and the price someone is willing to accept to sell a Lexis. I need not tell you that a Lexis has a higher price than a Schwinn bike!

Price, as the method used to express value, also allocates our resources. Our economy will allocate our resources which will fetch the highest price. Just think of wages: the higher the value that society places on someone's labor, the higher the wage one will be paid for that labor. Concerning the allocation of labor, why do some people allocate their labor in getting a medical degree? Because society values physician's labor highly, physicians are highly paid. And because of that relatively high compensation, many people allocate (or try to) allocate their efforts to getting into medical school. For the same reason, not too many people try to enter the museum curator graduate program at NYU. The number of positions available and the compensation for such occupations are low. The pay is low because our society does not value this service as much as the physician.

For example, when platinum first began to be used in catalytic converters to reduce pollution from automobile exhaust, new buyers entered the market. As automakers began to compete with makers of jewelry and other traditional users, platinum became more difficult to acquire. Competition for available supplies bids up the price of platinum. This provided buyers with a cue that the value of platinum had increased and provided an incentive to be careful with its use. At the same time, producers learned that, where possible, they should increase the quantity of platinum mined.

Instead, suppose a new technology were to reduce the cost of producing platinum, for example, by allowing extraction of platinum from mine wastes that used to be discarded. Information about the reduced cost would be transmitted by markets in the form of a lower price. People could then consider increasing the quantity of platinum they use.

In addition to knowing the best use for resources, people must also have incentives to act on that information. Markets provide incentives to sell goods and productive resources where they will bring the highest prices and to buy them where they can be obtained at the lowest prices. Profits motivate business managers to improve production methods and to design goods that match consumer needs. Workers who stay alert to opportunities and work where they are most productive receive the highest wages. Consumers are motivated to use less expensive substitutes where feasible.

Adam Smith, often considered the father of economics, saw the achievement of coordination through markets as the foundation of prosperity and progress. In a famous passage in *The Wealth of Nations,* he called markets an "invisible hand" that nudges people into the economic roles they can play best (see *Who Said It? Who Did It? 1.2*). To this day, an appreciation of markets as a means of coordinating choices remains a central feature of the economic way of thinking.

The Role of Hierarchy

Important as markets are, they are not the only means of achieving economic coordination. Some decisions are guided by direct authority within organizations, that is, by the mechanism of hierarchy. Decisions made by government agencies are one

WHO SAID IT? WHO DID IT? 1.2
ADAM SMITH ON THE INVISIBLE HAND
(See The Worldly Philosophers, Chapter III)

Adam Smith is considered to have been the founder of economics as a distinct field of study, even though he wrote only one book on the subject: *The Wealth of Nations*, published in 1776. Smith was 53 years old at the time. His friend David Hume found the book such hard going that he doubted that many people would read it. But Hume was wrong—people have been reading it for more than 200 years.

The wealth of a nation, in Smith's view, was not a result of the accumulation of gold or silver in its treasury, as many contemporary theorists believed. Rather, it was the outcome of the activities of ordinary people working and trading in free markets. To Smith, the remarkable thing about the wealth produced by a market economy is that it is not a result of any organized plan, but rather the unintended outcome of the actions of many people, each of whom is pursuing the incentives the market offers with his or her own interests in mind. As he put it:

> It is not from the benevolence of the butcher, the brewer, or the baker that we expect our dinner, but from their regard to their own interest ... Every individual is continually exerting himself to find out the most advantageous employment for whatever capital he can command ... By directing that industry in such a manner as its produce may be of the greatest value, he intends only his own gain, and he is in this, as in many other cases, led by an invisible hand to promote an end which was no part of his intention.*

Much of the discipline of economics as it has developed over the past two centuries consists of elaborations on ideas found in Smith's work. The idea of the "invisible hand" of market incentives that channels people's efforts in directions that are beneficial to their neighbors remains the most durable of Smith's contributions to economics. (Refer to *The Worldly Philosophers* by Heilbroner, Chapter III.)

*Adam Smith, *The Wealth of Nations* (1776), Book 1, Chapter 2.

important example. Government decisions are made not through the spontaneous choices of individuals, but via directives issued by a central authority. Business firms, especially large corporations, are another important example of the hierarchical form of organization. The Toyota Motor Corporation uses directives from a central authority to make many important decisions, for example, the decision to build the new hybrid version of its popular Camry in Kentucky rather than in Japan.

Although governments and corporations use hierarchical methods to make choices within their organizations, they deal with one another and with individual consumers through markets. Markets and hierarchies thus play complementary roles in achieving economic coordination. Some economies rely more on markets, others on government or corporate planning. At one extreme, the centrally-planned economy of North Korea places heavy emphasis on government authority. Market economics, such as that of the United States, make greater use of markets. But no economy uses one means of coordination to the exclusion of the other. Government regulatory agencies in the United States establish laws to control pollution or protect worker safety; on the other hand, North Korea uses small-scale markets to distribute some goods. Large corporations use commands from higher authority to make many decisions, but they also often subcontract with outsiders through the market, and they sometimes encourage their own divisions to deal with one another on a market basis.

In short, wherever one turns in economics, the question of coordination arises. Understanding economic coordination means understanding the complementary roles of markets, on the one hand, and of government and corporate hierarchies, on the other.

ECONOMIC METHOD

The economic way of thinking is a very broad concept; economic method is a somewhat narrower idea having to do with the way economists go about their work. The chapter would be incomplete without a few comments about method.

Theories and Models

Theory

A representation of the way in which facts are related to one another.

Model

A synonym for theory; in economics, often applied to theories that are stated in graphical or mathematical form.

Economists are always trying to understand how the choices people make are related to the situations in which the choices are made.

Any representation of the way in which facts are related can be called a **theory** or a **model**. The terms are synonyms, although economists tend to use the term *theory* to refer to more general statements about economic relationships and the term *model* to refer to more particular statements, especially those that take the form of graphs or mathematical equations.

Economics needs theories and models because facts do not speak for themselves. Take, for example, the fact that in 2005, for the first time in more than a decade, people bought fewer large SUVs and more ordinary passenger cars. Why did they do that?

Economists have a theory. They relate the change in car-buying choices to the 50 percent rise in the retail price of gasoline over the preceding two years. The relationship between the price of gasoline and the choice of cars is seen as a particular instance of a broader theory according to which an increase in the price of any good, other things being equal, leads consumers to seek ways to reduce their consumption of the good.

The theory as stated is a simple one. It relates car choices to just one other fact, the price of gasoline. A more complete theory would bring in other factors that influence consumer choice, such as the prices of goods other than gasoline, consumers' incomes, changes in the social image of SUV owners, and so on. Where does one draw the line? How much detail does it take to make a good theory?

There is no simple answer to this question, because adding detail to a theory involves a trade-off. On the one hand, if essential details are left out, the theory may fail altogether to fit the facts. On the other hand, adding too much detail defeats the purpose of understanding because key relationships may become lost in a cloud of complexity. The only real guideline is that a theory should be just detailed enough to suit the purpose for which it is intended, and no more.

By analogy, consider the models that aircraft designers use. The wind-tunnel models made to test the aerodynamics of a new design need to represent the shapes of the wings, fuselage, and control surfaces accurately, but they do not need to include tiny seats with tiny tables and magazine racks. On the other hand, a full-scale model built for the purpose of training flight attendants to work on the new plane would need seats and magazine racks, but it would not need wings.

In much the same way, the theories and models presented in this book are designed to highlight a few key economic relationships. They are helpful in understanding economics in the same way that playing a flight simulation game on a computer is helpful in understanding the basics of flying. Professional economists use more detailed models, just as professional pilots train with complex flight simulators rather than with simple computer games. Nevertheless, the basic principles learned from the simple models do not contradict those that apply to the more complex ones. In the simple games, just as in the complex simulators, adjusting the rudder makes the plane turn and adjusting the elevators makes it climb or dive.

The Use of Graphs[3]

The theories introduced so far have been stated in words. Words are a powerful tool for developing understanding, but they are even more powerful when they are supplemented by pictures. Economists support their words with pictures called graphs. An example will illustrate how economists use graphs to represent theories.

THE PRODUCTION POSSIBILITY FRONTIER Recall our earlier discussion of the trade-off between education and cars. Figure 1.1 shows the trade-off in graphical form for an economy in which only those two goods are produced. The horizontal

FIGURE 1.1 **PRODUCTION POSSIBILITY FRONTIER**

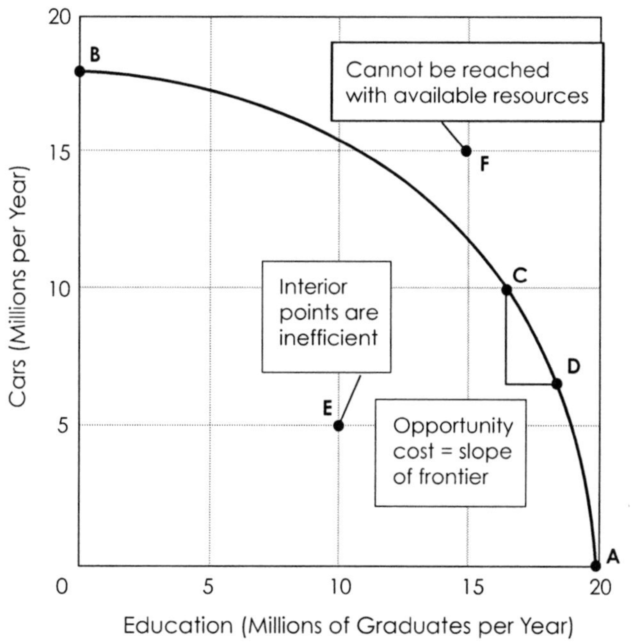

This figure shows combinations of cars and education that can be produced in a simple economy in which they are the only two products. Quantities of available factors of production and the state of existing knowledge are assumed to be fixed. If all factors are devoted to education, 20 million college graduates can be produced each year (point A). If all factors are devoted to making cars, 18 million cars can be produced each year (point B). Other combinations of the two goods that can be produced using available factors efficiently, such as those represented by points C and D, lie along a curve called a production possibility frontier. The slope of the frontier indicates the opportunity cost of education in terms of cars. Interior points, such as E, represent inefficient use of resources. Beginning from such a point, more of one good can be produced without producing less of the other. Points outside the frontier, such as F, cannot be reached using available factors of production and knowledge.

axis measures the quantity of education in terms of the number of college graduates produced per year; the vertical axis measures the production of cars. Any combination of education and cars can be shown as a point in the space between the two axes. For example, production of 10 million graduates and 5 million cars in a given year would be represented by point E.

Production possibility frontier

A graph that shows possible combinations of goods that can be produced by an economy given available knowledge and factors of production.

In drawing this graph, supplies of productive resources and the state of knowledge are assumed to remain constant. Even if all available resources are devoted to education, there is a limit to the number of graduates that can be produced in a year: 20 million. The extreme possibility of producing 20 million graduates and no cars is shown by point A. Likewise, the maximum number of cars that would be produced if no resources were put into education is 18 million cars, shown by point B. Between those two extremes is a whole range of possible combinations of education and cars. Those intermediate possibilities are shown by points such as C and D, which fall along a smooth curve. The curve is known as a **production possibility frontier**.

EFFICIENCY AND ECONOMIC GROWTH The production possibility frontier is a boundary between the combinations of education and cars that can be produced and those that cannot, using given knowledge and productive resources. As such, it serves nicely to illustrate the concept of efficiency in production. Points inside the frontier, such as point E, represent inefficient production. Beginning from such a point, more cars can be made without cutting the output of education (shown by a vertical move toward the frontier); more education can be produced without cutting the output of cars (a horizontal move toward the frontier); or the output of both goods can be increased (a move up and to the right toward the frontier).

Points such as A, B, C, and D that are on the frontier represent efficient production. Starting from any of those points, it is not possible to produce more of one good without producing less of the other. For example, in moving from C to D, output of education is increased but output of cars falls. Points such as F that lie outside the frontier cannot be reached even when the currently available knowledge and factors of production are used efficiently.

Over time, however, economic growth can stretch the production possibility frontier outward so that points such as F become possible. As mentioned earlier, the discovery of new ways of using available factors of production is one source of growth. So are additions to the total stock of factors of production—for example, through growth of the labor force. The case under discussion points to still yet another source of growth: Over time, the educational process itself improves the quality of the labor force, thus making a given number of people capable of producing more.

OPPORTUNITY COST AND COMPARATIVE ADVANTAGE The production possibility frontier can also be used to represent the concept of opportunity cost. As we have seen, once the economy is producing efficiently at a point on the frontier, choosing to make more of one good means making less of the other. For example, suppose we start at point C, where 16 million students graduate each year and 10 million cars are being made. If we want to increase the output of graduates to 18 million per year, we must give up some cars and use the labor, capital, and natural resources freed in this way to build and staff classrooms. In moving from point C to point D, we trade off production of 4 million cars for the extra 2 million graduates. Over that range of the frontier, the opportunity cost of each extra graduate is about two cars. The opportunity cost of graduates, measured in terms of cars, is shown by the slope of the frontier.

As more graduates are produced, and the economy moves down and to the right along the frontier, the frontier becomes steeper and the opportunity cost of producing graduates increases. A major reason is that not all factors of production—especially not all workers—are alike. Suppose we start all the way up at point B, where no education is produced, and transfer enough resources to education to open one small college. The first people we would pull off the assembly line to staff the classrooms would be those who have a comparative advantage in teaching. By the time enough resources have been transferred to education from the auto industry to reach point D, the most suitable recruits for academic life have already been used. Increasingly, to produce still more education we have to take some of the best production workers with no assurance that they will be good teachers. The opportunity cost of increasing the output of education (shown by the slope of the frontier) is correspondingly greater.

Theory and Evidence

Theories are of no use in explaining relationships among facts unless they fit those facts. Theory building is a matter of constantly comparing proposed explanations with evidence gleaned from observations of the actual choices people make—that is, with **empirical** evidence. When empirical evidence is consistent with the relationships proposed in a theory, confidence in the validity of the theory is increased. When evidence is not consistent with the theory, the theory needs to be reexamined. The relationships proposed in it may be invalid, or they may be valid only under circumstances different from those that prevailed when the observations were made. The theory then needs to be modified by changing the proposed relationships or adding detail.

Empirical
Based on experience or observation.

Government agencies and private firms generate mountains of empirical data on economic activity. Economists constantly examine those data in an effort to confirm theories or find inconsistencies that point the way to better theories. Statistical analysis of empirical economic data is known as **econometrics**—literally, the science of economic measurement.

Econometrics
The statistical analysis of empirical economic data.

Theories and Forecasts

Economic theories can help us understand things that happened in the past—trends in gasoline consumption since the 1970s, the effects of the information revolution of the 1990s, and so on. But understanding the past is not always enough. People also want forecasts of future economic events.

Within limits, economic theory can be useful here, too. Any theory that purports to explain a relationship between past events provides a basis for predicting what will happen under similar circumstances in the future. To put it more precisely, economic theory can be used to make **conditional forecasts** of the form "If A, then B, other things being equal." Thus, an economist might say, "If gasoline prices rise, and if at the same time consumer incomes and the prices of other goods do not change, purchases of low-mileage vehicles will fall."

Conditional forecast
A prediction of future economic events in the form "If A, then B, other things being equal."

Thousands of economists make a living from forecasting. Decision-makers in business and government use economic forecasts extensively. Forecasts are not perfect, however, and forecasters sometimes make conspicuous mistakes. There are at least three reasons for the mistakes.

First, insufficient attention is sometimes paid to the conditional nature of forecasts. The news might report, for example, that "economists predict a drop in SUV sales," yet people keep right on buying big vehicles. In such a case the news report may have failed to note the forecasters' precautionary comments. The forecasters may have said that SUV sales would drop in response to a gas price increase if consumer incomes and technology remained the same, but consumers got richer and new technology made SUVs less gas-hungry, so SUV sales did not fall after all.

Second, a forecast may be invalid because the theory on which it is based is incorrect or incomplete. Economists do not always agree on what theory best fits the facts. Some theories give more weight to one fact, others to different facts. The competing theories may imply conflicting forecasts under some conditions. At least one of the forecasts will then turn out to be wrong. Finding out which theories yield better forecasts than others is an important part of the process through which valid theories are distinguished from inadequate ones.

Third, economic forecasts can go wrong because some of the things that business managers and government officials most want to know are among the hardest to predict. For example, a competent economist could produce a fairly accurate forecast of vehicle sales, making certain assumptions about incomes and the prices of gasoline and other goods. However, what the marketing people at General Motors would like to know is what will happen to the social image of SUVs—will they continue to be a symbol of high status, or will they become an embarrassment in a more environmentally conscious society? Social attitudes are not among the variables that economists can forecast accurately.

Despite these limitations, most economists take the view that well-founded conditional forecasts, for all their limitations, are a better basis for business and public policy decisions than whims and guesswork. Still, they caution against relying too heavily on forecasts.

Theory and Policy

Economists are often asked to use their theories to analyze the effects of public policies and forecast the effects of policy changes. The government may, for example, be considering new measures to aid unemployed workers, new approaches to improving air quality, or new measures to regulate international trade. How will the effects of such policies be spread through the economy? How will they affect people's lives?

Economists have their own characteristic way of thinking about public policy, just as they have their own way of thinking about other topics. In particular, economists are concerned with identifying both the direct and indirect effects of policy, as well as any indirect or unintended consequences. They are also constantly alert to both the long-run and short-term effects of policy. For example:

- Unemployment compensation has the intended effect of aiding unemployed workers, but it also has the unintended effect of increasing the number of workers who are unemployed, because workers receiving compensation can afford to take their time finding just the right new job. Many observers see generous unemployment compensation in Germany and other European countries as one reason unemployment rates there are higher than in the United States.

- Regulations intended to improve the fuel efficiency of automobiles encourage production of cars that weigh less, but the lighter cars are somewhat less safe. Increased highway deaths among drivers of the lighter cars may thus be an unintended consequence of efforts to save fuel.
- After widespread banking failures in the 1980s, U.S. regulators made rule changes intended to strengthen the balance sheets of commercial banks. Those regulations also raised the cost of bank loans relative to loans from other sources outside the banking system. As an unintended consequence, banks lost their most credit-worthy customers to other lenders and ended up with balance sheets that held higher percentages of risky loans than before.

While policies may have unintended consequences, public policy still plays an important role in the economy. It would be wrong to conclude that the government should never act simply because its actions may do some harm as well as some good. Rather, economists simply urge that policy makers look at the whole picture, not just part of it, before they make a decision. As Henry Hazlitt once put it, the whole of economics can be reduced to a single lesson:

> *The art of economics consists in looking not merely at the immediate but at the longer effects of any act or policy; it consists in tracing the consequences of that policy not merely for one group but for all groups.*[4]

As you progress through your study of economics—both the macro and micro branches—you will encounter repeated examples of the way economic theory can help understand the choices people make and the complex effects of policies intended to regulate those choices.

SUMMARY

1. **What is the subject matter of economics?** Economics is a social science that seeks to understand the choices people make in using scarce resources to meet their wants. Scarcity is a situation in which there is not enough of something to meet everyone's wants. *Microeconomics* is the branch of economics that studies choices that involve individual households, firms, and markets. *Macroeconomics* is the branch of economics that deals with large-scale economic phenomena, such as inflation, unemployment, and economic growth.
2. **What considerations underlie the choice of what an economy will produce?** Producing more of one good requires producing less of something else because productive resources that are used to produce one good cannot be used to produce another at the same time. Productive resources are tradi-

tionally classified into three groups, called *factors of production*. *Labor* consists of the productive contributions made by people working with their hands and minds. *Capital* consists of all the productive inputs created by people. *Natural resources* include anything that can be used as a productive input in its natural state. The *opportunity cost* of a good or service is its cost in terms of the forgone opportunity to pursue the best possible alternative activity with the same time or resources.

3. **What considerations underlie the choice of how to produce?** Goods and services can be produced in many different ways, some of which are more efficient than others. *Economic efficiency* refers to a state of affairs in which it is impossible to make any change that satisfies one person's wants more fully without causing some other person's wants to be satisfied less fully. *Efficiency in production* refers to a situation in which it is not possible, given the available productive resources and existing knowledge, to produce more of one good or service without forgoing the opportunity to produce some of another good or service. Once efficiency has been achieved, production potential can be expanded by increasing the availability of resources or by improving knowledge. The process of increasing the economy's stock of capital is known as *investment*. The process of looking for new possibilities—making use of new ways of doing things, being alert to new opportunities, and overcoming old limits—is known as *entrepreneurship*.

4. **What considerations underlie the choice of who will do which work?** Although a person can survive apart from all human contact, economic efficiency is greatly enhanced by cooperation with others. Three things make cooperation worthwhile: teamwork, learning by doing, and comparative advantage. Teamwork can enhance productivity even when there is no specialization. Learning by doing improves productivity even when all workers start with equal talents and abilities. Comparative advantage comes into play when people have different innate abilities or, after learning by doing, have developed specialized skills. Having a *comparative advantage* in producing a particular good or service means being able to produce it at a relatively lower opportunity cost than someone else.

5. **What considerations underlie the choice of for whom goods will be produced?** In part, deciding for whom goods will be produced revolves around issues of efficiency. *Efficiency in distribution* refers to a state of affairs in which, with a given quantity of goods and services, it is impossible to satisfy one person's wants more fully without satisfying someone else's less fully. Efficiency is part of *positive economics*, the area of economics that is concerned with facts and the relationships among them. *Normative economics* is the area of economics that is devoted to judgments about which economic conditions and policies are good or bad.

6. **What mechanisms are used to coordinate economic choices?** The two principle methods of coordinating choices are *hierarchy* and *spontaneous order*. Markets are the most important example of spontaneous order. The internal decisions made by large corporations and units of government are the most important examples of hierarchy.

7. **How do economists use theory, graphs, and evidence in their work?** A *theory* or *model* is a representation of the ways in which facts are related to one another. Economists use graphs to display data and make visual representations of theories and models. For example, a *production possibility frontier* is a graph that shows the boundary between combinations of goods that can be produced and those that cannot, using available factors of production and knowledge. Economists refine theories in the light of *empirical* evidence, that is, evidence gleaned from observation of actual eco-

nomic decisions. The economic analysis of empirical evidence is known as *econometrics*. Economic models are often used to make *conditional forecasts* of the form "If A, then B, other things being equal."

KEY TERMS

Scarcity
Economics
Microeconomics
Price theory
Macroeconomics
Employment theory
Factors of production
Labor
Capital
Land
Opportunity cost
Economic efficiency
Efficiency in production
Investment
Entrepreneurship
Comparative advantage
Distribution
Efficiency in distribution
Positive economics
Normative economics
Spontaneous order
Hierarchy
Market (*The Market*)
Theory
Model
Production possibility frontier
Empirical
Econometrics
Conditional forecast

PROBLEMS AND TOPICS FOR DISCUSSION

1. **Opportunity cost.** Gasoline, insurance, depreciation, and repairs are all costs of owning a car. Which of these can be considered opportunity costs in the context of each of the following decisions?
   a. You own a car and are deciding whether to drive 100 miles for a weekend visit to a friend at another university.
   b. You do not own a car but are considering buying one so that you can get a part-time job located 5 miles from where you live.

   In general, why does the context in which you decide to do something affect the opportunity cost of doing it?

2. **Comparative advantage in international trade.** Suppose that in the United States a car can be produced with 200 labor hours, while a ton of rice requires 20 labor hours. In Japan, it takes 150 labor hours to make a car and 50 labor hours to grow a ton of rice. What is the opportunity cost of producing rice in each country, stated in terms of cars? What is the opportunity cost of cars, stated in terms of rice? Which country has a comparative advantage in cars? Which in rice?

3. **Efficiency in distribution and the food stamp program.** The federal food stamp program could have been designed so that every low-income family would receive a book of coupons containing so many bread coupons, so many milk coupons, and so on. Instead, it gives the family an allowance that can be spent on any kind of food the family prefers. For a given cost to the federal government, which plan do you think would better serve the goal of efficiency in distribution? Why?

   Now consider a program that would allow families to trade their food stamps for cash (some such trading does occur, but it is restricted by law) or one in which poor families are given cash, with which they can buy whatever they want. Compare these alternatives with the existing food stamp program in terms of both positive and normative economics.

4. **Spontaneous order in the cafeteria.** Suppose that your college cafeteria does not have enough room for all the students to sit down to eat at once, so it stays open for lunch from 11:30 A.M. to 1:30 P.M. Consider the following three methods of distributing diners over the two-hour lunch period in such a way that everyone can have a seat.
   a. The administration sets a rule: Freshmen must eat between 11:30 and 12:00, sophomores between 12:00 and 12:30, and so on for juniors and seniors.
   b. The lunch period is broken up into half-hour segments, with green tickets for the first shift,

blue tickets for the second, and so on. An equal number of tickets of each color is printed. At the beginning of each semester an auction is held in which students bid for the ticket color of their choice.

c. Students can come to the cafeteria whenever they want. If there are no empty seats, they have to stand in line.

Compare the three schemes in terms of the concepts of (i) spontaneous order and hierarchy; (ii) information and incentives; and (iii) efficiency.

5. **A production possibility frontier.** Bill Swartz has four fields spread out over a hillside. He can grow either wheat or potatoes in any of the fields, but the low fields are better for potatoes and the high ones are better for wheat. Here are some combinations of wheat and potatoes that he could produce:

Number of Fields Used for Potatoes	Total Tons of Potatoes	Total Tons of Wheat
All 4	1,000	0
Lowest 3	900	400
Lowest 2	600	700
Lowest 1	300	900
None	0	1,000

Use these data to draw a production possibility frontier for wheat and potatoes. What is the opportunity cost of wheat, stated in terms of potatoes, when the farmer converts the highest field to wheat production? What happens to the opportunity cost of wheat as more and more fields are switched to wheat?

CASE FOR DISCUSSION

Zimbabwe's Land Questions

HARARE, November 2003—President Mugabe continued seizure of primarily white-owned land in urban areas. The country's white farmers own much of the country's best agricultural land; according to government figures, 4,400 whites owned 32% of Zimbabwe's agricultural land, while about one million black peasant families farmed 38%. Furthermore, whites own a disproportionate share of the country's most fertile land. The situation was created in colonial times when blacks were forced off their ancestral lands. "The land question" was the source of discontent among the majority of Zimbabweans and a major cause of the guerrilla war that led to Zimbabwe's independence in 1980. When Mugabe came to power in 1980, he promised to balance the scales for black farmers through land reform.

Land reform and redistribution is expensive. Not only does the government need to compensate farmers giving up their property, but it also needs to provide infrastructure—such as roads, schools, and hospitals—for land redistribution to be beneficial. There is also the difficulty of taking large, sophisticated farms and then subdividing them into plots to give to people without the means to farm them effectively.

President Mugabe says Britain should pay because the British government colonized the region, seizing land from African farmers in the late 19th century. While the U.K. and others have provided some aid to help the government purchase land from "willing" white farmers, donors have refused further support unless President Mugabe's land program is more clearly defined.

The white farmers themselves do not see why they should have to pay because of what happened in the past. Many say they bought their farms at market rates since Zimbabwe's independence and reject arguments rooted in colonization. While Zimbabwe's government has paid some farmers, a new law requires farmers to leave their farms before receiving compensation.

Despite promises to target the seizure of the least-productive farms, many of those on the so-called "hit-list" have been the most efficient growers of tobacco. President Mugabe's opponents accuse him of exploiting the land question to win support amid Zimbabwe's current economic crisis.

The threat of land seizures has led to a steep decline in agricultural production on white-owned farms, exacerbating food shortages and unemployment in Zimbabwe. This coupled with two years of drought threaten a famine in which up to six million of Zimbabwe's citizens could go hungry. Aid agencies estimate over one-third of the population will be unable to feed themselves by the end of the year.

Consider the following hypothetical situations involving individuals and the government in Zimbabwe:

- Shekan currently owns 100 hectares of land that he uses for tobacco farming. On this land he has hired several hands to assist in harvesting and curing the tobacco leaves. He owns capital equipment to assist in curing the tobacco leaves. Shekan pays his workers 5 Zimbabwean dollars per pound of tobacco. Shekan then sells tobacco at the market price of 7 Zimbabwean dollars per pound.
- Amadika is a middle-aged woman who works on Shekan's farm. Using Shekan's curing equipment, she gathers and cures 50 pounds of tobacco each year.
- Tatenda is a young woman who was able to gather and cure 60 pounds of tobacco on Shekan's farm. She has decided to leave the farm and attend college in the United States. Tatenda has received a full scholarship and financing from the school to cover her expenses.
- Dakarai is a young man who currently works on Shekan's farm. He is able to gather and cure 75 pounds of tobacco each year using the available capital equipment. Instead of giving all 75 pounds to Shekan, he sells 25 pounds of tobacco illegally to a cigarette manufacturer for 6 Zimbabwean dollars per pound.

QUESTIONS

1. What might explain why Shekan pays his workers 5 Zimbabwean dollars per pound of cured tobacco while he sells it for 7 Zimbabwean dollars? What is Shekan's contribution to the tobacco production process?
2. Under President Mugabe's land management plan, Amadika is to receive 10 hectares of Shekan's property, but she receives none of the capital equipment she currently uses on Shekan's farm. When Amadika receives 10 hectares of land from Shekan's farm, will she be able to gather and cure the same amount of tobacco? Why or why not?
3. In terms of Zimbabwean dollars, what is Tatenda's opportunity cost of attending college? Why is there still a cost, even though Tatenda receives a scholarship? If she were to receive land under President Mugabe's plan, how might this affect her decision to attend school?
4. Assume that a gallon of milk costs 2 Zimbabwean dollars. What is the cost of a gallon of milk in terms of pounds of tobacco?
5. Suppose Zimbabwe's government decides that 2 dollars is too expensive for milk, and imposes a law that sets the price of milk at 1 Zimbabwean dollar per gallon. How will this affect the availability of milk in Zimbabwe?
6. Why might Dakarai sell some of his tobacco crop to Shekan at 5 Zimbabwean dollars per pound, when he can receive 6 dollars from an illegal trader?
7. President Mugabe recently denounced people, such as Dakarai, who engage in illegal trade. The government, and many Zimbabweans, see people like Dakarai as an exploiter who robs from Shekan. Discuss this issue in terms of fairness and efficiency.

END NOTES

1. Efficiency, defined this way, is sometimes called *Pareto efficiency* after the Italian economist Vilfredo Pareto.
2. Armen A. Alchian and Harold Demsetz, "Production, Information Cost, and Economic Organization," *American Economic Review* (December 1972): 777–795.
3. Some basic graphical concepts—axes, points and number pairs, slopes, and tangencies—are discussed in the appendix to this chapter.
4. Henry Hazlitt, *Economics in One Lesson* (New York: Arlington House, 1979), 17.

Appendix to Chapter 1: WORKING WITH GRAPHS

Graphs are an invaluable aid in learning economics precisely because they make use of these three special abilities of the human brain. Graphs are not used to make economics harder, but to make it easier. All it takes to use graphs effectively as a learning tool is the inborn human skill in working with pictures plus knowledge of a few simple rules for extracting the information that graphs contain. This appendix outlines those rules in brief. Additional details and exercises can be found in the *Study Guide* that accompanies this textbook.

Pairs of Numbers and Points

The first thing to master is how to use points on a graph to represent pairs of numbers. The table in Figure 1A.1 presents five pairs of numbers. The two columns are labeled "x" and "y." The first number in each pair is called the *x value* and the second the *y value*. Each pair of numbers is labeled with a capital letter. Pair A has an *x* value of 2 and a *y* value of 3; pair B has an *x* value of 4 and a *y* value of 4; and so on.

The diagram in Figure 1A.1 contains two lines that meet at the lower left-hand corner; they are called *coordinate axes*. The horizontal axis is marked off into units representing the *x* value and the vertical axis into unit representing the *y* value. In the space between the axes,

FIGURE 1A.1 NUMBER PAIRS AND POINTS

	x	y
A	2	3
B	4	4
C	6	5
D	8	6
E	10	7

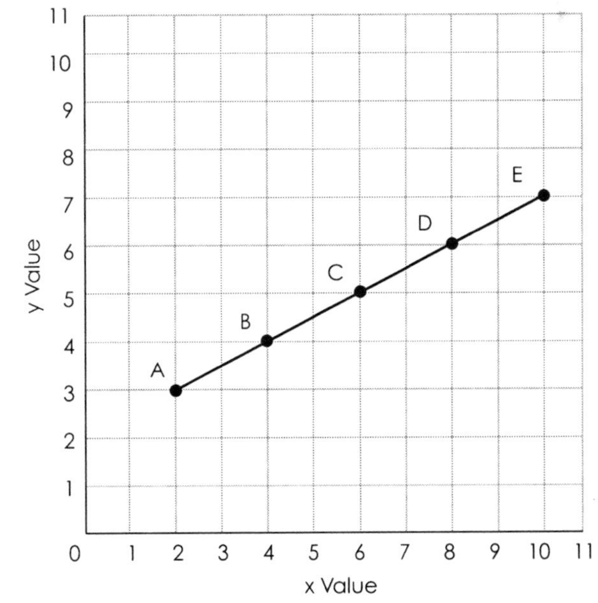

Each lettered pair of numbers in the table corresponds to a lettered point on the graph. The x value of each point corresponds to the horizontal distance of the point from the vertical axis; the y value corresponds to its vertical distance from the horizontal axis.

FIGURE 1A.2 SLOPES OF LINES

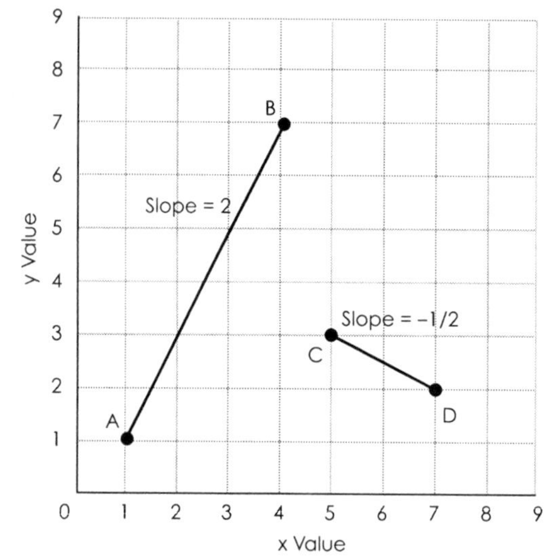

The slope of a straight line drawn between two points is defined as the ratio of the change in the y value to the change in the x value as one moves from one point to the other. For example, the line between points A and B in this Figure has a slope of +2, whereas the line between points C and D has a slope of −1/2.

each pair of numbers from the table can be shown as a point. For example, point A is found by going two units to the right along the horizontal axis and then three units straight up, parallel to the vertical axis. That point represents the *x* value of 2 and the *y* value of 3. The other points are located in the same way.

The visual effect of a graph usually can be improved by connecting the points with a line or a curve. By doing so, the relationship between *x* values and *y* values can be seen at a glance: as the *x* value increases, the *y* value also increases.

Slope

For a straight line, the ratio of the change in the y value to the change in the x value between any two points on the line.

Positive slope

A slope having a value greater than zero.

Direct relationship

A relationship between two variables in which an increase in the value of one variable is associated with an increase in the value of the other.

Slopes and Tangencies

The lines or curves used in graphs are described in terms of their slopes. The **slope** of a straight line between two points is defined as the ratio of the change in the *y* value to the change in the *x* value between the two points. In Figure 1A.2, for example, the slope of the line between points A and B is 2. The *y* value changes by six units between these two points, whereas the *x* value changes by only three units. The slope is the ratio 6/3 = 2.

The slope of a line between the points (x_1, y_1) and (x_2, y_2) can be expressed in terms of a simple formula that is derived from the definition just given:

$$\text{Slope} = (y_2 - y_1)/(x_2 - x_1)$$

Applied to the line between points A and B in Figure 1A.2, the formula gives the following result:

$$\text{Slope} = (7 - 1)/(4 - 1) = 6/3 = 2$$

A line such as that between A and B in Figure 1A.2 is said to have a **positive slope**, because the value of its slope is a positive number. A positively sloped line represents a **direct relationship** between the variable represented on the *x* axis and that represented on the *y* axis—that is, a relationship in which an increase in one variable is associated with an increase in the other. The relationship of the age of a tree to its height is an example of a direct relationship. An example from economics is the relationship between family income and expenditures on housing.

When a line slants downward, such as the one between points C and D in Figure 1A.2, the *x* and *y* values change in opposite directions. Going from point C to point D, the *y* value changes by –1 (that is, decreases by one unit) and the *x* value changes by +2 (that is, increases by two units). The slope of this line is the ratio –1/2.

Negative slope

A slope having a value less than zero.

When the slope of a line is given by a negative number, the line is said to have a **negative slope**. Such a line represents an **inverse relationship** between the *x* variable and the *y* variable—that is, a relationship in which an increase in the value of one variable is associated with a decrease in the value of the other variable. The relationship between the temperature in the room and the time it takes the ice in your lemonade to melt is an example of an inverse relationship. To give an economic example, the relationship between the price of gasoline and the quantity consumers purchase, other things being equal, is an inverse relationship.

Inverse relationship

A relationship between two variables in which an increase in the value of one variable is associated with a decrease in the value of the other.

The concepts of positive and negative slopes, and of direct and inverse relationships, apply to curves as well as to straight lines. However, the slope of a curve, unlike that of a straight line, varies from one point to the next.[1] We cannot speak of the slope of a curve in general, but only of its slope at a given point. The slope of a curve at any given point is defined as the slope of a straight line drawn tangent to the curve at that point. (A **tangent** line is one that just touches the curve without crossing it.) In Figure 1A.3, the slope of the curve at point A is 1 and the slope at point B is –2.

Tangent

A straight line that touches a curve at a given point without intersecting it.

[1]Economists try to be consistent, but in talking about lines and curves, they fail. They have no qualms about calling something a "curve" that is a straight line. For example, later we will encounter "demand curves" that are as straight as a stretched string. Less frequently, they may call something a line that is curved.

FIGURE 1A.3 SLOPES OF CURVES

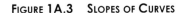

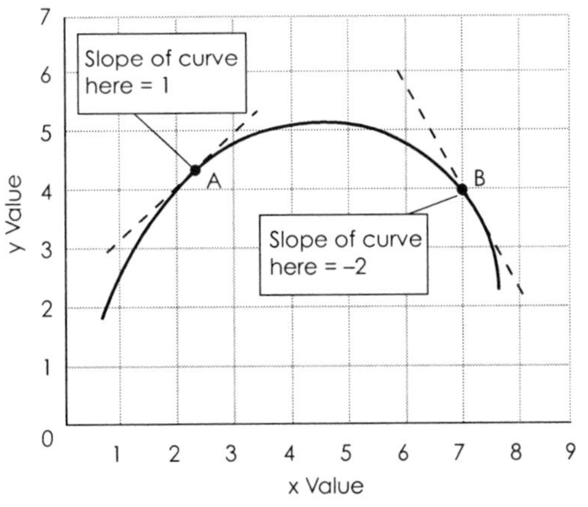

The slope of a curve at any point is defined as the slope of a straight line drawn tangent to the curve at that point. A tangent line is one that just touches the curve without crossing it. In this figure, the slope of the curve at point A is 1 and the slope at point B is –2.

Using Graphs to Display Data

Graphs are used in economics for two primary purposes: for visual display of quantitative data and for visual representation of economic relationships. Some graphs are primarily designed to serve one purpose, some the other, and some a little of both. We begin with some common kinds of graphs whose primary purpose is to display data.

Figure 1A.4 shows three kinds of graphs often used to display data. Part (a) is *pie chart*. Pie charts are used to show the relative size of various quantities that add up to a total of 100 percent. In this case, the quantities displayed are the percentages of U.S. foreign trade accounted for by various trading partners. In the original source, the graph was drawn as part of a discussion of U.S. trade with Canada, Japan, and Western Europe. The author wanted to make the point that trade with these countries is very important. Note how the graph highlights Canadian, Japanese, and Western European trade with the U.S., and at the same time omits details not relevant to the discussion by lumping together the rest of Europe, Africa, the rest of Asia, and many other countries under the heading "rest of the world." In reading graphs, do not just look at the numbers, but ask yourself, "What point is the graph trying to make?"

Part (b) of Figure 1A.4 is a *bar chart*. Bar charts, like pie charts, are used to display numerical data (in this case, unemployment rates) in relationship to some nonnumerical classification of cases (in this case, educational attainment). Bar charts are not subject to the restriction that data displayed must total 100 percent. What point do you think the author of this graph was trying to make?

Part (c) of Figure 1A.4 is an example of a data display graph very common in economics—the *time-series graph*. A time-series graph shows the values of one or more economic quantities on the vertical axis and time (years, months, or whatever) on the horizontal axis. This graph shows the ups and downs of the U.S. unemployment rate by month over the period 1980 through 1991.

Note one feature of this time-series graph: the scale on the vertical axis begins from 3 percent rather than from 0. By spreading out the data points in the range 3 to 11 percent, one can show the trend of unemployment in greater detail. The advantage of greater detail has an offsetting danger, however. Careless reading of the graph could cause one to exaggerate the amount by which unemployment rises during a recession. For example, the unemployment line is more than three times higher above the horizontal axis in 2003 than in 2000. However, careful reading of the graph shows that the unemployment rate in December 1991 was actually only about half again as high (6% vs. 4%) in 2003 as in 2000. The moral of the story: Always examine the vertical and horizontal axes of a graph carefully.

Using Graphs to Display Relationships

Some graphs, rather than simply recording observed facts, attempt to represent theories and models—that is, to show the relationships among facts. Figure 1A.5 shows two typical graphs whose primary purpose is to display relationships.

Part (a) of Figure 1A.5 is the production possibility frontier that we encountered in Chapter 1. The graph represents the inverse relationship between the quantity of cars that can be produced and the quantity of education that can be produced, given available knowledge and productive resources.

FIGURE 1A.4 USING GRAPHS TO DISPLAY DATA

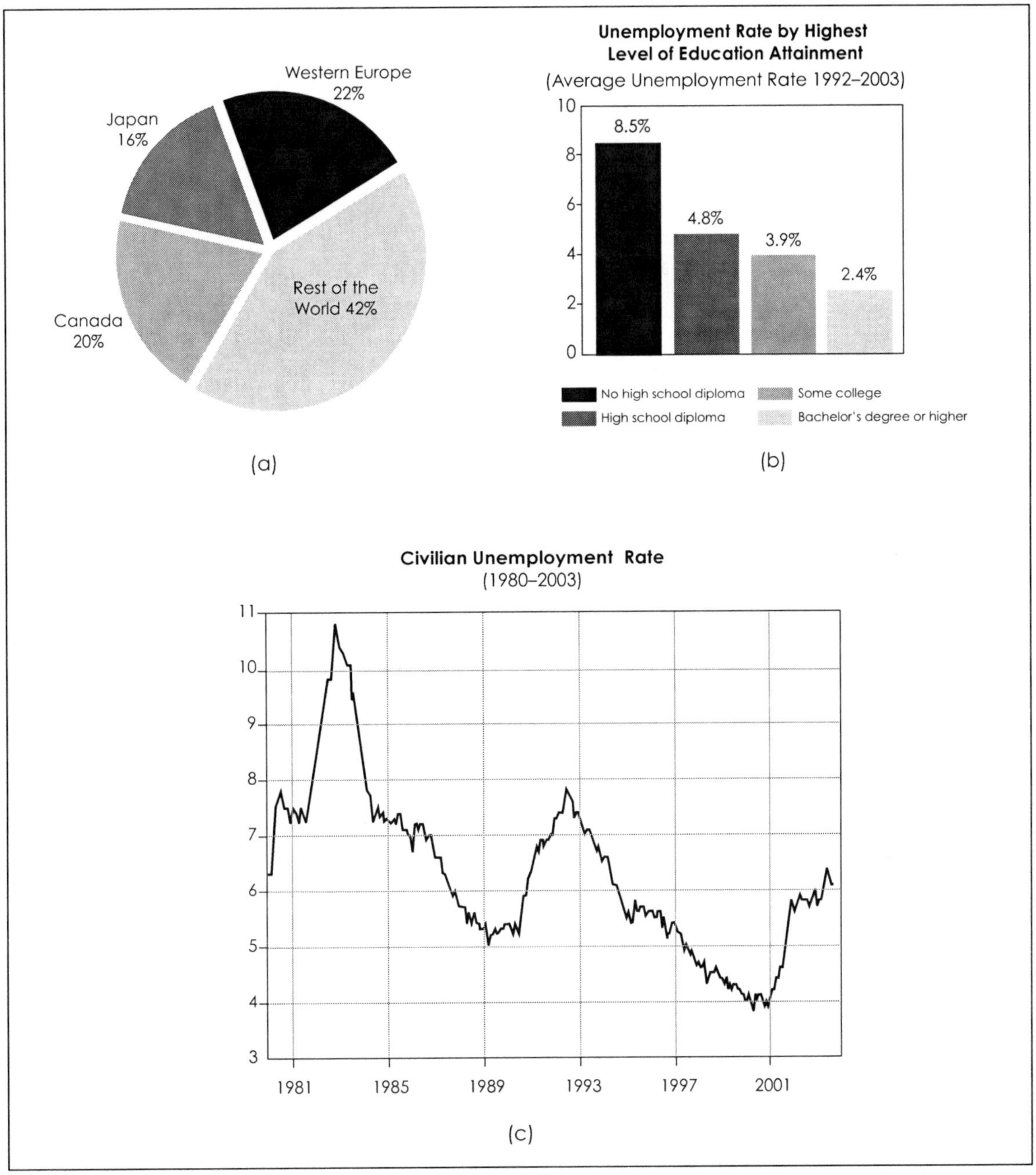

This figure shows three common kinds of data display graphs. The *pie chart* in part (a) is used when the data items sum to 100 percent. The *bar chart* in part (b), like the pie chart, is used when reporting numerical data that are associated with nonnumerical categories (in this case educational attainment). The bar chart does not require data items to sum to 100 percent. The *time-series graph* in part (c) shows the values of one or more economic quantities on the vertical axis and time on the horizontal axis.

Source: Part (a), U.S. Council of Economic Advisers, *Economic Report of the President* (Washington, D.C.: Government Printing Office, 2002), Table B-105, 397; part (b), Bureau of Labor Statistics, *Current Population Survey*; and part (c), Bureau of Labor Statistics, *The Employment Situation*.

FIGURE 1A.5 USING GRAPHS TO SHOW RELATIONSHIPS

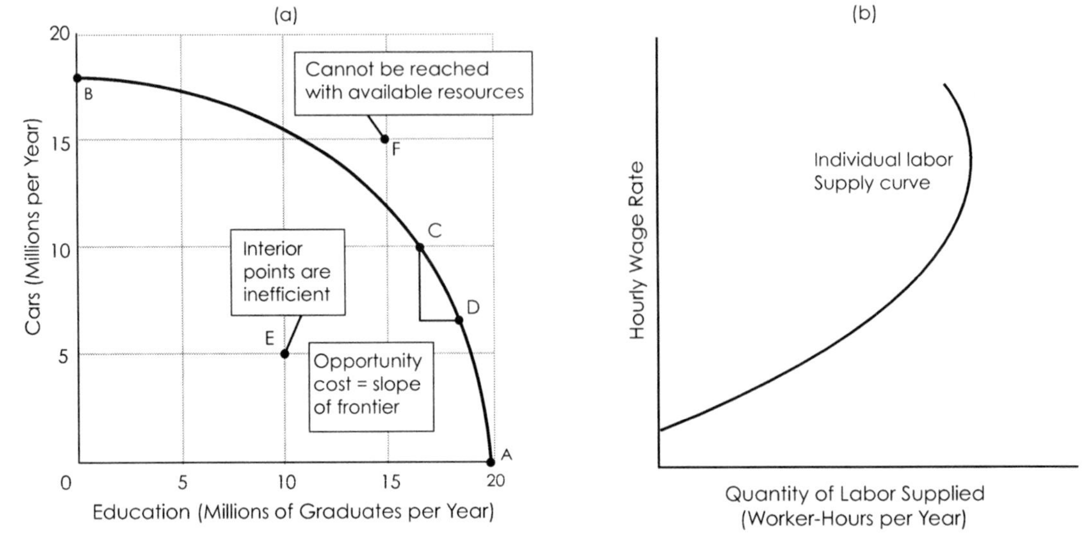

Relational graphs are visual representations of theories, that is, of relationships among facts. Two typical relational graphs are shown here. Part (a) is the production possibility frontier discussed in Chapter 1. It relates quantities of cars to quantities of education that can be produced with given factors of production and knowledge. Part (b) represents a theory of individual labor supply, according to which an increase in the hourly wage rate, after a point, will cause a person to reduce the quantity of labor supplied. Part (b) is an abstract graph in that it shows only the general nature of the relationship, with no numbers on either axis.

Part (b) of Figure 1A.5 represents a relationship between the quantity of labor that a person is willing to supply (measured in worker-hours per year) and the wage rate per hour the person is paid. According to the theory portrayed by the graph, raising the wage rate will, up to a point, induce a person to work more hours. But beyond a certain point (according to the theory), a further increase in the wage will actually cause the person to work fewer hours. Why? Because the person is so well off, he or she prefers the luxury of more leisure time to the reward of more material goods.

Note one distinctive feature of this graph: There are no numbers on the axes. It is an abstract graph that represents only the qualitative relationships between the hours of labor supplied per year and the wage rate. It makes no quantitative statements regarding how much the number of hours worked will change as a result of any given change in wage rate. Abstract graphs are often used when the point to be made is a general one that applies to many cases, regardless of quantitative differences from one case to another.

Packing Three Variables into Two Dimensions

Anything drawn on a flat piece of paper is limited to two dimensions. The relationships discussed so far fit a two-dimensional framework easily, because they involve just two variables. In the case of the production possibility frontier, the two are the quantity of education (horizontal axis) and the quantity of cars (vertical axis). In the case of the labor supply, they are hours worked per year (horizontal axis) and wage rate per hour (vertical axis). But reality does not always cooperate with geometry. Often one must take three or more variables into account in order to understand relationships among facts.

A number of methods have been devised to represent relationships involving three or more variables. For example, a map of the United States might use coordinates of latitude and longitude to indicate position, contour lines to indicate altitude, and shadings of various colors to indicate vegetation. An architect might use a perspective drawing to give the illusion of three dimensions—height, width, and depth—on a flat piece of paper. This section deals with one simple method of packing three variables into two dimensions. Although the method is a favorite of economists—it will be used in dozens of graphs in this book—we will show its generality by beginning with a noneconomic example.

A NONECONOMIC EXAMPLE The example concerns heart disease, the leading cause of death in the United States. In recent years, medical researchers have discovered that the risk of heart disease is closely linked to the quantity of cholesterol in a person's blood. Studies have indicated, for example, that a 25 percent reduction in cholesterol can cut the risk of death from heart attack by nearly 50 percent. Knowing this, millions of people have had their cholesterol levels tested, and if they were found to be high, have undertaken programs of diet, exercise, or drug therapy to reduce their risk of heart disease.

Important though cholesterol is, however, just knowing your cholesterol level is not enough to tell you your risk of dying of a heart attack in the coming year. Other variables also enter into the risk of heart disease. One of the most important of these variables is age. For example, for men aged 20 with average cholesterol levels, the mortality rate from heart disease is only about 3 per 100,000. For men aged 60, the mortality rate rises to over 500 per 100,000, still assuming average cholesterol. We thus have three variables to deal with: mortality, cholesterol, and age. How can we represent these three variables using only two-dimensional graphs?

A possible approach would be to draw two separate graphs. One would show the relationship between age and heart disease for the male population as a whole, without regard to differences in cholesterol counts. The other would show the relationship between cholesterol and heart disease for the male population as a whole, without regard to age. By looking from one diagram to the other, we could get an idea of the three-variable relationship as a whole.

However, such a side-by-side pair of graphs would be clumsy. There must be a better way to represent the three variables in two dimensions. The better way, shown in Figure 1A.6, is to use cholesterol and mortality as the *x* and *y* axes, and to take age into account by plotting separate lines for men of various ages. That chart is far easier to interpret than the side-by-side pair would be. If you are a man and know your age and cholesterol count, you just pick out the appropriate line and read off your risk of mortality. If you do not like what you see, you go on a diet.[2]

The multi-curve graph is a lovely invention. One of the great things about it is that it works for more than three variables. For example, we could add a fourth variable, gender, to the graph by drawing a new set of lines in a different color to show mortality rates for women

[2]We could instead have started with the age-mortality chart and drawn separate lines for men with different cholesterol levels. Such a chart would show exactly the same information. We could even draw a chart with cholesterol and age on the axes, and separate contour lines to represent various levels of mortality. The choice often depends on what one wants to emphasize. Here, we emphasize the cholesterol-mortality relationship because cholesterol is something you can do something about. You cannot do anything about your age, so we give age slightly less emphasis by not placing it on one of the two axes.

FIGURE 1A.6 THREE VARIABLES IN TWO DIMENSIONS

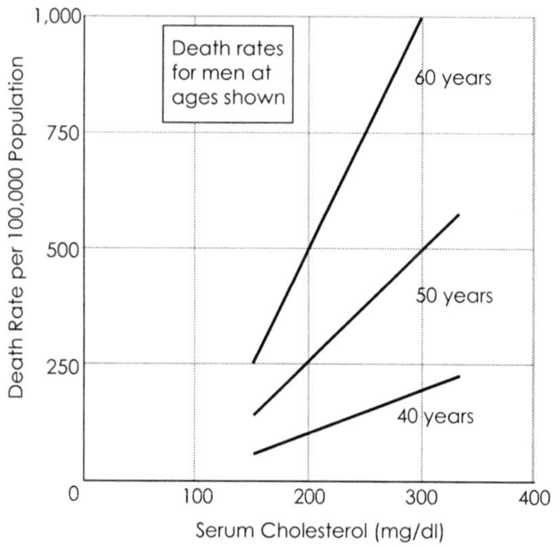

This graph shows a common way of representing a three-variable relationship on a two-dimensional graph. The three variables in this case are serum cholesterol (a measure of the amount of cholesterol in the blood), age, and death rate from heart disease for the U.S. male population. The relationship among the three variables is most easily interpreted, if all three variables are included in one graph, by drawing separate cholesterol-death rate lines for each age group. As a man ages, his cholesterol-death rate line shifts upward.

of various ages. Each line for women would have a positive slope similar to the men's lines, but would lie somewhat below the corresponding line for men of the same age, because women, other things being equal, experience lower mortality from heart disease.

SHIFTS IN CURVES AND MOVEMENTS ALONG CURVES Economists use three-variable, multi-curve graphs often enough that it is worth giving some attention to the terminology used in discussing them. How can we best describe what happens to a man as he ages, given the relationship shown in Figure 1A.6?

One way to describe the effects of aging would be to say, "As a man ages, he moves from one curve to the next higher one on the chart." There is nothing at all wrong with saying that, but an economist would tend to phrase it a bit differently, saying "As a man ages, his cholesterol-mortality curve shifts upward." The two ways of expressing the effects of aging have exactly the same meaning. Preferring one or the other is just a matter of habit.

If we express the effects of aging in terms of a shift of the cholesterol-mortality curve, how should we express the effects of a reduction in cholesterol for a man of a given age? An economist would say it this way: "Cutting a man's cholesterol count through diet or exercise will move him down along his cholesterol-mortality curve."

Before you finish this book, you will see the phrases "shift in a curve" and "movement along a curve" a great many times. How can you keep them straight? Nothing could be easier.

- If you are talking about the effect of a change in a variable that is shown on one of the coordinate axes of the diagram, the effect will be shown as a movement along one of the curves.

- If you are talking about the effect of a change in a variable that is not shown on one of the coordinate axes of the diagram, the effect will be shown by a shift in one of the curves.

Study Hints

So much for the basic rules of graphics. Once you master them, how should you study a chapter that is full of graphs?

The first—and most important—rule is to avoid trying to memorize graphs as patterns of lines. In every economics course, at least one student comes to the instructor after failing an exam and exclaims, "But I learned every one of those graphs! What happened?" The reply is that the student should have learned economics instead of memorizing graphs. Following are some hints for working with graphs.

After reading through a chapter that contains several graphs, go back through the graphs one at a time. Cover the caption accompanying each graph, and try to express the graph's "picture" in words. If you cannot say as much about the graph as the caption does, reread the text. Once you can translate the graph into words, you have won half the battle.

Next, cover each graph and use the caption as a guide. Try to sketch the graph on a piece of scratch paper. How are the graph's axes labeled? How are the curves labeled? What are the slopes of various curves? Are there important points of intersection or tangencies? If you can go back and forth between the caption and the graph, you will find that the two together are much easier to remember than either one separately.

Finally, try going beyond the graph that is shown in the book. If the graph illustrates the effect of an increase in the price of butter, try sketching a similar diagram that shows the effect of a decrease in the price of butter. If the graph shows what happens to the economy during a period of rising unemployment, try drawing a similar graph that shows what happens during a period of falling unemployment. This is a good practice that may give you an edge on your next exam.

MAKING YOUR OWN GRAPHS For some students, the hardest test questions to answer are ones that require original graphs as part of an essay. Suppose the question is, "How does a change in the number of students attending a university affect the cost per student of providing an education?" Here are some hints for making your own graph.

1. Write down the answer to the question in words. If you cannot, you might as well skip to the next question. Underline the most important quantities in your answer, such as "The larger the *number of students* who attend a college, the lower the *cost per student* of providing them with an education, because fixed facilities, such as libraries, do not have to be duplicated."

2. Decide how you want to label the axes. In our example, the vertical axis could be labeled "cost per student" and the horizontal axis "number of students."

3. Do you have specific numbers to work with? If so, the next step is to construct a table showing what you know and use it to sketch your graph. If you have no numbers, you must draw an abstract graph. In this case, all you know is that the cost per student goes down when the number of students goes up. Your graph would thus be a negatively sloped line.

4. If your graph involves more than one relationship between quantities, repeat steps 1 through 3 for each relationship you wish to show. When constructing a graph with more than one curve, pay special attention to points at which you think the curves should intersect.

(Intersections occur whenever both the x and y values of the two relationships are equal.) Also note the points at which you think two curves ought to be tangent (which requires that their slopes be equal), the points of maximum or minimum value, if any, and so on.

5. When your graph is finished, try to translate it back into words. Does it really say what you want it to?

A REMINDER As you read this book and encounter various kinds of graphs, turn back to this appendix now and then. Do not memorize graphs as meaningless pictures; if you do, you will get lost. If you can alternate between graphs and words, the underlying point will be clearer than if you rely on either one alone. Keep in mind that the primary focus of economics is not graphs; it is people and the ways in which they deal with the challenge of scarcity.

CHAPTER 2

Supply and Demand: The Basics

After reading this chapter, you will understand:	1. How the price of a good or service affects the quantity demanded by buyers 2. How other market conditions affect demand 3. How the price of a good affects the quantity supplied by sellers 4. How other market conditions affect supply 5. How supply and demand interact to determine the market price of a good or service 6. Why market prices and quantities change in response to changes in market conditions 7. How price supports and price ceilings affect the operations of markets
Before reading this chapter, make sure you know the meaning of:	1. Spontaneous order 2. Markets 3. Opportunity cost 4. Law of unintended consequences

WE BEGAN THE preceding chapter with an example of the way rising gasoline prices affected sales of gas-guzzling SUVs in 2005. Automobiles are just one category among millions of goods and services for which prices, quantities sold, and other market conditions vary from day to day and from year to year. Whether they are goods that we ourselves buy and sell, or goods that our employers, neighbors, or family members buy and sell, the changing market conditions affect our lives in many ways. The factors determining market prices and quantities are thus a good starting point for any discussion of economics.

Supply

The willingness and ability of sellers to provide goods for sale in a market.

Demand

The willingness and ability of buyers to purchase goods.

Law of demand

The principle that an inverse relationship exists between the price of a good and the quantity of that good that buyers demand, other things being equal.

This chapter outlines a model of price determination in a market economy, the supply-and-demand model. Economists use the term **supply** to refer to sellers' willingness and ability to provide goods for sale in a market. **Demand** refers to buyers' willingness and ability to purchase goods.

DEMAND

The **law of demand**, one of the foundation stones of economics, can be stated formally as follows: In any market, other things being equal, an inverse relationship exists between the price of a good and the quantity of the good that buyers demand—that is, the amount they are willing and able to buy. Thus, the quantity demanded tends to rise as the price falls and to fall as the price rises.

We expect this to happen for two reasons. First, if the price of one good falls while the prices of other goods stay the same, people are likely to substitute the cheaper good. Second, when the price of one good falls while incomes and other prices stay the same, people feel a little richer. They use their added buying power to buy a bit more of many things, including, in most cases, a little more of the good whose price went down.

The terms *demand* and *quantity demanded,* as used in economics, are not the same as *want* or *need.* For example, I think a Porsche is a beautiful car. Sometimes when I see one on the street, I think, "Hey, I want one of those!" Alas, my income is limited. Although in the abstract I might want a Porsche, there are other things I want more. Thus, the quantity of Porsches I demand at the going price is zero.

On the other hand, I might *need* dental surgery to avoid losing my teeth. But suppose I am poor. If I cannot pay for the surgery or find someone to pay for it on my behalf, I am out of luck. The quantity of dental surgery I demand, therefore, would be zero, however great my need for that service. Demand, then, combines both willingness and ability to buy. It is not desire in the abstract, but desire backed by the actual intent to buy.

The Demand Curve

The law of demand states a relationship between the quantity of a good that people are willing and able to buy, other things being equal, and the price of that good. Figure 2.1 represents this one-to-one relationship for a familiar consumer good, chicken. It would be possible to discuss the demand for chicken of a single consumer, but more frequently, as in the following discussion, we focus on the total demand for the good by all buyers in the market.

The figure shows the demand relationship in two different ways. First look at part (a). The first row of the table shows that when the price of chicken is \$3.00 a pound, the quantity demanded per year is 1 billion pounds. Reading down the table, we see

FIGURE 2.1 A DEMAND CURVE FOR CHICKEN

(a)

	Price of Chicken (Dollars per Pound)	Quantity of Chicken Demanded (Billions of Pounds per Year)
	$3.50	0.5
	$3.00	1
	$2.50	1.5
A	$2.00	2
	$1.50	2.5
B	$1.00	3
	$0.50	3.5

(b)

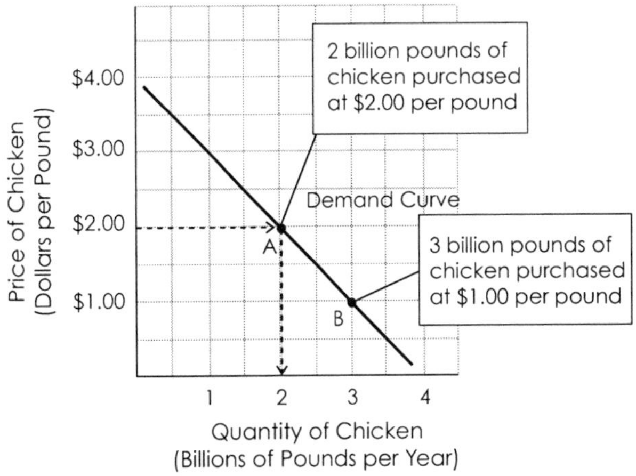

Both the table and the chart show the quantity of chicken demanded at various prices. For example, at a price of $2.00 per pound, buyers are willing and able to purchase 2 billion pounds of chicken per year. This price-quantity combination is shown by row A in part (a) and point A in part (b).

Demand curve

A graphical representation of the relationship between the price of a good and the quantity of that good that buyers demand.

Change in quantity demanded

A change in the quantity of a good that buyers are willing and able to purchase that results from a change in the good's price, other things being equal; shown by a movement from one point to another along a demand curve.

that as the price falls, the quantity demanded rises. At $2.50 per pound, buyers are willing and able to purchase 1.5 billion pounds per year; at $1.50, 2.5 billion pounds; and so on.

Part (b) of Figure 2.1 presents the same information in graphical form. The graph is called a **demand curve** for chicken. Suppose we want to use the demand curve to find out what quantity of chicken will be demanded at a price of $2.00 per pound. Starting at $2.00 on the vertical axis, we move across, as shown by the arrow, until we reach the demand curve at point A. Continuing to follow the arrow, we drop down to the horizontal axis. Reading from the scale on that axis, we see that the quantity demanded at a price of $2.00 per pound is 2 billion pounds per year. That is the quantity demanded in row A of the table in part (a).

The effect of a change in the price of chicken, other things being equal, can be shown as a movement from one point to another along the demand curve for chicken. Suppose that the price drops from $2.00 to $1.00 per pound. In the process, the quantity that buyers plan to buy rises. The point corresponding to the quantity demanded at the new, lower price is point B (which corresponds to row B of the table). Because of the inverse relationship between price and quantity demanded, the demand curve has a negative slope. (One variable increases causing the other variable to decrease.)

Economists speak of a movement along a demand curve as a **change in quantity demanded**. Such a movement represents buyers' reaction to a change in the price of the good in question, other things being equal.

Shifts in the Demand Curve[1]

The demand curve in Figure 2.1 represents a relationship between two variables: the price of chicken and the quantity of chicken demanded. But changes in other variables can also affect people's purchases of chicken. In the case of chicken, the prices of beef and pork would affect demand. Consumer incomes are a second variable that can affect demand. Changes in expectations about the future are a third, and changes in consumer tastes, such as an increasing preference for foods with a low carbohydrate content, are a fourth. The list could go on and on—the demand for ice is affected by the weather; the demand for diapers is affected by the birthrate; the demand for baseball tickets is affected by the won-lost record of the home team; and so on.

How are all these other variables handled when drawing a demand curve? In brief, two rules apply:

1. When drawing a single demand curve for a good, such as the one in Figure 2.1, all other conditions that affect demand are considered to be fixed or constant under the "other things being equal" clause of the law of demand. As long as that clause is in force, the only two variables at work are quantity demanded (on the horizontal axis) and price (on the vertical axis). The effect of a change in price on quantity demanded thus is shown by a *movement along* the demand curve.

2. When we look beyond the "other things being equal" clause and find that there is a change in a variable that is not represented on one of the axes, such as the price of another good or the level of consumer income, the effect is shown as a *shift* in the demand curve. In its new position, the demand curve still represents a two-variable price-quantity relationship, but it is a slightly different relationship than before because one of the "other things" has changed.

These two rules for graphical representation of demand relationships are crucial to understanding the theory of supply and demand as a whole. It will be worthwhile to expand on them through a series of examples.

CHANGES IN THE PRICE OF ANOTHER GOOD We have already noted that the demand for chicken depends on what happens to the price of beef, as well as what happens to the price of chicken. Figure 2.2, which shows demand curves for both goods, provides a closer look at this relationship.

Suppose that the price of beef is initially \$3.00 per pound and then increases to \$4.50 per pound. The effect of this change on the quantity of beef demanded is shown in part (a) of Figure 2.2 as a movement along the beef demand curve from point A to point B. Part (b) of the figure shows the effect on the demand for chicken. With the price of beef higher than before, consumers will tend to buy more chicken *even if the price of chicken does not change*. Suppose the price of chicken is \$2.00 per pound. When beef was selling at \$3.00 a pound, consumers bought 2 billion pounds of

FIGURE 2.2 EFFECTS OF AN INCREASE IN THE PRICE OF BEEF ON THE DEMAND FOR CHICKEN

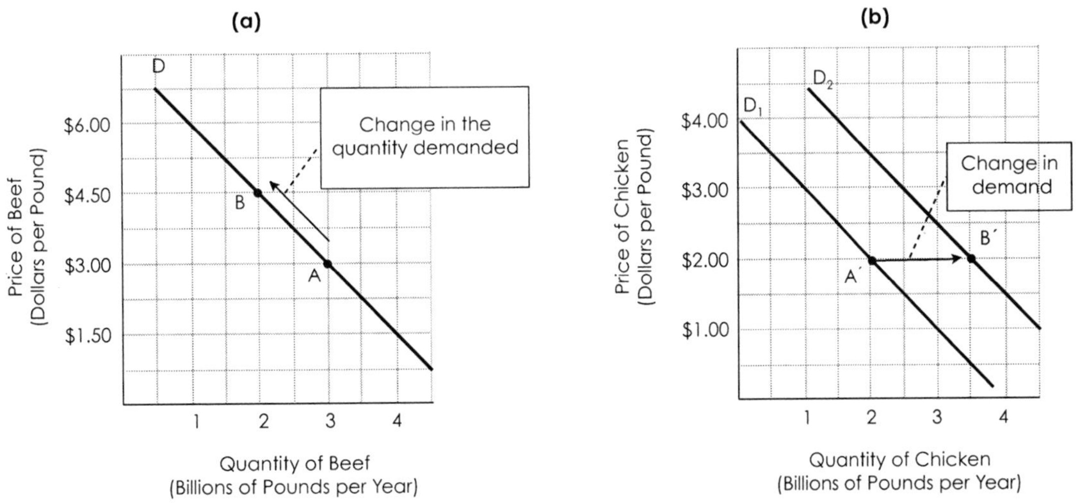

An increase in the price of beef from $3.00 to $4.50 per pound, other things being equal, causes a movement from point A to point B on the beef demand curve—a decrease in the quantity of beef demanded. With the price of chicken unchanged at $2.00 per pound, consumers will substitute chicken for beef. That will cause an increase in the demand for chicken, which is shown as a shift in the chicken demand curve from D_1 to D_2.

chicken a year (point A´ on demand curve D_1). After the price of beef goes up to $4.50 a pound, they will buy 3.5 billion pounds of chicken a year, assuming that the price of chicken does not change (point B´ on demand curve D_2).

A rise in the price of beef would cause consumers to buy more chicken regardless of the initial price of chicken. If the price of chicken had started out at $3.00 a pound and remained there while the price of beef went up, consumers would have increased their chicken consumption from 1 billion pounds a year to 2.5 billion pounds a year. At a price of $1.00 a pound for chicken, the quantity would have risen from 3 billion pounds to 4.5 billion pounds, and so on. We see, then, that a change in the price of beef causes the entire demand curve for chicken to shift. The "other things being equal" clause of the new demand curve, D_2, incorporates a price of $4.50 a pound for beef, rather than the price of $3.00 a pound assumed in demand curve D_1.

Change in demand

A change in the quantity of a good that buyers are willing and able to purchase that results from a change in some condition other than the price of that good; shown by a shift in the demand curve.

Earlier we explained that economists refer to a movement along a demand curve as a "change in quantity demanded." The corresponding term for a shift in a demand curve is a **change in demand**. A change in quantity demanded (a movement along the curve) is caused by a change in the price of the good in question (the variable on the vertical axis). In contrast, a change in demand (a shift in the demand curve) is caused by a change in some variable other than the price of the good in question (one that does not appear on either axis).

In the example in Figure 2.2, people bought more chicken when the price of beef went up, replacing one meat with the other in their dinners. Economists call such

Substitute goods

A pair of goods for which an increase in the price of one causes an increase in demand for the other.

Complementary goods

A pair of goods for which an increase in the price of one results in a decrease in demand for the other.

pairs of goods **substitutes**, because an increase in the price of one causes an increase in the demand for the other—a rightward shift in the demand curve.

Consumers react differently to price changes when two goods tend to be used together. One example is cars and gasoline. When the price of gasoline goes up, people's selection of cars will be affected. In particular, they will buy fewer low-mileage, large SUVs even if there is no change in the price of those vehicles. An increase in the price of gasoline thus causes a movement upward along the gasoline demand curve and a *leftward* shift in the demand curve for SUVs. Pairs of goods that are related in this way are known as **complements**.

Whether a given pair of goods are substitutes or complements depends on buyers' attitudes toward those goods; these terms do not refer to properties of the goods themselves. Some people might regard cheese and beef as substitute sources of protein in their diets; others, who like cheeseburgers, might regard them as complements.

One more point regarding the effects of changes in the prices of other goods is also worth noting: In stating the law of demand, it is the price of a good *relative to those of other goods* that counts. During periods of inflation, when the average level of all prices rises, distinguishing between changes in *relative prices* and changes in *nominal prices*—the number of dollars actually paid per unit of a good—is especially important. When the economy experiences inflation, a good can become relatively less expensive even though its nominal price rises, provided that the prices of other goods rise even faster.

Consider chicken, for example. Between 1950 and 2005 the average retail price of a broiler rose by almost 40 percent, from $.59 per pound to $1.05 per pound. Over the same period, however, the average price of all goods and services that consumers bought rose by about 600 percent. The relative price of chicken thus fell during the period even though its nominal price rose. The drop in the relative price of chicken had a lot to do with its growing popularity on the dinner table.

CHANGES IN CONSUMER INCOMES The demand for a good can also be affected by changes in consumer incomes. When their incomes rise, people tend to buy larger quantities of many goods, assuming that the prices of those goods do not change.

Figure 2.3 shows the effect of an increase in consumer incomes on the demand for chicken. Demand curve D_1 is the same as the curve shown in Figure 2.1. Suppose now that consumer incomes rise. With higher incomes, people become choosier about what they eat. They do not just want calories, they want high-quality calories from foods that are tasty, fashionable, and healthful. These considerations have made chicken increasingly popular as consumer incomes have risen.

More specifically, suppose that after their incomes rise, consumers are willing to buy 2.5 billion pounds of chicken instead of 1 billion pounds at a price of $3.00 per pound. The change is shown as an arrow drawn from point A to point B in Figure 2.3. If the initial price of chicken had been $2.00 per pound, even more chicken would be bought at the new, higher level of income. At the original income level and a price of

FIGURE 2.3 EFFECTS OF AN INCREASE IN CONSUMER INCOME ON THE DEMAND FOR CHICKEN

Demand curve D_1 assumes a given level of consumer income. If their incomes increase, consumers will want to buy more chicken at any given price, other things being equal. That will shift the demand curve rightward to, say, D_2. If the prevailing market price at the time of the demand shift is $3.00 per pound, the quantity demanded increases to 2.5 billion pounds (B) from 1 billion (A); if the prevailing price is $2.00 per pound, the quantity demanded will increase to 2 billion pounds (D) from 3.5 billion (C); and so on.

$2.00, the amount purchased would be 2 billion pounds, as shown by point C. After the increase in incomes, buyers would plan to purchase 3.5 billion pounds, shown by the arrow from point C to point D.

Whatever the initial price of chicken, the effect of an increase in consumer incomes is shown by a shift to a point on the new demand curve, D_2. The increase in demand for chicken that results from the rise in consumer incomes thus is shown as a shift in the entire demand curve. If consumer incomes remain at the new, higher level, the effects of any changes in the price of chicken will be shown as movements along the new demand curve. There is, in other words, a chicken demand curve for every possible income level. Each represents a one-to-one relationship between price and quantity demanded, given the assumed income level.

In the example just given, we assumed that an increase in income would cause an increase in the demand for chicken. Experience shows that this is what normally happens. Economists therefore call chicken a **normal good**, meaning that when consumer incomes rise, other things being equal, people will buy more of it.

Normal good

A good for which an increase in consumer incomes results in an increase in demand.

There are some goods, however, that people will buy less of when their incomes rise, other things being equal. For example, among your classmates, those with higher incomes are likely to go out for pizza more often than those with lower incomes. On nights when they eat pizza, they do not eat in the cafeteria, so the demand for cafeteria food falls as income rises. Similarly, when their incomes rise, people tend to buy less flour for baking at home and to buy more baked goods instead. People tend to buy fewer shoe repair services when their incomes rise; instead, they buy new shoes. Goods such as cafeteria food, flour, and shoe repair services are termed **inferior goods**. When consumer incomes rise, the demand curve for an inferior good shifts to the left instead of to the right. As in the case of substitutes and complements, the notions of inferiority and normality arise from consumer choices; they are not inherent properties of the goods themselves.

Inferior good

A good for which an increase in consumer incomes results in a decrease in demand.

CHANGES IN EXPECTATIONS Changes in buyers' expectations are a third factor that can shift demand curves. If people expect the price of a particular good to rise relative to the prices of other goods, or expect something other than a price increase to raise the opportunity cost of acquiring the good, they will step up their rate of purchase before the change takes place.

For example, suppose that in May, consumers rush to buy airline tickets in response to a series of news reports indicating that prices will be raised for tickets ordered after June 1. The people who buy their tickets in May will probably include many who were planning to travel late in the summer and ordinarily would have waited several more weeks before making their purchase. Thus, many more tickets will be sold in May than would have been sold at the same price if consumers had not anticipated the June price rise. We can interpret the surge in ticket sales in May as a temporary rightward shift in the demand curve.

CHANGES IN TASTES Changes in tastes are a fourth source of changes in demand. Sometimes these changes occur rapidly, as can be seen, for example, in such areas as popular music, clothing styles, and fast foods. The demand curves for these goods and services shift often. In other cases, changes in tastes take longer to occur but are more permanent. For example, in recent years consumers have been more health conscious than they were in the past. The result has been reduced demand for cigarettes and foods with high content of refined carbohydrates, along with increased demand for fish, whole grain foods, and exercise equipment.

CHANGES IN THE NUMBER OF BUYERS IN A MARKET (POPULATION). As the population increases, the demand in general and the demand for specific products will increase. As more and more people move to Carroll County, demand increases. Though population is increasing, in some areas there is an outward migration. Places such as Iowa and South Dakota along with major metropolitan areas have experienced population decreases as people seek out opportunities and better quality of life in other regions of the country. (Baltimore was once the third largest city in the U.S., but as the attractiveness of city living has declined, the population of Baltimore had declined as the suburban counties have seen increased population. These declines in population will cause demand in general to decline.

SUPPLY

The Supply Curve

We now turn from the demand side of the market to the supply side. As in the case of demand, we begin by constructing a one-to-one relationship between the price of a good and the quantity that sellers intend to offer for sale. Figure 2.4 shows such a relationship for chicken.

Supply curve

A graphical representation of the relationship between the price of a good and the quantity of that good that sellers are willing to supply.

The positively sloped curve in Figure 2.4 is called a **supply curve** for chicken. Like demand curves, supply curves are based on an "other things being equal" condition. The supply curve for chicken shows how sellers change their plans in response to a change in the price of chicken, assuming that there are no changes in other conditions—the prices of other goods, production techniques, input prices, expectations, or any other relevant condition.

Why does the supply curve have a positive slope? Why do sellers, other things being equal, plan to supply more chicken when the prevailing market price is higher than they plan to supply when the price is lower? Without going too deeply into a discussion of microeconomic theory, we can consider some common-sense explanations here.

FIGURE 2.4 A SUPPLY CURVE FOR CHICKEN

(a)

	Price of Chicken (Dollars per Pound)	Quantity of Chicken Demanded (Billions of Pounds per Year)
	$4.00	4
	$3.50	3.5
A	$3.00	3
	$2.50	2.5
B	$2.00	2
	$1.50	1.5
	$1.00	1

(b)

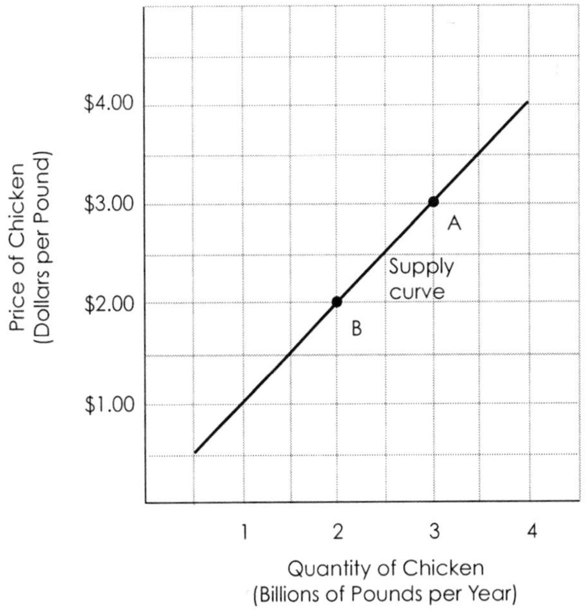

Parts (a) and (b) of this figure show the quantity of chicken supplied at various prices. As the price rises, the quantity supplied increases, other things being equal. The higher price gives farmers an incentive to raise more chickens, but the rising opportunity cost of doing so limits the supply produced in response to any given price increase.

One explanation is that the positive slope of the supply curve represents *producers' response to market incentives.* When the price of chicken goes up, farmers have an incentive to devote more time and resources to raising chickens. Farmers who raise chickens as a sideline may decide to make chickens their main business. Some people may enter the market for the first time. The same reasoning applies in every market. If parents are finding it hard to get babysitters, what do they do? They offer to pay more. If a sawmill cannot buy enough timber, it raises the price it offers to loggers, and so on. Exceptions to this general rule are rare.

Another explanation is that the positive slope of the supply curve reflects *the rising cost of producing additional output in facilities of a fixed size.* A furniture factory with a fixed amount of machinery might be able to produce more chairs only by paying workers at overtime rates to run the machinery for more hours. A farmer who is trying to grow more wheat on a fixed amount of land could do so by increasing the input of fertilizer and pesticides per acre, but beyond a certain point each unit of added chemicals yields less additional output.

Labor is a commodity not much different than chicken or lumber. Think of your personal reaction to higher wages. If your wage increases, then it is likely you will be more willing and able to increase the number of hours for work as the pay you receive increases.

Finally, the positive slope of the supply curve can be explained in terms of *comparative advantage and opportunity cost.* Figure 2.5a shows a production possibility frontier for an economy in which there are only two goods, tomatoes and chicken. Farmers can choose which product they will specialize in, but some farmers have a comparative advantage in growing tomatoes, others in raising chickens. Beginning from a situation in which only tomatoes are produced, farmers with the strongest comparative advantage in raising chickens—that is, those who are able to produce chicken at relatively the lowest opportunity cost—will switch from tomatoes to chicken even if the price of chicken is low. As the point of production moves along the frontier, the price of chicken must rise to induce farmers with relatively higher opportunity costs to make the switch. The slope of the frontier at any point represents the opportunity cost of producing more chicken for a farmer who finds it worthwhile to switch from tomatoes to chicken just at that point.

In Figure 2.5 the slopes at points A, B, and C in part (a) are graphed on a new set of axes in part (b). The graph can be interpreted as a supply curve if it is noted that the price of chicken must rise relative to the price of tomatoes to induce more farmers to switch to chicken as the opportunity cost rises.

Each of these common-sense explanations fits certain circumstances. Together, they provide an intuitive basis for the positive slope of the supply curve.

Change in quantity supplied

A change in the quantity of a good that suppliers are willing and able to sell that results from a change in the good's price, other things being equal; shown by a movement along a supply curve.

Shifts in the Supply Curve

As in the case of demand, the effects of a change in the price of chicken, other things being equal, can be shown as a movement along the supply curve for chicken. Such a movement is called a **change in quantity supplied**. A change in a condition other

FIGURE 2.5 THE PRODUCTION POSSIBILITY CURVE AND THE SUPPLY CURVE

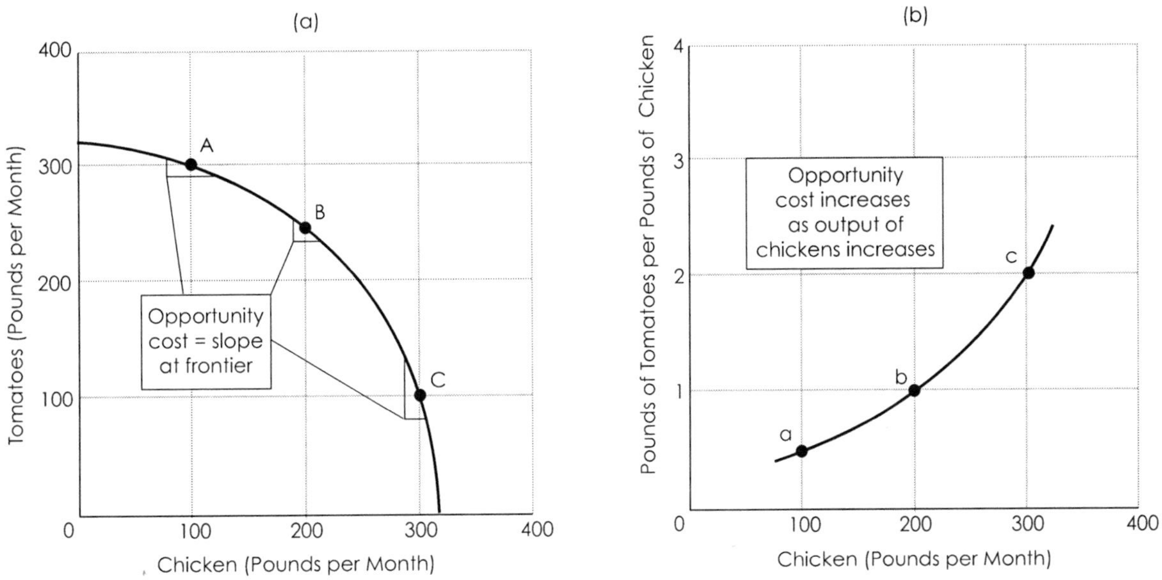

This figure offers an interpretation of the supply curve in terms of the production possibility frontier for an economy in which two goods are produced, tomatoes and chicken. Part (a) shows a production possibility frontier. The slope of the frontier at any point shows the opportunity cost of producing an additional pound of chicken measured in terms of the quantity of tomatoes that could have been produced using the same factors of production. The frontier curves because some operators have a comparative advantage in producing tomatoes and others have a comparative advantage in producing chicken. As more chicken is produced, those with the greatest comparative advantage in producing chicken are the first to stop producing tomatoes. Because the frontier gets steeper as more chicken is produced, the opportunity cost rises, as shown in part (b). The curve in part (b) can be interpreted as a supply curve, in the sense that an incentive, in the form of a higher price, will cause factors of production to be shifted from tomatoes to chicken despite the rising opportunity cost of producing chicken.

Change in supply

A change in the quantity of a good that suppliers are willing and able to sell that results from a change in some condition other than the good's price; shown by a shift in the supply curve.

than the price of chicken can be shown as a shift in the supply curve. Such a shift is referred to as a **change in supply**. Four sources of change in supply are worth noting. Each is related to the notion that the supply curve reflects the opportunity cost of producing the good or service in question.

CHANGES IN TECHNOLOGY A supply curve is drawn on the basis of a particular production technique. When entrepreneurs reduce the opportunity costs of production by introducing more efficient techniques, it becomes worthwhile to sell more of the good than before at any given price. (Think of the Purdue operations on the Eastern Shore of Maryland and the resulting increase of the available and grocery store freezer space devoted to chicken.) Figure 2.6 shows how an improvement in production technology affects the supply curve for chicken.

Supply curve S_1 is the same as the one shown in Figure 2.4. It indicates that farmers will plan to supply 3 billion pounds of chicken per year at a price of $3.00 per pound (point A). Now suppose that the development of a faster-growing bird reduces the amount of feed used in raising chickens. With lower costs per unit, farmers will

FIGURE 2.6 SHIFTS IN THE SUPPLY CURVE FOR CHICKEN

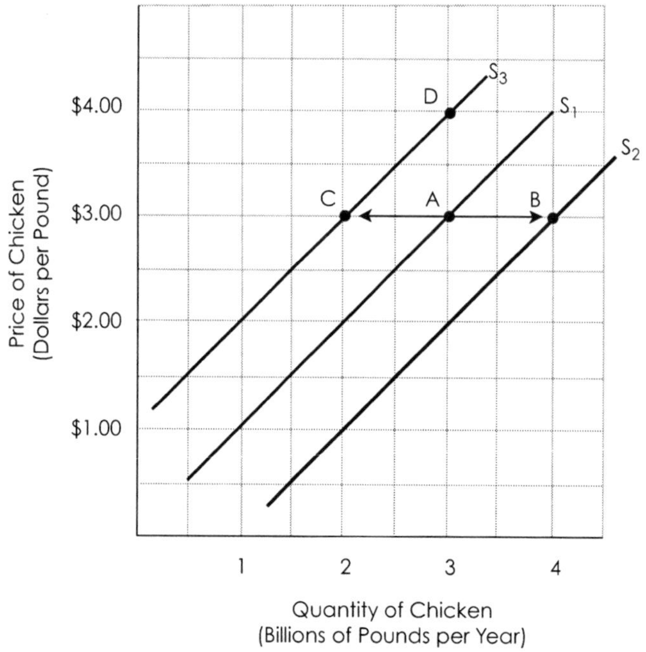

Several kinds of changes can cause the supply of chicken to increase or decrease. For example, a new production method that lowers costs will shift the curve to the *right,* from S_1 to S_2. The shift is to the right because, taking into account the new, lower cost of production per unit, producers will be willing to supply more chicken at any given price. An increase in the price of inputs, other things being equal, will shift the curve to the *left,* from S_1 to S_3. The shift is to the left because, taking into account the new, higher price of inputs, producers will be willing to supply less chicken at any given price. Changes in sellers' expectations or in the prices of competing goods can also cause the supply curve to shift.

be willing to supply more chicken than before at any given price. They may, for example, be willing to supply 4 billion pounds of chicken at $3.00 per pound (point B). The move from A to B is part of a shift in the entire supply curve from S_1 to S_2. Once the new techniques are established, an increase or decrease in the price of chicken, other things being equal, will result in a movement along the new supply curve.

CHANGES IN INPUT PRICES Changes in input prices are a second item that can cause supply curves to shift. An increase in input prices, other things being equal, increases the opportunity cost of producing the good in question, and hence it tends to reduce the quantity of a good that producers plan to supply at a given price. Refer again to Figure 2.6. Suppose that starting from point A on supply curve S_1, the price of chicken feed increases and no offsetting changes occur. Now, instead of supplying 3 billion pounds of chicken at $3.00 per pound, farmers will supply, say, just 2 billion pounds at that price (point C). The move from A to C is part of a leftward shift in the supply curve, from S_1 to S_3.

If the price of feed remains at the new level, changes in the price of chicken will cause movements along the new supply curve. For example, farmers could be induced to supply the original quantity of chicken—3 billion pounds—if the price of chicken rose enough to cover the increased cost of feed. As you can see in Figure 2.6, that would require a price of $4.00 per pound for chicken (point D).

CHANGES IN THE PRICES OF OTHER GOODS Changes in the prices of other goods that could be produced using the same factors of production can also produce a shift in the chicken supply curve. In our earlier example, farmers could use available resources to produce either chickens or tomatoes. Suppose that the price of tomatoes rises while the price of chicken stays at $3.00. The rise in the price of tomatoes gives some farmers who would otherwise have produced chickens an incentive to shift the use of their labor, land, and capital to the production of tomatoes. Thus, the effect of an increase in the price of tomatoes can be shown as a leftward shift in the chicken supply curve.

CHANGES IN EXPECTATIONS Changes in expectations can cause supply curves to shift in much the same way that they cause demand curves to shift. Again, we can use farming as an example. At planting time, a farmer's selection of crops is influenced not so much by current prices as by the prices expected at harvest time. Expectations over a time horizon longer than one growing season also affect supply. Each crop requires special equipment and know-how. We have just seen that an increase in the price of tomatoes gives farmers an incentive to shift from chicken to tomatoes. The incentive will be stronger if the price of tomatoes is expected to remain at the higher level. If it is, farmers are more likely to buy the special equipment needed for that crop and to learn the necessary production techniques.

TAXES, SUBSIDIES AND REGULATIONS Increased taxes will cause supply to decline. Reduced taxes will cause supply to increase. If for whatever reason, Maryland levied a tax on the chicken sales, then the willingness of farmers to devote their resources and labor to chicken production would decline. If there is concern over the waste from chicken farms and the legislature levies a tax to regulate the run off, then the supply of chicken would decline.

This is most obvious with the excise taxes placed on certain products. (An excise tax is a sales tax levied on a specific product only.) Both the federal and state government has excise taxes on gasoline, alcoholic beverages, tobacco products just to name a few. As the American public becomes less and less tolerant of tobacco use and continues to increase the tax on cigarettes, the tobacco companies are steadily looking to other markets to sell their product and are slowly abandoning the American domestic market. Also, tobacco companies have been diversifying away from tobacco and moving into other non-tobacco products. As the tax on alcohol and gasoline increase, the willingness to supply these products declines. Though less obvious, an increase on income causes the willingness to produce income to decline.

The opposite of a tax is a subsidy. A subsidy is a payment from the government for the production of a specific product. If the state of Maryland was concerned with unemployment on the Eastern Shore, they could consider paying entrepreneurs to start up chicken farm operations to increase the demand for construction and farm labor and thus, decrease unemployment. Our government does subsidize agriculture and other products.

Consider childcare. If it were determined that there was a critical shortage of child care facilities, the state could subsidize child care operations. For example, instead of paying taxes on the income derived from child care, the state would pay a provider an amount, say $20 per day, for each child. This subsidy, along with the fee paid by the parent, would encourage more providers to enter the market and current providers to expand their operations.

Consider this college. Your tuition covers about one third of the cost of operating this institution. Because of the generous support of the tax payers of the county and state, the supply of classes offered by Carroll is dramatically higher and your tuition price is much lower than otherwise would be.

Regulations act the same as taxes in that they reduce supply or the reduction of regulations increase supply. Should Maryland department of the Environment establish more stringent requirements on chicken farms on the Eastern Shore, this added imposition would discourage new farmers from entering the market and current farmers to reduce their operations.

Again, consider child care. No one disputes for the need for safety in the area of child care. But as the state imposes ever more requirements, such as nutrition guides for snacks, proper exercise regiments, specific nap facilities, training for employees, fences , soap requirements in washing facilities, safety furniture etc. the willingness to start a child care business declines.

THE INTERACTION OF SUPPLY AND DEMAND

Markets transmit information on what is valued, and that information is expressed in the form of prices. Not only is price an expression of what you the buyer is willing to give up to get a product, it is also an expression of what a seller is willing to accept to give up that same product. Taking these prices into account, along with other knowledge they may have, buyers and sellers make their plans.[2] As shown by the demand and supply curves, buyers and sellers plan to buy or sell certain quantities of a good at any given price.

Each market has many buyers and sellers, each making plans independently and without coercion. When they meet to trade, some of them may be unable to carry out their plans on the terms they expected. Perhaps the total quantity of a good that buyers plan to purchase is greater than the total quantity that suppliers are willing to sell at the given price. In that case, some of the would-be buyers must change their plans.

Or, perhaps planned sales exceed planned purchases at the given price. In that case, some would-be sellers will be unable to carry out their plans.

Market Equilibrium

Equilibrium

A condition in which buyers' and sellers' plans exactly mesh in the marketplace, so that the quantity supplied exactly equals the quantity demanded at a given price.

Sometimes no one is surprised: The total quantity of a good that buyers plan to purchase exactly matches the total quantity that producers plan to sell. When buyers' and sellers' plans mesh when they meet in the marketplace, no buyers or sellers need to change their plans. Under these conditions, the market is said to be in **equilibrium**, and commerce takes place!

Supply and demand curves, which reflect the plans of sellers and buyers, can be used to give a graphical demonstration of market equilibrium. Figure 2.7 uses the same supply and demand curves as before, but this time both curves are drawn on the same diagram. If the quantity of planned sales at each price is compared with the quantity of planned purchases at that price (either the table or the graph can be used to make this comparison), it can be seen that there is only one price at which the two sets of plans mesh. That price—$2.00 per pound—is the equilibrium price. If all buyers and sellers make their plans with the expectation of a price of $2.00, no one will be surprised and no plans will have to be changed.

Shortages

Excess quantity demanded (shortage)

A condition in which the quantity of a good demanded at a given price exceeds the quantity supplied.

Inventory

A stock of a finished good awaiting sale or use.

But what will happen if for some reason people base their plans for buying or selling chicken on a price other than $2.00 a pound?[3] Suppose, for example, that they base their plans on a price of $1.00. Figure 2.7 shows that at that price buyers will plan to purchase chicken at a rate of 3 billion pounds per year, but farmers will plan to supply only 1 billion pounds. When the quantity demanded exceeds the quantity supplied, as in this example, the difference is an **excess quantity demanded** or, more simply, a **shortage**. In Figure 2.7 the shortage is 2 billion pounds of chicken per year when the price is $1.00 per pound.

In most markets the first sign of a shortage is a drop in the **inventory**, that is, in the stock of the good in question that has been produced and is waiting to be sold or used. Sellers plan to hold a certain quantity of goods in inventory to allow for minor changes in demand. When they see inventories dropping below the planned level, they change their plans. Some may try to rebuild their inventories by increasing their output, if they produce the good themselves; or, if they do not make it themselves, they may order more from the producer. Some sellers may take advantage of the strong demand for their product to raise the price, knowing that buyers will be willing to pay more. Many sellers will do a little of both. If sellers do not take the initiative, buyers will—they will offer to pay more if sellers will supply more. Whatever the details, the result will be an upward movement along the supply curve as both price and quantity increase.

FIGURE 2.7 EQUILIBRIUM IN THE CHICKEN MARKET

(a)

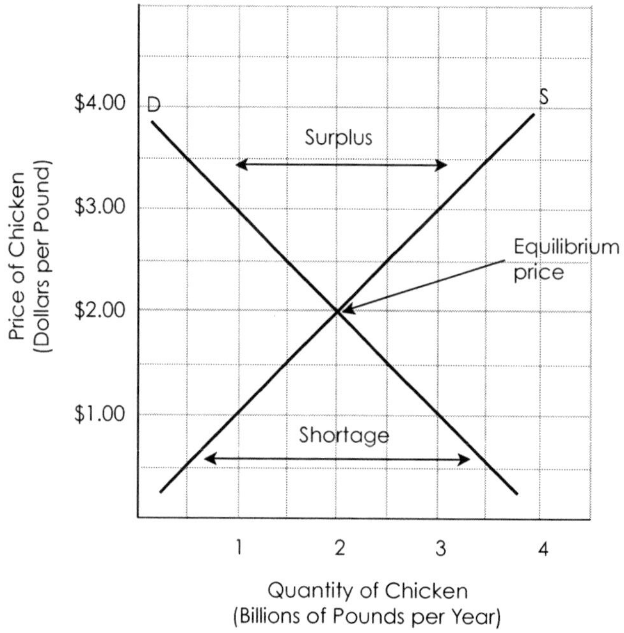

(b)

Price (per Pound)	Quantity Demanded (Billions of Pounds)	Quantity Supplied (Billions of Pounds)	Shortage (Billions of Pounds)	Surplus (Billions of Pounds)	Direction of Pressure on Price
$3.50	0.5	3.5	—	3	Downward
$3.00	1	3	—	2	Downward
$2.50	1.5	2.5	—	1	Downward
$2.00	2	2	—	—	Equilibrium
$1.50	2.5	1.5	1	—	Upward
$1.00	3	1	2	—	Upward
$0.50	3.5	0.5	3	—	Upward

This figure shows the supply and demand curves for chicken presented earlier in graphical and numerical form. The demand curve shows how much buyers plan to purchase at a given price. The supply curve shows how much producers plan to sell at a given price. At only one price—$2.00 per pound—do buyers' and sellers' plans exactly match. That is the equilibrium price. A higher price causes a surplus of chicken and puts downward pressure on price. A lower price causes a shortage and puts upward pressure on price.

As the shortage puts upward pressure on price, buyers will change their plans too. Moving up and to the left along their demand curve, they will cut back on their planned purchases. As both buyers and sellers change their plans, the market will move toward equilibrium. When the price reaches $2.00 per pound, both the shortage and the pressure to change buying and selling plans will disappear.

In the markets for most goods, sellers have inventories of goods ready to be sold. There are exceptions, however. Inventories are not possible in markets for services—haircuts, tax preparation, lawn care, and the like. Also, some goods, such as custom-built houses and machine tools that are designed for a specialized need, are not held in inventories. Sellers in these markets do not begin production until they have a contract with a buyer.

In markets in which there are no inventories, the sign of a shortage is a queue of buyers. The queue may take the form of a line of people waiting to be served or a list of names in an order book. The queue is a sign that, given the prevailing price, buyers would like to purchase the good at a faster rate than that at which producers have planned to supply it. However, some plans cannot be carried out—at least not right away. Buyers are served on a first-come, first-served basis.

The formation of a queue of buyers has much the same effect on the market as a decrease in inventories. Sellers react by increasing their rate of output, raising their prices, or both. Buyers react by reducing the quantity they plan to purchase. The result is a movement up and to the right along the supply curve and, at the same time, up and to the left along the demand curve until equilibrium is reached.

Surpluses

Having considered what happens when buyers and sellers initially expect a price below the equilibrium price, we now turn to the opposite case. Suppose that for some reason buyers and sellers of chicken expect a price that is higher than the equilibrium price—say, $2.50 per pound—and make their plans accordingly. Figure 2.7 shows that farmers will plan to supply 2.5 billion pounds of chicken per year at $2.50, but their customers will plan to buy only 1.5 billion pounds. When the quantity supplied exceeds the quantity demanded, there is an **excess quantity supplied**, or a **surplus**. As Figure 2.7 shows, the surplus of chicken at a price of $2.50 per pound is 1 billion pounds per year.

Excess quantity supplied (surplus)

A condition in which the quantity of a good supplied at a given price exceeds the quantity demanded.

When there is a surplus of a product, sellers will be unable to sell all that they had hoped to sell at the planned price. As a result, their inventories will begin to grow beyond the level they had planned to hold in preparation for normal changes in demand.

Sellers will react to the inventory buildup by changing their plans. Some will cut back their output. Others will lower their prices to induce consumers to buy more and thus reduce their extra stock. Still others will do a little of both. The result of these changes in plans will be a movement down and to the left along the supply curve.

As unplanned inventory buildup puts downward pressure on the price of chicken, buyers change their plans too. Finding that chicken costs less than they had expected, they buy more of it. In graphical terms, they move down and to the right along the demand curve. As that happens, the market is restored to equilibrium.

In markets in which there are no inventories, surpluses lead to the formation of queues of sellers looking for customers. Taxi queues at airports are a case in point. At some times of the day the fare for taxi service from the airport to downtown is more than high enough to attract a number of taxis that is equal to the demand. A queue of cabs waiting for passengers then forms. In some cities drivers who are far back in the queue try to attract riders by offering cut-rate fares. Often, though, there are rules against fare cutting. The queue then grows until the next peak period, when a surge in demand shortens it.

Changes in Market Conditions

On a graph, finding the equilibrium point looks easy. In real life, though, it is a moving target. Market conditions, by which we mean all the items that lie behind the "other things being equal" clause, change frequently. When they do, both buyers and sellers revise their plans, and market prices and quantities adjust.

RESPONSE TO A SHIFT IN DEMAND We will first consider a market's response to a shift in demand. Suppose, for example, that television news broadcasts a warning that eating chicken meat might transmit a new virus. The result would be an immediate decrease in demand for chicken. Part (a) of Figure 2.8 interprets this case in terms of the supply-and-demand model.

As the figure is drawn, the chicken market is initially in equilibrium at E_1. There the price is $3.00 per pound and the quantity produced is 2 billion pounds per year. Now the temporary change in tastes caused by the health warning shifts the demand curve to the left, from D_1 to D_2. (There is a shift in the demand curve rather than a movement along it, because a change in tastes is not one of the items represented by the axes of the diagram.) What will happen next?

At the original price of $3.00 per pound, there will be a surplus of chicken. The supply curve shows that at that price chicken farmers will plan to produce 2 billion pounds per year. However, according to the new demand curve, D_2, consumers will no longer buy that much chicken at $3.00 per pound. Instead, given their new tastes, they will buy only 1billion pounds at that price.

But the price does not stay at $3.00 for long. As soon as the demand curve begins to shift and the surplus begins to develop, chicken inventories rise above their planned levels, putting downward pressure on the price. As the price falls, producers revise their plans. They move down and to the left along their supply curve, reducing the quantity supplied. (There is a movement along the supply curve, not a shift in the curve, because the producers are responding to a change in the price of chicken, the variable shown on the vertical axis. Nothing has happened to change the "other things being equal" condition, such as technology, input prices, and so on, which could cause the supply curve to shift.)

As farmers move downward along their supply curve in the direction shown by the arrow in part (a) of Figure 2.8, they eventually reach point E_2, where their plans again mesh with those of consumers. At that point the price has fallen to $2.25 per pound and production to 1.5 billion pounds. Although health-conscious consumers

FIGURE 2.8 EFFECTS OF CHANGING CONDITIONS IN THE CHICKEN MARKET

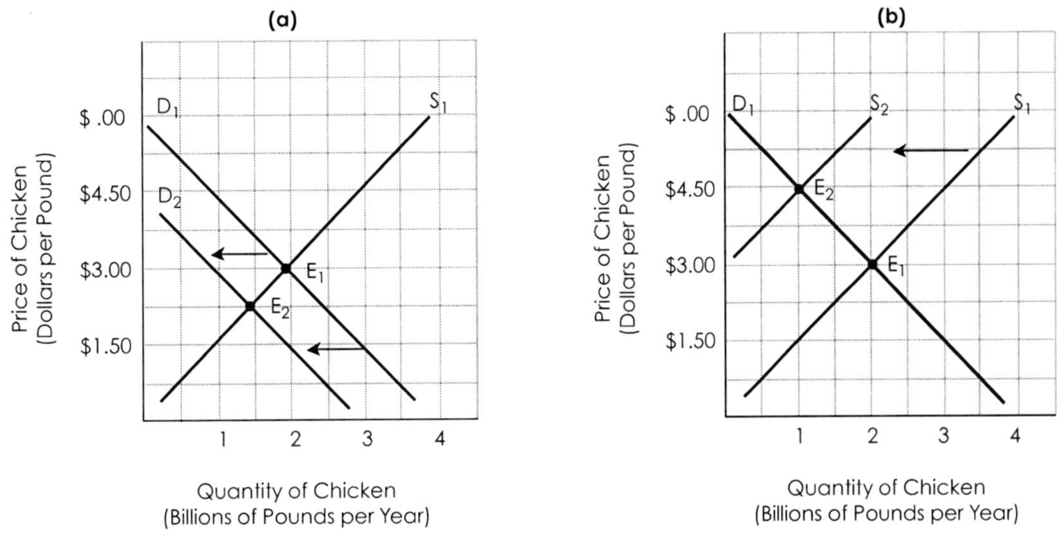

Part (a) of this figure shows the effects of a decrease in demand for chicken caused by a health warning about the safety of eating chicken. Initially the market is in equilibrium at E_1. The change in tastes causes a shift in the demand curve. At the original equilibrium price of $3.00 per pound, there is a temporary surplus of chicken. This causes inventories to start to rise and puts downward pressure on the price. As the price falls, producers move down along their supply curve to a new equilibrium at E_2. There both the price and quantity of chicken are lower than before the shift in demand. Part (b) shows the effects of a decrease in supply caused by a drought, which raises the price of corn used to feed chicken. The shift in the supply curve causes a shortage at the initial price of $3.00 per pound. The shortage puts upward pressure on price. As the price rises, buyers move up and to the left along the demand curve until a new equilibrium is reached at E_2. In each case, note that only one curve needs to shift to bring about the new equilibrium.

would not have bought that much chicken at the old price, they will do so at the new, lower price. E_2 thus is the new equilibrium point. Later, if the health scare proves to be baseless, the demand curve will shift back D_1 and the market price and quantity will return to their original values.

RESPONSE TO A SHIFT IN SUPPLY The original equilibrium might be disrupted by a change in supply rather than by a change in demand. For example, beginning from a condition of equilibrium, a drought in the Midwest might result in a higher price for grain for chicken feed. That would shift the supply curve to the left while the demand curve remained unchanged, as shown in part (b) of Figure 2.8.

Given the new supply curve, there will be a shortage of chicken at the original price. Inventories will decline and the prices will rise in response. As the price increases, producers will move upward and to the right along their new supply curve, S_2, and consumers will move upward and to the left along their demand curve, D_1, which remains in its original position. A new equilibrium is established when the price reaches $4.50 per pound.

One of the most frequent mistakes people make in learning the supply-and-demand model is to think that *both* curves always must shift in order to restore equilibrium. The examples given in Figure 2.8 show clearly that this is not the case. In part (a), after the demand curve shifts, a movement along the supply curve is enough to establish the new equilibrium. No shift in the supply curve is needed. Similarly, in part (b), after the supply curve shifts, the demand curve does not need to shift to reach the new equilibrium.

However, in the turmoil of real-world markets, cases can be found in which both curves do shift at once. This will happen when two separate changes in conditions occur at the same time, one acting on the supply curve and the other on the demand curve. *Economics in the News 2.1* provides a real-world example. It shows how beef prices were pushed upward in 2003 by two simultaneous changes in market conditions. One was a swing in consumer tastes toward beef because of the popularity of low-carbohydrate, high-protein diets. That shifted the demand curve to the right. At the same time a cutoff of beef imports from Canada shifted the supply curve to the

ECONOMICS IN THE NEWS 2.1

BEEF PRICES UP; FAST FOOD CHAINS SWITCH TO CHICKEN

Stock up the freezer if you like steak because beef prices at the supermarket are on their way up. And they're likely to stay there for a while.

U.S. cattle prices are at a record high, say economists with the U.S. Department of Agriculture . They've increased 34% since July, and this month the benchmark price of Nebraska choice steers went from $90 to $116 per 100 pounds. A year ago, the price per 100 pounds was $64.

"We've seen increases in the last 10 days," said Jim Robb, director of the Livestock Marketing Information Center in Denver. "Choice T-bone steak and New York strip steak, those prices are double what they were three weeks ago."

"Those prices will ease off a little bit but not much," said David Kay of *Cattle Buyers Weekly*. "We look as if we're going to have even tighter cattle supplies for slaughter in 2004 and even into 2005."

Prices are up because of a set of circumstances that Robb calls "completely unprecedented." First, consumer demand for beef has increased nearly 10% since 1998 after declining for 20 years.

Recent increases in consumption may be due in part because of the increasing popularity of high-protein diets, such as this summer's blockbuster South Beach diet, and the venerable Atkins diet.

Second, as Wayne Purcell of the Research Institute on Livestock Pricing at Virginia Tech points out, the U.S. banned imports of Canadian cattle and beef five months ago. The ban was imposed because of the discovery of a case of mad cow disease there last spring and reduced cattle and meat imports to the United States by 9%.

Consumers already may be feeling the impact, whether they're eating out or at home. U.S. restaurant chains such as McDonald's and Wendy's have been hyping salads and lean chicken pieces lately, and industry observers say it's no coincidence that the switch coincides with rising beef prices. Experts expect cost-cutting by other restaurant companies to offset rising food prices.

It is not clear how long it will take for the impact of the price increases to be felt at local meat counters. Retail beef prices typically trail the price paid at the stockyard anywhere from two weeks to two months. So last week's increase will not show up at supermarkets until the first weeks of November or until Christmas.

If grocers think the price hike is temporary, they may eat the difference rather than risk aggravating customers. But if grocers do raise prices, "they'll raise their everyday prices only a little, but they will keep them up for a year or so. And we just won't see beef featured in sales very much," Kay said.

Source: Elizabeth Weise, "Beef Prices On the Way Up," *USA Today*, October 24, 2003.

left. Either change acting alone would have been enough to raise the price. Both changes acting together had an especially sharp impact.

Equilibrium as Spontaneous Order

The way that a market moves toward a new equilibrium following a disturbance is an example of economic coordination through spontaneous order. In the case we have been following, the disturbance began either with a change in health consciousness among consumers or with a change in the weather. To make the adjustment to new conditions, the decisions of thousands of farmers, wholesalers, retailers, as well as that of millions of consumers, must somehow be coordinated. How can that be done?

In a *market* economy, no central planning agency or regulatory bureaucracy is needed. The required shift in the use of scarce resources is brought about through information and incentives transmitted in the form of changing market prices. The trend toward low-carbohydrate, high-protein diets in the early 2000s is a typical example. As demand for beef, chicken, and other high-protein foods rose, farmers responded to higher prices by raising more chickens and cattle. Labor, capital, natural resources, and entrepreneurial energy flowed into chicken and beef production without any central authority giving an order. At the same time, investments in donuts, a high-carb food that had boomed in the 1990s, slowed substantially.

The process was remarkably smooth for so vast a shift in resource use. Behind the scenes, surpluses and shortages nudged choices in the needed directions, but at no time did shortages occur in the acute form of empty meat coolers at the supermarket or lines of chicken-hungry consumers stretching down city streets. Similarly, slack demand for donuts signaled entrepreneurs to turn away from building new outlets, but it did not give rise to mountains of rotting donuts that had to be dumped into landfills. (However, there are a few abandoned and empty Krispy Kreame stores.)

No one *intended* this process of adjustment. Equilibrium is not a compromise that must be negotiated by a committee of consumers and producers. Just as shoppers manage to equalize the length of supermarket checkout lines without the guidance of a central authority, markets move toward equilibrium spontaneously, through the small, local adjustments that people make in their efforts to serve their own interests. As Adam Smith might have put it, we have not the benevolence of Frank Perdue or the Beef Industry Council to thank for our dinner; instead it is their self-interest that puts the right food on our table.

PRICE FLOORS AND CEILINGS: AN APPLICATION

Economics—both macro and micro—encompasses a great many applications of the concepts of supply and demand. Although each situation is unique, each to some extent draws on ideas developed in this chapter. This section, which uses the model to analyze the effects of government-imposed price floors and ceilings, provides some examples. Many more will be added in later chapters.

Price Supports: The Market for Milk

In our earlier example of the market for beef, a decrease in demand caused a surplus, which in turn caused the price to decrease until the surplus was eliminated. Markets are not always free to respond by adjusting prices, however. The market for milk is a case in point.

Figure 2.9 shows the market for milk in terms of supply and demand curves. The quantity of milk is measured in hundredweight, the unit used for bulk milk sales, equal to roughly 12 gallons. Suppose that initially the market is in equilibrium at point E_1. The wholesale price of milk is $13 per hundredweight, and 110 million hundredweight is produced per year. Then suppose that a trend in taste away from high-cholesterol foods shifts the demand curve for milk to the left. The result would be a surplus of milk at the $13 price, as shown by the arrow in Figure 2.9.

FIGURE 2.9 PRICE SUPPORTS FOR MILK

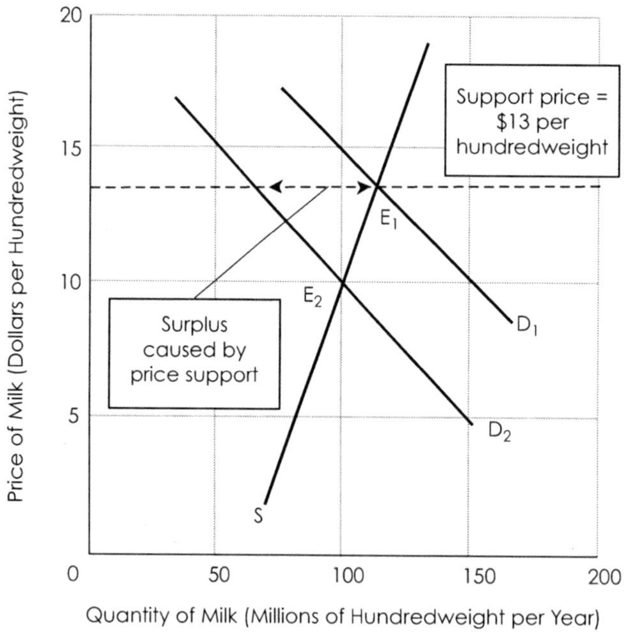

Suppose that initially the market for milk is in equilibrium at E_1. A shift in tastes away from high-cholesterol foods then shifts the demand curve to D_2. If the price were free to fall, there would be a temporary surplus that would push the price down to a new equilibrium at $10 per hundredweight. Instead, suppose that the government maintains a support price for milk at a level higher than the equilibrium price, as it did for many years ($13 per hundredweight in this example). The government would then need to buy the surplus milk and stores it in the form of powdered milk, butter and cheese to keep the price from falling.

At this point a new factor comes into operation that was not present in our earlier discussion of the chicken market. In that case, chicken prices were free to fall in response to a surplus, but in the milk market they are not. Instead, an elaborate set of government-imposed controls and subsidies puts a floor under the price of milk. As part of the controls, the government agrees to pay a minimum price for all milk that cannot be sold at that price on the open market. In our example, the support price is assumed to be $13.

With the demand curve in its original position D_1, there was no surplus and the government did not need to buy any milk. But with the demand curve in position D_2, there is a surplus of 40 million hundredweight per year. Under the price support law the government must buy this surplus and store it in the form of powdered milk, cheese, butter, and other products with long shelf lives.

Without price supports, the shift in demand would cause the price of milk to fall to the new equilibrium price of $10 per hundredweight. When price supports are applied to a product at a level higher than the equilibrium price, however, the result is a persistent surplus. The effects of the price support can be understood in terms of conflicting signals sent to producers and consumers. To consumers, the price of $13 says, "Milk is scarce. Its opportunity cost is high. Hold your consumption down." To producers, it says, "All is well. Incentives are unchanged. Feel free to continue using scarce resources to produce milk." Without price supports, a drop in the price to $10 would send a different set of messages. Consumers would hear: "Milk is cheaper and more abundant. Although it is not cholesterol free, give in to temptation! Drink more of it!" Producers would hear: "The milk market is not what it once was. Look at your opportunity costs. Is there perhaps some better use for your labor, capital, and natural resources?"

In response to the milk price supports in Pennsylvania, Maryland in the 1990s adopted price supports too. Because of the Pennsylvania surpluses which was being *dumped* (sold at a lower price in Maryland than allowed in Pennsylvania) in Maryland at low prices, the small dairy farms of Carroll and Frederick counties petitioned the legislature to place price ceilings on milk so as to keep the small Maryland dairy farms profitable. This government action has resulted in the over production of dairy products by the small Maryland dairy industry. These price supports cause you,(schools, families, children) the dairy consumers,to pay a higher price for dairy products than you otherwise would.

During the 1980s and 1990s, the government's price support was consistently higher than the equilibrium price. The program became very expensive, more than $1,000 per U.S. family by some estimates, enough to buy each family its own cow. From time to time the government has tried to eliminate the milk surplus by shifting the supply curve to the left so that it would intersect the demand curve near the support price. Under one program, for example, farmers were encouraged to sell their cows to be slaughtered for their meat, thereby reducing the size of dairy herds. But such programs have failed to eliminate the milk surplus. The chief reason is the dairy farmers' entrepreneurial response to the high price of milk. The government's efforts to cut the size of herds were largely offset by increased output per cow as a result of genetic improvements and better farm management practices. (technology improvements increase supply).The government accumulated mountains of surplus dairy products paid for through higher taxes levied on the general public. So not only does the general public pay higher prices for butter, milk and cheese, they also must pay higher taxes to purchase the surplus. And in another sense, the public pays through the mis allocation of land resources. Because there is too much acreage devoted to dairy farming, there is less land available for other purposes, such as new housing. Though Maryland has adopted the Smart Growth idea of land zoning, these programs result in higher real estate prices that in the near future, you will encounter.

Then, during the early years of the 21st century, conditions in the milk market changed. By 2005, the support price had fallen below the market price and the surplus had disappeared. This, too, had unintended consequences for public policy. Under the U.S. Department of Agriculture's Commodity Supplemental Food Program, as many as 100,000 mothers, children, and elderly people had received packages of free milk powder drawn from government surpluses. Suddenly these vast stocks were threatened with exhaustion, and officials were left scrambling to find other ways to aid needy citizens. Meanwhile, across the Atlantic, the European Union continues to operate a price support system that produces an ongoing surplus of more than 30 million tons per year. The European milk market is still in a position much like that shown in Figure 2.9.

Price Ceilings: The Case of Rent Control

In the milk market, the government maintains a support price that has often been above the equilibrium price. In certain other markets, a price ceiling below the equilibrium price is imposed. An example of the latter situation is rent control in housing markets.

Rent control in one form or another has been used in several major U.S. cities, including New York, Washington, D.C., San Francisco, and Los Angeles. The controls vary from one city to another, but in all cases maximum rents, at least for some categories of apartments, are established by law. The purpose of rent control is to aid tenants by preventing landlords from charging "unreasonably high" rents. What is unreasonably high is determined by the relative political strength of landlords and tenants rather than by the forces of supply and demand.

INTENDED EFFECTS Figure 2.10 interprets the effects of rent control in terms of supply and demand. For the sake of simplicity it is assumed that the supply of rental housing consists of units of equal size and rental value. Part (a) of the figure shows the effects of rent control in the short run. Here the short run means a period that is too short to permit significant increases or decreases in the supply of rental

FIGURE 2.10 EFFECTS OF RENT CONTROL

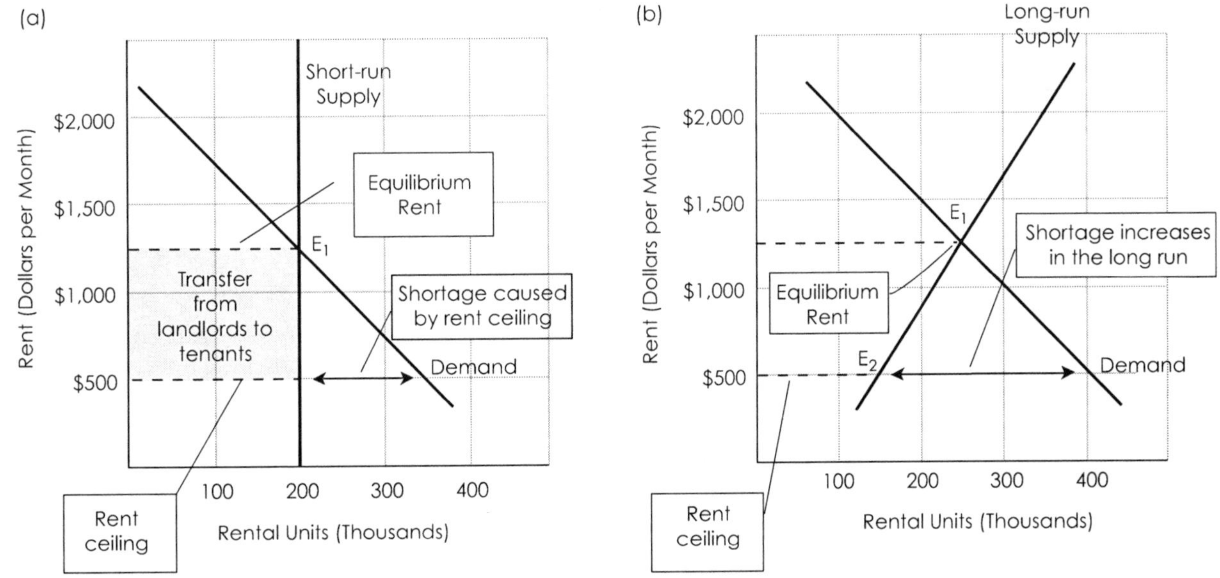

Part (a) shows the short-run effects of rent control. In the short run, the supply of rental apartments is considered to be fixed. The equilibrium rent is $1,250 per month. A rent ceiling of $500 per month is then put into effect. One possible outcome is that landlords will charge disguised rent increases, which will bring the true price back to $1,250 per month. If such disguised increases are prohibited, there will be a shortage of 350,000 units at the ceiling price. Part (b) shows the long-run effects when there is time to adjust the number of units in response to the price. If the ceiling price is enforced, landlords move down their supply curve to E_2. The shortage then becomes even more severe than in the short run.

housing. (The short-run supply curve, which is drawn as a vertical line, indicates that a change in price will not result in any change in the quantity of apartments supplied in the short run.[4])

Under the conditions shown, the equilibrium rent per standard housing unit is $1,250 per month for each of the 200,000 units in the city. Now suppose that a rent ceiling of $500 is imposed. The result is a gain to tenants of $750 per unit per month. The total sum transferred to tenants (that is, the benefit to them from below-market rents) is $750 per unit times 200,000 units, or $150 million, in all. In graphical terms, that sum is equal to the area of the shaded rectangle in Figure 2.10. The benefit to tenants at the expense of landlords is the principal intended effect of rent control.

UNINTENDED EFFECTS The policy of rent control, which does accomplish its goal of benefiting tenants at the expense of landlords, provides a classic illustration of the law of unintended consequences. In the short run, when the stock of apartments is fixed, the unintended consequences stem from the apartment shortage created by the controls. The shortage occurs because the quantity demanded is greater at the lower ceiling price than at the higher equilibrium price.

The greater quantity demanded has several sources. First, people who would otherwise own a house or condominium may now want to rent. Second, people who would otherwise live in non–rent-controlled suburbs may now seek rent-controlled units in the city. Third, each tenant may want more space, which results in a demand for more of the standardized units shown in Figure 2.10.

The shortage creates a problem for both landlords and tenants: How will the limited supply of apartments be rationed among those who want them? Both landlords and tenants devise a number of creative responses—*entrepreneurial* responses, as an economist would say.

One response on the part of landlords is to seek disguised rent increases. These may take the form of large, nonrefundable "key deposits" or security deposits. As an alternative, they may sell old, used furniture or drapes at inflated prices as a condition for renting the apartment. Finally, the costs of certain maintenance or security services that the landlord might otherwise have paid for may be transferred to tenants.

Tenants too may get into the act. When they decide to move, they may sublet their apartments to other tenants rather than give up their leases. Now it is the tenant who collects the key money or sells the old drapes to the subtenant. The original tenant may have moved to a distant city but maintains a bank account and a post office box for use in paying the rent. The subtenant is instructed to play the role of a "guest" if the landlord telephones. (the plot of the movie *Bonfire of the Vanities* and an episode of TV's *Seinfeld,* were set by New York City's rent control laws. Remember George and Elaine literally running to get in line to rent a rent controlled apartment and the fighting, arguing, and negotiating that ensued when they were both on the list for the apartment with a patio?

Advocates of rent control view these responses as cheating and often try to outlaw them. If prohibitions are enforced, the landlord will find that there are many applicants for each vacant apartment. In that case, the landlord must decide to whom to rent the apartment. The result will often be discrimination against renters who are from minority groups, who have children, or who have unconventional lifestyles.

In the long run, rent control has other unintended effects. The long run in this case means enough time for the number of rental units to grow through construction of new units or shrink through abandonment of old ones (or their conversion to condominiums). Other things being equal, the higher the rent, the greater the rate of construction, and the lower the rent, the greater the rate of abandonment or conversion. This is reflected in the positively sloped long-run supply curve in part (b) of Figure 2.10.

If rent controls are enforced in such a way that there are no disguised charges by landlords, the number of rental units shrinks and the market moves from E_1 to E_2. At E_2, the unintended effects that appeared in the short run become more pronounced. The intensity of housing discrimination increases relative to the short-run case, because the difference between the number of units available and the number sought by renters increases. Graphically, that difference is shown by the horizontal gap between the supply and demand curves at the ceiling price. In the short run, there is a shortage of 50,000 units; in the long run, the shortage increases to 75,000 units.

Rent controls are often defended as being beneficial to the poor. But when all of the unintended effects of rent control are taken into account, one may question whether poor families really benefit. In cases in which disguised rent increases are possible, the true cost of rental housing is not really decreased. Further, it is hard to believe that landlords' tendency to discriminate against minority group members, single-parent families, and tenants with irregular work histories will benefit the poor. The most likely beneficiaries of rent control are stable, middle-class families who work at the same jobs and live in the same apartments for long periods. There are numerous examples of well-paid entertainers who benefit from plush, Central Park, rent-controlled apartments. Because of the housing shortages in New York City, the nearby cities of Patterson, New Jersey, and Newark, New Jersey have seen a renaissance and gentrification.

Why does rent control persist as a policy, given its many seemingly perverse unintended consequences? Some economists explain the popularity of rent control in terms of the political power of the middle-class tenants who are most likely to benefit from rent controls and who see helping the poor as nothing more than a convenient cover for simple self-interest. Some explain their popularity in terms of the short time horizon of government officials: The adverse effect on tenants of ending rent control would appear very quickly, whereas such benefits as increased construction of new apartments would materialize only long after the next election. And some attribute the popularity of rent control to the simple fact that many voters do not give much thought to the policy's unintended consequences. Whatever the reason, it appears that very gradually rent control is weakening its hold, even in New York, long home of the strongest controls. In the past decade, more than 10 percent of the 1 million apartments once covered by New York's rent controls have left the system, and the trend is expected to continue.

In Praise of Price Gouging

Whenever a hurricane hits south Florida or anywhere, there seems to be a run on specific commodities (plywood, bottled water, batteries, canned foods, etc.) And inevitably, we'll see new reports of merchants raising the prices of these commodities to levels much higher than recently before the bad weather. The merchant accused of price increases is portrayed as an immoral profiteer, immorally gouging the unlucky public. But if we consider a Carroll county entrepreneur who rents a truck, and fills it with plywood, and hires a laborer, and drives this cargo to the affected area to provide

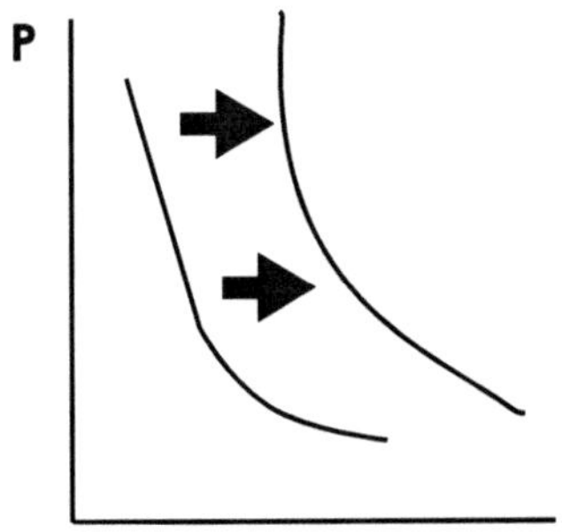

Demand for plywood (etc.) increases because of hurricane.

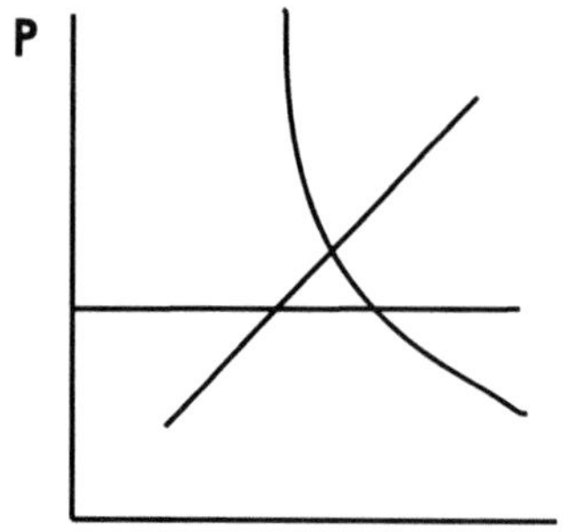

Unless price is permitted to increase, shortages will result. What's better, to have supplies at a higher price, or having nothing, but knowing the price is not allowed to increase on non-existing items?

this commodity that people need. However, to rent the truck, pay the laborer purchase the plywood, gas the truck, and journey to the hurricane area will cost the entrepreneur. Along with these costs, the entrepreneur expects enough return above his costs to make this effort worthwhile. Because of this expectation, the entrepreneur must charge a higher price than what Lowes or Home Depot charges. If the state authorities prohibit these price increases, then it is likely the entrepreneur will not take the bother to obtain and transport these commodities to a public who so desperately want them. Though the buyers who must pay a higher than normal price view this merchant as a wicked opportunist, nevertheless, without the opportunist charging higher prices, the public would not have access to vital supplies. So ask yourself, what's more desirable: no products but a lower price, or products available for sale but at a higher price?

A final word on Price Controls (ceilings). If you remember the gasoline lines of 1974 and 1979, you see the direct effect of non market forces influencing prices. The mid east OPEC oil states embargoed the United States for our support of the state of Israel (1973) and our support of the Shaw of Iran (1979). In the early 1970s, President Nixon imposed wage and price controls on the economy. These controls had been lifted on most products by 1979 except on the price of gasoline. As the supply of gasoline decreased because of the OPEC embargo, the price should have increased. But because of the price controls imposed by the government, shortages results. The method of distribution employed in the absence of price was queuing or waiting in line. Those who were willing to wait the longest received the scarce gasoline. During the first Gulf War in 1990 and after Hurricane Katrina hit the Gulf Coast, the price of gasoline spiked. Some quarters of society called for government intervention and setting price controls. To its credit, government refrained from restrictions on price increases. Had the government given in and imposed price restrictions, the pump price would not have gone up, however, there would have been less gasoline available for sale which would have caused the lines of the 70s and other disruptions to social peace that we have experienced. (The author did witness a gas riot in 1979 when young people actually vandalized and set fire to several gas stations before the police, in mass, dispersed the crowd.) So ask yourself—would you rather pay \$3.00+ per gallon of gas, or wait in line for three hours and be allowed to buy five gallons only for \$2.50 a gallon?

THIS CHAPTER HAS covered the basics of the supply-and-demand model and described a few applications of that model. There are many more applications in both macro- and microeconomics. In macroeconomics, the supply-and-demand model can be applied to financial markets, labor markets, and the problem of determining the rate of inflation and real output for the economy as a whole. In microeconomics, the model can be applied to product markets, markets for productive resources, and policy issues ranging from pollution to farm policy to international trade, to name just a few. As the great economist Alfred Marshall once put it, nearly all of the major problems of economics have a "kernel" that reflects the workings of supply and demand (see *Who Said It? Who Did It? 2.1*).

When one takes a detailed look at the underpinnings of the model, it appears to fit some kinds of markets more closely than others. The fit is best for markets in which there are many producers and many customers, the goods sold by one producer are much like those sold by others, and all sellers and buyers have good information on market conditions. Markets for farm commodities, such as wheat and corn, and financial markets, such as the New York Stock Exchange, meet these standards reasonably well.

However, even in markets that do not display all of these features, the fit is often close enough so that the supply-and-demand model provides useful insights into what is going on. The rental housing market is an example: Not all rental units are, in fact, alike, even when measurement is standardized for objective characteristics such

WHO SAID IT? WHO DID IT? 2.1

ALFRED MARSHALL ON SUPPLY AND DEMAND

Alfred Marshall, often considered to have been the greatest economist of his day, was born in London in 1842. His father was a Bank of England cashier who hoped the boy would enter the ministry. Young Marshall had other ideas, however. He turned down a theological scholarship at Oxford to study mathematics, receiving his M.A. from Cambridge in 1865.

While at Cambridge, Marshall joined a philosophical discussion group. There he became interested in promoting the broad development of the human mind. He was soon told, however, that the harsh realities of economics would prevent his ideas from being carried out. Britain's economic potential as a country, it was said, could never allow the masses sufficient leisure for education. This disillusioning episode appears to have triggered Marshall's fascination with economics.

At the time, British economics was dominated by the classical school founded by Adam Smith and David Ricardo. Marshall had great respect for the classical writers. Initially he saw his own work as simply applying his mathematical training to strengthen and systematize the classical system. Before long, however, he was breaking new ground and developing a system of his own. By 1890, when he brought out his famous *Principles of Economics*, he had laid the foundation of what we now call the neoclassical school.

In an attempt to explain the essence of his approach, Marshall included the following passage in the second edition of his *Principles:*

> In spite of a great variety in detail, nearly all the chief problems of economics agree in that they have a kernel of the same kind. This kernel is an inquiry as to the balancing of two opposed classes of motives, the one consisting of desires to acquire certain new goods, and thus satisfy wants; while the other consists of desires to avoid certain efforts or retain certain immediate enjoyment . . . in other words, it is an inquiry into the balancing of the forces of demand and supply.

Marshall's influence on economics—at least in the English-speaking world—was enormous. His *Principles* was the leading economics text for several decades, and modern students can still learn much from it. As a professor at Cambridge, Marshall taught a great many of the next generation's leading economists. Today his neoclassical school continues to dominate the profession. It has received many challenges, but so far it has weathered them all.

as floor space. Nevertheless, most economists would agree that valid conclusions about the effects of rent control can be arrived at by applying the supply-and-demand model to that market. Thus, the supply-and-demand model serves a precise analytical function in some cases and a broader, more metaphorical function in others. That flexibility makes the model one of the most useful items in the economist's tool kit.

SUMMARY

1. **How does the price of a good or service affect the quantity of it that buyers demand?** Economists use the term *demand* to refer to the willingness and ability of buyers to purchase goods and services. According to the *law of demand,* there is an inverse relationship between the price of a good and the quantity of it that buyers demand. The *quantity demanded* is the quantity that buyers are willing and able to pay for. The law of demand can be represented graphically by a negatively sloped *demand curve.* A change in the quantity demanded is shown by a movement along the demand curve.

2. **How do other market conditions affect demand?** A change in any of the variables covered by the "other things being equal" clause of the law of demand causes a shift in the demand curve; this is known as a *change in demand.* Examples include changes in the prices of goods that are *substitutes* or *complements* of the good in question as well as changes in consumer incomes, expectations, and tastes.

3. **How does the price of a good affect the quantity supplied by sellers?** *Supply* refers to sellers' willingness and ability to offer products for sale in a market. In most markets an increase in the price of a good will increase the quantity of the good that sellers are willing to supply. This relationship can be shown as a positively sloped *supply curve.* The higher price gives producers an incentive to supply more, but rising opportunity costs set a limit on the amount they will supply at any given price.

4. **How do changes in other market conditions affect supply?** A change in any of the items covered by the "other things being equal" clause of the supply curve will shift the curve. Examples include changes in technology, changes in the prices of inputs, changes in the prices of other goods that could be produced with the same resources, and changes in expectations.

5. **How do supply and demand interact to determine the market price of a good or service?** In a market with a positively-sloped supply curve and a negatively-sloped demand curve, there is only one price at which the quantity of a good that sellers plan to supply will exactly match the quantity that buyers plan to purchase. That is known as the *equilibrium* price. At any higher price there will be a *surplus,* and at any lower price there will be a *shortage.*

6. **Why do market prices and quantities change in response to changes in market conditions?** A change in any market condition that shifts the supply or demand curve will change the equilibrium price and quantity in a market. For example, the demand curve may shift to the right as a result of a change in consumer incomes. This causes a shortage at the old price, and the price begins to rise. As the price rises, suppliers move up along the supply curve to a new equilibrium. No shift in the supply curve is required. On the

other hand, better technology may shift the supply curve to the right. In that case, there is a surplus at the old price, and the price will fall. As the price decreases, buyers will move down along their demand curve to a new equilibrium. No shift in the demand curve is required.

7. **How do price supports and price ceilings affect the operation of markets?** A price support prevents the market price from falling when the demand curve shifts to the left or the supply curve shifts to the right. The result may be a lasting surplus. A price ceiling prevents the price from rising to its equilibrium level. The result may be a permanent shortage. The total quantity supplied may then be less than the quantity that buyers would like to purchase at the ceiling price or even at the equilibrium price.

KEY TERMS

Supply	Supply curve
Demand	Change in quantity supplied
Law of demand	Change in supply
Demand curve	Equilibrium
Change in quantity demanded	Excess quantity demanded (shortage)
Change in demand	Inventory
Substitute goods	Excess quantity supplied (surplus)
Complementary goods	
Normal good	
Inferior good	

PROBLEMS AND TOPICS FOR DISCUSSION

1. **A shifting demand curve.** A vending machine company has studied the demand for soft drinks sold in cans from machines. On a 70-degree day consumers in the firm's territory will buy about 2,000 cans at a price of $0.75. For each $.05 rise in price, the quantity sold falls by 200 cans per day; for each 5-degree rise in the temperature, the quantity sold rises by 150 cans per day. The same relationships hold for decreases in price or temperature. Using this information, draw a set of curves showing the demand for soft drinks on days when the temperature is 60, 70, and 85 degrees. Then draw a separate diagram with temperature on the vertical axis and quantity on the horizontal axis. Draw a line representing the relationship between temperature and quantity when the price is $0.75. Next draw additional temperature-quantity lines for prices of $0.50 and $1.00. Do the two diagrams give the same information? Discuss. (Note: If you have any trouble with this exercise, review the appendix to Chapter 1, "Working with Graphs," especially the section entitled "Packing Three Variables into Two Dimensions.")

2. **Demand and the relative price of motor fuel in the 1980s.** In 1979 and 1980 the nominal price of motor fuel rose much more rapidly than the general price level, pushing up the relative price of motor fuel. As we would expect, the quantity sold decreased. In 1981 and 1982 the relative price leveled off and then began to fall, but the quantity sold continued to fall. Which one or more of the following hypotheses do you think best explains the behavior of motor fuel sales in 1981 and 1982? Illustrate each hypothesis with supply and demand curves.
   a. In the 1970s the demand curve had the usual negative slope. However, in 1981 and 1982 the demand curve shifted to an unusual positively sloped position.
   b. The demand curve had a negative slope throughout the period. However, the recession of 1981 and 1982 reduced consumers' real incomes and thus shifted the demand curve.

c. The demand curve has a negative slope at all times, but the shape depends partly on how much time consumers have to adjust to a change in prices. Over a short period, the demand curve is fairly steep because few adjustments can be made. Over the long term, it has a somewhat flatter slope because further adjustments, such as buying more fuel-efficient cars or moving closer to the job, can be made. Thus, the decreases in fuel sales in 1981 and 1982 were delayed reactions to the price increases that occurred in 1979 and 1980.

3. **Shortages, price controls, and queues.** During the late 1980s and early 1990s, economic reforms initiated by Soviet President Mikhail Gorbachev began to raise consumer incomes, but the Soviet government continued to impose price ceilings on basic goods like food, clothing, and household goods. As a result, there were severe shortages of many goods and long lines at all kinds of stores became common. Then, in January 1992, the new Russian government, under President Boris Yeltsin, removed retail price controls on most goods. Within a month, prices more than doubled on average and lines disappeared. Analyze these events using the supply and demand model. First draw a supply and demand diagram for some common good, say, toilet paper, showing the market in equilibrium before the beginning of the Gorbachev reforms. Next, use shifts of the appropriate curves to show why the combination of rising incomes plus price ceilings produced shortages and lines. Finally, show what happened when price controls were removed in 1992.

4. **Eliminating queues through flexible pricing.** You are a member of the Metropolitan Taxi Commission, which sets taxi fares for your city. You have been told that long lines of taxis form at the airport during off-peak hours. At peak hours, on the other hand, few taxis are available and there are long lines of passengers waiting for cabs. It is proposed that taxi fares from the airport to downtown be cut by 10 percent during off-peak hours and raised by 10 percent during peak hours. How do you think these changes would affect the queuing patterns of taxis and passengers? Do you think the proposal is a good one from the passengers' point of view? From the cabbies' point of view? From the standpoint of economic efficiency? Discuss.

5. **Rent control.** Turn to part (b) of Figure 2.10, which shows the long-run effects of rent control. If the controls are enforced and there are no disguised rent charges, landlords move down the supply curve to E_2. Buildings are abandoned or converted because of the low rent they bring in. Now consider some alternative possibilities.
   a. Suppose that the controls are poorly enforced so that landlords, through key deposits, furniture sales, or some other means, are able to charge as much as the market will bear. What will the resulting equilibrium price and quantity be, taking both open and disguised rental charges into account?
   b. Now suppose that the controls are enforced so that landlords really cannot collect more than $500 per month. However, the controls are not enforced against tenants who sublet. What will the equilibrium quantity and price be, including both the rent paid to landlords and the disguised rental payments made by subtenants to their subleasors?

CASE FOR DISCUSSION

The hottest topic at a recent exposition for suppliers and users of off-road heavy equipment was tire shortages. Booming Chinese demand for raw materials meant that mining companies in China, Russia, and Indonesia were stocking up on new earth moving equipment and wearing tires our faster on equipment they already owned.

While demand soared, supply had a hard time keeping up. Building a new production line for large tires can take more than two years. The *Financial Times* reported that some tire makers were reactivating mothballed production lines for old-fashioned bias-ply tires. While not as good as modern radial tires, they were good enough to satisfy demand from customers who just wanted something "black and round," according to Prashant Prabhu, president of the earth-mover and industrial tire business of Michelin, the French tire maker. Prabhu also said his company was revising its pricing for large tires to take the shortage into account.

According to *Light and Medium Truck Magazine,* the shortages of huge off-road tires were spilling over into the market for heavy-duty truck tires. In addition to sharply increased demand, it blamed rising prices for materials, including both natural and synthetic rubber. The magazine predicted that the shortage would last two years or more.

Expectations, based on past experience, were a significant factor slowing the adjustment of supply to the shortage. In 2000–2003, demand for heavy-duty tires from equipment makers had dropped by more than 50%, leaving some tire makers with serious overcapacity. The fear that recent high demand might not last was leading some manufacturers to take a "wait-and-see" attitude.

Sources: *Financial Times,* Materials squeeze leads to tyre shortage, By James Mackintosh Published: April 28 2005 03:00; *Light and Medium Truck Magazine,* May 2005, http://www.ttnews.com/lmt/May05/tire.asp (May 22, 2005); and *Rental Management Online,* http://www.rentalmanagementmag.com/newsart.asp?ARTID=1776, May 22, 2005.

QUESTIONS

1. Beginning from a position of equilibrium, use supply and demand curves to show how the tire market is affected by an increase in demand for earth-moving equipment. Does the supply curve shift? The demand curve? Both? Explain.
2. Using a scheme similar to Figure 2.10, distinguish between long-run and short-run supply in the tire market. What do you expect to happen to the price and quantity of tires in the short run? The long run?
3. Why are expectations a factor determining the position of the supply curve? How would the path of price and quantity over time differ with and without the element of supplier caution based on the experience of 2000–2003?

END NOTES

1. Before continuing, the reader may want to review the Chapter 1 appendix "Working with Graphs," especially the section entitled "Packing Three Variables into Two Dimensions."
2. The "plans" referred to need not be formal or thought out in detail, and are subject to change. A consumer might, for example, make out a shopping list for the supermarket based on the usual prices for various foods, but then revise it to take into account unexpected price increases or sales on certain items. On specific occasions, consumer decisions may even be completely impulsive, with little basis in rational calculation. The model of supply and demand does not require that every decision be based on precise analysis, but only that consumer intentions, on the average, are influenced by prices and other economic considerations.
3. Why might buyers and sellers enter the market expecting a price other than the one that permits equilibrium? It may be, for example, that market conditions have caused the supply or demand curve to shift unexpectedly, so that a price that formerly permitted equilibrium no longer does so. It may be that buyers or sellers expect conditions to change, but they do not change after all. Or, it may be that government policy has established a legal maximum or minimum price that differs from the equilibrium price. Later sections of the chapter will explore some of these possibilities.
4. This is a fairly restrictive assumption. In practice, a small number of housing units can move into or out of the rental market quickly in response to changing conditions. "Mother-in-law apartments" in private homes are an example. If conditions in the rental market are unfavorable, the owners of such units may simply leave them vacant. Allowing for such fast-

reaction units means that the short-run supply curve, while still quite steep, would not be vertical. However, a vertical short-run curve simplifies the geometry while capturing the essential features of the situation.

CHAPTER 3

Economic Theory, Markets, and Government

After reading this chapter, you will understand:

1. The basic structure of economic theory
2. Why rationality is of central importance in economics
3. The meaning of market performance and market failure
4. Some alternative theories of the economic role of government

Before reading this chapter, make sure you know the meaning of:

1. Positive and normative economics
2. Entrepreneurship
3. Law of unintended consequences
4. Supply and demand

THE PRECEDING TWO chapters introduced the theory of supply and demand. The theory is a useful one, with immediate applications not only to microeconomics but to macroeconomics as well. However, before seeking further practical applications, or developing some of the more detailed theories that lie behind the deceptively simple concepts of supply and demand, it will be worth taking the time to ask some more general questions about the structure of economic theory, the reliability with which markets work, and the nature of the individuals and organizations that populate the economist's world. That will be the job of this chapter.

THE STRUCTURE OF ECONOMIC THEORY

To *analyze* something means to break it down into its component parts. A literary critic might analyze a novel in terms of such basic components as plot, character, and dialog. A detective might analyze a murder in terms of motive, means, and opportunity. Similarly, economists look for certain common elements when they analyze the choices people make in using scarce resources to meet their wants.

Objectives, Constraints, and Choices

The elements of which every economic theory is composed are three types of statements: statements about objectives, statements about constraints on opportunities, and statements about choices.

STATEMENTS ABOUT OBJECTIVES An *objective* is anything people want to achieve. A business owner may have the objective of earning the greatest possible profit. A consumer may strive for the greatest possible material satisfaction with a given income. People in any situation may blend their pursuit of narrowly "economic" objectives with family values, social responsibilities, and so on. Terms such as *aims*, *goals*, and *preferences* are interchangeable with *objectives*.

STATEMENTS ABOUT CONSTRAINTS ON OPPORTUNITIES A key part of every economic theory is a statement of the constraints on the set of opportunities that are available to choose among in a given situation. In a world of scarcity, alternatives are never unlimited, and constraints are universal. Some constraints relate to what is physically possible, given available resources and knowledge. Only so many bales of hay can be loaded into a truck that can hold 1,000 cubic feet of cargo. Only so many pounds of iron can be smelted from a ton of ore of a given quality.

Other constraints take the form not of physical limits but of opportunity costs, often defined in terms of prices. For example, there is no physical limit to the number of pairs of shoes a person can own, but if shoes cost $60 a pair and sweaters cost $30 apiece, each pair of shoes purchased means forgoing the opportunity to buy two sweaters (or something else of equal value).

Still other constraints take the form of legal rules. For example, it may be physically possible and worthwhile, in terms of costs and benefits, for a farmer to control insect pests by spraying DDT; however, it is illegal to do so. A particularly important set of legal constraints are those that define *property rights*. **Property rights** are legal rules that establish what things a person may use or control and the conditions under which that use or control may be exercised. In short, they establish what a person *owns*.

Property rights

Legal rules that establish what things a person may use or control, and the conditions under which such use or control may be exercised.

As an everyday example, consider the property rights that establish a person's ownership of a house. Those rights include the right to live in the house, to modify its structure, and to control the arrangement of furniture in its rooms. In some communities, ownership may include the right to park a boat trailer in the driveway and to have a swing set on the front lawn. In others, those particular rights may be limited by zoning laws or restrictive covenants.

Property rights extend to more abstract relationships as well. For example, ownership of a share of common stock in ConocoPhillips Corporation gives the stockholder a complex package of rights, including the rights to vote on issues affecting the firm and to share in the firm's profits. As another example, a software firm's copyright on a program it has produced gives it control over the conditions under which the program may be licensed for use by others.

STATEMENTS ABOUT CHOICES The final component of an economic theory is a statement of the choice that is most likely to be made, given particular objectives and constraints on opportunities. For example, Chapter 5 will look at the choices that underlie the law of demand. There, consumers will be seen as having the objective of obtaining the greatest possible satisfaction, given the constraints placed on their opportunities by their budgets, the range of goods available, and the prices of those goods. Given those objectives and constraints, the law of demand states that people can be expected to choose to increase their purchases of a good when its price is reduced, other things being equal.

Economic Theory and Rationality

Although all economic theories contain the three types of statements just listed, a successful theory is more than just a list—its elements need to form a coherent whole. Our understanding of the structure of economic theory would be incomplete without a discussion of a key assumption that serves to hold the three elements of a theory together: the assumption that people choose the *best* way of accomplishing their objectives, given the constraints they face. In other words, people are *rational.*

Rationality

Acting purposefully to achieve an objective, given constraints on the opportunities that are available.

Rationality means acting purposefully to achieve an objective, given constraints on available opportunities. Rationality also means that people behave in a way that benefits them. Note that it does not necessarily mean they behave legally. In certain environments, illegal behavior may be rational, in that, it could benefit the individual. (This assumption is not universal. All of us at times and some us routinely behave irrationally. Ask yourself how many of us smoke, over drink, over eat. These behaviors are irrational in that they harm us, but we continue to do them none the less.) The concept of rationality is built into the definition of economics given at the beginning of this book, which speaks of choosing the best way to use scarce resources to meet human wants. To say that some ways of using scarce resources are better than others, and that those are the ones people tend to choose, is to express the essence of rationality.

The assumption of rationality, so central to economics, is sometimes misunderstood as a psychological or philosophical assertion about human nature—an assertion that people are always coolly calculating, not emotional or impulsive. A critic once ridiculed economists for seeing the human individual as a "lightning calculator of pleasures and pains, who oscillates like a homogeneous globule of desire under the impulse of stimuli . . . [who] spins symmetrically about his own spiritual axis until the parallelogram of forces bears down upon him, whereupon he follows the line of the resultant. "[1] But as used in economics, the rationality assumption has nothing to do with that sort of caricature of "economic man."

The rationality assumption, properly understood, is simply a tool for giving structure to theories about the choices people make. Economists then fill in the specifics of the structure by observing what people do in various situations, that is, what choices they make when faced with certain opportunities.

Consider a very simple example. Suppose Bundy Hall, a dormitory, and Carpenter Hall, where economics classes are held, are located at opposite corners of a grassy quadrangle in the middle of a college campus. Across the diagonal of the quad between Bundy and Carpenter, a well-worn path has been beaten into the grass. Why is the path there, even though there are perfectly good sidewalks around all four sides of the quad?

If you ask an economist that question, the answer you get will probably be something like this: "The student's objective is to minimize the time it takes to get to class so that they can sleep as late as possible. Of the alternative routes to class, the diagonal path is the shortest one, so that's the path they choose to take."

Most people would probably accept that theory as a reasonable explanation of the path across the quad. Why? First and most important, because it is consistent with the observation that the path is there and students use it. Second, adding to its appeal, the theory corresponds with our intuition about what we would do in the given situation. Although economists are wary of relying too heavily on their own experience to verify their theories, in practice introspection plays a significant role. Finally, our theory about the path across the quad is likely to be accepted partly because it is simple. Economists, like their colleagues in other social and natural sciences, tend to prefer simple theories to complex ones when both are consistent with given observations. (The preference for simple theories over complex ones is known as **Ockham's razor**, after a fourteenth-century philosopher who urged its use to "shave away" unnecessary theoretical complexities.)

Ockham's razor

The principle that simpler theories are to be preferred to more complex ones when both are consistent with given observations.

So far, so good. But suppose now that a transfer student arrives from another campus and says, "At Treelined University there is a big quad just like this one, and there is no diagonal path across it. Here's a picture to prove it. What do you say to that, O Wise Economist?"

This is not a far-fetched possibility. Observations that are inconsistent with previously accepted theories cross economists' desks frequently. When that happens, they look for a way to modify the theory so that it provides a rational basis for the new observation. Given the structure of economic theory, we can expect the search to take one of two directions.

First, closer investigation will often show that the original theory failed to allow for some *constraint* on the opportunities available to people in the situation under study. For example, it might be that the campus police at Treelined University have a nasty practice of slapping a \$20 fine on any student caught walking on the grass. A modified theory is then formulated that takes this constraint into account: "Even when the shortest distance to class is a diagonal across the quad, a fine for walking on the grass will induce a certain percentage of students to take the sidewalk. The percentage taking the sidewalk will increase as the fine increases, so that with a sufficiently large fine, not enough students will take the shortcut to wear a path in the grass." This more general theory is consistent with observations made on both campuses.

Second, if closer investigation fails to turn up some previously unnoticed constraint on opportunities, it may turn out that the original theory was based on a mistaken understanding of the *objectives* of the people involved. In the case under discussion, it was assumed that students on both campuses placed a high priority on getting to class on time. However, perhaps the students of Treelined University take great pride in the appearance of their campus. They would rather be late to class than trample on the grass. Thus, there is a path on one campus and not on the other because students at the two schools rank their objectives differently.

Clearly differing choices can sometimes properly be attributed to differing objectives. For example, if Marcia buys pistachio ice cream while Mark buys chocolate ice cream, and the two flavors cost the same, we are comfortable concluding that their choices differ because their preferences do. However, as a rule, economists like first to see whether an explanation of different choices can be framed in terms of differing constraints on opportunities—prices, regulations, climate, and so on. If constraints are not checked first, explaining things in terms of differing preferences is simply too easy. Take, for example, the fact that people in the United States drive larger cars, on average, than people in Italy. Who would be satisfied just to say that Italians prefer little cars, without noting that drivers in Italy face different constraints—narrower streets, more expensive gasoline, and so on?

Something similar can be said about the rationality assumption. Just as economists are wary of relying too much on differences in preferences to explain choices, they are also wary of explaining choices in nonrational terms. Suppose, for example, that an economist sees a student, obviously late for class, who, instead of cutting across the quad or even hurrying around by the sidewalk, is walking slowly in circles in the middle of the grass. The economist questions the student, seeking a rational explanation. "Have you lost a contact lens? Are you exercising?" If an explanation cannot be found in terms of constraints and the rational pursuit of objectives, the economist is faced with a dilemma. One alternative would be to give up on studying this particular aspect of human behavior and call in some other specialist, perhaps a psychotherapist. The other would be to consider whether the concept of rationality itself needs to be rethought in order to understand what is going on. Increasingly, economists are choosing the alternative of rethinking the concept of rationality.

Full and Bounded Rationality

One way in which the rationality assumption can be modified is to distinguish full and bounded rationality.

Full rationality

The assumption that people make full use of all available information in calculating how best to meet their objectives.

Bounded rationality

The assumption that people intend to make choices that best serve their objectives, but have limited ability to acquire and process information.

Theories based on **full rationality** assume that people make full use of all available information in calculating how best to meet their objectives. The cost of making decisions, the possibility of error, and often, the cost of acquiring information are put to one side in theories based on full rationality.

On the other hand, some theories assume *bounded* rather than full rationality. To assume **bounded rationality** means to assume that people *intend* to make choices that best serve their objectives, but that they have limited ability to acquire and process information. They typically have to rely on partial information and use rules of thumb that do not make full use of the information they have.

For example, consider the task of choosing which university to attend. If college applicants strictly followed the assumption of full rationality, they would make full use of all sources of information available. They would carefully study the information on the Web site of every college in the country. On the basis of the information, they would outline preferred four-year programs of study at each school. They would systematically interview people who had attended all of the schools that rated near the top of their list and would perhaps visit those schools. Only when all information was in hand would they make a choice; in doing so, they might weigh such factors as the probable grades they would earn at each school, the influence of grades and choice of school on their lifetime incomes, and so on.

On the other hand, if applicants followed the assumptions of bounded rationality, they would conduct a more limited search. Perhaps they would arbitrarily limit their search in advance to schools from a certain region. They would listen to what friends and relatives said about schools they had attended and perhaps visit the nearest schools. Their final choice might be based more on advice from people they trusted and less on systematic balancing of objective information.

In the chapters that follow, we will encounter examples of theories based both on full and on bounded rationality.

Self-regarding preferences

A set of objectives that depend only on the material welfare of the decision maker.

Other-regarding preferences

A set of objectives that includes not only the material welfare of the decision maker, but also the material welfare of others and their attitudes toward the decision maker.

Self-Regarding Versus Other-Regarding Preferences

Another way to modify the assumption of rationality is to expand the definition of objectives to include human feelings like fairness, altruism, trust, spite, and envy. These feelings can be captured by distinguishing between **self-regarding** and **other-regarding** preferences. People who are concerned only with their own material welfare are said to have self-regarding preferences. People who balance considerations of their own material welfare with the welfare of others and also take into account what others think about them are said to have other-regarding preferences.

One simple example of other-regarding preferences is revealed in the "ultimatum game" described in *Applying Economic Ideas 3.1*. Results from repeated experiments around the world suggest that people often behave in ways that are better explained on the basis of other-regarding rather than strictly self-regarding preferences. Somewhat more controversial is the issue of whether to describe choices based on altruism, envy, and similar feelings as rational. The tendency in economics today seems to be

APPLYING ECONOMIC IDEAS 3.1
ULTIMATUMS, DICTATORS, AND OTHER GAMES

In recent years, games have become increasingly popular as a tool of economic research. One game that consistently produces results that contradict narrow definitions of economic rationality is the so-called *ultimatum game*.

The game works like this. Player A is given a sum of money, say $10. She is then asked to offer some share of the money to Player B. Next Player B has the option of accepting the offer or rejecting it. If B rejects A's offer, neither player gets to keep anything. If player B accepts, they divide the money according to the terms that A proposed. The name of the game comes from the fact that there is only one offer and only one chance to refuse—no extended bargaining is allowed, no repeated play during which an objective of developing a reputation or building trust might come into play.

Under the assumption of full rationality and self-regarding preferences, the outcome of the game is easy to predict. First, we conclude that Player B will never rationally reject any nonzero offer. To do so would give up a certain (although perhaps small) reward in favor of getting nothing at all. Second, we conclude that Player A, knowing that B will never reject any nonzero offer, no matter how small, will rationally make the smallest offer allowed. (Sometimes the rules might say this is one cent, sometimes one dollar, or whatever.)

But that is not at all what happens when the game is actually played. In practice, Player A typically offers a substantial amount, say 30 to 50 percent of the total. Furthermore, B typically rejects offers that are too low, with the frequency of rejection rising sharply for offers below 20 percent or so of the total. The experiment has been repeated thousands of times, not only with American college students but with African hunter-gatherers, Wall Street brokers, residents of Mongolia, and almost any group one can think of. The average amount offered and the threshold for rejection differ somewhat from one society to another, but it seems that the narrowly rational result is never observed.

What is going on? One hypothesis is that, when placed in the Player A position, people behave altruistically. They take pleasure from pleasing Player B. Another hypothesis is that Player A is not altruistic, but rather, strategically motivated by the fear that a too-low offer will be rejected. But if so, what motivates Player B? Why are low offers rejected when there is nothing material to gain by doing so? Is B motivated by some innate aversion to inequality? By a spiteful desire to draw pleasure from punishing an insufficiently generous Player A?

One way to try to sort out the motives is to play the related *dictator game* with a similar group of subjects. In the dictator game, Player A gets to keep her share regardless of whether B accepts or rejects the offer. Since there is no fear of rejection, any nonzero offer must be motivated purely by altruism. Interestingly, although the dictator game typically produces smaller offers than the ultimatum game, the offers are still substantially above zero. Seemingly, both altruism and fear of rejection play a role.

There are many, many variants of the games. Sometimes the players are known to each other, sometimes anonymous. Sometimes the game is played in a "double-blind" form where neither the players nor the experimenter knows the individual identities of the players or amount specific individuals offer or reject. (The double-blind variant is supposed to eliminate the possibility that Player A might be ashamed of appearing "too selfish" in the eyes of the experimenter.) No matter what, the offers never fall to zero. Human behavior is stubbornly more complex than narrowly rational, self-regarding preferences can account for!

toward expanding the concept of rationality in a way that allows for other-regarding preferences.

Richard H. Thaler of the University of Chicago suggests that including ideas like bounded rationality and other-regarding preferences will once again make economics more of a social science, as it was in the past. In the 19th and early 20th centuries, economists seemed comfortable with discussing emotional and psychological elements of economic behavior. As a preference for rigorous mathematical modeling came to dominate economics in the second half of the 20th century, these elements were eliminated. Almost all models of the period were based on full rationality and self-regarding preferences. While admitting that it is harder to construct models that incorporate the full range of human behavior, Thaler is hopeful that today's generation of economists are up to the task.[2]

MARKET PERFORMANCE AND MARKET FAILURE

Economic choices are not made in a vacuum. They are made within the context of a set of institutions, of which markets and government are two of the most important. This section offers a preview of what coming chapters will have to say about markets, especially the key concepts of *market performance* and *market failure*. The next section will preview the role of government in the economy.

Market Performance

Market performance

The degree to which markets work efficiently in providing arrangements for mutually beneficial trade.

Earlier, we defined a *market* as any arrangement that people have for trading with one another. When economists speak of **market performance**, then, they are referring to how efficiently markets do their job of providing arrangements for mutually beneficial trade.

Ideally, markets would make it possible to carry out every exchange that is to the mutual benefit of the parties involved. Suppose we are talking about the market for peaches. The parties to peach trading are farmers and consumers. An exchange will benefit consumers if the satisfaction they get from a peach is at least as great as the satisfaction they would get from spending the same amount on the next most attractive good (say, an apple). The exchange will benefit producers if the price paid for a peach is at least high enough to cover the opportunity cost of producing it. If there is a price that makes the trade beneficial both to consumers and to producers, then carrying out the trade will be *efficient* inasmuch as it will leave at least one party better off and neither worse off.

Although the details will require several chapters to work out, a simple diagram can give an intuitive idea of efficient market performance. Figure 3.1 shows two curves that represent the market for peaches. The demand curve represents the benefit of peaches to consumers as reflected by their willingness to buy peaches, given the price of peaches, the prices of alternative goods, and so on. The supply curve represents the opportunity costs of producing an additional peach as reflected by the willingness of farmers to produce and sell the product under given conditions.

At any point to the left of the intersection of the two curves, the price consumers would willingly pay for a peach (as indicated by the height of the demand curve) is greater than the minimum needed to cover farmers' costs (as indicated by the height of the supply curve). Thus, to the left of the intersection, trades carried out at any price between the two curves are mutually beneficial to consumers and producers. However, to the right of the intersection, the maximum consumers would find it worthwhile to pay for still more peaches is less than what is needed to cover farmers'

FIGURE 3.1 PERFORMANCE OF THE MARKET FOR PEACHES

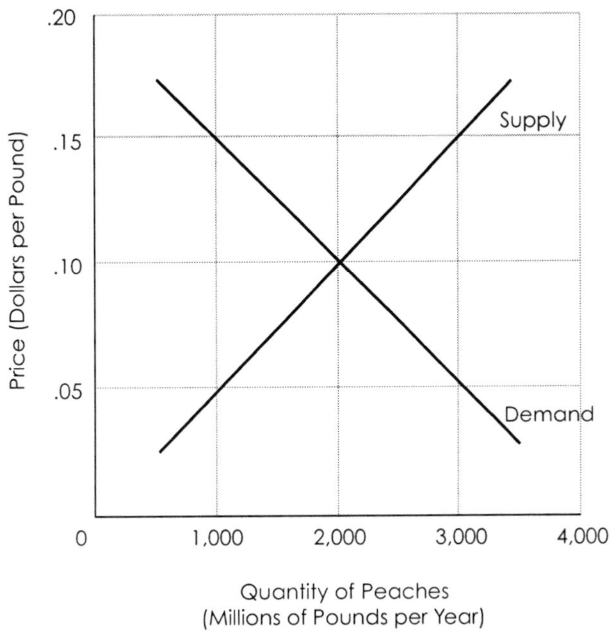

This exhibit shows hypothetical supply and demand curves for peaches. The demand curve reflects the willingness of consumers to buy peaches, given the price of peaches and the prices of alternative goods. The supply curve represents the willingness of farmers to sell peaches, given the price of peaches and the opportunity costs of production. At any point to the left of the intersection of the curves, the price that consumers would willingly pay for a peach (as indicated by the height of the demand curve) is greater than the minimum needed to cover farmers' costs (as indicated by the height of the supply curve). Thus, up to that point, exchanges carried out at a price between the two curves are mutually beneficial to consumers and producers. At any point to the right of the intersection, the maximum amount that consumers would be willing to pay for still more peaches is less than the amount needed to cover farmers' costs. Thus, production beyond the intersection point would not be efficient. It follows, then, that a market in which production is carried out just up to but not beyond the intersection point performs efficiently.

costs. There is no price at which further trades would benefit both parties, and therefore production beyond the intersection point would not be efficient.

It follows, then, that a market in which production is carried out just up to but not beyond the intersection point performs efficiently. At a lower quantity, some mutually beneficial exchanges would not occur. At a higher quantity, no price could be found that would benefit both parties. Not only is the quantity indicated by the intersection of the two curves just right, but the price is, too. Any higher price would lead to a wasteful surplus of peaches, whereas any lower price would lead to a shortage in which some consumers' wants would not be satisfied.

It is hard to exaggerate the enthusiasm that economists have for markets that generate such efficient outcomes. From those pursuing economic reform in the nations of the former Soviet Union to candidates touting new solutions to problems of American capitalism, there is widespread agreement that within large areas of economic life, markets can be an efficient means of solving basic economic problems. Yet even the most enthusiastic fans of markets recognize that they do not always function perfectly. Several conditions must be met before markets reach a stable equilibrium exactly at the intersection of the supply and demand curves. Let's look briefly at some of the situations in which market performance falls short of the ideal, again leaving details to later chapters.

Market Failure

Market failure

A situation in which a market fails to coordinate choices in a way that achieves efficient use of resources.

A **market failure** is a situation in which a market fails to coordinate choices in a way that achieves efficient use of resources. Of the many possible sources of market failure, three deserve special attention. We will discuss them under the headings of *externalities, public goods,* and *insufficient competition.* Other sources of market failure will be mentioned more briefly.

Externalities

The effects of producing or consuming a good whose impact on third parties other than buyers and sellers of the good is not reflected in the good's price.

EXTERNALITIES One type of market failure is failure to transmit information about scarcity in the form of prices. For markets to perform their job efficiently, prices should reflect the opportunity costs of producing the goods or services in question. Ordinarily, market prices do reflect at least a reasonable approximation of opportunity costs. However, situations arise in which producers' (and consumers') actions have effects on third parties, that is, people other than the buyer and seller who carry out a transaction. These third-party effects, which are not reflected in prices, are known as **externalities**. When externalities are present, the price system does not transmit accurate information about opportunity costs.

The classic example of a negative externality is pollution. Suppose a utility burns coal in its boilers to generate electricity. The costs of fuel, capital, and labor come to $.05 per kilowatt hour of electricity produced. They are called *internal costs* because they are borne by the utility itself. Those costs are reflected in market transactions—payments to coal producers, workers, stockholders and bondholders, and so on. Internal costs are part of the opportunity cost of making electricity because they represent the forgone opportunities of using the same natural resources, capital, and labor in some other industry. To stay in business, the utility must receive a price of at least $.05 per kilowatt hour, that is, a price at least equal to the internal opportunity costs.

But the internal costs are not the only costs of making electricity, as we saw in the case study at the beginning of the chapter. In the process of burning coal, the utility spews out clouds of sulfur dioxide, soot, and other pollutants. The pollution damages health, kills trees, and corrodes buildings in areas downwind from the plant. Those effects are referred to as *external costs* of generating electricity because they are borne by third parties—people who are neither buyers nor sellers of electricity or any of the inputs used in making it. From the viewpoint of the economy as a whole, external costs are also part of the opportunity cost of generating power. They represent the value of the factors of production that are destroyed by the pollution (such as dead trees or workers in other firms taking extended sick leave) or required in order to repair its effects (repainting houses, treating pollution-related diseases).

Suppose that pollution damage of all kinds comes to \$.02 per kilowatt hour of power produced. Added to the \$.05 in internal costs, the \$.02 of external costs brings the overall opportunity cost of steel to \$.07 per kilowatt hour. This figure reflects the value of the factors of production used directly by the utility plus those that are destroyed or diverted from other uses by the pollution.

If the price of electric power is set by supply and demand, its equilibrium value will tend toward the level of \$.05 per kilowatt hour that just covers internal costs. But this sends a false signal to users of electricity: It tells them that producing a kilowatt hour puts a smaller drain on the economy's scarce factors of production than is really the case. Thus, electricity users will use more power than they should. They will be less inclined to buy new, more efficient machinery, to design products so as to use less electricity, to shift to cleaner natural gas, and so on. In short, the market will fail to achieve efficient resource allocation because prices will have sent users the wrong information.

In a later chapter, in which we return to the economics of pollution, we will see that externalities can be interpreted as defects in the economy's system of property rights. For example, air pollution arises because no one has clear ownership rights to air. If landowners had the right to control the use of air above their property, they could, in principle, prevent utilities and other pollution sources from using their airspace to dispose of wastes unless they were paid appropriate compensation. Following this reasoning, some economists advocate restructuring property rights to control pollution.

There are circumstances that producers' actions have beneficial effects on third parties that the beneficiaries do not pay for, the classic *free rider* situation. This situation is referred to as a positive externality. Consider the benefit we all derive from public health inoculations. Don't we all benefit from someone not spreading tuberculosis or a child not spreading measles? In cases of positive externalities, when those who don't pay the price yet receive the benefit, society expects other institutions (government) to compensate the source of the benefit. Along with public health, public education is a positive externality. Every citizen, regardless if they went to public school or have children in public schools, benefit from universal education. (Think of what it would be like if 40% of the labor force was illiterate?)

Public goods

Goods that (1) cannot be provided for one person without also being provided for others, and (2) when provided for one person can be provided for others at zero additional sum.

PUBLIC GOODS The goods and services discussed in all the examples used to this point—chicken, cars, apartments, and so on—share two characteristics or *properties:* (1) The supplier can decide to supply the good to some people and to exclude others; this is termed the *property of exclusion.* (2) Use of a unit of the good by one person limits the possibility of use of that unit by other people; this is termed the *property of rivalry.* Some goods do not possess the properties of exclusion and rivalry, however. These are known as **public goods.** Lacking the property of exclusion, they cannot be provided for one person without also being provided for others. Lacking the property of rivalry, once they are provided for one person, they can be provided for others at no extra cost. Public goods, like externalities, are a potential source of market failure.

Perhaps the closest thing to a pure public good is national defense and public broadcasting (PBS/NPR). One person cannot be protected against nuclear attack or invasion without the protection being extended to everyone. And your watching *Sesame Street* or listening to *Prairie Home Companion* does not deny someone else that same experience. Also, it costs no more to protect a single resident of an area than to safeguard an entire city or region. And it doesn't cost more to have 100 radio or TVs tuned in to PBS/NPR than 1,000,000. Although pure public goods are rare, other goods may lack the properties of exclusion or rivalry to some extent. These can be called impure public goods. Police protection provides one example: In their functions of promoting public safety in general and deterring street crime, the police are providing a public good. But in their function of solving an individual crime, such as a burglary, they are providing a private good to the person who hopes to recover the stolen property. Maintenance of urban streets, the provision of parks, even the space program have been cited as examples of goods that are neither purely public nor purely private. The library and public schools are similar. If you borrow the one copy of the *Da Vinci Code* from the library, or if you register for a popular nursing class at Carroll, then you will exclude someone else from the reading of the novel or access to the course.

Private firms have difficulty making a profit selling products that, once they are provided to one customer, become available to others at no additional cost. To see why the market may fail in such cases, imagine that someone tries to set up a private missile defense system—call it Star Wars, Inc.—to be paid for by selling subscriptions to people who want protection from a nuclear attack. There are two reasons I might choose not to subscribe. First, I know that if my neighbors subscribed and got their homes protected, my home would be protected too, even if I did not pay; I could take a *free ride* on a public good paid for by others. Second, I might be willing to contribute if I had *assurance* that at least, say, 1,000 of my neighbors did so. That would raise enough money to buy at least one missile. But I would not contribute without the assurance that this minimum would be met. Contributing along with just 500 neighbors would buy only half a missile, which would be useless, and my contribution would be completely wasted.

Economists have long argued that the *free-rider problem* and the *assurance problem*, which make people reluctant to contribute voluntarily to the support of public goods, mean that government may have to provide those goods if they are to be provided at all. (We say *may* because, as *Applying Economic Ideas 3.2* illustrates, some things that have the characteristics of public goods are provided by private firms.) However, many goods and services that are provided at public expense are public goods only to a small extent, if at all. Take education, for example. The principal beneficiaries of public education are students. It is not impossible to exclude students from the schools. Only a few schools, public or private, operate on an "open admission" basis. Others select their students according to neighborhood, ability to pay, or scholastic achievement.

APPLYING ECONOMIC IDEAS 3.2

PRIVATE PROVISION OF PUBLIC GOODS

Many economists argue that private firms cannot supply public goods because of the assurance and free rider problems that arise whenever goods have the properties of nonexclusion and nonrivalry. In practice, however, private firms and voluntary organizations often do find methods of providing goods that have these properties. Examples include broadcast radio and television, computer software, and amenities like streets and parks in residential neighborhoods.

In some cases private firms simply alter the product in a way that makes it possible to exclude free riders. Thus, television signals can be scrambled so that they can be received only by subscribers who rent a decoder; computer software can be copy protected so that the original purchasers cannot make free copies for their friends; and streets can be equipped with toll booths. In this case, the good ceases to be a public good, even though it continues to have the property of nonrivalry.

Exclusion has its disadvantages, however. The necessary technology may be expensive and less than fully reliable, and the attempt to exclude may be offensive to customers the firm would like to attract. To avoid these disadvantages, private firms and voluntary organizations often use other techniques to provide public goods.

- One approach is to link the public good to an ordinary good, offering the two as a package deal. Thus, public radio stations send their contributors magazines with movie reviews and program guides; computer software companies provide advice via telephone to legitimate registered purchasers; and real estate developers find it worthwhile to build residential streets as part of a package included with the sale of private homes.
- Another approach is to build on the psychological satisfaction of contributing to a good cause or the psychological discomfort of being recognized as a free rider. This works best in small communities where everyone knows everyone else. But organizations like public radio stations can achieve something of the same effect by publicly thanking contributors over the air.
- Still another device is the "assurance contract." Sometimes people hesitate to contribute to a good cause because they fear their contribution will be in vain unless others join them. In such a case, the provider can accept pledges of support that will be activated only if an agreed minimum of support is received. Thus, families might be asked to contribute checks to a fund to build a neighborhood playground on the understanding that the checks will be returned uncashed if the necessary minimum is not raised.

As these examples show, the economic category of "public good" does not always mean a good that must be provided by the government.

Moreover, education clearly has the property of rivalry in consumption. Students cannot be added to a school without some additional expense. The more students a school admits, the more teachers, classrooms, laboratories, and other facilities it must provide. Thus, education fits the definition of a public good, if at all, only to the extent that it has some overall benefit such as promoting good citizenship.

Think of gated communities or colleges with private security forces and colleges. These institutions provide private police forces for the protection of those within the community who have paid the fee. Towson and Carroll security won't leave the campus to pursue a suspect. Nor will they protect students or staff anywhere off campus.

INSUFFICIENT COMPETITION A third source of market failure is insufficient competition. As we have seen, market prices should reflect opportunity costs if they are to guide resource allocation efficiently. In the case of harmful externalities, market failure occurs because prices fall below opportunity costs. Where competition is insufficient, however, market failure can occur because prices are too high.

Monopoly

A situation in which there is only a single seller of a good or service.

As an extreme case, consider a market in which there is only a single seller of a good or service; such a market is termed a **monopoly**. Residential electric service is a frequently cited example. Suppose that Metropolitan Electric can generate power at an opportunity cost of $10 per kilowatt hour. Selling electric power at that price would guide customers in choosing between electricity and other energy sources, such as oil or coal, and in undertaking energy-saving investments, such as home insulation and high-efficiency lighting.

If homeowners could buy electricity from anyone they chose the way they buy eggs or gasoline, the forces of competition, acting through supply and demand, would push the market price toward the level of opportunity costs. The utility would not sell power at a price below opportunity costs because doing so would put it out of business. Further, in a competitive market any seller that tried to raise prices much above opportunity costs would be undercut by others.

However, utilities do not compete in selling to residential customers. Every home, after all, is connected to only one set of power lines. In this case, if not restrained by government regulation, a utility could substantially increase its profits by charging a price higher than opportunity costs. Of course, raising the price would mean that less power would be sold as customers moved up and to the left along their demand curves. But up to a point, the greater profit per kilowatt hour sold would more than outweigh the effects of the reduction in quantity demanded.

If too high a price is charged, homeowners will get a false message regarding the opportunity cost of electricity. They may make substitutions that are not economically justified. For example, they may switch from electricity to oil for heat even in regions where cheap hydroelectric power is available, or from electric air conditioning to gas air conditioning even in areas where the opportunity cost of electricity is below that of gas.

Market failures due to insufficient competition are not necessarily limited to the extreme case of monopoly. Under some circumstances, competition among a small number of firms may also lead to prices that are above opportunity costs, especially if the firms engage in collusion. The circumstances under which competition is or is not sufficient to ensure the efficient operation of markets is the subject of an enormous body of economic research and of more than a few controversies, as we will see in coming chapters.

OTHER MARKET FAILURES Some economists would list other sources of market failure in addition to the three just discussed. For example, the macroeconomic phenomena of inflation and cyclical unemployment are sometimes considered to be market failures. Certainly, an economy that is subject to excessive inflation and unemployment provides a poor environment in which to coordinate the actions of buyers and sellers of individual goods and factor services. However, the effects of inflation and unemployment, together with policies intended to keep them under control, lie outside the scope of the microeconomics course.

As we have defined it, market failure means failure to achieve an *efficient* allocation of scarce resources. In addition, the market may or may not achieve an *equitable* allocation of resources. Whether unfairness, inequality, and economic injustice in a market economy should be given the label *market failure* is more a matter of terminology than of substance. In this book, market failure is defined in a way that makes it an issue of efficiency alone. But this definition is not meant to deny the importance of issues of economic justice. Such issues will be discussed extensively at several points in the following chapters, although not under the heading of market failure.

THE ECONOMIC ROLE OF GOVERNMENT

Although markets play an enormous role in answering the key questions of who, what, how, and for whom, not all economic decisions are made in markets. Some important economic decisions are made in hierarchies. Allocation of resources within a business firm is one example of hierarchical decision making; we will focus on that later. Here we are concerned with the role of government, the other major example of hierarchy in economics.

If we want to understand the microeconomic role of government, a good place to begin is by asking, Why does government play any role in the economy at all? Why, that is, cannot all decisions be made by households and private firms coordinating their actions through markets? Economists offer two answers, one based on the notion of market failure, the other on that of *rent seeking*. The answers are partly contradictory and partly complementary. Each will figure prominently in coming chapters, and each deserves a brief preview here.

The Market Failure Theory of Government

According to the market failure theory of government, the principal economic role of government is to step in where markets fail to allocate resources efficiently and fairly. Each type of market failure calls for a particular type of governmental intervention.

Take the case of pollution. Earlier we gave the example of a utility whose contribution to air pollution caused $.02 worth of damage for every kilowatt hour of electricity. Government can do a number of things to correct the resulting market failure, for example, it can require the utility to install pollution control equipment that will prevent poisonous gas from escaping into the atmosphere.

When markets fail to supply public goods, government also is called in. Often, as in the case of national defense, the government simply becomes the producer of the public good. In other cases, such as education, which some economists consider to be in part a public good, the government need not be the sole producer. Private schools and colleges are encouraged with subsidies and tax benefits to add to the supply of education produced by public institutions.

Government has attempted to remedy market failures arising from insufficient competition in a variety of ways. In some cases government uses *antitrust laws* to preserve competition by preventing mergers of competing firms, or even by breaking large firms up into a number of smaller ones. In other cases, such as the electric power industry, *regulation* is used to control prices charged by a monopoly firm. In a few cases, such as the Tennessee Valley Authority's electric power facilities, the government itself may become a monopoly producer of a good or service.

The Public Choice Theory of Government

The market failure theory of government is sometimes criticized for being more of a theory about what the government ought to do than about what it actually does. The problem, say the critics, is that too many government programs, rather than correcting market failures, seem to promote inefficiency or inequality in markets that would function well without government intervention. Price supports for milk are an example. That program holds the price of milk above its equilibrium level, thus causing persistent surpluses. That is hardly efficient. Further, although some benefits go to farmers who are in financial difficulty, thus serving the goal of fairness, many of the subsidies go to farmers who are financially well off.

Critics of the market failure theory maintain that government policies should be understood not in terms of broad social goals like efficiency and fairness but in terms of how people use the institutions of government to pursue their own self-interest. This approach to policy analysis is known as **public choice theory**. Another example is a highly paid professional athlete. What would the opportunity cost (highest alternative salary) Ray Lewis could earn if he were not on the Ravens?

Public choice theory
The branch of economics that studies how people use the institutions of government in pursuit of their own interests.

Economic rent
Any payment to a factor of production in excess of its opportunity cost.

RENTS AND RENT SEEKING One of the key concepts of public choice theory is *economic rent*. In everyday language, a *rent* is simply a payment made for the use of something, say, an apartment or a car. Public choice theorists use the term in a more specialized sense, however. An **economic rent** is any payment to a factor of production in excess of its opportunity cost. An example is the huge income a popular author like J. K. Rowling or Dan Brown earns from a new novel—an income much higher than the author could earn working the same amount time in any other line of work.

When rents are earned through competition in markets, they are called *pure economic profits*. Entrepreneurs are always on the lookout for earning such profits, for example, by introducing a new product superior to that of rival firms, or by being the first to implement a cost-saving production method. When they are successful, the income they earn may be substantially higher than what others are able to earn by employing similar factors of production in less imaginative ways.

Pure economic profit that entrepreneurs earn through private market activity is not the only category of economic rents, however. Firms, workers, and resource owners often turn to government in search of rents, rather than trying to outwit their rivals in the marketplace. A dollar earned through a government program that raises the price at which a firm sells its output or lowers the prices at which it buys its inputs is worth just as much as a dollar of profit earned through purely private efforts at innovation. In some cases it may even be better. Profits earned from innovation in a competitive market may be short lived because rivals will soon come out with an even better product or introduce an even cheaper production method. However, government regulations can not only create opportunities to earn rents but also shield those opportunities from competitors. Obtaining and defending rents through government action is known as **political rent seeking**, or often simply as **rent seeking**, with the political aspect implied.[3]

Political rent seeking (rent seeking)

The process of seeking and defending economic rents through the political process.

Consider publicly funded stadiums. The people of Maryland, through the Maryland Stadium Authority, paid for and own M M & T Bank Stadium where the Ravens play. The Ravens have exclusive rights to use the stadium and can veto or allow whoever they want to use the stadium. It is the Ravens' management who decides if Navy will play Notre Dame in Baltimore. Along with the prerogative of whom plays there, the Ravens' receive all the revenue from the parking lots regardless of whom is playing. So if Navy plays Army in Baltimore, it is only with the permission of the Ravens' management with the Ravens' receiving all the parking fees! The Cleveland Browns, by moving to Baltimore at the request of the Maryland state and Baltimore city governments, is an excellent example of political rent seeking.

Consider the case of milk price supports, which, as we saw earlier, are hard to explain in terms of the market failure theory of government. Public choice theorists see this policy as a classic case of *political rent seeking*. Because a large portion of the benefits of price supports go to farmers who are not in trouble, broad-ranging programs generating rents for all farmers will draw much wider political support than programs more narrowly targeted only on needy farmers. Without the political support of the relatively prosperous farmers who draw the bulk of the subsidies, say public choice theorists, programs for farmers in trouble would not get the votes they need in Congress.

Government restrictions on competition are another way of generating rents. For example, tariffs and import quotas on clothing, cars, sugar, steel, and other products shield domestic firms and their employees from foreign competition. The firms thus are able to earn rents by raising prices above the competitive market level, and the employees are able to earn rents in the form of higher wages. Examples of government restrictions on competition can be found within the domestic economy as well. For example, licensing fees and examinations restrict the number of competitors who can enter such professions as law and medicine and often even such occupations as manicuring and hair styling.

FROM THE LAW OF UNINTENDED CONSEQUENCES TO GOVERNMENT FAILURE The notion that government policies do not always promote efficiency and equity is not new. Economists have long been aware of the law of unintended consequences—the tendency of government policies to have effects other than those desired by their proponents. But public choice theory goes beyond the notion of unintended consequences, which could be traced simply to incomplete analysis on the part of policy makers. Rather, the element of rent seeking in the formulation of government policy suggests that there is a systematic tendency for government programs to cause rather than to cure economic inefficiencies—a tendency, that is, toward **government failure**.

Government failure

A situation in which a government policy causes inefficient use of resources.

In introducing the notion of government failure, public choice theorists do not intend to imply that government always makes a mess of things or that the market always functions perfectly; rather, they demonstrate that both the market and government are imperfect institutions. In deciding whether a given function is better performed by government or the market, the possibilities of government failure must be weighed against those of market failure.

Concerning government failure, consider the government school system. Though the Carroll County public schools do have very good outcomes at a low per student cost, many government schools are less than satisfactory. If we would look at the outcome of major cities such as Baltimore or Washington, D.C. we would have to conclude that the government school system is a failure. The dropout rate and the lack of academic achievement from the graduates is an obvious and disgraceful example of government failure. Ask yourself, would a different model of delivering public education be in order in these areas?

Looking Ahead

This chapter has provided an overview of microeconomics in terms of theory and institutions. All economic theory has a common core: the analysis of rational choice given certain objectives and constraints. The great variety within economics comes in large part from the wide range of institutional settings within which these common elements of theory are applied.

Looking ahead, Chapters 5 through 9 and 13 focus almost exclusively on market institutions. The topics covered in those chapters constitute the core of what is commonly called *neoclassical*. The origins of the neoclassical school of economics can be traced to the work of Alfred Marshall at the end of the 19th century (see *Who Said It? Who Did It? 2.1*) It has long been the dominant school of economics in the United States and many other countries. In keeping with the neoclassical tradition, the models presented in later chapters will incorporate several simplifying assumptions:

1. An assumption of full rationality. Decision makers are seen as having well-defined objectives (for example, profit maximization) and as being competent to make use of all available information in choosing how best to pursue those objectives.
2. An assumption of self-regarding preferences. In these models, decision makers are understood as being motivated by material gain for themselves.
3. An emphasis on the price system as the economy's key mechanism for transmitting information. The prices of all goods and services are typically assumed to be public information available free to all households and firms. For the most part, costs of acquiring information are ignored.
4. An emphasis on formal models of economic behavior that can be stated in graphical or mathematical terms, and a focus on conditions of equilibrium.

Comparatively little attention is paid to disequilibrium, change, and innovation, especially when formulating formal models.

5. Treatment of households, firms, and where considered, government agencies as "black boxes." The main focus is on the interactions of these units in the marketplace. Relatively little attention is paid to the workings of their internal hierarchies.

The very restrictiveness of these assumptions is the source of much of the success of neoclassical theory. Neoclassical economics is like a searchlight that is able to illuminate objects brightly precisely because it is focused narrowly. In the following chapters, we will encounter one situation after another, ranging from highway safety to negotiations among OPEC oil ministers, where neoclassical economics provides insights of striking clarity and predictions that stand up remarkably well to the test of experience.

Despite the century-old success of neoclassical microeconomics, in recent decades economists have become interested in a number of problems that its narrowly focused searchlight cannot adequately illuminate. Chapters 12, 14, and 15 take up a number of extensions of neoclassical theory, and, in some cases, challenges to it. In these chapters, many of the simplifying assumptions of the neoclassical tradition are modified.

Chapters 12, 14, and 15 then apply both traditional neoclassical tools and their more recent extensions to five areas of government policy—antitrust and regulation, labor policy, poverty and income distribution.

SUMMARY

1. **What is the basic structure of economic theory?** Economic theories are constructed from statements about people's objectives, aims, and preferences; statements about the constraints on available opportunities; and statements about how people choose among the available opportunities so as to best meet their objectives.

2. **Why is rationality of central importance to economics?** To be rational means to act purposefully to achieve one's objectives, given the available opportunities. In some cases, economists assume *full rationality,* which means that they assume that people make full use of all available information in calculating how best to meet their objectives. In other cases, they assume *bounded rationality,* which means that they assume that people intend to make the choices that best serve their objectives, but have limited ability to acquire and process information. The assumption of rationality is sometimes further modified to allow for other-regarding as well as self-regarding preferences.

3. **What is the meaning of market performance and market failure?** *Market performance* refers to how efficiently markets do their job of providing arrangements for mutually beneficial trade. Ideally, markets would make it possible to carry out every possible mutually beneficial trade, in which case they would operate perfectly efficiently.

Sometimes, however, *market failure* occurs, in which case markets fail to carry out their job efficiently. *Externalities, public goods,* and insufficient competition (leading to *monopoly*) are among the most widely discussed sources of market failure.

4. **What are some alternative theories of the economic role of government?** According to the market failure theory of government, everything that markets can do efficiently should be left to them. Government should intervene only to correct market failures, whether narrowly or broadly defined. Another theory maintains that many government policies are not efforts to correct market failure but, instead, result from *political rent seeking.* Rent seeking refers to the process of seeking payments in excess of opportunity costs.

KEY TERMS

Property rights
Rationality
Ockham's razor
Full rationality
Bounded rationality
Self-regarding preferences
Other-regarding preferences
Market performance
Market failure
Externalities
Public goods
Monopoly
Public choice theory
Economic rent
Political rent seeking (rent seeking)
Government failure

PROBLEMS AND TOPICS FOR DISCUSSION

1. **Alternative path theories.** The chapter proposes a simple theory to explain the existence of a path across a grassy area on a certain college campus. Here is another theory that might also explain the path: "Economics lectures are so boring that students prefer to be late to them. However, near the sidewalk on one side of the quad there is a beehive, and many students have suffered stings; and on the other side of the quad is the chemistry building, which smells bad when the wind blows a certain way. Sometimes if you cut across the middle of the quad, you find four-leaf clovers that give you good luck on your exams. Those are the reasons that there is a path across the quad." Applying the principle of Ockham's razor, which theory do you think is better? Why? Would you reject the more complex theory out of hand, or would you first want to make some observations? What observations would you make?

2. **Italians in America.** According to a theory suggested in the chapter, people drive smaller cars in Italy than in the United States not because of different preferences but because they face different constraints on their opportunities—higher gasoline prices, narrower streets, and so on. On the basis of that theory, what prediction would you make about the cars driven by Italians who move to the United States? What kind of observations would you suggest to test whether preferences or constraints are the key factor in the choice of car size?

3. **An alternate definition of economics.** David Friedman has said that economics can be defined as "that way of understanding behavior that assumes that people are rational." Compare Friedman's definition with the one presented in Chapter 1 of this book. What similarities or differences do you see?

4. **The economics of voting.** Did you vote in the most recent state or national election? If so, how was your choice of a candidate influenced by your objectives and constraints? If you did not vote, was your decision not to vote influenced by objectives and constraints? Do you think your choice of a candidate (or your choice not to vote) was a rational one? Discuss.

5. **Government failure versus market failure.** When the possibilities of both government failure and market failure are taken into account, does the fact that a government policy causes inefficiency necessarily mean that abolishing the policy would result in greater efficiency? Does the fact that a certain market fails to work efficiently necessarily mean that intervention by government would improve the situation? Discuss.

CASE FOR DISCUSSION

A Price That's Too Good to Be Bad

Almost any aisle of any supermarket is a battleground in the never-ending war between house brands and national brands. The weapons of the national brands are advertising, reputation, and brand recognition. The big gun on the side of the house brands is price. One day recently, for example, shoppers at a Virginia Safeway store could take their choice of Johnson & Johnson baby powder for $3.29 or a can of Safeway brand at $2.59; of Kellogg's cornflakes at $1.97 per box or the house brand at $1.59; of Wesson vegetable oil at $4.59 per bottle or Safeway's product at $3.39 per bottle; or of Heinz distilled vinegar at $1.93 per quart or Safeway's Townhouse brand at $1.23.

What logic lies behind this competition? One's first thought might be that it all depends on the law of demand. If so, one would think, the lower the price of the house brand, the higher its sales relative to the national brand. But marketers of consumer products have found that the law of demand applies only up to a point in the competition between house brands and national brands. Paradoxically, a price that is *too* low can actually hurt the sales of the house brand.

Consider the case of Pathmark supermarkets' Premium All Purpose cleaner. This house brand product was designed to compete head-to-head with Fantastik, the leading national brand. The two products were chemically identical. The house brand's packaging mimicked that of the national brand. And Pathmark's product was priced at just $.89, versus $1.79 for Fantastik.

Yet, from its first introduction, Premium All Purpose cleaner was a slow seller. Frustrated Pathmark marketers even added a sticker to the label that said, "If you like Fantastik, try me!" But the sticker did not help. Finally Pathmark decided to drop the product.

What went wrong? Interviewed by *The Wall Street Journal,* Robert Wunderle, a spokesman for Supermarket General Corporation, Pathmark's corporate parent, blamed the failure on a price "so low that it discredited the intrinsic value of the product."

Many retailers consider it risky to price their house brands more than 20 to 25 percent below the national brand. But there are exceptions. If the product is so simple and familiar that consumers believe there can be no quality difference, it is safe to establish a bigger discount. Thus, for example, Safeway puts a bigger discount on its house brand vinegar and vegetable oil than on its house brand baby powder or cornflakes.

Peter Schwartz, president of Daymon Associates, Inc., a private-label research and marketing firm, explains the problem this way: "The further the distance from the national brand, the higher the credibility problem for consumers. Once you get outside the customer's comfort zone, the consumer psychology becomes, 'Gee, they must have taken it out in quality.'"

Source: Based in part on Alix M. Freedman, "A Price That's Too Good May Be Bad," *The Wall Street Journal,* November 15, 1988, B1.

QUESTIONS

1. Would you characterize the behavior of consumers who buy Fantastik brand cleaner instead of Pathmark's Premium All-Purpose cleaner as full rationality, irrationality, or bounded rationality? Explain.

2. The case suggests that in choosing among alternative brands of goods, consumers sometimes rely on the rule of thumb that higher prices tend to be associated with higher quality. From your own experience as a shopper, do you think that this rule of thumb is valid on the average? Valid always? Rarely valid? Give examples.
3. A consumer who followed the assumptions of bounded rationality would be most likely to apply the preceding rule of thumb, rather than seeking independent information on product quality, in purchasing which kinds of goods?
   a. Major purchases such as automobiles.
   b. Goods that are purchased frequently and can easily be inspected, such as clothing.
   c. Goods like household cleaners that are purchased infrequently constitute a small part of the consumer's budget and cannot easily be inspected or tested before purchase. Discuss why the rule of thumb is more reasonable in some cases than others, and give additional examples of each case.

END NOTES

1. Thorstein Veblen, "In Dispraise of Economists," in *The Portable Veblen,* ed. Max Lerner (New York: Viking Press, 1958), 232–233.
2. See Richard H. Thaler, "From Homo Economicus to Homo Sapiens," *Journal of Economic Perspectives,* Volume 14, No. 1 (Winter 2000): 133–141.
3. For a representative collection of papers on the theory of rent seeking, see James M. Buchanan, Robert D. Tollison, and Gordon Tullock, eds., *Toward a Theory of the Rent-Seeking Society* (College Station: Texas A&M Press, 1980).

CHAPTER 4

Supply, Demand, and Elasticity

After reading this chapter, you will understand:

1. How the responsiveness of quantity demanded to a price change can be expressed in terms of elasticity
2. How elasticity applies to situations other than the responsiveness of the quantity of a good demanded to a change in its price
3. How elasticity is useful in interpreting issues of taxation and other public policies

Before reading this chapter, make sure you know the meaning of:

1. Supply and demand
2. Demand, quantity demanded
3. Supply, quantity supplied
4. Substitutes and complements
5. Normal and inferior goods

HOW MUCH DID you pay for this textbook? Was it more expensive or less expensive than the books you buy for other courses? As a student, you probably have a strong desire to pay less for your books if you can. Have you ever wondered why your professor sometimes chooses books that are so expensive? (Or maybe written by himself?)

This chapter will help you understand the effect of price on choices that people make among alternative goods, like different textbooks, different foods, or different modes of transportation. It will focus on the concept of *elasticity,* a word economists use to say how sensitive such choices are to price. As a student, your choice of textbook is probably very sensitive to price—your demand is *elastic,* to use the economist's term. However, your professor, who does not pay for the books, cares less about how much they cost. Your professor's demand may be *inelastic*. In the following pages you will learn how to define, measure, and apply the important concept of elasticity.

ELASTICITY

The responsiveness of quantity demanded to a change in price can be expressed in many ways, depending on the units of measurement that are chosen. Consider the demand for chicken, an example used in a preceding chapter. A study of the budget of a single American household might find that an increase of ten cents per pound would decrease consumption by 1 pound per week. A study done in France might find that a price increase of 1 euro per kilogram decreased consumption of all consumers in the city of Lille by 25,000 kilos per month. Are the findings of these studies similar? It is hard to tell, because the units used are different. It would require more information, and some calculations, to know whether the sensitivity of demand to price as measured in different countries using different currencies, are the same. The same would be true of two studies in one country if one measured price in dollars per ton and tons per year, while the other used dollars per pound and pounds per week.

To avoid confusion arising from the choice of different units of measurement, it is useful to standardize. One common way of doing so is to express all changes as percentages. Suppose, for example, that the studies of both American and French consumers found that a 20 percent increase in price was associated with a 10 percent decrease in quantity demanded. These percentages would stay the same regardless of whether the original data were stated in dollars per pound, euros per kilo, or any other measurement.

Elasticity

A measure of the response of one variable to a change in another, stated as a ratio of the percentage change in one variable to the associated percentage change in another variable.

The use of percentages to express the response of one variable to a change in another is widespread in economics. The term **elasticity** is used to refer to relationships expressed in percentages. Like equilibrium, elasticity is a metaphor borrowed from physics. Much as equilibrium calls to mind a pendulum that has come to rest hanging straight down, elasticity conjures up the image of a rubber band that stretches by a certain proportion of its length when the force applied to it is increased by a given percentage. This chapter introduces several applications of elasticity in economics.

Price Elasticity of Demand

Price elasticity of demand

The ratio of the percentage change in the quantity of a good demanded to a given percentage change in its price, other things being equal.

We begin with the relationship between price and quantity demanded. The **price elasticity of demand** is the ratio of the percentage change in the quantity of a good demanded to a given percentage change in its price. Figure 4.1 presents five demand curves showing different degrees of price elasticity of demand. In part (a), the quantity demanded is strongly responsive to a change in price. In this case, a decrease in price from $5 to $3 causes the quantity demanded to increase from three units to six. Because the percentage change in quantity demanded is greater than the percentage

FIGURE 4.1 PRICE ELASTICITY OF DEMAND

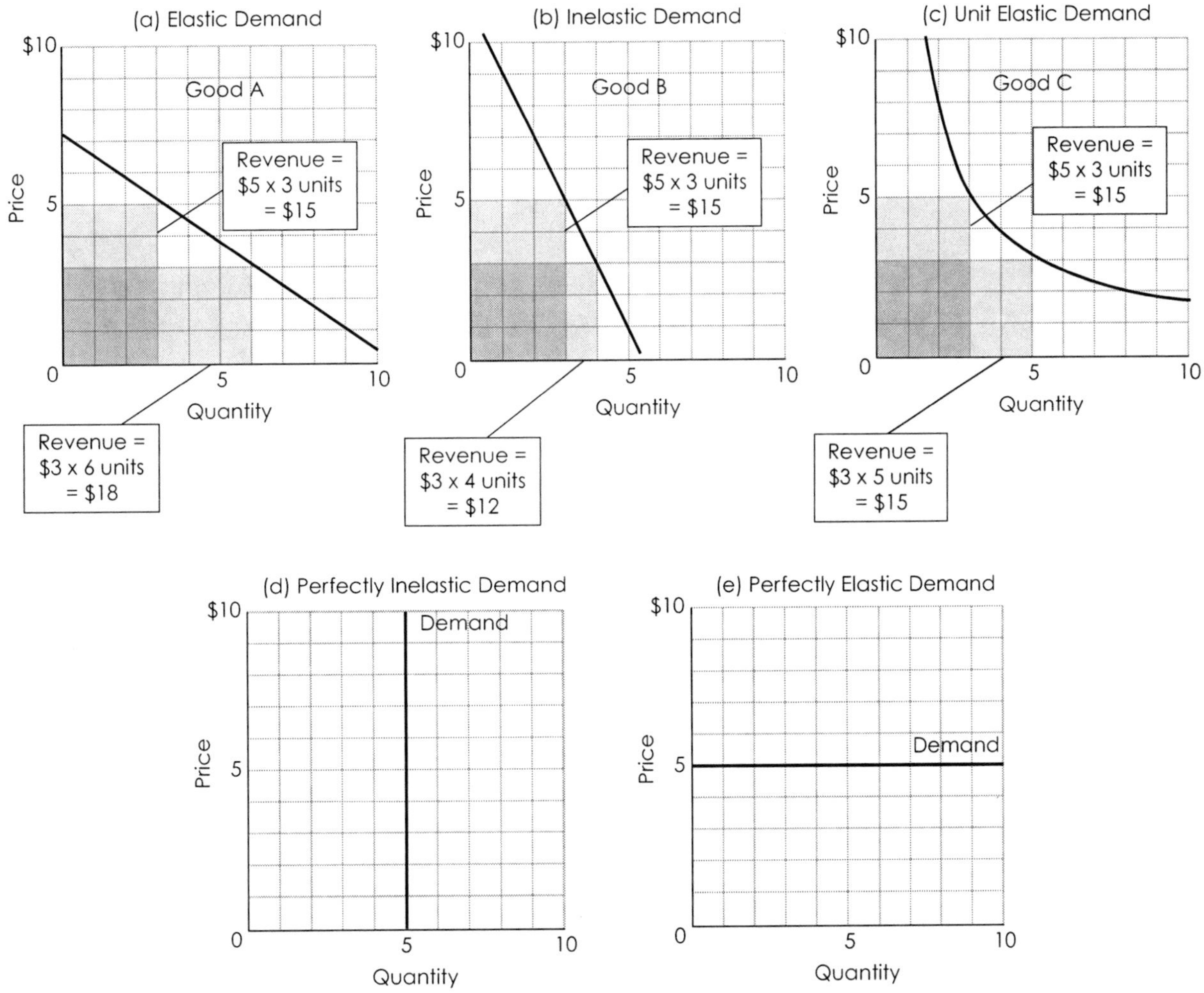

This figure shows five examples of demand curves with various degrees of elasticity over the indicated range of variation of price and quantity. The examples illustrate elastic, inelastic, unit elastic, perfectly inelastic, and perfectly elastic demand. For the first three cases, the revenue change associated with a change in price is shown. When demand is elastic, a price decrease causes revenue to increase. When demand is inelastic, a price decrease causes revenue to decrease. When demand is unit elastic, revenue does not change when price changes.

Revenue

Price times quantity sold.

change in price, the drop in price causes total revenue from sales of the good to increase. **Revenue** is the price times the quantity sold. (TR = P × Qs) On a supply-and-demand diagram, revenue can be shown as the area of a rectangle drawn under the demand curve, with a height equal to price and a width equal to quantity demanded. In this case comparison of the shaded rectangles representing revenue before the price reduction ($5 per unit × 3 units = $15) and afterward ($3 per unit × 6 units = $18) shows that revenue is greater after the price has been reduced. When the

Elastic demand

A situation in which quantity demanded changes by a larger percentage than price, so that total revenue increases as price decreases.

Inelastic demand

A situation in which quantity demanded changes by a smaller percentage than price, so that total revenue decreases as price decreases.

Unit elastic demand

A situation in which price and quantity demanded change by the same percentage, so that total revenue remains unchanged as price changes.

Perfectly inelastic demand

A situation in which the demand curve is a vertical line.

Perfectly elastic demand

A situation in which the demand curve is a horizontal line.

quantity demanded changes by a greater percentage than price, so that a price decrease causes total revenue to increase, demand is said to be **elastic**.

Part (b) of Figure 4.1 shows a case in which the quantity demanded is only weakly responsive to a change in price. Here, a $2 decrease in price, from $5 to $3 per unit, causes the quantity demanded to increase by just one unit—from three to four. This time the percentage change in quantity demanded is less than that in price. As a result, the decrease in price causes total revenue to fall (again note the shaded rectangles). In such a case demand is said to be **inelastic**.

Part (c) shows a case in which a change in price causes an exactly proportional change in quantity demanded, so that total revenue does not change at all. When the percentage change in quantity demanded equals the percentage change in price, demand is said to be **unit elastic**.

The final two parts of Figure 4.1 show two extreme cases. Part (d) shows a vertical demand curve. Regardless of the price, the quantity demanded is five units—no more, no less. Such a demand curve is said to be **perfectly inelastic**. Part (e) shows a demand curve that is perfectly horizontal. Above a price of $5, no units of the good can be sold; but as soon as the price drops to $5, there is no limit on how much can be sold. A horizontal demand curve like this one is described as **perfectly elastic**. The law of demand, which describes an inverse relationship between price and quantity, does not encompass the cases of perfectly elastic and inelastic demand, and we do not expect market demand curves for ordinary goods and services to fit these extremes. Nevertheless, we will see that perfectly elastic and inelastic curves sometimes provide useful reference points for theory building, even though they do not resemble real-world market demand curves.

Calculating Elasticity of Demand

In speaking of elasticity of demand, it is often enough to say that demand is elastic or inelastic, without being more precise. At other times, though, it is useful to give a numerical value for elasticity. This section introduces the most common method used to calculate a numerical value for elasticity of demand.

The first step in turning the general definition of elasticity into a numerical formula is to develop a way to measure percentage changes. The everyday method for calculating a percentage change is to use the initial value of the variable as the denominator and the change in the value as the numerator. For example, if the quantity of California lettuce demanded in the national market is initially 10,000 tons per week and then decreases by 2,500 tons per week, we say that there has been a 25 percent change (2,500/10,000 = .25). The trouble with this convention is that the same change in the opposite direction gives a different percentage. By everyday reasoning, an increase in the quantity of lettuce demanded from 7,500 tons per week to 10,000 tons per week is a 33 percent increase (2,500/7,500 = .33).

Decades ago the mathematical economist R. G. D. Allen proposed an unambiguous measure of percentage changes that uses the midpoint of the range over which change takes place as the denominator. Allen's formula is not the only possible one, but it caught on and remains the most popular.

To find the midpoint of the range over which a change takes place, we take the sum of the initial value and the final value and divide by 2. In our example, the midpoint of the quantity range is (7,500 + 10,000)/2 = 8,750. When this is used as the denominator, a change of 2,500 units becomes (approximately) a 28.6 percent change (2,500/8,750 = .286). Using Q_1 to represent the quantity before the change and Q_2 to represent the quantity after the change, the midpoint formula for the percentage change in quantity is

$$\text{Percentage change in quantity} = \frac{Q_2 - Q_1}{(Q_1 + Q_2)/2}$$

The same approach can be used to define the percentage change in price. In our case, the price of lettuce increased from about \$250 per ton to about \$1,000 per ton. Using the midpoint of the range, or \$625, as the denominator [(\$250 + \$1,000)/2 = \$625], we conclude that the \$750 increase in price is a 120 percent increase (\$750/\$625 = 1.2). The midpoint formula for the percentage change in price is

$$\text{Percentage change in price} = \frac{P_2 - P_1}{(P_1 + P_2)/2}$$

THE MIDPOINT FORMULA FOR ELASTICITY Defining percentage changes in this way allows us to write a useful formula for calculating elasticities. With P_1 and Q_1 representing price and quantity before a change, and P_2 and Q_2 representing price and quantity after the change, the midpoint formula for elasticity is

$$\text{Price elasticity of demand} = \frac{(Q_2 - Q_1)/(Q_1 + Q_2)}{(P_2 - P_1)/(P_1 + P_2)} = \frac{\text{Percentage change in quantity}}{\text{Percentage change in price}}$$

Here is the complete calculation for the elasticity of demand for lettuce when an increase in price from \$250 per ton to \$1,000 per ton causes the quantity demanded to fall from 10,000 tons per day to 7,500 tons per day:

P_1 = price before change = \$250
P_2 = price after change = \$1,000
Q_1 = quantity before change = 10,000
Q_2 = quantity after change = 7,500

$$\text{Elasticity} = \frac{(7{,}500 - 10{,}000)/(7{,}500 + 10{,}000)}{(\$1{,}000 - \$250)/(\$1{,}000 + \$250)}$$

$$= \frac{-2{,}500/17{,}500}{\$750/\$1{,}250}$$

$$= \frac{-.142}{.6}$$

$$= -.24$$

Because demand curves have negative slopes, this formula yields a negative value for elasticity. The reason is that the quantity demanded changes in the direction opposite to that of the price change. When the price decreases, ($P_2 - P_1$), which appears in the denominator of the formula, is negative, whereas ($Q_2 - Q_1$), which appears in the numerator, is positive. When the price increases, the numerator is negative and the denominator is positive. However, in this book we follow the widely used practice of dropping the minus sign when discussing price elasticity of demand. Thus, the elasticity of demand for lettuce would be stated as approximately .24 over the range studied.

A numerical elasticity value such as .24 can be related to the basic definition of elasticity in a simple way. That definition stated that price elasticity of demand is the ratio of the percentage change in quantity demanded to a given percentage change in price. Thus, an elasticity of .24 means that the quantity demanded will increase by .24 percent for each 1 percent change in price. An elasticity of 3 would mean that quantity demanded would change by 3 percent for each 1 percent change in price, and so on.[1]

ELASTICITY VALUES AND TERMINOLOGY Earlier in the chapter we defined *elastic, inelastic, unit elastic, perfectly elastic,* and *perfectly inelastic* demand. Each of these terms corresponds to a numerical value or range of values of elasticity. A perfectly inelastic demand curve has a numerical value of 0, since any change in price produces no change in quantity demanded. The term *inelastic* (but not perfectly inelastic) *demand* applies to numerical values from 0 up to, but not including, 1. *Unit elasticity,* as the name implies, means a numerical value of exactly 1. *Elastic demand* means any value for elasticity that is greater than 1. *Perfectly elastic* demand, represented by a horizontal demand curve, is not defined numerically; as the demand curve becomes horizontal, the denominator of the elasticity formula approaches 0 and the numerical value of elasticity increases without limit.

Determinants of Elasticity of Demand

The fact that elasticity often varies along the demand curve means that care must be taken in making statements about *the* elasticity of demand for a good. In practice, what such statements usually refer to is the elasticity, measured by the midpoint formula or some alternative method, over the range of price variation that is commonly observed in the market for that good. With this understanding, we can make some generalizations about what makes the demand for some goods relatively elastic and the demand for others relatively inelastic.

SUBSTITUTES, COMPLEMENTS, AND ELASTICITY One important determinant of elasticity of demand is the availability of substitutes. When a good has close substitutes, the demand for that good tends to be relatively elastic, because people willingly switch to the substitutes when the price of the good goes up. Thus, for example, the demand for corn oil is relatively elastic, because other cooking oils can usually be substituted for it. On the other hand, the demand for cigarettes is relatively inelastic, because for a habitual smoker there is no good substitute.

This principle has two corollaries. One is that the demand for a good tends to be more elastic the more narrowly the good is defined. For example, the demand for lettuce in the numerical example given earlier was relatively inelastic. This could be because many people are in the habit of eating a salad with dinner and do not think of spinach or coleslaw as completely satisfactory substitutes. At the same time, however, it could be that the demand for any particular variety of lettuce is relatively elastic. If the price of Boston lettuce rises while the prices of iceberg, romaine, and red-leaf lettuce remain unchanged, many people will readily switch to one of the other varieties, which they see as close substitutes.

The other corollary is that demand for the product of a single firm tends to be more elastic than the demand for the output of all producers operating in the market. As one example, the demand for cigarettes as a whole will be less elastic than the demand for any particular brand. The reason is that one brand can be substituted for another when the price of a brand changes.

The complements of a good can also play a role in determining its elasticity. If something is a minor complement to an important good (that is, one that accounts for a large share of consumers' budgets), demand for it tends to be relatively inelastic. For example, the demand for motor oil tends to be relatively inelastic, because it is a complement to a more important good, gasoline. The price of gasoline has a greater effect on the amount of driving a person does than the price of motor oil.

PRICE VS. OPPORTUNITY COST Elasticity measures the responsiveness of quantity demanded to the monetary price of a good. In most cases, the price, in money, is an accurate approximation of the opportunity cost of choosing a good, but that is not always the case. We mentioned one example at the beginning of the chapter: The price of a textbook is an opportunity cost to the student who buys it, but it is not an opportunity cost to the professor who assigns it, because the students pay for the book, not the professor. As a result, publishers have traditionally assumed that professors will pay little attention to the price of the text, and demand will be highly inelastic. This is changing. One motivation for me to publish this book was because of the ever higher prices you pay for texts. Some competitive texts would retail to you at over $130. Along with the high prices, some publishers bundle study guides, CD ROMs and other under-used products that the student must purchase as part of the package that the teacher may seldom (never) use. Also, some state legislatures are considering regulations on what and how state university professors select books and how departments choose those texts. However, in recent years students have increasingly been making their influence felt, so that price-elasticity of demand for textbooks may be increasing. (Ebay purchases and other NET sites for texts.)

The textbook market is a relatively small one, but there are other much more important markets where the responsibility for choice does not lie with the party who bears the opportunity cost. Medical care provides many examples. Doctors choose what drug to offer to patients, but either the patient or the patient's insurance company pays for the drug. As a result, demand for drugs is very inelastic, and doctors sometimes prescribe expensive brand-name drugs when cheaper generic drugs are available to do the same job.

Business travel is still another example of the separation of price and opportunity cost. Business travelers do not pay for their own airline tickets, hotels, and meals, so their demand for these services tends to be inelastic. When vacationers purchase the same services, they bear the full opportunity cost themselves. Not surprisingly, business travelers often choose more expensive options. In many cases airlines and hotels take advantage of the separation of price and opportunity cost by charging different rates to business and vacation travelers.

TIME HORIZON AND ELASTICITY One of the most important considerations determining the price elasticity of demand is the time horizon within which the decision to buy is made. For several reasons, demand is often less elastic in the short run than in the long run.

One reason is that full adjustment to a change in the price of a good may require changes in the kind or quantity of many other goods that a consumer buys. Gasoline provides a classic example. When the price of gasoline jumped in the early 2000s, many people's initial reaction was to cut out some nonessential driving, but the total quantity of gasoline demanded was not much affected. As time went by, though, consumers began adjust in many ways. One important adjustment, as mentioned in Chapter 1, was to buy fewer fuel-hungry SUVs and more higher-mileage cars. If this trend continues, the total amount of gasoline purchased could fall substantially.

Another reason elasticity tends to be greater in the long run than in the short run is that an increase in the price of one good encourages entrepreneurs to develop substitutes—which, as we have seen, can be an important determinant of elasticity. To take an example from history, consider the response to what has been called America's first energy crisis, a sharp increase in the price of whale oil, which was used as lamp fuel in the early nineteenth century. At first candles were the only substitute for whale-oil lamps, and not a very satisfactory one. People therefore cut their use of whale oil only a little when the price began to rise. But the high price of whale oil spurred entrepreneurs to develop a better substitute, kerosene. Once kerosene came onto the market, the quantity of whale oil demanded for use as lamp fuel dropped to zero.

A final reason for greater elasticity of demand in the long run than in the short run is the slow adjustment of consumer tastes. The case of beef and chicken, featured in a preceding chapter, provides an example. Chicken, originally the more expensive meat, achieved a price advantage over beef many years ago, but eating lots of beef was a habit. Gradually, though, chicken developed an image as a healthy, stylish, versatile food, and finally it overtook beef as the number-one meat in the United States.

In the 1970's the American demand for gasoline was very inelastic. However as time passed, our demand became more elastic as smaller cars and our tastes changed. As the price of gasoline remained relatively low, our demand for it slanted upward to a more inelastic situation.

In the Spring of 2008, gas prices increased toward $4 a gallon. As time passed, the quantity of gasoline decreased as Americans carpooled and drove less. Also, the popularity of SUVs and other low-efficiency cars declined and the appeal of smaller hybrids increased. The sales of silly scooters even increased. (Though a man in a business suit may appear silly as he rides up and down Rt. 140, he may get the last laugh as he fills up the scooter tank for less than $8.

Income Elasticity of Demand

Determining the response of quantity demanded to a change in price is the most common application of the concept of elasticity, but it is by no means the only one. Elasticity can also be used to express the response of demand to any of the conditions covered by the "other things being equal" assumption on which a given demand curve is based. As we saw in a preceding chapter, consumer income is one of those conditions.

Income elasticity of demand

The ratio of the percentage change in the quantity of a good demanded to a given percentage change in consumer incomes, other things being equal.

The **income elasticity of demand** for a good is defined as the ratio of the percentage change in the quantity of that good demanded to a percentage change in income. In measuring income elasticity, it is assumed that the good's price does not change. Using Q_1 and Q_2 to represent quantities before and after the change in income, and y_1 and y_2 to represent income before and after the change, the midpoint formula for income elasticity of demand can be written as follows:

$$\text{Income elasticity of demand} = \frac{(Q_2 - Q_1)/(Q_1 + Q_2)}{(y_2 - y_1)/(y_1 + y_2)} = \frac{\text{Percentage change in quantity}}{\text{Percentage change in income}}$$

For a normal good, an increase in income causes demand to rise. Because income and demand change in the same direction, the income elasticity of demand for a normal good is positive. For an inferior good, an increase in income causes demand to decrease. Because income and demand change in opposite directions, the income elasticity of demand for an inferior good is negative.

Some of the considerations that determine price elasticity also affect income elasticity. In particular, whether a good is considered to be normal or inferior depends on how narrowly it is defined and on the availability of substitutes. For example, a study by Jonq-Ying Lee, Mark G. Brown, and Brooke Schwartz of the University of Florida looked at the demand for frozen orange juice.[2] Orange juice considered as a broad category is a normal good; people tend to consume more of it as their income rises. However, when the definition is narrowed so that house-brand and national-brand frozen orange juice are treated as separate products, the house-brand product turns out to be an inferior good. As their incomes rise, consumers substitute the higher-quality national brands, which have a positive income elasticity of demand.

The demand for gasoline is based more on the income of the buyer than the price at the pump. As American income increases, our demand to use gasoline becomes ever more inelastic. More important than the price of a gallon of gasoline is our income. Because of ever higher incomes in 2005–2006, Americans continued to fill up and drive their large cars. One alarming aspect of the recent run up in gas prices and our inelastic demand for gasoline, is the American savings rate. Americans are putting gas purchases on credit cards, and as the price increases, the amount of money borrowed to fund our driving increases. As we borrow ever more for gasoline, our savings rate continues to decline. This is troubling since our ability to grow is potentially reduced as the available resources for investment are reduced.

It is important to understand income elasticity from a management's point of view. If you're the buyer for Cox Ford Dealership and must make a decision on what and how many types of cars to order from the factory, If you know the income is rising in Carroll County, then you'd be more inclined to order top of the line models for your showroom and lot. On the other hand, if the income of an area was declining, then you would be more inclined to order less expensive cars, or maybe try to find used cars to offer to your customers.

Cross-Elasticity of Demand

Another condition that can cause a change in the demand for a good is a change in the price of some other good. The demand for chicken is affected by changes in the price of beef, the demand for SUVs by changes in the price of gasoline, and so on. Such relationships can be expressed as elasticities: The **cross-elasticity of demand** for a good is defined as the ratio of the percentage change in the quantity of that good demanded to a given percentage change in the price of another good. The midpoint formula for cross-elasticity of demand looks just like the one for price elasticity of demand, except that the numerator shows the percentage change in the quantity of one good while the denominator shows the percentage change in the price of some other good.

Cross-elasticity of demand

The ratio of the percentage change in the quantity of a good demanded to a given percentage change in the price of some other good, other things being equal.

Cross-elasticity of demand is related to the concepts of substitutes and complements. Because lettuce and cabbage are substitutes, an increase in the price of cabbage causes an increase in the quantity of lettuce demanded; the cross-elasticity of demand is positive. Because SUVs and gasoline are complements, an increase in the price of gasoline causes a decrease in the quantity of SUVs demanded; the cross-elasticity of demand is negative. The previously mentioned study of frozen orange juice found a positive cross-elasticity of demand between house-brand and national-brand juices, indicating that the two are substitutes.

From a manager's point of view, again this is important to understand, if you're a buyer for the Ford dealership in Westminster, you should have more than a general idea about what will happen to the demand for your Explorers if General Motors is reducing the price of their SUVs. You wouldn't want to over buy the now more expensive Ford's and have them sitting on your lot for weeks as you watch the cars fly off the lot at the nearby Chevy dealership.

Price Elasticity of Supply

Price elasticity of supply

The ratio of the percentage change in the quantity of a good supplied to a given percentage change in its price, other things being equal.

Elasticity is not confined to demand; it can also be used to indicate the response of quantity supplied to a change in price. Formally, the **price elasticity of supply** of a good is defined as the percentage change in the quantity of the good supplied divided by the percentage change in its price. The midpoint formula for calculating price elasticity of supply looks like the one for determining price elasticity of demand, but the Qs in the numerator of the formula now refer to quantity *supplied* rather than quantity *demanded*. Because price and quantity change in the same direction along a positively sloped supply curve, the formula gives a positive value for the elasticity of supply.

In later chapters we will look in detail at the considerations that determine the elasticity of supply for various products. Two of those considered are especially important, however, and deserve some discussion here.

One determinant of the elasticity of supply of a good is the mobility of the factors of production used to produce it. As used here, *mobility* means the ease with which factors can be attracted away from some other use, as well as the ease with which they can be reconverted to their original use. The trucking industry provides a classic example of mobile resources. As a crop such as lettuce or watermelons comes to harvest in a particular region of a country, hundreds of trucks are needed to haul it to market. Shippers compete for available trucks, driving up the price paid to truckers in the local market. Independent truckers throughout the country learn—from their own experience, from trucking brokers, and from Internet sites—where they can earn the best rates for hauling produce. It takes only a modest rise in the price for hauling a load of Georgia watermelons to attract enough truckers to Georgia to haul the crop to market. When the harvest is over, the truckers will move elsewhere to haul peaches, tomatoes, or whatever.

In contrast, other products are produced with resources that are not so mobile. Petroleum provides a good example. When oil prices rise, producers have an incentive to drill more wells. However, given limited numbers of drilling rigs and other highly specialized equipment, not to mention limited numbers of sites worth exploring, even a doubling of oil prices has only a small effect on oil output. Factor mobility in this industry is limited in the other direction, too. Once a well has been drilled, the investment cannot be converted to a different use. Thus, when world demand falls, as it did in 1998, prices fall sharply but the quantity of oil produced falls by much less than price.

A second determinant of elasticity of supply is time. As in the case of demand, price elasticity of supply tends to be greater in the long run than in the short run. In part, the reason for this is connected with mobility of resources. In the short run, the output of many products can be increased by using more of the most flexible inputs—

for example, by adding workers at a plant or extending the hours of work. Such short-run measures often mean higher costs per unit for the added output, however, because workers added without comparable additions in other inputs (such as equipment) tend to be less productive. If a firm expects market conditions to warrant an increase of supply in the long run, it will be worthwhile to invest in additional quantities of less mobile inputs such as specialized plants and equipment. Once those investments have been made, the firm will find it worthwhile to supply the greater quantity of output at a lower price than in the short-run case because its costs per unit supplied will be lower. The Case for Discussion at the end of Chapter 2, which discussed the market for heavy-duty tires, provides an example of the difference between short-run and long-run elasticity of supply.

APPLICATIONS OF ELASTICITY

Elasticity has many applications in both macro- and microeconomics. In macroeconomics, it can be applied to money markets, to the aggregate supply and demand for all goods and services, and to foreign-exchange markets, to name just a few. In microeconomics, elasticity plays a role in discussions of consumer behavior, the profit-maximizing behavior of business firms, governments' regulatory and labor policies, and many other areas. To further illustrate elasticity, we conclude this chapter with applications featuring the problems of tax incidence and drug policy.

Elasticity and Tax Incidence

Who pays taxes? One way to answer this question is in terms of *assessments*—the issue of who bears the legal responsibility to make tax payments to the government. A study of assessments would show that property owners pay property taxes, gasoline companies pay gasoline taxes, and so on. However, looking at assessments does not always settle the issue of who bears the economic burden of a tax—or, to use the economist's term, the issue of **tax incidence**.

Tax incidence

The distribution of the economic burden of a tax.

The incidence of a tax does not always coincide with the way the tax is assessed, because the economic burden of the tax, in whole or in part, often can be passed along to someone else. The degree to which the burden of a tax may be passed along depends on the elasticities of supply and demand. Let's consider some examples.

INCIDENCE OF A GASOLINE TAX First consider the familiar example of a gasoline tax. Specifically, suppose that the state of Virginia decides to impose a tax of $1 per gallon on gasoline beginning from a situation in which there is no tax. The tax is assessed against sellers of gasoline, who add the tax into the price paid by consumers at the pump.

Figure 4.2 uses the supply-and-demand model to show the effects of the tax. Initially, the demand curve intersects supply curve S_1 at E_1, resulting in a price of $2 per

FIGURE 4.2 INCIDENCE OF A TAX ON GASOLINE

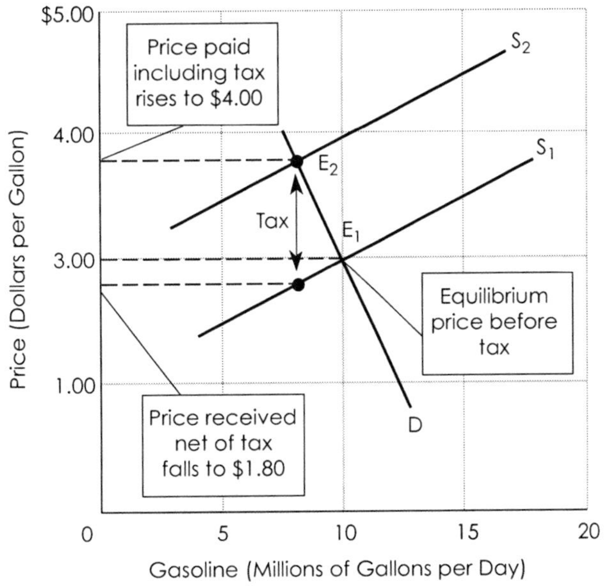

S_1 and D are the supply and demand curves before imposition of the tax. The initial equilibrium price is $2 per gallon. A tax of $1 per gallon shifts the supply curve to S_2. To induce sellers to supply the same quantity as before, the price would have to rise to $3. However, as the price rises, buyers reduce the quantity demanded, moving up and to the left along the demand curve. In the new equilibrium at E_2, the price rises only to $2.80. After the tax is paid, sellers receive only $1,80 per gallon. Thus, buyers bear $.80 of the tax on each gallon and sellers the remaining $.20. Buyers bear the larger share of the tax because demand, in this case, is less elastic than supply.

gallon. The supply curve is elastic in the region of the initial equilibrium. The elasticity of supply reflects the fact that we are dealing with the gasoline market in just one state; only a slight rise in the price in Virginia is needed to divert additional quantities of gasoline from elsewhere in the nation, because of the wide geographic reach of the wholesale gasoline market. The retail gasoline market is more local. If the price in Virginia rises, some consumers living near the border may cross a state line to fill up in Maryland or North Carolina, but most people will continue to fill up in Virginia. In the short run, they have only limited ways to save gas, such as cutting back on nonessential trips. As a result, demand for gasoline is less elastic than the supply in the region of the initial equilibrium.

The effect of the tax is to shift the supply curve to the left until each point on the new supply curve is exactly $1 higher than the point for the corresponding quantity on the old supply curve. (We could instead say that the supply curve shifts *upward* by $1.) Because sellers must now turn over $1 to the state government for each gallon of gas sold, they would have to get $3 per gallon to be willing to sell the same quantity (10 million gallons per day) as initially. However, when sellers attempt to pass the tax on to motorists, motorists respond by reducing the amount of gas they buy. As the quantity sold falls, sellers move down and to the left along supply curve S_2 to a new equilibrium at E_2.

In the new equilibrium, the price is $2.80 per gallon—just $.80 higher than the original price. The new price includes the $1 tax, which sellers add to their net price of $1.80 per gallon—a net price that is $.20 less than before. The amount of the tax—$1 per gallon—is shown by the vertical gap between the supply and demand curves. The economic burden of the tax is divided between buyers and sellers, but in this case it falls more heavily on the buyers.

INCIDENCE OF A TAX ON APARTMENT RENTS In the preceding example, the incidence of the gasoline tax falls more heavily on buyers than on sellers because demand is less elastic than supply. If the elasticities are reversed, the results will also be reversed, as can be seen in the case of a tax on apartment rents.

In Figure 4.3, the market for rental apartments in Ogden, Utah (a small city) is initially in equilibrium at $500 per month. The supply of rental apartments is inelastic. An increase in rents will cause a few new apartments to be built, whereas a reduction will cause a few to be torn down, but in either case the response will be moderate. On the other hand, demand is fairly elastic, because potential renters consider houses or condominiums a fairly close substitute for rental apartments.

FIGURE 4.3 INCIDENCE OF A TAX ON APARTMENT RENTS

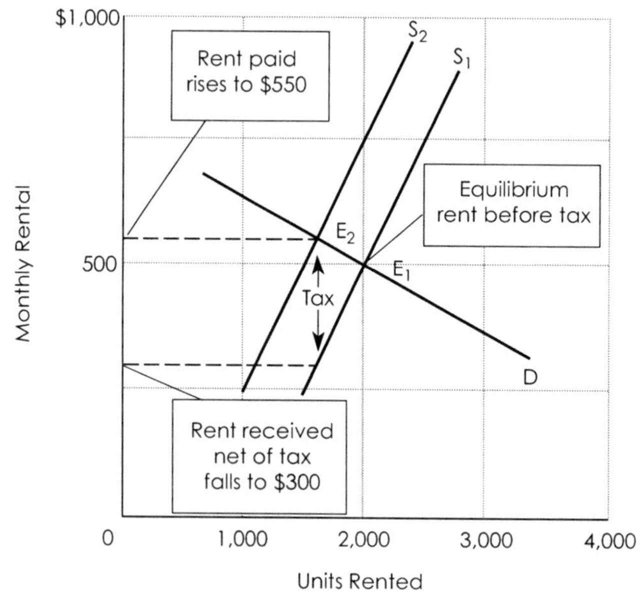

This figure shows the incidence of a tax imposed in a market in which supply is less elastic than demand. Initially, the equilibrium rent is $500 per month. A $250-per-month tax on apartment rents shifts the supply curve to S_2. The new equilibrium is at E_2. Landlords end up absorbing all but $50 of the tax. If they tried to pass more of the tax on to renters, more renters would switch to owner-occupied housing, and the vacancy rate on rental apartments would rise.

Given this situation, suppose that the local government decides to impose a tax of $250 per month on all apartments rented in Ogden. This tax, like the gasoline tax, is assessed against landlords, who include the tax payment in the monthly rental they charge to tenants. As in the previous example, the tax shifts the supply curve to the left until each point on the new supply curve lies above the corresponding point on the old supply curve by the amount of the tax. (Again, we could instead say the supply curve shifts upward by the amount of the tax.) After the shift, the market reaches a new equilibrium at E_2. There the rental price paid by tenants rises to only $550 per month, as indicated by the intersection of the new supply and demand curves. Landlords succeed in passing only $50 of the $250 monthly tax along to tenants. Their net rental income, after turning over the tax receipts to the town government, is now just $300, down from $500 before imposition of the tax. In this case, because supply is inelastic and demand is elastic, suppliers bear most of the incidence of the tax and buyers only a little.

INCIDENCE AND TAX REVENUE When the government considers imposing a tax on gasoline, cigarettes, apartments, or any other item, the price elasticity of demand and supply is important not only for how the burden is shared between buyers and sellers, but also for how much tax revenue the government collects. When buyers or sellers are more responsive to changes in price (when demand or supply is more elastic), a tax will generate less revenue for the government.

Figure 4.4 compares the markets for two items: milk and pork. The elasticities of supply are similar, but the price elasticities of demand differ. Pork has many obvious substitutes—beef, chicken, turkey, and other meats. Milk has few substitutes, so its demand is more inelastic. The markets for milk and pork are shown in Figure 4.4. The equilibrium price of milk is $0.50 per gallon and 12 million gallons are sold each year at this price. The milk market equilibrium is point E_1 on the left panel of Figure 4.4. The equilibrium (shown by the point E_1 on the right panel of Figure 4.4) is $0.75 per pound and 12 million pounds are sold each year.

Suppose now that the government imposes a $1.00 tax on each product. In the milk market, where demand is inelastic, the tax leads to a small decrease in the quantity, from 12 to 10 million gallons. The government collects $1.00 on each gallon of milk sold, for a tax revenue of $10 million on the 10 million gallons sold after the tax. In the market for pork, the tax leads to a larger reduction in the quantity people buy, from 12 to 6 million pounds. The government will collect a total of $6 million from the tax on pork, collecting $1.00 on each of the 6 million pounds sold. When comparing the two taxes, the government collects more revenue from the tax on milk. Today, governments rely for most of their revenue on broad-based taxes like income taxes, sales taxes, and value-added taxes. In past centuries, however, taxes on individual goods were more important than they are now. In those days, taxes on goods with highly inelastic demand, like salt, tobacco, and matches, were especially popular.

FIGURE 4.4

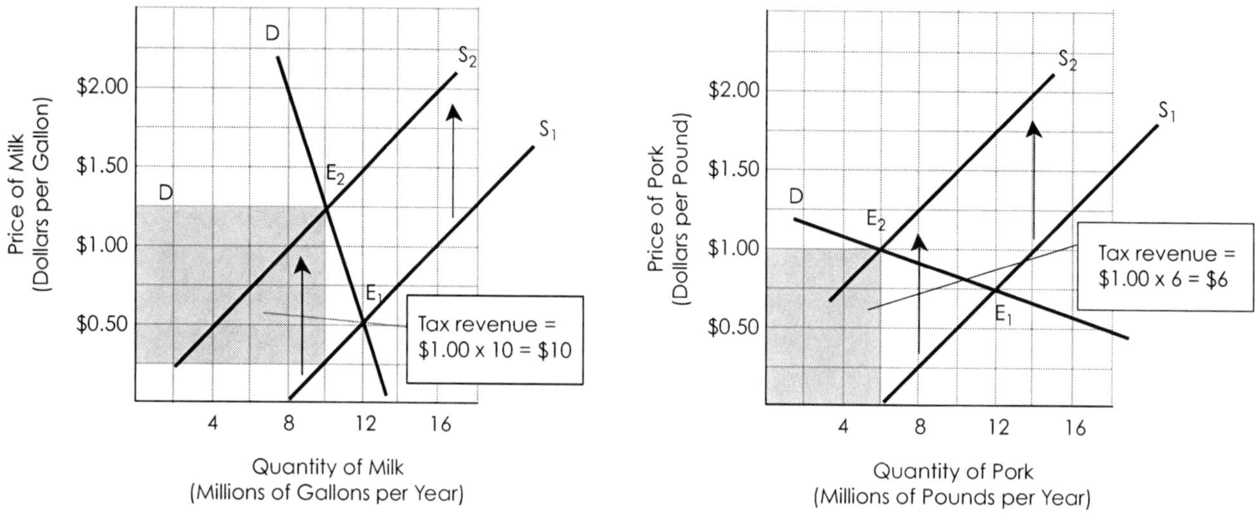

A tax imposed on a good that has an inelastic demand will generate more tax revenue than a tax on a good with elastic demand, assuming similar supply conditions. The diagrams above compare the effects of a $1.00 tax on the markets for milk (inelastic demand) and pork (elastic demand). In the market for milk, the tax reduces the equilibrium quantity by 2 million gallons, from point E_1 (12 million gallons) to E_2 (10 million gallons). Therefore, the government collects a total of $10 million from the milk tax. The same $1.00 tax on pork causes a large reduction in the quantity sold, from 12 million pounds (point E_1) to 6 million pounds (point E_2). This means the government will only collect $6 million, as only 6 million pounds of pork are sold at the new equilibrium.

In the 1990's the federal government levied a tax on luxury yachts, the thinking being that only rich people bought yachts and they should pay their fair share. Because the demand for yachts was much more elastic than the tax writers understood, the tax collected on the sale of big, private boats was minimal, but the consequences to the boat building industry was devastating. Hundreds of good, upper middle class jobs were eliminated as the sales of these boats declined dramatically. The revenue collected was so much lower than the costs of the unemployment compensation that had to be paid, as well as the disruption to several local communities along the Eastern Shore and other states along the North East coast (Maine, New Jersey, etc.).

Elasticity and Prohibition

In the case of gasoline and apartment rents, a tax led to a reduction in the quantity consumed, which we characterized as an unintended consequence of the tax. In a few cases, the reduction in quantity consumed may be an *intended* consequence of the tax. Modern taxes on tobacco products are one example: because tobacco is regarded as harmful, a reduction in quantity consumed is seen as desirable. Taxes on environmentally harmful products, such as the chemicals responsible for ozone depletion, are another example.

Prohibition is a more extreme policy aimed at reducing the quantity of a product consumed. Alcoholic beverages were subject to prohibition in the United States during the 1920s, and drugs like marijuana, heroin, and cocaine are subject to prohibition today. Prohibition is a common method of environmental regulation as well, with the pesticide DDT and lead additives for gasoline serving as examples.

On the surface, a policy of prohibition may seem very different from a tax, since unlike a tax, prohibition raises no tax revenue for the government. However, if we use economic analysis to look below the surface, we see some similarities as well as differences between taxation and prohibition.

First, passage of a law prohibiting production and sale of a good does not make it impossible to supply the good, but simply more expensive. After the prohibition is in effect, the supplier must consider not only the direct costs of production, but the extra costs of covert transportation and distribution systems, the risk of fines or jail terms, the costs of hiring armed gangsters to protect illegal laboratories, and so on. From the law-breaking supplier's point of view, these costs can be seen as an implicit tax. If the price rises by enough to cover them, the good will still be supplied. Thus, the effect of prohibition of a good is to shift its supply curve to the left until each point on the new supply curve lies above the corresponding point on the old curve by a distance equal to the extra costs associated with evading the prohibition.

Second, the effects of the prohibition, like those of a tax, depend on the elasticities of demand and supply. This is illustrated in Figure 4.5, which compares the effects of prohibition on the U.S. markets for DDT and cocaine. The demand for DDT is shown as relatively elastic, because fairly effective substitutes are available at a price only a little higher than the banned pesticide. The demand for cocaine is shown as relatively inelastic, in part because once people become addicted, they will be very reluctant to curtail their use of the drug even if its price rises sharply.

In the case of elastic demand for DDT (Figure 4.5a), even a weakly enforced prohibition, which raises costs of illegal supply only a little, will sharply reduce the quantity sold. Such a weak prohibition, represented by a shift in the supply curve from S_1 to S_2, is already enough to reduce the total revenue (price times quantity sold) earned by producers from \$14,000 per week to \$8,500 per week. A more vigorously enforced prohibition, as represented by supply curve S_3, raises the cost of supply by enough to eliminate use of the product altogether.

In the of case cocaine, with its inelastic demand, even a strongly enforced prohibition has relatively little effect on quantity sold. This case is represented in Figure 4.5b by a shift in the supply curve to S_2. Because quantity demanded is not much affected by the price increase, total revenue from the sale of cocaine rises substantially, from \$130,000 per week at equilibrium E_1 to \$300,000 per week at equilibrium E_2. As long as demand is inelastic, increasing strictness of enforcement, which drives the supply curve still higher, will make the sales revenue of drug suppliers increase still further.

Elasticity of demand is important in understanding the intended and unintended consequences of prohibition. The intended consequence, of course, is to reduce or

FIGURE 4.5 ELASTICITY AND THE EFFECTS OF PROHIBITION

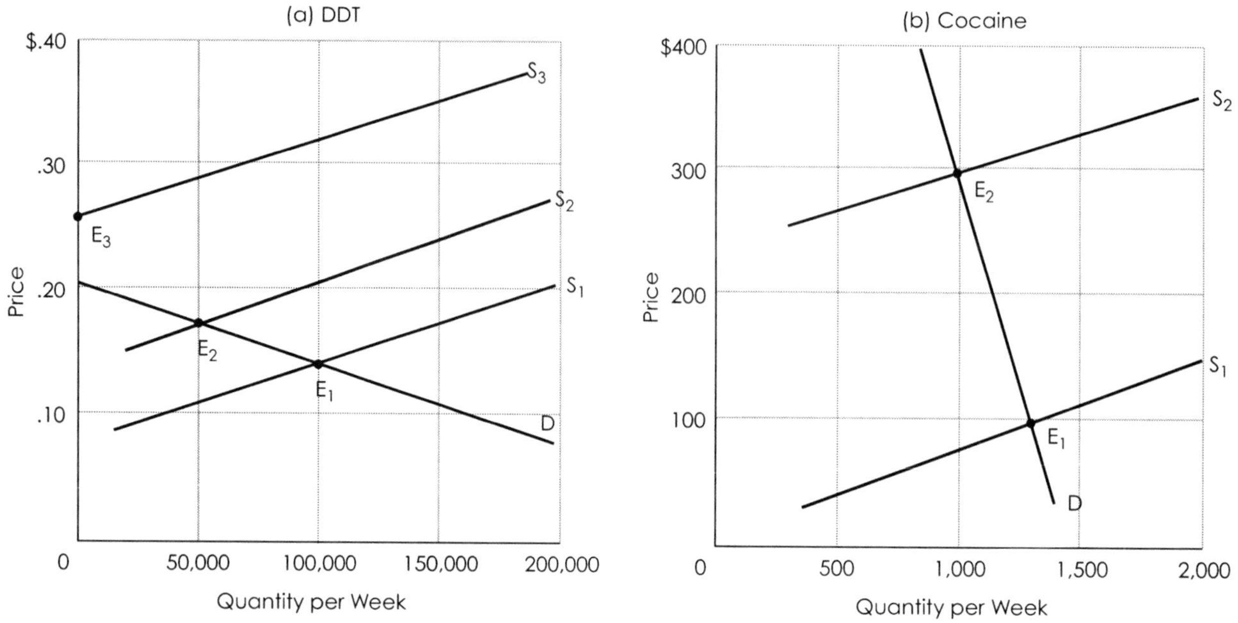

A law prohibiting production and sale of a good, like a tax on the good, shifts its supply curve to the left. The new supply curve will lie above the old supply curve at any given quantity by a distance equal to the cost of evading the prohibition. The effects on price, quantity, and revenue depend on the elasticity of demand. Part (a) uses DDT to illustrate prohibition of a good with elastic demand. A weakly enforced prohibition (S_2) raises the price, reduces the quantity, and reduces total revenue earned by producers from sale of the product. A strongly enforced prohibition reduces quantity and revenue to zero (S_3). Part (b) uses cocaine to illustrate prohibition of a good with inelastic demand. In this case, even strong efforts to enforce prohibition do not reduce quantity sold to zero. Because quantity sold increases by a smaller percentage than price increases, there is an increased total revenue and expenditure on the good.

eliminate use of the product. As we see, the more elastic the demand for the product, the more successful is the policy of prohibition in achieving its intended effects. The unintended effects of prohibition are those associated with the change in revenue that the policy produces. These are very different in the case of elastic and inelastic demand.

Where demand is elastic, the unintended consequences are a loss of profit to DDT producers, and a small rise in the cost of growing crops as farmers switch to more expensive pesticides. Neither has major social consequences. The loss of profit from producing DDT will be offset by profits from production of substitutes, very likely by the same companies. And the increased cost of growing crops is offset by the benefits of a cleaner environment.

On the other hand, where demand is inelastic, prohibition increases total expenditure on the banned product. The social consequences of this are severe. First, users of cocaine must spend more to sustain their habit. At best this means impoverishing themselves and their families; at worst it means an increase in muggings and armed robberies by users desperate for cash. Second, the impact of the prohibition on suppliers must be considered as well. For suppliers, the increase in revenue does not just mean an increase in profit (although profits may increase), but also an increase in expenditures devoted to evading prohibition. In part, the result is simply wasteful, as when drug suppliers buy an airplane to make a single one-way flight rather than using normal transportation methods. Worse, another part of suppliers' increased expenditures take the form of hiring armies of thugs to battle the police and other suppliers, further raising the level of violence on city streets, or bribing government officials, thereby corrupting the quality of government.

The issue of drug prohibition, of course, involves many normative issues that reach far beyond the concept of elasticity. One such issue is whether people have a right to harm themselves through consumption of substances such as tobacco, alcohol, or cocaine, or whether, instead, the government has a duty to act paternalistically to prevent such harm. Another concerns the relative emphasis that should be placed on prohibition versus treatment in allocating resources to reduce drug use. The analysis given here cannot answer such questions. However, it does suggest that the law of unintended consequences applies in the area of drug policy as elsewhere, and that elasticity of demand is important in determining the nature and severity of those consequences.

SUMMARY

1. **How can the responsiveness of quantity demanded to a price change be expressed in terms of elasticity?** *Elasticity* is the responsiveness of quantity demanded or supplied to changes in the price of a good (or changes in other factors), measured as a ratio of the percentage change in quantity to the percentage change in price (or other factor causing the change in quantity). The *price elasticity of demand* between two points on a demand curve is computed as the percentage change in quantity demanded divided by the percentage change in the good's price.

2. **How is the elasticity of demand for a good related to the revenue earned by its seller?** If the demand for a good is elastic, a decrease in its price will increase total revenue. If it is inelastic, an increase in its price will increase total revenue. When the demand for a good is unit elastic, revenue will remain constant as the price varies.

3. **How can elasticity be applied to situations other than the responsiveness of the quantity of a good demanded to a change in its price?** The concept of elasticity can be applied to many situations besides movements along demand curves. The *income elasticity of demand* for a good is the ratio of the percentage change in quantity demanded to a given percentage change in income. The *cross-elasticity of demand* between goods A and B is the ratio of the percentage change in the quantity of good A demanded to a given percentage change in the price of good B. The *price elasticity of supply* is the ratio of the percentage change in the quantity of a good supplied to a given change in its price.

4. **What determines the distribution of the economic burden of a tax?** The way in which the economic burden of a tax is distributed is known as the *incidence* of the tax. The incidence depends on the relative elasticities of supply and demand. If supply is relatively more elastic than demand, buyers will bear the larger share of the tax burden. If demand is relatively more elastic than supply, the larger share of the burden will fall on sellers. If the good is subject to prohibition rather than to a tax, elasticity of demand will determine how many resources are likely to be devoted to enforcement and evasion of the prohibition.

KEY TERMS

Elasticity
Price elasticity of demand
Revenue
Elastic demand
Inelastic demand
Unit elastic demand
Perfectly inelastic demand
Perfectly elastic demand
Income elasticity of demand
Cross-elasticity of demand
Price elasticity of supply
Tax incidence

PROBLEMS AND TOPICS FOR DISCUSSION

1. Recently, the Maryland legislature and Gov. O'Malley raised the tax on a pack of cigarettes by $1.00. The law of demand will tell us that quantity demanded will decline. But the concept of elasticity is needed to understand how and why the tax revenue will change. Draw a rough sketch of what you think the demand curve looks like for cigarettes and how this tax will impact the revenues collected by Annapolis.

QUESTIONS

1. On the basis of this article, do you think that price elasticity of demand for cigarettes in Indonesia is elastic, inelastic, unit elastic, perfectly elastic, or perfectly inelastic? Cite the specific passages supporting your conclusion, and note any apparent contradictions in the article.
2. According to the article, 64 percent of the people of Indonesia, where cigarette prices are among the lowest in the world, are smokers, compared to less than 25 percent in the United States, where prices are higher. What does this suggest about the price elasticity of demand for tobacco in the long run? Why might the long-run elasticity of demand for cigarettes be greater than the short-run demand?
3. According to Angky Camaro of Sampoerna, a tax increase that reduced quantity sold would hurt producers. Using a diagram similar to Figure 4.2, explain why this would be true even if the percentage decrease in quantity were less than the percentage increase in price.
4. According to the article, in 2004, cigarette sales increased as income increased, while taxes were unchanged. What does this tell you about the income elasticity of demand?

CHAPTER 5

Consumer Choice

After reading this chapter, you will understand:	1. The elements involved in consumers' rational choices 2. How consumers balance their choices of goods and services to achieve an equilibrium 3. What lies behind the effect of a price change on the quantity of a good demanded 4. Why demand curves have negative slopes 5. Why both consumers and producers gain from exchanges 6. Why the burden of a tax exceeds the revenue raised by government
Before reading this chapter, make sure you know the meaning of:	1. Substitutes and complements 2. Normal and inferior goods 3. Incidence of a tax

THIS CHAPTER EXPLORES the theory of rational choice as applied to choices made by consumers. No doubt the first image that comes to mind when you read the words "consumer choice" is one of people filling their shopping carts in a supermarket. The theory of consumer choice does apply in a supermarket, but it is broader than that. It extends to choices involving health and safety, like whether to smoke or whether to wear a seatbelt when driving. It extends to life choices like whether to marry and have children. As we will see in this chapter, it applies to any scenario in which people make choices so as to obtain the most satisfaction they can in a situation of scarcity, given the alternatives and opportunity costs that they face. This chapter begins by outlining a theory of rational choice by consumers. Later, it will explore a number of applications of the theory, some of them quite ordinary, others more surprising.

UTILITY AND THE RATIONAL CONSUMER

Economic theories have a typical structure that can be described in terms of statements about objectives, constraints, and choices. Theories of consumer choice fit this pattern. The study of consumer choice thus gives us a chance to fill in the general structure of economic theory with some specific content.

Utility

We begin with the question of consumer *objectives*—why is it that people consume goods and services at all? The answer that people usually give when they think about their own motivations is that consumption of goods and services is a source of pleasure and satisfaction. A loaf of bread to eat, a warm bed to sleep in, a book to read—each serves a particular consumer want or need.

Utility

The pleasure, satisfaction, or need fulfillment that people obtain from the consumption of goods and services.

Economists use the term **utility** to refer to the pleasure or satisfaction people get from the consumption of goods and services. The term goes back some 200 years to the work of the eccentric English social philosopher Jeremy Bentham (1748–1832). Bentham, who studied English law and came to hate it, was obsessed with reforming the law in a way consistent with the principle of the "greatest good for the greatest number." He thought ordinary words such as *pleasure, satisfaction,* or *happiness* were too weak to convey the power of his vision of maximum bliss, so he coined the new word *utility* and established a quasi-religious movement called utilitarianism to promote the idea. Over the centuries, the term *utility* has lost the mystical overtones that it had for Bentham and his followers, but economists still use it in preference to its more ordinary synonyms when they refer to the objective that consumers pursue when choosing among goods and services.

Constraints on Opportunities

Having established utility as the objective, the next step in constructing the theory of consumer choice is to find a way of describing the constraints on the set of opportunities available to consumers. Those constraints encompass all the circumstances that, in a world of scarcity, prevent people from consuming all they want of everything they want.

The most important constraints are limits on the types of goods available, the prices of those goods, and the size of the consumer's budget. A restaurant menu provides a classic example of a constrained opportunity set. You may want tofu salad for lunch, but it is not on the menu. Among the dishes that are on the menu, your favorite might be the filet mignon, but the filet is $18 a serving, and your budget constrains you to spend no more than $5 on lunch. In the end, you settle for a cheeseburger.

To be sure, there are situations in which constraints other than budgets and market prices may be the most important ones. In choosing how fast to drive your car, the "price" (opportunity cost) of greater safety may be taking more time to get where you are going. In choosing a spouse, one constraint is the law that says you can be married to only one person at a time. Later in the chapter, we will look at some examples of nonmarket choices, but choices made in markets remain the central focus of consumer theory.

In constructing a theory of the choices consumers make to maximize utility within their budget constraints, we will proceed in two steps. First, we look at a traditional version of the theory based directly on the notion of utility; then we look at a more modern version in which utility plays a less explicit role.

Diminishing Marginal Utility and Consumer Choice

Jeremy Bentham's notion of "the greatest good for the greatest number" was anything but scientific. In the late nineteenth century, William Stanley Jevons and other economists, working independently, took a major step forward in their understanding of rational choice by consumers when they developed the principle of diminishing marginal utility (see *Who Said It? Who Did It? 5.1*). That step was based on the insight that most of the choices consumers make are not all-or-nothing matters (such as whether to take up smoking or to swear off smoking forever); instead, they are incremental decisions (such as whether to eat chicken one more time a month). Whenever economists refer to the effects of doing a little more or a little less of something, they apply the adjective *marginal*. Thus, the **marginal utility** of a good is the amount of added utility that a consumer gains from consuming one more unit of that good, other things being equal.

Marginal utility

The amount of added utility gained from a one-unit increase in consumption of a good, other things being equal.

The most important principle arrived at by Jevons and others is that of **diminishing marginal utility**. According to this principle, the greater the quantity of any good consumed, the less the marginal utility derived from consuming one more unit of that good.

Principle of diminishing marginal utility

The principle that the greater the consumption of some good, the smaller the increase in utility from a one-unit increase in consumption of that good.

Let us look at how the principle of diminishing marginal utility can be applied to an everyday situation. Assume that you are seated at a lunch counter where pizza is being sold at a price of $2 for a rather skimpy slice and lemonade is being sold at a price of $1 for a small glass. You have $10 to spend on lunch. What will you order?

Your objective is to choose a lunch that will give you the greatest possible utility. Will you spend all your money to buy five pieces of pizza? Probably not. However much you like pizza, you will not get as much satisfaction out of the fifth piece as the first—at least not according to the principle of diminishing marginal utility. Probably you will be willing to pass up the fifth piece of pizza to have a couple of glasses of lemonade with which to wash the first four down. Doing so will increase your total

WHO SAID IT? WHO DID IT? 5.1
WILLIAM STANLEY JEVONS AND MARGINAL UTILITY THEORY

The English economist William Stanley Jevons is credited with the first systematic statement of the theory of marginal utility. Jevons was trained in mathematics and chemistry. With this background, it is not surprising that when his interest turned to economics he tried to restate economic theories in mathematical terms. It was this effort that led him to the theory of marginal utility.

In his *Theory of Political Economy*, published in 1871, Jevons set forth the principle of diminishing marginal utility:

> *Let us imagine the whole quantity of food which a person consumes on an average during twenty-four hours to be divided into ten equal parts. If his food be reduced by the last part, he will suffer but little; if a second tenth part be deficient, he will feel the want distinctly; the subtraction of the third part will be decidedly injurious; with every subsequent subtraction of a tenth part his sufferings will be more and more serious until at length he will be upon the verge of starvation. Now, if we call each of the tenth parts an increment, the meaning of these facts is, that each increment of food is less necessary, or possesses less utility, than the previous one.*

Jevons was the first economist to put the new theory into print, but he shares credit for the "marginal revolution" with at least three others who were working along the same lines simultaneously. The Austrian economist Carl Menger also published his version of marginal utility theory in 1871. Three years later, the Swiss economist Leon Walras, who was not aware of Jevons's or Menger's work, came out with still another version. Finally, Alfred Marshall worked out the basics of marginal utility theory at about the same time in his lectures at Cambridge, although he did not publish his version until 1890.

utility, because the first two lemonades will give you a lot of satisfaction and the last piece of pizza only a little. How about the fourth piece of pizza? Maybe you will be willing to give up half of it for one more glass of lemonade. As you cut back on pizza and increase your consumption of lemonade, the marginal utility of pizza rises and that of lemonade falls. Finally you get to the point at which you cannot increase your utility by spending less on one good and more on the other within a given budget. You have reached a point of **consumer equilibrium**.

Consumer equilibrium

A state of affairs in which a consumer cannot increase the total utility gained from a given budget by spending less on one good and more on another.

You reach consumer equilibrium when the marginal utility you get from a dollar's worth of one good equals the marginal utility you get from a dollar's worth of the other. Another way to state this is that the ratio of the marginal utility of a good to its price must be the same for all goods. Thus:

$$\frac{\text{Marginal utility of good A}}{\text{Price of good A}} = \frac{\text{Marginal utility of good B}}{\text{Price of good B}}$$

This formula can be applied using an imaginary unit of utility, the "util." Suppose, for example, that you have adjusted the quantities of pizza and lemonade you buy so that you get 10 utils from another slice of pizza at a price of $2 per slice and 5 utils from another glass of lemonade at a price of $1 per glass. At these ratios, you get no more added satisfaction from an extra dollar's worth (one half-slice) of pizza than from an extra dollar's worth (one glass) of lemonade. It is not worthwhile to trade off some of either good for some of the other. You are in consumer equilibrium.

On the other hand, suppose you get 18 utils from another slice of pizza (9 utils per half-slice) and 4 from another glass of lemonade, still given the same prices. Now you are not in consumer equilibrium. Cutting back by one lemonade would lose you just 4 utils. You could then use the dollar you saved to buy another half-slice of pizza, thereby gaining 9 utils. By making this adjustment in your consumption pattern, you would not only gain total utility, but also move closer to consumer equilibrium, because the marginal utility you would get from pizza would fall slightly as you consumed more and the marginal utility you would get from lemonade would rise a little as you consumed less.

Attaching numbers to things in this way helps explain the principle involved. Remember, though, that in practice consumer choice is a much more subjective process. Some people count calories when they sit down to lunch; some count the pennies in their pockets; but no one counts "utils"—they cannot really be counted. Utility is something we feel, not something we think about. Because some people feel differently about what they eat than others do, they make different choices. Perhaps you would rather have a cold squid salad and a glass of iced coffee than either pizza or lemonade. Although your choice might differ from someone else's, the logic of the decision—the calculation of utility, the concept of equilibrium—is the same.

$$\frac{MU(x)}{P_{(x)}} = \frac{MU\infty}{P\infty}$$

The rational consumer will continue to consume a good until the marginal utility derived from the last unit consumed in relation to the price of that item is equal to the marginal utility of everything else consumed in relation to the consumer's budget constraint.

From Consumer Equilibrium to the Law of Demand

The concepts of consumer equilibrium and diminishing marginal utility can be combined to give an explanation of the law of demand. The explanation, which is useful even though it is not entirely precise, goes as follows: Suppose you have adjusted your pattern of consumption until you have reached an equilibrium in which, among other things,

$$\frac{\text{MU of pizza}}{\$2} = \frac{\text{MU of lemonade}}{\$1}$$

As long as this equality holds, you will not benefit from increasing your consumption of pizza; doing so would soon push down the marginal utility of pizza. The marginal utility per dollar's worth of pizza would drop below the marginal utility per dollar's worth of lemonade, making you better off if you switched back to more lemonade.

But what if the price of pizza were to drop to, say, $1.50 per slice, upsetting the equality just given? To make the two ratios equal again, given the new price of pizza, either the marginal utility of lemonade would have to rise or that of pizza would have to fall. According to the principle of diminishing marginal utility, one way to get the marginal utility of pizza to fall is to consume more pizza, and one way to get the marginal utility of lemonade to rise is to consume less lemonade. Perhaps you would do a little of both—that is, cut back a little on lemonade and consume a little more pizza. In so doing, you would be acting just as the law of demand would predict: A decrease in the price of pizza would have caused you to buy more pizza.

This line of reasoning connects the law of demand with the principle of diminishing marginal utility in a way that appeals to common sense. However, that is not good enough for all economists. In the next section, we will look at an alternative line of reasoning.

SUBSTITUTION AND INCOME EFFECTS

In the view of some economists, the whole concept of utility is suspect because of its subjective, unmeasurable nature. Instead, they favor an explanation of the law of demand based on the concepts of substitution and income effects of a change in price. The two approaches to demand are, in a broad sense, consistent, but the explanation based on income and substitution effects avoids direct dependence on marginal utility and the measurement of utility.

The Substitution Effect

One reason people buy more of a good whose price falls is that they tend to substitute a good with a lower price for other goods that are relatively expensive. In our earlier example, we looked at the effects of a drop in the price of pizza. The change in price will cause people to substitute pizza for other foods that they might otherwise have eaten—hamburgers, nachos, whatever. Broader substitutions are also possible. With the price of pizza lower than before, people may substitute eating out for eating at home or a pizza party for an evening at the movies. The portion of the increase in the quantity demanded of a good whose price has fallen that is caused by the substitution of that good for other goods, which are now relatively more costly, is known as the **substitution effect** of a change in price.

Substitution effect

The part of the increase in quantity demanded of a good whose price has fallen that is caused by substitution of that good for others that are now relatively more costly.

The Income Effect

A second reason that the change in a good's price will cause a change in the quantity demanded has to do with the effect of price changes on real income.

In economics, the term *nominal* is used to refer to quantities measured in the ordinary way, in terms of the dollar prices at which transactions actually take place. The term *real* is used to indicate quantities that have been adjusted to take into account the effects of price changes. The distinction between real and nominal income is a typical application of these terms: If your monthly paycheck is $1,000, that is your nominal income—the number of dollars you earn. If your nominal income stays at \$1,000 while inflation doubles the average prices of all goods and services, your *real* income—your ability to buy things taking price changes into account—will fall by half. If your nominal income stays at \$1,000 while the average prices of goods and services drop by half, your real income will double.

In macroeconomics the distinction between real and nominal income is widely used in connection with inflation, which involves changes in the prices of many goods at once. But the distinction can also be applied in microeconomics, which tends to emphasize the effects of price changes for one good at a time. The reason is that if the price of even one good changes while the prices of other goods remain constant, there will be some effect on the average price level and, hence, on real income.

With this in mind, let us return to our example. Again suppose that the price of pizza falls while your nominal income and the prices of all other goods and services remain the same. Although pizza occupies only a small place in your budget, a fall in its price means a slight fall in the average level of all prices and, hence, a slight increase in your real income. If you continued to buy the same quantity of pizza and other goods and services as before, you would have a little money left over. For example, if the price of pizza goes down by \$.50 a slice and you usually buy ten slices a month, you would have \$5 left over after making your usual purchases. That is as much of an increase in your real income as you would get if your paycheck were increased by \$5 and all prices remained constant.

The question now is: What will you spend the \$5 on? The answer: You will use it to buy more of things that are normal goods. If pizza is a normal good, one of the things you will buy with your increased real income is more pizza. The portion of the change in quantity demanded of a good whose price has fallen that is caused by the increase in real income resulting from the drop in price is known as the **income effect** of the price change.

Income effect

The part of the change in quantity demanded of a good whose price has fallen that is caused by the increase in real income resulting from the price change.

Income and Substitution Effects and the Demand Curve

In the case of a normal good, the income effect is an additional reason for buying more of a good when its price falls. With both the income and substitution effects causing the quantity demanded to increase when the price falls, the demand curve for a normal good will have a negative slope. We can reach this conclusion with no reference to the awkward concept of utility. So far, so good.

If we are dealing with an inferior good, however, the situation is a little different. Let us say that hot dogs are an inferior good for you. You eat them if you are hungry and they are all you can afford, but if your income goes up enough to buy pizza, you phase out hot dogs. Now what will happen if the price of hot dogs goes down while the prices of all other goods and services remain constant?

First, there will be a substitution effect. Hot dogs now are relatively cheaper compared with lemonade, pizza, pretzels, haircuts, or whatever. Taken by itself, the substitution effect will cause you to buy more hot dogs. Other things (including real income) being equal, the rational consumer will always buy more rather than less of something when its opportunity cost (in this case, its price relative to other goods) goes down. But here other things are not equal. At the same time that the fall in the price of hot dogs tempts you to substitute hot dogs for other things, it also raises your real income slightly. Taken by itself, the increase in your real income would cause you to buy fewer hot dogs because hot dogs are an inferior good for you. Thus, in the case of an inferior good, the substitution and income effects work at cross-purposes when the price changes.

What, then, is the net effect of a decrease in the price of hot dogs? Will you buy more or fewer of them than before? In the case of a good that makes up only a small part of your budget, such as hot dogs, it is safe to assume that a fall in price will cause you to buy more and a rise in price to buy less. The reason is that a change in the price of something of which you buy only a little anyway will have only a miniscule income effect, which will be outweighed by the substitution effect. Thus, when the substitution effect is larger than the income effect, the demand curve for an inferior good will still have a negative slope.

However, there is a theoretical possibility that the demand curve for an inferior good might have a positive slope. For this to be the case, the good would have to make up a large part of a person's budget so that the income effect would be large. Imagine, for example, a family that is so poor that they spend almost all of their income on food, and almost the only foods they can afford to buy are bread and oatmeal. They eat bread as a special treat on Sunday, but the rest of the week they must make do with inferior-tasting but cheaper oatmeal. One day the price of oatmeal goes up, although not by enough to make it more expensive than bread. The rise in the price of oatmeal is devastating to the family's budget. They are forced to cut out their one remaining luxury: The Sunday loaf of bread disappears and is replaced by oatmeal. The paradoxical conclusion, then, is that a rise in the price of oatmeal causes this family to buy more, not less, oatmeal. The family's demand curve for oatmeal has a positive slope. A good that has a positively sloped demand curve for such reasons is called a **Giffen good** after a nineteenth-century English writer, Robert Giffen, who supposedly mentioned the possibility.[1]

Giffen good

An inferior good accounting for a large share of a consumer's budget that has a positively sloped demand curve because the income effect of a price change outweighs the substitution effect.

The conditions required for a positively sloped demand curve—an inferior good that makes up a large portion of the consumer's budget—are very special. Such conditions are unlikely to be encountered in the markets in which people usually conduct transactions. If you are in the pizza business—or even in the oatmeal business—you can be virtually certain that, taking the world as it really is, raising the price of any good or service will cause people to buy less of it and cutting the price will cause them to buy more of it. The Giffen-good phenomenon has been demonstrated under carefully controlled experimental circumstances. And nothing in the pure logic of rational choice disproves the possibility of such a situation occurring in an actual market situation.

Applications of Income and Substitution Effects

The law of demand and the concepts of income and substitution effects can be applied to any situation in which a consumer seeks to maximize utility in the face of established alternatives and constraints, even when the "goods" in question are not "for sale," and even when constraints and the opportunity costs of the available alternatives are not stated in money. This section will look at some of the wider applications of the theory of consumer choice.

Children as Durable Consumer Goods

University of Chicago economist Gary Becker, winner of the 1992 Nobel Memorial Prize for economics, has made his reputation by applying economic reasoning to areas of choice that many people think of as noneconomic. Some of his best-known research concerns choices made within the family. As an example, consider Becker's analysis of the number of children a family chooses to have.

Children, in Becker's view, are durable consumer goods. They return benefits to parents over many years in such forms as love, family pride, and mowing the lawn. But there are opportunity costs associated with having children. Those costs include the goods and services forgone to pay the extra grocery bills, clothing bills, and doctors' bills for the children. But in Becker's view, the biggest opportunity cost of having children is the time parents spend caring for them. That time, too, has an opportunity cost. Time not spent caring for children could be spent working to earn income. Thus the higher the parents' earning power, the greater the opportunity cost of having children.

What does this imply about the number of children a family chooses to have? It has been widely observed in many societies that as family income rises, the number of children per family tends to fall. Does this mean that children are inferior goods? Not at all, says Becker. Children are normal goods; other things being equal, the income effect would cause a family to want more children as its income increases. But other things are not equal. As Becker notes, there is also a substitution effect because, if the higher income reflects a higher hourly wage, it increases the opportunity cost of each hour spent caring for children. On the average, the substitution effect outweighs the income effect, so higher-income families end up having fewer children.

As confirmation of his analysis, Becker notes that the income and substitution effects can be partially distinguished by looking separately at the effects of changes in men's and women's incomes. Traditionally, women perform a greater proportion of child care than men. In a family where this is the case, an increase in a woman's income would have a stronger substitution effect than an increase in a man's income. The reason is that, in such a family, a woman with a high income would encounter a high opportunity cost for each hour taken off from work to devote to child care, whereas, by assumption, the man would take few hours off for child care regardless of his income. Empirical data in fact reveal such a pattern to be prevalent: Birth rates tend to vary directly with incomes earned by men because the income effect outweighs the relatively weak substitution effect. But birth rates vary inversely with incomes earned by women, who experience a relatively stronger substitution effect.

And what is it that parents substitute for a greater quantity of children when their incomes rise? Some, no doubt, substitute ski vacations in Austria, BMWs, and other luxuries. But, Becker notes, they have another reaction as well, one that is consistent with the theory of consumer choice. In place of a greater number of children, he says, upper-income families substitute investment in higher-quality children: piano lessons from the age of five; tutors to help cram for SAT exams; tuition payments to Yale Law School. It's all so *rational,* says Becker.

CONSUMER SURPLUS

This chapter has related consumer choice to the demand curve from two perspectives—that of utility theory and that of income and substitution effects. In both cases, the demand curve was viewed as answering the question, How much of a good will consumers wish to purchase at any given price? In this section, we turn to a different question to which the demand curve also can provide an answer: How much will consumers be willing to pay for an additional unit of a good given the quantity they already have?

The Demand Curve as Willingness to Pay

Figure 5.1 shows a demand curve for apples for a college student, Hannah Lee. Lee stocks up on snack foods at a local supermarket and often includes apples in her purchases. The demand curve given in the figure shows that the number of apples she eats each month depends on their price. Currently the price of an apple is \$.40. At this price, she buys ten per month. On other days she substitutes an orange or a banana.

The demand curve indicates that \$.40 is the maximum that Lee would be willing to pay for the tenth apple. If the price rose to \$.45, she would substitute some other fruit for the tenth apple. However, she would not cut out apples altogether. Although \$.40 is the maximum she is willing to pay for the tenth apple, she would not give up the ninth apple unless the price rose above \$.45. Similarly, she would be willing to pay up to \$.50 before giving up the eighth apple, up to \$.55 before giving up the seventh, and so on. The height of the demand curve at each point (emphasized here by a vertical bar) shows the maximum that she would willingly pay for each unit consumed. That maximum decreases as the quantity consumed increases, in accordance with the principle of diminishing marginal utility.

Measuring the Surplus

Figure 5.1 shows the maximum that Lee is willing to pay for various quantities of apples, but it also shows that she need not actually pay this amount. At the going price of

FIGURE 5.1 CONSUMER SURPLUS

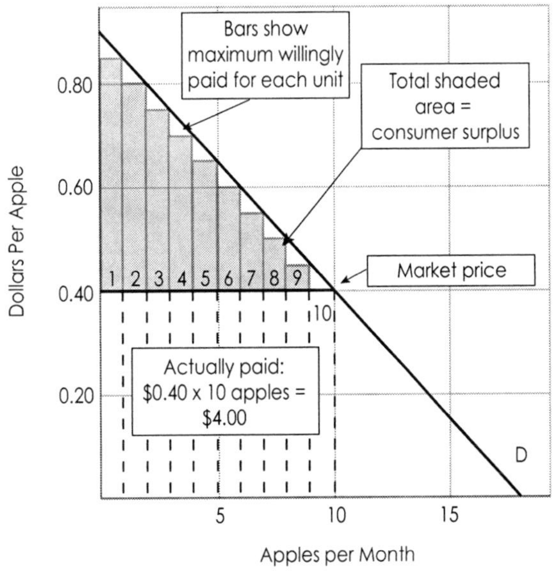

The height of a demand curve shows the maximum that this consumer would be willing to pay for an additional unit of a good. For example, she would be willing to pay up to $.85 for the first apple bought each month but only $.55 for the seventh. The maximum she would willingly pay for each unit is shown by a vertical bar. In this case, the market price is $.40; thus, she buys 10 apples a month, paying a total of $4.00. The difference between what she actually pays at the market price and the maximum she would have been willing to pay, shown by the shaded area, is called consumer surplus.

$.40, she pays only a total of $4 for the ten apples she buys each month. Except in the case of the last unit purchased, she gets each unit for less than what she would willingly have paid for it. The difference between what she would willingly have paid for each unit and the amount actually paid at the market is called the **consumer surplus** for that unit. The consumer surplus on each unit is shown by the shaded portion of the corresponding vertical bar. For example, the surplus on the first apple, for which Lee would have willingly paid $.85 if necessary, is $.45, because she actually paid only $.40. The total consumer surplus on all units purchased is shown by the sum of the shaded portions of the bars. The area of the triangle between the demand curve and the market price is an approximate measure of consumer surplus.[3]

Consumer surplus

The difference between the maximum that a consumer would be willing to pay for a unit of a good and the amount that he or she actually pays.

Consumer Surplus, Producer Surplus, and Gains from Exchange

The reasoning behind the notion of consumer surplus can be extended to the producers' side of the market as well. Consider Figure 5.2, which shows a typical market operating according to principles of supply and demand. The equilibrium market price is established at the point where the supply and demand curves cross. The

FIGURE 5.2 GAINS FROM EXCHANGE

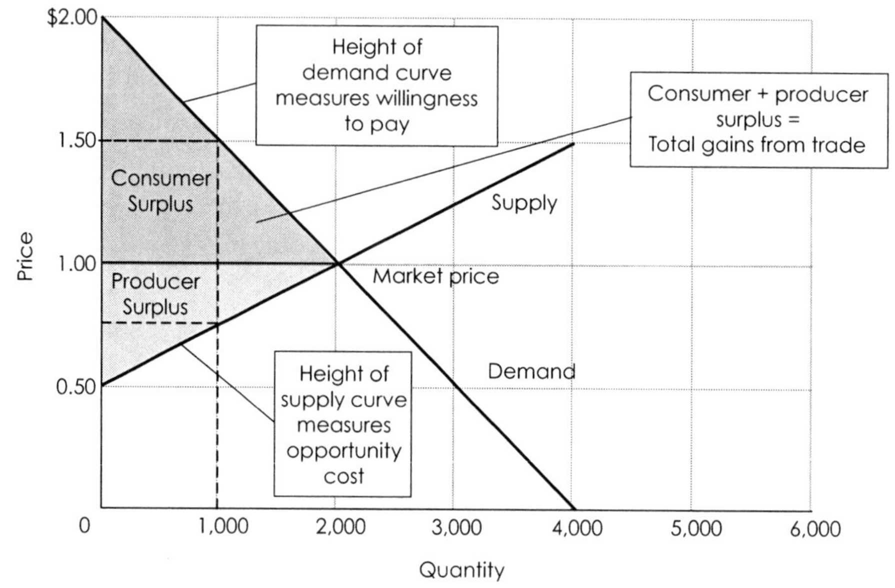

This figure shows that both consumers and producers gain from exchange. Here the equilibrium market price is $1 per unit. The demand curve shows the maximum that consumers would willingly pay for each unit. Consumers' gain from exchange takes the form of consumer surplus, shown by the area between the demand curve and the market price. The supply curve shows the minimum that producers would willingly accept rather than put their resources to work elsewhere. Producers earn a surplus equal to the difference between what they actually receive at the market price and the minimum they would have been willing to accept. The producer surplus is shown by the area between the supply curve and the market price. Assuming an equilibrium is reached at the point of intersection of the two curves, total gains from exchange are thus the entire area between them up to the intersection.

demand curve, as we have seen, measures the maximum amount that consumers would be willing to pay for each unit sold; for example, they will pay no more than $1.50 for the one thousandth unit. Consumer surplus is a measure of the difference between the maximum that consumers would have been willing to pay and what they actually pay at the market price.

Now turn to the supply curve. The height of the supply curve at any point represents the minimum that producers would willingly accept for the unit. For example, producers would be unwilling to accept less than $.75 for the one thousandth unit sold. If they could not get at least that much, the producers would divert their resources to an alternative use rather than produce the one thousandth unit of this product.

Producer surplus

The difference between what producers receive for a unit of a good and the minimum they would be willing to accept.

However, as the figure is drawn, producers receive the market price of $1 per unit for all units sold, including the one thousandth. On that unit, they earn a producer surplus of $.25. The **producer surplus** earned on each unit is the difference between the market price and the minimum that the producers would have been willing to accept in exchange for that unit—the difference between $1 and $.75 for the one thousandth unit in our example. The total producer surplus earned on all units is shown by the area between the supply curve and the market price.

We see, then, that the concept of surplus in the market is symmetrical. Consumers buy the goods, except for the very last unit, for less than the maximum amount they would have been willing to pay, and producers sell the goods, except for the very last unit, for more than the minimum amount they would have been willing to accept. Thus, *both buyers and sellers gain from exchange*. That is why markets exist. As long as participation is voluntary, they make everyone who buys and sells in them better off than they would be if they did not participate. Assuming an equilibrium at the intersection of the supply and demand curves, as in Figure 5.2, the total of the mutual gains from exchange—consumer surplus plus producer surplus—is equal to the entire shaded triangle between the supply and demand curves to the left of their intersection point.

SUMMARY

1. **What elements are involved in consumers' rational choices?** Objectives and constraints on opportunities provide the setting for rational choice by consumers. Consumers choose rationally when they set goals and make systematic efforts to achieve them. The objective of consumer choice is *utility*—the pleasure and satisfaction that people get from goods and services. The added utility obtained from a one-unit increase in consumption of a good or service is its *marginal utility*. The greater the rate of consumption of a good, the smaller the increase in utility from an additional unit consumed.

2. **How do consumers balance their choices of goods and services to achieve an equilibrium?** *Consumer equilibrium* is said to occur when the total utility obtained from a given budget cannot be increased by shifting spending from one good to another. In equilibrium, the marginal utility of a dollar's worth of one good must equal the marginal utility of a dollar's worth of any other good.

3. **What lies behind the effect of a price change on the quantity of a good demanded?** The change in quantity demanded that results from a change in a good's price, other things being equal, can be separated into two parts. The part that comes from the tendency to substitute cheaper goods for more costly ones is the *substitution effect*. The part that comes from the increase in real income that results from a decrease in the price of the good, other things being equal, is the *income effect*.

4. **Why do demand curves have negative slopes?** For a normal good, the substitution and income effects work in the same direction. The demand curves for normal goods therefore have negative slopes. For inferior goods, the income effect and the substitution effect work in opposite directions. For inferior goods, therefore, the demand curve will have a negative slope only if the substitution effect outweighs the income effect. In practice, this is virtually always the case, although *Giffen goods* with positively sloped demand curves are a theoretical possibility.

5. **Why do both consumers and producers gain from exchange?** When consumers buy a product at a

given market price, they pay the same amount for each unit purchased. However, because of the *principle of diminishing marginal utility,* the first units purchased are worth more to them than the last ones purchased. The difference between what consumers actually pay for a unit of a good and the maximum they would be willing to pay is the *consumer surplus* gained on that unit of the good. Similarly, the difference between what sellers actually receive for a good and the minimum they would have accepted is known as *producer surplus.*

6. **Why does the burden of a tax exceed the revenue raised by government?** When a tax is imposed on a good or service, the equilibrium price including the tax rises while the equilibrium price net of the tax falls. As a result, the equilibrium quantity falls, making both consumers and producers forgo some surplus. The forgone surplus is not captured in the form of tax revenue and is called the *excess burden of the tax.* It is a burden on consumers and producers over and above the sum that the government collects as tax revenue.

KEY TERMS

Utility	Substitution effect
Marginal utility	Income effect
Principle of diminishing utility	Giffen good
	Consumer surplus
Consumer equilibrium	Producer surplus

PROBLEMS AND TOPICS FOR DISCUSSION

1. **Externalities of automobile safety.** The increase in deaths of pedestrians and bicyclists resulting from drivers' use of seat belts or air bags is an example of an *externality*, a concept introduced in Chapter 3. What could the government do to prevent this externality while still achieving the goal of increased driver safety? Bonus question: If you complete the appendix to this chapter, analyze the trade-off between speed and safety using an indifference curve diagram. How does the installation of seat belts in a car change the budget line?

2. **Can there be increasing marginal utility?** Can there be increasing marginal utility in some cases? For example, suppose it would take eight rolls of wallpaper to decorate your kitchen. If someone gave you seven rolls of wallpaper, you would get only limited utility from them. An eighth roll, however, would give you great utility. Do you think this is a valid exception to the principle of diminishing marginal utility?

3. **Consumer equilibrium, marginal utility, and prices.** Martha Smith consumes two pounds of pork and five pounds of beef per month. She pays $1.50 a pound for the pork and $2 per pound for the beef. What can you say about the ratio of the marginal utility of pork to the marginal utility of beef, assuming that this pattern represents a state of consumer equilibrium for Smith? Is the ratio 3/4, 4/3, 5/2, 2/5, or none of these?

4. **A Giffen good.** A Giffen Good is a good that experiences increased demand for when the price rises and decreased demand for when the price falls. Mainly a theoretical concept, but there have arguable been goods with this property. A family living in Minnesota vacations in Florida each January. One year the price of home heating fuel goes up sharply. The family turns the thermostat down a little, but even so the heating bills go up so much that the family cannot afford to go to Florida that year. Staying home in January means that the house must be kept heated during that month. The extra fuel burned during January is more than what the family has been able to save

by lowering the thermostat setting in other months. Thus, the total quantity of fuel burned in the winter rises as a result of the increase in the price of heating fuel. Analyze this case in terms of the income and substitution effects. Is home heating fuel a Giffen good for this family? (Hint: Winter vacations in Minnesota are an inferior good for this family. Heating fuel is a complement to winter vacations in Minnesota and hence is also an inferior good.)

5. **Excess burden of a tax.** Figure 4.5 in Chapter 4 demonstrates the incidence of a tax on apartment rents. Using the approach outlined in this chapter, calculate the revenue raised by this tax and the excess burden of the tax. How much of the excess burden is borne by landlords? How much by tenants?

END NOTES

1. The positive slope of the demand curve for a Giffen good does not depend on an assumption of bounded rationality. A fully rational consumer would have a negatively sloped demand curve for house-brand cleaner.
2. Sam Peltzman, "The Effects of Automobile Safety Regulation," *Journal of Political Economy* 83 (August 1975): 677–725. In a follow-up study, Robert W. Crandall and John D. Graham ("Automobile Safety Regulation and Offsetting Behavior: Some New Empirical Estimates," *American Economic Review* 74 (May 1984): 328–331) also found that safety regulation had unintended consequences on driving behavior. In distinction to the original Peltzman study, some researchers claim that the effects are small, and that safety regulation has a net beneficial effect.
3. An intermediate-level microeconomics course would explain that for reasons associated with the income effect, the triangle does not provide a precise measure of consumer surplus. However, the approximation is close for goods that make up only a small part of consumers' total expenditures.

CHAPTER 6

The Dilemma of American Health Care

After reading this chapter, you will understand:	1. What factors are pushing the demand for health care. 2. Why there are restrictions to the increase of supply of health care. 3. The market for transplants

AMERICA HAS THE best health care available. Unfortunately, there may be problems with accessibility; not everyone has access to the doctor when she is in need of medical treatment. Though every hospital, by law, must treat anyone who presents herself for treatment to ensure life, many less than life-threatening disorders are not treated and progress to life-endangering situations. It is argued that if the minor illnesses were treated, and not allowed to progress to dangerous levels, the system could save billions of dollars. But this is not the only, and maybe not the primary, problem pushing up the costs (price) of health care.

SITUATIONS PUSHING UP HEALTH CARE PRICES

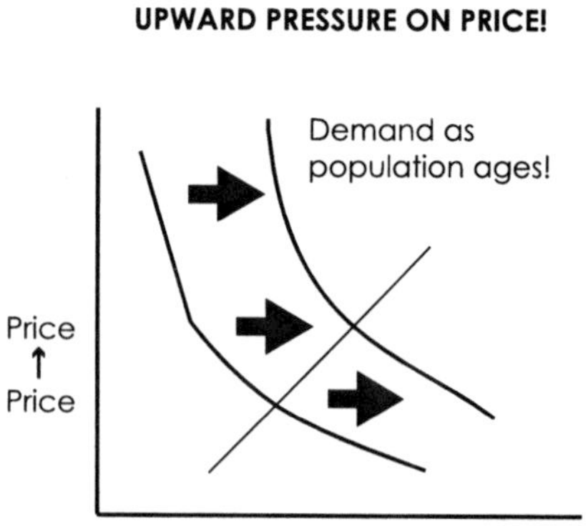

Situation #1

The American population is aging. It is the aged who consume the majority of the health care resources. Because of this aging population, the demand for health care is increasing, thus pushing the price up!

Situation #2

Health care is a normal good. This means that as our income increases, our demand for health care increases. The standard of living and income of Americans is increasing, both individually and collectively. As our incomes increase, our demand for health care increases, thus putting further upward pressure on price.

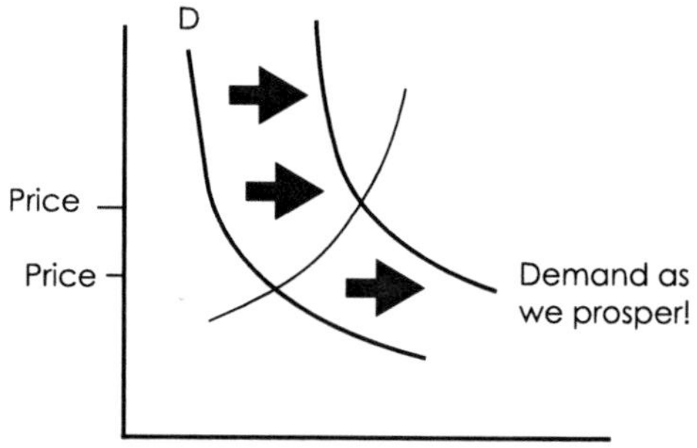

Situation #3

Since most Americans receive their health insurance from their employer, they are removed from the true cost and thus, the price of the care they consume. Americans perceive that their care has no marginal cost since they do not have to write a check for the care they consume. Thus, since they perceive price to be close to free, the law of demand comes into play. When the price is perceived to be very low, in this case almost free, then the quantity demanded increases. Thus, most American may OVER DEMAND when it comes to health care. Because they don't feel any financial loss, they are more likely to use the health care system for illness, or fear of illnesses, that otherwise they wouldn't. This over consumption pushes demand out and thus stresses the system and tends to increase price further.

AMERICAN HEALTH CARE DEMANDS

When it comes to health care, American's demand three things. First, we demand that we receive the BEST health care possible. When we are in the doctor's office or hospital we will not tolerate any treatment that is not the most up-to-date, state-of-the-art, and modern as possible.

Second, we demand that we receive our health care IMMEDIATELY. We will not wait! If you've ever had a severe toothache, you know of the impatience you feel to get in the dentist's chair and get that pain gone! Imagine how anxious you are when you feel poorly. You demand the physician make room in her appointment schedule for you NOW!

Finally, in the area of health care, we demand CHEAP care. We don't want to pay for it. We demand that someone else pay for our health care, or that no one pays for it. We are outraged by the costs that the doctor, nurse, pharmacist, and x-ray technician charges us for their products and services.

As you should realize, we can't have all three. Because the BEST, by definition is the most expensive, it is impossible to have the most expensive health care at a CHEAP price! That is, unless we are willing to wait for the care. So, if we want the best possible health care but at a low price, we'll have to wait for it because everyone else with that same need will be demanding the service and we'd have to get in line behind them and wait our turn.

Traditionally, Americans have chosen the first two options, best care, and fast care. But as the price (and quality) of health care increased, we've started to move toward the HMOs.

The insurance premiums may be lower at HMOs, but the services they promise are not the best possible available. Some HMO members were surprised to realize that not all of the wonderful treatments, transplants, cancer procedures, pharmaceuticals, etc. were covered by their plan. So, the care was fast, the care was cheap (relatively), but it was not the best. Some other plans may come with higher premiums, but they will provide better treatment.

Other countries have chosen different options than America. Canada's government payer system offers good care at low cost, funded by taxes, and it covers every Canadian, but the Canadian system cannot offer the care quickly. There are horror stories of Canadians waiting for months for certain treatments, or coming south to America for medical treatment.

In the Spring of 2008, Carroll showed the film SICKO made by Michael Moore. The film depicted horror stories about things gone wrong with specific incidents to Americans and then showed some aspects of foreign health care. During the film, Moore constantly informed the viewers that no one paid for health care in the nations Moore filmed in. His theme was that care was free. Only once, and with no emphasis, Moore stated that taxes may be a slight amount higher in these countries. After the film, a panel of physicians and health care professions (a pharmaceutical sales rep and a medical instrument sales rep) discussed the film. During the discussion they brought out many of the shortcomings of the American system, but they all agreed that the film was one sided at best and most agreed that Moore intentionally left out true positive aspects of the American system as well as major shortcomings of foreign systems.

As of May, 2008, both Democratic candidates for president have proposed much greater national government intervention in the health insurance system. The two democratic candidates favor a centralized national plan. Sen. Clinton has said she would require every person to enroll in some care system regardless of their desires. Sen.

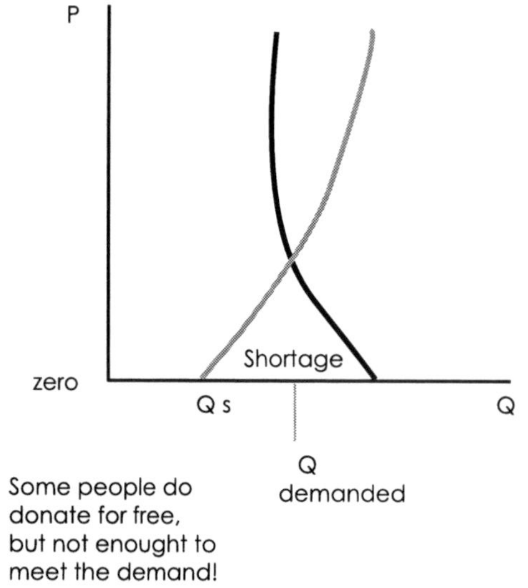
P
Shortage
zero
Q s
Q
Q
demanded
Some people do
donate for free,
but not enought to
meet the demand!

As the price paid to donors, would the amount of blood supplied increase?

Would the number of organs available increase if there was some form of compensation for becoming an organ donor?

Blood for Pay?

New meaning to the term

Blood Money!

McCain, the Repulican candidate, has proposed a market system with tax credits paying the large portion of the premiums for those who could not afford them, while leaving the plans in private hands. In November of 2008, once again the American people will decide which philosophy they want: central planned, national care or decentralized, market oriented care.

SHOULD THE MARKET BE USED TO DETERMINE ORGAN TRANSPLANTS?

There is a shortage of organs for needed transplants, as well as blood needed for transfusions and for surgeries. Why is this? An economic explanation for shortages is that the price paid is too low, thus causing a lower quantity supplied. An economic solution for this is to increase the price paid for organs and blood donations. If people had something to gain (people are motivated by incentives) would more people sign organ donation cards and donate blood regularly to the Red Cross? Some people have signed donation cards and voluntarily donate blood, but there are not enough people willing to give away their blood and/or organs to meet the demand. So, ask yourself: Do I GIVE blood to the Red Cross? If not, would I for \$25, \$50, or \$75? How much pay would it take for you to increase your donations? And ask if you've signed a donation card in case of accident? If not, would you for a \$2,000 life insurance policy?

PROBLEMS AND TOPICS FOR DISCUSSION

1. **Is health care a RIGHT?**

CHAPTER 7

Production and Cost

After reading this chapter, you will understand:	1. How economists view the concepts of cost and profit 2. The distinction between short-run and long-run time horizons 3. How costs vary in response to changes in the quantity of a variable input 4. How a firm's cost structure can be represented in geometric terms 5. The choices a firm faces in the course of long-run expansion
Before reading this chapter, make sure you know the meaning of:	1. Opportunity cost 2. Entrepreneurship 3. Economic rent 4. Rational choice

BUSINESS FIRMS, WHETHER giants like Microsoft or midgets like a local lawn service, are one of the basic units of microeconomic analysis. They can be studied from many perspectives: as expressions of their owners' personalities, as social systems within which owners and workers interact, as organizations with complex communication structures, as systems of contracts and property rights. Volumes have been written on each of these aspects. In this chapter, however, we will look at firms from a more material point of view: as mechanisms for transforming inputs of labor, capital, and natural resources into outputs of goods and services to meet human needs. The firm as a production organization is a key element of the neoclassical tradition in microeconomics. Understanding the firm as a user of inputs to produce outputs will provide a foundation for exploring other perspectives on the firm in later chapters.

COSTS AND PROFITS

As in our discussion of consumer choice, we can begin by looking at the firm's objectives and constraints. Our theory will assume that the principal objective of any private firm is to maximize its profit. The principal constraints on its opportunities are, first, its costs of production, and second, the demand for its output. We will bring demand into the picture beginning in the next chapter. In this one we will explore costs and their relationship to profit.

The Profit Motive

The assumption that profit is the principal objective of the business firm often meets an objection similar to that raised against the assumption of rationality: It implies too narrow a view of human nature. To be sure, critics say, profit is important, but it is hardly the only thing businesses are interested in. Managers of some firms seem to display other-regarding preferences. They spend large amounts on supporting the arts or aiding the homeless, in excess of any amounts that might enhance profit via good publicity. Other firms are led by egotists who will risk all, including profit itself, in pursuit of building a personal empire. Still others are run by people who prefer to take Wednesday afternoons off for golf as long as their firms earn a minimum level of profit needed to survive.

After our discussion of rational choice in Chapter 3, it should not be hard to guess how economists answer these objections.

One answer, true to the spirit of neoclassical economics, is that the assumption of profit maximization is not intended to serve as a comprehensive description of the motives behind business decisions. Rather, it is a simplification whose purpose is to give a sharper structure to theories about the way decisions are affected by changes in costs or demand. A simple theory should be discarded for a more complex one only if it fails to explain behavior observed in the real world. In practice, theories based on the assumption of profit maximization are able to explain a great deal of what firms are observed to do. In later chapters we will encounter some special situations in which theories can be improved by taking into account objectives other than profit. But such situations are few.

A second defense of the profit maximization assumption is the so-called survivorship principle. To understand this principle, imagine that ownership of firms is at first distributed randomly among people who are inclined to pursue the objective of profit and others who favor the objectives of charity, ego satisfaction, or the easy life. Over time, the firms that maximized profit would increase their capital and grow steadily through investment or acquisition. Those that pursued other objectives would at best have fewer profits to invest in expansion and at worst might be forced out of business by losses. As time went on, then, the survivors of the competitive process would tend to be the profit maximizers.

The Nature of Costs

Profit is the difference between revenue and costs, so we cannot get far in discussing profits without looking at costs. As we learned in Chapter 1, economists think first and foremost in terms of *opportunity cost*. Because of scarcity, no production can take place without an opportunity cost. There are never enough resources to satisfy all wants, and therefore the decision to produce any one thing implies the need to forgo using the same resources to produce something else. The opportunity costs of production are a fundamental constraint on a firm's ability to maximize its profits. In this section, we will explore several aspects of production costs and explain their relationship to one another.

IMPLICIT AND EXPLICIT COSTS The opportunity costs that a firm faces include the compensation it must pay to workers, investors, and owners of natural resources in order to attract factors of production away from alternative uses, as well as the payments it must make to other firms that supply it with intermediate goods, such as parts, semifinished materials, and business services. Those costs can be classified in several ways. We begin with the distinction between explicit and implicit costs.

Explicit costs

Opportunity costs that take the form of explicit payments to suppliers of factors of production and intermediate goods.

Implicit costs

Opportunity costs of using resources contributed by the firm's owners (or owned by the firm itself as a legal entity) that are not obtained in exchange for explicit payments.

Explicit costs are opportunity costs that take the form of explicit payments to suppliers of factors of production and intermediate goods. They include workers' wages, managers' salaries, salespeople's commissions, payments to banks and other suppliers of financial services, fees for legal advice, transportation charges, and many other things. Explicit costs are familiar to accounting majors and accountants easily relate to hard, objective numbers.

Long as this list is, explicit costs do not include all of the opportunity costs that a firm bears when it engages in production. There are also **implicit costs**—opportunity costs of using resources contributed by the firm's owners (or owned by the firm itself as a legal entity) that are not obtained under contracts calling for explicit payments. For example, if the proprietor of a small firm works along with the firm's hired employees without receiving a salary, he or she gives up the opportunity to earn a salary by working for someone else. As another example, when a firm uses a building that it owns, it need not make a payment to anyone, but it gives up the opportunity to receive payments from someone else to whom it could rent the building. Firms normally do not record implicit costs in their accounts, but this does not make those costs any less real. A self employed person once opened a health club—gym and gave up a well paying insurance position. After the first year of operation, the entrepreneur had a profit (revenues—explicit costs) of $12,000. His accountant congratulated him on his profit. However, his economist consoled him on his loss. His economist pointed out that he gave up a $60,000 per year salary in order to earn $12,000. Taking in account the implicit costs, or the loss of insurance salary, this gym owner lost $48,000!

COSTS AND PROFITS The distinction between explicit and implicit costs is important in understanding what economists mean by profit—the firm's chief objective. Economists use the term profit to mean the difference between a firm's total revenues and all of its opportunity costs, including both explicit and implicit costs. To distinguish this meaning from other possible meanings, we will call it **pure economic profit.** Special care must be taken to distinguish economic profit from two other uses of the term profit.

Pure economic profit

The sum that remains when both explicit and implicit costs are subtracted from total revenue.

Accounting profit

Total revenue minus explicit costs.

First, in the business world, *profit* is often used to mean revenue minus explicit costs only, without giving consideration to implicit costs. Economists call this concept **accounting profit** because it considers only the explicit payments that appear in the firm's written accounts. (If you have studied accounting, you will know that in real life accountants are not quite that simple minded. However, perhaps because economists don't always know much about accounting, they continue to use the term.) The relationship between accounting profit and pure economic profit is as follows

$$\text{Pure economic profit} = \text{Accounting profit} - \text{Implicit costs}$$

or alternatively

$$\text{Accounting profit} = \text{Pure economic profit} + \text{Implicit costs.}$$

Normal profit (normal return on capital)

The implicit opportunity cost of capital contributed by the firm's owners (equity capital).

Second, pure economic profit needs to be distinguished from so-called **normal profit**, a term that is sometimes used to refer to the opportunity cost of capital contributed by the firm's owners (*equity capital,* in financial terminology). **Normal return on capital** is an equivalent term. Suppose that you use \$200,000 of your own savings as capital for their new business. You could instead have invested in securities that paid a 10 percent rate of return, or \$20,000 per year. That \$20,000 would be your opportunity cost of capital. It represents the return your funds would have earned in their best alternative use.

To understand how the opportunity cost of owners' capital comes to be called *normal profit,* consider a firm that has no other implicit costs. In order for such a firm to earn zero economic profit, its accounting profit would have to be equal to its implicit opportunity cost of capital. Such a rate of accounting profit could be called "normal" in the sense that it is just enough to make it worthwhile for owners to invest their capital in this firm, rather than in the best alternative line of business available. Lines of business that earned more than this (that is, a positive pure economic profit), would be perceived as "abnormally" profitable, and would swiftly attract new investors and competitors. Those that earned less would be perceived as less than "normally" profitable, and would tend to shrink as investors channeled their capital elsewhere.

If a firm has other implicit costs in addition to those of owners' capital, its accounting profit must be sufficient to cover them, too, in order to earn zero economic profit. This idea can be expressed in terms of any of the following equations, all of which are equivalent:

Accounting profit = Pure economic profit + Implicit costs
= Pure economic profit + Implicit cost of capital + Other implicit costs
= Pure economic profit + Normal profit + Other implicit costs.

COSTS ARE SUBJECTIVE A final word is in order regarding the nature of costs. In turning from the theory of consumption set forth in the previous chapter to the theory of production costs, it may at first appear that we are moving from an area of economics governed by subjective valuations to one of objective valuations. But this is true only in part, if at all.

It is true that business managers and their accountants do make serious efforts to record costs in numerical form, and in doing so, to apply consistent, rational methods that are as free as possible from wishful thinking and intentional bias. In this sense, the process of cost accounting is objective.

In a deeper sense, however, the theory of cost is just as much rooted in subjective judgments as is the theory of consumer choice. That is because all costs, as explained above, are *opportunity costs*. Opportunity costs reflect the value that would have been produced by resources in the best alternative use. But opinions can differ as to what the best alternative is, and what its value is. For example, what really is the opportunity cost to the Martins of investing their $200,000 savings in their computer firm? Ralph might think that the best alternative use would have been to purchase a portfolio of international stocks paying a 10 percent rate of return. Andrea might think the best alternative use would have been to buy shares in an aggressive hedge fund, a riskier use of their savings, but one yielding an expected return of 11 percent. Who is to say which one is right? Which alternative use of the $200,000 is best depends not only on subjective estimates of the likely return from alternative investments, but also on the subjective attitude toward risk of the person making the investment.

The same is true of the opportunity costs of resources other than capital. For example, an assessment of the opportunity cost of assigning a talented worker to one task must take into account not just what the worker is paid, but also what he or she could have contributed elsewhere in the firm. It will rarely be possible to measure the worker's productivity objectively in both tasks, so the decision will usually be made on the basis of a manager's subjective judgment. In short, because choices are subjective, costs are subjective, too.

Profit, Rents, and Entrepreneurship

Pure economic profit, as we have defined it, is the difference between what a firm receives for the products it sells and the opportunity cost of producing those products. Previously we encountered the notion of payments in excess of opportunity costs, where we called them *economic rents*. Pure economic profit, then, is a type of economic rent. Nevertheless, the two terms are not fully interchangeable.

For one thing, economic rent is a broader notion than profit. *Profit* is usually used in connection with the activities of a business firm, whereas *rents* can be said to be earned by any factor of production. Consider, for example, the income of rock stars, sports professionals, and other people with exceptional talents in a certain line of work. Their opportunity cost of pursuing their chosen line of work may be low, in the sense that their income from their most attractive alternative occupation (say, selling insurance or working as a lifeguard) may be far lower than what they actually earn. The amount by which their extraordinary income as a rock star, sports professional, or whatever exceeds their income from their best alternative occupation can properly be called economic rent, but that income would not usually be called profit.

A distinction is also sometimes made between *profit seeking* and *rent seeking*. Profit seeking is commonly associated with the activity of entrepreneurship. Entrepreneurs seek profits by finding ways to use factors of production, purchased at market prices, to create goods and services of greater value or at a lower cost compared with their competitors. Our imaginary Martins are an example of entrepreneurs seeking profits by finding a new way to satisfy customer needs. Thus, *profit seeking* means finding ways to create new value.

However, some firms seek to increase their revenues not through innovation and cost reduction but by seeking restrictions on competition. For example, the Martins might try to boost their firm's earnings by persuading Congress to ban imports of similar PDAs made in China and Korea. This is an example not of entrepreneurship but of political rent seeking.[1]

The distinction between profits earned by entrepreneurs and rents earned by rent seekers is certainly not watertight. In both cases, we are dealing with revenues that exceed opportunity costs. Data like those presented in Figure 7.1 do not tell us all we might want to know about the origin of the $20,000 of pure economic profit. Was that $20,000 earned by entrepreneurial creation of a new product superior to the products of competitors, or was it earned by rent seeking in the form of restrictions that drove the superior products of foreign competitors out of the market? The issues raised by this kind of question go beyond the cost and revenue data that we deal with in this chapter and the next one, but we will return to them in later chapters.

Fixed Costs, Variable Costs, and Sunk Costs

> In all cases, a *normal profit* will be considered a cost of doing business and be included in all cost functions.

The implicit-explicit distinction provides one way to classify costs, but it is not the only one. Another important classification of costs is based on the time horizon within which production decisions are made.

The amounts of the inputs a firm uses vary as the amounts of output change. The amount of some inputs used can be adjusted quickly, for example, the amount of electricity used can be increased just by turning on a switch. Quantities of other inputs take longer to adjust; for example, con-

FIGURE 7.1 ACCOUNTS OF FIELDCOM, INC.

Total Revenue	$600,000
Less explicit costs:	
Wages and salaries	300,000
Materials and other	100,000
Equals accounting profit	$200,000
Less implicit costs:	
Forgone salary, Andrea Martin	80,000
Forgone salary, Ralph Martin	80,000
Opportunity cost of capital	20,000
Equals pure economic profit	$ 20,000

This figure shows the implicit and explicit costs of the imaginary firm Fieldcom, Inc., owned by entrepreneurs Ralph and Andrea Martin. Total revenue minus explicit costs equals accounting profit. Subtracting implicit costs from this quantity yields pure economic profit. The opportunity cost of capital contributed by the Martins is sometimes referred to as normal profit.

Fixed inputs

Inputs that cannot be increased or decreased in a short time in order to increase or decrease output.

Fixed costs

The explicit and implicit opportunity costs associated with providing fixed inputs.

Variable inputs

Inputs that can be varied within a short time in order to increase or decrease output.

Variable costs

The explicit and implicit costs of providing variable inputs.

Short run

A time horizon within which output can be adjusted only by changing the amounts of variable inputs used while fixed inputs remain unchanged.

Long run

A time horizon that is long enough to permit changes in both fixed and variable inputs.

structing a new office building takes many months, even years. In general, inputs that take longer to adjust can be thought of as those that define the size of the firm's plant, such as the physical size of structures and the production capacity of machinery. They are known as **fixed inputs**. The cost of providing fixed inputs are called **fixed costs**.

In addition to fixed inputs, the firm uses **variable inputs** that can be adjusted quickly and easily within a plant of a given size as output changes. The costs of providing variable inputs are called **variable costs**. Raw materials energy, and hourly labor are variable inputs for most firms. However, which inputs are fixed and which are variable depends on the situation. For example, a firm that hires workers on an hourly basis may treat wages as a variable cost. Another firm that hires workers on a yearly contract, subject to a "no layoff" agreement, would treat wages as a fixed cost, at least within the time limits of the contract.

The difference between fixed and variable inputs is the basis for the distinction between two time horizons: the short run and the long run. The **short run** is a length of time in which output can be changed by changing the quantity of variable inputs used, but that is too short to permit changes in the size of a firm's plant (that is, fixed inputs). For example, an automaker can vary output from month to month by adding extra shifts of workers without installing additional equipment or building new factories. The **long run** is a length of time that is long enough to permit changes in the amounts of fixed inputs. For example, an automaker can increase capacity to meet expected growth of demand over a period of a few years by building new plants, as well as by adding extra shifts of workers within its old plants. The college's long run is the time that it may take to increase the size of campus or construct new buildings. We are in the process of building a new classroom building near the amphitheater. There is some discussion that the YMCA building may be acquired by the college. Because of the funding process and the politics involved with the county and the state, the community college's long run is much longer than, say, the building of a new McDonald's restaurant or an new Starbucks franchise.

IMPLICIT AND EXPLICIT FIXED COSTS In all cases, cost means opportunity cost and therefore includes both implicit and explicit costs. Particular attention must be paid to this fact in dealing with fixed costs.

Fixed costs are "fixed" in the sense that they do not vary with the firm's rate of output. However, they are ongoing costs that must be borne by the firm each day it continues to lease or own the facilities it needs in order to stay in business. If those ongoing costs take the form of periodic payments, they are explicit fixed costs. If they reflect the opportunity cost of ownership of facilities that have been purchased by the firm, they are implicit costs.

As an example, consider a trucking firm. One of the facilities it needs is a warehouse. The warehouse is a fixed cost that the firm incurs regardless of how much freight is hauled in a given month, but it might take either an explicit or an implicit form. The firm might, for example, lease the warehouse for an annual payment of \$12,000 in installments of \$1,000 per month. That would make the warehouse an explicit cost. But the firm might instead choose to buy the warehouse for a price of \$120,000. The \$120,000 in cash used to buy the warehouse could have been used for some other purpose—say, to buy securities yielding 10 percent interest. The income (\$12,000 a year or \$1,000 a month) that could have been earned with these funds if they had not been used to buy the warehouse is an opportunity cost of owning the warehouse—an implicit fixed cost. The cost continues as long as the firm keeps the warehouse, even if it goes a month without carrying any freight at all. But if the firm decides to quit the trucking business, it can sell the warehouse and recover the \$120,000 for use elsewhere. In that case it would cease to bear the \$1,000-a-month fixed cost of the facility.

Sunk costs

Once-and-for-all costs that, once incurred, cannot be recovered.

SUNK COSTS Fixed costs, especially implicit fixed costs, should not be confused with **sunk costs**. Sunk costs reflect once-and-for-all expenditures that, once made, cannot be recovered even if the firm leaves its line of business. For example, the trucking firm just mentioned may have paid \$1,000 to have "Taylor Trucking" painted on the wall of its warehouse. That is a sunk cost. If the firm sells the warehouse (or terminates its lease), the sign becomes worthless. There is no way to recover the \$1,000 that was paid for it, because the next owner or tenant will want a different sign.

If a firm is planning to enter a new line of business or to expand its operations, the sunk costs of doing so are an opportunity cost associated with entry into the new venture. Thus, in considering serving a new city, the trucking firm must think, "$120,000 to buy the warehouse plus $1,000 to paint the sign." But because they cannot be recovered, sunk costs, unlike fixed and variable costs, are *not* counted as part of the firm's ongoing costs of doing business. Once the commitment has been made, the sunk cost is no longer an opportunity cost to the firm because the firm has, once and for all, lost the opportunity to do anything else with the funds in question. In deciding whether to remain in business, the firm should think only, "We could get $120,000 by selling the warehouse." The $1,000 paid for the sign would not enter into the decision at all. In business, the irrelevance of sunk costs to ongoing operations is often expressed in the phrase "bygones are bygones."

The remainder of this chapter will be concerned only with firms' ongoing fixed and variable costs of doing business; sunk costs will not enter into the picture. In later chapters we will return to the subject of sunk costs when discussing the processes through which firms enter and leave particular markets.

PRODUCTION AND COSTS IN THE SHORT RUN

Now that we have pinned down the meaning of cost, our next task is to build a theory to explain how a firm's costs vary with its level of output. The cost that a firm must bear to produce a given level of output is, as we have said, one of the basic constraints that shape a firm's decisions. Our discussion of cost theory will be divided into two parts, corresponding to the time horizons that we have called the short run and the long run.

Production with One Variable Input in the Short Run

Although most firms have several inputs that can be varied even in the short run, it will simplify matters to begin with a case in which only one input—the quantity of labor employed—can be varied. Let us turn once again to Fieldcom for an example.

Total physical product

The total output of a firm, measured in physical units.

Figure 7.2 shows what happens to the daily production rate measured in physical terms, or **total physical product**, as the number of workers is varied from zero to eight. If no workers are employed, no production can take place. In this firm, one worker alone cannot produce anything either—some parts of the job require a minimum of two people working together. Two workers can get production moving, but because they use a lot of time setting up jobs and changing from one job to another, they are able to produce at a rate of only one PDA per day. When a third worker is added, some degree of specialization becomes possible, and production increases to three units per day. A fourth worker gets things moving really

FIGURE 7.2 RESPONSE OF OUTPUT TO CHANGES IN ONE VARIABLE INPUT

(a)

(1) Input (Workers per Day)	(2) Total Physical Product (Units per Day)	(3) Marginal Physical Product (Units per Worker)
0	0	
1	0	0
2	1	1
3	3	2
4	7	4
5	10	3
6	12	2
7	13	1
8	13	0

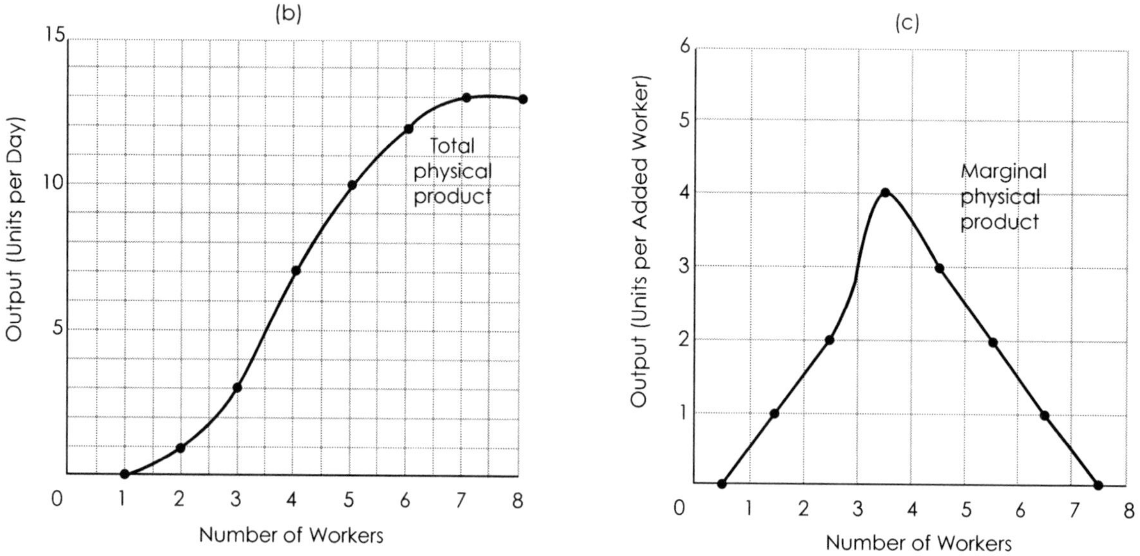

This figure shows how the output of PDAs at Fieldcom, Inc., responds to changes in one variable input—labor. All other inputs remain constant while the number of workers is varied. One worker can produce nothing, since some equipment takes a minimum of two employees to operate. Output increases—at first rapidly, then more slowly—as more workers are used. After seven workers are on the job, all equipment is in use; thus additional workers add nothing more to output. Column 3 of part (a) and the chart in part (c) show the amount of added output that results from each added worker. This is known as the ***marginal physical product*** of the variable input.

smoothly, and production rises to seven units per day. Adding workers five, six, and seven boosts the plant's output to its maximum of thirteen PDAs per day. At that point it does no good to add more workers; all the tools and equipment are in use, and the extra workers would have to stand around waiting for a turn to use them.

Of course, output could be increased by adding *other* inputs in addition to workers—more assembly tables, more testing equipment, and so on. But for the moment we are looking at the effects of increasing just one variable input, other things being equal.

Marginal physical product

The increase in output, expressed in physical units, produced by each added unit of one variable input, other things being equal.

MARGINAL PHYSICAL PRODUCT The chart in part (b) and columns 1 and 2 in part (a) of Figure 7.2 show the relationship between labor inputs and daily output. In the range of one to seven workers, output rises as labor input increases, but not at a constant rate. Column 3 of the table and the chart in part (c) of the figure show how much output changes for each successive worker. The amount by which output changes in each instance is called the **marginal physical product** of the variable input. (As elsewhere, the adjective *marginal* refers to the effect of a small change in a quantity—here, the quantity of a variable input.) Adding one full-time worker at a time, as in the table, gives the progression of marginal physical products shown in part (c).

THE LAW OF DIMINISHING RETURNS The example just given shows a pattern that economists consider typical for the marginal product of a single variable input such as labor. At first, as workers are added, marginal product increases. Increasing marginal product reflects the advantages of cooperation: the superiority of team production and the benefits of specialization by comparative advantage. After a point, however, as more workers are added, marginal product stops rising and begins to fall. In the case of a single variable input, the principal reason for the eventual decline in marginal physical product is the overcrowding of complementary fixed inputs—in our example, such things as work space, tools, and testing equipment.

Part (c) of Figure 7.2 shows the relationship of marginal physical product to the number of workers in the form of a graph called the *marginal physical product curve*. The part of the curve with a negative slope illustrates a principle known as the **law of diminishing returns**. According to this principle, as the amount of one variable input is increased while the amounts of all other inputs remain fixed, a point will be reached beyond which the marginal physical product of the input will decrease.

Law of diminishing returns

The principle that as one variable input is increased while all others remain fixed, a point will be reached beyond which the marginal physical product of the variable input will begin to decrease.

The law of diminishing returns applies to all production processes and to all variable inputs. The example just given is drawn from manufacturing, but the law could be demonstrated just as well with an example from, say, farming, with fertilizer as the variable input: As more fertilizer is added to a field, output increases, but beyond some point the gain in output brought about by an additional ton of fertilizer tapers off. (In fact, too much fertilizer could poison the plants, in which case marginal physical product would become negative.) Oil refineries, power plants, barber shops, government bureaus—indeed, *any* production process—could be used to illustrate the law of diminishing returns. There can be no exceptions.

If you are in an evening class, you experience diminishing returns at about 8:00 PM. As each minute of instruction passes, you retain or remember less and less of the information presented. Maybe by 9:00 PM your memory starts to forget the information from 6:45 and thus, you're now in the negative zone. This may also happen to the day students, but this may start at the Thanksgiving holiday in the Fall term, or after Spring break for the Spring students.

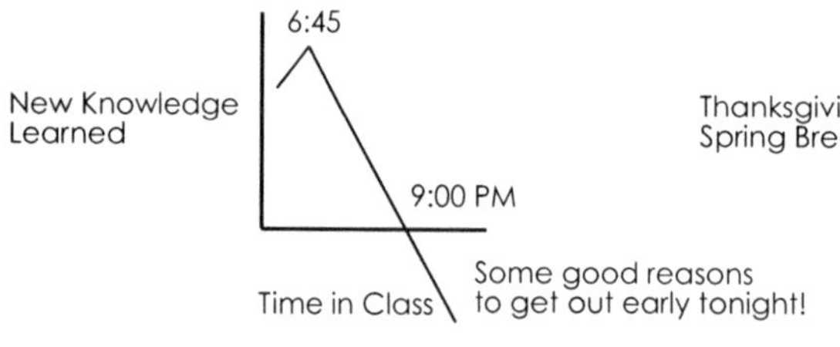

From Marginal Physical Product to Marginal Costs

The relationship between inputs and output in terms of physical units is an important constraint on a firm's profit-maximizing activities. However, most business decisions are not made in terms of physical units but in terms of money. Our next step, then, is to restate the constraint implied by the marginal physical product curve in money terms, that is, to ask how much each added unit of output *costs*.

Marginal cost

The increase in cost required to raise the output of some good or service by one unit.

The change in cost associated with a one-unit change in output is called **marginal cost**. To make the conversion from marginal physical product to marginal cost, we proceed as follows, again using Fieldcom as an example.

The first step is to rearrange the data given in Figure 7.2 in terms of input per unit of output. This is done in Figure 7.3. The table in part (a) of the figure reverses the order of the first two columns. Also, the charts in parts (b) and (c) are flipped so that units of output, rather than units of labor input occupy the horizontal axis.

The next step is to convert physical units of input into costs stated in dollars. To do so, we need to know the cost per unit of input. To keep things simple, this example assumes that the variable input, labor, carries an explicit price of $100 per day. Multiplying the labor inputs in column 2 of the figure by the $100-per-day wage yields total labor costs, which are shown in column 3. Those data are used to plot a total labor cost curve in part (b) of the figure. Taking the rearrangement of the axes and the change in units into account, that curve can be recognized as the mirror image of the total physical product curve shown in Figure 7.2.

Finally, column 4 of the table in Figure 7.3 is filled in to show marginal cost, that is, the change in cost, stated in dollars per unit change in output. Increasing output from zero to one requires adding two workers, so the added cost per unit in that range is $200; increasing output by two more units (from one to three) requires one more worker at $100 per day, so the cost per added unit of output in that range is $50; and so on. The marginal cost curve shown in part (c) of the figure is plotted from columns 1 and 4 of the table. As in the case of marginal product, the effect of adding one full-time worker at a time becomes a smooth curve if smaller increments are considered. Again considering the change in units and rearrangement of the axes, part (c) of Fig-

FIGURE 7.3 COST AND OUTPUT WITH ONE VARIABLE INPUT

(a)

(1) Output (Units per Day)	(2) Labor Input	(3) Total Labor Cost (Dollars per Day)	(4) Marginal Cost (Dollars per Unit)
0	0	0	
1	2	200	200
3	3	300	50
7	4	400	25
10	5	500	33
12	6	600	50
13	7	700	100

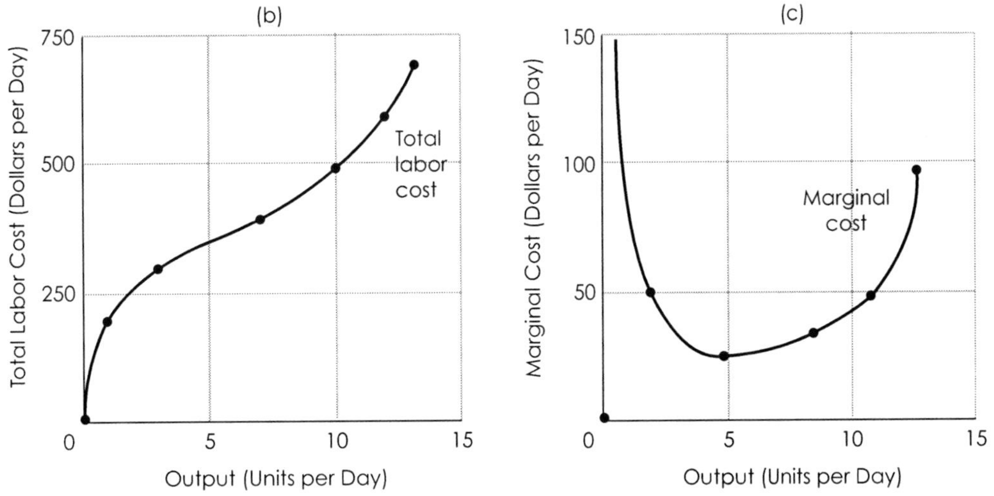

This figure shows how the cost of production at Fieldcom, Inc., changes as output varies. The table and graphs are based on the data used in Figure 7.2, but here they are recast to stress cost assuming a daily wage of $100 per worker. Column 3 of the table and the chart in part (b) show total labor cost for various output levels. Column 4 of the table and the chart in part (c) show marginal cost—the amount by which cost increases per added unit of output. For example, increasing the number of workers from three to four raises output by four units, from three to seven PDAs per day. Over this range, then, the cost of each added PDA is one-quarter of a day's wage, or $25.

ure 7.3 is the approximate mirror image of the marginal physical product curve shown in part (c) of Figure 7.2.

More Than One Variable Input

The Fieldcom example assumes that only one input is varied. In practice, short-run increases or decreases in Fieldcom's output would require changes in many—though not all—of its inputs. For example, if the firm wanted to raise its output, in addition to hiring more workers it might burn more fuel to keep the shop heated longer each day and double the rate at which it orders parts.

The appendix to this chapter outlines a way of analyzing changes in two or more variable inputs. Without going into detail, it can be stated that as long as at least some inputs remain fixed, the law of diminishing returns continues to apply. Also, a region of increasing marginal physical product will probably exist at low levels of output. When such a relationship between variable inputs and physical product is combined with a constant price for each input, the result is a total cost curve with a reverse-S shape and a U-shaped marginal cost curve, as in the case of a single variable input.

A Set of Short-Run Cost Curves

Variable cost and marginal cost curves with the shapes just described are shown in Figure 7.4. The figure gives the full set of curves in both graphical and tabular form and also contains some often-used formulas and abbreviations that pertain to cost curves.

Total variable cost is shown graphically in part (a) of Figure 7.4 and numerically in column 2 of part (c). The total variable costs in this example are analogous to the costs shown in the preceding example, except that these allow for more than one variable input. In addition to variable costs, *total fixed costs* (office staff, testing equipment, rent, and so on), which are assumed to be $2,000 per day, are shown in column 3 of part (c). Adding columns 2 and 3 gives short-run *total cost* (variable plus fixed costs), which is shown in column 4. The total fixed cost and total cost curves are plotted together with the total variable cost curve in part (a). Because by definition total fixed cost does not vary as output changes, the total fixed cost curve is a horizontal line $2,000 above the horizontal axis. Total fixed cost is the amount by which total cost exceeds total variable cost, so the total cost curve parallels the total variable cost curve at a higher level. The vertical distance between the total cost and total variable cost curves equals total fixed cost.

The next column in part (c) of Figure 7.4 is marginal cost. Marginal cost data appear on lines between the total cost entries in order to stress that marginal cost shows how total cost changes as the level of output varies. The marginal cost curve is plotted in part (b) of the figure.

All of the cost concepts shown in total terms in part (a) of the figure can also be expressed on a per-unit basis. This is done in the last three columns in the table and the chart in part (b) of Figure 7.4. *Average variable cost* equals total variable cost divided by quantity of output; *average fixed cost* equals total fixed cost divided by output; and *average total cost* equals total cost divided by output. The three average cost curves are drawn together with the marginal cost curve in part (b) of the figure.

Some Geometric Relationships

Parts (a) and (b) of Figure 7.4 demonstrate some important geometric relationships among the cost curves. First, compare the marginal cost curve with the total variable

FIGURE 7.4 A SET OF SHORT-RUN COST CURVES

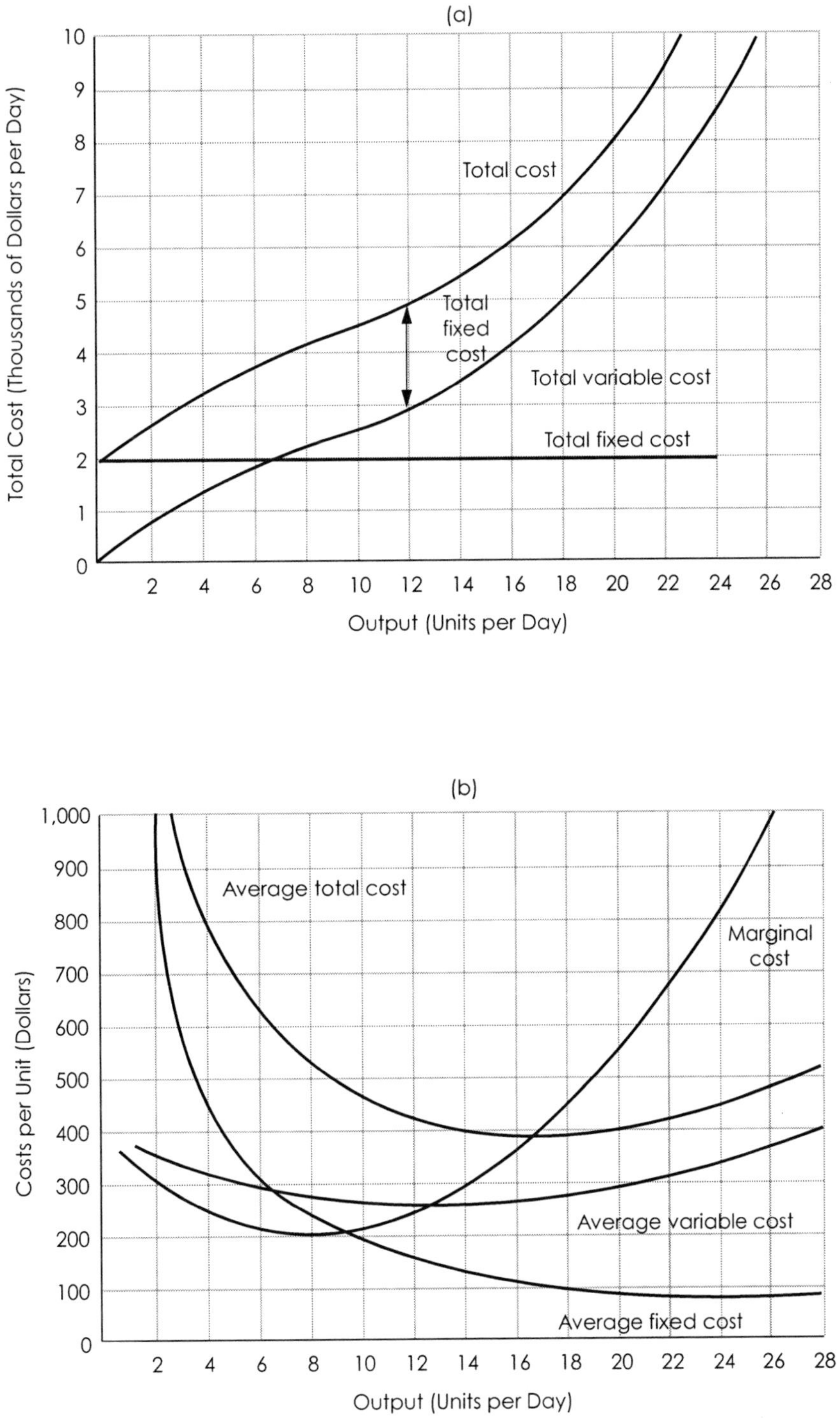

(continues)

FIGURE 7.4 A SET OF SHORT-RUN COST CURVES, CONTINUED

(c)

Quantity of Output (Units per Day) (1)	Total Variable Cost (Dollars per Day) (2)	Total Fixed Cost (Dollars per Day) (3)	Total Cost (Dollars per Day) (4)	Marginal Cost (Dollars per Unit) (5)	Average Variable Cost (Dollars per Unit) (6)	Average Fixed Cost (Dollars per Unit) (7)	Average Total Cost (Dollars per Unit) (8)
0	$ 0	$2,000	$ 2,000		—	—	—
1	380	2,000	2,380	$380	$380	$2,000	$2,380
2	720	2,000	2,720	340	360	1,000	1,360
3	1,025	2,000	3,025	305	342	667	1,009
4	1,300	2,000	3,300	275	325	500	825
5	1,550	2,000	3,550	250	310	400	710
6	1,780	2,000	3,780	230	296	333	629
7	1,995	2,000	3,995	215	285	286	571
8	2,200	2,000	4,200	205	275	250	525
9	2,400	2,000	4,400	200	266	222	488
10	2,605	2,000	4,605	205	260	200	460
11	2,820	2,000	4,820	215	256	181	437
12	3,050	2,000	5,050	230	254	169	421
13	3,300	2,000	5,300	250	254	154	408
14	3,575	2,000	5,575	275	255	143	398
15	3,880	2,000	5,880	305	259	133	392
16	4,220	2,000	6,220	340	264	125	389
17	4,600	2,000	6,600	380	271	118	389
18	5,025	2,000	7,025	425	279	111	390
19	5,500	2,000	7,500	475	289	105	394
20	6,030	2,000	8,030	530	302	100	402
21	6,620	2,000	8,620	590	315	95	410
22	7,275	2,000	9,275	655	331	91	422
23	8,000	2,000	10,000	725	348	87	435
24	8,800	2,000	10,800	800	367	83	450

(d)

Common abbreviations

Q	Quantity of output
TC	Total cost
TFC	Total fixed cost
TVC	Total variable cost
MC	Marginal cost
AVC	Average variable cost
AFC	Average fixed cost
ATC	Average total cost

Useful formulas:

$$TC = TFC + TVC$$

$$MC = \frac{\text{Change in TC}}{\text{Change in Q}} = \frac{\text{Change in TVC}}{\text{Change in Q}}$$

$$AVC = \frac{TVC}{Q}$$

$$AFC = \frac{TFC}{Q}$$

$$ATC = \frac{TC}{Q}$$

A whole set of short-run cost curves can be derived from data on fixed and variable costs, as this figure shows. The data are presented in the form of a table and a pair of graphs. The figure also lists a number of useful abbreviations and formulas.

cost curve. The bottom of the U-shaped marginal cost curve lies at exactly the level of output at which the slope of the reverse-S-shaped total variable cost curve stops flattening out and starts getting steeper. (In the language of geometry, this is the *inflection point* of the total variable cost curve.) This relationship holds because the slope of the total variable cost curve shows the rate at which total variable cost changes as output changes, and that is the definition of marginal cost. In graphical terms, then, the *height* of the marginal cost curve always equals the *slope* of the total variable cost curve.

A second feature of the cost curves in Figure 7.4 also deserves comment. The marginal cost curve intersects both the average variable cost and the average total cost curves at their lowest points. This is not a coincidence; it is a result of a relationship that can be called the **marginal-average rule**, which can be explained as follows: Beginning at any given point, ask what the cost of making one more unit of output will be. The answer is given by marginal cost. Then ask whether that cost is more or less than the average cost of all units produced up to that point. If the added cost of the next unit made is less than the average cost of all the previous units, making that unit will have the effect of pulling down the average. If the next unit costs more, making that unit will pull the average up. It follows that whenever marginal cost is below average variable cost, the average variable cost curve must be falling (negatively sloped), and whenever marginal cost is above average variable cost, the average variable cost curve must be rising (positively sloped). This, in turn, implies that the marginal cost curve cuts the average variable cost curve at its lowest point. The same is true of the relationship between marginal cost and average total cost.

Marginal-average rule

The rule that marginal cost must equal average cost when average cost is at its minimum.

The marginal-average rule is not unique to economics; it can be seen in many everyday situations. Consider, for example, the effect of your grade in this course on your grade point average. You could call this grade your "marginal grade," because it represents the grade points earned by taking one more course. If your grade in this course (that is, your marginal grade) is higher than your average grade in other courses, the effect of taking this course will be to pull up your average. Your grade point average thus must be rising if your marginal grade exceeds your average grade. If you do worse than average in this course, your grade point average will fall. When your marginal grade falls short of your average grade, your grade point average must be falling. This relationship is the same as the one between marginal cost and aver-age cost. If the cost of making one more unit is less than the average cost of making previous units, the average will be pulled down; if it is more, the average will be pulled up.

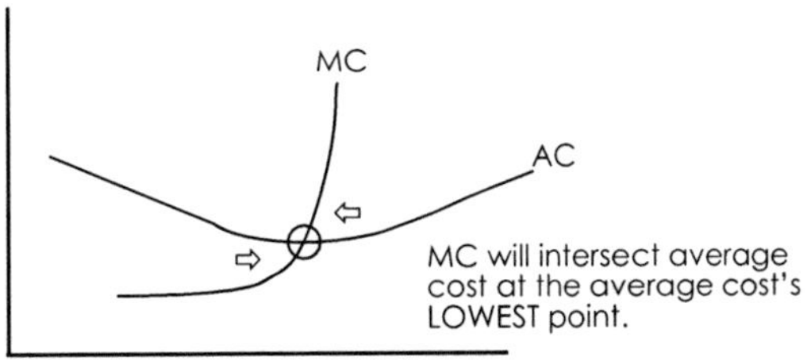
MC
AC
MC will intersect average cost at the average cost's LOWEST point.

Some people find it easier to remember the relationships among the various cost concepts if they are presented as formulas. If you are one of those people, you may find the formulas in part (d) of Figure 7.4 useful. The figure also presents some common abbreviations. They are not used in this text, but you may want to use them in your note taking, and your instructor will probably use them on the blackboard.

LONG-RUN COSTS AND ECONOMIES OF SCALE

In the first part of the chapter, we pointed out that different kinds of costs are relevant to different kinds of decisions. The costs that we call variable are relevant to decisions regarding short-run changes in output using a given quantity of fixed inputs. For example, how much corn should a farmer grow, given a certain available acreage and stock of farm equipment? Any change in prices or quantities supplied that does not involve a change in the quantity of fixed inputs used will be made with reference to the position of the firm's short-run cost curves.

In other cases, however, attention centers on plans for lasting expansion or contraction of the firm's stock of fixed inputs. For example, dairy farmers might adjust to a permanent elimination of milk price supports by selling some of their land or farm equipment. Such questions must be answered with reference to long-run costs, to which we turn in this section. For the time being, we consider only fixed costs that are recoverable in the event that the firm leaves its line of business or permanently scales back its operations. Sunk costs are assumed to be zero.

Planning for Expansion

Put yourself in the position of an entrepreneur about to set up a small firm. You think it would be wise to start with a small plant, but you want to do some long-range planning, too. In consultation with specialists, you put together information on plants of five possible sizes, each of which could represent a stage in the future growth of your firm. Short-run average total cost curves for each of the plants are drawn in Figure 7.5. The first one shows short-run average total costs for the range of output that is possible given the firm's first small plant, the one in the converted gas station; the second curve corresponds to a slightly larger plant; and so on.

The size of plant you actually choose will depend on the level of output you plan to produce over a time horizon long enough to change from one size of plant to the next. Choosing a plant of a certain size does not commit a firm forever, but the choice is not a trivial one. As *Applying Economic Ideas 7.1* shows, a small firm cannot afford to take on the costs of a permanently larger plant just to fill a single order. It may not make sense to expand the size of your plant unless these fixed costs can be spread out over a long enough period at the output level for which a plant is designed. Only

FIGURE 7.5 SHORT- AND LONG-RUN AVERAGE COST CURVES

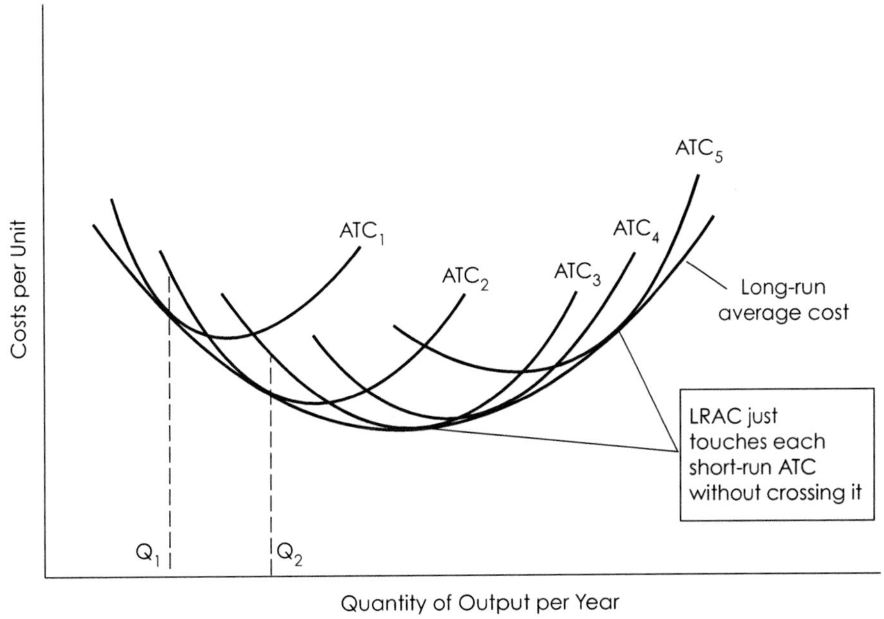

The position of the short-run average total cost curve for a firm depends on the size of the plant. In the long run, the firm has a choice of operating with any size of plant it chooses. Each plant size can be represented by a U-shaped short-run average total cost curve. Five such curves are shown in this graph. A new firm might begin with a plant that can be represented by a short-run average total cost curve such as ATC$_1$. Then, as demand for its product expands, it might move to one of those farther to the right. The firm's long-run average cost curve is the "envelope" of these and other possible short-run average total cost curves; that is, it is a smooth curve drawn so that it just touches the short-run curves without intersecting any of them.

when the firm expects a long-term increase in its output should it move from one of the short-run curves shown in Figure 7.5 to the next.

The five short-run cost curves in the figure represent only a sampling of possible plant sizes. Taking into account the short-run curves that correspond to intermediate-sized plants as well as those shown, we can draw a *long-run average cost curve* such as the one in the figure. Such a curve is the "envelope" of all the possible short-run average cost curves, meaning that it just touches each of the possible short-run curves without crossing them. The size of plant chosen for each output in the long run will be the one that corresponds to a short-run average total cost curve that is just tangent to the long-run average total cost curve at that point.

Figure 7.5 shows that there is one best plant size for any given level of output that the firm plans to produce in the long run. It may be physically possible to produce a given level of output in a larger or smaller plant, but that would involve a penalty in terms of cost per unit. For example, in Figure 7.5 the output level Q_1 is produced at

APPLYING ECONOMIC IDEAS 7.1

SONY CORPORATION FACES COSTS AND OPPORTUNITIES

Several years ago Akio Morita, chairman of the Japanese electronics giant, Sony Corporation, was asked to talk about the early days of his firm. Here he describes what it was like to be just a small company.

Our first transistor radio of 1955 was small and practical—not as small as some of our later efforts, but we were very proud of it. I saw the United States as a natural market. I took my little $29.95 radio to New York and made the rounds of possible retailers.

While making the rounds, I came across an American buyer who looked at the radio and said he liked it very much. He said his chain, which had about 150 stores, would need large quantities. He asked me to give him a price quotation only on quantities of 5,000, 10,000; 30,000, 50,000 and 100,000 radios. What an invitation!

But back in my hotel room, I began pondering the possible impact of such grand orders on our small facilities in Tokyo. We had expanded our plant a lot since we outgrew the unpainted, leaky shack on Gotenyama [a hill on the southern edge of Tokyo]. We had moved into bigger, sturdier buildings adjacent to the original site and had our eye on some more property, but we did not have the capacity to produce 100,000 transistor radios a year and also make the other things in our small product line. Our capacity was less than 10,000 radios a month. If we got an order for 100,000, we would have to hire and train new employees and expand our facilities even more. This would mean a major investment, a major expansion and a gamble.

I was inexperienced and still a little naive, but I had my wits about me. I considered all the consequences I could think of, and then I sat down and drew a curve that looked something like a lopsided letter U. The price for 5,000 would be our regular price. That would be the beginning of the curve. For 10,000 there would be a discount, and that was at the bottom of the curve. For 30,000 the price would begin to climb. For 50,000 the price per unit would be higher than for 5,000, and for l00,000 units the price would have to be much more per unit than for the first 5,000.

My reasoning was this: If we had to double our production capacity to complete an order for 100,000 and if we could not get a repeat order the following year we would be in big trouble, perhaps bankrupt, because how in that case could we employ all the added staff and pay for the new and unused facilities?... In Japan, we cannot just hire people and fire them whenever our orders go up or down. We have a long-term commitment to our employees and they have a commitment to us.

I returned the next day with my quotation. The buyer looked at it and blinked as though he couldn't believe his eyes. He put down the paper and said, patiently, "Mr. Morita, I have been working as a purchasing agent for nearly thirty years and you are the first person who has ever come in here and told me that the more I buy the higher the unit price will be. It's illogical!" I explained my reasoning to him and he listened carefully to what I had to say. When he got over his shock, he paused for a moment, smiled, and then placed an order for 10,000 radios—at the 10,000 unit price—which was just right for him and for us.

Source: Akio Morita, "When Sony Was an Up and Comer," **Forbes,** October 6, 1986, 98–102. Adapted from ***Made in Japan: Akio Morita and Sony*** by Akio Morita with Edwin M. Reingold and Mitsuko Shimomura. Copyright 1986 by E. P. Dutton, a division of NAL Penguin, Inc. Reprinted by permission of the publisher, E. P. Dutton.

least cost in a plant of the size corresponding to the short-run curve ATC_1. The same level of output could also be produced in the larger plant corresponding to ATC_2, but only at a higher cost per unit, because the larger plant would not be used to its designed capacity. On the other hand, the larger plant represented by ATC_2 is the best plant size for output Q_2. That larger output could be produced in the smaller plant, but only by running it at a rate higher than the one for which it is designed. The penalty, in terms of unit cost, is shown by the fact that ATC_1 lies above ATC_2 at the output level Q_2.

If a firm wants to produce at an unusually high or low rate for a short time, it may make sense to do so by moving along the short-run average total cost curve corresponding to its present plant size. An example would be a firm that decides to run overtime to fill an exceptionally large order, or one that cuts back to half-shifts to weather a temporary business downturn. But when sustained increases in output level are under consideration, costs are minimized by building a larger plant, as a young firm such as Sony will do when it has enough confidence in long-term demand for its product to expand. Likewise, a firm that is planning to reduce its output permanently will eliminate some plant rather than keep production facilities operating at lower levels of output than those for which they were designed. Decisions of that kind represent movements out or back along the firm's long-run average cost curve.

Economies of Scale

Movements along a firm's long-run average cost curve, during which the firm is free to adjust quantities of all the inputs it uses, are referred to as changes in the *scale* of production. Some special terminology is used to describe the way long-run average cost changes as the scale of production changes. In any output range in which long-run average cost *decreases* as output increases, the firm is said to experience **economies of scale**. In any output range in which long-run average cost *increases*, the firm is said to experience **diseconomies of scale**. Finally, if there is any range of output for which long-run average cost does not change as output varies, the firm is said to experience **constant returns to scale** in that range.

Economies of scale
A situation in which long-run average cost decreases as output increases.

Diseconomies of scale
A situation in which long-run average cost increases as output increases.

Constant returns to scale
A situation in which there are neither economies nor diseconomies of scale.

Minimum efficient scale
The output level at which economies of scale cease.

The long-run average cost curve in Figure 7.5 is smoothly U-shaped, so there is no range of constant returns to scale. However, empirical studies suggest that the long-run cost curves of actual firms may have long flat sections in the middle over which average cost changes relatively little as output changes. Economies of scale for such a firm appear only over a range of rather low output levels, and diseconomies appear only over a range of very high output levels. For a firm with such a long-run average cost curve, the level of output at which economies of scale end and constant returns to scale begin can be called the firm's **minimum efficient scale**.

SOURCES OF ECONOMIES OF SCALE Where do economies of scale come from? If firms grew simply by increasing fixed and variable inputs in exact proportion, so that a large plant amounted to nothing more than a lot of small plants built side by side, one might expect changes in scale to have no effect at all on average cost. But that is not the way firms expand. As they grow, they tend to change the technologies they use and their methods of internal organization to take advantage of new opportunities offered by the higher output level. Those changes give rise to economies of scale.

In part, economies of scale stem from the human factors mentioned before—the advantages of team production and specialization according to comparative advantage. A firm can get very large before it completely exhausts the possibilities for cooperation and specialization. In a small firm, for example, the marketing function may be something the owner does from 3:00 P.M. to 4:00 P.M. after touring the plant floor and perhaps taking a turn running a machine. A somewhat larger firm can afford to hire a marketing manager who devotes full time to the job. In a still larger firm, subspecialties develop—a sales manager, a director of product development, an advertising specialist, all under the direction of the marketing manager.

Other economies of scale have origins in technology. In many lines of production, for example, a machine that is capable of doing twice the work of a smaller one costs less than twice as much to build and operate. A pizza oven that is big enough to bake 60 pizzas an hour costs less than twice as much as a 30-pizza-per-hour model. A tractor that can plow 50 acres a day costs less than twice as much as one that can plow only 25 acres, and the large model still requires only one driver. For a firm that is too small to utilize a large piece of equipment fully, the smaller model can still be the appropriate choice. But as the firm grows, technological economies lower its average costs.

What is more, growth of a firm does not just mean constant expansion of a single plant. Operation of multiple plants can yield further economies of scale even after each plant reaches the minimum efficient scale at which technical economies are exhausted. The McDonald's hamburger chain provides a good example. The minimum efficient scale for a single plant (restaurant) is very small in the fast-food industry. Yet McDonald's gains some important economies by running a large number of restaurants as a system. Some of these are production economies: Individual food items and ingredients can be made in central kitchens; managers can be trained at "Hamburger University"; and so on. A multiplant firm such as McDonald's also realizes economies of scale in such areas as finance and marketing.

Economies of Scale

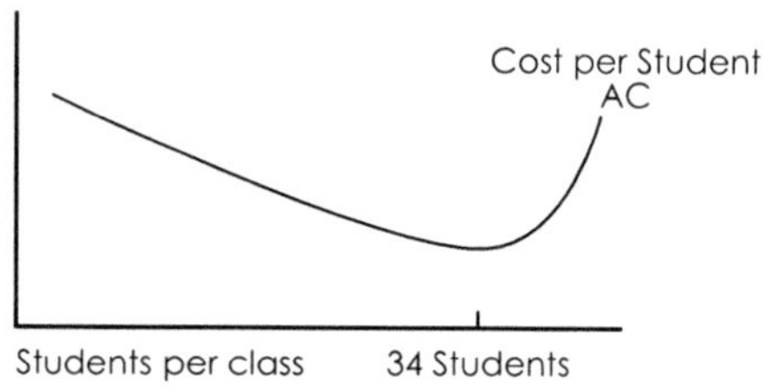

As the number of students enrolled in this Econ class increases, the cost per student declines—until the 35th student registers. At this point, the college must open a new section of the course, which means a new teacher must be hired and paid. The increased salary expenses makes the total costs increase dramatically. For this reason, the school may not welcome the 35th student!

SOURCES OF DISECONOMIES OF SCALE Although there are many sources of economies of scale, they are not limitless. As a firm expands, it encounters diseconomies of scale as well as economies. Technological sources of diseconomies can often be avoided. For example, as an airline grows, at first it may buy larger and larger planes, but rather than keep this up until its planes get so big that they cannot fly, it starts buying more and more planes of optimal size. In other lines of business, firms can avoid potential technical diseconomies by building multiple plants of optimal size.

The most important diseconomies are organizational. As a firm grows, it finds itself depending more and more on hierarchical means of coordinating its employees' activities. As a hierarchy grows, the cost of channeling information to key decision makers tends to rise. Moreover, individual incentives tend to get diluted in a large hierarchical organization. More and more managerial skill has to be devoted to maintaining employee loyalty and motivation. There is an increasing risk that departments and divisions will pursue parochial interests that diverge from those of the firm as a whole.

In some lines of business, firms can grow to a very large size before the diseconomies start to outweigh the economies. Huge firms, such as General Motors, AT&T, and IBM, successfully manage hierarchies that are bigger than the governments of all but a handful of countries. But the very mention of such corporate giants calls to mind their vulnerability to smaller, more aggressive rivals. All three of the companies just listed have lost sales in recent years to smaller competitors in important product lines.

In other lines of business, comparatively small firms seem to have the edge. In farming, services, and retail trade, small units predominate. In still other industries, franchising is used to combine economies of scale in a few functions such as marketing and product development with the production advantages of small-unit operation.

Much more could be written about costs and production functions, but we have now covered the most important points. Coming chapters will repeatedly make use of the concepts of marginal and average costs, economies of scale, and profit maximization to show how firms make decisions in a variety of market contexts.

SUMMARY

1. **How do economists view the concepts of cost and profit?** *Explicit costs* are opportunity costs that take the form of explicit payments to suppliers of factors of production and intermediate goods. *Implicit costs* are the opportunity costs associated with using resources contributed by the firm's owners (or owned by the firm itself as a legal entity) that are not obtained under contracts calling for explicit payments. Implicit costs include the opportunity cost of capital needed to attract owners' capital to the firm. If only explicit costs are subtracted from revenue, the result is *accounting profit*. Revenue minus all costs, both implicit and explicit, is *pure economic profit*.

2. **What is the distinction between short-run and long-run time horizons?** *Fixed inputs* cannot be increased or decreased in a short time; they are linked with the size of the firm's pl
of such inputs are term
inputs can be varied quick
or decrease output; they

energy, and raw materials. The costs of those inputs are termed *variable costs*. *Sunk costs* are once-and-for-all expenditures that cannot be recovered once they have been made. The *short run* is a period within which only variable inputs can be adjusted. In the *long run* changes can be made in fixed inputs, including plant size.

3. **How do costs vary in response to changes in the quantity of a variable input?** As the amount of one input to a production process increases while the amounts of all other inputs remain fixed, output will increase, at least over some range. The amount of output added by each one-unit increase in the variable input is known as the *marginal physical product* of that input. According to the *law of diminishing returns,* as the amount of one variable input used in a production process increases (with the amounts of all other inputs remaining fixed), a point will be reached beyond which the amount of output added per unit of added variable input (that is, the marginal physical product of the variable input) will begin to decrease. The principle applies to all production processes.

4. **How can a firm's cost structure be represented in geometric terms?** A whole set of cost curves can be constructed for a firm, given data on its fixed and variable costs. The most commonly used cost curves are total cost, total fixed cost, total variable cost, average fixed cost, average variable cost, average total cost, and marginal cost. According to the *marginal-average rule,* the marginal cost curve intersects the average variable cost and average total cost curves at their lowest points.

5. **What choices does a firm face in the course of long-run expansion?** In the long run a firm can adjust the amounts of fixed inputs that it uses by expanding or reducing its plant. Each possible plant size has a U-shaped short-run average total cost curve. The firm's long-run average cost curve is a shallower U-shaped curve based on a set of short-run curves. When long-run average cost decreases as output increases, the firm is said to experience *economies of scale.* When long-run average cost increases as output increases, the firm is said to experience *diseconomies of scale.* If there are neither economies nor diseconomies of scale, the firm is said to experience *constant returns to scale.*

KEY TERMS

Explicit costs
Implicit costs
Pure economic profit
Accounting profit
Normal profit (normal return on capital)
Fixed inputs
Fixed costs
Variable inputs
Variable costs
Short run
Long run
Sunk costs
Total physical product
Marginal physical product
Law of diminishing returns
Marginal cost
Marginal-average rule
Economies of scale
Diseconomies of scale
Constant returns to scale
Minimum efficient scale

PROBLEMS AND TOPICS FOR DISCUSSION

1. **Entrepreneurship and risk.** One of the opportunity costs borne by anyone who starts a new business, whether it is Akio Morita of Sony or our imaginary Ralph and Andrea Martin, is that of exchanging the secure life of employees of large firms for the risky life of entrepreneurs. Do you think they would be willing to do this if they expected to earn no more than their previous salaries plus a "normal profit" on the capital they invested in the firm? Do you think that pure eco-

nomic profit can be viewed as compensation to entrepreneurs for the risk they bear? Discuss.

2. **Implicit and explicit costs.** List the basic costs of owning and operating an automobile. Which are explicit costs? Which are implicit costs? Does driving an automobile impose any external opportunity costs on the economy as a whole that do not show up on your list as either implicit or explicit costs? If so, what are they?

3. **Fixed and variable costs.** Divide the costs of owning and operating an automobile into fixed and variable costs. Suppose that you were deciding whether to drive to a football game at a nearby college or to take the bus instead. Would you take both fixed and variable costs into account? Suppose that you were deciding whether to buy a house in a neighborhood where you could walk to work or a house in a neighborhood where you would have to buy a second car to drive to work every day. Would you take both fixed and variable costs into account? Explain the difference between the two situations.

4. **Economies and diseconomies of scale.** Do you think the business of running a college is subject to economies or diseconomies of scale? Which parts of the college's operation (such as library, dormitories, faculty salaries, moving students between classes, and so on) are subject to economies of scale, diseconomies of scale, or constant returns to scale?

5. **Total cost curves.** Draw a set of coordinate axes on a piece of graph paper. Label the *x* axis "Output" (0 to 20 units) and the *y* axis "Cost" (0 to 20 units). Plot the following (x, y) points on your graph: (0, 4); (2, 6); (4, 7); (7, 8); (9, 9); (11, 11); (13, 14). Connect these points with a smooth curve and label it "total cost." Working from this curve, construct a total fixed cost curve and a total variable cost curve for the same firm.

6. **Marginal and average cost curves.** Draw a second set of coordinate axes on another piece of graph paper. Label the horizontal axis "Output" (0 to 20 units) and the vertical axis "Cost per Unit" (0 to 2 units, in tenths of a unit). Using as a basis the total cost, total variable cost, and total fixed cost curves you drew for problem 5, construct the following curves on your new graph: marginal cost, average total cost, average variable cost, and average fixed cost.

7. **Relating the long- and short-run cost curves.** Turn to Figure 7.5 and copy the diagram onto a sheet of graph paper, drawing the long-run average total cost curve and one of the short-run average total cost curves. Use these curves to construct the corresponding long- and short-run total cost curves. Both total cost curves should be reverse-S shaped and tangent to each other at the same output level for which the average total cost curves are tangent.

8. **Diminishing returns.** Suppose that you examine the relationship between the amount of coal burned per week in a certain power plant and the amount of electricity generated per week. You find that for small amounts of coal—too small even to bring the boiler up to the temperature needed to make steam—no electricity can be produced. After a certain minimum amount of coal is burned, the plant begins to operate. From that point on, the added amount of electricity generated per added ton of coal burned is constant over a wide range. Then a point is reached beyond which burning more coal produces no more electricity. Sketch the total physical product curve for this plant, and draw a graph showing how marginal physical product varies as output changes. Does this production process obey the law of diminishing returns?

9. **More on diminishing returns.** It has been said that were it not for the law of diminishing returns,

all the food that the world needs could be grown in a flowerpot. Discuss this statement. (Suggestion: Think of land as the only fixed factor and fertilizer as the only variable factor. How much food could be grown in the flowerpot if the marginal physical product of fertilizer were constant regardless of the amount used per unit of land?)

CASE FOR DISCUSSION

Tennis at the Grand Slam

The Grand Slam Sport and Health Club is a large, modern facility in the suburbs of a medium-sized American city. The club offers many activities, including swimming, weight training, and aerobics, but its leading attraction is excellent indoor tennis courts. Members may play on clay or two types of hard-surface courts. To add to members' enjoyment of the sport, the club offers private and group lessons; tournament, ladder, and team competitions; and numerous social events.

To join the club, a single individual pays a $1,000 nonrefundable initiation fee. In addition, there is an $88 monthly membership charge, which must be paid whether or not the member uses the facilities. Those two fees cover most of the club's costs, so it is able to keep the charge for actual playing time quite low. The fee for an hour's use of a court is only $2.

At first the low hourly court fee created a problem for the club. The fee was so low that members would not bother to call to cancel a court reservation if they changed their minds about playing. Other members would then be told that no reservations were available, when in fact the courts stood empty.

To overcome this problem, the club introduced a new rule: Members who make reservations and use the court pay the usual $2 per hour. But a member who makes a reservation and does *not* show up pays a penalty rate of $10 per hour for the unused time. A reservation can be canceled nine hours or more in advance with no charge at all. This rule has proved successful in reducing abuses of the reservation system and making court time more readily available to all members.

QUESTIONS

1. Classify the costs of membership in the Grand Slam as fixed, variable, and sunk.
2. Suppose that you are thinking about joining the Grand Slam to play indoor tennis. Which of the costs of membership are opportunity costs that would be relevant to your decision?
3. Suppose you are a member of the Grand Slam but are considering dropping your membership so that you can afford to do other things, such as traveling. Which of the costs of membership in the club are opportunity costs that would be relevant to your decision?
4. Suppose that you are a member of the club and are deciding whether to spend next Saturday afternoon playing tennis there. Which of the costs of membership are opportunity costs that would be relevant to your decision?
5. Suppose that it is noon on Saturday. You have made a reservation for an hour of court time at 5:00 P.M. A friend asks you to join a pickup basketball game at that time instead. What is the opportunity cost associated with abandoning the tennis reservation to join the basketball game?

END NOTES

1. See James M. Buchanan, "Rent Seeking and Profit Seeking," in *Toward a Theory of the Rent-Seeking Society*, eds. James M. Buchanan, Robert D. Tollison, and Gordon Tullock (College Station: Texas A&M University Press, 1980), 3–15.

Appendix to Chapter 7: COST AND OUTPUT WITH TWO VARIABLE INPUTS

In this chapter we looked at the relationship between cost and output when just one input is varied and all other inputs are kept constant. In this appendix, we extend the theory of cost to the case in which more than one input is varied.

Substitution of Inputs

The main new feature of situations in which more than one input is varied is the possibility of substituting one input for another. Consider the case of Henry Hathaway, a farmer who grows corn. Hathaway spends all his time working on his farm and does not hire anyone to help him. For him, the amount of labor used in growing corn is a fixed input. In addition to fixed amounts of labor and machinery, he uses two variable inputs: land and fertilizer.

Hathaway can grow a given quantity of corn—say, 200 bushels—in many different ways. Some of the possibilities are shown in Figure 7A.1. One way to grow 200 bushels of corn is to use 2.5 tons of fertilizer and 10 acres of land. This is represented by point P on the graph. If Hathaway wants to grow the same amount of corn on less land, he can substitute fertilizer for land. For example, at point Q he can grow 200 bushels of corn on 5 acres by using 5 tons of

FIGURE 7A.1 AN ISOQUANTITY LINE

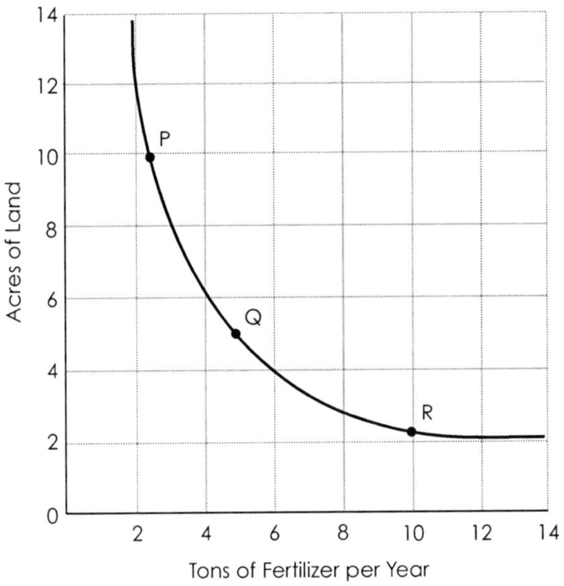

This graph shows an isoquantity line, or isoquant, for the production of 200 bushels of corn. The variable inputs are land and fertilizer; the other inputs, labor and machinery, are assumed to be fixed. Points P, Q, and R represent various ways of growing the given quantity of corn. A movement downward along the isoquant represents the substitution of fertilizer for land while output is maintained at 200 bushels per year. As more and more fertilizer is substituted for land, the isoquant becomes flatter because of diminishing returns.

fertilizer. By substituting still more fertilizer for land, he can move to point R, where the 200 bushels are grown on just 2.5 acres using 10 tons of fertilizer.

Diminishing Returns in Substitutions

In this chapter, we defined the law of diminishing returns as it applies to a situation in which one input is varied while all others remain constant. In that situation, after a certain point the amount of the variable input needed to make an extra unit of output increases. (This is another way of saying that the marginal physical product of the variable input decreases.) A similar principle applies when one input is substituted for another in such a way as to keep output at a constant level: As the amount of input x is increased, the amount of x needed to replace one unit of y increases.

The example in Figure 7A.1 illustrates this principle. In moving from point P to point Q, 2.5 tons of fertilizer replace 5 acres of land while output stays constant at 200 bushels. But in moving from point Q to point R, 5 more tons of fertilizer are needed to replace just 2.5 acres of land.

As a result of the law of diminishing returns in substituting one input for another, a curve connecting points P, Q, and R becomes flatter as one moves downward and to the right along it. This reflects the decreasing ratio of the marginal physical product of fertilizer to the marginal physical product of land as more fertilizer is substituted for land.

Choosing the Least-Cost Production Method

Isoquantity line (isoquant)

A line showing the various combinations of inputs with which a given quantity of output can be produced.

The line connecting points P, Q, and R in Figure 7A.1 is called an **isoquantity line** or **isoquant**, because it shows the combinations of inputs that can be used to produce a given amount of output. (The prefix *iso* comes from a Greek word meaning "equal.") Although all the points on the isoquant are equal in terms of output, they are not equal in terms of cost. To see how a producer can choose the least-cost method of producing a given level of output, we need to know the prices of the inputs.

In the appendix to Chapter 5, we used budget lines as a graphical device to represent the prices of consumer goods. As Figure 7A.2 shows, the same technique can be used to represent the prices of inputs. The graph assumes a cost of $50 a ton for fertilizer and a rental price of $50 per year for land. The sum of $400 can buy 8 tons of fertilizer and no land, 8 acres of land with no fertilizer, or any of the other points on line A; the sum of $500 will buy 10 tons of fertilizer, 10 acres of land, or any of the other points on line B; and so on.

When the isoquant for 200 bushels of corn is drawn on top of a set of budget lines for the inputs, it is easy to see the least-cost method of producing that output level: It is the method that uses 5 tons of fertilizer and 5 acres of land. This corresponds to point Q on the graph, where the isoquant just touches budget line B. Points P and R are possible ways of growing 200 bushels of corn, but they lie on budget line C, which corresponds to a cost of $625. Note also that a budget of less than $500 (say, $400, as shown by budget line A) is not enough to reach the 200-bushel isoquant no matter how it is split between fertilizer and land.

Responses to Changes in Input Prices

If input prices change, the least-cost combination of inputs is likely to change as well. Suppose that the suburbs begin to expand in the direction of Hathaway's farm, driving up the price of land. Now land that used to rent for $50 per acre per year rents for $200 per acre. The price of fertilizer remains unchanged at $50 a ton.

FIGURE 7A.2 FINDING THE LEAST-COST PRODUCTION METHOD

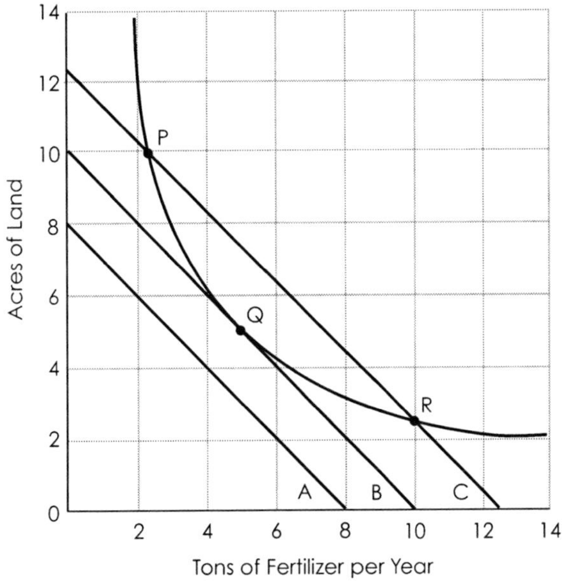

This graph shows how the least-cost method of production can be found from among the points on an isoquant given the prices of the variable inputs. Here the price of fertilizer is assumed to be $50 a ton and the rental price of land $50 per year. A set of budget lines is drawn to represent various levels of spending on inputs. Line A, which corresponds to a total variable cost of $400, does not provide enough inputs to produce 200 bushels of corn. Line C, which corresponds to a total variable cost of $625, provides enough inputs to grow 200 bushels of corn using methods P or R. Line B, which corresponds to a total variable cost of $500, permits the 200 bushels to be grown using method Q, which is the least-cost method given these input prices.

The results of the increase in the price of land are shown in Figure 7A.3. Now $500 will not be enough to buy the combinations of inputs that fall along budget line B. Even if all the money were spent on land, only 2.5 acres could be rented. The new $500 budget line is C, which does not reach the 200-bushel isoquant at any point.

To grow 200 bushels, Hathaway must now spend more than $500. As he increases his budget for land and fertilizer, the budget line shifts upward but stays parallel to C. When the budget line reaches D, which corresponds to spending $1,000 on inputs, it just touches the isoquant at R. We see that now $1,000 is the lowest cost at which 200 bushels of corn can be grown, given a price of $50 a ton for fertilizer and $200 an acre for land. With those prices, R is the least-cost combination of inputs.

In this case, the effect of an increase in the price of an input is typical. Less of the input whose price has gone up is used, and the other input, which has become relatively less costly, is substituted for it. We will return to this topic in later chapters, where we discuss the markets for productive resources.

Varying Output

The isoquant technique can also be used to analyze variations in output with two variable inputs. Part (a) of Figure 7A.4 shows an isoquant "map" with three sets of points that correspond to three

FIGURE 7A.3 EFFECTS OF A CHANGE IN INPUT PRICES

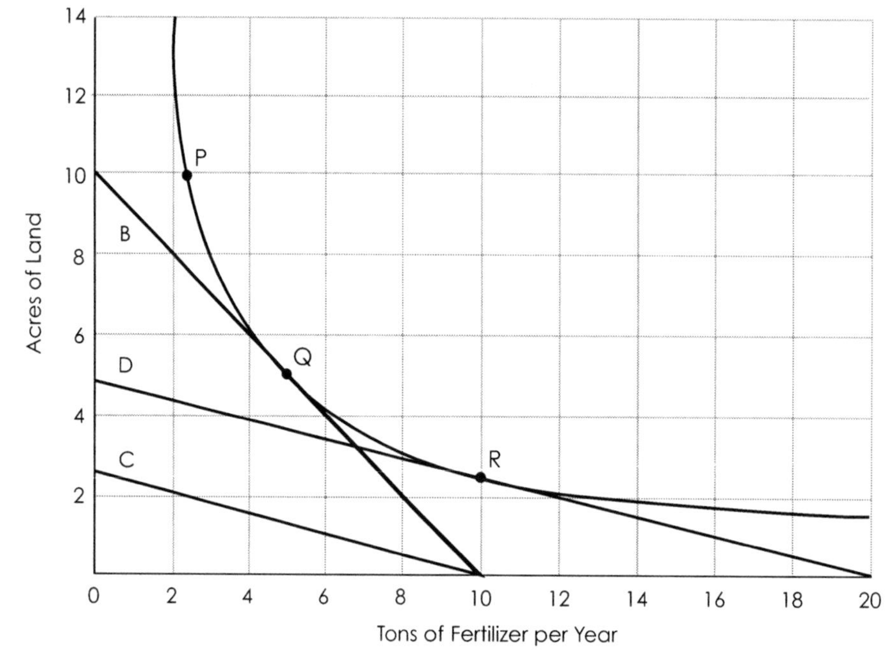

If the rental price of land increases from $50 to $200 per year while the price of fertilizer remains fixed at $50 a ton, 200 bushels of corn can no longer be produced for $500. The $500 budget line shifts from position B to position C and now falls short of the 200-bushel isoquant. Increasing the amount spent on variable inputs to $1,000 shifts the budget line up to position D, where it just touches the isoquant at point R. The increase in the price of land thus not only raises the total variable cost of growing 200 bushels of corn but also causes fertilizer to be substituted for land, which is now relatively more costly.

output levels. As before, P, Q, and R represent three ways of growing 200 bushels of corn. Points S, T, and U represent three ways of growing 100 bushels, and points V, W, and X are three ways of growing 300 bushels. An isoquant has been drawn through each set of points.

In this figure, we return to the assumption that land costs $50 an acre and fertilizer $50 a ton. Using these prices, a set of budget lines has been drawn, each corresponding to a different total variable cost, $300, $500, and $1,000.

As the graph clearly shows, there is a least-cost method for producing each output level given these prices. Point T is the best way to produce 100 bushels; Q is best for 200 bushels; and W is best for 300 bushels. Other output levels would be possible as well; these would lie along the line drawn from the origin through points T, Q, and W. This line is called the firm's **expansion path**. As the firm moves along its expansion path, more of both the variable inputs, land and fertilizer, is used. Meanwhile, the fixed inputs—labor and machinery, in Hathaway's case—remain constant.

Expansion path

A line on an isoquant diagram showing the least-cost combinations of inputs used to produce various levels of output, for given input prices.

Deriving a Cost Curve from the Isoquant Map

Once the expansion path has been identified, we can easily construct a total variable cost curve. All we need do is construct a graph that links each output point on the expansion path

FIGURE 7A.4 EXPANSION OF OUTPUT AND TOTAL VARIABLE COSTS

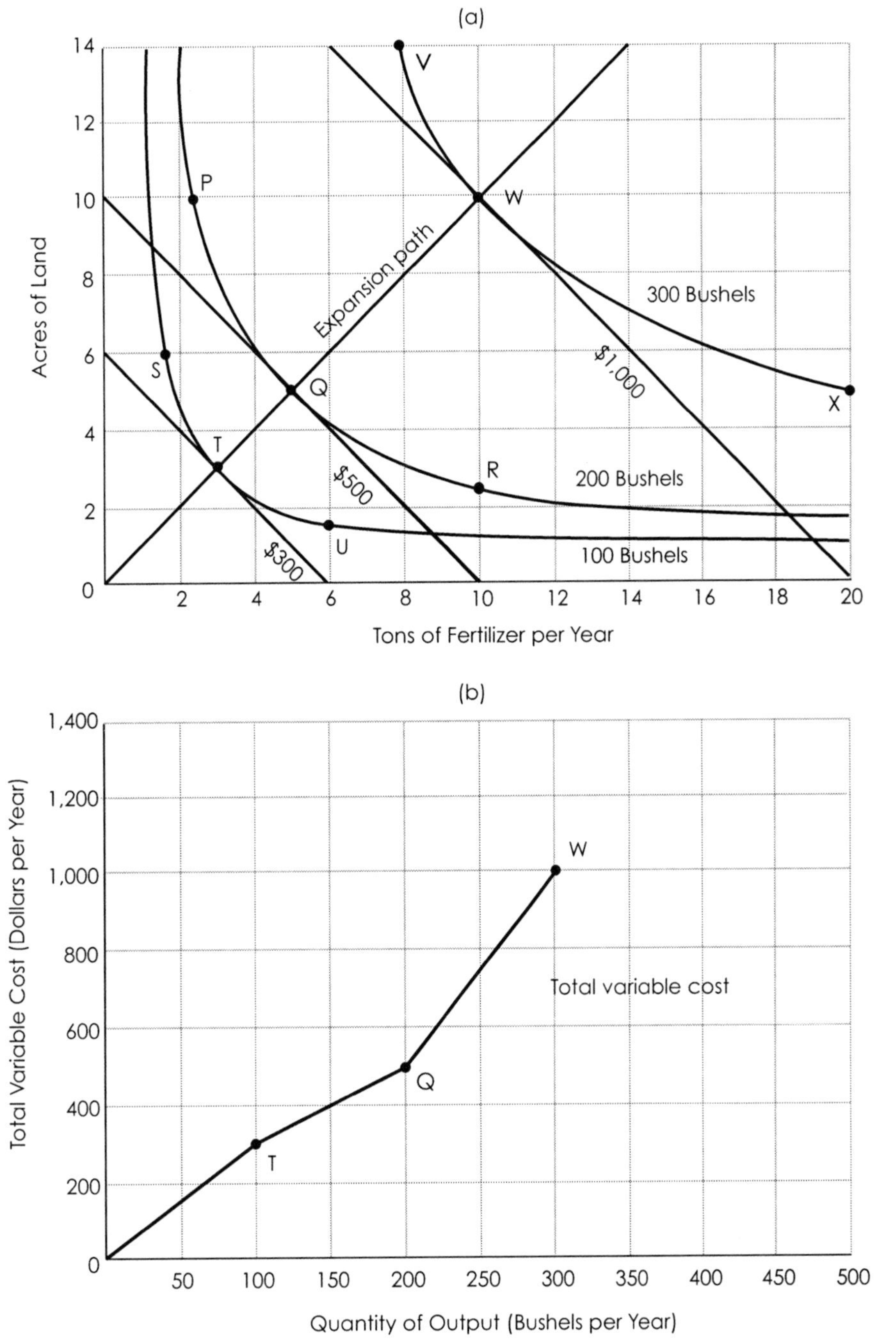

Part (a) of this figure shows three isoquants for the production of corn corresponding to outputs of 100, 200, and 300 bushels per year. Assuming input prices of $50 an acre for land and $50 a ton for fertilizer, budget lines can be drawn to show the minimum total variable cost for each output level. As output expands, the firm will move from T to Q and then to W along the expansion path. Part (b) of the figure plots the amount of output and the total variable cost for each of these points. The result is a reverse-S-shaped total variable cost curve that shows the effects of diminishing returns for output levels above 200 bushels per year.

with the variable cost level of the corresponding budget line. This is done in part (b) of Figure 7A.4. At the origin, both output and total variable cost are zero. At point T, output is 100 bushels per year and total variable cost is $300 per year; at Q, we have 200 bushels and $500; and at W, 300 bushels and $1,000. Plotting these points and connecting them give the firm's total variable cost curve.

This curve has the same reverse-S shape as the cost curve of Fieldcom, Inc., discussed earlier in this chapter. This shape results from the law of diminishing returns, here applied to the case in which two inputs vary while all others remain fixed. Beyond point Q, the amounts of inputs needed to produce each added unit of output begin to rise, just as they did when only one input was allowed to vary. Only if all inputs are allowed to vary and none is allowed to remain fixed can a firm escape the effects of the law of diminishing returns.

CHAPTER 8

Price Charged and Quantity Supplied Under Perfect Competition

After reading this chapter, you will understand:

1. What characteristics define the structure of a market
2. What determines the profit-maximizing output level in the short run for a perfectly competitive firm
3. Under what conditions a firm will continue to operate even if it sustains a loss
4. How a firm's short-run supply curve is related to its cost curves
5. The conditions for long-run equilibrium in a perfectly competitive industry
6. What determines the shape of the long-run supply curve for a perfectly competitive industry
7. How efficiently markets perform under perfect competition

Before reading this chapter, make sure you know the meaning of:

1. Entrepreneurship
2. Efficiency
3. Theories and models
4. Perfectly elastic demand
5. Objectives, constraints, and choices
6. Market performance
7. Monopoly
8. Short- and long-run costs

In the last chapter we looked at the structure of costs for an individual firm taken in isolation. However, in the real world firms do not operate alone; they face competition. Competition may take the form of giants such as General

Motors and Toyota struggling to dominate a market, or advertising campaigns by rivals wooing fickle consumers. Sometimes it takes the form of rapid increases in the number of brands and styles, as in markets for breakfast cereal and clothing. Sometimes it takes the form of many small firms selling essentially identical products in a market in which entry and exit are easy. In this chapter, we take a first look at the phenomenon of competition.

Market structure

The key traits of a market, including the number and size of firms, the extent to which the products of various firms are different or similar, ease of entry and exit, and availability of information.

Economists refer to the conditions under which competition occurs in a market as **market structure.** Market structure is defined in terms of the number and size of firms, the nature of the product, ease of entry and exit, and availability of information.

Perfect competition

A market structure that is characterized by a large number of small firms, a homogeneous product, freedom of entry and exit, and equal access to information

In this book we will look at four market structures that have traditionally been emphasized in neoclassical economics. The first, to which this chapter is devoted, is **perfect competition**. The defining characteristics of perfect competition are the presence of many firms, none with a significant share of the market; a product that is homogeneous; easy entry into the industry and exit from it; and equal access to information by buyers and sellers. By a "significant" share of the market, we mean a share that is large enough so that the actions of a single firm are enough to noticeably affect the market price. Because this small market share firm cannot influence the price of the product by its one decisions (increase/decrease the amount supplied) they are referred to as a *price taker.* By a "homogeneous product," we mean that the various firms' products are alike in all important respects. By "ease of entry," we mean that firms that are just starting to produce the product can do so on an equal footing with existing firms in terms of the prices paid for inputs, access to government permits or licenses, and so on. By "ease of exit," we mean that firms face no legal barriers to leaving the market and are able to find buyers or other uses for their fixed inputs. Finally, by "equal access to information," we mean that all buyers and sellers have complete information about the price of the product and of the inputs used to produce it, that buyers know all they need to know about product characteristics, and that all producers have equal knowledge of production techniques.

Oligopoly

A market structure in which there are a few firms, at least some of which are large in relation to the size of the market.

Monopolistic competition

A market structure in which there are many small firms, a differentiated product, and easy entry and exit.

A second market structure, *monopoly,* is at the opposite extreme from perfect competition. A monopoly, as defined previously, is a market in which a single firm accounts for 100 percent of sales of a product that has no close substitutes. Monopoly will be examined in detail in the next chapter.

Perfect competition and monopoly are "ideal type" market structures. Few if any markets exactly fit the definitions, although many approximate them. The next two market structures are more descriptive. **Oligopoly** means a market with a few firms, at least some of which have a significant share of the market. The product may be either homogeneous or differentiated; there may or may not be significant barriers to entry; and buyers and sellers need not have equal access to all kinds of information. Most familiar markets for branded products, from automobiles to toothpaste, fit in this category. **Monopolistic competition** resembles perfect competition in that there are many small firms and easy entry and exit, but under monopolistic competition the various firms' products are differentiated from one another. Many sectors of retail trade and small service firms fit this category.

The characteristics of the four market structures are summarized in Table 8.1.

PERFECT COMPETITION AND SUPPLY IN THE SHORT RUN

In building a model to fit the market structure of perfect competition, our objectives are (1) to show how the profit-maximizing decisions of individual firms determine the quantity they will supply at various prices and (2) to show how individual firms' decisions generate market supply curves. We will look first at the short run and then at the long run.

The Constraints

With a few brief exceptions (discussed in a later chapter), all models considered in this book assume that, regardless of market structure, the firm's objective is to maximize profit. That means that differences in the choices that firms make under various market structures must be traced to differences in the constraints they face rather than to differences in objectives.

COST CONSTRAINTS One set of constraints, those imposed by costs, was discussed in the preceding chapter. In the case of perfect competition, we make three special assumptions regarding costs:

TABLE 8.1 MARKET STRUCTURES

	Number and Size of Firms	Nature of Product	Entry and Exit Conditions	Information Availability
Perfect Competition	Many firms, all small	Homogenous	Easy	Equal access to all information
Monopolistic Competition	Many firms, all small	Differentiated	Easy	Some restrictions
Oligopoly	Few firms, at least some of them large	Differentiated or homogeneous	May be some barriers to entry	Some restrictions
Monopoly	One firm	Unique product	Barriers to entry are common	Some restrictions

The structure of a market refers to the conditions under which firms compete in it—the number and size of firms, the nature of the product, the ease of entry and exit, and the availability of information. Perfect competition and monopoly are "ideal" types of structures. Few—if any—markers fit their definitions perfectly. Monopolistic competition and oligopoly are descriptive of most markets in the U.S. economy.

1. All firms in the market have access to the same technology and know where to buy inputs at the same prices. These conditions are implied by the assumptions of a homogeneous product and equal access to information by all firms. As a result, all firms have identical long- and short-run cost curves.
2. Economies of scale are exhausted at a small level of output relative to the quantity demanded in the market at the prevailing price so that there is room for many firms producing at the minimum long-run average cost. Without this assumption, it would not be possible to maintain many firms, each small relative to the market, as is required in this market structure.
3. There are no sunk costs. Firms that leave the market are able to recover implicit fixed costs by selling their plant and equipment to other firms. This is part of the requirement of free entry and exit.

DEMAND CONSTRAINTS: THE FIRM AS PRICE TAKER The other principal constraint on the choices made by a profit-maximizing firm is the demand for the product that the firm produces. The perfectly competitive market structure imposes a very special demand constraint on the firm: Because all firms in such an industry are small and have homogeneous products, each firm is a **price taker**. This means that the price at which each firm sells its output is determined by forces beyond the firm's control, namely, supply and demand conditions in the market as a whole. If an individual firm raised its price even a fraction above the prevailing market price, it could sell nothing at all. Equally, there would be no point in lowering its price even a fraction below the prevailing market price. If it did so, it would be overwhelmed by more orders than it could possibly fill. Demand conditions under perfect competition for the individual firm and for the market as a whole are illustrated in Figure 8.1. Note that the demand facing the individual seller is perfectly elastic.

Price taker

A firm that sells its output at prices that are determined by forces beyond its control.

Part (a) of Figure 8.1 shows the supply and demand curves for the market for chicken as given in earlier chapters. The equilibrium price is $2.00 per pound, and the equilibrium quantity is 2 billion pounds per year. Part (b) shows how the market looks from the viewpoint of an individual producer. The range of possible outputs is measured in terms of thousands rather than billions of pounds. The range of choice over which any one firm can vary its output is so small relative to the total quantity demanded that the market price will not be perceptibly affected whether the firm produces 10,000, 20,000, or 40,000 pounds of chicken a year. A 10,000-pound movement is too small even to see on the scale of the market supply and demand curves. As far as the individual firm is concerned, then, the demand curve it faces appears to be perfectly elastic (horizontal) at the market price, even though, when viewed from the perspective of the market as a whole, the demand curve has the usual negative slope.

Previously we introduced the term *marginal cost* to refer to the amount by which total cost changes when output changes by one unit. Now we can introduce a similar term, **marginal revenue**, to refer to the amount by which total revenue changes as a result of a one-unit change in output. Recall that *revenue* means price times quantity

Marginal revenue

The amount by which total revenue changes as a result of a one-unit increase in quantity sold.

FIGURE 8.1 MARKET DEMAND AND DEMAND FOR THE PERFECTLY COMPETITIVE FIRM

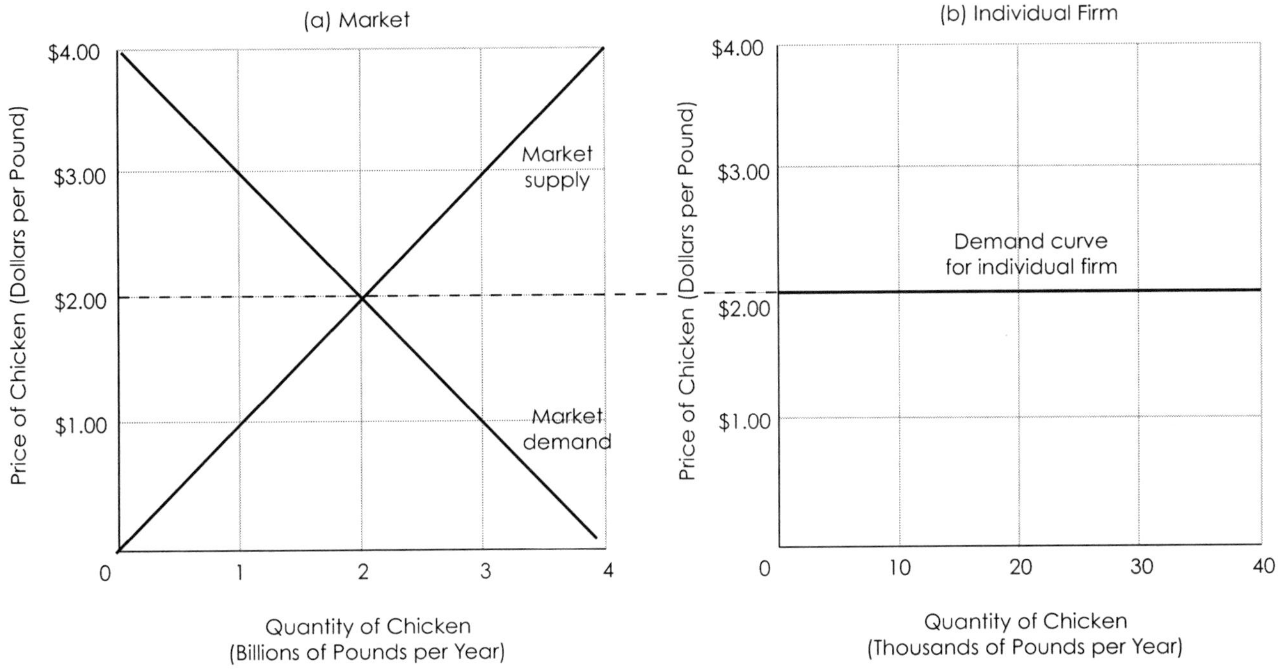

The perfectly competitive firm is a price taker. It is so small relative to the market as a whole that its decisions do not significantly affect the market price. In this example, the market equilibrium price is $2.00 per pound. The price will not be much affected if the individual firm shown in part (b) produces 20,000 rather than 40,000 pounds out of the billions of pounds produced in the market as a whole. Because the individual competitive firm is a price taker, the demand curve it faces is perfectly elastic. As a result, revenue equals price for a perfectly competitive firm.

sold. For a firm with a perfectly elastic demand curve, marginal revenue simply equals price. For example, if the price of chicken is $2 per pound, the firm will receive a revenue of $200 from the sale of 100 pounds of chicken and a revenue of $202 from the sale of 101 pounds. A 1-pound increase in output yields a $2 increase in revenue, that is, an increase in revenue equal to the product's price. Under perfect competition, then, marginal revenue and price are equal for the individual firm. (In the next chapter, we will see that marginal revenue and price are not equal in market structures where the firm's demand curve is not perfectly elastic.)

Short-Run Profit Maximization for the Firm

Now that we have introduced some basic concepts, we can apply them to the problem of how an individual firm chooses a level of output that yields the maximum profit, given the constraints imposed by its cost and demand curves. In doing so, it will be convenient to refer to a specific numerical example. Our example will be based on the imaginary firm Fieldcom introduced in the preceding chapter. Bear in mind, however, that neither this nor any other real-world firm exactly fits the ideal type.[1]

Part (a) of Figure 8.2 shows short-run cost data for Fieldcom as given in the last chapter. It also shows the revenue Fieldcom earns from the sale of each quantity of output, assuming a market price of $500 per unit.

Subtracting total cost in column 3 from total revenue in column 2 yields the total profit the firm earns at each output level. The maximum is reached at 19 units per day, where a profit of $2,000 per day is earned. The profit-maximizing output level is

FIGURE 8.2 SHORT-RUN PROFIT MAXIMIZATION UNDER PERFECT COMPETITION

(a)

Quantity of Output (1)	Total Revenue (2)	Total Cost (3)	Total Profit (2) − (3) (4)	Marginal Cost (5)	Marginal Revenue (6)
0	$ 0	$2,000	−$2,000		
1	500	2,380	−1,880	$380	$500
2	1,000	2,720	−1,720	340	500
3	1,500	3,025	−1,525	305	500
4	2,000	3,300	−1,300	275	500
5	2,500	3,550	−1,000	250	500
6	3,000	3,780	−780	230	500
7	3,500	3,955	−495	215	500
8	4,000	4,200	−200	205	500
9	4,500	4,400	100	200	500
10	5,000	4,605	395	205	500
11	5,500	4,820	680	215	500
12	6,000	5,050	950	230	500
13	6,500	5,300	1,200	250	500
14	7,000	5,575	1,425	275	500
15	7,500	5,880	1,620	305	500
16	8,000	6,220	1,780	340	500
17	8,500	6,600	1,900	380	500
18	9,000	7,025	1,975	425	500
19	9,500	7,500	2,000	475	500
20	10,000	8,030	1,970	530	500
21	10,500	8,620	1,880	590	500
22	11,000	9,275	1,725	655	500
23	11,500	10,000	1,500	725	500
24	12,000	10,800	1,200	800	500

(continues)

This figure shows the profit-maximizing level of output chosen by a perfectly competitive firm, Fieldcom, Inc., given a market price of $500 per unit. That level of output can be found by comparing total cost and total revenue, as shown in parts (a) and (b). It can also be found by comparing marginal cost and marginal revenue. (Because the firm is a price taker, marginal revenue is equal to price.) Profit increases up to the point at which rising marginal cost begins to exceed marginal revenue; after that point, it declines. Regardless of the approach used, the profit-maximizing output is 19 units per day and the maximum profit per day is $2,000.

shown graphically in part (b) of Figure 8.2. There the firm's total profit is indicated by the distance between the total revenue and total cost curves. That distance is greatest at 19 units of output.

Instead of comparing total cost and total revenue, we can find the profit-maximizing output level by comparing marginal cost and marginal revenue. Look first at columns 5 and 6 of part (a) of Figure 8.2. Column 5 gives data on marginal cost. (As

FIGURE 8.2 SHORT-RUN PROFIT MAXIMIZATION UNDER PERFECT COMPETITION, CONTINUED

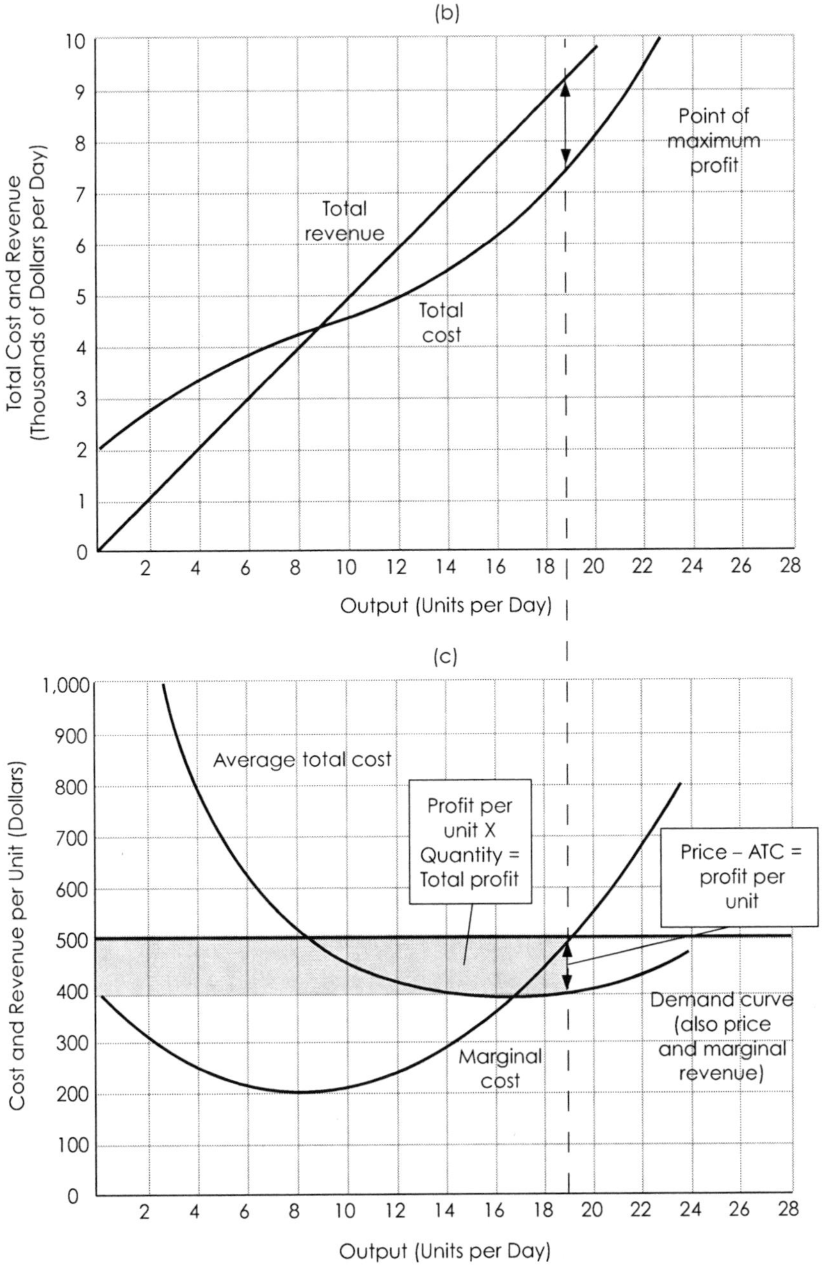

before, the data are printed on lines between the entries in the first four columns to show that marginal cost is the change in cost as output moves from one level to another.) Column 6 shows marginal revenue, which, as explained, is equal to the product's price. Each PDA that Fieldcom sells adds $500 to its total revenue.

As the table shows, both total cost and total revenue rise as output increases. If the increase in revenue exceeds the increase in cost (that is, if marginal revenue is greater than marginal cost), boosting output by one unit increases total profit. If the increase in cost exceeds the increase in revenue (that is, if marginal cost is greater than marginal revenue), raising output by one unit reduces total profit. Therefore, to maximize profit a firm should expand its output as long as marginal revenue exceeds marginal cost and should stop as soon as rising marginal cost begins to exceed marginal revenue. A comparison of columns 5 and 6 of Figure 8.2 shows that for Fieldcom this means producing 19 units of output per day—the same number we arrive at when we compare total cost and total revenue.

The marginal approach to short-run profit maximization is shown graphically in part (c) of Figure 8.2. At up to about 19 units of output, the marginal cost curve lies below the marginal revenue curve, so each added unit of output increases profit. (The graph, unlike the table, pictures output as a continuous quantity so that profit maximization need not occur exactly at an even number of units.) Beyond that point, the marginal cost curve rises above the marginal revenue curve so each added unit of output reduces profit. The point of profit maximization—the point at which the rising section of the marginal cost curve intersects the marginal revenue curve—matches the point in part (b) at which the spread between total revenue and total cost is greatest.

In part (c), the vertical distance between the demand curve, which shows price, and the average total cost curve represents the profit per unit. Profit per unit multiplied by the number of units gives total profit. Thus, from the standpoint of part (c), total profit equals the area of the shaded rectangle.

Minimizing Short-Run Losses

In the example just given, Fieldcom was able to make a profit at a price of $500. However, market conditions might not always be so favorable. Suppose, for example, that the market price drops to $300. A lower market price means a downward shift in the firm's perfectly elastic demand curve. Being a price taker, the firm can do nothing about the price and will have to adjust its output as best it can to meet the new situation. The required adjustments are shown in Figure 8.3.

There is no output level at which the firm can earn a profit given a price of $300. Unable to earn a profit, the firm must focus on keeping its losses to a minimum. With a price of $300 per unit, the minimum loss occurs at 14 units of output. As in the previous case, that is the output level beyond which marginal cost begins to exceed the product's price.

FIGURE 8.3 MINIMIZING SHORT-RUN LOSSES UNDER PERFECT COMPETITION

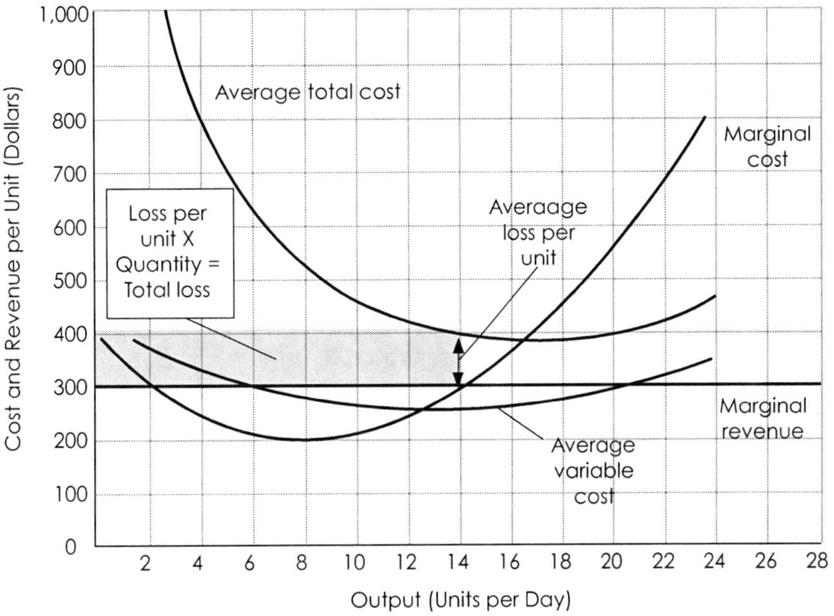

If the product's market price is too low to permit earning a profit, the firm must try to keep its losses to a minimum. For Fieldcom, Inc., given a price of $300 per unit, the point of minimum loss is 14 units of output per day. The marginal cost curve intersects the marginal revenue curve at a point higher than average variable cost but lower than average total cost. Each unit of output sold earns more than its share of variable cost but not enough to pay for its share of total cost when its share of fixed cost is included.

In graphical terms, we note that the point at which the rising section of the marginal cost curve intersects the marginal revenue curve lies between the average total cost and average variable cost curves.[2] Because the demand curve is below the average total cost curve, there is a loss on each unit sold. The total loss is equal to the shaded rectangle (loss per unit times quantity of output). However, the demand curve lies above the average variable cost curve. This means that revenue per unit is more than enough to cover variable cost and, hence, that each unit sold makes at least some contribution to covering fixed cost. Thus, losses are smaller than they would be if no output were produced, assuming that fixed costs must be paid even when output drops to zero.

As an aid to understanding the logic of the loss-minimizing decision, suppose for a moment that wages are the firm's only variable cost and that rent on its building is its only fixed cost. At the point shown, the firm is bringing in more than enough revenue to pay its wage bill (variable costs); the remainder will help pay the rent. If the firm shuts down temporarily, it will have to pay the rent with no help at all from current revenue. That would mean a loss equal to fixed cost—even more of a loss than at 14 units of output per day.

The logic of continuing operations in order to minimize losses applies only in the short run, when the costs of fixed inputs must be borne regardless of how much output is produced. A firm would not continue to operate indefinitely with the price below average total cost as shown in Figure 8.3. In the long run, a firm can free itself of fixed costs by selling its equipment, allowing long-term leases to expire, and so on. We will return to the conditions under which firms will leave the industry later in the chapter.

Shutting Down to Cut Short-Run Losses

What would happen if the price of PDAs dropped even lower than $300? Would it then still be worthwhile for the firm to keep making them even though it was losing money? The answer, as shown in Figure 8.4, is no.

The figure assumes a price of $225 per unit. With such a low price the firm cannot make a profit at any output level. But this time the best thing for the firm to do in the short run is to shut down. As illustrated by *Economics in the News 8.1*, brief shutdowns are a normal way of adjusting inventories to changing supply and demand

FIGURE 8.4 SHUTTING DOWN TO MINIMIZE SHORT-RUN LOSS

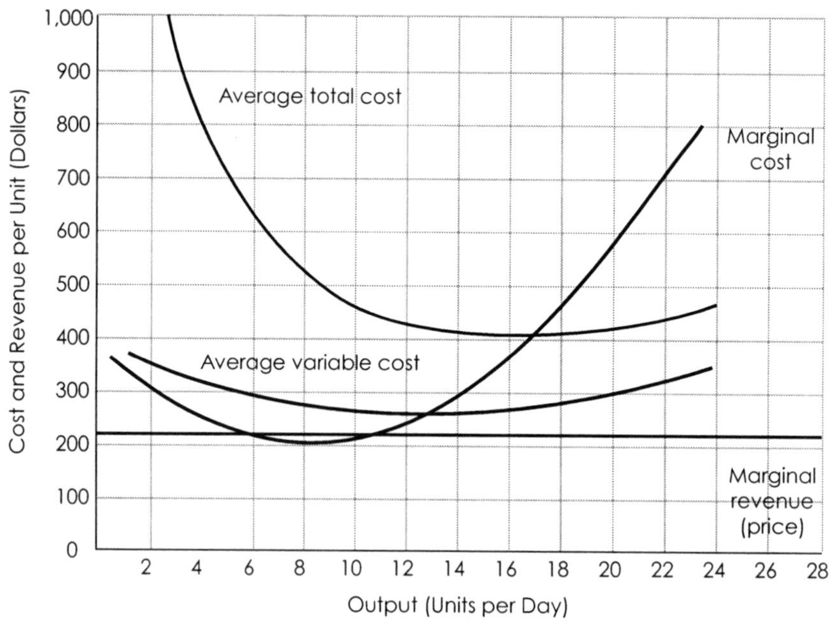

The price of a firm's output may drop so low that the firm must shut down in order to keep short-run losses to a minimum. As illustrated here, such a situation occurs for Fieldcom at a price of $225 per unit. Marginal cost rises above marginal revenue at about 11 units of output. That output yields a smaller loss ($2,345) than those slightly greater or lower. However, the loss can be reduced to just $2,000 a day if the firm shuts down. The marginal cost curve in this case intersects the marginal revenue curve at a point below average variable cost. That is the signal to shut down.

ECONOMICS IN THE NEWS 8.1

CHANGING WITH THE SEASONS

Croatia is a small, newly independent country that must make the most of its resources as it hurries to catch up to the living standards of the rest of Europe. Luckily it has one big asset: a stunning Adriatic coastline with brilliant sun, sparkling clear water, and hundreds of islands, perfect for get-away weekends by Parisians or Berliners.

In the opinion of some, the crown jewel among the Croatian islands is Hvar. The tiny port of Hvar Town is a tourist paradise of ancient red-roofed houses cascading down a steep hill from an old fort at the top to a quaint fishing harbor below. Taking advantage of some fine, clear weather in mid-March, a recent visitor found the streets of Hvar Town lined with hotels, restaurants, and souvenir shops—all of them closed! Although it has facilities to serve thousands of tourists in the summer, all but one hotel and all but three or four restaurants close for the season each winter, to open again in the late spring.

At first it seems like such a waste. All that natural beauty is still there, and the water is just as clear even if the air is a few degrees cooler. Why don't the hotels and restaurants just offer low, off-season rates in order to stay busy all winter? With a little thought, though, the economic logic of the decision to shut down becomes clear. Hotel and restaurant owners have to take a close look at their costs when deciding whether to operate on a year-round or seasonal basis. Some costs, like property taxes and interest on bank loans can't be avoided by shutting down, but others, especially labor costs for clerks and kitchen staff, can be eliminated when the establishment is closed. To a certain point, it pays to stay open by offering lower, off-season rates, but when those rates fall so low that they don't even cover the wages of the cooks and cleaners, it is time to put up the shutters and wait for spring.

And what about the one hotel that stays open in the winter? Is the owner just ignorant of economics? No, there's an economic logic behind this hold-out strategy, too. If just one hotel stays open while all others shut, the small number of visitors to the town are enough to push its revenues above the break-even point. It's all an example of competition in action.

conditions. The example illustrates the point that shutting down is not at all the same as going out of business. Provided that the outlook for the future is good, it makes sense for a firm to keep its plant intact, pay its rent, and even continue some benefits for employees to ensure that they will be ready to come back when called. The firm therefore does not escape its fixed costs. When market conditions improve, inventories are brought into line with demand, and as the market price rises again, the firm can resume operations. Only if market conditions are never expected to improve will the firm consider winding up its affairs and going out of business.

In the case of a temporary shutdown, it can be misleading to follow the rule of expanding output until marginal cost begins to exceed marginal revenue. With the price at $225, such a point is reached at about 11 units of output per day. That output level does give the firm a lower loss than a level slightly higher or slightly lower. But in this case the firm takes an even smaller loss by not producing at all.

The reason 11 units of output does not minimize loss is that the demand curve lies below the average variable cost curve at that point. Suppose again that wages are the firm's only variable cost and rent is its only fixed cost. At 11 units of output, revenue is not enough even to meet the firm's payroll. The firm will do better to send its workers home and save the cost of wages, even though when it does this the owners will have to pay the entire rent from reserves, without any help from current sales revenue.

Should an Ocean City hotel remain open in the Winter? Only if it can cover its variable costs!

The Firm's Short-Run Supply Curve

The examples just given provide the information needed to draw a short-run supply curve for a perfectly competitive firm. Let's work through an example like the one shown in Figure 8.5 starting with a price of $500. As we saw earlier, Fieldcom will turn out 19 devices a day at that price. Point E_1 of the firm's short-run marginal cost curve thus is a point on its supply curve.

Now suppose that the demand for PDAs slackens and the market price begins to fall. As it does so, the point at which marginal revenue equals marginal cost moves downward along the firm's marginal cost curve. Soon point E_2 is reached—the point at which marginal cost and average total cost are equal. This occurs at an output of about 17 units and a price of about $385. At that price, the best the firm can do is break even; either a greater or a smaller output will result in a loss.

If the price falls still lower, the firm's objective becomes one of keeping its loss to a minimum. At a price of $300, for example, the firm minimizes its loss by making 14 units (point E_3). In the range of prices between minimum average total cost and minimum average variable cost, the supply curve continues to follow the marginal cost curve.

FIGURE 8.5 DERIVATION OF THE SHORT-RUN SUPPLY CURVE

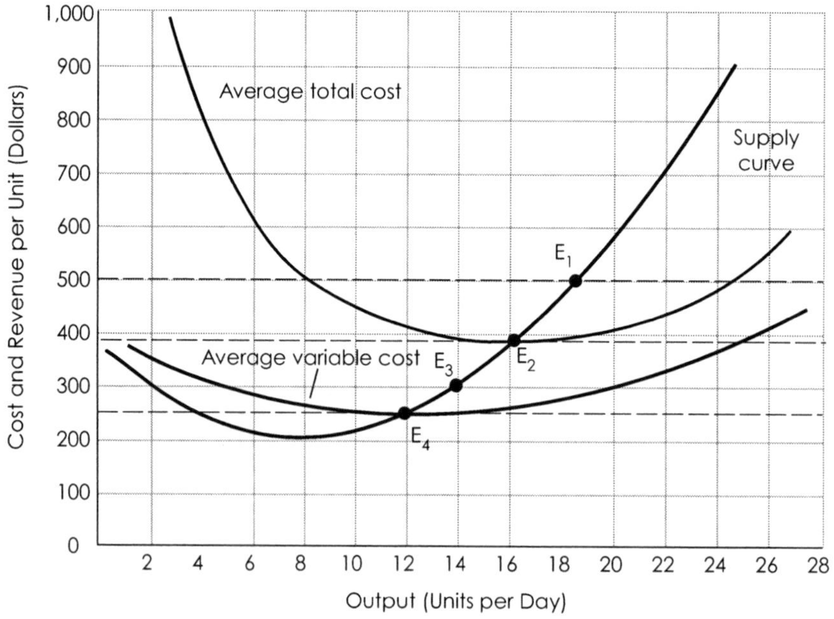

This graph shows how a short-run supply curve for Fieldcom, Inc. can be derived from its cost curves. When the price and marginal revenue is $500, the firm will produce at point E_1. As the price falls the firm will move downward along its short run marginal cost curve as shown by points E_2 and E_3. The firm will continue to produce at the point at which price equals marginal cost until marginal cost falls below average variable cost. E_4 thus is the lowest point on the firm's supply curve. Below that price the firm will shut down.

At about $250 the price reaches the lowest point on the average variable cost curve. There the firm is just on the edge of shutting down—it is covering its variable costs with nothing to spare. Its loss is equal to its fixed costs. At any lower price the firm will minimize its losses by shutting down. Thus, point E_4 is the lowest point on the marginal cost curve that can be considered part of the firm's supply curve.

The preceding discussion of the firm's short-run supply decision can be summed up as follows: *The short-run supply curve of a profit-maximizing firm operating in a perfectly competitive market coincides with the upward sloping part of the marginal cost curve lying above its intersection with the average variable cost curve.*

The Industry's Short-Run Supply Curve

Once we have a supply curve for each firm in an industry, we can add them together to construct a supply curve for the industry as a whole. Figure 8.6 shows how this can be done, beginning with the supply curves for three firms. To get the total supply of the three firms at each price, the quantities supplied by each firm are added together. In graphical terms this means adding the supply curves horizontally. To generalize the process to an industry with many firms, the individual supply curves of the remaining firms in the industry would be added to the three shown.

In adding the firms' supply curves together, we assumed that input prices did not change as output expanded. For a small firm in a perfectly competitive industry, this is a realistic assumption. However, if all firms in an industry try to grow at the same time, the assumption may not hold. In fact, input prices will rise unless a greater quantity of inputs can be purchased without paying higher prices, that is, unless the

FIGURE 8.6 DERIVATION OF A SHORT-RUN INDUSTRY SUPPLY CURVE

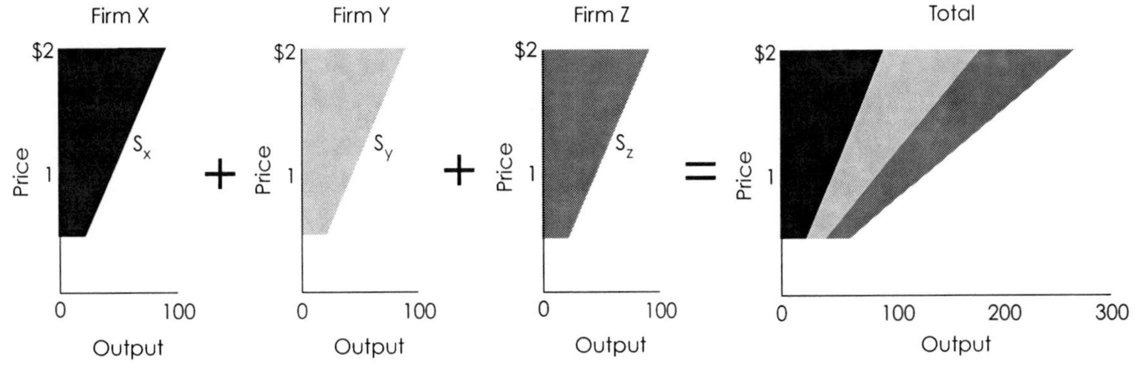

A short-run industry supply curve can be obtained by summing the supply curves of individual firms.Here this method is shown for the first three firms in an industry. The supply curves of additional firms would be added in the same way. If the prices of inputs change as industry output varies, the industry supply curve will need to be adjusted.

short-run supply curves for inputs to the industry are perfectly elastic. If input prices rise as the industry's total output grows, each firm's cost curves will shift upward as the output of all firms increases. That will make the short-run industry supply curve somewhat steeper than the sum of the individual supply curves.

LONG-RUN EQUILIBRIUM UNDER PERFECT COMPETITION

Up to this point we have considered changes in industry output that result from firms' decisions to produce more or less as the market price changes. In doing so, however, we have neglected an important part of a competitive industry's response to changes in demand: the processes of entry and exit.

Consideration of entry and exit moves us from the short run to the long run. In the last chapter we distinguished between the long run, when all inputs can be varied, and the short run, when some inputs are fixed. The ability to vary all inputs in the long run—even durable ones such as land, structures, and major pieces of equipment—allows firms to enter a market for the first time, starting with a new plant and work force. It also means that they can leave a market for good, releasing all their employees and selling their plant and equipment. (Sometimes firms leave peacefully, with the owners selling the firm's assets and dividing up the proceeds. Other times they leave the market only when forced to do so, such as when creditors resort to a bankruptcy court to force a sale of the firm's assets in order to pay its debts.) Typically, as an industry expands and contracts, many firms enter and leave it.

Free entry and exit of firms is one of the basic traits of a perfectly competitive market. Free entry does not mean that firms can enter at no cost. They may have to pay a great deal to purchase equipment, hire key employees, and so on. Free entry simply means that if they are willing to make the necessary investment, new firms are free to compete with existing ones on a level playing field. They are not kept out by patents or licensing requirements, trade secrets, collusion by firms already in the industry, or lack of raw materials. Likewise, free exit means that firms face no legal barriers to shutting down or moving if they find that they cannot make a profit. Strictly interpreted, free exit also means that firms have no sunk costs. When they leave the industry, they can put fixed assets to other uses or find buyers for them.

Free entry and exit did not play a direct role in our discussion of a firm's short-run supply decision. However, as we will now see, it is crucial to understanding how a competitive market works in the long run.

Long-Run Equilibrium for a Competitive Firm

At numerous points we have used the term *equilibrium* to refer to a state of affairs in which economic decision makers have no incentive to change their plans. Three conditions are required for a perfectly competitive firm to be in equilibrium in the long run:

1. The firm must have no incentive to produce a larger or smaller output given the size of its plant (that is, the amount of fixed inputs it uses). That requires that short-run marginal cost be equal to short-run marginal revenue, which means that the short-run equilibrium condition is also a condition for long-run equilibrium.
2. Each firm must have no incentive to change the size of its current plant (that is, with the amount of fixed inputs it uses).
3. There must be no incentive for new firms to enter the industry or for existing firms to leave it.

Figure 8.7 shows a perfectly competitive firm for which these three requirements are met. First, short-run marginal cost equals price at 25 units of output per day, which is the level of output the firm will choose in order to make the maximum profit. Second, the firm has a plant that is just the right size to make short-run average total cost equal to the lowest possible long-run average cost at the chosen output level. The short-run average total cost curve for a plant of any other size would give a higher average total cost for the chosen output. Third, both long-run average cost and short-run average total cost are equal to price at the equilibrium level of output. This guarantees that there

FIGURE 8.7 A PERFECTLY COMPETITIVE FIRM IN LONG-RUN EQUILIBRIUM

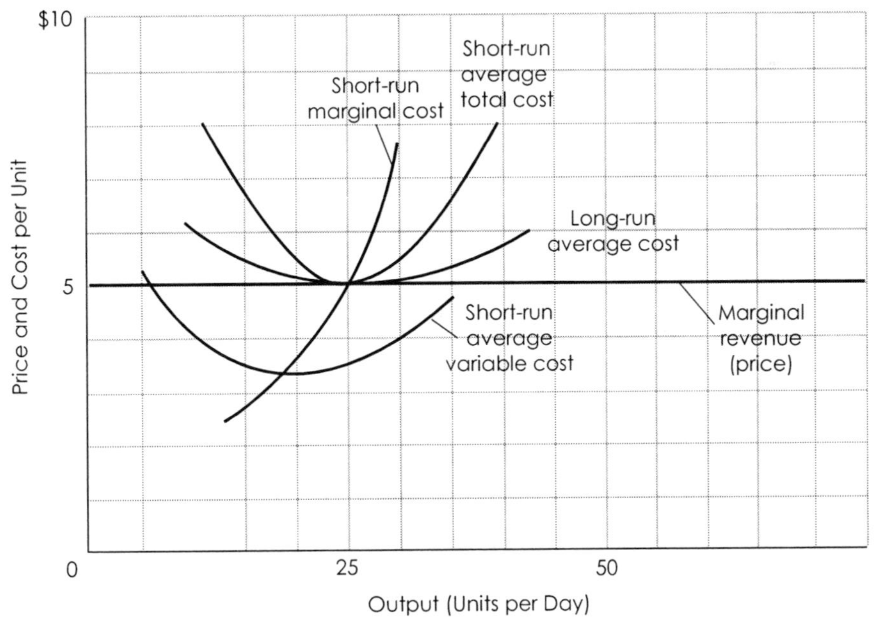

Long-run equilibrium in a perfectly competitive industry requires that the typical firm (1) have no short-run incentive to change the level of its output; (2) have no long-run incentive to change the size of the plant used to produce its output; and (3) have no long-run incentive to enter or leave the industry. This requires that price, short-run marginal cost, short-run average total cost, and long-run average cost all have the same value in equilibrium as shown here.

is no incentive for entry or exit. As always, average total cost comprises both explicit and implicit costs, including the opportunity cost of capital, or "normal profit." When price equals average total cost, then, firms are earning zero economic profit. Any positive economic profit would attract new firms into the industry, whereas negative economic profits (economic losses) would cause firms to leave the industry.

Maximize Profit Point
At the quantity where
MC = MR

All firms will maximize profits at the quantity where MC = MR. Look at the banner in the back of the classroom, understand this concept and memorize this formula!

The three conditions for long-run equilibrium are summarized in the following equation.

Price = Marginal cost = Short-run average total cost = Long-run average cost

If any part of this equation does not hold, firms will have a reason to change their plans. If price does not equal short-run marginal cost, they will have an incentive to change their output levels by changing the quantity of variable inputs used, even if they cannot, in the short run, change the size of their plants. If short-run average total cost does not equal long-run average cost, their current plant is too large or too small to produce their current level of output at the least possible cost. They will want to change the size of the plants they are using, so their plant will be the ideal size to produce their current output. And if price is lower than long-run average cost, firms in the industry will want to leave it; if price is above long-run average total cost, firms outside the industry will want to enter it.

Industry Adjustment to Falling Demand

A state of long-run equilibrium, such as that shown in Figure 8.7, exists only as long as outside conditions do not change. Suppose, though, that those conditions do change—for example, there is a long-run decrease in the market demand for the firm's product. Figure 8.8 shows what will happen.

Part (a) of Figure 8.8 shows a set of cost curves for a typical firm. Part (b) is a supply-and-demand diagram for the market as a whole. The short-run industry supply curves shown are built up from those of the individual firms in the market (see Figure 8.6). The demand curves in part (b) are market demand curves.

Suppose that initially the short-run market supply and demand curves are in the positions S_1 and D_1. The equilibrium price is \$5. Each firm takes this price as given and adjusts its output on that basis, producing 25 units. At that price and output, a

FIGURE 8.8 LONG-RUN ADJUSTMENT TO DECLINING DEMAND

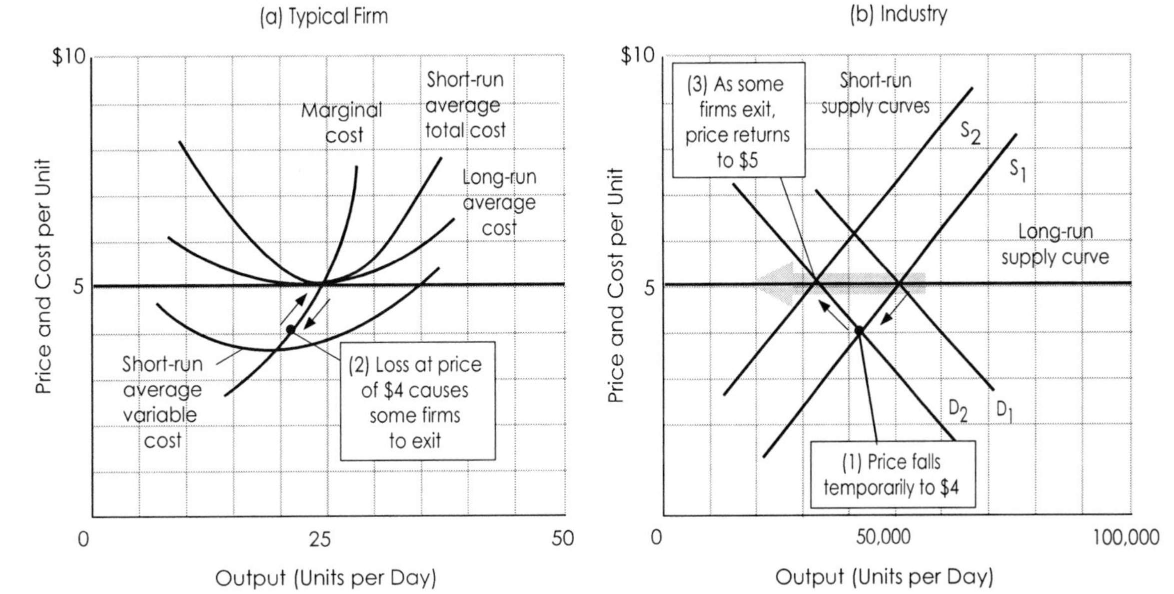

Part (a) represents a typical firm in a perfectly competitive industry; part (b) represents the industry as a whole. At first, both the firm and the industry are in long-run equilibrium at a price of $5. Then something happens to shift the market demand curve leftward from D_1 to D_2. In the short run, the price falls to $4 at the intersection of D_2 and S_1. The firm's short-run response is to move downward along its marginal cost curve. Because the price is still above average variable cost, the firm does not shut down. After a while, some firms (not the one shown) get tired of taking losses and leave the industry. This causes the market supply curve to shift toward S_2 and the market price to recover. The typical firm returns to the break-even point. The market has traced out part of its long-run supply curve as shown by the large arrow.

typical firm would just break even. (Remember, though, that "breaking even" in the economic sense means earning enough to cover all costs, including the opportunity cost of capital.)

Now something happens—say, a change in consumer tastes or incomes—that shifts the demand curve to a new position, D_2. The short-run result is a drop in the market price, to $4. Each firm, being a price taker, will view the decline in price as beyond its control and will adjust to it as best it can. As shown in part (a) of Figure 8.8, this means cutting back output slightly in order to keep losses to a minimum, but not shutting down completely. Each firm's movement downward along its short-run marginal cost curve is what causes the movement of the market as a whole downward and to the left along the short-run supply curve.

However, the new situation cannot be a long-run equilibrium, because each firm is operating at a loss. The firms' owners are not earning a normal rate of return, that is, they are not earning enough to cover the opportunity costs of keeping their capital invested in the industry. If the market demand curve shows no hope of shifting back to the right, some owners will pull their capital out of the industry. They may go bankrupt, abandoning their fixed assets to their creditors. They may sell their plant and equipment and get out while they can. Or they may keep their firms running but convert their plants to make goods for other, more profitable markets.[3]

For the sake of the example, suppose that the typical firm shown in Figure 8.8 is not one of the first to leave. As some other firms withdraw, industry output falls by the amount of their output. The short-run market supply curve, which now comprises fewer individual supply curves, shifts to the left toward S_2. As it does so, the market price begins to move upward along demand curve D_2. When the price gets all the way back to \$5, the firms remaining in the industry will no longer be losing money. Firms will stop leaving the industry, and the market will have reached a new long-run equilibrium. At the new equilibrium price, short-run marginal cost, short-run average total cost, and long-run average cost will once again be equal.

This sequence of events has traced out a portion of the industry's *long-run supply curve,* as shown by the large horizontal arrow. A long-run supply curve for an industry shows the path along which equilibrium price and quantity move when there is a lasting change in demand. Movement along this curve requires enough time for firms to adjust the sizes of their plants or enter or leave the market.

With the economic slowdown of 2008, Starbucks is suffering and has announced the closing of 100 stores. As more competitors enter the gourmet coffee market, (McDonald's with their coffee bistros, Starry Night at the 140 center, The Pour Hours on Main St. in Westminster, etc.) the price of fancy coffee is declining. Since gourmet coffee is a normal good (as income declines, demand will decline) and coffee, a homogenous product, as more firms enter the market and price is lowered, some Starbucks are no longer making the normal profit needed to keep them open.

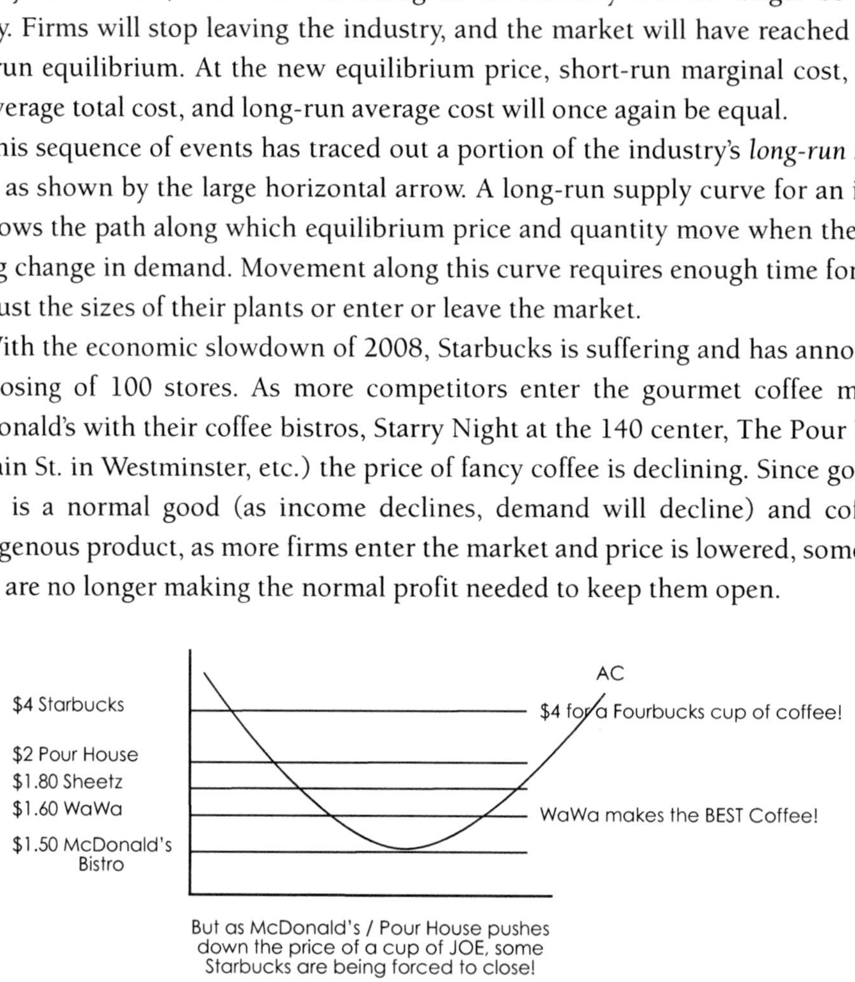

Industry Adjustment to Rising Demand

When there is a long-run increase in demand, freedom of entry plays the same role that freedom of exit plays when demand falls. Such a case is shown in Figure 8.9. The starting position in this figure is the same as that in Figure 8.8. Short-run supply curve S_1 and demand curve D_1 result in an equilibrium price of \$5. The individual firm breaks even at an output of 25 units. Now watch what happens as the demand curve shifts to the right, to D_2. The short-run result is an increase in the market price, to \$6. The typical firm adjusts to the new price by moving up along its short-run mar-

FIGURE 8.9 LONG-RUN ADJUSTMENT TO AN INCREASE IN DEMAND

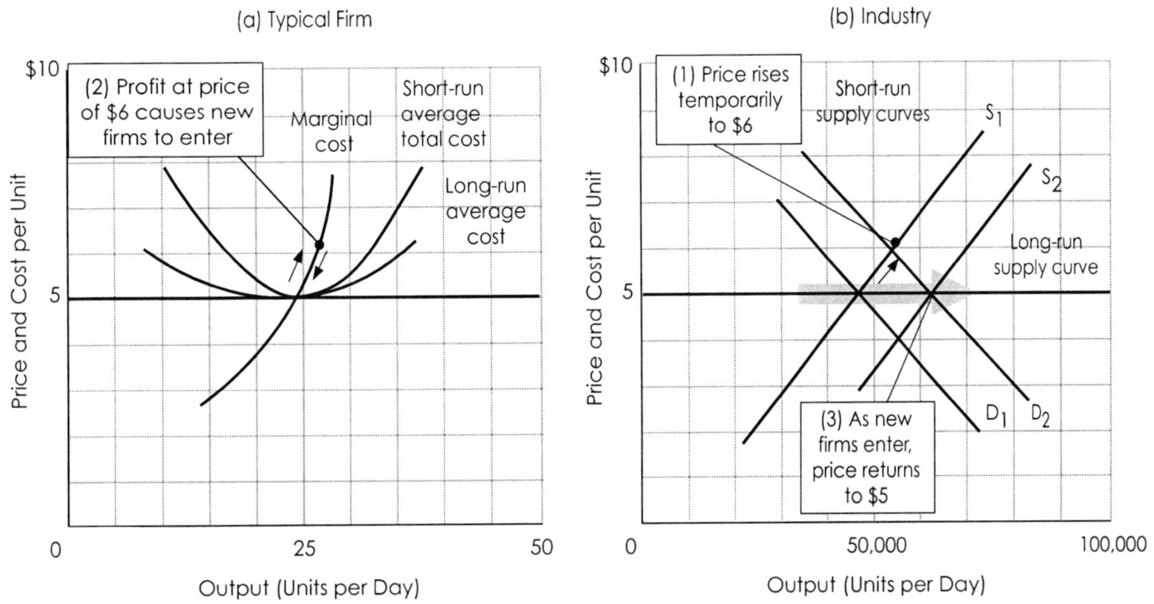

In this figure, both the firm and the industry start out in equilibrium at a price of $5. Then something happens to shift the market demand curve rightward to D_2. In the short run, the price rises to $6 at the intersection of D_2 and S_1. The firm's short-run response is to move upward along its marginal cost curve, earning better-than-normal profits. After a while, the high profits attract new firms into the industry. As those firms enter, the market supply curve shifts toward S_2. Profits for the typical firm return to zero, and new firms stop entering the industry. Again the market has traced out part of its long-run supply curve as shown by the large arrow.

ginal cost curve. As all firms do this, the market moves up and to the right along short-run supply curve S_1.

But again the short-run position is not the new long-run equilibrium, because now all firms are making an economic profit. Entrepreneurs will soon spot this healthy, growing market as a good one in which to invest. Some of them may start new firms in this market; others may shift plant and equipment from making something else to making goods for this industry. Whether the entry is by new firms or by existing ones that are producing for this market for the first time, new entries will cause the supply curve to shift to the right, toward S_2.

As the short-run market supply curve shifts to the right, the price falls. It does not fall far enough to drive the new entrants out of the market, but it does fall far enough to drive pure economic profits back to zero. Entry of firms into the market will stop, and the market will reach a new long-run equilibrium at the intersection of S_2 and D_2.

Once again a portion of the long-run supply curve for the industry has been traced out, as shown by the large horizontal arrow in Figure 8.9. This long-run supply curve again is perfectly elastic. A rightward shift in the demand curve has, in the long run, produced an increase in quantity supplied but no rise in price.

As a final detail, note the importance of the assumption that there are no sunk costs in the industry. If entering the industry required specialized investments that could not be recovered later, firms would view them as opportunity costs when deciding whether to enter the market. They would not enter unless the price was high enough (and was expected to stay high enough) to give them a normal rate of return on the nonrecoverable investments. Once in the industry, however, those sunk costs would no longer affect decisions, according to the "bygones are bygones" principle. They would not count as part of the fixed (but not sunk) costs that must be covered by revenue for continued operation to be worthwhile. Thus, existing firms may *stay* in business indefinitely even if the price falls somewhat below what would be needed to attract new firms. When sunk costs are present, then, the industry supply curve is no longer a two-way street. Such an industry would, in effect, follow one supply curve when expanding and a different, lower one when contracting.

Although the theoretical model of perfect competition does not allow for sunk costs, such costs are common in the real world. Consider the history of that uniquely American entertainment establishment, the drive-in theater. In the early years after World War II, drive-in theaters were a growing business. With demand high, many entrepreneurs entered the industry. Later, demand for this form of entertainment declined. But even when market demand dropped well below the level needed to make it worthwhile to construct new drive-ins, existing operators stayed in business. They did so even though they were no longer earning enough to cover the original sunk cost of their screens and projection houses because those facilities could neither be moved nor converted to any other use. Only when demand fell still lower, so that revenues no longer covered recoverable fixed costs (such as the cost of land) and variable costs (such as wages, electricity, and film rentals) did drive-in theater operators finally leave the market.

The Elasticity of Long-Run Supply

The long-run industry supply curve in Figures 8.8 and 8.9 is perfectly elastic. Given such a curve, a change in demand affects only the equilibrium quantity, not the price, in the long run. However, that is not the only possible case. Supply curves that are positively sloped, negatively sloped, and U-shaped are also possible.

The shape of the long-run industry supply curve depends mainly on what happens to the industry's input prices in the long run as output expands. If the long-run supply curves for all inputs to the industry are perfectly elastic, the prices of those inputs will not change as the quantities of them demanded by the industry increase. It may also be that the industry uses such a small part of the total supply of each input that any change in input prices that does occur will be slight. For example, cookie stores use such a small part of the total supply of flour and eggs that expansion or contraction of such stores will have no perceptible effect on the market prices of those inputs. Industry output can therefore expand without affecting the costs of the individual firms, and the supply curve will be perfectly elastic.

Suppose, however, that the industry is a heavy user of relatively specialized inputs whose outputs can be boosted only at an increasing cost. For example, consider the home construction business, which uses a substantial portion of all the lumber produced in the country. An expansion of the construction industry will cause lumber suppliers to exhaust the lowest-cost stands of trees and begin harvesting higher-cost timber. The home construction industry also employs a significant proportion of all carpenters in the country. If the industry expands, carpenters' wages may have to rise relative to those of, say, auto mechanics in order to attract additional workers into the occupation.

Figure 8.10 shows what happens in such an industry as a permanent increase in demand causes output to expand. As in the preceding case, the shift in demand first pushes up price along the short-run supply curve. New firms enter the market. However, the expansion of the industry raises input prices. Each firm's short-run marginal cost and average total cost curves are shifted upward from MC_1 to MC_2 and from ATC_1 to ATC_2 as shown. As a result, the new long-run equilibrium is at a higher price than the initial equilibrium. The long-run industry supply curve, drawn through the two points of short-run equilibrium, therefore has a positive slope.

It is also possible for the price of an input to decrease as the industry's total output increases. For example, as sales of electronic equipment expand, the firms that

FIGURE 8.10 A POSITIVELY SLOPED LONG-RUN INDUSTRY SUPPLY CURVE

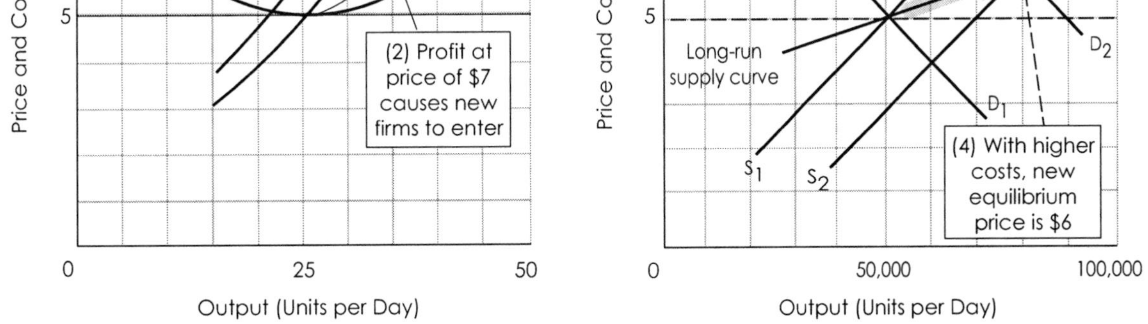

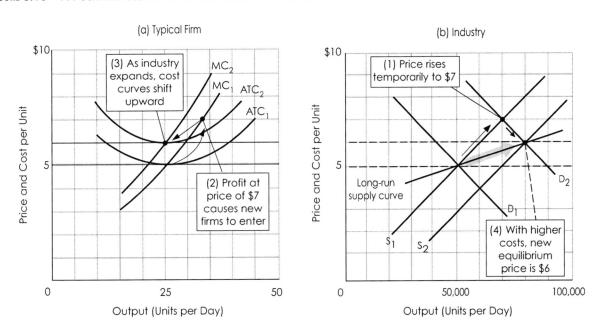

In Figures 8.8 and 8.9, it was assumed that input prices do not change as industry output expands. This pair of diagrams shows what happens if industry expansion causes input prices to rise. As output expands, rising input prices push up the firm's marginal cost curve from MC_1 to MC_2 and its average total cost from ATC_1 to ATC_2. The result is a new long-run equilibrium price that is higher than the initial price. The long-run industry supply curve thus has a positive slope.

make components for such equipment may be able to use cheaper production methods. If that occurs, the short-run cost curves for all firms will drift downward as new firms enter the industry. The long-run supply curve then will be negatively sloped.

Finally, it is possible for these various forces to operate together. At first long-run supply is influenced by the falling price of one special input, but beyond a certain point some other special input becomes a limiting factor that causes the long-run supply curve to bend upward. The long-run industry supply curve then becomes U-shaped.

As we have seen, many variations are possible. Only through direct observation of the industry in question can we tell which possibility applies.

MARKET PERFORMANCE UNDER PERFECT COMPETITION

Earlier in the text we introduced the notion of *market performance* in reference to how efficiently exchanges within markets resolve the basic economic questions of what, how, who, and for whom. Perfectly competitive markets have long earned high marks for several aspects of performance. In this section we look at market performance under perfect competition as it relates to the questions of *what* should be produced and *how* it should be produced.

What Should be Produced

When the concept of market performance was introduced, we used a diagram similar to Figure 8.11 to show the quantity of a good (peaches, in this case) that must be produced for a market to perform efficiently. The demand curve, we said, represents the amount consumers are willing to pay for an additional pound of peaches, given any level of output. That amount reflects the benefit of the marginal pound as perceived by consumers. The supply curve represents the amount suppliers require if they are to produce an additional pound of peaches. That amount corresponds to the opportunity cost to producers of supplying the marginal pound. As long as the demand curve is higher than the supply curve, trade at a price between the two curves can potentially benefit both parties. Accordingly, opportunities for mutually beneficial trades are exhausted (and efficiency is achieved) only if production is carried out to the point of intersection between the supply and demand curves, but not beyond that point.

In this chapter we have shown that the supply curve in a perfectly competitive market is the summation of the marginal cost curves of the individual firms. At any given market price, producers will supply the quantity that makes marginal cost equal to marginal revenue, which in turn is equal to the market price. Thus, the price-quantity combination at which transactions take place in a competitive market will be some point on the supply curve.

FIGURE 8.11 EFFICIENT OUTPUT UNDER PERFECT COMPETITION

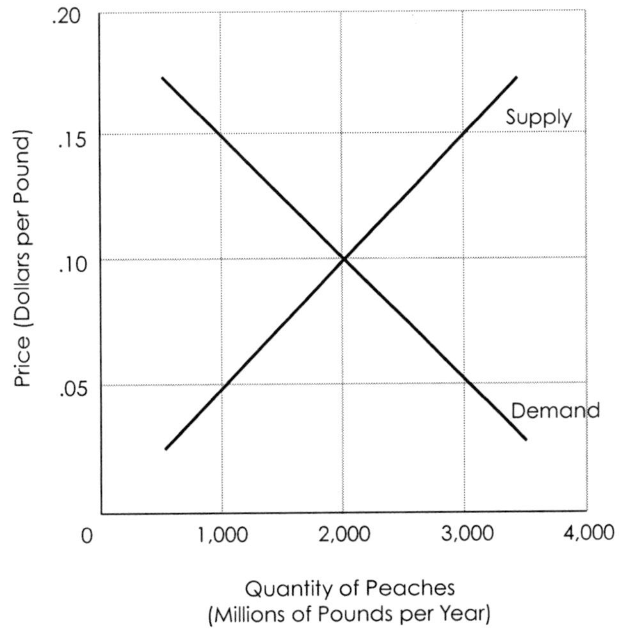

This figure shows supply and demand curves for a perfectly competitive market for peaches. Under perfect competition, each firm's efforts to keep marginal cost equal to marginal revenue ensure that the industry will produce at some point on the supply curve. Equilibrium for the market as a whole can occur only at the point where the supply and demand curves intersect. That represents an efficient resolution to the question, What should be produced?

For the market to end up at the right point on the supply curve, the market price must correspond to the intersection of the supply curve with the demand curve. To see why this will happen in a competitive market, we can put Chapter 2's analysis of market equilibrium together with this chapter's conclusions regarding perfect competition. From Chapter 2, we know that a price that is higher than the intersection of the supply and demand curves results in a surplus. Unplanned accumulation of inventory causes the price to fall. As the price falls, firms move down along the supply curve so as to keep marginal cost equal to marginal revenue. Similarly, a price that is lower than the intersection of the supply and demand curves results in a shortage. Depletion of inventories causes the market price to rise. Firms move up along the supply curve to keep marginal cost and marginal revenue equal. Thus, in a perfectly competitive market the equilibrium point will correspond to the intersection of the supply and demand curves. That is the efficient outcome.

Generalizing from these conclusions, we can see that in an economy in which all markets were perfectly competitive and in which there were no externalities the efficient quantity of every good would be produced. That would represent an efficient solution to the overall question of what should be produced—how many peaches, apples, tomatoes, and so on. Beginning from a situation in which the competitive markets for all products were in equilibrium, it would not be possible to substitute any one good for another (say, by producing more peaches at the expense of using fewer resources to produce apples) in a way that would make any person better off without making at least one other person worse off.

How to Produce

The preceding conclusion about what should be produced holds in both short- and long-run equilibrium. In addition, in the long run only, perfectly competitive markets ensure that each good is produced at the lowest possible cost—a key aspect of how goods should be produced.

To understand why goods are produced at the lowest cost in a situation of long-run competitive equilibrium, review Figures 8.8 and 8.9. In those figures the point of long-run equilibrium is shown to occur at the point where the typical firm operates at the minimum point of both the short-run average total cost curve and the long-run average cost curve.

Starting from such a point, a decrease in demand causes the market price to fall. In response, each firm reduces its output to the point where short-run marginal cost equals the new price. Although short-run marginal cost is lower at that output, short-run average total cost is higher because the firm moves up and to the left along the average total cost curve as output falls. Thus, at this point in the adjustment to falling demand, the given level of output is not being produced at the lowest possible cost. That is inefficient.

However, the inefficient situation does not last. Because short-run average total cost exceeds the market price, the firms suffer an economic loss, and some of them will leave the industry. Assuming no further change in demand, as the number of firms in the industry decreases, each firm is able to increase its output and move back toward its point of least-cost production. Similar reasoning applies to the expansion of industry output in response to an increase in demand.

Under perfect competition, firms are led not only to produce at the lowest possible short-run average total cost, given the size of their plants, but also to select the correct plant size to minimize average cost in the long run. To see why, suppose that one firm had a plant that was not the optimal size. As we saw in the last chapter, the short-run average total cost curve for such a firm would be tangent to its long-run average cost curve at a point above and to the right of the point of long-run minimum cost (if the plant were too large) or above it and to the left (if the plant were too small). The firm with the wrong size plant would thus be at a cost disadvantage relative to its competitors. As competition drove the market price toward a level equal to minimum long-run average cost, the firm would either adjust the size of its plant to the cost-minimizing level or leave the industry because of economic losses.

Other Aspects of Market Performance

The tendency of perfectly competitive markets to produce the efficient quantity of each good and to produce those quantities at the lowest cost are important strengths of this market structure. In a future chapter we will extend the analysis of perfect competition to factor markets. In doing so, we will see that perfectly competitive markets perform efficiently with regard to the questions of *who* and *for whom* as well as those of *what* and *how*. In these respects, long-run equilibrium in perfectly competitive markets sets a standard against which the performance of other market structures can be judged.

Nevertheless, it would be claiming far too much to say that perfect competition is the ultimate in market performance under all conditions. It would be premature to condemn every respect in which real-world markets depart from the structural characteristics of perfect competition. Before we write off all markets that are not made up exclusively of small firms, all markets in which products are not homogeneous, all markets in which newly entering firms encounter entry barriers or incur sunk costs, or all markets in which some participants know things that others do not, many questions must be asked. Among them are the following:

- Are there conditions in which other market structures equal or at least approximate the efficiency of perfect competition?
- How do alternative market structures perform when attention is focused on innovation and entrepreneurship rather than on equilibrium under conditions where technology and product characteristics are assumed to be unchanging?
- When markets fail to perform efficiently, what public-policy options are available? How should the dangers of government failure be weighed against the dangers of market failure?

Only when these additional aspects of the problem have been explored will we be in a position to make a balanced judgment of market performance under various market structures.

Think of examples of businesses which fit this model and think of the prices they charge. The fast food industry fits this model. The prices of the happy meals don't vary much from Wendy's, Burger Kin,g or McDonald's. They are not exact, but there isn't much difference between the Big Mac or the Whooper. There is relative ease of entry into this business. (You and I could open a hot dog cart similar to the one in front of Lowe's or Home Depot.) Individual restaurants really don't have pricing power in that if one raised the price of their meal combination, shortly the volume would decline dramatically. Also the retail gasoline industry would fit this model. (Not the refining industry.)

SUMMARY

1. **What characteristics define the structure of a market?** A *market structure* is defined in terms of the number and size of firms in the market, the nature of the product, ease of entry and exit, and availability of information. A *perfectly competitive market* has the following traits: (1) There are many buyers and sellers, each of which is small compared with the market as a whole; (2) the product is homogeneous; (3) it is easy to enter or leave the market; and (4) all buyers and sellers have equal access to information. Other market structures to be studied in this course include *monopoly, oligopoly,* and *monopolistic competition.*

2. **What determines the profit-maximizing output level in the short run for a perfectly competitive firm?** In the short run the relationship between marginal cost and *marginal revenue* (price) determines the profit-maximizing output level for a perfectly competitive firm. The firm should expand output up to, but not beyond, the point at which marginal cost rises to the level of marginal revenue, provided that marginal revenue is at least equal to average variable cost at that point.

3. **Under what conditions will a firm continue to operate even if it sustains a loss?** If marginal revenue is below average total cost at the point at which marginal cost and marginal revenue are equal, the firm cannot earn a profit. It will minimize loss in the short run by staying open if marginal revenue is above average variable cost. If marginal revenue is below average variable cost at the same point, the firm will minimize loss by shutting down.

4. **How is a firm's short-run supply curve related to its cost curves?** The short-run supply curve for a perfectly competitive firm is the upward-sloping part of the marginal cost curve lying above its intersection with the average variable cost curve.

5. **What are the conditions for long-run equilibrium in a perfectly competitive industry?** Long-run equilibrium in a perfectly competitive industry requires (1) that price be equal to short-run marginal cost so that each firm is content with the level of output it is producing; (2) that short-run average total cost be equal to long-run average cost so that firms are satisfied with the size of their plants, given their output rate; and (3) that price be equal to long-run average cost so that there is no incentive for new firms to enter the industry or for existing firms to leave it.

6. **What determines the shape of the long-run supply curve for a perfectly competitive industry?** A perfectly competitive industry adjusts to long-run changes in demand through exit of firms (in the case of a drop in market demand) or entry of new firms (in the case of a rise in market demand). If input prices do not change as the industry's output changes, the industry's long-run supply curve will be perfectly elastic. If input prices rise, the long-run supply curve will have a positive slope; if they fall, it will have a negative slope.

7. **How efficiently do markets perform under perfect competition?** Under conditions of equilibrium, a perfectly competitive market produces a quantity of output that corresponds to the intersection of the market's supply and demand curves. In an economy in which all markets are in perfectly competitive equilibrium and there are no externalities, the question of what to produce is thus resolved efficiently. Also, in a situation of long-run equilibrium the output of a perfectly competitive market is produced at the lowest possible cost. This means that the question of how to produce is also resolved efficiently.

KEY TERMS

Market structure
Perfect competition
Oligopoly
Monopolistic competition
Price taker
Marginal revenue

PROBLEMS AND TOPICS FOR DISCUSSION

1. **Market structures.** Give examples (other than those presented in the text) of industries that fit, or approximate, the market structures of perfect competition, monopoly, oligopoly, and monopolistic competition.

2. **Buyers as price takers.** The concept of price taking can apply to buyers as well as to sellers. A price-taking buyer cannot influence prices by changing the amount purchased. Are you a price taker for the goods you buy? Can you give an example of a firm that might not be a price taker in the market in which it buys one or more of its inputs?

3. **Changes in fixed cost and the supply curve.** Fieldcom buys some automated equipment to speed up production of its PDAs. The equipment adds $500 per day to the firm's fixed costs, but it saves $50 per unit in variable costs. Rework the graph in Figure 8.5 to show how the new equipment affects Fieldcom's supply curve. (You may want to rework part (a) of Figure 8.2 as a basis for the new supply curve.) What is the minimum price the firm must now charge to continue operating in the short run? What is the lowest price at which it can break even?

4. **Long- and short-run elasticity of supply.** In Chapter 4 it was asserted that, other things being equal, the elasticity of supply of a good tends to be greater the more time firms have to adjust to new market conditions. Using the theory of perfect competition as presented in this chapter, explain the basis for that assertion.

5. **Long-run supply with falling input prices.** Figure 8.10 shows the long-run adjustment of a competitive industry to an increase in demand in the case in which input prices rise as industry output increases. Assume instead that input prices fall as output rises. Draw a new set of diagrams to show how a typical firm and the industry as a whole would respond to an increase in demand.

CASE FOR DISCUSSION

Independent Truckers as a Perfectly Competitive Industry

The next time you are out on the highway, take a look at the trucks that are passing you. You will see many that belong to large firms, such as Yellow Freight, that haul large numbers of small shipments all over the country on regular schedules. You will also see trucks that bear the names of companies such as Sears or Sun Oil, for which transportation is a sideline.

If you look closely, though, you will see that about one truck in four looks a little different. The tractors, many of which are brightly painted and highly chromed, often have sleepers attached to them. The trailers, often refrigerated, are likely to be filled with farm produce moving to market. These are the trucks of independent owner-operators, who move much of the nation's output of farm goods and some manufactured goods.

Each firm in this market consists of a person who owns and drives just one truck. There are many such firms—as many as 35,000, by some estimates.

From the shipper's point of view, one refrigerated truck is about as good as another as long as it is headed in the right direction. And most independent truckers will go wherever their loads take them.

Entry into the market is easy. Some people go into business with a used truck and as little as $5,000. Most operators buy their trucks on credit. Exit is also easy—too easy, some say. Many independent truckers go broke every year, and the number of firms rises and falls with the state of the economy.

People who run the giant trucking companies that haul manufactured goods often look down their noses at the independent truckers with their loads of apples and potatoes. They call them gypsies or worse. But this system succeeds in putting fresh produce on dinner tables in every town every day.

QUESTIONS

1. In what ways does the independent trucking industry approximate the requirements of perfect competition? Are there any ways in which it does not meet those requirements?
2. On the average, the firms in a perfectly competitive industry earn no pure economic profits. However, average conditions do not always apply. What would you expect to happen to the profits of independent truckers when the economy enters a recession? When it enters a period of prosperity? What do you think would happen to the number of firms in the industry at such times?
3. Diesel fuel is a major input for independent truckers. What would you expect to happen to the profits of independent truckers and the number of firms in the industry as the price of fuel rises and falls? Outline the sequence of events in each case. (Drawing a graph may help.)

END NOTES

1. The description of Fieldcom in Chapter 7 implied that the firm's PDAs had special qualities of "ruggedization" that set them apart from other computers. This would violate the assumption of product homogeneity. For the purposes of this chapter, we will imagine that the idea of "ruggedized" PDAs did not work out, but that the Martins instead have discovered that they can survive by making "generic" PDAs that function just like others on the market.
2. This graph shows why we emphasize that profit maximization occurs where the *rising* section of the marginal cost curve intersects the marginal revenue curve. There is sometimes also an intersection of the *falling* section of the marginal cost curve with the marginal revenue curve, as is the case at about 3 units of output in Figure 8.3. That intersection is *not* a point of profit maximization, but rather, one of loss maximization.
3. The discussion of exit from a perfectly competitive market seems to pose a paradox: If all firms are *exactly* alike, why don't they all stay in the market as long as conditions are favorable, and then all leave the market at the same instant when conditions become unfavorable? However, real-world markets only approximate the conditions of perfect competition. In such markets, small differences in firms' circumstances of cost or demand, or in the temperaments of their owners, will cause some to leave the market before others do.

CHAPTER 9

The Price Charged and Quantity Supplied by Monopoly

After reading this chapter, you will understand:

1. The circumstances in which monopoly can exist
2. How the profit-maximizing price and output for a monopoly are determined
3. How long-run equilibrium is achieved under monopoly
4. What kinds of pricing strategies are used by monopolies and other price-searching firms
5. How monopoly affects market performance

Before reading this chapter, make sure you know the meaning of:

1. Market performance and market failure
2. Rent seeking
3. Consumer and producer surplus
4. Market structure

As defined earlier in the text, a monopoly is a market structure in which a single firm is the sole supplier of a product that has no close substitute. There are few firms that meet this requirement, if it is taken literally. Is Microsoft a monopolist in the market for operating systems? No, it has a large market share, but Mac and Linux users would deny a lack of substitutes. Does the U.S. Postal Service have a monopoly on delivery of mail? Yes, if narrowly defined as first-class postal mail, but Federal Express, e-mail, and fax are substitutes. Does your local electric company have a monopoly? Probably yes, if you mean delivery of electric power by wire, but industrial users of co-generation equipment and green consumers with off-the-grid systems represent substitutes. Is Major League Baseball a monopoly, or for that matter, all of the major sports leagues? Still, we can learn much from studying the market structure that we call monopoly, even if we have a hard time finding perfect real-world examples. One thing we will learn in this chapter is a version of the profit maximization models that applies to all firms that are not price takers, whether pure monopolists or not. Another thing we will learn is why pure monopoly is rare and, where it exists, why it does not last forever.

MONOPOLY

Like the model of perfect competition presented in the preceding chapter, the model of monopoly aims to explain the operation of markets in terms of the firm's objectives and constraints. For monopoly, as for perfect competition, standard neoclassical models assume that profit maximization is the firm's objective. The differences in market outcomes between the two cases, then, stem from differences in the constraints that are assumed to define the set of opportunities open to the firm.

Constraints Faced by Monopoly

The monopolist's ability to earn a profit, like that of other firms, is constrained in part by its production costs. The model presented here is based on the theory of cost presented in an earlier chapter. The special restrictions imposed in perfect competition (a minimum efficient scale that is small relative to the size of the market and no sunk costs) do not apply to monopoly.

The other principal constraint on the monopolist's profit-making opportunities is the demand for its product. Because a monopolist is by definition the only firm in its market, the demand curve faced by the firm is the same as the market demand curve for the product. The monopolist's demand curve, then, is negatively sloped—the quantity of output that can be sold increases as the price decreases. Consider the Bull Fight Matador Red Cape Company of Taneytown. This was the ONLY American bull fight accessory company in the United States. It had a monopoly on all bullfighting items in the United States. But because the demand for authentic matador capes made in the USA was so small, the monopoly had to shut down because the firm was unable to cover its costs.

The monopolist is assumed to know, at least roughly, the characteristics of the demand curve for its product, whether from econometric studies, trial and error, or simple intuition. Because both price and quantity vary along the negatively sloped demand curve, the monopolist, unlike a perfectly competitive firm, is not a price taker. Instead, its demand curve represents a menu of possible price-quantity combinations, from which it selects the combination that will yield the maximum profit. Because it searches for the most profitable price in a range of possible prices, a monopolist can be called a **price searcher**, or a *price maker.* (Unlike the perfectly competitive firm which is a *price taker.*)

Price searcher

Any firm that faces a negatively sloped demand curve for its product.

The model of monopoly presented in this section incorporates one additional constraint: The monopolist is assumed to offer its output at a single price that is uniform for all customers and allow all buyers to purchase as much or as little as they want at that price. A monopoly that follows this pricing policy can be termed a **simple monopoly**. Other pricing strategies will be discussed later in the chapter.

Simple monopoly

A monopoly that offers its output at a single price that is uniform for all customers and allows all buyers to purchase as much or as little as they want at that price.

Output, Price, and Marginal Revenue Under Simple Monopoly

We first noted the relationship between price and total revenue along the demand curve earlier in this book, when the concept of elasticity was introduced. There we showed that when demand is *elastic* a drop in price causes total revenue to rise. (The reason is that in percentage terms the quantity sold rises by more than the price falls; thus, the product of price times quantity, which equals revenue, increases.) In contrast, when demand is *inelastic* revenue falls when the price drops. (This occurs because with inelastic demand the percentage increase in quantity is less than the percentage decrease in price.) With a straight-line demand curve, such as the one in part (b) of Figure 9.1, the upper half is elastic and the lower half inelastic. That accounts for the shape of the "revenue hill" in part (c).

$$\frac{\Delta TR}{\Delta Q}$$

Earlier we defined *marginal revenue* as the change in total revenue that results from a one-unit increase in a firm's output. Column 4 in part (a) of Figure 9.1 presents data on marginal revenue for the firm in this example. The figures in the column are the differences between the entries in column 3. Part (b) of the exhibit shows the firm's marginal revenue curve. The marginal revenue curve is above the horizontal axis when total revenue is increasing (elastic demand) and below it when total revenue is decreasing (inelastic demand). It intersects the horizontal axis at the point of maximum total revenue.

An easy rule can be used to sketch the marginal revenue curve corresponding to any straight-line demand curve: *The marginal revenue curve for a straight-line demand curve always cuts the horizontal distance from the demand curve to the vertical axis exactly in half.* Following this rule, the point where the marginal revenue curve intersects the horizontal axis can be placed halfway between the origin and the horizontal intercept of the demand curve (that is, the point where the demand curve intersects the horizontal axis). (In Figure 9.1 the marginal revenue curve cuts the horizontal axis at 17.5, half of 35.) The vertical intercept of the marginal revenue curve is the same as that of the straight-line demand curve. (The vertical intercept is at $10 in Figure 9.1.) (This rule does not apply to curved demand curves, but the examples in this book are kept simple.)

The marginal revenue curve is always below the demand curve. For a simple monopolist, the marginal revenue that the firm gets from the sale of one additional unit is *less* than the price at which the unit is sold, not equal to the price as in a perfectly

FIGURE 9.1 DEMAND, TOTAL REVENUE, AND MARGINAL REVENUE UNDER SIMPLE MONOPOLY

(a)

Quantity of Output (1)	Price (2)	Total Revenue (3)	Marginal Revenue (4)
1	$10.00	$10.00	
2	9.70	19.40	$9.40
3	9.40	28.20	8.80
4	9.10	36.40	8.20
16	5.50	88.00	
17	5.20	88.40	.40
18	4.90	88.20	–.20
33	.40	13.20	
34	.10	3.40	–9.80
35	.00	.00	–3.40

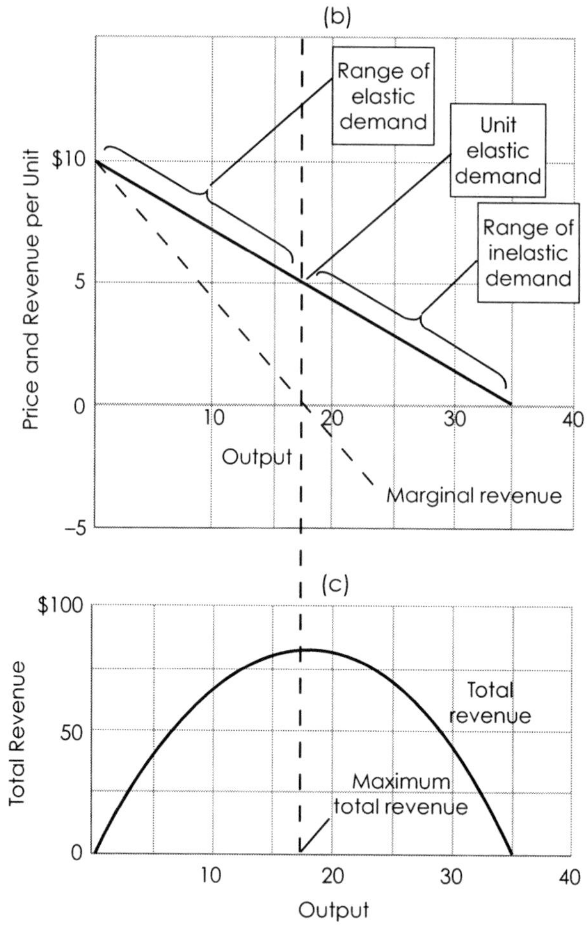

This figure shows how demand, total revenue, and marginal revenue are related under simple monopoly. Total revenue is found by multiplying price by output at each point on the demand curve. Marginal revenue is the increase in total revenue that results from a one-unit increase in output. When demand is elastic, marginal revenue is more than zero and total revenue is increasing. When demand is inelastic, marginal revenue is less than zero and total revenue is decreasing. Marginal revenue is less than price at all levels of output.

competitive firm. The gap between price and marginal revenue stems from the fact that the firm sells all units supplied in a given period at the same price. This means that it must cut the price on all units sold per period, not just on the last one, in order to increase the quantity sold. For example, if our monopolist wants to increase sales from 10 units per period to 11 units per period, it must cut the price on all 11 units from $7.30 to $7. Although the firm gains $7 in revenue from the sale of the eleventh unit, its total revenue increases by only $4, from $73 to $77. The added revenue from the eleventh unit is partly offset by a $3 reduction ($.30 per unit) in total revenue from the other 10 units.

The fact that the marginal revenue curve for a monopolist lies below its demand curve illustrates the marginal-average rule discussed in the preceding chapter. The average revenue realized by the simple monopolist, as represented by the height of the demand curve for any given level of output, must be falling if marginal revenue is less than average revenue.

Finding the Point of Maximum Profit

Figure 9.2 adds the monopolist's cost curves to its demand and marginal revenue curves. The data presented there can be used to identify the price-quantity combination that will yield the maximum profit. As in the preceding chapter, this can be done either by comparing total cost with total revenue or by taking a marginal approach.

A monopolist maximizes profits by producing the quantity of output for which marginal cost equals marginal revenue. The price it charges for the product is determined by the height of the demand curve (rather than the height of the marginal revenue curve) at the profit-maximizing output. Note that maximizing profit is not the same as maximizing revenue. Beyond 13 units of output (the profit-maximizing level in this case), total revenue continues to rise for a while, but profit falls because total cost rises even more rapidly.

Maximize Profit Point
At the quantity where
MC = MR

Total cost for the firm at various output levels is given in column 6 of part (c) of Figure 9.2. Subtracting total cost from total revenue (column 3) gives total profit (column 7). A glance at column 7 shows that the profit-maximizing output level is 13 units. The total revenue–total cost approach to profit maximization is shown graphically in part (a) of the exhibit. Total profit equals the vertical gap between the total cost and total revenue curves. It reaches a maximum at about 13 units of output, where the two curves are farthest apart. (As in the preceding chapter, the graphs, unlike the tables, are continuous, so maximums and minimums need not occur exactly at whole-number quantities of output.) Note that maximizing profit is not the same as maximizing revenue. Between 13 and 17 units of output, total revenue continues to rise. But because total cost rises even more rapidly, profit falls.

The marginal approach to profit maximization is illustrated by the data in columns 4 and 5 in part (c) of Figure 9.2. Marginal revenue is the amount by which total revenue increases when output is increased by one unit; marginal cost is the amount by which total cost increases. It follows that as long as marginal revenue exceeds marginal cost, adding one more unit of output adds more to total revenue than to total cost and hence adds to total profit. Beyond 13 units of output, marginal

FIGURE 9.2 PROFIT MAXIMIZATION FOR A MONOPOLIST

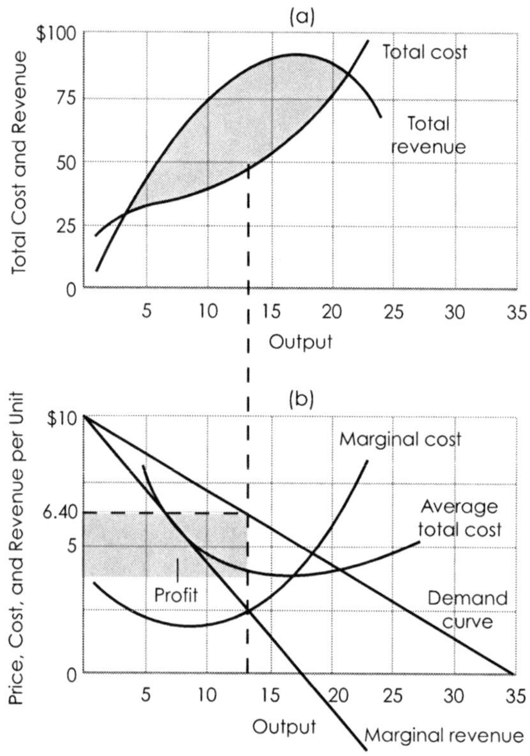

(c)

Quantity of Output (1)	Price (2)	Total Revenue (3)	Marginal Revenue (4)	Marginal Cost (5)	Total Cost (6)	Total Profit (7)
1	$10.00	$10.00			$23.80	–$13.80
2	9.70	19.40	$9.40	$3.40	27.20	–7.80
3	9.40	28.20	8.80	3.05	30.25	2.05
4	9.10	36.40	8.20	2.75	33.00	3.40
5	8.80	44.00	7.60	2.50	35.50	8.50
6	8.50	51.00	7.00	2.30	37.80	13.20
7	8.20	57.40	6.40	2.15	39.95	17.45
8	7.90	63.20	5.80	2.05	42.00	21.20
9	7.60	68.40	5.20	2.00	44.00	24.40
10	7.30	73.00	4.60	2.05	46.05	26.95
11	7.00	77.00	4.00	2.15	48.20	28.80
12	6.70	80.40	3.40	2.30	50.50	29.90
13	**6.40**	**83.20**	**2.80**	**2.50**	**53.00**	**30.20**
14	6.10	85.40	**2.20**	**2.75**	55.75	29.65
15	5.80	87.00	1.60	3.05	58.80	28.20
16	5.50	88.00	1.00	3.40	62.20	25.80
17	5.20	88.40	.40	3.80	66.00	22.40

MC = MR A monopolist maximizes profits by producing the quantity of output for which marginal cost equals marginal revenue. The price it charges for the product is determined by the height of the demand curve (rather than the height of the marginal revenue curve) at the profit-maximizing output. Beyond 13 units of output (the profit-maximizing level in this case), total revenue continues to rise for a while, but profit falls because total cost rises even more rapidly.

revenue falls below marginal cost; therefore, any further expansion of output reduces total profit. The logic here is exactly the same as for a perfectly competitive firm, except that now marginal revenue is variable rather than constant.

Part (b) of Figure 9.2 compares marginal revenue and marginal cost in graphical terms. The profit-maximizing output is found at the point where the positively sloped section of the marginal cost curve intersects the marginal revenue curve; that is, at about 13 units of output. Profit per unit at that output is equal to the vertical gap between the demand curve (which shows the price at which the product is sold) and the average total cost curve. Profit per unit times quantity of output equals total profit, as shown by the shaded rectangle.

The intersection of the marginal cost and marginal revenue curves in Figure 9.2 gives the profit-maximizing *output* for the firm, but the profit-maximizing *price* is given by the height of the demand curve for that level of output. For a monopolist, that price is always above marginal cost when profit is being maximized. For the firm in our example, marginal cost at 13 units of output is $2.50 per unit, but according to the demand curve consumers are willing to buy 13 units at a price as high as $6.40 per unit. Therefore, $6.40, not $2.50, is what the monopolist will charge for the 13 units of output in order to earn the maximum profit.

Profit Maximization or Loss Minimization?

If market conditions are unfavorable, a monopolist, like a perfectly competitive firm, may be unable to earn a profit in the short run. (Think of a firm that has a monopoly on the sale of peanuts at the local baseball stadium; such a firm might well suffer losses during a season when the home team is playing badly and attendance is low.) In such a case, it will aim to minimize losses. Whether a profit is possible depends on the position of the demand curve relative to the firm's average total cost curve.

The possibility of a loss is shown in Figure 9.3. The demand curve lies below the average total cost curve at all points. The monopolist might find itself in such a position during a recession, when a drop in consumer income temporarily shifts the demand curve to the left. Following the usual rule, the profit-maximizing (or loss-minimizing) level of output is found at the point where the marginal cost and marginal revenue curves intersect, that is, at about 10 units. According to the demand curve, that much output cannot be sold for more than $4 per unit, even though average total cost at 10 units of output is $4.60. At a price of $4 per unit, then, the firm will lose $.60 on each unit sold. The total loss is shown by the shaded rectangle.

Although the firm suffers a loss at 10 units of output, no other output level will yield a smaller loss. In Figure 9.3, the price of $4 per unit is more than enough to cover average variable costs. A monopolist, like a perfect competitor, is better off staying in business in the short run, even at a loss, as long as the price at which it can sell its output is greater than the average variable cost. But if the demand curve shifts so

FIGURE 9.3 A MONOPOLIST SUFFERING A SHORT-RUN LOSS

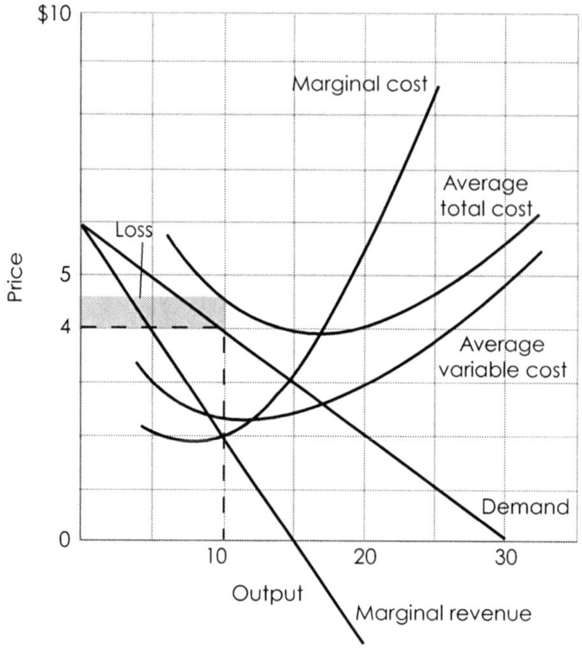

Sometimes demand may not be high enough to allow a monopolist to earn a profit. In this graph, for example, the demand curve lies below the average total cost curve at all points. The best the monopolist can do in the short run is cut losses by producing at the point at which marginal cost equals marginal revenue. If the demand curve were to shift downward even further, preventing the firm from obtaining a price that would cover average variable cost, the short-run loss-minimizing strategy would be to shut down.

far to the left that it falls below the average variable cost curve at all points, the firm will minimize its short-run losses by shutting down.

We see, then, that being a monopolist does not guarantee that a firm will be able to earn a profit. It can do so only if demand conditions allow the product to be sold at a price that exceeds the cost of producing it. (Do you remember the Bull Fight Matador Red Cape Company of Taneytown?) The situation shown in Figure 9.3 was assumed to be only temporary, in which case the firm would ride it out, waiting for better times to return. Sometimes, however, a monopolist faces a permanent decline in demand. A privately owned, profit-maximizing monopolist will then leave the industry, freeing itself of its fixed costs by selling its assets, terminating its long-term leases, and so on. *Applying Economic Ideas 9.1* illustrates this possibility with the case of urban mass transit systems, which, in many cities, formerly operated as privately owned closed monopolies. When the demand for mass transit services fell, the systems could no longer operate at a profit and might have disappeared entirely but for public subsidies.

APPLYING ECONOMIC IDEAS 9.1

SUBSIDIZED MONOPOLY: THE CASE OF MASS TRANSIT (SOCIALLY OPTIMAL PRICING)

To many people, monopoly is synonymous with vast profits. Not all monopolies are profitable however. A case in point is the mass transit systems of most large U.S. cities.

Until the 1960s, the majority of urban bus lines in the United States were privately owned. Often there was more than one transit firm in a city—Chicago had more than thirty at one point. However, city governments granted each firm a closed monopoly over the routes it operated, so that people were often unable to choose among transit systems to get to any given destination.

In 1950 this largely private transit system carried some 17 billion passengers. Gradually, however, more and more commuters and shoppers begin to travel by car. By 1970 ridership on urban mass transit systems had fallen to just 7 billion. Along the way, the business became unprofitable for most private firms, despite their monopoly status. In 1963, for the first time, urban mass transit as a whole experienced an operating loss. Since that date it has never regained profitability.

City governments could simply have let the private transit systems go out of business. In some cases, especially trolley systems, they did so. However, all subway and most urban bus systems were gradually transferred to city ownership where they remain to this day.

These government-owned monopoly transit systems like their private predecessors, must decide how to price their product. One possible rule would be to equate marginal cost and marginal revenue in order to minimize losses and keep subsidies for the system to a minimum. However, because of several considerations, many cities offer fares lower than what would be dictated by the rule of equating marginal cost and marginal revenue. Consequently, they must offer larger subsidies than would result from a simple loss-minimization strategy.

One such consideration is efficiency. It could be argued that for commuters to choose efficiently between mass transit and driving their own cars, the transit fare should be equal to the marginal cost of providing an additional ride on the public transit system A subsidy-minimizing price would be higher than marginal cost and, thus, higher than the efficient level.

Second, it can be argued that a further adjustment of the fare should be made to allow for traffic congestion, a form of negative externality that in itself results in inefficient use of transportation resources. A low fare that causes people to choose mass transit rather than travel by car can be defended as a means of offsetting the adverse effects of traffic congestion. Have you ever driven the Johns Falls or Rt 695 at 7:15 on a regular week day morning. Would it not be in society's interest if there were 10% less cars on the road and more people in the near empty Metro or light rail cars?

Also, low transit fares are often defended as a means of benefiting low income households, which tend to be heavy users of public transportation. Without affordable public transportation as a means of getting to work, it is argued, some lower-income people would not be able to keep their jobs and instead would have to depend on the assistance of public welfare payments.

Finally, consider the BUS in Ocean City. In the early hours of an August Sunday morning, isn't in society's best interest to keep the 22 year old men out of their cars and not behind the wheel of their cars after several hours or enjoying the clubs and provide them with a method of getting back to their motels or apartments? Do you think the fare charged for a bus ride equals the cost of running the big bus up and down the street most of the night? (It doesn't.)

In practice, then, most mass transit systems do not set fares to minimize subsidies. To do so would require operating at a point at which marginal revenue is positive, indicating that the system is operating on the elastic part of its demand circle. However, fare increases on most systems result in higher revenues, showing that they are on the inelastic portion of the demand curve. As a rule, city governments leave transit fares low until taxpayers start complaining about the size of the necessary subsidies. Then they raise fares to the point at which the strength of the marginal complaint from transit riders balances that of the marginal complaint from taxpayers.

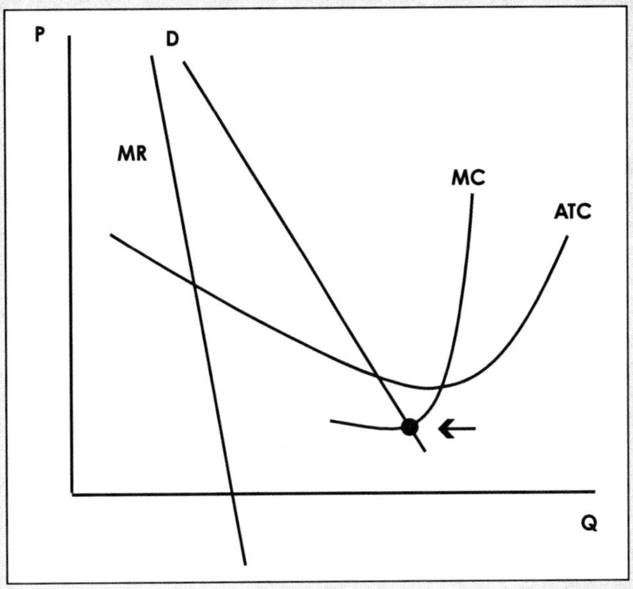

PROFIT MAXIMIZATION IN THE LONG RUN

In presenting the model of perfect competition, we distinguished between two time horizons. In the short run, each firm had a plant of fixed size, and the number of firms in the industry was also fixed. In the long run, each firm was free to adjust the size of its plant, and firms were free to enter or leave the industry. Each case gave rise to a clearly defined equilibrium. The simple model of monopoly presented in the preceding section is oriented toward the short run. The issues raised by consideration of the long run under monopoly conditions are more complex. Not all of them can be resolved in terms of simple equilibrium solutions. Nevertheless, some of the issues are worth considering.

Long-Run Equilibrium Without Threat of Entry

The simplest situation is that of a monopolist that faces no threat of entry into its market by competitors. For such a firm, a graph such as Figure 9.2 can represent long-run as well as short-run profit maximization. Only the interpretation of the curves changes. The curve that is labeled average total cost in Figure 9.2 would now be interpreted as the firm's long-run average cost curve, allowing for free adjustment of fixed inputs as in the long-run competitive case. The marginal cost curve would be the corresponding long-run marginal cost curve, and the demand curve would be the long-run demand curve. The long-run equilibrium would occur at the output where long-run marginal cost equals long-run marginal revenue, and the long-run equilibrium price would be given by the height of the long-run demand curve at that point. Beyond what has already been said about the short run, three things are worth noting about such a long-run equilibrium.

1. The firm must at least break even in the long-run equilibrium. The loss-minimizing situation shown in Figure 9.3 cannot be a long-run equilibrium because the firm would leave the market if it could not at least recover its long-run average cost.

2. Unlike the case of perfect competition, long-run equilibrium under monopoly need not occur at the minimum point on the firm's long-run total cost curve. It could occur at an output below minimum long-run average cost (as shown in Figure 9.2), or at an output greater than minimum long-run average cost (as would be the case if the demand curve in Figure 9.2 were to shift strongly to the right). Whatever its long-run equilibrium output, the monopolist will select the size of plant that is best suited to that level of output. In graphical terms, this would mean a short-run average total cost curve tangent to the long-run average cost curve at the equilibrium output.

3. The price that will maximize long-run profit for the firm will be lower than the price that will maximize short-run profit if, as is usually the case, demand

is more elastic in the long run than in the short run. Beginning from a point of long-run equilibrium, a monopolist could temporarily increase its profit by raising its price and cutting output to move up along its less elastic short-run demand curve. But, given that higher price, customers would make long-run adjustments in their consumption patterns, reducing the quantity demanded until they were back on the long-run demand curve at a correspondingly lower level of output. The monopolist's profit at the higher price would then be less than at the original long-run equilibrium price.

Open Monopoly, Entrepreneurship, and Limit Pricing

In the case just examined it is easy to identify an equilibrium point, but only because the case excludes an essential element of reality: entrepreneurship. It treats short- and long-run demand curves as given, whereas in practice any firm that earns a pure economic profit for any length of time is sure to attract the attention of entrepreneurs eager to get a piece of the action. They will have their own ideas about what is given and what is subject to change.

Consider long-run equilibrium for an open monopolist. Such a firm is currently the sole supplier of its product but is not protected by the decisive cost advantages of a **natural monopoly** or the legal barriers to entry of a closed monopoly. With little or no built-in protection from would-be rivals, what options does it have?

Natural monopoly

An industry in which long-run average cost is minimized when only one firm serves the market.

One option is to push the price all the way up to the short-run profit-maximizing level, enjoy pure economic profits while they last, and accept the fact that sooner or later other firms will enter the market and take away part or all of those profits. In many cases that is just what firms do. The consumer electronics industry provides many familiar examples. The first firm to reach the market with a DVD player, a flat-screen TV, or a telephone that takes and transmits pictures typically sets a high initial price. Soon other firms enter with products that closely imitate the original one. The market then becomes an oligopoly in which the first firm may still hold a significant market share, but at a much lower price level. With luck, by the time pure economic profits disappear entirely, the firm's research department will come up with a new product from which the firm can again reap temporary monopoly profits. Often the hope of even short-lived monopoly profits is a strong spur to innovation.

But there is a second option available to an open monopolist. Instead of setting the price at the short-run profit-maximizing level, it may set a somewhat lower price, one that gives it a moderate profit but at the same time makes the market a less attractive target for would-be competitors. Such a strategy is called **limit pricing** because it limits short-run profits in the hope of limiting entry.

Limit pricing

A strategy in which the dominant firm in a market charges less than the short-run profit-maximizing price in order to limit the likelihood of entry by new competitors.

Speaking in general terms, a limit pricing strategy tends to be more attractive if the monopolist enjoys any cost advantage, even a small one, over potential entrants. For example, a new entrant may need to incur sunk costs, say, to recruit a network of dealers or acquaint consumers with a new brand name. Or perhaps through "learning by doing" the first firm in the market has achieved lower production costs than another firm can achieve when it first enters the market. Given such a cost advantage, the first firm may be able to earn a pure economic profit at a price that is still low enough to deter other entrants.

There need not be an all-or-nothing choice between short-run profit maximization and limit pricing. A firm may set an intermediate price that merely slows entry without entirely preventing it. It may introduce its product at a high price and then "slide down the demand curve" as other firms enter. The variations are endless. As the firm's attention turns away from the marginal cost–marginal revenue calculus of the simple monopolist to strategic moves and countermoves against actual and potential rivals, the market structure that we have called **open monopoly** shades into oligopoly. And that is a subject for another chapter.

Open monopoly

A monopoly in which one firm is, at least for a time, the sole supplier of a product but has no special protection from competition.

Closed Monopoly and Rent Seeking

Let us turn now to the implications of entrepreneurship for a **closed monopoly**—one that is protected by a legal barrier, such as a government permit or a patent. If the market is truly closed to competition in any form, there is nothing to add beyond what was said earlier in the section on long-run equilibrium without threat of entry. However, few if any monopolies are closed that tightly. Instead, they face threats to their profits on two fronts: (1) the development of substitute products and (2) challenges to the legal barriers that close the market to competition.

Closed monopoly

A monopoly that is protected by legal restrictions on competition.

First consider substitute products. Although the market structure of monopoly assumes that the product has no "close" substitutes, closeness is clearly a matter of degree. There is no such thing as a product with no substitutes at all. Moreover, a monopolist must consider not only existing substitutes, but also the development of new ones. If one firm has a monopoly on a patented drug, rival researchers will strive to develop alternate therapies for the condition. If a railroad charges a monopoly price on a route that has no competing rail service, it will encourage competition from pipelines, barges, and trucks.

Over time, then, the higher the price set by the monopolist and the longer that price is maintained, the more rival entrepreneurs will attempt to supply varied and attractive substitutes. As they do so, the monopolist's demand curve will gradually be pushed to the left.

Meanwhile, the same or other rivals will be at work on another front. The closed monopolist's hold on the market may be protected by law, but lobbyists can persuade legislatures to change laws, and lawyers can find loopholes in them. If the closed monopoly is earning pure economic profits, lawyers and lobbyists become attractive investments for potential rivals. To combat them, the monopolist will have to invest in lawyers and lobbyists of its own.

The efforts of firms to break into or protect closed monopolies are examples of rent seeking. The "rents" being sought in this case are the pure economic profits that the monopolist earns over and above the opportunity costs of producing its product.

But rent seeking and defenses against rent seeking are costly. They require a firm to hire lawyers, lobbyists, and researchers, and divert the time of its managers from other tasks. These costs must be added to production costs when computing profit. In terms of our model, expenditures that arise from rent seeking and defenses against it push a firm's cost curves upward.

Rent seeking need not be limited to rivals that seek to enter the firm's market. The firm's own employees may get in on the act. Monopoly profits earned by a protected employer—say, a municipal transit company or a firm with a monopoly contract to collect a city's garbage—are an attractive target for unions. Unions do not always depend only on their own bargaining power; sometimes they may seek legislative intervention in labor disputes. Rent seeking by a monopolist's suppliers and even by its customers may also occur.

The closed monopolist thus is caught in a vise. Entrepreneurs developing substitute products push its demand curve to the left, and at the same time the need to defend itself against rent seekers pushes its costs upward. Even if no rivals enter the monopolist's market directly, it will gradually be forced toward the position shown in Figure 9.4, where it just breaks even. When it reaches a situation of zero economic profit, an equilibrium will finally be established in which the rate of introduction of substitutes and the level of rent-seeking expenditures stop increasing.

FIGURE 9.4 THE BREAKEVEN POSITION FOR A MONOPOLIST

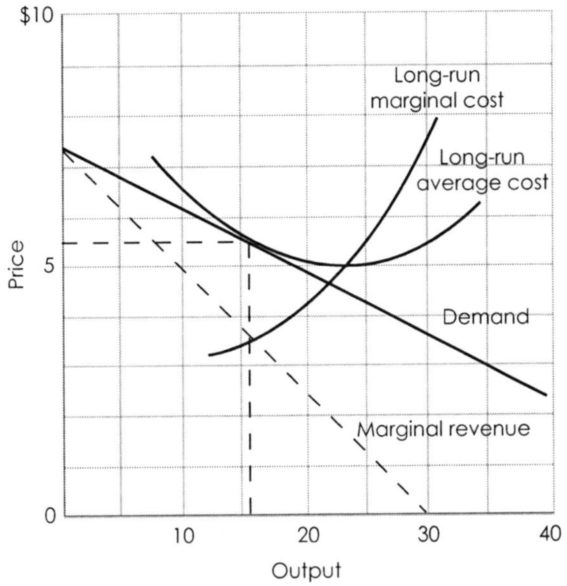

This exhibit shows a monopolist that is just breaking even. The firm earns enough revenue to cover all costs, including the opportunity cost of capital, but not enough to permit an economic profit. A closed monopoly could be driven to this position in the long run through erosion of demand as substitutes are developed or by the costs of defending its monopoly position against rent seekers.

As an example of a monopolist caught in such a squeeze, consider the U.S. Postal Service. For two centuries it has fought for and held on to its closed monopoly on delivery of first-class mail. Yet the postal service, far from being richly profitable, is lucky if it breaks even. A large part of the explanation is found in the vigorous expansion of substitutes (UPS, Federal Express, electronic transmission of documents via fax or Internet), and the highly successful rent-seeking activities of postal employee unions.

To summarize, the life of a monopolist is not a bed of roses. True, extraordinary short-run profit opportunities may arise, but a monopolist must not be overly aggressive in exploiting them. New substitute products, newly entering firms, and rent-seeking all pose threats. In real life, being a monopolist is a lot more work than finding the point where a couple of lines cross on a graph.

COMPLEX PRICING STRATEGIES

The model of simple monopoly assumes that all units sold in a given period must be sold at the same price, and all customers are allowed to buy as much or as little as they want at that price. Not all monopolists use this simple pricing strategy, however. Neither do oligopolies or firms in monopolistically competitive markets. In this section, we look at two more complex pricing strategies that go beyond that of simple monopoly.

Price Discrimination

The first complex pricing strategy we will consider is that of charging different prices to different buyers for the same product. When the prices charged to different buyers do not simply reflect differences in the costs of serving them, the firm is said to practice **price discrimination**. For example, a theater that charges adults $8 for a seat and children just $6 is practicing price discrimination; the cost of providing a seat to a child and to an adult is the same. However, a gas station that charges $.04 per gallon less for cash purchases than for credit card purchases is not practicing price discrimination. It is simply passing along the lower cost of cash transactions to its cash customers.

Price discrimination

The practice of charging different prices for various units of a single product when the price differences are not justified by differences in cost.

CONDITIONS FOR PRICE DISCRIMINATION Three conditions must be met for a price searcher to engage in price discrimination. First, it must be impossible or at least inconvenient for buyers to resell the product. For example, it is unlikely that your campus bookstore could get away with selling economics texts at list price to seniors and at a 25 percent discount to everyone else. If it tried to do so, some clever sophomore would soon go into business buying books for resale to seniors at a split-the-difference price. The bookstore's list-price sales would soon fall to zero. Second, the seller must be able to classify buyers into groups on the basis of the elasticity of their demand for the good. Those with highly inelastic demand can then be charged high prices and those with more elastic demand can be charged lower prices. If the firm could not tell whose demand was more and whose was less elastic, it would not know who should be asked to pay the higher price. Finally, there must be some market power. That means though a firm isn't a perfect monopoly, there must be some barriers to entry and only a very limited number of firms in the market.

Although it is convenient to discuss price discrimination in conjunction with monopoly, the practice may appear in other market structures, as well. Consider, for example, price discrimination by colleges and universities, which are certainly not monopolies. First, the school's business office sets tuition and fees at a level that it thinks is about as high as anyone would be willing to pay. Next, the admissions office gives its approval to a certain number of qualified applicants. Finally, the financial aid office gives selective price rebates, called scholarships, to students who would be unwilling or unable to attend if they were charged the full tuition. A student I know applied to and was accepted to Frostburg University. She didn't respond right away to the acceptance letter since Frostburg was not her first choice. As the deadline approached and the University still had not heard from this candidate, they offered her a *scholarship* which amounted to a 5% reduction in tuition.. It turned out that the University had not yet filled its dorms or class rooms for the following Fall term and realized it would be better to receive discounted tuition payment than nothing at all. Since the marginal cost of this student attending the university was close to zero, receiving 95% of tuition is better than nothing This award was no scholarship at all, but rather a price reduction, no different than a car dealer reducing a price to close a sale to an unsure customer.

A college or university is in an ideal position to practice price discrimination. For one thing, the product cannot be resold. If you are admitted to both Harvard and Dartmouth, and choose to attend Harvard, you cannot sell your Dartmouth admission to someone who did not get into either place. Also, the school insists that applicants supply a great deal of information on families' willingness and ability to pay. Because the demand for a good tends to be less elastic the smaller the share of income a family spends on it, rich families are likely to have less elastic demand for college education than poor families. Finally, an applicant's high-school grades and test scores also help in estimating his or her elasticity of demand. A student with relatively high grades probably has many alternatives and, hence, relatively elastic demand. A student with lower grades may be lucky to get into just one school. For this reason, it makes sense to charge lower prices (that is, give larger scholarships) to students with good grades.

In this case, as in others where markets can be divided into separate submarkets with distinct demand curves, the firm sets marginal cost equal to marginal revenue in each market. The result is a higher equilibrium price for customers whose demand is less elastic. Consider a student whose parent attended the same school. It is likely she would be more inelastic in her desire to attend the alma mater of her mother than another school.

Fairness and Price Discrimination

Price discrimination is often viewed as unfair, especially by those who pay the higher prices. Many people, for example, are annoyed if they learn that the person sitting next to them on an airplane paid less than they did for a ticket on the same flight. In fact, many people think it is unfair for a firm to charge different prices to different customers even when the difference is justified by considerations of cost and does not count as price discrimination in the economic sense. An example is the practice of charging young men more than young women for automobile insurance. Insurance companies insist that the different rates are justified by the fact that men are involved in more accidents, but this does not end the perception that the difference in rates is unfair.

Economists, on the other hand, tend to look more kindly on price discrimination. They not only see it as a practice that promotes efficiency, but, properly understood, as one that often promotes fairness, as well. The example of college scholarships illustrates some of the reasons that price discrimination can be beneficial. This form of price discrimination makes it possible for some students to attend colleges that they otherwise could not afford, while shifting part of the cost, in the form of high tuition, to the students who can most afford to pay. Similarly, price discrimination makes it easier for parents to take young children to the movies. It makes it possible for students who are willing to buy tickets in advance and stay at their destinations over a Saturday night to fill airline seats that business travelers would leave empty.

These examples emphasize that price discrimination may, in some circumstances, be beneficial in terms of fairness. Later in the chapter we will see that it can also allow markets to perform more efficiently. For these reasons, although price discrimination will always have its critics, economists often rise to its defense.

Two-part pricing

A pricing strategy in which people must pay for the right to become a buyer before choosing how much to buy at a given price.

Access fee

The part of a two-part pricing strategy paid for the right to become a customer.

User charge

The per-unit price offered in a two-part pricing strategy to qualified customers who have paid the access charge.

TWO-PART PRICING

Price discrimination is more complex than the pricing strategy used by simple monopoly in that it charges different prices to different customers. A different type of more complex pricing strategy departs from the rule that once a price is set, everyone must be allowed to buy as much or as little as they want at that price. Instead, people must first pay for the right to become a buyer, and only then choose how much they want to buy at a per-unit price offered by the firm. We will call this the **two-part pricing** strategy. We will call the amount paid to become a buyer the **access fee**, and we will call the amount charged per unit once the access fee has been paid the **user charge**.

Examples of two-part pricing are easy to find. Here are just a few examples that everyone is familiar with:

- Night clubs often impose a cover charge (the access fee) for admission, and then sell food and drinks at prices (user charges) stated on a menu.

- Utilities like electricity, telephone, and sometimes cell-phone service often charge a flat monthly connection charge (the access fee), which sometimes includes a fixed minimum amount of use, plus a charge per kilowatt hour or minute of phone service (the user charge) beyond any amount covered by the access fee.

- Country clubs charge large membership fees (access fees), sometimes reaching tens of thousands of dollars, for the right to join. Members then pay small "greens fees" (user charges) each time they play golf. In pro sports, teams are requiring season ticket buyers to purchase a Personal Seating License (PCL) which is an upfront payment for the privilege of buying a season ticket. The justification for this fee is to cover the upfront costs of building a stadium, putting the cost on the beneficiary of the stadium over the general tax paying public. Major universities will require a donation to the school foundation for the privilege of buying a season football or basket ball ticket. Notre Dame reserves large sections of their stadium for *Contributing* Alumni.

- The popular discount chain Price Club charges an annual membership fee (access fee) that gives admission to its stores. Members are then offered very low prices on merchandise (user fees).

The two-part pricing strategy helps a firm get around a dilemma that faces the simple monopolist. If a simple monopolist maximizes profit by setting a price equal to marginal cost, it must turn away some potentially profitable business. The potentially profitable business represents extra units that could be sold by cutting the price below the simple monopoly price, but still leaving it above marginal cost. Price discriminators get around this dilemma by cutting the price for some, but not all units sold. Two-part pricing gets around the dilemma in a different way. By charging a price below that of a simple monopoly, it "gives up" some revenue, but it recoups the "lost" revenue by charging an access fee.

Customers are often happy with two-part pricing because it gives them lower prices (at the margin), and sometimes higher quality, as well, compared with simple monopoly. For example, Price Club, because of its membership fee, is able to offer merchandise at a lower mark-up over cost than rival Wal-Mart, which has no membership requirement. And country clubs that require membership fees provide higher-quality, less-crowded courses and clubhouses compared with public golf courses that rely on greens fees alone. Also, there is a prestige or snob appeal of belonging to the correct country club or having good seats at the Maryland-Duke or Penn State-Michigan game.

Two-part pricing is especially popular in markets where fixed costs are high and marginal costs are comparatively low. Electric power companies, telephone companies, and golf courses all fit this model. Without access fees, per-unit prices would have to be very high relative to marginal costs in order for the firm to break even.

Sometimes fixed costs constitute almost all the cost of a service, and marginal costs are nearly zero. In that case, the access fee may provide all of a firm's revenue and the user fee may be set to equal zero (that is, equal to marginal cost). Most internet service providers follow this variant of the two-part pricing model, and in recent years, it has become more common for cell phones, as well.

MARKET PERFORMANCE UNDER MONOPOLY

In the last chapter we looked at market performance under perfect competition. That market structure received high marks for two aspects of market performance. First, we noted that in competitive equilibrium marginal cost is equal to market price. Production thus proceeds to the point at which no further mutual gains for buyers and sellers are possible. In that sense an economy of competitive markets provides an efficient solution to the question of what to produce. Second, we noted that in long-run equilibrium a perfectly competitive firm produces at the lowest point on its long-run average cost curve. This is a key aspect of efficiency in the choice of how to produce.

In this section we look at market performance under monopoly. First, we compare simple monopoly with perfect competition in terms of the questions of what and how to produce. We then look briefly at the question of for whom goods are produced. Finally, we explore some unresolved issues.

What to Produce: Consumer and Producer Surplus

The concepts of consumer and producer surplus, which were introduced in a previous chapter, provide a useful tool for analyzing market performance with regard to the quantity of each good that is produced. Figure 9.5 makes the comparison between perfect competition and simple monopoly.

Part (a) of the exhibit shows a perfectly competitive market. As we saw in Chapter 6, the height of the demand curve measures the maximum amount that consumers would willingly pay for a given quantity of output. The height of the supply curve measures the minimum amount that suppliers would willingly accept for a given output. Because the supply curve is based on the marginal cost curves of individual firms, it reflects the opportunity cost of producing each additional unit. The equilibrium price is $20 and the equilibrium quantity 200 units. Consumers, who would be willing to pay more than $20 for all but the two hundredth unit, earn a consumer surplus equal to the area beneath the demand curve but above the market price. Producers, who produce all but the two hundredth unit at an opportunity cost of less than $20, earn a producer surplus equal to the area above the supply curve but beneath the market price. These surpluses represent consumers' and producers' mutual gains from exchange.

Under competitive conditions production is carried to the point at which all potential gains from exchange are exhausted. Nothing would be gained from produc-

FIGURE 9.5 MARKET PERFORMANCE UNDER MONOPOLY AND COMPETITION

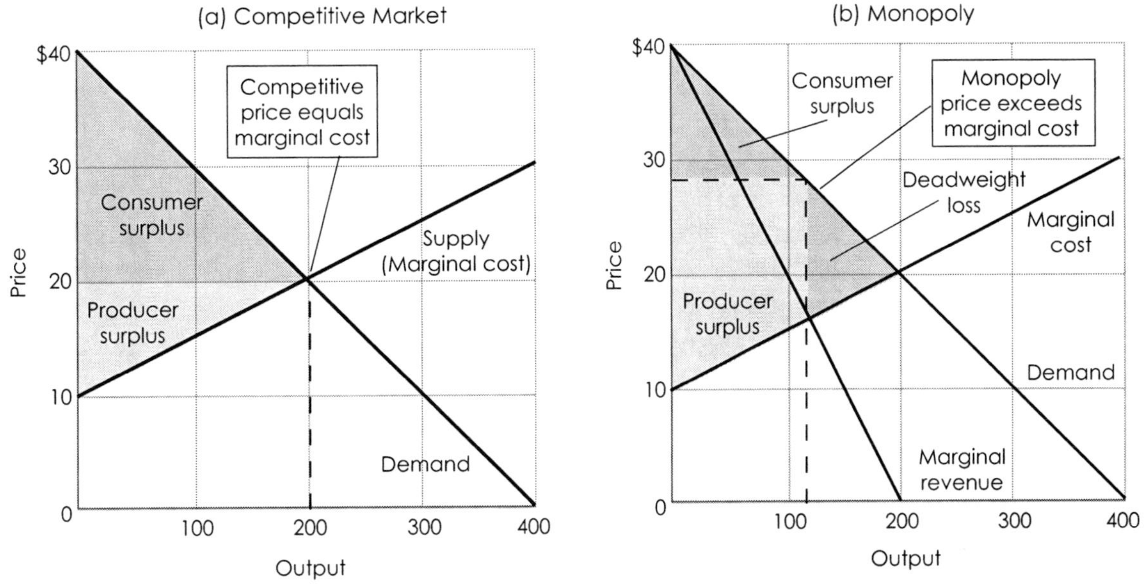

Under perfect competition, shown in part (a), production is carried out to the point at which the price consumers are willing to pay for the last unit produced just equals the opportunity cost of producing it. All possible gains from trade are realized in the form of producer and consumer surplus. Under monopoly, production stops short of that point. Consumer surplus is smaller and producer surplus larger than under competition, but the total of the two is smaller. Some potential gains from trade go unrealized. This deadweight loss is the reason monopoly is considered a form of market failure.

ing beyond the 200-unit mark. From the 201st unit on, the opportunity cost of the unit to producers as measured by the supply curve would exceed its value to consumers as measured by the demand curve.

Now consider the situation under simple monopoly, as shown in part (b) of the exhibit. To make the comparison easy, the demand and marginal cost curves for the monopolist in question are assumed to be the same as the market demand and supply curves for the competitive industry.

To maximize its profits, the simple monopolist limits production to 120 units and charges a price of $28 per unit. Even at that price, consumers are better off than they would be if the good were entirely unavailable. They realize a surplus equal to the area beneath the demand curve but above the $28 price. The monopolist, on the other hand, realizes a substantial producer surplus. The 120th unit, which is sold for $28, costs only $16 to produce, yielding a producer surplus of $12. Surpluses on earlier units, which are produced at a lower opportunity cost, are correspondingly greater. The total producer surplus equals the shaded area above the marginal cost curve but below the $28 price, bordered on the left by the vertical axis and on the right by the profit-maximizing quantity.

Comparison of the competitive case with the monopoly case reveals these three differences.

1. Consumer surplus is smaller under simple monopoly.
2. Producer surplus is larger under simple monopoly.
3. The total of producer and consumer surpluses is smaller under simple monopoly.

The third difference reveals the inefficiency of monopoly. It indicates that some potential gains from exchange are not realized. Other things being equal, production of units 121 through 200 would provide benefits to consumers that exceed their costs. This would make both producers and consumers better off. The potential gains from trade that are "wasted" are shown by the triangle lying between the supply and demand curves and bordered on the left by the monopolist's profit-maximizing quantity. That area represents a **deadweight loss**—a term that is often used to refer to any benefit that is lost by one party but not gained by another. The excess burden of a tax, illustrated in Chapter 5, is another example of a deadweight loss.

Deadweight loss

A loss of consumer or producer surplus that is not balanced by a gain to someone else.

If producing another 80 units of output would make both producers and consumers better off, one might ask why this is not done. The answer lies in the assumption that a simple monopolist offers a single price per unit to all buyers. The complex pricing strategies examined above are designed to overcome this disadvantage of simple monopoly. Under price discrimination, the monopolist might be able to hold the price of the first 120 units at $28 while selling units 121 through 200 at a price of $20. If it did so, both the firm and its customers would benefit. A firm using two-part pricing could charge the marginal-cost price of $20 to its members, and make up the lost revenue through an access fee. In either case, the deadweight loss would then be recaptured. A simple monopolist, on the other hand, must sell all units at a uniform price. Such a firm cannot cut the price on units 121 through 200 without also cutting the price on units 1 through 120. The intersection of the marginal cost and marginal revenue curves marks the limit of the simple monopolist's willingness to produce.

To summarize, the fact that a simple monopoly's price exceeds its marginal cost in a situation of equilibrium means that too little of the good is produced to realize all potential gains from trade. Under monopoly, the consumer does not pay the lowest possible price, under a perfectly competitive, the consumer pays the lowest possible price. Simple monopoly therefore distorts the choice of what to produce. Compared with perfectly competitive industries, simple monopolies produce goods in inefficiently small quantities. Perfectly competitive firms produce a quantity at the lowest average cost. Monopolies do not since increasing their output would reduce profits even though they would reduce (eliminate) waste as they achieve economies of scale. However, in the real world monopolies, monopolistic competitors, and oligopolists often use more complex pricing strategies that keep prices closer to marginal cost. The deadweight loss is thus less than implied by Figure 9.5.

How to Produce: Average Total Cost in Monopoly Equilibrium

A second favorable trait of perfect competition, as we saw in the preceding chapter, is the fact that its equilibrium output is produced at the least possible long-run average cost. This trait is not shared by monopoly. As we saw earlier in this chapter, equilibrium output for a monopoly can occur at any point along its long-run average cost curve. Thus, monopoly cannot lay claim to minimization of average total cost and in this respect can be said to be less efficient than perfect competition.

How serious the inefficiency is in practice depends on circumstances. Three cases need to be considered.

1. In the case of a natural monopoly, equilibrium will usually occur at an our-put at which the firm is still experiencing economies of scale. Dividing the industry's total output between two or more firms would mean that each of them would have to operate at an even lower, and hence less efficient, level of output. Thus, although the natural monopoly produces an inefficiently low level of output, it produces that output at the lowest possible cost given the demand and cost curves for the product.
2. Empirical cost studies indicate that many firms experience approximately constant returns to scale after a minimum efficient scale has been reached. If demand for the product is sufficient so that the profit-maximizing equilibrium output for such a firm is greater than that minimum efficient scale, that output will be produced at the minimum possible cost. This will be so even if the chosen output is smaller than the efficient level, that is, the level that would make price equal to marginal cost.
3. The equilibrium output may lie on the rising portion of the monopolist's average cost curve, where it encounters decreasing returns to scale. Dividing total output among two or more smaller firms would then decrease average total cost. In this case the monopolist not only produces an output that is too small to realize all potential consumer and producer surplus, but also produces that output at an inefficiently high cost.

Failure to minimize average total cost appears to be a problem only when the monopolist experiences diseconomies of scale at the equilibrium output. This can happen only in a closed monopoly. A natural monopoly experiences economies of scale at its equilibrium output. And an open monopoly could not survive in the long run if it operated at a significant cost disadvantage relative to smaller firms entering the market. A limit pricing strategy would not work for such a firm, and a short-run profit-maximizing price would only speed the entry of rivals.

In addition to operating at an inefficient point on its long-run average cost curve, there is another reason that a closed monopolist's costs may be inefficiently high. Earlier we noted that closed monopolists may have to spend heavily on lobbying and legal battles to defend themselves against rent-seeking rivals that want to break down the legal protections the monopoly enjoys. Those costs add little or nothing to output or consumer satisfaction. Loss of the output that the lawyers or lobbyists could have produced if they had worked elsewhere, it can be argued, is another form of deadweight loss from closed monopoly.

For Whom Does Monopoly Promote Inequality?

Cartoonists draw monopolists as fat men with big cigars and long limousines. For good measure, they may sketch in a child in rags watching the limousine drive by. Such cartoons reflect a common view that monopoly promotes inequality. To the extent that noneconomists worry about monopolists at all, they are more likely to dislike them because they are seen as rich and powerful than because they are seen as inefficient.

Sometimes monopoly does confer wealth and power. The "robber barons" who tried to monopolize the oil, steel, and tobacco industries at the turn of the century were a case in point. The richest person in the world today is Microsoft's Bill Gates. Although Microsoft's market is properly considered an oligopoly, its market share is so large that the term "monopoly" is often applied in popular discussion. But aside from such anecdotal evidence, does the theory of monopoly provide any reason to associate the market structure of monopoly with large private fortunes? Not necessarily.

For one thing, we must ask who owns the monopoly. If the monopoly is a giant corporation, much of its stock may be owned by such institutions as insurance companies and union pension funds. If so, the monopoly's profits will benefit widows and orphans as well as fat cats with big cigars. Other monopolies are small operations such as, say, the only gas station or theater in an isolated small town. The owners may barely earn enough to cover costs. In still other cases, monopolies are owned by government—the U.S. Postal Service, the retail liquor monopolies of many states, and the Tennessee Valley Authority's monopoly of electric power in an area covering several states are examples. Any profits made by those monopolies become available to finance other areas of government activity rather than creating private fortunes. In other cases, such as public transit systems, monopoly profits are actually negative, and customers receive the benefit of subsidies.

Finally, as we have seen, there is no guarantee that monopolists will earn pure economic profits in the long run. Competition from substitute products erodes the profits of some monopolies. Closed monopolies may spend potential profits on measures to fend off rent seekers. Open monopolies may limit their profits in order to deter other firms from entering the market.

This is not to say that a market economy does not produce large inequalities of wealth and income. Instead, the point is that monopoly, as a market structure, is neither a necessary nor a sufficient condition for inequality. There are poor monopolists, and there are people who grow rich under oligopoly, monopolistic competition, and even perfect competition.

SUMMARY

1. **In what circumstances can monopoly exist?** A monopoly is a firm that is the sole supplier of a product that has no close substitutes. Three classes of monopoly can be distinguished: *closed monopolies,* which are protected by legal restrictions on competition; *natural monopolies,* which are protected by economies of scale; and *open monopolies,* which have no special protections against the entry of potential competitors.
2. **How are the profit-maximizing price and output for a monopoly determined?** A *simple monopoly* (one that does not practice price discrimination) earns a maximum profit by producing the quantity of output that makes marginal cost equal to marginal revenue. The price is determined by the height of the demand curve at the profit-maximizing level. If a monopoly cannot earn a profit in the short run, it will try to keep its loss to a minimum. If the loss-minimizing price is above average variable cost, the firm will continue to operate in the short run. If the loss-minimizing price is below average variable cost, it will shut down.
3. **How is long-run equilibrium achieved under monopoly?** In the long run, a monopoly that faces no threat of competition maximizes its profit at the level of output for which long-run marginal cost is equal to long-run marginal revenue. Because demand tends to be more elastic in the long run, the long-run profit-maximizing price may be lower than the price that would maximize short-run profit. An open monopoly may discourage other firms from entering the market by charging a price below that which would maximize short-run profit. Such a strategy is known as *limit pricing.*
4. **What pricing strategies are available to monopolies and other price-searching firms?** A monopolist or other firm that is not a price taker can practice *price discrimination* if its product cannot be resold by buyers and if it has some way of classifying buyers on the basis of elasticity of demand. Although price discrimination is resented by buyers who must pay higher prices, it may increase efficiency by allowing customers who value the product more than its marginal cost but less than the price that a simple monopolist would charge to buy the product. An alternative strategy is two-part pricing, which involves charging an access fee for the right to become a customer plus a per-unit user fee.
5. **How does monopoly affect market performance?** Monopoly can be a source of market failure in that the amount of output it produces is less than the amount that would make marginal cost equal to the price charged. As a result, some consumers who would be willing to pay a price that is higher than marginal cost are unable to buy from a monopolist. Because some gains from trade (consumer and producer surplus) are not realized under a simple monopoly, there is a *deadweight loss* to the economy. Also, under long-run equilibrium conditions a monopoly does not necessarily produce at the point of minimum long-run average cost.

KEY TERMS

Price searcher
Simple monopoly
Natural monopoly
Limit pricing
Open monopoly
Closed monopoly
Price discrimination
Two-part pricing
Access fee
User fee
Deadweight loss

PROBLEMS AND TOPICS FOR DISCUSSION

1. **Charging any price you like.** "A monopolist can always make a profit because with no competition it can charge any price it likes." Do you think

this statement is true? Suppose you own the only movie theater in a small town. Because your corrupt uncle is on the town's zoning board, you feel confident that no competitors will be allowed into the market. What factors might limit your ability to "charge any price you like"?

2. **Short-run shutdown for a monopolist.** Redraw the graph in Figure 9.3, shifting the demand and marginal revenue curves to illustrate the case in which a monopolist will shut down in the short run rather than continue to produce at a loss.

3. **Price discrimination.** Air travelers are sometimes surprised and annoyed to find that the price of a ticket for a short flight may exceed the price for a long flight. For example, a round-trip ticket from Washington, D.C., to Seattle on one airline costs $235, compared with the same airline's price of $278 from Washington, D.C., to Dayton, Ohio, less than a third of the distance. Travelers complain that such prices represent unfair discrimination against the residents of medium-sized cities such as Dayton. They say that airlines should be forced to charge prices that are scaled in proportion to the distance flown. The airlines answer that major city pairs such as Washington, D.C.–Seattle can be served at a lower cost (with larger planes and fewer empty seats) than less frequently traveled city pairs such as Washington, D.C.–Dayton. Discuss the merits of the current price structure and the proposed alternative in terms of fairness and efficiency.

4. **Mass transit pricing and market failure.** Reread the sections of Chapter 3 that deal with market failure and rent seeking. Can it be argued that the market failure theory of government justifies public ownership and subsidy of mass transit systems? What particular types of failure are involved here? What pricing policy would be called for under the market failure theory? Do you think there are any elements of mass transit policy that can be explained under the theory of rent seeking?

CASE FOR DISCUSSION

The Postal Monopoly

The U.S. Post Office was organized in 1789 and immediately began losing money. One of the reasons that it lost money was competition. The post office charged the same price to deliver a letter anywhere in the country, but its costs were not the same in every case. For letters mailed between points in the East, the post office charged more than cost; for letters mailed to points in the West, it charged less than cost.

Competitors flocked to the routes on which costs were low. For example, in the 1840s Henry Wells, who later founded the famous Wells-Fargo Company, set up a mail service between Philadelphia and New York. He charged $.06 for a first-class letter, compared to the post office's rate of $.25. By the early 1840s private firms were carrying at least one-third of the mail in the United States.

To fight off the competition, the post office turned to Congress. In 1845 Congress strengthened the restrictions on private first-class mail service. This saved the post office from extinction and allowed it to continue its policy of uniform rates regardless of the cost of service. This policy remains in force for first-class mail: The price for mailing a letter to any address in the United States is the same, whatever the distance. However, the cost of delivering a letter clearly is not the same for all addresses. Deliveries to post office boxes are least expensive; deliveries to homes in suburban neighborhoods are a bit more costly; and rural free delivery service is more expensive still.

Source: Based in part on *Economics of Public Policy,* 2nd ed. (Chapter 11), by John C. Goodman and Edwin G. Dolan (St. Paul, MN: West Publishing Company, 1982).

QUESTIONS

1. On the basis of information given in the case, should the postal monopoly on first-class mail be classified as closed, open, or natural? Why?
2. Do you think the practice of charging all customers the same price when costs differ from one customer to another should be viewed as price discrimination? Do you think it has any benefits? Discuss in terms of efficiency and fairness.
3. Although the U.S. Postal Service (USPS) has retained its monopoly on ordinary first-class mail, it allows competition from such firms as United Parcel Service (UPS) and Federal Express (FedEx) in carrying overnight and third-class mail (parcels). In these cases both the USPS and its private competitors charge different prices according to weight and distance and according to whether pickup and delivery services are provided. Why does a policy of charging a single price regardless of cost not work in a market in which competition exists?

CHAPTER 10

Industrial Organization, Monopolistic Competition, and Oligopoly

After reading this chapter, you will understand:

1. How the structure of markets in the U.S. economy has changed over time
2. How the interdependence of firms under oligopoly affects price and output decisions
3. Why oligopolistic firms sometimes collude to increase profits, and the problems they encounter as a result
4. The conditions that affect market performance under oligopoly
5. How equilibrium is achieved under monopolistic competition, and how well monopolistically competitive markets perform

Before reading this chapter, make sure you know the meaning of:

1. Consumer and producer surplus
2. Economies of scale
3. Market structure
4. Types of monopoly
5. Limit pricing

WHAT IS THE most competitive market in the world? Some people might choose the market for commercial aircraft. Every order placed comes down to a hard-fisted slugfest between two heavyweights, U.S.-based Boeing and E.U.-based Airbus. In 2004, Airbus delivered 320 planes to Boeing's 285. But many industry observers saw Boeing as poised to retake the lead with its 787 Dreamliner. Due to be introduced in 2008, Boeing already had 128 firm orders as of the 2005 Paris Air Show. Airbus was offering its rival 350 model, but the 350 is not an all-new plane, and what is more, it will be later getting into service. Tens of thousands of jobs in Europe and the United States hang in the balance.

The Boeing-Airbus example highlights the fact that the term *competition* has more than one meaning. In the phrase "perfect competition" it refers to *market structure*. A market is perfectly competitive if it has large numbers of small firms, the product is homogeneous, all firms share information equally, and it is easy to enter or leave the market. In contrast, competition in the form of Boeing versus Airbus refers to *business rivalry*. In this sense "rivalry" refers to the activities of entrepreneurs, not just those of business managers who are responding to conditions that they accept as given.

In the market structure of *oligopoly*, to which much of this chapter is devoted, rivalry becomes a central issue. Rivalry is also an important issue for the market structures that border on oligopoly. At one end of the spectrum, oligopoly shades into what we have called open monopoly, a market structure in which a single firm, although it is the sole supplier of a product at the moment, is threatened by the entry of potential rivals. At the other end, oligopoly shades into *monopolistic competition*. In monopolistically competitive markets, rivalry is likely to be strong among firms that are near neighbors. For example, rivalry among vendors on an urban street corner can be as sharp in its way as the rivalry between giant firms in the tobacco or breakfast cereal industry, or the wholesale electricity providers in the case above.

This chapter will take in the whole spectrum of market structures that fall somewhere between the ideal types of monopoly and perfect competition. It will begin with a look at some empirical data on the organization of industry. The next section will take up oligopoly, and the last section will discuss monopolistic competition.

MARKET STRUCTURE IN THE U.S. ECONOMY

The structure of markets has long been of interest not only to economic theorists, but also to those who look at actual markets. A particular focus of this work has been the degree to which the largest firms dominate the economy as a whole or particular markets within it. In this section, we will take a look at some data relating to the structure of markets in the United States, today and in the past.

Aggregate Concentration

Aggregate concentration

The degree to which the economy as a whole is dominated by the largest firms.

One way to gauge the influence of the largest firms is to measure **aggregate concentration**, the degree to which the economy as a whole is dominated by the largest firms. There is a popular fear that large corporations have disproportionate power and influence. Social Critic Ralph Nader has made a career by appealing to people who feel powerless against perceived corporate dominance of their lives. Statements such as, "Today, the increasing size and wealth of corporations point to more concentration of wealth and of political and economic power and influence than before," are commonplace on anticapitalist and antiglobalization Web sites.[1] Frequent news of mergers of giant corporations with one another to form even larger entities fuel fears of corporate dominance. Do economic data on aggregate concentration back up these views?

Apparently not. Lawrence J. White of New York University surveyed a wide range of available data on aggregate concentration in the U.S. economy. However measured, the data show little change over time in the relative economic influence of the largest firms.

The broadest measure of aggregate concentration is the share of total value added contributed by the largest firms. (Value added measures the value of output adjusted for the value of inputs bought from other firms.) Figure 10.1 shows trends in value added by the top 50 and top 200 corporations in the United States. The share of the top 50 firms increased from the end of World War II until the early 1960s, and has changed little since then. The share of the top 200 manufacturing firms reached a peak in the 1970s, and has declined since then. Data on shares of total sales, total assets, and total employment also show no strong trend toward greater aggregate concentration in recent decades.[2] These data do not by themselves exclude the possibility that large corporations may have increased their political or social power without increasing their relative economic size, but neither do they support such a view.

FIGURE 10.1 TRENDS IN AGGREGATE CONCENTRATION IN THE UNITED STATES

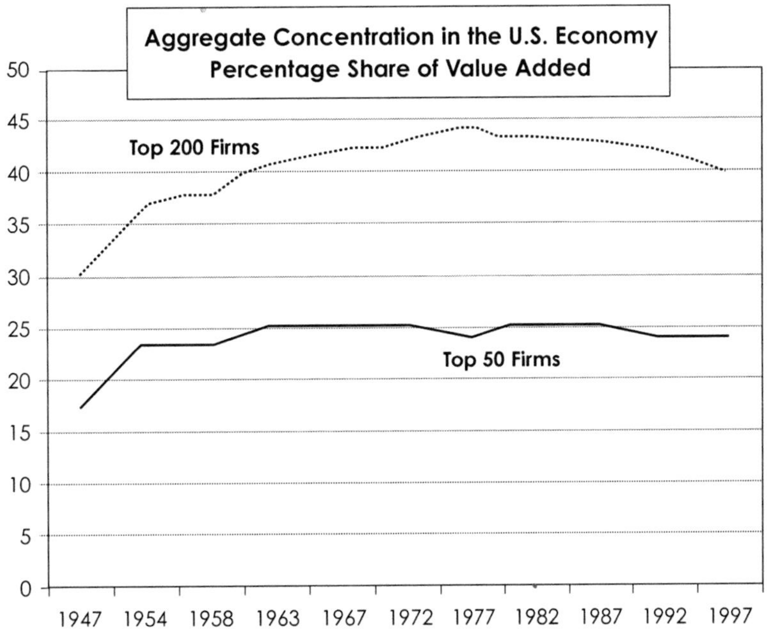

The relative size of the largest manufacturing corporations in the U.S. economy increased in the first two decades following World War II. Since that time, the relative size of the top 50 firms has changed little, and that of the top 200 firms, after peaking in the 1970s, has decreased.

Source: Lawrence J. White, "Trends in Aggregate Concentration in the United States," *Journal of Economic Perspectives*, Volume 16, No. 4, Fall 2002, Table 1.

Measures of Market Concentration

Market concentration

The degree to which a market is dominated by a few large firms.

Concentration ratio

The percentage of all sales that is accounted for by the four or eight largest firms in a market.

Herfindahl-Hirschmann index (HHI)

An index of market concentration that is calculated by squaring the percentage market shares of all firms in an industry then summing the squared-values.

If our interest is market structure rather than overall corporate power, we need to look not at aggregate concentration but **market concentration**, the degree to which a market is dominated by one or a few large firms. Market concentration gives us a clue as to whether a given sector of the economy more closely fits the structures of monopoly, oligopoly, monopolistic competition, or perfect competition.

A **concentration ratio** is the simplest measure of market concentration. A concentration ratio gives the percentage of all sales in a market that are accounted for by a specified number of firms in that market. The most commonly used such ratio is the four-firm concentration ratio, which shows the combined market share of the top four firms as a percent of sales in the market as a whole.

Concentration ratios have a number of limitations. Obviously they do not distinguish between an industry in which a single firm dominates the market and one in which four or more top firms share it more or less equally. A market in which one firm held 77 percent and twenty-three others held 1 percent each would have the same four-firm concentration ratio as one in which five firms each held 20 percent.

A measure of market concentration that overcomes this drawback is the **Herfindahl-Hirschmann index (HHI)**. The HHI of market concentration is calculated by squaring the percentage market shares of each firm in the market and summing the squares. For an industry with n competing firms, the formula is

$$H = p_1^2 + p_2^2 + \ldots + p_n^2,$$

where p_k is the percentage market share of firm k.

The Herfindahl-Hirschmann index rises as the market becomes more concentrated, reaching a maximum value of 10,000 for a monopoly. Thus, an industry with one hundred equal-sized firms would have a HHI of 100; one with ten equal-sized firms would have an index of 1,000; one with five equal-sized firms would have an index of 2,000; and so on. Unlike concentration ratios, the HHI can distinguish between degrees of concentration in markets with equal numbers of firms. For example, a market with eight firms of equal size has the same eight-firm concentration ratio as one in which one firm has 30 percent and seven others have 10 percent each. But the HHI for the latter market is 1,600 compared with 1,250 for the former. The difference in HHIs for the two markets reflects a widespread view that the presence of one dominant firm in a market makes that market less competitive in the sense that the dominant firm can exercise more influence over price and quantity than other firms in the market. Table 10.1 gives data on concentration ratios and HHIs for selected U.S. manufacturing industries.

The U.S. Department of Justice (DOJ) uses the HHI when evaluating how a merger between two or more companies will affect the industry's competition. As a rule of thumb, mergers within industries that have an HHI value of 1,000 or less are permitted without much intervention from the DOJ. Companies seeking mergers within indus-

TABLE 10.1 MARKET CONCENTRATION FOR SELECTED U.S. MANUFACTURING INDUSTRIES

Industry Description	Number of Companies	Share of Sales Accounted for by Largest Companies			HHI
		4 Largest	8 Largest	50 Largest	
Wood kitchen cabinets	4,303	19%	25%	46%	156
Book publishing	2,504	23%	38%	77%	251
Petroleum refining	131	30%	49%	97%	414
Meatpacking-plant products	1,296	50%	66%	88%	1,123
Household refrigerators and freezers	52	82%	98%	100%	1,891
Motor vehicles and car bodies	398	84%	91%	99%	2,676

The table above shows manufacturing industry concentration data based on the 1992 U.S. Census. Note that the number of companies is not the only important determinant of the degree of competition in industries. Even though there are only 131 petroleum refiners in the United States, this is a relatively competitive industry. The largest four petroleum refiners account for only 30 percent of all sales in this industry. This is reflected in the low HHI value for petroleum refining. On the other hand, there were almost 400 motor-vehicle and car-body manufacturers in the United States, but more than three-fourths of this industry is dominated by the four largest companies. The top 50 motor-vehicle and car-body companies account for nearly all sales. The high concentration in the motor-vehicle and car-bodies industry is shown by the relatively high HHI value of 2,676.

Source: U.S. Census, *1992 Census—Concentration Ratios in Manufacturing.*

tries with index values above 1,000 will draw the DOJ's attention. The DOJ then analyzes the market to determine whether the merger will adversely affect competition.

Blending Structural and Behavioral Evidence

Many economists think that structural evidence, such as concentration ratios or the Herfindahl-Hirschmann index, is not enough to judge the competitiveness of a market. In addition, they say, attention must be paid to the way firms actually behave. Can they block the entry of rivals into the market? Do domestic firms face competition from imports? Do they collude or compete in making pricing decisions? Do they compete vigorously in product innovation and other nonprice areas? Information about such issues should be considered along with structural data in determining competitiveness.

The results of one study that combined structural and behavioral evidence are given in *Applying Economic Ideas 10.1*. That study, conducted by William C. Shepherd, concluded that more than three-quarters of the U.S. economy was at the time "effectively competitive," a category that takes in perfect competition, monopolistic competition, and loose forms of oligopoly. Less than 3 percent of the economy was classified as pure monopoly, with most of that category consisting of public utilities.

Shepherd's results are interesting in that they indicate a strong trend toward increased competitiveness in the U.S. economy from 1958 to 1980. U.S. industries experienced an increase in business consolidation in the 1980s, but this lead to only

APPLYING ECONOMIC IDEAS 10.1

TRENDS IN COMPETITION IN THE U.S. ECONOMY

Economists have followed trends in competition and concentration in the U.S. economy for more than fifty years. In 1982, William C. Shepherd attempted to view all of these studies from a historical perspective. Relying on recent data as well as on older published studies, he classified U.S. markets into four categories for the years 1939, 1958, and 1980. The categories, which combine measurements of market structure with information on the behavior of firms, are as follows:

1. *Pure monopoly:* Market share at or near 100 percent, plus effectively blocked entry, plus evidence of effective monopoly control over the level and structure of prices. In practice, this category includes mainly utilities and patented goods.
2. *Dominant firms:* A market share of 50 percent to over 90 percent, with no close rival. High barriers to entry. Ability to control pricing, set systematic discriminatory prices, influence innovation, and (usually) earn rates of return well above the competitive rate of return.
3. *Tight oligopoly:* Four-firm concentration above 60 percent, with stable market shares. Medium or high barriers to entry. A tendency toward cooperation, shown especially by rigid prices. Excess profits are neither necessary nor sufficient to establish the existence of tight oligopoly.
4. *Effective competition:* Four-firm concentration below 40 percent, with unstable market shares and flexible pricing. Low barriers to entry, little collusion, and low profit rates.

The data in the table below show that the competitiveness of U.S. markets increased slightly from 1939 to 1958 and dramatically from 1958 to 1980. Shepherd attributes the change to three factors: increased international competition, deregulation, and enforcement of antitrust laws. Increased international competition and further deregulation have probably resulted in a continuation of the trend toward competitiveness in the 1980s. Enforcement of antitrust law has played a reduced role in shaping market structure in the 1980s, but it has continued to play an active role in discouraging collusive behavior on the part of rival firms.

Sectors of the Economy	National Income in Each Sector, 1978 ($ billions)[a]	The Share of Each Sector That Was Effectively Competitive		
		1939 (%)	1958 (%)	1980 (%)[a]
Agriculture, Forestry, and Fisheries	54.7	91.6	85.0	86.4
Mining	24.5	87.1	92.2	95.8
Construction	87.6	27.9	55.9	80.2
Manufacturing	459.5	51.5	55.9	69.0
Transportation and Public Utilities	162.3	8.7	26.1	39.1
Wholesale and Retail Trade	261.8	57.8	60.5	93.4
Finance, Insurance, and Real Estate	210.7	61.5	63.8	94.1
Services	245.3	53.9	54.3	77.9
TOTAL	1,506.5	55.0	61.7	79.5

The Share of Each Category in Total National Income	($ billions)	Percentage Shares		
		1939	1958	1980
1. Pure Monopoly	38.2	6.2	3.1	2.5
2. Dominant Firm	42.4	5.0	5.0	2.8
3. Tight Oligopoly	272.1	36.4	35.6	18.0
4. Effectively competitive	1,157.9	52.4	56.3	76.7
TOTAL	1,510.6	100.0	100.0	100.0

[a] 1980 figures reflect competitive conditions as of 1980. The industry weights are based on 1978 data for national income, the latest year available.

Source: William G. Shepherd, "Causes of Increased Competition in the U.S. Economy, 1939–1980," *Review of Economics and Statistics* (November 1982), Table 2.

modest increases in business concentration.[3] The trend toward greater competitiveness has continued, partially because of international pressure. From 1990 to 2002, total imports of goods and services, adjusted for inflation, more than doubled. In addition, many foreign firms entered U.S. markets through purchases of U.S. companies or construction of manufacturing facilities in the United States. Also, 1980 marked the beginning of the trend toward deregulation in transportation, communications, and finance. In structural terms, regulatory reform has decreased concentration in some industries (such as telephone service) while increasing it in others (such as airlines). However, even when reform has been accompanied by numerous mergers of firms, thus increasing the concentration ratio, structural changes have been outweighed by greater freedom to compete, with the result that regulated markets are, on the whole, more competitive than before.

Causes of Market Concentration

Given the evidence that some markets are more concentrated than others, it is natural to ask why. No single theory explains market concentration, but a variety of hypotheses have been proposed. We will discuss these under the headings of economies of scale, barriers to entry, and sunk costs.

ECONOMIES OF SCALE A firm is said to experience economies of scale if its long-run average cost declines as its output increases. At one extreme is the case of natural monopoly, in which economies of scale are so strong that minimum-cost production requires that the entire market supply be produced by a single firm. In less extreme cases, the *minimum efficient scale* for a firm—the point at which the average total cost curve stops falling and begins to flatten out—is so large that only a few firms can efficiently coexist in the market.

Suppose, for example, that the minimum efficient scale for a single plant producing refrigerators is 15 percent of U.S. consumption. The theoretical minimum four-firm concentration ratio implied by the minimum efficient plant size would then be 60 percent. The industry could not be any less concentrated than this without forcing some firms to use plants that are too small to produce at minimum long-run average cost. However, empirical studies suggest that economies of scale *at the plant level* clearly are not enough to explain the observed degree of market concentration.

Of course, as emphasized previously, there are many sources of economies of scale above the plant level. Operating more than one plant may result in savings in scheduling, transportation, research and development, finance, marketing, and administration costs. In addition to economies of scale in the ordinary sense, which pertain to a plant's rate of output per unit of time, a firm with a larger market share can also carry out longer production runs at an efficient rate of output. To the extent that cost savings can be achieved through "learning by doing," a plant with a large market share benefits from greater accumulated experience with each product than does one with a small market share. These kinds of economies may lie beyond the ability of economists and accountants to measure using the techniques commonly applied in studies of economies of scale.[4] The auto industry, cigarette industry, appliance industry, air craft industry all fit the model of Barriers to Entry.

Even after all such qualifications are taken into account, however, it appears that economies of scale alone do not fully account for the degree of concentration found in U.S. industry. Let's turn, then, to the role of barriers to entry.

Barrier to entry

Any circumstance that prevents a new firm in a market from competing on an equal footing with existing ones.

BARRIERS TO ENTRY For our purposes, a **barrier to entry** may be defined as any circumstance that prevents a new firm from competing on an equal footing with existing firms in a particular market.[5] In a market with neither large economies of scale nor high barriers to entry, growth will tend to occur mainly through the entry of new firms, leading to a decrease in concentration over time. With the presence of barriers to entry, the first firms in the industry may be able to maintain their market shares as the industry grows, even without the help of economies of scale.

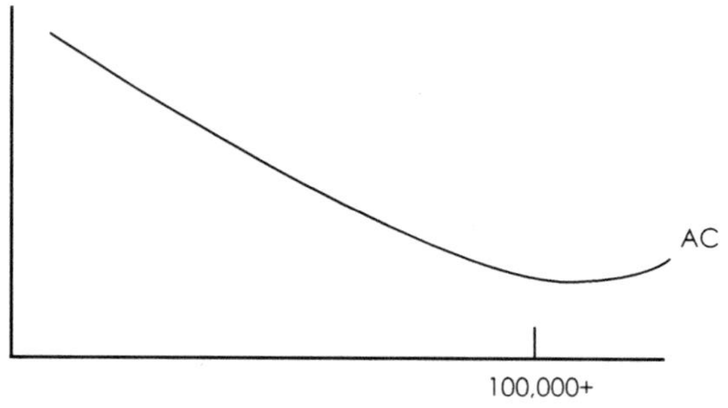

Because of the high fixed costs to enter certain industries, firms must produce and sell a large amount of items to achieve economies of scale. Auto manufacturers and pharmaceutical producers must sell millions of items to reduce their cost per unit (AC) to a profit-earning level.

Sometimes barriers to entry are deliberately created by federal, state, or local governments. The markets that were referred to as closed monopolies in previously are examples, but governments often let more than one firm into a market without opening it to all competitors. For example, to establish a new federally chartered bank, one must obtain permission from a federal agency, the Comptroller of the Currency. One factor that is considered in granting the permit is whether there are already enough banks in the area—in the judgment of the comptroller, not that of the market. The expense of obtaining the permit and the risk that the permit will be denied are significant barriers to competition in the banking industry.

A second kind of barrier to entry is control of a nonreproducible resource. The market for caviar, long controlled by the Soviet Ministry of Fishing, is an example. Ownership of a nonreproducible resource gives existing firms an advantage over new ones and in this way acts as a barrier to entry. (Diamonds from DeBeers of South Africa.)

Patents and copyrights, another class of barriers to entry, are important in both oligopoly and monopoly. A patent or copyright can be treated as a restrictive regulation. As an alternative, it can be treated like ownership of any other nonreproducible resource. In either case, patents and copyrights clearly can make entry difficult and contribute to market concentration. For example, patents held by Xerox Corporation slowed (but did not stop) entry of competing firms into the market for office copiers. Aspartame (NutraSweet) was patented and no other company could legally copy or reproduce this product.

As the term is used here, a *barrier to entry* is something that keeps new firms from duplicating the performance of existing ones in terms of cost or product quality. It does not mean that every effort or expense that a firm must undertake to enter a market should be thought of as a barrier to entry. To start a new firm, an entrepreneur must take risks, find investors, recruit workers, attract customers, and so on. All of these activities are hard work—hard enough to discourage some people from making the effort. But the need for hard work is not a barrier to entry in the economic sense. When entrepreneurs are free to buy the building blocks for their new firms on the same terms as existing firms buy them, even huge markets can be penetrated by new entrants. Examples include Honda's entry into the automobile market, starting from the base of its motorcycle business or the entry of Russia's Lukoil brand into the U.S. retail gasoline market via its purchase of Getty Petroleum Marketing.

MERGERS At some times, firms find it beneficial to merge. This allows firms to take advantage of economies of scale as their market share increases. By increasing quantity sold, firms can move down the average cost curve and reduce the cost per unit all the while they are reducing the competitive pressure to keep prices low. In the 1990s there were several oil company mergers, most notable the Mobil Oil merger with Exxon reforming part of John D. Rockefeller's Standard Oil Company and the merger of British Petroleum with Amoco and ARCO, along with Chevron and Texaco. In 2008 there was the merger of Northwest Airlines with Delta Air and there is speculation (May of 2008) of further concentration of the airlines as UAL (United Air) and US Air negotiate their merger.

SUNK COSTS AND CONTESTABILITY OF MARKETS Sunk costs are another consideration that can play a role in determining market structure. Entry into many industries does require substantial sunk costs. The new firm may need to purchase custom-made equipment with little resale value, construct a plant in a place where it would have no other obvious use, or spend heavily on advertising and promotion to establish a new brand name in the minds of consumers.

As we have defined the term, sunk costs are not necessarily barriers to entry provided that firms that are already in the market had to undertake the same expenses when they entered. In a market in which the demand for a product is growing and is expected to remain high enough to enable a new firm with at least the minimum efficient scale to cover all of its opportunity costs, including sunk costs, entry can take place just as it would in an industry in which there are no sunk costs.

However, the situation may be different in markets in which there is a temporary increase in demand. In such a market, sunk costs affect the feasibility of what has been called hit-and-run entry—entry by firms that expect to leave the market again once demand conditions return to normal. A firm will not enter such a market on a temporary basis unless it is sure it can recover its fixed costs when it leaves.

In some cases, firms will not be sure whether changes in demand conditions justify entry. Under conditions of uncertainty, firms will be bolder about entering if sunk costs are low. Low sunk costs encourage firms to "test the water" in a new market. For example, a computer retailer might rent a store in a new shopping center to test demand in that area, knowing that the lease can be terminated if the store turns out to be unprofitable. Another category of retailer might have to build a special building that could not be used for anything else, so it would be more cautious about entering a new market.

Contestable market

A market in which barriers to entry and exit are low.

A market in which there are neither barriers to entry nor sunk costs, and which therefore is open to hit-and-run entry, is known as a **contestable market**. The airline industry is often cited as an example of a contestable market. In that industry, starting a whole new airline may entail sunk costs, but the relevant market is usually considered to be a city pair, such as Baltimore–Miami. Entry into an established city-pair market by a carrier not previously operating there may require little more than renting a few gates and reassigning some airplanes and crews.

THEORY OF OLIGOPOLY: INTERDEPENDENCE AND COLLUSION

Earlier chapters presented simple models of profit maximization for perfect competition and monopoly. Those models were based on the analysis of rational responses of managers to cost and demand constraints. In contrast, there is no single, general model of oligopoly. Instead, the theory of oligopoly consists of some broadly applied generalities plus a collection of more specific models that apply to special cases. This section looks at the general principles; the appendix to the chapter discusses some of the special-case models.

The Constraint of Oligopolistic Interdependence

The chief difficulty in analyzing oligopoly concerns the nature of the constraints the firm faces in a market in which there are just a few rival firms. Those firms, like firms in perfectly competitive and monopolistic markets, face constraints in the form of cost curves and market demand conditions. In addition, however, they face another constraint: the reactions of rival firms. The change in the profit that any one firm realizes as a result of a change in price, output quantity, or product characteristics depends not only on how customers respond (as is the case in the other market structures) but also on how other firms in the market respond. The linkage of each firm's choices to its rivals' reactions is called **oligopolistic interdependence**.

Oligopolistic interdependence

The need to pay close attention to the actions of rival firms in an oligopolistic market when making price or production decisions.

The problem of oligopolistic interdependence can be illustrated by how street vendors operate. Consider a hot-dog vendor named Suzy who sells hot dogs at the Westminster Home Depot. If she were the only hot-dog vendor in the market, her profit-maximizing strategy would be based on calculations of marginal cost and marginal revenues—or at least on Suzy's seat-of-the-pants estimates of those variables. If, on the other hand, there were enough firms in the market for perfect competition to exist, each firm would care only about an impersonal market price and would not care about individual rivals' reactions. The price would be treated as a given and output would be adjusted by each firm until the price equaled marginal cost.

Now, consider what happens when Suzy faces competition from only three other vendors at Lowes, Kohl's and BJ's. Suppose that, initially, all four vendors charge $2 per hot dog. With only four hot-dog vendors on the corner of 15th and L, however, the pricing decision depends not only on each vendor's estimates of marginal cost and marginal revenue but also on each one's estimates of its rivals' actions. Suzy may decide to raise her price, say to $2.50 instead of $2, banking on the loyalty of her customers. This strategy is based on the hunch that the other vendors will get tired of working so hard for so little profit. before all the customers who are loyal to Suzy's hot-dog cart shift to the cheaper vendors just across the street. Another vendor may try to undercut the market, charging $1.75 instead of $2. This vendor's strategy is based on the guess that the $2 customers are not so loyal after all, and that a higher sales volume will allow the low-price seller to earn a profit even at the low price. Thus, the price charged and quantity produced in an oligopoly can change not only as a result of changes in "objective" conditions, such as cost and demand, but also as a result of purely subjective estimates of human traits, such as stubbornness, loyalty, patience, and anger.

An implication of oligopolistic interdependence is that any model of oligopoly must begin by specifying how each firm expects its rivals to react to changing conditions. We can begin with the special case in which the rival firms in a market agree to cooperate in the pursuit of profit. (A hot dog cart outside of a big box store would much better fit the perfect competition model than oligopoly because of *ease of entry* into the market.)

Cartels

Oligopolistic interdependence may lead to intense rivalry, as in the case of the popcorn vendors, but it can also result in collusion. *Collusion* occurs when the firms in an oligopoly realize that they can jointly increase their profits by raising the product's price and working out an agreement for dividing the market among them. When collusion is open and formal and involves all or most of the producers in the market, the result is called a **cartel**.

Cartel

A group of producers that jointly maximize profits by fixing prices and limiting output.

A simple example will show how cartels work. Imagine an industry made up of one hundred small firms. Assume that the marginal cost of production for all firms in the industry is $1 per unit, regardless of the amount produced. Because marginal cost is the same for all units of output, the marginal cost curve also serves as the long-run average cost curve and the long-run supply curve for the industry. This perfectly elastic long-run supply curve is shown in Figure 10.2, along with a demand curve for the industry.

Consider further, the gas stations along Rt. 140. If one station lowers her price, then the others match the price reduction. In order to maintain market share, another lowers her price further and temporarily they enjoy higher market share and sales, but only until the other stations match the price reduction. But, say the owners all meet for lunch at Denny's on Engler Rd. near the Super Fresh grocery store, and inevitably they discuss PRICE and ask each other "why are we cutting our own throats with this price war?" Then they could all agree NOT to lower price and further agree to slowly raise their prices together. Since it is likely that their combined quantity sold won't increase, then combined total revenues will only rise with the price increases and each firm, as long as they all agree and stick to the agreement, will realize higher profits.

The industry's equilibrium price and level of output depend on how the market is organized. Initially, suppose that all firms act like perfect competitors. According to the theory set forth in a previous chapter, this will result in an equilibrium in which

FIGURE 10.2 PROFIT MAXIMIZATION FOR A CARTEL

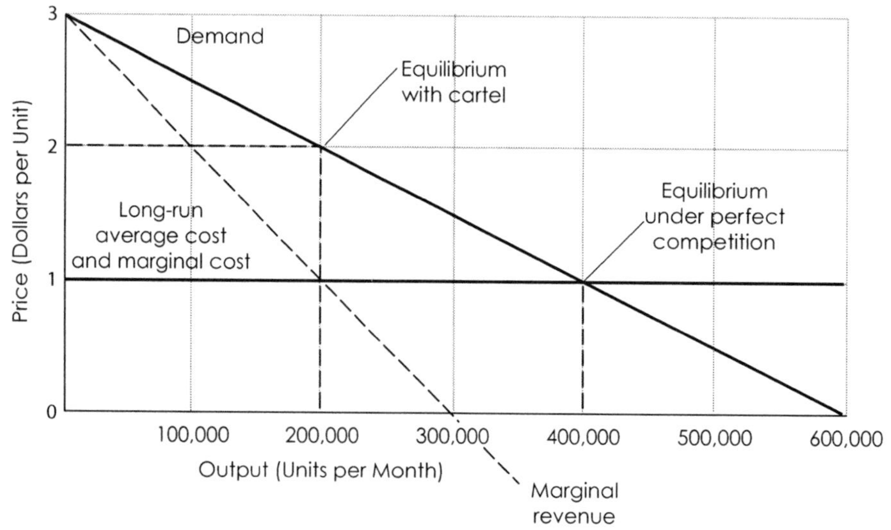

This graph shows an industry made up of one hundred firms, each producing at a constant long-run average and marginal cost. If the firms act like perfect competitors, the industry will be in equilibrium at the point at which the demand and marginal cost curves intersect. If the firms form a cartel, however, they can jointly earn profits by restricting output to the point at which marginal cost equals marginal revenue and raising the price from $1 to $2.

the market price is $3.90 per gallon (equal to long-run average cost and long-run marginal cost) and sell 400,000 gallons of gas each month. In that equilibrium, firms earn no economic profit.

Now suppose that one day the heads of the one hundred firms meet to form a cartel. They elect a cartel manager, who is asked to work out a production and marketing plan that will result in the maximum possible total profits for the industry, and to divide them fairly among the members.

The profit-maximizing problem that the cartel manager faces is exactly the same as the one faced by a monopolist. Industry profits are highest at the output level at which marginal revenue equals marginal cost—200,000 units per month. If output is restricted to that quantity, the price can be raised to $4.45 per unit, which will yield $200,000 per month of pure economic profit.

To divide this profit among all the cartel members, the manager will give each firm an output quota of 2,000 units a month, half as much as each was producing before the cartel was formed. In that way the member firms will reap the benefits of pure monopoly despite their small size and large number.

THE STABILITY PROBLEM Although cartels are good for their members, they are not so good for consumers. For them, cartels mean a smaller supply of goods and higher prices. Fortunately for consumers, cartels have some built-in problems that make them hard to form and unstable over time.

The first problem faced by cartels is control over entry. As we have seen, any industry in which prices are higher than long-run average cost tends to attract new firms. Because the whole point of a cartel is to raise prices above the competitive level, a cartel acts as a magnet for entrepreneurs. Remember the law of supply: as prices increase, the quantity supplied increases. Cartel members must limit their output, but non-cartel members will be encouraged to enter the market. But the entry of new firms into the market does not increase the total amount that the cartel can sell at the profit-maximizing price. More firms only mean that the profits must be divided into smaller shares. It is not enough simply to say that new producers cannot join the cartel. If they enter as independent producers, selling outside the framework of the cartel's market sharing agreement, they still depress the cartel's profits. Any cartel, then, needs to find a way to control entry into its market if it is to serve the interests of its founding members.

A second—and even more serious—inherent problem faced by cartels is enforcing output quotas. In a cartel each member has an incentive to cheat. The cheating takes the form of producing output beyond its quota, and the reward, if the cheating is successful, is greater profit. Take the cartel in Figure 10.2. As noted earlier, the quota for each of the one hundred members is 2,000 units per month—just half of what each would produce under perfect competition.

What would happen if one firm cheated on its quota by stepping up its output while the others went on playing by the rules? The answer is simple: Production of an extra 2,000 units per month would have only a small effect on the market price, because it would represent only a 1 percent increase in total industry output. By producing 4,000 units a month, the cheater would double its monthly profit—as long as other firms in the market did not cheat too.

But what if ninety-nine firms cheated and stepped up their output to 4,000 units while the remaining firm stuck to its quota? With industry output at 398,000 units, the price would be forced down toward the competitive level of $1. The firm that played fair would gain nothing for having done so.

The conclusion to which this leads is that every member of a cartel will have an incentive to cheat if it expects other members to play fair—and it will also have an incentive to cheat if it expects others to cheat as well.

CARTELS IN PRACTICE The problems of entry and cheating affect all cartels. The Organization of Petroleum Exporting Countries (OPEC) is a well-known case. In 1973, OPEC controlled about 60 percent of the oil imports of the industrialized countries. Taking advantage of its market power, in the next eight years it increased crude oil prices about tenfold, to a level approaching $40 per barrel (equivalent to over $100 a barrel in 2005 dollars). Output was divided among the cartel's members in proportion to formulas that were agreed upon at meetings of the oil ministers of the various OPEC countries. Saudi Arabia, the largest producer, had the greatest influence and the largest quota.

The price increase brought the OPEC countries fabulous wealth in the short run. However, it also spurred output in non-OPEC areas, such as Alaska, the North Sea, and Mexico (Law of Supply: higher prices increase higher quantity coming to market). Moreover, the demand for oil proved more elastic in the long run than in the short run as factories installed energy conservation equipment and consumers bought more fuel-efficient cars. As a result of these changes, OPEC lost half of its former market share. Saudi Arabia cut back its own output to less than 25 percent of capacity and tried to persuade smaller member countries to accept lower quotas as well. But cheating in terms of both price and quantity became widespread. By 1986 the OPEC cartel was in disarray; at one point the market price of oil plunged below $10 a barrel.

Since that time, oil prices have recovered. One reason is a slowing pace of new oil discoveries. Another is booming oil demand in China and India. As a result, oil prices have risen to record highs in nominal terms, and near their historic highs measured in constant dollars. Whether this latest increase can be attributable to supply restriction by OPEC rather than supply and demand conditions on the world market is open to question, however.

Because cartels that depend on voluntary cooperation among members run into problems, some cartels have enlisted the government to enforce quotas and restrict entry. (One justification Sadam Hussein used to explain his 1990 invasion of Kuwait was that Kuwait was exceeding their oil quota and thus pushing down the price of Iraqi oil. Sad am stated that his invasion of Kuwait was justified because Kuwaiti over production was stealing oil revenue from the people of Iraq. In the United States, agricultural cartels known as *marketing orders* are a case in point. However, as can be seen from *Economics in the News 10.1*, even government-assisted cartels may eventually collapse.

With crude oil prices hitting record highs over $125 a barrel (Spring, 2008) economic theory and the law of supply predicts the entry of new suppliers into the market. There is discussion of opening the Alaska wilderness to oil drilling and the search for new sources of oil in the oceans off America's coasts is becoming ever closer. Also, at these high prices, the profitability of alternatives to oil become more realistic. We are aware of the battery technology that is quickly developing and improving as well as the use of agriculture to produce ethanol to fuel our Yukon Corneliuses, Suburban Assault Vehicles, our Lake Tahoe, and our, oh so necessary, HUMMERS.

ECONOMICS IN THE NEWS 10.1

BIG TOBACCO, LAWSUITS, AND COMPETITION

The U.S. Department of Justice attempts to monitor industry competitiveness using industry concentration ratios and HHI values. This does not entirely prevent cartels among U.S. producers, especially those protected by regulations dating back to the early twentieth century. For instance, many people know that they are dealing with a cartel when they buy gasoline. But few people realize that for years they were doing the same whenever they bought a pack of cigarettes.

The U.S. tobacco industry is, to a large degree, controlled by the four largest cigarette companies: Altria, R. J. Reynolds, Brown & Williamson, and Lorillard. While not legally permitted to fix prices on tobacco products, these companies have implicitly colluded in the way they have dealt with their recent lawsuit settlements. For years, Big Tobacco fought off lawsuits claiming the companies concealed the true health risks associated with smoking, but a new wave of successful suits led to a large settlement between the big-four companies and state attorneys general in 1998. The settlement required that the companies pay about $200 billion over twenty-five years to cover the states' costs of health care for smokers. If the big four could not be sure of continued high revenues, they would have had a hard time paying these enormous sums, so the settlement enlisted states to support a big-brand cartel that keeps prices high by imposing fees on small rivals not covered by the settlement.

The agreement highlights an important relationship between regulation and competition: the big tobacco producers might not have settled unless the states tried to stop small rivals from undercutting its prices; and the states stood to reap higher payments if the major brands fared well. So, many states passed laws requiring tobacco upstarts to pay the states fees equivalent to—or, after taxes, even more than—what the big four companies pay in the settlement.

The settlement led to new anti-smoking ads, funded by the large tobacco producers themselves. While it appeared to the public a penalty on the big cigarette companies and a coup for state prosecutors, it actually benefits Altria, R. J. Reynolds, Brown & Williamson, and Lorillard. The increased fees paid by smaller tobacco companies make it harder for them to undercut the majors' prices.

Two small tobacco producers have filed a federal lawsuit challenging the settlement, claiming it violates federal antitrust laws. "This is not some bedroom conspiracy to fix prices that we have to prove. It's all there in the settlement," says lawyer David Dobbins, who represented the Las Vegas–based cigarette importer, Freedom Holdings. The big brands' "treble-damage liability is astronomical," he notes. "Eventually this cartel will be abolished and competition will return to the cigarette market."

The settlement may not be working out as well as the states and the big tobacco producers had hoped, however. States expect their settlement fees to fall 16 percent this year to a total $7.8 billion. The reason—entry of cheap, previously unknown brands, whose share has risen to nearly 10 percent of the market, up from 1 percent five years ago. This doesn't come as a surprise: The big brands raised their wholesale price $1.10, to over $3 a pack, several times the sum needed to fund their payments to the states.

Source: Scott Woolley, "A Cozy Cancer Cartel," *Forbes*, January 29, 2004.

Coordination Without Collusion

Formal cartels are not unknown, but they are rare. They are uncommon partly because of their inherent instability, as explained in the preceding section. Also—at least in the United States—most cartels are illegal under the antitrust laws. (Those laws will be described in a later chapter.) But we are left with the question of whether the firms in an oligopoly can, even without open collusion, tacitly coordinate their price and output decisions in a way that will jointly maximize their profit. To put it another way, will an industry in which there are only a few firms but no formal cartel perform more nearly like the model of perfect competition or like that of monopoly?

There have been a number of attempts to answer this question with formal models similar to those of perfect competition and monopoly. Those attempts have not been particularly successful, however, because there is no simple way to handle the problem of oligopolistic interdependence—the dependence of each firm's behavior on its rivals' decisions.

To construct a formal model, one must make a specific assumption about how each firm reacts to what its rivals do and how it expects them to react to what it does. One model, for example, assumes that each firm reacts to its rivals' changes in prices or output but expects them not to respond to changes in its own prices and output. Another model assumes that rivals will always match price cuts but never match price increases. Still another assumes that each firm expects its rivals to do the worst thing possible and plans accordingly.

Several formal models are described in the appendix to this chapter. None of them, however, offers a general solution to the question of how price and output decisions are made under oligopoly. In the absence of a general, formal model, much of the writing on oligopoly deals with informal theories consisting of conjectures about the conditions that tend to make cooperation by oligopolists easier or more difficult. Under conditions that facilitate formal, tacit coordination, price and output may tend to more closely resemble the results of a cartel. Under conditions that make coordination more difficult, price and output may tend to more nearly approximate the result of perfect competition. Some of the most common themes of the informal theories are described next.

NUMBER AND SIZE OF FIRMS There is little doubt that the number and size of the firms in a market make a big difference. Tacit coordination is easier in a market with only two or three large firms of roughly equal size than in a market in which a dozen equal-sized firms control half the market and the rest is controlled by smaller firms. If the number of firms is large enough and the size of the largest firms is sufficiently small, the market ceases to be an oligopoly. With a homogeneous product and easy entry and exit, it becomes perfectly competitive, as discussed in an earlier chapter. With a differentiated product and easy entry and exit, it becomes monopolistically competitive, a case that we will analyze later in this chapter.

The relative size and number of the various firms in the market are considered to be important on the ground that cooperation is easier in an industry in which there is one dominant firm. That firm may be able to act as a price leader. Under the strongest form of **price leadership**, firms are no longer uncertain about how their rivals will react to price changes. The leader knows that the others will follow it, whether it raises or lowers the price. The others know that if they follow the leader others will too, but not if they raise or lower prices on their own. When it works, this arrangement is tantamount to a cartel in that the dominant firm's efforts to maximize its own profit will also maximize the entire industry's profits. U.S. Steel and General Motors are examples of companies that were once thought to play the role of price leaders in their markets, although neither of these firms occupies the dominant position today that it once did.

Price leadership

A situation in which price increases or decreases by a dominant firm in an oligopoly, known as the price leader, are matched by all or most of the other firms in the market.

THE NATURE OF THE PRODUCT The nature of the product also affects the ease or difficulty of coordination. A homogeneous product for which there is a smooth flow of orders tends to make coordination easier; widely used steel products, such as railroad rails and wire, are examples. A variable product for which the flow of orders is irregular tends to make coordination more difficult; the ship building industry is a case in point. In such an industry, there are simply too many things to coordinate. It is not enough that all firms tacitly agree to sell at the same price; they must also agree on a set of price variations based on changes in quality, speed of delivery, size of order, and so on. Under these conditions an agreement to raise the price above the competitive level, even if it can be sustained, is unlikely to lead to higher profits. It is more likely to lead to an outbreak of competition by firms offering higher quality, more convenient scheduling, volume discounts, and so on. These factors will add to the cost of doing business or reduce revenue until excess profits disappear.

GROWTH AND INNOVATION The rates of growth and innovation in a market are another factor that is likely to affect the ease or difficulty of coordination among rival oligopolists. In a market in which product features, production techniques, and buyers' and sellers' personalities do not change from year to year, an agreement among firms, whether it is tacit or overt, will never have to be revised. In a market with rapidly changing elements, any agreement will soon be made obsolete by changing conditions or be disrupted by the entry of new buyers or sellers. Given the uncertainties of tacit agreements and the fact that overt ones are illegal, one would expect that the faster the pace of growth and change, the less successful rival firms will be in coordinating their activities.

EASE OF ENTRY AND EXIT Barriers to entry play an important role in the price and output decisions of an oligopoly. Even if there are only a few firms in the market, the threat of entry by new firms may force existing ones to practice limit pricing to avoid attracting new rivals. Under limit pricing, as explained in Chapter 9, the price is set below the profit-maximizing level implied by short-run demand, marginal revenue, and marginal cost.

Barriers to entry are also important in considering the effect of mergers on price and output decisions in an oligopoly. A merger within an oligopoly reduces the number of firms in the industry and, if the larger members are involved, increases the concentration ratio. Taken in isolation, a reduction in the number and an increase in the size of firms would tend to make coordination easier, perhaps leading to a more cartel-like result. Often, however, new firms quickly enter to fill any gaps left by mergers. The publishing industry is an example of one in which there have been several mergers of leading firms, but also many entries of new small firms, so that the degree of competition remains substantial. Also, as pointed out earlier in the chapter, sunk costs that cannot be recovered when the firm leaves the market can be as important as ease of entry in determining price and output decisions under oligopoly.

Market Performance Under Oligopoly

Neither the formal theories discussed in the appendix to this chapter nor the informal rules of thumb just presented give conclusive answers to the question of market performance under oligopoly. Depending on the situation, some oligopolies may behave much like perfectly competitive markets, with prices equal or close to marginal cost. Others, with or without open collusion, may behave more like a monopoly, with prices higher than marginal cost and a resulting deadweight loss.

When they cannot answer questions about market performance by means of pure theory, economists turn to statistical methods. Ideally, one would like to measure the gap between price and marginal cost at the point of market equilibrium, but it is rarely possible to do so. In the absence of reliable data on marginal cost, an indirect approach can be used. If firms in concentrated industries can be shown, on average, to earn returns that exceed the opportunity cost of capital, one can infer that they are behaving more like monopolists than like perfect competitors. If, on the other hand, firms in concentrated industries earn only "normal profits"—that is, rates of return on capital that are no higher, on average, than those earned by firms in less concentrated industries—one can conclude that oligopolies perform about as well as more competitive industries. Following this reasoning, much of the debate about market performance under oligopoly focuses on rates of return.

The first person to try this approach in a systematic way was University of California professor Joe Bain. In 1951 Bain published the results of a study of forty-two selected industries for the years 1936 to 1940. According to Bain's analysis of the data, industries with concentration ratios of over seventy earned higher profits than less concentrated ones. The link between profits and concentration was neither perfect nor strong, but it did exist.

During the 1950s and 1960s many of Bain's students and followers repeated his studies for other industries and years. Most of them got the same results: a weak but persistent link between profits and concentration. Economists concluded that in general, the more highly concentrated an industry, the more it will tend to perform like a cartel or a monopoly. This would be true even if there were no agreement among rivals to raise prices and divide up markets.

As faith in this idea grew, economists tried as hard as they could to prove it, using the more advanced statistical techniques and better data that became available each year. But the harder they tried, the more elusive the connection became. Some studies showed that if the data are adjusted for the size of firms in different markets, the link between concentration and profits tends to disappear. Others indicated that if the data are adjusted for differences in advertising expenditures, the connection evaporates. Still others suggested that results like Bain's hold only in periods of recession and disappear with the return of prosperity.

Moreover, as the link between concentration and profits was becoming more ambiguous, economists were growing less certain about how such a link should be interpreted even if it could be confirmed. New reasons were found to explain why firms in more concentrated industries might appear to earn higher profits than firms in less concentrated ones. Those reasons had nothing to do with monopoly pricing or tacit coordination. For example, a concentrated industry that was growing rapidly might need to earn high profits to attract capital. Perhaps the high profits of the largest firms in each concentrated industry might simply reflect those firms' superior efficiency relative to smaller firms in the same industry. Finally, the higher profits that some concentrated industries appeared to earn might not be pure economic profits; they might merely reflect the fact that the categories used by accountants to record business transactions do not accurately reflect implicit costs.

Price and Quantity Under Equal Market Share

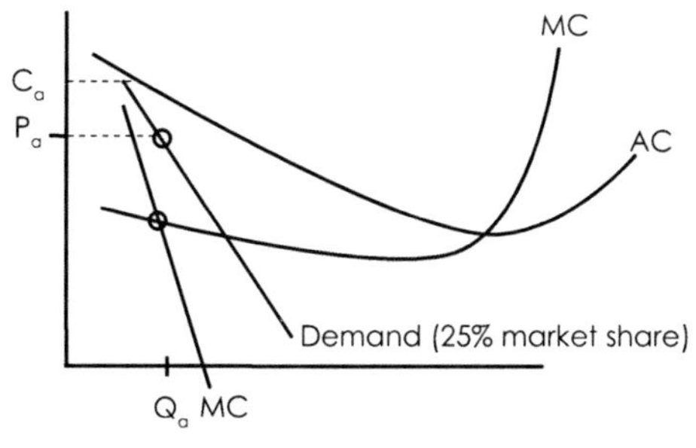

Assuming there are only a small number of firms in the market and each firm has an equal market share, but each firm's share is too small to enjoy significant economies of scale, then each firm could suffer losses as shown here. Each firm will follow the MC = MR rule for profit maximization, but in this case, at Q_a, each firm will charge price P_a but the cost to produce each unit is C_a which is greater than the revenue derived and therefore, each firm is losing money.

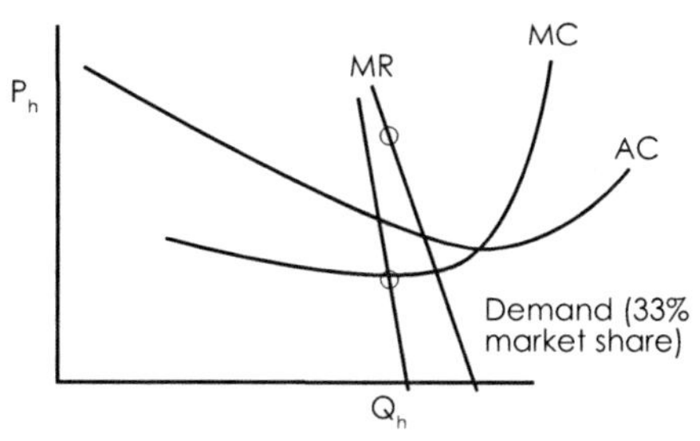

No firm will stay in a business where they are losing money for any extended period of time. After the first firm leaves the industry, the market share can be divided by the three remaining firms. This increase in share allows each firm to move down its cost curve all the while it can increase its price. Again using the

MR = MC rule now but on the one third market share, each firm produces Q_h but charges P_h, which is higher now than the cost to produce, thus, each firm earns an economic profit, where previously the four firms all incurred losses.

The Kinked Demand Curve Theory

In 1939, a century after Cournot, another major oligopoly theory was proposed. Known as the *kinked demand curve theory,* it was proposed at about the same time by the British economists R. L. Hall and C. J. Hitch and the American economist Paul M. Sweezy. Like the Cournot theory, the kinked demand curve theory begins from a simple assumption about oligopolists' reactions to price changes by rivals: Each firm expects that if it cuts its price, its rivals will match the cut, but that if it raises its price, no other firms will follow.

Figure 10.3 shows how the market looks to an oligopolist who makes these two assumptions. Let P be the price ($1.70, in this case) that happens to prevail in the market. If the firm cuts its price below P, other firms will lower their prices in turn. Sales in the industry as a whole will expand. The firm in question will keep about the same share of the market and will move down the lower slope of the demand curve. In con-

FIGURE 10.3 THE KINKED DEMAND CURVE THEORY OF OLIGOPOLY

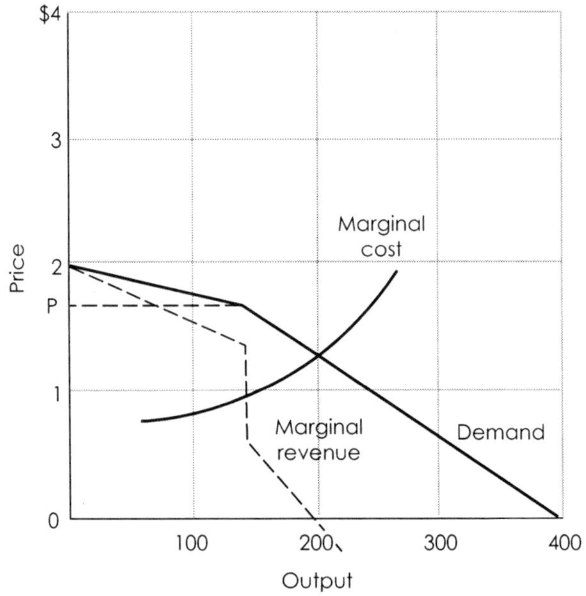

An oligopolist will have a kinked demand curve if its rivals will follow any price decrease it makes but will not follow price increases. There is a sharp step in the marginal revenue curve that corresponds to the kink in the demand curve. Here the marginal cost curve crosses the marginal revenue curve at the step. This makes the equilibrium very stable.

trast, if the firm raises its price, the others will not follow suit. Instead of keeping its share of the market, our firm will lose customers to its rivals. As a result, the part of the firm's demand curve above price P is much more elastic than the part below it.

Now bring marginal cost and marginal revenue into the picture. Give the firm a short-run marginal cost curve with the usual positive slope. The marginal revenue curve contains a step that corresponds to the kink in the demand curve. To the left of the step, marginal revenue is very high, showing that revenue will be lost quickly if the firm moves up the very elastic part of the demand curve. To the right of the step, marginal revenue is much lower, indicating that little extra revenue can be obtained by moving down the less elastic part of the demand curve. As drawn, the marginal cost curve cuts the marginal revenue curve right at the step. The prevailing price is an equilibrium price for the firm, because it will be unprofitable to move in either direction.

The kinked demand curve equilibrium for an oligopolist is a very stable kind of equilibrium. Unlike a pure monopolist, the oligopolist with a kinked demand curve will not change its price or output in response to small- or medium-sized changes in cost. The level of marginal cost shown in Figure 10.3 can move by as much as $.30 in either direction, and the firm will not change its price or output. The marginal cost curve will still cross the marginal revenue curve at the step. Only if marginal cost changes by more than $.30 will the firm break with the prevailing price.

Like the Cournot theory, the kinked demand curve theory is simple and elegant. Its assumptions about the way each oligopolist views its rivals' actions are clearly more plausible than Cournot's. But the kinked demand curve theory has a major limitation of its own. Although it explains why an oligopolist might be reluctant to change its price once it has set that price, it fails to show how the price comes to be set at any particular level in the first place. The theory thus provides an answer to a question that is not central to the analysis of oligopoly. In addition, some empirical studies have failed to confirm the theory's prediction that prices will be changed less often under oligopoly than under monopoly.

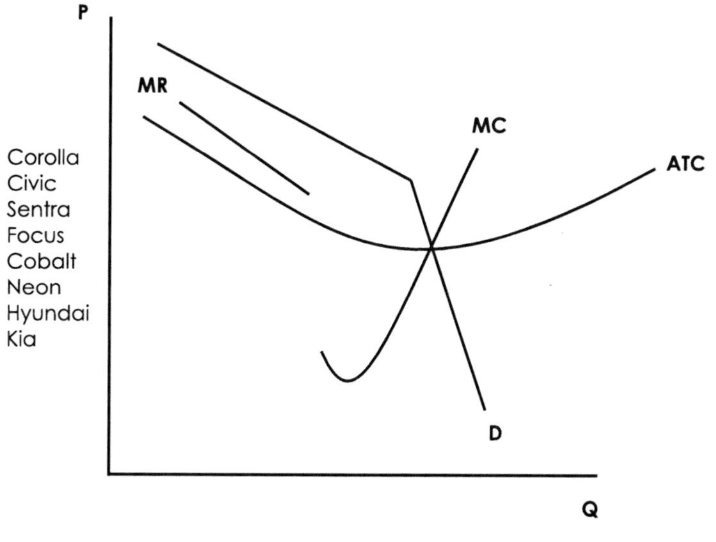

Think of the auto industry. A Toyota may cost more that a Neon, but not much more. The reason for this is that if Toyota would increase the price of their Corolla then even loyal Toyota customers would consider buying a now relatively lower priced Civic or some other substitute. As the Toyota price rises above the kink, it enters the elastic portion of the demand curve and therefore, quantity sold will decline dramatically as will total revenue to Toyota as consumers purchase the cheaper substitutes. (This is assuming the other competitors will NOT match the price increase of Toyota. Should If Toyota decreases their price below the kink, then it enters the inelastic portion of the demand curve causing only slight increase in quantity demanded and it is likely the competitors will match the price reduction of Toyota to maintain their market share. Thus we see sticky prices, that is, prices that don't fluctuate. In this case, non price competition may take place. Call manufactures will compete on image, marketing, style, not on price.

In some cases, a dominant firm may take the role of price leader. One firm will experiment with price increases and watch carefully the reaction of their competitors. Other firms in the industry may match the increase of the leader in an attempt to increase profits. However, if they don't, then the leader will retreat immediately and lower their price. This pricing behavior is evident in the airline industry. Prices are often raised by on firm, (sometimes late on a Friday afternoon) and the leader watches the reaction of the other competing firms. By Monday, the other firms will match the increase or the leader will lower their price. As long as these firms don't conspire to set or change price, this activity is legal. However, should competitors meet on a golf course or a country club and discuss pricing and agree to match prices increase, they are in violation of the Anti Trust laws and liable to prosecution and imprisonment. There are numerous examples of competitors conspiring and being punished.

THE THEORY OF MONOPOLISTIC COMPETITION

Up to this point we have looked at industries in which many small firms produce a homogeneous product and at others in which a few large firms make products that need not be alike. Those cases leave out a very large class of markets in which there are many small firms, each of which makes a product that differs slightly from those of its competitors. This market structure is known as *monopolistic competition*. Examples include restaurants, service stations, bakeries, some types of publishing companies, and countless others.

Characteristics of monopolistic competition:

1. Ease of entry/exit to market similar to perfect competition
2. Aggressive product differentiation by advertising
3. Price takers

Profit Maximization Under Monopolistic Competition

Although there is no general agreement on a formal model for oligopoly, there is a widely accepted model of monopolistic competition. As its name implies, this model, which dates from work done in the 1930s by Edward H. Chamberlin and independently by Joan Robinson, blends monopolistic and competitive aspects. Like a monopolist, the monopolistically competitive firm is a price searcher facing a negatively sloped demand curve. However, like the perfectly competitive firm, the monopolistic competitor is assumed to share the market with many other small firms. For this reason, the model of monopolistic competition ignores oligopolistic interdependence. It assumes that each firm in the market is so small that no one firm is significantly affected by what another one does.

The theory can be understood with the help of Figure 10.4, which shows short- and long-run equilibrium positions for a typical firm under monopolistic competition. The demand curve has a negative slope because each firm's product is a little different from its competitors' products. Each firm therefore can raise its price at least slightly without losing all its customers, because some customers attach more importance than others to the special style, location, or other marketing advantage the firm offers. Given this negatively sloped demand curve, the short-run profit-maximizing position shown in part (a) of the figure is found in the same way as that for a simple monopolist: The output level is determined by the intersection of the marginal cost and marginal revenue curves, and the price charged is determined by the height of the demand curve at that point.

However, this particular short-run equilibrium cannot also be long-run equilibrium under monopolistic competition. The reason is that monopolistically competi-

FIGURE 10.4 SHORT-RUN AND LONG-RUN EQUILIBRIUM UNDER MONOPOLISTIC COMPETITION

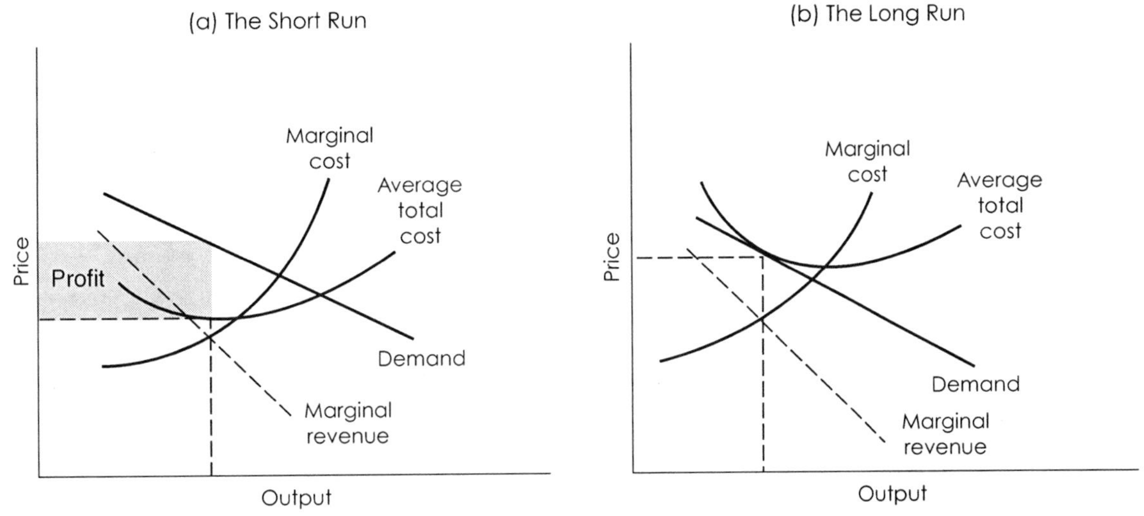

Under monopolistic competition, each firm is a price searcher with a negatively sloped demand curve but there are no barriers to entry by new firms. In the short run, a firm that produces at the point at which marginal cost equals marginal revenue can earn pure economic profits, as shown in part (a). In the long run, however, new firms are attracted to the market. This diverts part of the demand from firms that are already in the market, thus lowering each one's demand curve. Also, those firms may fight to keep their share of the market, using means that will increase their costs. Entry by new firms will continue until a long-run equilibrium is reached in which profits are eliminated, as shown in part (b).

tive markets are highly contestable, with easy entry and exit. In the short-run position shown in part (a) of Figure 10.4, the firm is earning a pure economic profit; this is shown by the fact that price exceeds average total cost.

But profits attract new firms. As new firms enter the market, two things happen. First, the demand curves of existing firms shift downward. This happens because the new firms' products, although they are not identical to those of the original firms, are substitutes for them. Second, in response to the new competition, firms that are already in the market may step up their advertising, improve their product in some way, or take other steps to win back customers. These efforts cause the firms' average total cost curves to shift upward. The downward shift in the original firms' demand curves, or the upward shift in their cost curves, or both, continue until there are no more profits to attract new firms. The result is the long-run equilibrium position shown in part (b) of Figure 10.4.

The Theory of Advertising

If asked, why firms advertise, your response would correctly be to increase sales. However, the further purpose would be to reduce costs. But how would spending millions of dollars for Michael Jordon, or Brittany Spears, or Tiger Woods, reduce costs? If the advertising campaign is successful, the new, higher cost curve will result in a point that is actually lower than the previous lower average cost. The total costs will increase as the firm pays for the celebrity and the TV/radio time is incurred. But the ATC will decline if the advertising campaign is successful.

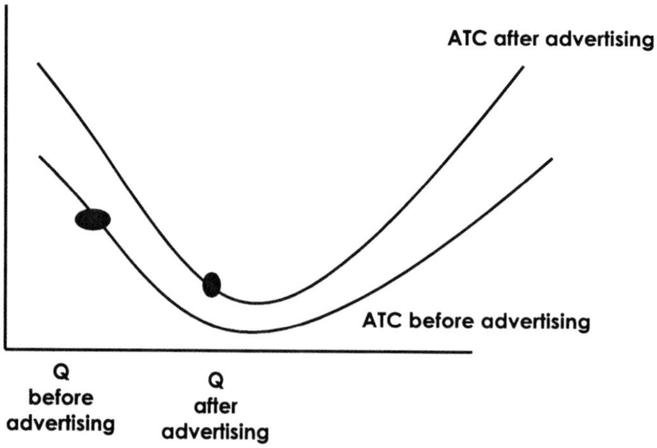

The Performance of Monopolistically Competitive Industries

Some economists have argued that the long-run equilibrium position shown in Figure 10.4 indicates poor performance by monopolistically competitive industries. For one thing, as in the case of pure monopoly, each firm stops short of the output level that would maximize the sum of producer and consumer surplus. Likewise, the gap between price and marginal cost indicates potential added production that would benefit both the firm and its customers. In addition, under monopolistic competition a firm does not operate at the lowest point on its long-run average cost curve. If there were fewer firms, each producing a greater amount of output, the same quantity of goods could be provided at a lower total cost. Following this reasoning, it has been argued that monopolistic competition results in too many gas stations, supermarkets, and restaurants, each operating at less than full capacity and each charging inefficiently high prices. Yet despite the high prices, each earns only the minimum return it needs to stay in business.

The problem with this critique is that it ignores the value of the product variety that is the hallmark of monopolistic competition. It is beside the point to argue that prices would be a little lower if there were fewer barbershops, each somewhat less conveniently located; or fewer supermarkets, each a little more crowded; or fewer ice cream flavors, even if some people could not have their favorite flavor. Would a move in that direction benefit consumers? Not if consumers are willing to pay something for variety. The Market—you and I—are willing to pay higher prices and accept inefficiency for variety.

When all is said and done, the prevailing view is that monopolistic competition and perfect competition are not all that different and that both serve customers reasonably well. Both fall into the category that Shepherd refers to as "effectively competitive." And it is encouraging to consider, as reported earlier in *Applying Economic Ideas 10.1*, that more than three-quarters of the economy fits into this broad category.

SUMMARY

1. **How has the structure of markets in the U.S. economy changed over time?** Aggregate concentration of U.S. industry has changed little in recent decades. *Concentration ratios* and the *Herfindahl-Hirschmann index* are two measures of the degree to which a market is dominated by a few firms. They can be used together with information about the behavior of firms to estimate the degree of competition in a market. More than three-quarters of U.S. output is produced in effectively competitive markets. The share of output produced by monopolies, oligopolies with dominant firms, and tight oligopolies appears to be declining.

2. **How does the interdependence of firms under oligopoly affect price and output decisions?** *Oligopolistic interdependence* refers to the need for each firm in an oligopoly to pay close attention to its rivals' actions when making decisions regarding price, output, or product characteristics. Oligopolistic interdependence makes it difficult to construct simple, generally applicable models of oligopoly.

3. **Why do oligopolistic firms sometimes collude to increase profits, and what problems do they encounter as a result?** A group of producers that jointly maximize profits by fixing prices and limiting output is known as a *cartel*. A cartel's profits are maximized by setting output at a level corresponding to the intersection of the marginal cost and marginal revenue curves for the industry as a whole. The chief problems encountered by cartels are controlling entry and preventing members from cheating on prices and output quotas.

4. **What conditions affect market performance under oligopoly?** Among the factors that are thought to affect market performance under oligopoly are the number and size of firms in the market, the presence or absence of *price leadership*,

the nature of the product (homogeneous or varied), the pace of growth and innovation, and the ease or difficulty of entry and exit. If barriers to entry and exit are low, a market is said to be *contestable*. Contestable markets are thought to perform well even if they are highly concentrated.

5. **How is equilibrium achieved under monopolistic competition, and how well do such markets perform?** A monopolistic competitor maximizes profit at the output level at which marginal cost equals marginal revenue. In the long run competition in such an industry results in an equilibrium in which price equals average total cost for each firm. In this equilibrium, price does not equal marginal cost and production does not take place at the point of minimum average total cost; nevertheless, consumers enjoy the benefit of product variety.

KEY TERMS

Market concentration
Concentration ratio
Herfindahl-Hirschmann index (HHI)
Barrier to entry
Contestable market
Oligopolistic interdependence
Cartel
Price leadership

PROBLEMS AND TOPICS FOR DISCUSSION

1. **Oligopolistic interdependence in action.** Look around your community for a case in which a firm is conducting a special sale or product promotion. To what extent, if at all, is the firm's action a response to something its rivals have done? To what extent, if at all, have its rivals reacted with their own sales or promotions?

2. **Barriers to entry.** "Barriers to entry are lower in the restaurant industry than in the airline industry because a restaurant requires only a few workers and a few thousand dollars in capital, whereas even a small airline requires many workers and millions of dollars in capital." Do you agree? Why or why not?

3. **The market for college education.** What market structure do you think best fits the market for college education? What factors do you believe affect the structure of the college education industry? How important are economies of scale? How important are barriers to entry and exit?

4. **Labor unions as cartels.** In what ways do labor unions resemble cartels? In what ways do they differ from cartels? Do you think labor unions ever suffer from the problems of instability that plague cartels?

CASE FOR DISCUSSION

All Things Begin Small

In 1994, the German automobile maker BMW acquired Rover Group, adding the British Mini Cooper to its collection of cars. In 2001, the Mini Cooper premiered at the Detroit auto show and was available for sale in the U.S. the following year. Despite the phenomenal growth in sport-utility vehicles in the U.S., the compact Mini has been extremely popular.

The rest of the world seems to share this sentiment. In the fall of 2003, BMW was considering plans to increase production of its Mini plant at Oxford to about 200,000 a year to meet growing demand. BMW's chief executive Helmut Panke estimated Mini sales could top 165,000 this year after hitting a record of 144,000 in 2002. By 2003 annual output was about 160,000.

There have been fears that capacity constraints at the Oxford plant could force some Mini production abroad, but Panke said the car would be built only at Oxford, where BMW planned to streamline production to remove bottlenecks. One option being considered is to lengthen workers' shifts from the traditional eight to nine or ten hours.

Panke said that output at BMW car plants could grow by between 40,000 and 50,000 units a year—with minimum investment. Increased output and sales of the Mini are integral to BMW's plans to lift global sales from 1 to 1.4 million between 2003 and 2008.

Panke held up the Mini as "a UK manufacturing success story," destroying the myth that Britain's manufacturing sector would never make a comeback.

Source: Based on David Gow, "BMW to boost production of 'UK success story,'" *Guardian Unlimited,* November 13, 2003.

QUESTIONS

1. How would you best characterize the market in which the Mini is sold: Perfectly competitive, oligopolistic, monopolistically competitive, or oligopoly? Why?
2. If the Mini enjoys strong demand, do you think that will allow BMW to charge a price higher than marginal cost? Why or why not?
3. How might BMW's rivals react to the introduction and success of the Mini? Do you think BMW must take this into account when planning its marketing strategy?
4. What sunk costs does BMW encounter when bringing out a new car like the Mini? What does this say about the degree to which the automobile market is contestable?

END NOTES

1. Anup Shah, "The Rise of Corporations," Globalissues.org, (http://www.globalissues.org/TradeRelated/Corporations/Rise.asp), July 16, 2005.
2. Lawrence J. White, "Trends in Aggregate Concentration in the United States," *Journal of Economic Perspectives,* Volume 16, No. 4 (Fall 2002): 137–160.
3. Julia Porter Liebeskind, Tim C. Opler, and Donald E. Hatfield, "Corporate Restructuring and the Consolidation of US Industry," *The Journal of Industrial Economics* 11(2) (March–April 1996).
4. See John S. McGee, "Efficiency and Economies of Size," in *Industrial Concentration: The New Learning,* eds. Harvey J. Goldschmid, Michael H. Mann, and Fred J. Weston (Boston: Little, Brown, 1974), 55–96.
5. Economists have struggled for decades to find consensus on the definition of "barrier to entry." For a survey of proposed definitions, see R. Preston MacAfee et. al., "What is a Barrier to Entry," *American Economic Review,* Papers and Proceedings (May 2004): 461–465.

CHAPTER 11

Oil

After reading this chapter, you will understand:

1. How the market structure of petroleum refining influences the price of gasoline at the pump.
2. How the demand for gasoline plays an equal part in determining the price of gasoline at the pump.

GASOLINE

Price at the Pump

By now, you should know that gasoline prices are increasing. Also, by now, you should know these price increases are not a result of a conspiracy of white, rich men in New York City plotting to separate you from your money. What's going on can be explained by the theory presented so far this semester.

First: Gasoline price is a function of the market: you and I deciding along with everyone else what the price is. So lets analysis DEMAND for gasoline.

Our Demand

We (you and I and everyone else who drives or expects products to be trucked or shipped to stores, etc.) want gasoline. Gas allows us mobility and increases our access to goods and services. This fuel that transports us and products we purchase improves our standard of living. Because of the value we place on our mobility the demand for gasoline is very inelastic. That is to say, we will do without many other things before we do without driving when and to where our whims dictate.

Also, demand is increasing. There are more of us wanting to drive. (Just look at the student parking lot of our high schools.) And, we want bigger cars! And, the Chinese and Indians are getting more affluent and cars and gasoline are normal goods. So, not only are we, Americans demanding ever more and more oil, those in developing nations also are demanding ever more petroleum.

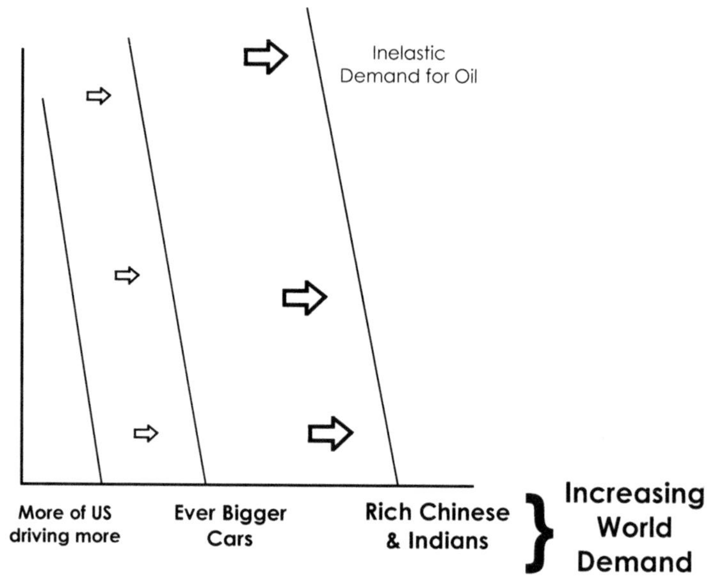

Next, our personalities are linked to our automobiles. How often do we hear that our personality is reflected in the type of car we buy? Because of the importance the car and the fuel to move the car is to our personalities and daily life functions, the utility derived from these products is relatively high!

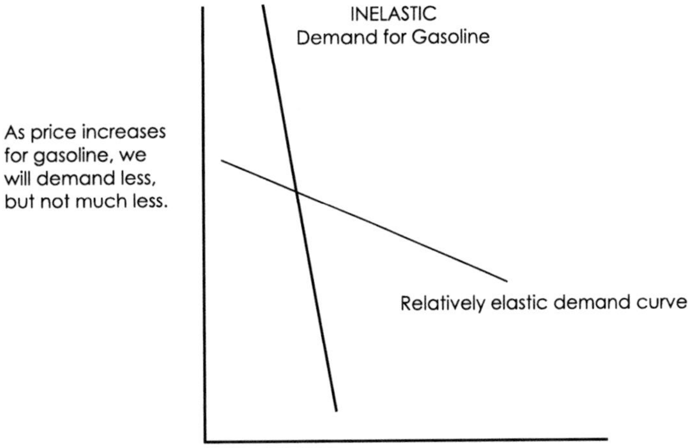

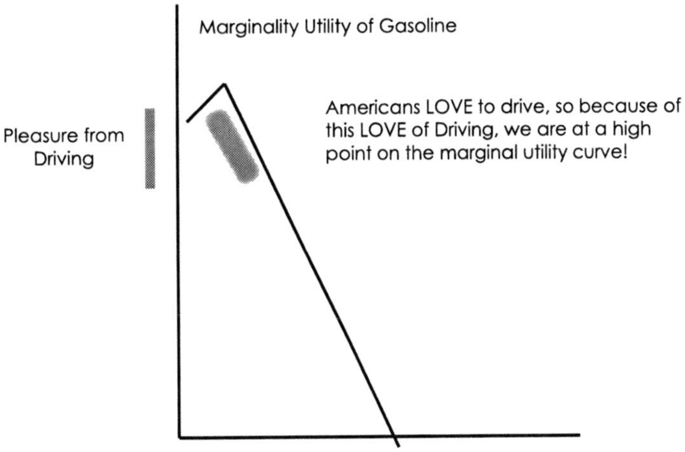

The Supply

As you should know, there are few refiners of gasoline because of high fixed costs and mergers and other barriers to entry. So, the gasoline refining industry fits perfectly the oligopoly model of price behavior. So, because of the lack of competition in this market, there is much less pressure to reduce prices and thus reduce profits. Because of the inelastic demand for gasoline, the higher prices of crude can be easily passed on to us, the burners of gasoline.

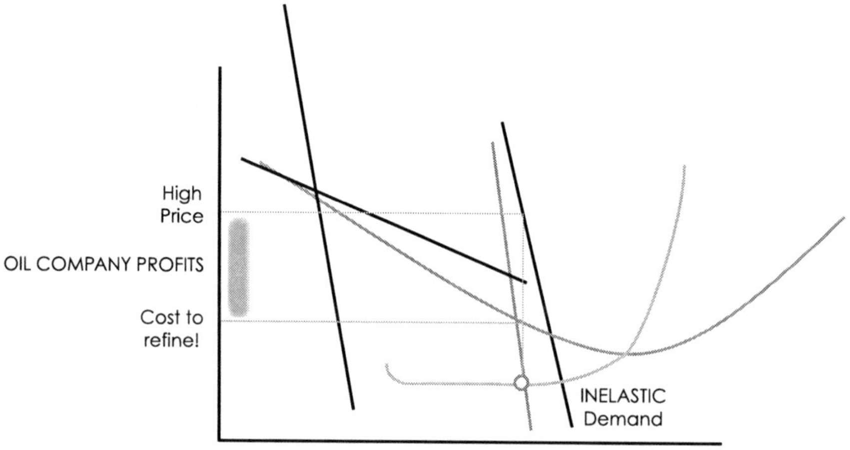

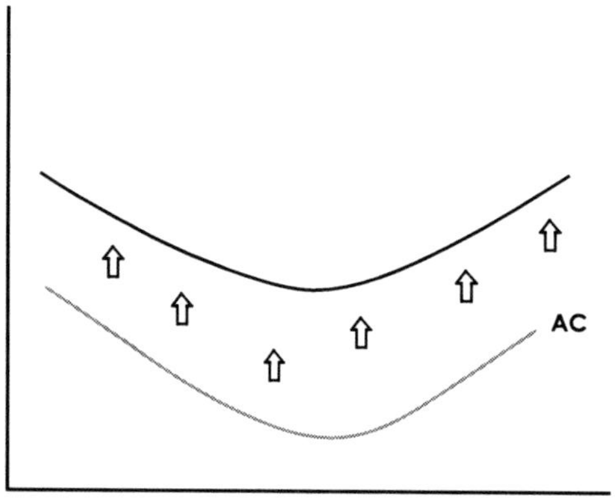

Costs to the Big Oil Companies

Today, there are political problems in Nigeria, Iran, and Venezuela. Also, Russian supply has not increased as predicted. Russian output disappointments are due to either political leverage of the Russian government to influence western nations, or technological inefficiency. Iran may come under UN economic sanctions because of their nuclear power developments and Nigerian rebels are disrupting oil pipelines. Because of these pressures on supply, the cost to American refineries are increasing.

Additionally, the government has required a different additive for domestic gasoline. Some states also require different blends of additives for gasoline for pollution, environmental reasons. This requirement for additives increases the cost of refining and transporting gasoline which causes the retail price to be higher.

Finally, it cannot be ignored that the states and national government tax gasoline. The tax collected by all levels of government on each gallon of gas sold is greater than the profits earned by the oil company on each gallon of gas sold.

So, the conclusion is that WE, the consumers, by our demand, play an equal role in the price of gasoline along with the suppliers (oil companies) and we bear an equal responsibility in the ever higher prices we are forced to pay. Also, our governments play a role in the price we pay by the taxes they levy.

The recent runup in prices of crude oil may be explained by the possibility of speculation. Because American stock market values have been declining and the real estate markets have been declining, investors are looking for places to invest with the most upside potential. Commodities have been the place where capital gains can be found, therefore, gold and oil have been favorite places for players of the market to invest. But a word of warning, if the spike in oil prices are a result of a rush to speculation, then just as the housing market crashed and just as the dot com internet stock market crashed, so too could the oil bubble burst and oil prices could come back down. As of Memorial Day of 2008, it is yet to be seen if this will happen.

Earth's Supply of Oil Declining??

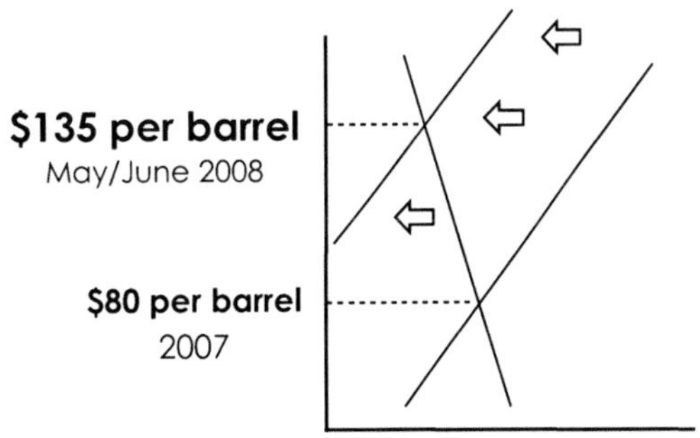

Another possible explanation for the runup in gas prices is the weak dollar. We must pay, in dollars for imported oil. As the dollar weakens, we must trade ever more dollars to obtain the oil we want to burn. One factor for the weak dollar is the action of the Federal Reserve. To protect American home prices and protect the American banking industry and the real estate and construction markets, the Fed has turned on the money spigots and have forced the interest rates down. Low American interest rates discourage foreigners from demanding our dollars thus weaking our currency. For the dollar to strengthen, the Fed will have to push rates up, thus causing problems for real estate and mortgage companies and home construction.

Finally, there is a gloomy theory that oil supplies have or will soon peak. Some believe that the earth has only a finite amount of crude oil and that humans have used so much and regardless of ever-improving technology, there just isn't any more oil to be found. This decline in supply could be the explanation in the recent spike of oil prices. If this is correct, we have a difficult adjustment period and the lower standard of living that higher transportation prices entail. But, (silver lining) ever higher prices with no expectation of lower adjustments will be an incentive for smart chemists and engineers to perfect and improve alternative technology to replace oil. Only trouble is that the new technology will cost more than oil in 2006 and won't be available until who knows when.

CHAPTER 12

Antitrust and Regulation

After reading this chapter, you will understand:

1. Which business practices are illegal under the antitrust laws
2. How economists' views on antitrust policy have changed over time
3. How natural monopolies are regulated and what problems are posed by regulation
4. Why some industries are regulated despite their inherently competitive structure
5. The effects of regulatory reform
6. Current trends in health and safety regulation

Before reading this chapter, make sure you know the meaning of:

1. Political rent seeking
2. Market failure
3. Public choice theory
4. Natural monopoly
5. Herfindahl index and concentration ratios
6. Transaction costs

Antitrust laws

A set of laws, including the Sherman Act and the Clayton Act, that seek to control market structure and the competitive behavior of firms.

IN EARLIER CHAPTERS we discussed the market failure and public choice theories of policy in general terms. Now we turn our attention to two specific areas of government policy to which these theories can be applied. We begin with a discussion of **antitrust laws**—a set of laws that seek to improve market performance by regulating the competitive behavior of firms. Later in the chapter we turn to other regulatory policies that also attempt to influence the competitive behavior of firms and the performance of markets.

ANTITRUST LAWS AND POLICIES

The antitrust laws are a complex group of statutes, court decisions, and regulatory rulings that have developed over the past century. What they have in common is the aim of regulating competitive practices that are deemed unfair, inefficient, or otherwise harmful to the public interest. We can begin our discussion of the antitrust laws with a brief review of the major statutes in this area.

The Sherman Antitrust Act

The Sherman Antitrust Act of 1890 forms the core of antitrust policy in the United States. It outlaws "every contract, combination in the form of a trust or otherwise, or conspiracy in restraint of commerce among the several States, or with foreign nations." It also declares that "every person who shall monopolize, or attempt to monopolize, or combine or conspire with any other person or persons, to monopolize any part of the trade or commerce among the several States, or with foreign nations, shall be deemed guilty of a misdemeanor." (In 1974 the act was amended so that violations of its provisions would be treated as felonies.)

The government can sue firms that violate the provisions of the Sherman Act and ask for any of several types of penalties. It can request fines or jail sentences. (The latter, once rare in antitrust cases, have become much more common now that violations constitute felonies.) It can also obtain an *injunction* (a court order that bars the offending firm from continuing an action that is in violation of the act). In extreme cases it can ask the court to order the offending firm to be broken up into smaller units that would compete with one another, as was done in the case of the AT&T telephone monopoly.

In addition, private parties who claim to have been harmed by violations of the Sherman Act can bring suits of their own. If they win, they can obtain damages equal to three times the value of any loss they can prove to have suffered. Private antitrust suits are quite common today.

The Clayton Act and the Federal Trade Commission Act

Antitrust officials of the federal government won some notable early victories under the Sherman Act; the most dramatic of these were the breakups of Standard Oil and American Tobacco in 1911. Nevertheless, many people felt that the Sherman Act was not enough. Their concerns led to the Clayton Act of 1914, which has four major provisions: (1) It outlaws certain forms of price discrimination; (2) it limits *tying contracts* (contracts for the sale of a firm's products that include an agreement prohibiting the purchaser from using or dealing in a competitor's products); (3) it restricts mergers achieved through purchase of stocks when the effect is to reduce competition substantially; and (4) it restricts *interlocking directorates* (situations in which the same person is on the boards of directors of two or more firms).

In the same year that it passed the Clayton Act, Congress passed the Federal Trade Commission Act, which supplements the former. This act declares broadly that "unfair methods of competition in commerce are illegal." It leaves the decision as to what constitutes an unfair method to the Federal Trade Commission (FTC), which was formed by the act as an independent agency with the purpose of attacking unfair practices.

Antitrust Policy

In practice, U.S. antitrust policy is not determined by the antitrust statutes alone. The laws are written in broad terms. Congress left to the courts the questions of what constitutes an "attempt to monopolize," a "substantial lessening of competition," and an "unfair method of competition." The government's two major antitrust agencies—the Federal Trade Commission and the Antitrust Division of the Department of Justice—also have a great deal of discretion in setting antitrust policy. Within the framework of the laws and prior court decisions, it is their job to decide precisely what kinds of business conduct should be viewed as anticompetitive.

This section outlines the growth of antitrust policy over the years with respect to the subjects of price fixing, mergers, so-called vertical restraints, and price discrimination.

Price fixing

Any attempt by two or more firms to cooperate in setting prices.

PRICE FIXING Whatever else the Sherman Act may do, no one denies that it outlaws **price fixing.** Competing firms must make their pricing decisions on their own; they cannot cooperate to set prices that are more to their liking than those resulting from independent action. The recent tendency of the courts and antitrust officials has been to treat price fixing as a *per se* violation of the law—which means that only the fact of a price-fixing agreement need be proven in order to win a conviction. Thus, in a case such as the one discussed at the beginning of the chapter, it is not necessary to prove that the price-fixing attempt was successful or that the prices set were unreasonable. Also, accused price fixers cannot defend themselves on the ground that their action might have had beneficial effects.

Besides making price fixing illegal, the law has been interpreted as applying to other forms of cooperative conduct that might affect prices indirectly. For example, certain practices that cartels engage in, such as agreeing to restrict output or divide markets, have been treated just as severely as agreements on prices.

There are numerous examples of cooperation among competitors. The producers of matzo, the unleavened food consumed by Jewish families at their Seder, Passover celebration, were accused of price fixing when the Justice Department caught officials from two most prominent producers, meeting at the same Brooklyn, NY deli and conspiring to set prices. Also, the members of the Ivy League and other prestigious universities were also accused of price fixing when it became apparent that the Penns, Yales, and Harvards of the country didn't want tuition price to be a factor in the decision of where to attend college. So the financial aid officers would meet and discuss aid packages and, it turned out, that the aid packages offered to students had the effect of making the tuition price almost identical at these elite institutions.

Horizontal mergers

Mergers of firms that compete in the same market.

Vertical mergers

Mergers of firms with a supplier-purchaser relationship.

Conglomerate mergers

Mergers of firms in unrelated markets.

MERGERS The Clayton Act includes provisions designed to discourage mergers, but initially these provisions did not prove to be very effective. Not until the Clayton Act was amended by the Celler-Kefauver Act in 1950 did control of mergers become a major part of antitrust law enforcement. After that time the courts and antitrust agencies moved in a direction that brought virtually any merger under scrutiny. Besides opposing **horizontal mergers** (mergers of firms that compete in the same market), the government often challenged **vertical mergers** (mergers of firms with a supplier-customer relationship, such as an automaker and a spark plug manufacturer). **Conglomerate mergers** (mergers of firms in unrelated markets, for example, an oil company and a retail chain) were also frequent targets of antitrust enforcement. In some cases, the Court acted despite the fact that the companies involved had relatively small market shares. It viewed its mission as one of stopping anticompetitive trends before they could start. Office Depot wanted to merge with Staples and the Department of Justice saw this as a threat to competition and disallowed this. It is yet to be seen if the proposed merger of Sirius Satellite Radio and XM Radio will be permitted.

CURRENT POLICY ON MERGERS Although the Celler-Kefauver Act remains on the books, federal policy on mergers tends to be much less strict than it was in the 1960s. The more permissive policy stems partly from trends in economic theory. For several reasons, economists are less certain that increased market concentration leads to poor performance than they were a few years ago.

First, economists now have a broader understanding of the potential gains in efficiency that might result from a merger. Such gains were once viewed narrowly, in terms of economies of scale in manufacturing operations. Now, as explained previously, economists believe that redrawing the boundaries of firms through mergers may produce savings in transaction costs as well as in production costs; also, mergers may improve market performance in entrepreneurial respects as well as in terms of static efficiency. Second, mergers are now widely seen as an important mechanism through which shareholders are able to discipline corporate directors and managers. And third, whereas merger policy once focused exclusively on the domestic economy, today international competition is often taken into account. For example, the 1987 merger of Chrysler and American Motors reduced the number of U.S. auto makers by one, but created a company more able to compete with Japanese rivals.

Today horizontal mergers, even between large firms, may be permitted if there is "clear and convincing" evidence that the merger would result in increased efficiency in production or nonproduction operations, or if one of the firms is in danger of failing if the merger does not take place. In addition to considerations of international competition, another reason the government did not challenge the merger of Chrysler and American Motors, despite a Herfindahl index of well over 2,000 for the industry with the combined firm, was that American Motors was viewed as a failing firm. Later the government approved a further merger between Chrysler and Germany's Daimler motors. Since that time, many additional large mergers have been approved, including AOL with Time-Warner and Exxon with Mobil. But not all such mergers are approved. In the same year that Chrysler merged with American Motors, the government blocked the proposed merger of Coca-Cola with Dr Pepper, seeing no mitigating circumstances in that case. More recently, the government intervened to prevent a merger of defense giants Lockheed Martin and Northrop Grumman.

In most cases vertical and conglomerate mergers are less likely to be challenged than horizontal mergers by firms of equal size. However, several factors could cause the Justice Department to object to such mergers, including the elimination of potential market entrants, the creation of barriers to entry, a tendency to facilitate collusion, or the elimination of a firm that has not "played along" with tacit cooperative arrangements in the past.

VERTICAL RESTRAINTS Like vertical mergers, vertical restraints on trade involve agreements between a supplier and a customer. They are distinct from horizontal restraints, such as the price-fixing case discussed at the beginning of the chapter, which involve agreements between direct competitors. Many kinds of vertical restraints have been attacked under the antitrust laws, though not always successfully. Among the kinds that have been challenged most often are resale price maintenance agreements, territorial restrictions, tying agreements, and exclusive dealing.

Under *resale price maintenance agreements,* retailers agree not to sell a good below a price set by the manufacturer. Such agreements have been held to be unlawful restraints on trade because they limit price competition among the retailers that carry the manufacturer's product. In practice, the prohibition on resale price maintenance has never been watertight; some agreements that indirectly achieve the same thing have survived court tests.

Manufacturer-imposed limits on the area in which a retailer can sell a product also reduce competition at the retail level. Antitrust officials have viewed such *territorial restrictions* with suspicion; but, as in the case of resale price maintenance, the ban on such restrictions has not been complete.

The Clayton Act outlaws *tying agreements* when their effect is to substantially limit competition. These include agreements under which a buyer is required to purchase one product in order to purchase another, for example, to buy a company's supplies if it buys its equipment. The Supreme Court has found that "tying arrangements serve hardly any purpose beyond the suppression of competition."[1]

In an *exclusive-dealing agreement,* a manufacturer obtains from a retailer a promise that the latter will not deal in products supplied by the manufacturer's competitors. Many exclusive-dealing agreements have been overturned by the courts, although the practice of exclusive dealing has survived in some industries.

Tying agreements and exclusive dealing agreements were at the heart of two of the biggest antitrust suits in recent years, those filed by the U.S. Department of Justice and the European Commission against Microsoft. Those suits are described in *Economics in News 12.1*.

Although many vertical restraints remain illegal under the Clayton Act, antitrust authorities are less inclined than formerly to pursue such cases vigorously. A major reason is the now widely held view that some vertical restraints have the desirable effect of reducing transaction costs and controlling opportunistic behavior.

For example, a computer manufacturer might want to impose retail price maintenance requirements to encourage retailers to provide high-quality presale consulting services to potential customers. If retailers were free to compete on the basis of price, some would choose to skimp on service in order to sell at deeply discounted prices. Customers could turn to the full-service dealers for presale consultation but make the

ECONOMICS IN THE NEWS 12.1

MICROSOFT VS. THE TRUSTBUSTERS

Microsoft Corporation is one of the great entrepreneurial successes of our times. Founded in 1975 by Bill Gates and Paul Allen, it got its big break when it secured a license in 1981 to write an operating system for the new IBM PC. It used the success of the MS-DOS operating system it created for IBM to increase its market share among competing hardware makers until, by the end of the 1990s, it was selling more than 90% of all personal computer operating systems worldwide. In the process, Bill Gates became famous as the world's wealthiest individual.

Not surprisingly, a company with such a dominant position in the market became a target of antitrust investigations. In 1994, the U.S. Department of Justice brought a complaint against Microsoft based on the alleged illegal use of exclusionary contracts and predatory conduct to maintain its dominant market position. The heart of the case consisted of a series of allegations about the relationship between Microsoft's operating system and its Internet Explorer browser. The government considered Microsoft's decision to "bundle" the browser together with the operating system to be an illegal exclusionary agreement. In addition, it considered the practice of giving away Internet Explorer without charge to be a form of predatory pricing. Both were seen as having the principal objective of placing the rival Netscape browser at a disadvantage.

Microsoft countered that the software market was more competitive than the Justice Department claimed. Its 90 percent market share could be attributed to "network effects" that are at work in any market where there is an advantage for two users to share a product or standard. However, it saw its dominant position as constantly under threat of "catastrophic entry" by some new technology. As a result, Microsoft was driven to keep its prices low (just one-sixteenth of the theoretical profit maximizing price, by one estimate) and constantly innovate. Although a large firm, to be sure, it argued that it served is customers well.

After years of litigation, a final settlement with the Department of Justice was reached in 2004. The settlement did not prevent Microsoft from tying its browser to its operating system—the cornerstone of the government's original case. It did require Microsoft to be more generous in providing information on the details of its operating system to rival software developers. The final result has hardly had an earth-shattering impact on the software market.

The settlement with the DOJ did not end Microsoft's antitrust troubles, however. While the U.S. suit was in progress, the European Commission, which has antitrust authority for the European Union, brought its own case. In many ways it was similar to that of the U.S. Department of Justice, although it focused on Microsoft's media player and its rivals rather than Internet browsers.

On balance, the European Commission has been tougher on Microsoft than the U.S. government. Its proposed settlement will, if fully implemented, prevent bundling of the media player, require strict sharing of information on software systems, and impose a large fine. At this writing, the parties are still litigating the final interpretation of the settlement.

actual purchase from a discounter. Such opportunistic behavior could eventually drive full-service dealers out of the market, leaving nothing but discounters.

The current thinking is that customers do not need to fear agreements between manufacturers and retailers as long as there are competing manufacturers. In such industries some manufacturers may adopt a high-price, high-service marketing strategy while others use a low-price, minimal-service strategy. This pattern, which can be seen in industries ranging from computers to designer clothes, gives consumers a wide range of choices.

PRICE DISCRIMINATION In the original Clayton Act, price discrimination was listed as an illegal practice, but that section was not widely enforced at first. Things changed in 1936. In that year the Clayton Act was amended by the Robinson-Patman Act, which greatly strengthened the law against price discrimination. Although the Robinson-Patman Act is complex, its basic purpose is to prevent price discrimination by sellers of goods (but not services). To this end it prevents sellers from offering different prices to different buyers unless it can be shown that any discounts reflect cost savings or are efforts to meet competition.

The Robinson-Patman Act has been criticized by economists for the ease with which it can be turned from a tool for promoting competition into a means by which a firm can shield itself from competition by its rivals. *Applying Economic Ideas 12.1* shows what can go wrong under the Robinson-Patman Act.

Partly because of the tendency of the Robinson-Patman Act to produce bizarre results, the government has sharply cut back its enforcement efforts in recent years.

Price Discrimination is not uncommon. The airlines price discriminate as well as restaurants, hotels, movie theaters, and pharmaceutical companies. To be able to price discriminate a firm must be able to segment consumers by their elasticity of demand, have some market (monopoly) power, and ensure the product cannot be resold.

THE NEW ECONOMICS OF ANTITRUST

For many years vigorous enforcement of antitrust laws enjoyed widespread support among economists. The need for antitrust policy seemed to follow naturally from traditional neoclassical economics, in which any departure from perfect competition is seen as a potential source of market failure. F. M. Scherer expressed the traditional view when he wrote in 1980 that "the enforcement of antitrust laws is one of the more important weapons wielded by government in its effort to harmonize the profit-seeking behavior of private enterprises with the public interest."[2]

However, that view of antitrust action no longer predominates. Today many economists are increasingly skeptical of antitrust policy, at least as practiced in the past. The critics include reformers, who think that a revised antitrust policy can still contribute to the defense of the public interest; public choice theorists, who see

APPLYING ECONOMIC IDEAS 12.1

THE UTAH PIE CASE

In 1958 Utah Pie Company, a local bakery in Salt Lake City, built a new frozen-pie plant. The frozen-pie market in that city was growing rapidly; in fact, it more than quadrupled in size between 1958 and 1961. Through an aggressive campaign stressing low prices, Utah Pie was able to capture a full two-thirds of this market soon after building its plant.

Utah Pie's main competitors were three national food product companies—Pet Milk Company, Carnation Milk Company, and Continental Baking Company. Nowhere else had these firms faced the kind of competition that Utah Pie was giving them. But rather than pulling out of the Salt Lake City market, they decided to fight back. By cutting prices on their own pies and making special deals with supermarkets to sell their pies under house brands, they succeeded in cutting Utah Pie's slice of the market back to 45 percent by 1961. (In absolute terms, Utah Pie's sales grew steadily throughout the period because the size of the market as a whole was growing.)

Angered by the actions of the three outside companies, Utah Pie sued them under the Robinson-Patman Act. Its lawyers claimed that Pet, Carnation, and Continental were engaging in illegal price discrimination by selling pies at lower prices in Salt Lake City than elsewhere. When the case reached the Supreme Court, it was decided in favor of Utah Pie. In the words of the Court, Pet, Carnation, and Continental "contributed to what proved to be a deteriorating price structure over the period covered by this suit," thereby harming the local firm. And that, said the Court, was just the sort of action the Robinson-Patman Act was designed to prevent.

Economist Ward Bowman has sharply criticized the Court's decision. Initially, Bowman points out, Utah Pie had a virtual monopoly over its local market. Then Pet, Carnation, and Continental moved in, with the result that consumers benefited from lower prices and more pies, although prices stayed high enough to give all four companies a profit. True, the three national companies did engage in price discrimination—they sold their pies more cheaply in Salt Lake City than elsewhere. But if that was a sign that something was wrong, the solution surely should have been to encourage more competition in the other markets, not less competition in Salt Lake City.

Sources: Ward S. Bowman, "Restraint of Trade by the Supreme Court: The Utah Pie Case," *Yale Law Journal* 77 (1967): 70–85; and *Utah Pie v. Continental Baking Co.*, 386 U.S. 685 (1967).

antitrust policy as a tool of political rent seekers; and members of the Austrian school, who argue for outright repeal of the antitrust laws.

The Antitrust Reformers

Antitrust reformers share the traditional view that government should intervene in the economy where necessary to correct market failures. In their view, the flaws in past policy stem from its failure to take into account such considerations as transaction costs and the scarcity value of information. When interpreted in terms of the new extensions of neoclassical economics, many business practices that once seemed harmful now appear benign. The reformers propose that future antitrust efforts be guided by the following principles:

1. Consumer welfare should be the touchstone of antitrust policy. The potential benefits of any action in terms of efficiency of production or distribution should be weighed against possible anticompetitive effects in judging consumer welfare.
2. The main enforcement targets should be conspiracies to fix prices or divide markets, horizontal mergers that would create very large market shares, and

predatory actions aimed at harming competitors (with predation carefully distinguished from active competition). (Howard Stern and Oprah Winfrey on satellite radio?)

3. Enforcement actions should not overemphasize vertical restraints, nor should they be directed at small horizontal mergers or any vertical or conglomerate merger or at price discrimination.

In setting forth a similar program for antitrust policy, Robert Bork wrote in 1978 that these are "not prescriptions for the nonenforcement of the antitrust laws, but rather for their enforcement in a way that advances, rather than retards, competition and consumer welfare."[3] Beginning about that time, a number of academic critics of traditional antitrust policy left their universities for government posts. Among them were William Baxter, who headed the antitrust division of the Department of Justice during the first term of the Reagan administration, and James C. Miller III, who headed the Federal Trade Commission. Other critics, including Bork, Richard Posner, and Ralph Winter, were appointed to federal judgeships.

Meanwhile, trends in legal education were also having an effect on the thinking of antitrust lawyers. Legal education has long stressed learning from past cases and judicial opinions. Today, however, this aspect of legal training is often supplemented with formal training in economics. As a result, students of antitrust law are encouraged to focus more closely on the questions of efficiency and consumer welfare raised by the cases with which they deal.

Antitrust and Public Choice Theory

Public choice theorists look at antitrust policy from a different perspective. As in other areas of government policy, they reject the notion that government policy is driven primarily by pursuit of the general public interest. Instead, they see antitrust policy as rooted in the private interests of voters, lobbyists, legislators, and bureaucrats.

The history of antitrust policy offers more than a little support for such a view. At the time that the Sherman Antitrust Act was passed, neoclassical economics, with its concepts of efficiency and market failure, barely existed. Americans were hostile toward "trusts," as they called the large firms of their day, not because they were inefficient but because they were rich and powerful. If they were efficient as well, that made them still richer and more powerful. Consider the viewpoint reflected in the following passage from an 1897 Supreme Court decision:

> *[Large firms] may even temporarily, or perhaps permanently, reduce the price of the article traded in or manufactured, by reducing the expense inseparable from the running of many different companies for the same purpose. Trade or commerce under those circumstances may nevertheless be badly and unfortunately restrained by driving out of business the small dealers and worthy men whose lives have been spent therein and who might be*

> *unable to readjust themselves to their altered surroundings. Mere reduction in the price of the commodity dealt in might be dearly paid for by the ruin of such a class.*[4]

Modern public choice theorists believe that today, as in the past, antitrust policy is shaped by the interests of "small dealers and worthy men." The essence of the antitrust laws, they say, is to transfer rights from large economic entities to small ones.[5] The mechanism that brings this about can be described as follows.

First, it is said, small-business interests, which are expressed through community leaders in every congressional district, exercise substantial influence. Lawmakers accommodate those interests through broad measures such as antitrust laws while keeping their big-business constituents happy through more narrowly focused benefits such as corporate tax loopholes and military contracts. Having passed a set of broadly written antitrust laws, the legislatures turn enforcement over to the bureaucracy.

The second force shaping antitrust policy, then, is the self-interest of the enforcement agencies. These agencies, like other bureaus, seek to maximize their budgets, the size of their staffs, and the number of cases brought by the agencies. In the opinion of some observers, these universal bureaucratic tendencies have been sharpened by the unusual arrangement under which antitrust enforcement is divided between two competing federal agencies, the FTC and the Justice Department. The cases brought by these agencies, some say, have little if anything to do with the public interest. Rather, as Richard Posner once put it, they are undertaken "at the behest of corporations, trade associations, and trade unions whose motivation is at best to shift the costs of their private litigation to the taxpayer and at worst to harass competitors."[6] Thus, the bureaucratic interests of the enforcement agencies in creating more litigation dovetail neatly with those of political rent seekers in the business community.

From the perspective of public choice theory, such cases as *Utah Pie* are not products of mistaken economic theory or misinterpretations of the public interest by prosecutors and judges. Rather, they are a natural outcome of the political process that created the antitrust laws in the first place.

The Future of Antitrust Policy

As the discussion in the preceding section made clear, reformers succeeded in making a number of important changes in antitrust policy during the 1980s. In many respects, their once-radical ideas have become the new conventional wisdom. Does this mean that antitrust policy will play a permanently reduced role in economic affairs, with possible repeal of some of the more restrictive statutes? Perhaps, but perhaps not.

For one thing, outside the economics profession the old populist view of antitrust action remains alive. As one critic of recent reforms has put it, "antitrust [law] was intended also to further a social and moral vision of America. At the core of that vision was a conviction that the past greatness, and future potential, of the country depended on the kind of character—resourceful, practical, and determined—that only competitive individualism would foster."[8] (Consumer activist and former FTC Chairman Michael Pertschuk puts it more simply, characterizing the proper focus of antitrust policy as a "Jeffersonian preference for dispersed power" applied not only to the dispersion of power among various branches of government but also to the dispersion of economic power among a multitude of relatively small firms.)

At the same time, public choice theorists were skeptical as to whether the changes brought about by the reformers of the 1980s would last, given no change in the underlying constitutional arrangements and the influence of special-interest groups. For example, Robert Tollison characterized the idea that "better people make better government" as "tried and true nonsense." Government, he said, "cranks along by an internal logic of its own."[9] Tollison, it should be noted, was himself a top staff economist on the FTC under the chairmanship of reformer James Miller, so perhaps he knows whereof he speaks.

REGULATION OF NATURAL MONOPOLY

The aim of antitrust policy is to prevent one firm, or a few firms acting in concert, from gaining control of a market. However, there are some cases, known as natural monopolies, in which there is no practical way to avoid the dominance of one firm. In this section we examine policies intended to improve the performance of these markets, and also the unintended consequences such policies sometimes bring about.

The Policy Problem

A *natural monopoly* is an industry in which total costs are kept to a minimum by having just one producer serve the whole market. A natural monopoly is a situation where competition, *from society's point of view,* would be inconvenient, unworkable, or unmanageable. Local gas, electric, cable TV, and water services are often cited as examples. It is easy for one such utility to hook up more customers once it has run its lines into their neighborhood, but it is wasteful and costly for a number of different companies to run lines down the same street.

The policy problem raised by a natural monopoly is how to keep the firm from taking advantage of its position to raise prices and restrict output. Consider the example shown in Figure 12.1. That firm, an electric utility, has constant marginal costs and a negatively sloped long-run average cost curve. The demand curve intersects the long-run average cost curve at quantity Q_1, not far from the minimum efficient scale of production. If this output were divided between two firms, each of which produced half of quantity Q_1, the cost per unit would be a lot higher—and still more so if there were more than two firms.

If one unregulated firm operates in a market, it can be expected to act like a pure monopolist. Instead of producing Q_1 it will produce Q_2, which corresponds to the

FIGURE 12.1 REGULATION OF A NATURAL MONOPOLY

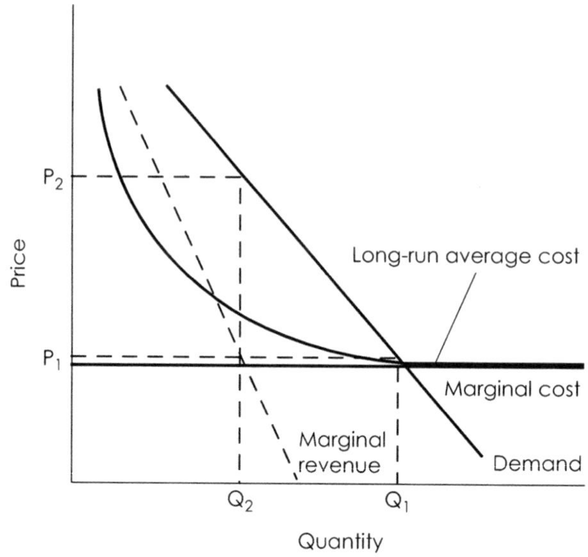

This graph shows the cost and demand curves for a natural monopoly such as an electric utility. As an unregulated monopolist, the firm would make the maximum profit by charging price P_2 and selling quantity Q_2. If regulators impose a maximum price of P_1, the firm will find it worthwhile to produce quantity Q_1.

intersection of the firm's marginal revenue and marginal cost curves. The price that corresponds to this output is P_2, which is far above marginal cost. This is too small an output and too high a price to permit efficient production.

The Regulatory Solution

It appears, then, that in a natural monopoly competition by two or more firms is inefficient, as is monopoly pricing by a single firm. The traditional solution is to allow just one firm to operate but to regulate the price at which it can sell its output. For example, the firm may be limited to a price of no more than P_1, the price at which the demand curve intersects the long-run average cost curve in Figure 12.1 With this price ceiling in force, the firm becomes a price taker for output levels up to Q_1, because even if it kept output below that level, it would be prevented from further raising the price. The maximum profit is earned under the regulated price by producing Q_1 units of output. This is a lower price and a greater quantity than would result either from an unregulated pure monopoly or from production by two or more competing firms.

For the market to be perfectly efficient, the price would have to be reduced to the level of marginal cost, which is slightly lower than P_1. At any price lower than P_1, however, the firm would suffer a loss. It could survive in the long run only if it were subsidized. By allowing the firm to charge price P_1, which is high enough to just cover all costs, the regulators would avoid the need for a subsidy while giving up only a small degree of efficiency.

FAIR RETURN TO INVESTMENT PRICE OF A REGULATED MONOPOLY

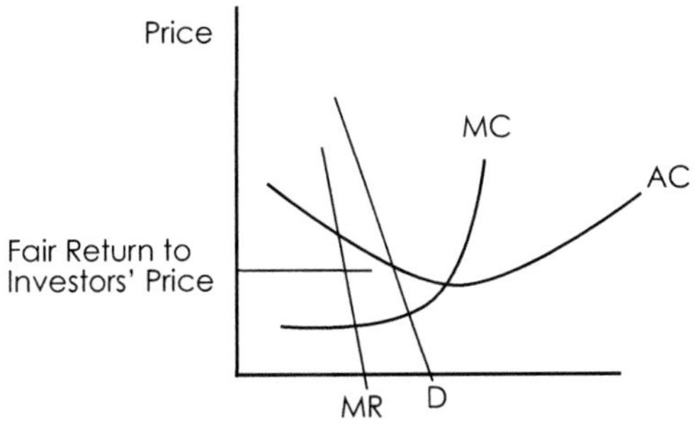

PSC sets price at the Q where AC + Demand

This price includes a normal profit, allowing the monopoly to earn what the PSC considers a fair return on investment.

FAIR RATE OF RETURN AS A FOCUS OF REGULATION The correct regulated price in Figure 12.1 is easy to identify because the shapes and positions of the demand and cost curves are right there on the page. In the real world, however, regulators do not have complete information about demand and cost. Lacking this information, they set the regulated price indirectly by focusing on the **rate of return** earned by the firm. The rate of return is the firm's accounting profit expressed as a percentage of its net worth.

Rate of return

A firm's accounting profit expressed as a percentage of its net worth.

To see why the rate of return is a useful focus of regulatory policy, consider the implications of setting various prices. If the price is set equal to average total cost, the firm will earn a "normal profit," that is, a rate of return equal to the opportunity cost of capital. If the price is higher than average total cost, the firm will earn more than a normal profit, that is, enough to cover the opportunity cost of capital with some left over as economic profit. If the price is set below average total cost, the firm will earn less than a normal profit. Because revenue is insufficient to meet all opportunity costs, including that of capital, the firm will suffer an economic loss.

Armed with this reasoning, the regulators proceed in five steps:

1. They measure the value of the firm's capital—say, $1.2 million. This is called the *rate base*.
2. They measure the average rate of return for the economy, that is, the normal rate of profit. Suppose this turns out to be 15 percent per year. (In practice, steps 1 and 2 are more difficult than they sound, but for our purposes the regulators can be given the benefit of the doubt.)
3. They multiply the rate base by the permitted rate of return to calculate a total cost of capital for the firm—in this case, $180,000 per year. This sum should be enough both to make interest payments on the portion of the firm's capital that was acquired by borrowing and to yield an accounting profit high enough to compensate the owners for their investment in the firm.
4. They ask the firm to propose a price or set of prices that it thinks will allow it to meet its capital costs.

5. As time goes by, they keep track of the firm's actual rate of return, cutting the price if it rises above the normal level and allowing it to rise if returns fall below the normal level.

LIMITATIONS OF RATE-OF-RETURN REGULATION For a number of reasons, rate-of-return regulation may not always achieve its goals of lower prices and greater output. One possible reason is that regulators may be influenced by political rent seekers. This may occur, for example, if regulated firms "capture" the regulatory agency by gaining control over the appointment of regulators, or if regulators follow lax policies in the hope of finding well-paid jobs in the industry after their terms as regulators expire. On the other hand, regulatory agencies in some areas have been captured by groups that represent consumers. They seek the short-run gains that come from keeping rates low without regard for the regulated firms' long-run need to attract capital in order to maintain capacity and service quality.

Another possible problem is that regulators may not know enough about the industry to control its rate of return. It is by no means easy to measure such factors as the regulated firm's stock of capital, its actual rate of return, and the opportunity cost of capital. The more regulators must rely on guesswork, the less likely they are to be effective.

Finally, by allowing the firm to charge a price equal to its costs plus a normal profit, regulation distorts incentives. If a firm is allowed to earn revenues that exceed its cost by a certain maximum amount, why should it try to minimize its costs at all? Minimizing costs is hard work for managers. Why not relax and take things easy? Why not take Wednesday mornings off for golf? Install new carpeting in the boardroom? Give the president's nephew a job? There is no incentive to try to keep costs down.

DISTORTIONS CAUSED BY THE WRONG RATE OF RETURN For several reasons, then, regulators may set rates of return that are either higher or lower than the opportunity cost of capital. Either case will cause problems. For example, a study by Harvey Averch and Leland Johnson suggested that in the 1950s and 1960s regulated rates for electricity tended to be too high.[10] They allowed utilities to achieve a rate of return that was higher than the opportunity cost of capital. This gave the utilities' stockholders an indirect way of taking advantage of their monopoly position. They could raise capital to build new plants whether they were needed or not, and then add the plants into their rate base. The regulators then would allow them to raise their rates enough not only to pass along the costs of the new plants but to earn a pure economic profit as well. The outcome—now known as the *A-J effect*—was that too high a rate of return led to wasteful overinvestment in the regulated industry.

By the 1980s the situation had changed. Some economists came to fear that rates of return had fallen too low. If this were so, it would cause the A-J effect to operate in reverse. Utilities would avoid investing in new plants even when the plants would be justified from the consumer's point of view. Such a policy of "rate suppression" might keep rates low for consumers for many years before problems become apparent. But as old plants wear out, the quality of service falls. Some writers predict serious shortages of electric power in the future if rate suppression continues.

Not all economists agree that rate suppression is widespread. It is no easier for outside observers to know whether a utility is charging just the right rates than it is for regulators to make this judgment. It is widely agreed, however, that the A-J effect cuts both ways: Either too high or too low an allowed rate of return is harmful. Thus, in their search for efficiency regulators must walk a narrow line between two kinds of errors.

Each state has its own system of natural monopoly regulation. In Maryland, the Public Service Commission has the responsibility of regulating (setting) utility prices. The members of the PSC are appointed by the governor. In 2006, the PSC appointed by then Gov. Erlich and the electric rate increase were very controversial and a factor which led to the election of Martin O'Malley.

SOCIALLY OPTIMAL PRICE OF A REGULATED MONOPOLY

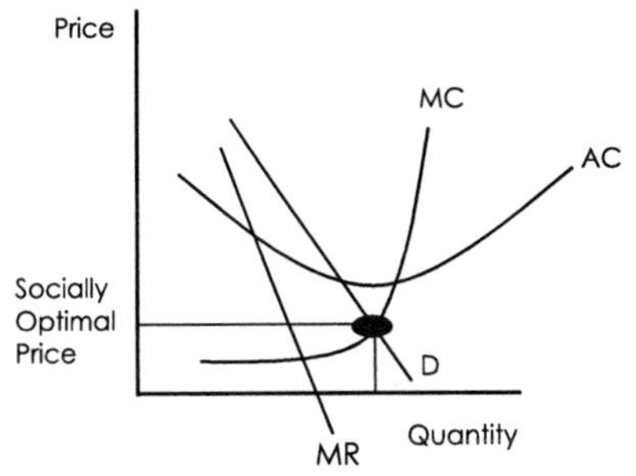

PSC sets price at the Q where MC = Demand

This low price is below the cost of producing, so this firm will LOSE money on each sale and therefore, require a government subsidy.

Another theory of regulation is the Social Optimal idea. Some industries and their products are considered to be in the best interest of society. If left unregulated, these industries would produce at a quantity and charge a price where marginal revenue is equal to marginal cost. This price would be much higher and this quantity would be much lower than is considered *best for society.* In this situation, the Public Service Commission will set the price charged where marginal cost is equal demand. (The fair return price was set where average cost is equal to demand.) As you can see from the graph, this would cause a situation where the cost to produce this product is greater than the revenue derived from each sale. Since firms cannot lose money indefinitely, it would be required that the government step in and provide a subsidy. This is the case with public transportation systems. For example, the bus that runs in Ocean City is a socially optimal natural monopoly. The state government has determined that it is in the best interest of society to have a means of transportation on a Friday or Saturday night at the Ocean. For parking reasons as well as DWI, DUI problems, it's in the interest of society to provide an alternative to private cars. So the price of the bus is set at $2 to encourage public transportation instead of driving by individuals who otherwise may be not capable of safe operation of motor vehicles. The $2 fare for the bus ride does not cover the cost of operating those buses in Ocean City. The same is true of the light rail and metro in Baltimore and the MVA. It is in the best interest of society to provide a means of transport for workers to get to work and also to reduce traffic on the Jonesalls and Route 695. So the MVA is funded by government subsidies more so than the fares charged. Do you think the $3.50 you pay to take the light rail to Camden Yards covers the cost of operating and maintaining the trolley cars to and from the stadium?

Or, does the fair you pay for riding the metro cover the costs of digging and maintaining the tunnel system under the city? No, it doesn't, and the taxpayers subsidize these transportation systems because it is believed it is in *society's best interest*.

REGULATION OF COMPETITIVE INDUSTRIES

Natural monopolies are not the only industries to come under regulation. There are many others—transportation, banking, finance, and communications, to name just a few—that have long been regulated even though their market structures, in the absence of regulation, are oligopolistic, monopolistically competitive, and in some cases, close to perfectly competitive. In this section we look at the regulation of competitive behavior in such industries.

Historical Origins

Railroads first came under regulation in the late nineteenth century, but the big surge in regulation came in the 1930s. One tends to think of the Great Depression mainly in terms of high unemployment; however, another major feature of the Depression was low prices. Between 1929 and 1933 the consumer price index dropped about 25 percent. Today most economists would explain both the high unemployment and the falling prices in macroeconomic terms, blaming them on low aggregate demand, inappropriate monetary policy, and so on. At the time, however, people tended to blame the high unemployment levels on low prices. If only prices could be raised, business leaders said, it would be possible to put more workers on the payroll.

It is not surprising that competition, which in many cases tends to keep prices low by comparison with monopolistic or oligopolistic market structures, was not popular during the Depression. In fact, too much competition was seen as a barrier to economic recovery. In 1933 Congress passed the National Recovery Act, which encouraged firms to use cartel-like methods to prop up prices. That act was declared unconstitutional by the Supreme Court, but other legislation that applied only to specific industries survived. Two of the most important industries that were regulated in order to limit competition were trucking, which was brought under the control of the Interstate Commerce Commission (ICC) in 1935, and airlines, which came under the regulation of the Civil Aeronautics Board (CAB) in 1938. As discussed in an earlier chapter, agricultural marketing orders, another way of limiting competition, date from the same period.

Rate and Entry Regulations in Transportation

The case of transportation regulation reveals some key differences between the regulation of competitive industries and that of natural monopolies. Two of these differences were a focus on controlling entry by new firms and a tendency to set minimum rather than maximum prices. The traditional argument for regulation of natural monopolies was that without regulation prices would rise too high. In the case of airlines and trucking, the concern was that without regulation prices would fall too low.

It is generally agreed that regulation of trucking and airlines achieved the goal of raising prices and limiting the number of firms in those industries. As the years passed, however, many economists began to have second thoughts as to whether high prices and limited competition were the proper goals of government policy. With the advent of high inflation rates in the 1970s, the doubts about regulation grew stronger, and economists turned almost unanimously against the regulation of entry and the setting of minimum rates in competitive industries.

Regulation and Political Rent Seeking

Critics of transportation regulation tended to view this area of policy as an example of political rent seeking. They saw regulation as a device that permits rival firms to form cartels, which enable them to raise prices above opportunity costs and earn profits in excess of those that would be possible in a more competitive environment.

REGULATED INDUSTRIES AS CARTELS It is easy to see why this theory developed. In an earlier chapter we saw that two major weaknesses of most cartels are inability to control competition by nonmembers and inability to keep members from cheating on price agreements. The laws that gave the ICC and the CAB authority over trucking and airlines were directed at these problems. Both agencies became highly restrictive in terms of entry by new firms. (The CAB did not let in a single new major airline for forty years, and the ICC was only slightly less restrictive.) Further, both agencies were granted, and used, the authority to prevent carriers from cutting prices below specified minimum levels, as well as the authority to regulate maximum rates.

A number of studies carried out in the 1960s and 1970s seemed to support the cartel theory of regulation. Many of them were based on comparisons of regulated and unregulated markets. One study, for example, showed that unregulated intrastate airline fares in California and Texas were only about half of regulated interstate fares for similar distances. Other studies compared regulated freight rates for industrial goods with those for agricultural produce, which had been exempted from regulation. Again the regulated rates seemed substantially higher.

IMPERFECTIONS IN THE CARTELS But certain aspects of regulation did not support the notion that regulators acted as cartel managers aiming solely to maximize the profits of regulated firms. For example, despite the CAB's best efforts, regulated airlines were not always able to earn high profits. In the trucking industry, the major users of freight service, which should have been hurt most by high rates, rarely complained—in fact, they tended to praise regulation for bringing about a high level of service.

In trying to explain these puzzling facts, economists began to pay more attention to imperfections in the cartels allegedly created by regulation. The most glaring of these was the fact that although airline and trucking regulations controlled *price* competition, they did not control *nonprice* competition. Both trucking firms and airlines were free to compete for customers by offering more frequent and convenient service, advertising more heavily, and engaging in active personal selling. This nonprice competition was very costly. In the case of airlines, for example, adding more flights every day meant that each flight would carry fewer passengers. Non-price competition thus pushed up the cost per passenger to a level so high that no matter what level of fares the CAB allowed, no more than a normal rate of return could be earned—and sometimes not even that.

As some of these effects of regulation became better understood, economists began to see that regulation could not be thought of simply in terms of a transfer of rents from users to producers. The effects of regulation were much more complicated than that. Some producers no doubt were sometimes able to earn higher profits than they otherwise would have. But most of the rents resulting from high fares went elsewhere.

Unionized workers were one group that seemed to benefit from regulation. Controls on entry reduced competition by nonunionized firms and made it possible for teamsters and airline pilots to bargain for higher wages. (Both of these unions strongly favored regulation.) Because nonprice competition sometimes put more planes in the sky and more trucks on the road than were actually needed, suppliers of trucks and planes may have enjoyed higher sales than they otherwise would have. Also, at least some customers were able to benefit from nonprice competition by getting a higher level of service than would have been likely without regulation. In particular, small shippers at out-of-the-way points may have benefited in that their rates did not always reflect the higher cost of their service compared with the cost of serving larger customers on heavily used routes.

Regulatory Reform

In the late 1970s long-standing criticisms of transportation regulation began to be translated into policy. Through legislation and the appointment of reform-minded regulators, restrictions on competition were eased for passenger airlines, air freight, trucking, and intercity bus service. There was also extensive deregulation of railroad rates and a relaxation of barriers to competition between railroads and motor freight. The CAB was abolished, and a few of its former powers were granted to the Federal Aviation Administration (FAA), whose main concern is air safety. The ICC stayed in business with a reduced staff and much more limited functions until 1995, when it, too, was terminated.

In addition to the reform of regulation in the transportation industries, there were significant regulatory reforms in other industries. In financial industries, banks were freed from regulations that had barred them from competing by offering higher interest rates and new services. In communications, the breakup of AT&T and the rise of cell phones brought competition to the telephone industry, and the Federal Communications Commission changed the regulatory atmosphere in radio and television broadcasting.

Certain results can be identified in nearly every industry in which regulatory reform has taken place. These include the following:

APPLYING ECONOMIC IDEAS 12.2

REGULATORY REFORM IN THE AIRLINE INDUSTRY

Airlines were the first major transportation industry to experience regulatory reform. The results, in terms of prices, service, and industry structure, have in many ways been typical of the experience of other industries undergoing regulatory reform.

Regulatory reform of the industry began in 1979. Over the next decade, average fares declined and passenger volume rose dramatically. Revenue per passenger mile, the broadest measure of air fares, declined from 4.5 cents per mile to 3,5 cents per mile on an inflation-adjusted basis. Over approximately the same period, passenger volume increased by 60 percent. The fact that the 60 percent increase in passenger volume was accompanied by just a 25 percent increase in takeoffs indicates that better utilization of equipment was a major source of savings.

Compared with the situation in the 1970s, air travelers today have a wider variety of options, ranging from ultra-discount tickets with severe restrictions on refunds and travel times to full-fare tickets with no restrictions. Southwest Airlines and other new low-fare carriers have offered a new, no-frills model that has challenged traditional carriers. However, despite many new entries, mergers of existing carriers left the market dominated by a relatively few "supercarriers" by the 1990s.

The airline situation is complicated by the fact that one part of the air travel system—the airlines—was deregulated and made more competitive, while two other parts—the air traffic control system and the airport—remained government monopolies. The growth in air traffic has placed great strains on air traffic control and the airports, leading to more flight delays and increased concern about safety. Despite legitimate safety concerns, however, the safety record, as measured by fatal accidents, remained superior to the record prior to 1980s deregulation, as shown in the accompanying chart.

The terrorist attacks on September 11, 2001, set off a new round of changes in the airline industry. One of the changes has been a complete overhaul of airport security. By 2004, the federal government assumed control of baggage screening and required random searches of individuals boarding planes. Also, the combination of the terrorist threat and the inconvenience caused by added airport security discouraged many individuals from traveling by air. Increased security requirements not only meant longer lines at security checkpoints, but it increased costs for the airlines. They needed to fund additional training for pilots and flight attendants and pay for added security features such as locks on cockpit doors. On top of these problems, fuel costs rose sharply in the early 2000s. The result was bankruptcy for many traditional carriers, including the industry's largest, United Airlines. The federal government has offered significant financial support, partly in the form of direct loan guarantees and partly by absorbing some of the major carriers' pension costs. As of this writing, the financial position of the traditional carriers remains extremely difficult, although some low-cost carriers are doing well. Even in this complex situation, there is little likelihood of a way out via restoration of CAB-style regulation.

Source: Early history of deregulation based, in part, on President's Council of Economic Advisers, *Economic Report of the President* (Washington, D.C.: Government Printing Office, 1988), Ch. 6. Source of safety information: FAA.

Airline Accident Rate (1983–2002)

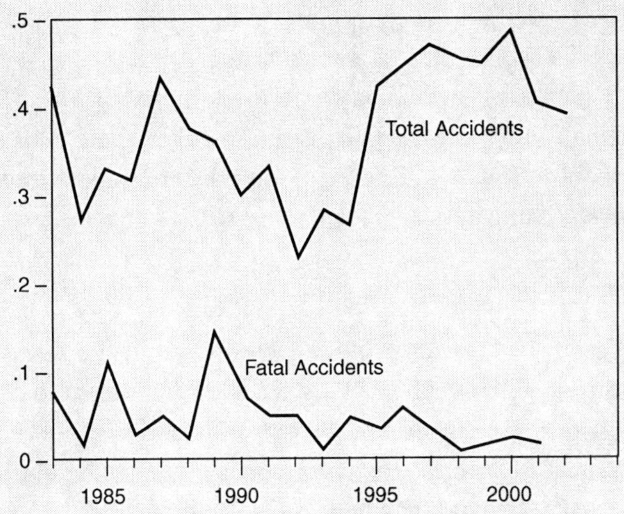

- Prices have fallen on the average, although not for all customers.
- A greater variety of services became available, including many low-price, no-frills choices that had not been offered under regulation.
- Many new firms entered the industries, and there were many mergers and business failures among firms that were not able to adapt to increased competition.

Applying Economic Ideas 12.2 illustrates these effects in the case of the airline industry. Despite these generally positive outcomes, it would be an exaggeration to characterize the deregulatory efforts of the early 1980s as unqualified successes.

In addition to the troubles of the airline industry, another example of the harmful effects of partial deregulation can be found in the banking industry. At the beginning of the 1980s, banks' policies regarding lending and deposits were substantially deregulated. However, one important element of the regulatory system—deposit insurance—remained untouched. This allowed some unscrupulous bankers to take a "free ride" on the government insurance scheme, and use depositors' money for excessively risky loans. In part for this reason, there was a major banking crisis in the 1980s. Many institutions failed, and taxpayers had to rescue the government deposit insurance agency to keep it from failing as well. The response to the banking crisis of the 1980s was, in most respects, to strengthen and improve regulations rather than to do away with them.

Finally, it must be said that even at the height of the deregulation movement, there was a trend toward increased regulation in the areas of health, safety, and the environment. Health and safety regulation is examined in the next section.

HEALTH AND SAFETY REGULATION

At the same time that regulatory reform was reducing the economic role of old-line regulatory agencies such as the ICC and the CAB, other areas of regulation were expanding. Among the agencies reflecting this trend are the Occupational Safety and Health Administration (OSHA), the Consumer Product Safety Commission (CPSC), the National Highway and Traffic Safety Administration (NHTSA), and the Environmental Protection Agency (EPA). In addition, some older agencies, such as the Food and Drug Administration (FDA), have become much more active than before. These agencies are not directly concerned with prices and competition; rather, their focus is on the kinds of goods that are produced and how they are produced. Let us take a look at what economists have to say about health and safety regulation, an issue that has provoked much debate.

Normative Issues

The goal of health and safety regulation is to make the world a safer, healthier, more pleasant place in which to live. Because this is a goal that no one can argue with, why are regulations designed to achieve it a matter of debate? Part of the answer is that even when goals are agreed upon, there can be disagreements about the best ways to pursue those goals. Such disagreements, which belong to the realm of positive economics, will be discussed shortly. Other major sources of controversy are normative. Although almost everyone believes that health and safety are good in themselves, there are disagreements about their relationship to other worthwhile goals. Two such normative disagreements often threaten to overshadow any consideration of the positive economics of health and safety regulation. They are the question of valuing health and safety and that of deciding whose values should shape policy when values differ.

CAN HEALTH AND SAFETY BE ASSIGNED AN ECONOMIC VALUE? The first issue is whether one should even consider trade-offs between human health and safety on the one hand and material well-being on the other. Many supporters of strong, strictly enforced health and safety regulations argue that there is no way to measure the value of human life. Regulations therefore should be set without regard to economic trade-offs or cost-benefit ratios of any kind.

Others, however, do not share this view. They do not belittle the value of human life; rather, they see no point in condemning something that people do every day—and people do sacrifice their own health and safety in favor of other goals daily. They choose the convenience of car travel over the discomforts of bus travel, even though buses are known to be many times safer than cars. They take high-paying jobs in cities rather than low-paying jobs in the country, even though city air is known to be much less healthful than country air. They have medical checkups once a year but not twice a year or once a month because the gain in terms of health is not worth the sacrifice in terms of time and money.

WHOSE VALUES? The second normative question remains to be answered even if one concedes that cost-benefit analysis can be reasonably applied in the areas of health and safety. That is the question of whose values should govern any trade-offs made between health and safety on the one hand and economic costs on the other. Should policy be guided by the values of the people who receive the benefits and bear the costs, or should it be left to the judgment of experts? In practical terms, this comes down to the question of when people should simply be warned about health and safety hazards and when they should be forced to be safe and healthy whether they want to or not.

Strictly speaking, economics as a science has nothing to say about these normative issues. Nevertheless, economists often strongly believe that it is reasonable to consider economic costs and benefits in making health and safety decisions and to allow well-informed people to make those choices for themselves whenever possible. When such an economist discusses health and safety regulation with someone who believes in health and safety at any cost, what is likely to take place is a fight rather than a rational debate. This is unfortunate, because there are some things that economics as a science—that is, positive economics—can contribute to the controversy over health and safety regulation.

Positive Issues

One area of positive economics on which economists and regulators should be able to agree is ensuring that regulatory goals, once chosen, are achieved at the lowest cost.

Consider the matter of giving local decision makers the greatest possible leeway in choosing the lowest-cost means of complying with regulation. One way to do this is to issue regulations in the form of performance standards rather than engineering controls. *Performance standards* are rules that specify the results to be achieved, whereas *engineering controls* are rules that specify particular techniques to be used or equipment to be installed.

Another issue on which positive economics can focus is evaluating the benefits of a proposed regulation relative to its costs. For example, in 1984 the EPA issued a study that showed that banning lead in gasoline would have benefits totaling $1.8 billion. In the EPA's view, this would more than offset the cost, which it estimated at about $.02 per gallon of gasoline. Ethyl Corporation, which produced the lead additive that the EPA sought to ban, said that the agency had left out a major cost. According to Ethyl, banning lead would mean that older cars (which had been designed before lead-free gasoline was widely available) would need valve repairs much more often. In Ethyl's estimate, the cost of these repairs would be $18 billion per year, far more than the benefits. In this case, cost-benefit analysis narrowed the grounds of the dispute over elimination of lead in gasoline and allowed progress toward agreement on terms of the phase-out.

Still another area of regulation in which positive economics can be helpful is tracing the unintended consequences of regulation. For example, Chapter 3 discussed the unintended consequences of auto safety regulation, which were suspected of having the unintended effect of increasing hazards to pedestrians and bicyclists. Similarly, regulations requiring safety caps on aspirin bottles had the unintended effect of making it more likely that people would leave the caps off altogether, thus, in some cases, increasing hazards to children. A study by Richard L. Stroup and John C. Goodman detailed dozens of other cases in which well-intentioned health and safety regulations have had unintended effects that endanger health and safety.[11]

Looking Ahead

This chapter has covered a lot of ground, from traditional antitrust policy to health and safety regulation. Everywhere it has turned, however, it has encountered a constant theme: Economists tend to be skeptical of government attempts to improve market performance through regulation. The economic case against regulation can be stated in the form of three basic propositions.

The first proposition is that, in practice, regulation tends to be dominated by questions of political rent seeking and income distribution rather than efficiency. In some cases, the goal may be to keep the owners of regulated firms from earning monopoly profits. In others, it may be to prevent such firms from competing so intensely that none of them can earn a profit. The goal may be to favor one group of customers or suppliers at the expense of others. It may be to give workers higher wages than they otherwise would earn or to give them a different balance between wages and a safe workplace. Economists do not argue with any of these goals; their complaint is that regulation is an inefficient way of benefiting one group at the expense of another. Many dollars in costs are incurred for every dollar in benefits gained by those whom the regulation is intended to help.

The second proposition is that regulation is less efficient than the market as a means for making decisions and using information. Regulators fail to keep prices down because they know too little about the cost and demand conditions under which firms operate. They try to second-guess the market in deciding which firms should be allowed to serve which markets. In this way they end up raising costs for everyone. They leave too little room for innovation and local initiatives aimed at satisfying special needs or suiting unique circumstances.

Third, regulations intended to serve the public interest often have unintended consequences. Sometimes those consequences can be traced to political rent seeking by special interests, as when antitrust laws are used by firms to harass their competitors, or when regulatory agencies are "captured" by the industries they are intended to regulate. In other cases the unintended consequences are simply a result of failure to think things through according to sound economic principles. Whatever the case, the unintended consequences of regulation have costs that tend to offset the intended benefits.

As we turn to other areas of microeconomic policy in the remaining chapters, we will encounter these themes again. They affect government policies in the areas of environment, labor markets, poverty, and international trade just as they do in the areas of antitrust and regulation examined in this chapter.

SUMMARY

1. **Which business practices are illegal under the antitrust laws?** *Antitrust laws* seek to control market structure and the competitive behavior of firms. The oldest of the antitrust laws is the Sherman Act of 1890, which outlaws combinations and conspiracies in restraint of trade and makes any attempt to monopolize a market illegal. The Clayton and Federal Trade Commission Acts of 1914 seek to control unfair trade practices. The Clayton Act, together with the Celler-Kefauver Act of 1950, controls mergers. The Robinson-Patman Act of 1935 regulates price discrimination.

2. **How have economists' views on antitrust policy changed over time?** For many years vigorous enforcement of antitrust laws had widespread support among economists. Recently, however, economists' views have changed. Reformers, armed with new views about the efficiency effects of business practices, urge greater consideration for consumer welfare, fewer restrictions on all but the largest horizontal mergers, and less attention to vertical restraints and price discrimination. Public choice theorists see antitrust laws in terms of political rent seeking by small economic entities at the expense of large ones. Economists of the modern Austrian school see antitrust laws as

injurious to economic freedom and justice and damaging to the entrepreneurial market process.

3. **How are natural monopolies regulated, and what problems are posed by regulation?** Natural monopolies, such as electric utilities, are subject to regulation that aims to prevent excessive *rates of return*. Regulation does not always work smoothly, however. If too high or too low a rate of return is set, the regulated firm's investment incentives will be distorted.

4. **Why are some industries regulated despite their inherently competitive structure?** Many industries have been regulated even though they are not natural monopolies. Some economists have seen such regulation as a form of rent seeking. In effect, regulation amounts to government imposition of a cartel. The rents generated by regulatory "cartels" are shared among firms, their workers, and their customers. Efficiency does not seem to be a major reason for the regulation of such industries.

5. **What are the effects of regulatory reform?** A great deal of regulatory reform has taken place in airlines, air freight, trucking, intercity bus service, and railroads as well as in some areas of banking and communications. The results are lower prices, though not for all customers; increased competition, with many new entrants and some failures of established firms; and greater variety in the products and services offered to consumers.

6. **What are the current trends in health and safety regulation?** Regulation has been growing in the areas of health and safety at the same time that it has been decreasing in such industries as transportation, communication, and financial services. Disputes in these areas of regulation raise both normative and positive issues. The normative issues include the question of whether one can place an economic value on health and safety, as well as the issue of whose values should guide regulatory policy. The positive issues include finding ways to keep down the costs of regulation, compare its costs and benefits, and trace its unintended consequences.

KEY TERMS

Antitrust laws	Vertical mergers
Price fixing	Conglomerate mergers
Horizontal mergers	Rate of return

PROBLEMS AND TOPICS FOR DISCUSSION

1. **Antitrust laws and economic rights.** "Everyone should have the unrestricted right both to sell goods and services in any market and to withhold goods or services from sale." Are the antitrust laws consistent with this statement? Why or why not?

2. **Public ownership of utilities.** In some cities utilities such as electric companies and gas distribution companies are owned by the city government. What do you think are the advantages and disadvantages of public ownership of a natural monopoly compared with regulated private ownership? With unregulated private ownership?

3. **Value of trucking permits.** Before 1980 the ICC limited the number of trucking firms that could serve any given route. Often the only way a new firm could get permission to serve a route was to buy the "certificate" (permit) of a firm that already served that route. Some of those permits were worth hundreds of thousands of dollars. Why were the permits worth so much? After deregulation the value of such permits fell to zero. Why do you think this happened?

4. **Regulation of taxis.** How are taxis regulated in the area where you live? Is there free entry into the market? Are minimum or maximum fares set? How easy is it to get a cab if you need one? Would you suggest any changes in regulatory policy for your area?

5. **Highway speed limits.** In 1987 states were given the option of raising the speed limit on rural interstate highways from 55 to 65 miles per hour. The move was controversial, because it was feared that the rate of highway fatalities would increase as a result of higher speeds. How would you go about judging whether a change in the speed limit is a good idea? Discuss both positive and normative aspects of the question.

CASE FOR DISCUSSION

Tipping the Balance

The growing popularity of sport utility vehicles (SUVs) and the widely publicized rollover deaths in Ford Explorers using Firestone tires in the 1990s have drawn the critical eye of government regulators. After the Ford-Firestone incident, Congress required the National Highway Traffic Safety Administration (NHTSA) to test automobiles on a track. Prior to the increased fear of rollovers, the NHTSA used a mathematical formula to estimate a vehicle's star rating. For instance, a five-star rating meant that an automobile has a less than 10 percent chance of rollover in a single accident.

The NHTSA track tests were incorporated into safety ratings beginning with the 2004 models. Compared with prior years, the 2004 results showed improvement for a few SUVs. This added fuel to lobbyists' arguments against increased regulations targeting the SUV, such as gas mileage restrictions and subsidies for promoting the development of hybrids. "SUV Rollover Hysteria Appears Misplaced," said a news release from the lobbyist group Sport Utility Vehicle Owners of America.

Others remained unconvinced. "I think there are many SUVs, probably a majority of SUVs that have stability issues," said Brian O'Neill, president of the Insurance Institute for Highway Safety. "What consumers really need to know, if they're bound and determined to buy an SUV, is which ones are more stable than others." People often equate the size of SUVs with increased safety, but their high center of gravity makes them more prone to rollover compared with other automobiles.

"You don't have to get the C.G. [center of gravity] very high to get the vehicle to a point where it's unstable," said Paul Mercurio, an engineer for Bosch. Bosch makes stability control technology that helps reduce rollovers in cars and trucks.

Are rollovers common? The SUV industry lobbyists often cite that only 2.5 percent of accidents involve a rollover. However, among drivers and passengers involved in a rollover accident, one-third of them die as a result of the accident. So, while rollovers are rare, the chances of surviving are less than comforting. According to statistics from the Insurance Institute for Highway Safety, SUVs had higher fatality rates compared with cars. Between 2000 and 2001, 1997–1999 model year cars weighing between 3,500 and 3,999 pounds had a fatality rate of 87 accidents per million registered vehicles. This compares with a fatality rate of 160 for SUVs in the same weight class and model years.

"Personally, I believe a minivan is as functional as an SUV without the handling questions," he said. "It's typically a less-expensive vehicle. It's just not trendy."

Source: Information from Danny Hakim, "The Tipping Point for Safety," *The New York Times*, February 22, 2004.

QUESTIONS

1. Suppose that Ford and Firestone offered to pay $1 million per fatal accident in the Ford Explorer. Is

this a reasonable figure? To put it in human terms, consider the following two ways of looking at the offer:

a. Imagine yourself in a hospital following a fatal rollover accident. A representative of the Ford Motor Company enters the room and offers you a choice:

   You can either have $1 million or be restored to health. Which option would you take?

b. Imagine that you are about to buy an SUV and that a stability control system is optional rather than required equipment. You expect to drive the car 100,000 miles before junking it. If the car has no stability control, your chances of being killed in a rollover accident over that period are about 16 in 10,000. If it has a stability control system and you use it regularly, your chances of being killed over the same period are about 2 in 10,000. If you value your life at $1 million, you should be willing to pay up to $1,000 for the stability control system. What is the maximum you would actually be willing to pay?

2. Setting aside the issue of whether $1 million is the "right" value for a human life, do you agree in principle that a cost-benefit formula is the proper framework for making the decision about modifying the stability design of SUVs? Or do you feel that cost doesn't really matter? If you were an SUV manufacturer, would you install stability-control safeguards at a cost of say $400 per vehicle? If you were a consumer rather than a manufacturer, how much would you pay for an optional, stability package that would prevent a rollover accident? More than $400? Less?

END NOTES

1. *Standard Oil Co. of California and Standard Stations, Inc, v. United States*, 337 U.S. 293, 305 (1949).
2. F. M. Scherer, *Industrial Market Structure and Economic Performance* (Chicago: Rand McNally, 1980), 491.
3. See Robert H. Bork, *The Antitrust Paradox* (New York: Basic Books, 1978), 405–406.
4. *United States v. Trans-Missouri Freight Ass'n.*, 166 U.S. 323 (1897).
5. See Bruce L. Benson, M. L. Greenhut, and Randall G. Holcombe, "Interest Groups and the Antitrust Paradox," *Cato Journal* (Winter 1987): 801–817.
6. Richard Posner, "The Federal Trade Commission," University of Chicago *Law Review* 37 (1969): 87.
7. For a short exposition of Armentano's views, see "Efficiency, Liberty, and Antitrust Policy," *Cato Journal* (Winter 1985): 925–931. Those views are developed at greater length in *Antitrust and Monopoly: Anatomy of a Policy Failure* (New York: Wiley, 1982).
8. Robert A. Katzman, "The Attenuation of Antitrust," *Brookings Review* (Summer 1984): 24.
9. Robert D. Tollison, "Public Choice and Antitrust," *Cato Journal* (Winter 1985): 905–906.
10. Harvey A. Averch and L. L. Johnson, "Behavior of the Firm under Regulatory Constraint," *American Economic Review* (December 1962): 1052–1069.
11. Richard L. Stroup and John C. Goodman, "Making the World Less Safe: The Unhealthy Trend in Health, Safety, and Environmental Regulation," National Center for Policy Analysis Policy Report no. 137, April 1989.

CHAPTER 13

Pricing in Resource Markets

After reading this chapter, you will understand:

1. The circumstances that determine demand for productive inputs
2. The circumstances that determine the supply curve for labor
3. The characteristics of equilibrium in a competitive labor market
4. The characteristics of labor market equilibrium with only one or a few employers
5. Why wages are not the same for all labor markets and for all individuals within a labor market

Before reading this chapter, make sure you know the meaning of:

1. Substitutes and complements
2. Elasticity
3. Income and substitution effects
4. Marginal physical product and diminishing returns
5. Perfect competition and price takers
6. Theory of monopoly and price searchers

Labor

The contributions to production made by people working with their minds and muscles.

THIS CHAPTER TURNS to an important set of markets that we have referred to only indirectly up to this point: the markets in which firms obtain the inputs they need to carry on production. Those markets have traditionally been termed *factor markets* because they provide **labor**, capital, and natural resources, the basic factors of production. Today, however, economists are just as likely to refer to them as *resource markets* or simply as *markets for inputs*. The more modern terms emphasize the fact that the basic theory applies not just to the three classic factors of production but to inputs of all kinds—everything from the labor of production workers to software for the firm's computers or electric power to light the parking lot.

The first part of this chapter outlines a general theory of demand for inputs. In the second part, attention is focused on markets for labor, which is the most important category of input.

DEMAND FOR RESOURCES

In many ways resource markets are similar to the product markets we have already studied. The theories of supply and demand and the tools of marginal analysis apply to resource markets just as they do to product markets. However, resource markets differ from product markets in one major respect: In many resource markets, firms are the buyers and households are the sellers rather than the other way around. A theory of the demand for resources therefore must be based on an analysis of profit maximization by firms.

Objectives and Constraints

As in other branches of microeconomic theory, the first step toward a theory of demand for resources is to specify the objectives and constraints faced by firms. We will continue to assume that the objective is profit maximization. Three types of constraints will be considered:

1. *Production technology.* The firm is constrained in part by technology, which determines how inputs can be combined to produce outputs. When one variable input is considered, technological constraints can be represented as marginal physical product curves. Technology with more than one variable input can be represented using the graphical technique explained in the Chapter 7 Appendix, "Cost and Output with Two Variable Inputs."

2. *Demand for the product.* Firms buy resources not for their own sake but to use them as inputs in producing goods and services for sale. This same holds true for labor. With very few exceptions, labor is purchased not for its own sake, but rather for the good or service that that labor produces. (An exception may be a performer. We may pay a high fee to watch a talented ball player or listen to a good singer for the joy of seeing (hearing) the performance. Does anyone pay for this Econ class just to watch or hear the professor? You have enrolled here for the service derived, the three transferable credits, not for the econ experience!) The demand for any input thus is said to be a **derived demand**, because it ultimately reflects demand for the product that the input is used to produce.

Derived demand

Demand for a productive input that stems from the demand for the product the input is used to produce.

3. *Resource cost.* The third constraint that a firm must consider in deciding how much of an input to purchase is the cost of obtaining that input. In com-

petitive input markets that cost is simply the market price of the resource in question. (Imperfectly competitive markets are considered later in the chapter.)

Marginal Physical Product

Previously we defined the *marginal physical product* of a resource as the increase in output that results from a one-unit increase in the input of that resource when the amounts of all other inputs used stay the same. For example, if using one additional worker-hour of labor to cultivate a turnip field yields an additional output of five turnips when no other input to the production process is changed, the marginal physical product of labor in that field is five turnips per labor hour.

As we have seen, the marginal physical product of a resource varies as the amount of it used changes, other things being equal. In particular, as the quantity of a single input increases while the quantities of all other inputs remain fixed, a point will be reached beyond which the marginal physical product of the variable input will decline. This principle is known as the *law of diminishing returns.*

Figure 13.1 shows total and marginal physical product curves for a firm that is subject to the law of diminishing returns over the range from 0 to 20 units of an input. (At this point, it does not matter whether the input in question is labor, a raw material, or something else; the principle is the same for all.) As the amount of this input is increased while the amounts of all other inputs used are held constant, output increases—but at a diminishing rate. The first unit of the input yields a marginal physical product of 20 units of output, the second a marginal physical product of 19 units of output, and so on. After the twentieth unit of input, marginal physical product drops to zero: A ceiling has been reached beyond which adding more of the variable input cannot produce more output unless the amounts of some of the fixed inputs are also increased. For example, if the variable input is labor, adding more than 20 workers may do nothing to increase output unless the amount of machinery available for the workers to use is increased as well. Beyond 20 units of input, where the marginal physical product of the variable input drops to zero, the total physical product curve becomes horizontal.

Marginal Revenue Product

Because the demand for a resource of production is a derived demand, the firm must consider the revenue it will earn from the sale of the output produced by an added unit of input as well as the input's marginal physical product. The change in revenue that results from the sale of the added output produced by a one-unit increase

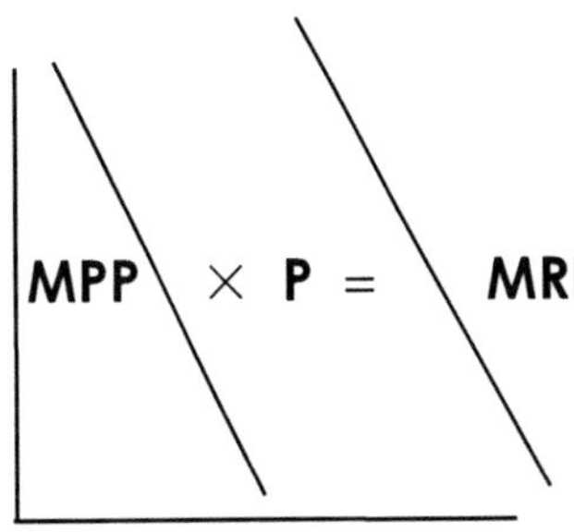

Marginal Physical Product × Price = Marginal Revenue Product

FIGURE 13.1 TOTAL AND MARGINAL PHYSICAL PRODUCT OF AN INPUT OF PRODUCTION

(a)

Quantity of Input (1)	Total Physical Product (2)	Marginal Physical Product (3)
0	0	
1	20	20
2	39	19
3	57	18
4	74	17
5	90	16
6	105	15
7	119	14
8	132	13
9	144	12
10	155	11
11	165	10
12	174	9
13	182	8
14	189	7
15	195	6
16	200	5
17	204	4
18	207	3
19	209	2
20	210	1

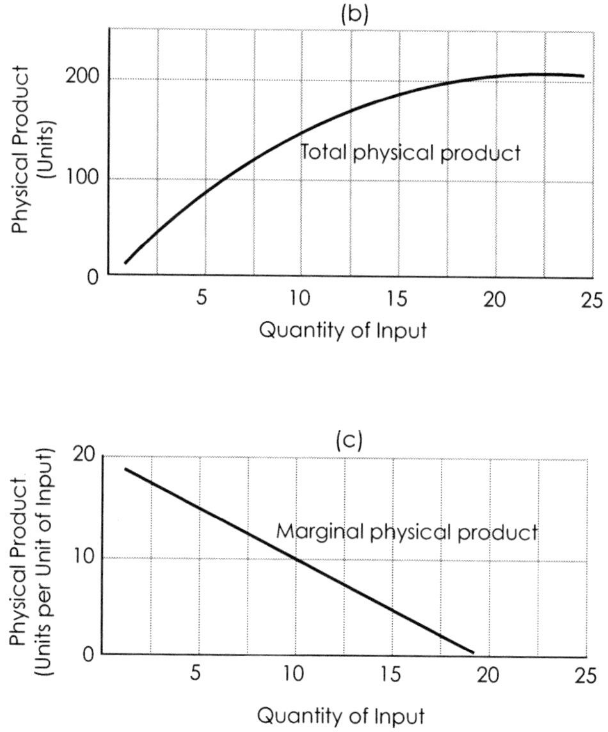

As the quantity of one resource input increases with the quantity of other inputs remaining unchanged, total physical product increases, but at a decreasing rate. As parts (a) and (c) of this figure show, marginal physical product decreases as the quantity of the employed input increases. This decrease is a direct result of the law of diminishing returns.

Marginal revenue product

The change in revenue that results from the sale of the output produced by one additional unit of an input.

Value of marginal product

Marginal physical product times the product's per-unit price.

in the input of a resource is the **marginal revenue product** of that resource. The relationship of marginal revenue product to demand for the product must be considered separately for firms that are *price takers* and for those that are *price searchers* in their output markets.

MARGINAL REVENUE PRODUCT FOR THE PRICE-TAKING FIRM A firm that is a price taker in its output market faces a perfectly elastic demand curve for the good it produces. The quantity of output it produces has no effect on the price at which its output is sold. Marginal revenue for the competitive firm thus equals the price of the firm's output, which is constant for all quantities of output. For such a firm, then, marginal revenue product equals the **value of marginal product**, that is, marginal physical product times the output's price.

Figure 13.2 gives an example. The marginal physical product schedule is the same as that given in Figure 13.1, and a constant price of $1 per unit of output is assumed.

FIGURE 13.2 MARGINAL REVENUE PRODUCT FOR A TYPICAL PRICE-TAKING FIRM

Quantity of Input (1)	Total Physical Product (2)	Marginal Physical Product (3)	Revenue per Unit (Price) (4)	Marginal Revenue Product (5)
0	0			
		20	$1	$20
1	20			
		19	1	19
2	39			
		18	1	18
3	57			
		17	1	17
4	74			
		16	1	16
5	90			
		15	1	15
6	105			
		14	1	14
7	119			
		13	1	13
8	132			
		12	1	12
9	144			
		11	1	11
10	155			
		10	1	10
11	165			
		9	1	9
12	174			
		8	1	8
13	182			
		7	1	7
14	189			
		6	1	6
15	195			
		5	1	5
16	200			
		4	1	4
17	204			
		3	1	3
18	207			
		2	1	2
19	209			
		1	1	1
20	210			

For a price-taking firm, the marginal revenue product of an input equals the value of marginal product, that is, the input's marginal physical product times the product's price. This figure assumes that the product price is $1 per unit and that marginal physical product is the same as in Figure 13.1.

Marginal Resource Cost

Marginal resource cost

The amount by which a firm's total resource cost must increase for the firm to obtain an additional unit of that resource.

The third constraint that the firm must consider in determining how much of each resource to employ as a productive input is the cost of obtaining each additional unit of that resource, that is, its **marginal resource cost**.

We can begin by considering the case in which the markets where the firm buys its inputs are perfectly competitive, so that the firm is a price taker in those markets. This will be the case if the firm is only one of a large number of firms that are competing to buy a particular resource and if the amount of the resource it uses is only a small fraction of the total used by all firms. For a firm that buys as a price taker, the marginal resource cost equals the market price of that particular input. For example, if the market wage rate for data-entry workers is $7 an hour, the marginal resource cost for data-entry workers' labor is $7 an hour for any firm that is a price taker in the market for data-entry workers.

Profit Maximization

To maximize profits, a firm must use just enough of each input to equalize marginal revenue product and marginal resource cost. If marginal revenue product exceeds marginal resource cost, hiring one more unit of the input will add more to revenue than to cost and, hence, will increase profit. If marginal resource cost exceeds marginal revenue product, *reducing* the amount of that input by one unit will reduce cost by more than revenue and thus increase profit. Only when marginal revenue product and marginal resource cost are equal will it be impossible for any change in the amount of the input to increase profit. In equation form, this rule can be stated as

$$\text{MRC} = \text{MRP},$$

where MRC stands for marginal resource cost and MRP for marginal revenue product. The rule applies both to firms that are price takers in their output markets and to those that are price searchers in their output markets.

Figure 13.3 illustrates the profit maximization rule. Both the table and the corresponding graph assume that the firm is a price taker in the output market and that the market price of the output is $1 per unit, as in Figure 13.2. The firm is also assumed to be a price taker in the resource market, buying inputs of that resource at $5 per unit. Note that profit rises as more of the resource is purchased, up to the 15th unit of input. The firm just breaks even on the purchase of the 16th unit of input, and thereafter profit declines. It is between the 15th and 16th units of input that marginal revenue product becomes exactly equal to marginal resource cost.

Resource Demand Curves

When a firm is a price taker in an input market, whether it is a price taker in the output market or not, its marginal revenue product curve for the input is also its demand curve for the input. A demand curve must indicate the quantity demanded at each price, and it has been shown that the quantity of the input demanded by such a firm will be whatever quantity makes the input's price (and, hence, its marginal resource cost) equal to marginal revenue product.

The same profit-maximizing concept that underlies the demand curves of individual firms for the resource can be extended to all firms hiring a given resource to create a market demand curve for that resource. The resulting curve, like those of the individual firms, is a derived demand curve. As we have seen, the demand for any input ultimately does not stem from the usefulness of the input itself but, rather, from the demand for the products the input is used to produce. The market demand for farmland is derived from the market demand for food, the market demand for typographical workers from the market demand for books, and so on.

Like the demand for outputs, the demand for inputs changes in response to changes in economic conditions. Suppose that demand curve D_0 in Figure 13.4 is the

FIGURE 13.3 PROFIT MAXIMIZATION FOR A PRICE-TAKING FIRM

(a)

Quantity of Input (1)	Marginal Revenue Product (2)	Marginal Input Cost (3)	Total Variable Cost (4)	Fixed Costs (5)	Total Revenue (6)	Total Profit (7)
1			$ 5	$100	$ 20	–$85
2	$19	$5	10	100	39	–71
3	18	5	15	100	57	–58
4	17	5	20	100	74	–46
5	16	5	25	100	90	–35
6	15	5	30	100	105	–25
7	14	5	35	100	119	–16
8	13	5	40	100	132	–8
9	12	5	45	100	144	–1
10	11	5	50	100	155	5
11	10	5	55	100	165	10
12	9	5	60	100	174	14
13	8	5	65	100	182	17
14	7	5	70	100	189	19
15	6	5	75	100	195	20
16	5	5	80	100	200	20
17	4	5	85	100	204	19
18	3	5	90	100	207	17
19	2	5	95	100	209	14
20	1	5	100	100	210	10

(b)

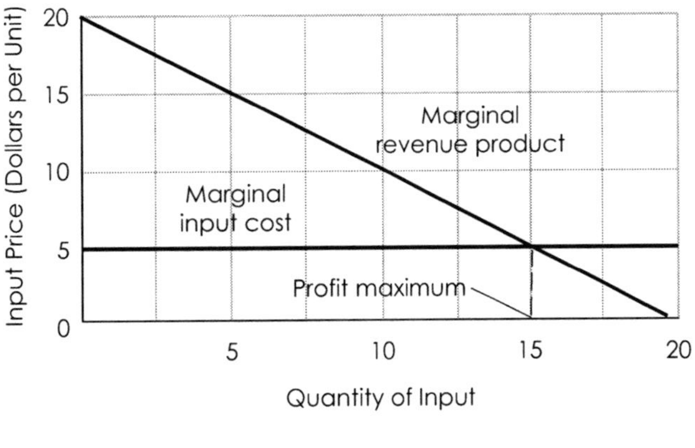

Maximizing profits requires that a firm buy just enough of each resource input to equalize marginal revenue product and marginal resource cost. Here it is assumed that the firm is a price taker, as in Figure 13.2. The point of profit maximization falls between 15 and 16 units of input.

FIGURE 13.4 MOVEMENTS ALONG A RESOURCE DEMAND CURVE AND SHIFTS IN THE CURVE

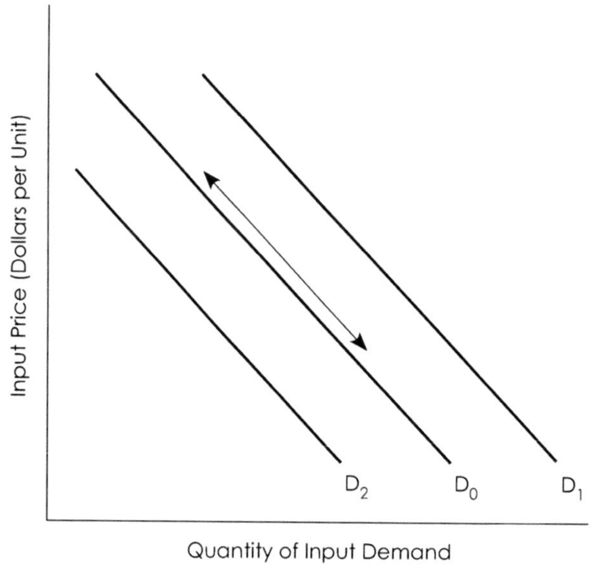

Changes in the price of a resource, other things being equal, will produce movements along a resource demand curve, as shown by the arrow. Other kinds of changes can shift the curve. An increase in demand for the product produced by the input might shift the curve from D_0 to D_1. An increase in the price of another input that is a complement to the given input might shift the curve from D_0 to D_2.

market demand curve for some input. A change in the market price of that input will cause the quantity of the resource demanded to change; this is represented by a *movement along* the demand curve, as shown by the arrow parallel to D_0. Changes in economic conditions other than a change in the input's price can cause a change in the demand for that input; this is shown by a *shift* in the demand curve—say from D_0 to D_1 or from D_0 to D_2. We will first consider the elasticity of demand for inputs in response to changes in their prices, and then examine conditions that can shift resource demand curves.

The Price Elasticity of Resource Demand

The price elasticity of demand for a resource, as for any other good, is the ratio of the percentage change in the quantity demanded of the resource to a given percentage change in its price, other things being equal. The degree of price elasticity of demand for a resource is influenced by several circumstances.

PRICE ELASTICITY OF DEMAND FOR THE PRODUCT Because the demand for any input is derived from the demand for the product it is used to produce, elasticity of demand for an input depends on the elasticity of demand for the product. Suppose, for example, that the demand for taxi services is relatively elastic. If taxi fares are forced up as a result of an increase in drivers' wages, the quantity of taxi service demanded will fall sharply and there will be a correspondingly large effect on the quantity of drivers demanded. On the other hand, suppose that the demand for neurosurgery is relatively inelastic. An increase in the price charged for neurosurgery caused by an increase in neurosurgeons' fees will have relatively little effect on the number of brain operations performed. The increase in fees will consequently have a relatively small effect on the demand for that specialized kind of labor.

THE INPUT'S SHARE IN TOTAL PRODUCTION COSTS Through similar reasoning, we can conclude that a change in the price of an input will have a greater effect on the demand for it the greater its share of total costs, other things being equal. The reason is that a change in the price of an input representing a large share of total costs will have a greater impact on the market price of the product. For example, the cost of coal represents a large share of the cost of generating electricity. Doubling the price of coal therefore will have a big percentage impact on the price of electricity and a correspondingly large effect on the quantity of electricity demanded. The resulting drop in the quantity of electricity demanded will, in turn, cause a substantial drop in the quantity of coal demanded. On the other hand, lubricating oil for a power station's generating equipment accounts for only a trivial share of the total cost of electricity. Doubling the price of lubricating oil would have only a tiny effect on the rates paid by the utility's customers and, thus, only a tiny effect on the quantity of electricity demanded. As a result, doubling the price of lubricating oil will have a smaller percentage impact on the quantity demanded of this input than was the case for the more important input, coal.

SUBSTITUTABILITY AMONG INPUTS Other things being equal, the demand for an input will be more elastic the more easily other inputs can be substituted for it. For example, clowns are an essential part of circus entertainment. If clowns' wages rise, a circus can substitute other inputs, such as trained animal acts, only to a limited degree without disappointing its customers. Thus, a doubling of clowns' wages would have a relatively small percentage effect on the quantity of clowns demanded. On the other hand, automatic elevators are a very satisfactory substitute for the labor of elevator operators. A rise in the wages of operators consequently has a major impact on the number of operators employed. Earlier in the century, as the wages of elevator operators and similar kinds of unskilled labor rose, automatic elevators almost universally replaced manually operated ones.

ELASTICITY OF SUPPLY OF OTHER INPUTS Finally, the elasticity of demand for an input depends not only on the technical substitutability of other inputs but also on the elasticity of supply of other inputs. In the case of elevator operators, automatic elevator equipment, like most manufactured goods, is available under conditions of relatively elastic supply, at least in the long run. In contrast, consider the business of parking cars. It is technically possible to substitute land for labor: The number of attendants used to park a given number of cars can be reduced by spreading a parking lot out over more land so that customers have room to park their own cars. But what is technically possible does not always make sense in economic terms. In small towns, where land for parking is easy to find, self-service lots do predominate. But in urban areas the supply of land is relatively inelastic. A rise in attendants' wages in Manhattan thus cannot practically be offset by an increase in the number of one-level, self-service parking lots. As a result, parking attendants have not gone the way of elevator operators, at least not in big cities.

Changes in Demand for Resources

Let's turn now from price elasticity of demand, which pertains to changes in quantity demanded (that is, to movements along the demand curve), to changes in demand (that is, to shifts in the demand curve). Three kinds of changes are capable of causing shifts in the demand curve for inputs of any productive resource.

A CHANGE IN DEMAND FOR OUTPUT In the case of shifts in the resource demand curve, as in the case of movements along the curve, the principle of derived demand plays a key role. In particular, a change in demand for the product produced by an input (that is, a shift in the product demand curve) will cause a change in demand for the input. The source of changes in product demand can be either microeconomic or macroeconomic in nature. A microeconomic example is the increase in demand for the labor of poultry workers as a result of a shift in consumer tastes from beef to chicken. A macroeconomic example is the rise and fall of the demand for labor as the economy experiences expansions and recessions over the course of the business cycle. Expansion brings tight labor markets and increased overtime work; recessions bring layoffs and unemployment.

A CHANGE IN THE PRICE OF ANOTHER INPUT A second source of shifts in the demand curve for an input is a change in the price of some other input. The notions of *substitutes and complements*, which were introduced in an earlier chapter, are applicable here. For example, consider labor and farm machinery, both of which are used to grow corn. In Mexico, where labor is relatively cheap, relatively little machinery is used per bushel of corn produced; more machinery is used in the United States, where labor is relatively expensive. Labor and machinery thus can be viewed as substitutes in the production of corn. On the other hand, consider diesel fuel and the labor of drivers, both of which are used to produce truck transportation. A drop in the price of fuel will lower total costs, increasing the quantity of transportation services demanded. As a result, the number of drivers hired will increase. Thus, labor and fuel are complements in the production of truck transportation.

CHANGES IN TECHNOLOGY Changes in technology are a third condition that affects the demand for inputs. As improving technology shifts firms' cost curves downward, the quantity of inputs needed to produce a *given* quantity of output is affected. Sometimes technology will cause the demand for one input to rise while the demand for another input falls. For example, the introduction of improved crop varieties in developing countries as part of the so-called green revolution has led to a decrease in the amount of land needed per unit of crop yield, but it has required an increase in the amount of chemical fertilizers required per unit of crop yield. Frequently, however, a new technology reduces the quantities of *all* inputs needed to produce a given unit of output. For example, the introduction of e-mail dramatically shortened the time needed to produce and circulate a memo to colleagues working on a project within a firm. As a result, an office could produce a given number of memos using both fewer labor hours and less specialized printing and copying equipment than before.

Over time, however, an increase in demand for the product, itself sometimes stimulated by improvements in technology, may more than offset the reduced quantity of an input used per unit of output. The end result of the whole process of technological change and growth may be an increased quantity demanded of a given resource. Consider the relationship between clerical workers and office equipment. In the eighteenth century, firms employed clerks to copy documents laboriously by hand. In the nineteenth century, pen and ink were replaced by the typewriter. In the twentieth century, word processors and photocopiers became available, and these in turn were supplanted by e-mail. Each technological innovation vastly reduced the number of clerical-worker hours needed to process a given volume of documents. But at the same time, the quantity of document processing demanded grew dramatically, with the result that the clerical labor force is larger now than at any time in the past.

RESOURCE SUPPLY AND DEMAND: THE LABOR MARKET

Up to this point, we have discussed marginal productivity and demand for resources in general terms that apply to any productive input. When we turn to the supply side of resource markets, however, we cannot be so general because the considerations affecting supply are somewhat different for various factors of production. In this section, we will discuss the supply curve for labor and then see how demand and supply together determine equilibrium in the labor market.

The Labor Supply Curve

Labor is supplied by the same individuals and households whose role as consumers was analyzed in a previous chapter. A similar approach can be applied here. We begin with the labor supply decision for an individual worker; we then turn to market labor supply curves.

LABOR SUPPLY FOR AN INDIVIDUAL Previously we showed that all consumer choices involve trade-offs. Individuals' decisions regarding how much labor to supply can be analyzed in terms of a trade-off between two "goods": leisure and purchased consumer goods. Leisure is valued for relaxation, recreation, and the completion of household tasks. Time spent at leisure is time taken away from work, however, and hence it is time diverted from earning income that could be used to buy consumer goods. In making the choice between the two, consumers are faced with two key constraints: (1) the limit of a 24-hour day to be divided between income-earning work and leisure, and (2) the wage rate that determines the purchasing power earned per hour of work.

The hourly wage rate can be thought of as the opportunity cost of leisure in that it represents the dollar equivalent of the goods and services that must be sacrificed in order to enjoy an added hour of leisure. As the wage rate increases, the work-versus-leisure decision is affected in two ways:

1. There is a *substitution effect* as the increased wage rate raises the opportunity cost of leisure, providing an incentive to substitute work (and the goods bought with the resulting income) for leisure.

2. The increase in the wage rate has an *income effect* that tends to reduce the number of hours worked. The higher wage rate—assuming that the prices of goods and services remain unchanged—increases workers' real incomes. With higher real incomes, workers tend to consume larger amounts of normal goods and smaller amounts of inferior goods. Leisure is a normal good. Other things being equal, people generally seek more leisure, in the form of shorter working hours and longer vacations, as their incomes rise. Taken by itself, then, the income effect of a wage increase is a reduction in the amount of labor supplied by workers.

As illustrated in Figure 13.5, the net effect of an increase in the wage rate depends on the relative strengths of the substitution and income effects. It is generally believed that for very low wages the substitution effect predominates; therefore, the quantity of labor supplied by an individual initially increases as the wage rises. As the wage rises still more, however, the income effect becomes stronger. People seem to treat leisure as a normal good; after they have assured themselves of a certain material standard of living, they begin to consider "spending" any further wage increases on more time off from work. If such a pattern prevails, the labor supply curve for an individual will have a backward-bending shape like the one shown in Figure 13.5. Over the positively sloped low-wage section, the substitution effect of wage changes predominates; over the negatively sloped high-wage section, the income effect prevails.

FIGURE 13.5 AN INDIVIDUAL'S LABOR SUPPLY CURVE

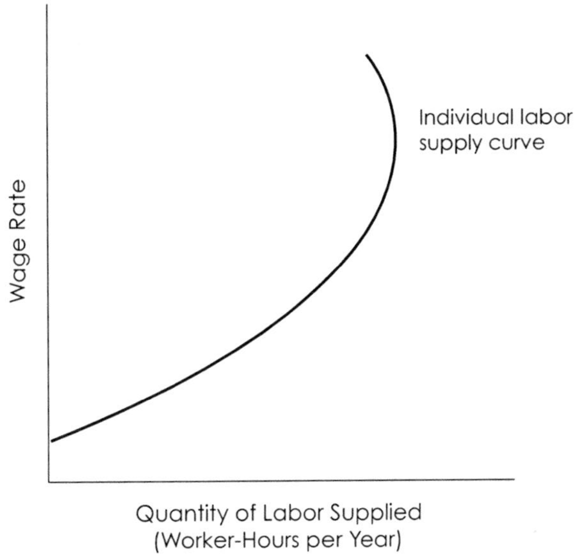

On the one hand, a higher wage tends to increase the amount of work that a person is willing to do, because the extra income compensates for time taken away from leisure pursuits. On the other hand, a higher wage allows a person to take more time off from work and still enjoy a high standard of living. Taken together, the two effects tend to give the individual labor supply curve the backward-bending shape shown here.

MARKET LABOR SUPPLY CURVES Although the labor supply curves for individual workers may bend backward, at least over some range of wages, the supply curve for any given type of labor as a whole is likely to be positively sloped throughout. Consider, for example, the supply of electrical engineers in New York, of data-entry workers in Chicago, or of farm laborers in Texas. Beyond some point, each individual engineer, data-entry worker, or laborer might respond to a wage increase by cutting back on the number of hours worked. For the market as a whole, however, this tendency would be more than offset by the entry of new workers from other occupations or areas. Thus, other things being equal, if the wage rate for electrical engineers in New York rose, more engineering students would take up that specialty; if the wage rate for data-entry workers in Chicago rose, more people would go into such work instead of, say, becoming receptionists; and if the wage rate for farm laborers in Texas rose, workers would be drawn in from Arizona, Florida, and Mexico.

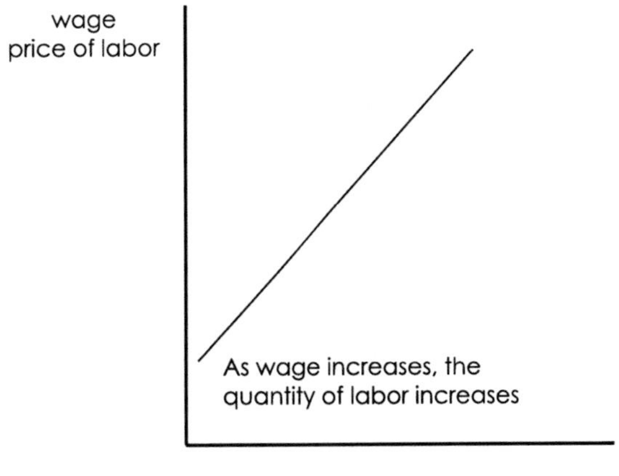

As a result, for any discussion of the market for a particular category of labor at a specific time and place, it is reasonable to draw the labor supply curve with the usual positive slope regardless of the shape of the individual labor supply curves underlying it.

Competitive Equilibrium

Determining the wage rate in a labor market that is perfectly competitive on both sides is a simple matter of supply-and-demand analysis. Figure 13.6, for example, shows supply and demand curves for the labor market for data-entry workers in Chicago. It assumes that a large number of workers compete for jobs and a large number of employers compete for them so that both are price takers. The market supply curve has a positive slope, and the market demand curve for data-entry workers is derived from the demand curves for individual firms.

Equilibrium in this market requires a wage rate of $7 an hour, with 200,000 workers employed. If the wage rate were lower, there would be a shortage of data-entry workers. Some firms, unable to fill all their job openings, would offer premium wages to workers from other jobs or regions. The wage rate would thus be driven up to the equilibrium level. If, on the other hand, the wage rate were above $7 an hour, there would be a surplus of data-entry workers. Many people would be looking for such jobs and not finding them. After a sufficiently long search, some would be will-

FIGURE 13.6 DETERMINATION OF THE EQUILIBRIUM WAGE IN A COMPETITIVE LABOR MARKET

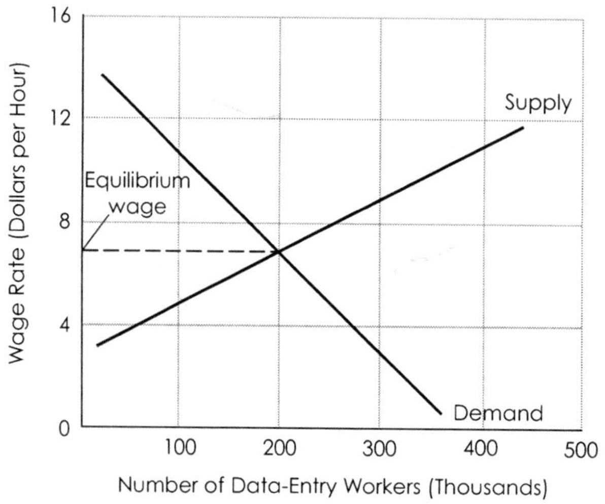

Although each individual worker may have a backward-bending supply curve, the supply curve for data-entry workers in any local market will have the usual positive slope. As the wage rises, people will be drawn into this occupation from other kinds of work or other localities. When both employers and workers are price takers in the labor market, the point of equilibrium is found where the supply and demand curves intersect. Here the equilibrium wage rate is $7 an hour and the equilibrium quantity of labor is 200,000 workers.

ing to accept work at lower-than-desired wages, thereby pushing the wage rate down toward equilibrium; others would move into other occupations or regions.

In a labor market such as this one—in which both employers and employees are price takers—the equilibrium wage rate equals the marginal revenue product of labor. In the special case in which all employers are price takers (perfect competitors) in the market where they sell their output as well as in the market where they purchase inputs, the equilibrium wage rate also equals the value of marginal product.

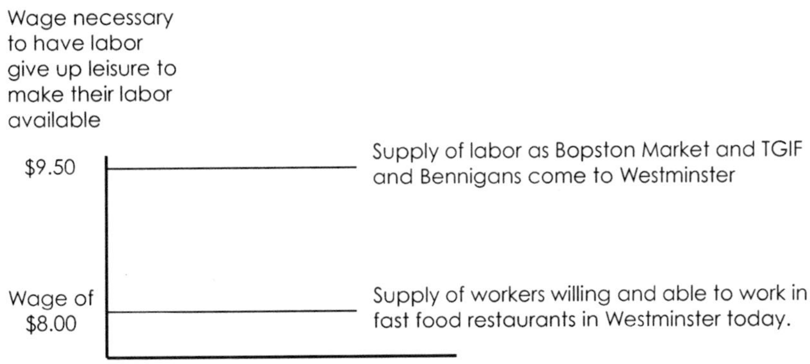

There are differences in perception of the labor supply. The individual sees the supply of labor as backward bending while the market supply is positively slopped. However, the employer sees the supply curve as horizontal. At current circumstances, an employer will have to pay the going rate but at that rate, she can employ an unlimited number of workers. But should other employers enter the market and increase demand for workers, the supply will shift up causing the wage to increase.

WAGES: The conclusion we can draw is that our wage and what most people are paid is the result of supply and demand. The demand for our labor is derived from the goods or services we produce which our employer then sells. The demand for us is the value of what we add to the total output (MPP) times the price charged for what we've contributed to the total (MRP). Thus, the demand for labor is equal to the MRP. The supply of labor is how much are we willing and able to supply at certain wage rates. The equilibrium wage is where the value of our labor (MRP) is equal to the number of hours we are willing and able to sell at the wage that is equal to our MRP.

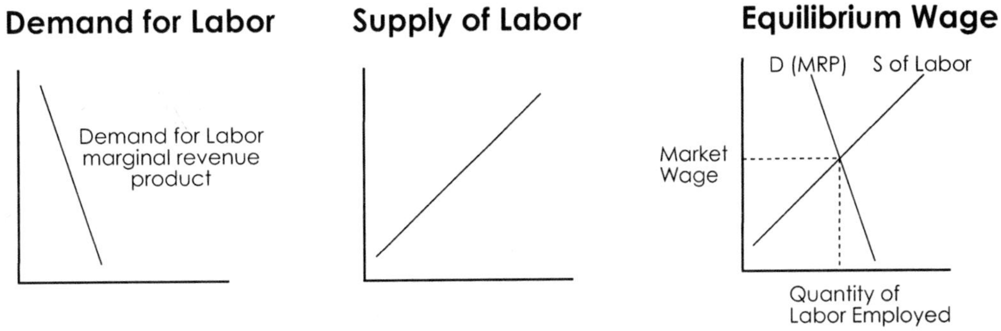

The Marginal Productivity Theory of Distribution

Supply and demand determine how much each worker earns as well as how much labor will be used in making each product. When employers are price takers in the markets in which they buy inputs, profit maximization requires that each resource be used up to the point at which its marginal revenue product will equal its price. This reasoning suggests that each unit of each resource receives a reward equal to the contribution it makes to the firm's revenue. The idea that resources are rewarded according to their marginal productivity is known as the **marginal productivity theory of distribution**.

Marginal productivity theory of distribution

A theory of income distribution in which each input of production receives a payment equal to its marginal revenue product.

In an economy in which all markets—output as well as input—are perfectly competitive, the marginal productivity theory applies even more directly. In this case marginal revenue product equals output price times marginal physical product. In such an economy the reward that each unit of each input receives is equal to the value of marginal product. Thus, if an extra hour spent pulling weeds in a cabbage patch increases production by 20 pounds and cabbage sells for $.50 per pound, the equilibrium wage rate must be $10 an hour—no more, no less.

The marginal productivity theory of distribution as we have defined it is a proposition of positive economics. However, some people find this principle of distribution appealing in a normative sense as well, in terms of both efficiency and fairness. Under the marginal productivity principle, the reward of every worker is exactly equal to that worker's contribution to the productive process. If a worker or other resource owner withholds a unit of productive services from the market, that person will suffer a loss of earnings exactly equal to the value of production that is lost to the economy as a whole. The normative version of the marginal productivity theory is, in effect, the old idea of "from each according to ability, to each according to work" restated in the language of neoclassical economics.

In the past, national labor markets were largely isolated from one another, so that the marginal productivity theory applied only within a given country. In countries where the supply of labor was abundant relative to demand, wages were lower than in countries where labor was relatively scarce. To some extent, such differences were mitigated by international migration of labor, but that was always a slow process. Today, modern means of communication allow some kinds of work to be performed anywhere in the world. The result has been the phenomenon of "outsourcing," which has led to greater integration of world labor markets. *Economics in the News 13.1* discusses some of the issues raised by outsourcing as it creates new opportunities and new challenges in both high-wage and low-wage countries.

What can you or I, or any of us get paid? For the college to pay me I must continue to sell seats in this class. My pay must equal the tuition (P) you pay times the number of students who register for this Econ class (MPP). You, my students, are my marginal physical product. The tuition you pay for this class is the price. Thus, the more of you in my classes, the more the college can pay me and the more I earn. Should my enrollment decline, then the school could not pay me the salary I enjoy.

ECONOMICS IN THE NEWS 13.1

WHERE ARE THE JOBS GOING?

One of the most dramatic changes in the U.S. labor market over the past three decades has been the decrease in high-paying jobs for workers with modest educational achievement. Once low-skill manufacturing jobs, whether in the automobile, steel, or textile industry, permitted high-school graduates, and even high-school dropouts, to live a middle-class lifestyle. Today this is much less often the case.

For years, U.S. manufacturers have been under pressure to raise productivity in order to remain competitive in world markets. From 1970 to 2002, while manufacturing output held roughly constant as a share of gross domestic product, manufacturing employment plunged from 27 percent of all nonfarm employment to just 13 percent. Meanwhile, employment in service-related industries reached 72 percent by 2000.

So where are all of the low-skill manufacturing jobs going? Many of them overseas. U.S. and multinational corporations have moved production out of the United States into countries where they are able to pay workers lower wages—"outsourcing," this is called. In early 2000, U.S. workers noted a new trend—not only were the factory jobs moving abroad, but those in the service industries as well. In July 2003, for instance, U.S. firms shipped 30,000 new service-sector jobs to India while eliminating some 226,000 in this country, according to researchers at the University of California, Berkeley. Forrester Research has estimated that 3.3 million U.S. service-sector jobs will head to foreign countries over the next fifteen years, along with $136 billion in wages.

Why? Simple economics. The U.C. Berkeley research study estimated that computer programming jobs that pay $60,000 to $80,000 per year in the United States can go for as little as $8,952 a year in China, $5,880 in India, or $5,000 in the Russian Federation.

On the other end, the newly outsourced jobs represent a tremendous opportunity. In India, where per capita GDP was just $2,900 in 2003, a $5,880 job puts a programmer firmly in the middle class. In some Indian cities, new American-style suburbs are springing up, fueled by outsourced jobs.

There is still another side to the outsourcing story. *New York Times* columnist Thomas Friedman went to India to do an exposé on outsourcing. He asked the owner of the 24/7 call center, a major outsourcing contractor, how can it be good for America to have Indians doing all these white collar jobs? He was surprised by the answer. "Look around the office," the Indian entrepreneur replied. The computers are from Compaq. The software is from Microsoft. The phones are from Lucent. Even the bottled water is supplied by Coca Cola, a trusted brand name in India. Overall, American exports to India have nearly doubled in the past decade. What goes around, comes around.

Small wonder outsourcing has drawn mixed reactions. On the one hand, by early 2004, eight states had taken up legislation aimed at preventing public dollars from going to companies with workers overseas, according to the National Conference of State Legislatures. On the other hand, Harris Miller, president of the Information Technology Association of America (ITAA), says the issue is overblown. He estimates that less than 2 percent of the 10 million jobs in the information technology industry, including government work, are performed overseas. Miller said that if the government prevents U.S. companies from outsourcing, other countries will retaliate with similar restrictions, "and the big losers are U.S. workers and U.S. industry."

Source: Based in part on Greg Schneider, "Anxious About Outsourcing," *Washington Post*, January 31, 2004; and Thomas L. Friedman, "What Goes Around . . . ," *New York Times*, February 26, 2004.

Therefore, it is in my best interest that you, and your friends, sisters, parents, children etc, continue to enroll in Econ classes at Carroll.

Monopsony

Not every input market meets the conditions required for the marginal productivity theory of distribution to apply. In particular, there are cases in which firms are price searchers rather than price takers in input markets. In labor markets, this will tend to occur when one or a few employers dominate the market in a particular location or for a particular skill. It can also happen when workers vary in their perceptions of nonwage characteristics of jobs with different employers. Some people might work for Acme because it is close to their neighborhood; some might prefer Zeus Company because the managers there are friendlier; and so on. Whatever the reason, the employer cannot hire unlimited numbers of workers at a constant wage. The labor supply curve faced by the individual employer is not horizontal as it is in a perfectly competitive labor market.

Monopsony

A situation in which there is only a single buyer in a market; more generally, any situation in which a firm is a price searcher in a market in which it is a buyer.

The extreme case, in which a single employer accounts for 100 percent of the demand in a resource market, is termed **monopsony**. In ancient Greek, from which these terms are derived, *monopsony* means "one buyer" just as *monopoly* means "one seller." In principle, we could also identify the resource market structures of *oligopsony* (a few buyers) and *monopsonistic competition* (many buyers perceived as different by sellers). However, it is common, although not very precise, to apply the term *monopsony* to all markets in which the buyers are price searchers.

In a monopsony labor market, then, the wage rate is not a given. Instead, the employer must choose among a set of price-quantity combinations lying along a positively sloped labor supply curve. As an example, compare the situation of a retail store in Albuquerque that wants to hire a few security guards with the situation of the U.S. government, which wants to hire soldiers for the army. The retail store is a price taker in the market for security guards. If the going wage for such guards is, say, $40,000 a year, it can call an agency or put an ad in the paper and get as many guards as it wants at that price. The situation of the government as the employer of volunteer soldiers is very different. Experience with military recruitment ever since the end of the draft has shown that the success of recruitment efforts depends on the level of military pay. At the turn of the twenty-first century, a slack job market made recruitment relatively easy. However, after the U.S. invasion of Iraq, the military services have found it harder and harder to meet their recruitment quotas. To attract more recruits, they have raised pay, usually in the form of increased enlistment bonuses.

The Monopsonist's Marginal Resource Cost Curve

In discussing monopoly we distinguished between price-discriminating monopoly and simple monopoly. The latter sells all units at the same price, whereas the former sells to different customers at different prices. The same distinction applies in the labor market. In this chapter we consider only the simple case in which an employer pays the same wage to all workers who do the same job. For example, the employer may have a policy of raising the wages of all workers on the payroll if market conditions make it necessary to pay more for new hires. To pay new workers more than old ones might be bad for morale.

Figure 13.7 shows the supply curve and the marginal resource cost curve faced by a hypothetical simple monopsonist—say, a large insurance company that employs most of the data-entry workers in a small town. The supply schedule for these workers shows that no one will work in this occupation at a wage rate of $3 an hour or

FIGURE 13.7 MARGINAL RESOURCE COST UNDER MONOPSONY

(a)

Quantity of Labor Supplied (Number of Workers) (1)	Wage Rate (Dollars per Hour) (2)	Total Resource Cost (Dollars per Hour) (3)	Marginal Resource Cost (Dollars per Hour) (4)
1	$3.02	$ 3.02	
2	3.04	6.08	$ 3.06
3	3.06	9.18	3.10
150	6.00	900.00	
151	6.02	909.02	9.02
152	6.04	918.08	9.06
200	7.00	1,400.00	
201	7.02	1,411.02	11.02
203	7.04	1,422.08	11.06

(b)

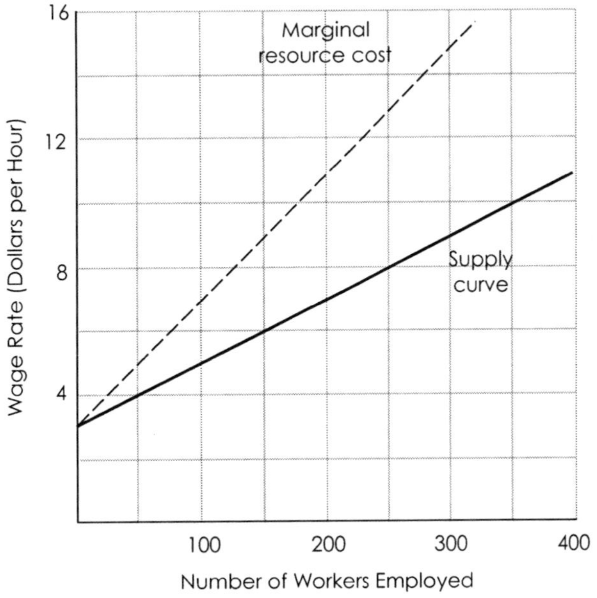

Under monopsony, marginal resource cost exceeds factor price. Consider an increase in quantity from 150 to 151 units of labor. The wage rate must be raised from $6 to $6.02 not just for the 151st employee but for all the previous 150 as well. Marginal resource cost in this range thus is $9.02 rather than $6.02 an hour.

less. Above the $3 wage, each extra $.02 per hour will attract one more worker. Suppose that the monopsonistic employer has hired 150 data-entry workers at a rate of $6 an hour, making the total labor cost for a labor force of this size $900 an hour.

Now consider what will happen to the firm's total labor cost per hour if it expands its labor force by one worker. According to the supply curve, hiring 151 data-entry workers requires a wage of \$6.02 an hour. That wage must be paid not just to the 151st worker but to all workers. The total cost of a labor force of 151 data-entry workers, then, is \$6.02 times 151, or \$909.02 per hour. The addition of one more worker has raised the total labor cost per hour from \$900 to \$909.02—a marginal resource cost of \$9.02. The result is much the same regardless of the chosen starting point. In every case the monopsonist's marginal resource cost exceeds the resource price (in this case, the wage rate).

Part (b) of Figure 13.7 shows a marginal resource cost curve based on the marginal resource cost column of the table in part (a). This curve lies above the supply curve at every point. The graph shows that the relationship between the supply curve and the marginal resource cost curve for the monopsonist is similar to that between a monopolist's demand and marginal revenue curves.

Monopsony Equilibrium

Given the monopsonist's marginal resource cost curve, which is derived from the market supply curve for that resource, the equilibrium level of employment for the firm is determined as follows: Figure 13.8 shows the monopsonistic employer's marginal revenue product curve along with the labor supply and marginal resource cost

FIGURE 13.8 DETERMINATION OF WAGES UNDER MONOPSONY

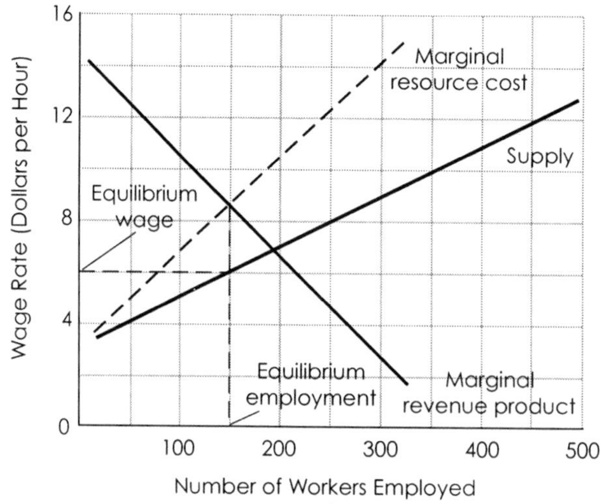

This figure shows the marginal revenue product of labor curve, labor supply curve, and marginal resource cost curve for a monopsonist. The quantity of labor required for maximizing profits is found at the point at which the marginal revenue product and marginal resource cost curves intersect. The equilibrium wage rate does not occur at this point. Instead, it is equal to the height of the supply curve directly below that intersection.

curves from Figure 13.7. Following the general rule that profit is maximized at the quantity of labor for which marginal resource cost equals marginal revenue product, the monopsonist will hire 150 data-entry workers at a wage rate of $6 an hour.

When a labor market is in monopsony equilibrium, the wage rate is lower than both the marginal resource cost and the marginal revenue product of labor. In the example just given, the equilibrium wage rate is $6 an hour (which is equal to the height of the labor supply curve), although the marginal revenue product is $9 an hour at the point at which the marginal revenue product and marginal resource cost curves intersect. Despite the gap between the wage rate and the marginal revenue product, adding to the amount of labor hired would not raise revenue enough to offset higher labor costs. The reason is that the cost of hiring another worker is not just the $6.02 an hour that must be paid to the 151st worker; instead, it is that sum plus the extra $.02 per hour by which the wages of all 150 previously hired workers must be raised. The complete marginal resource cost for the 151st worker thus is $6.02 + $3.00, or $9.02 an hour.

Examples of monopsony behavior would be a coal town in Kentucky or West Virginia. If there is only one buyer of labor in the region, then the employer can hire workers to a quantity where the MRP = MFC. At this level, the wage that must be paid to hire this quantity of labor is less than the value the workers are contributing to the business. Thus, the monopsonist underpays her employees. Consider the major sports leagues: since there is only one buyer of baseball players (MLB), the teams will only hire labor to the point where the MRP (value that each labor contributes) is equal to the MFC (change in total cost to the league to hire that player). Though it is difficult to be sympathetic to a man being paid hundreds of thousands of dollars to play a game, it is true that that man is underpaid!

WHY WAGE RATES DIFFER

According to a widely shared concept of justice, all people are created equal. But if that is so, why do people's earnings in labor markets differ so widely? Why do different people receive different wages within a given labor market, and why do the wage structures of some markets differ markedly from those of others? In this section we look at some extensions of conventional marginal productivity theory that help explain why wage rates differ.

Non-Wage Job Characteristics

One reason wage rates differ is that jobs differ in ways other than wages; they differ in such characteristics as safety, prestige, comfort, and challenge, as well. Other things being equal, workers are willing to supply their services at lower wages to employers that offer jobs with more attractive nonwage characteristics. Knowing this, many employers try to make the jobs they offer safe, attractive, and challenging. Employers who must attract workers to jobs that cannot be freed from risk and discomfort often have to pay higher wages.

But the proposition that employers must pay more to attract workers to jobs with less desirable nonwage characteristics applies only when *other things are equal.* In practice, it turns out that many tedious, unpleasant, and even dangerous jobs pay low wages, while the high-salaried occupants of the executive suite work in air-conditioned comfort and eat lunches served on fine china in special dining rooms. How can this seeming paradox be explained in terms of labor market theory?

Economists see nothing paradoxical in the contrast between the heat and noise of the factory floor and the cool calm of the executive suite. They simply interpret the observed pattern as evidence that comfort on the job is a *normal good.* As people's incomes rise, they want more comfort. An employer must take this into account when offering a package of wage and working conditions to various employees. Suppose that a firm offered a warehouse worker a cut in pay from $7 an hour to $6 an hour ($2,000 a year) in return for which it would replace the vinyl tile in the warehouse coffee room with wool carpet and replace the cheap posters on the wall with original artwork. Would it be surprising if the warehouse worker turned down the offer? But suppose the same firm offered its president a raise from $500,000 a year to $502,000 a year, in exchange for which the carpet in the president's office would be ripped out and its oil paintings replaced with cheap posters. Would it be surprising if the president turned down the offer?

This principle applies on an international scale, as well. Major U.S. multinationals with plants in developing countries are very often regarded as local leaders in terms of the wages and working conditions they offer. Their factories are, more often than not, cleaner, better lit, and safer than those of their small, local competitors. Yet when these overseas plants are compared in terms of working conditions with factories in the United States, they often are denounced as "sweatshops." What is the truth? Are multinational corporations ruthlessly exploiting foreign workers? Or are those workers, who are just making the first steps out of dismal poverty, less willing to trade off hard cash wages for improvements in workplace amenities? There is often no unambiguous answer to such questions.

Human Capital

Differences in the nonwage characteristics of jobs do not fully explain why wages differ. Ability also counts. If the supply of abilities needed for the job of corporate president were as abundant as the supply of abilities needed for the job of warehouse worker, we would not expect labor markets to give rise to such a big difference in pay to the two occupations.

Some people are born with special abilities, or at least with unusual potential for developing them. The enormous salaries of professional ballplayers, first-rate opera singers, and other superstars are a direct result of the scarcity of those abilities. But the abilities people are born with are only part of the story. Training and education are at least as important as innate ability for most occupations, from lawyers and accountants to glassblowers and hairdressers.

Economists view the costs of training and education as a form of investment. Taking courses to become an accountant, in this view, is much like buying a dump truck in order to go into the gravel-hauling business. In both cases one makes an expenditure now to acquire something that will increase one's future earning power. The main difference is that the dump truck operator acquires capital in the form of a machine, whereas the accountant acquires **human capital**—capital in the form of learned abilities.

Human capital

Capital in the form of learned abilities that have been acquired through formal training or education or through on-the-job experience.

According to human-capital theory, the earnings of each occupation that requires special training must be high enough to make up for the opportunity cost of getting the training. In the case of a person going to college to acquire a degree in accounting, the opportunity cost includes both the costs of getting the degree (tuition, books, and so on) and the income that could have been earned if the college years had been spent working in an occupation that required no college degree (see *Applying Economic Ideas 1.1* from Chapter 1). Other things being equal, we would expect occupations that require longer or more expensive training to pay more than those that require less. Thus, we would expect doctors to earn more than lawyers, lawyers to earn more than hairdressers, and so on—and that is in fact the case.[1] (You are attending this class, and reading this text, hopefully, to improve the value of your labor and as such, you are hoping to fetch a higher income after graduation.)

Of course, the nonwage characteristics of jobs may play a role in people's willingness to invest in various kinds of human capital. If certain occupations are more exciting or prestigious than others, people may be willing to enter them even if the pay alone is not enough to justify the investment in training. For example, the training required to become a ballet dancer may be as long and rigorous as that needed to become, say, an orthodontist, but dancers, on the average, earn less than orthodontists. The difference in pay presumably has something to do with the value placed by would-be dancers on the opportunity for artistic expression.

Formal education is by no means the only way to invest in human capital. As the case at the beginning of the chapter shows, on-the-job training is also important. In total, employers may spend as much for on-the-job training as is spent on formal education at all levels. Both employers and employees benefit from this vast investment in human capital. Employers benefit from the ability to fine-tune the skills of their work forces to the physical capital in which they have invested. In that sense, physical capital and human capital are often complementary inputs. At the same time, employees benefit, not only from immediate promotions and higher pay but also because training may broaden their options in the labor market.

Efficiency Wage Theory

Efficiency wage theory

The theory that wages above the minimum necessary to attract qualified workers can raise productivity by enough to increase profit.

Human-capital theory suggests that the ability to perform a job better results in an increase in the wage rate of a worker or group of workers. Another theory suggests that the opposite may also be true—higher pay may itself lead to better on-the-job performance. This line of reasoning is referred to as **efficiency wage theory**.

Efficiency wage theory poses the following question: Why do many firms pay a wage that is higher than necessary to attract workers with the desired minimum qualifications? Anyone who has ever looked for a job has probably had the experience of hearing about an employer who offers a high wage for particular skills and working conditions, only to learn that the employer has hundreds of applications on file and a low turnover rate. According to the simple supply-and-demand model, the profit-maximizing strategy for such a firm would be to lower the wage rate, allowing the backlog of job applications to shrink to just the level necessary to cover turnover. Yet this is not always done.

The explanation offered by efficiency wage theory is that the high wage stimulates increased productivity. Several reasons have been suggested, including improved morale, lower absenteeism, and lower employee turnover. Also, workers at a high-wage firm are likely to be less willing to risk losing their jobs because of poor performance and therefore may work to the best of their abilities with less supervision and monitoring.

Efficiency wages are not a new idea. In 1914, Henry Ford used efficiency wages when he cut turnover and increased productivity by raising his workers' pay to the unheard of level of $5 a day. *Applying Economic Ideas 13.1* gives a contemporary example. Efficiency wages are not uncommon. For instance, consider the West Coast fast-food restaurant In-N-Out Burger. While most fast-food restaurants often offer starting pay at the minimum wage, In-N-Out's starting wage is $8.25 per hour. It also provides paid vacations, food at work, and an optional 401(k) plan with a company match. Not surprisingly, In-N-Out ranks among the best in food quality and customer service.

ARE MOVIE STARS OR SPORTS PLAYERS OVERPAID?

APPLYING ECONOMIC IDEAS 13.1

COSTCO VS. SAM'S CLUB IN THE LABOR MARKET

Costco versus Sam's Club is one of the hottest rivalries in U.S. retail trade. Both companies follow the philosophy of "pile 'em high and sell 'em cheap." Both feature huge stores with rock-bottom prices for a wide range of merchandise, much of it top-of-the-line brand names.

However, in the labor market, where they compete for workers, the two companies take different approaches. Costco pays its U.S. full-time employees an average of $17.41 per hour, well above the industry average. An experienced cashier can make $40,000. Sam's Club is a division of Wal-Mart, which pays its employees an average of just $12 per hour, on the low end of the industry scale.

Benefits as well as wages differ at the two companies. According to the *Wall Street Journal*, 82% of Costco's employees are covered by insurance, compared with 44% for Wal-Mart. Costco pays 92% of insured workers' premiums, compared to 66% at Wal-Mart.

Costco also has a different attitude toward labor unions. Wal-Mart resists unionization vigorously. Costco does not actively encourage unionization, but it accepts workers' rights to unionize if they think doing so will improve their lot. About 20 percent of Costco's U.S. employees are unionized.

The result of these differences in policy is a dramatic difference in employee loyalty. According to the *Financial Times*, Costco has an annual labor turnover of just 17%. Wal-Mart's is near the industry average of 44%.

"Paying good wages is not in opposition to good productivity," says Costco Chief Executive and President, Jim Sinegal, speaking to a reporter from *Business Week*. "If you hire good people, give them good jobs, and pay them good wages, generally something good is going to happen."

Sources: "James Sinegal, Costco: The Bargain Hunter," *Business Week* Sept. 23, 2002; "Costco's Dilemma: Is Treating Employees Well Unacceptable for a Public Corporation?" *Wall Street Journal*, March 26, 2004; "Pile High, Sell Cheap, and Pay Well," *Financial Times*, July 11, 2005.

SUMMARY

1. **What circumstances determine demand for productive inputs?** For a firm that is a price taker in its output market, the *marginal revenue product* of any input is equal to the input's *value of marginal product*—that is, marginal physical product times the product's price. For a firm that is a price searcher in the output market, it is equal to marginal physical product times marginal revenue and thus is less than the value of marginal product. In both cases the firm makes the maximum profit by buying each input up to the point at which marginal revenue product equals *marginal resource cost*. Hence, the marginal revenue product curve is the resource demand curve for any firm that is a price taker in its input market. The demand for a resource is said to be derived from the demand for the goods it is used to produce.

2. **What circumstances determine the supply curve for labor?** Labor supply curves depend on the trade-off that people make between leisure and the goods and services they can buy with income earned in the labor market. The labor supply curve for an individual worker, and perhaps for the economy as a whole, may bend backward above a certain wage rate. However, the supply curve for a single labor market is positively sloped throughout its length.

3. **What are the characteristics of equilibrium in a competitive labor market?** In a labor market in which employers are price takers, the equilibrium wage rate will be equal to the marginal revenue product of labor, a proposition known as the *marginal productivity theory of distribution*. If employers are also price takers in the output market, the equilibrium wage rate also will be equal to the value of the marginal product.

4. **What are the characteristics of labor market equilibrium with only one or a few employers?** *Monopsony* refers to a situation in which employers are price searchers in the market in which they buy inputs. The marginal resource cost curve for such a firm lies above the supply curve for labor. The equilibrium input is established at the intersection of the marginal resource cost curve and the marginal revenue product curve. In such a market the equilibrium wage is below the marginal revenue product.

5. **Why are wages not the same for all labor markets and for all individuals within a labor market?** Wages differ among markets and among individuals for a variety of reasons. Some wage differences stem from differences in the nonwage characteristics of jobs or from differences in the *human capital* possessed by individuals. According to *efficiency wage theory* some employers pay more than the going wage because doing so results in higher productivity.

KEY TERMS

Derived demand
Marginal revenue product
Value of marginal product
Marginal resource cost
Marginal productivity theory of distribution
Monopsony
Human capital
Efficiency wage theory

PROBLEMS AND TOPICS FOR DISCUSSION

1. **Outsourcing.** How might increased outsourcing affect the quality of the U.S. labor force? If regulations preventing outsourcing were successful, how would this affect U.S. companies? What about consumers buying goods and services from these producers?

2. **Households as buyers in resource markets.** This chapter discusses only resource markets in which

the buyers are firms. Are households ever direct buyers of the basic factors of production? For example, are you the direct buyer of a factor of production when you hire someone to type a term paper? How would the theory of resource markets have to be modified to take into account cases in which the buyers of resources are households rather than firms?

3. **A case of backward-bending labor demand?** In his historical novel *Chesapeake* James Michener describes the unsuccessful efforts of early European colonists to run their plantations using hired Native American labor. Among the many factors that led to the breakdown of relationships between the planters and local inhabitants were economic problems. For example, Michener reports the frustration of a planter who finds that an offer of higher wages does not keep Native American workers from quitting their jobs in the fields after a few weeks of work; in fact, the workers seem to quit sooner when their pay is raised. Does what you have learned in this chapter shed any light on this situation? Discuss.

4. **Monopsony and monopoly.** Is a monopsonist always a monopolist, and vice versa? Try to imagine a firm that is a monopsonist in its factor market but a perfect competitor in its product market. Then try to visualize a firm that is a monopolist but not a monopsonist.

5. **The relationship between "how" and "or whom."** Discuss the following statement: "It is a good idea to let resource markets determine how things are produced, but the matter of for whom things are produced should be handled according to need, not according to supply and demand." Is it possible to separate the "how" and "for whom" functions of resource markets?

6. **Trends in the pay of men and women.** The wage gap between men and women has narrowed somewhat in the past ten years and is expected to narrow further. Do you think the narrowing of the wage gap has anything to do with the facts that (a) women are more than proportionately represented in service occupations and (b) demand for services is growing faster than demand for goods? Discuss.

7. **Wages and working conditions in the newly industrialized countries.** Evaluate the following statement: "We probably can't do much about the fact that workers in Korea, Taiwan, and other newly industrialized countries are paid less than U.S. workers doing similar jobs. However, we should not tolerate the fact that those workers are forced to work under conditions that fall far short of U.S. standards for health, safety, comfort, and hours of work. We should either insist on better working conditions or stop importing goods made by workers who are exploited in that way." How would this proposal affect workers in the newly industrialized countries (a) if the threat to cut off trade worked and labor conditions in those countries were brought up to U.S. standards, and (b) if the threat failed and trade with the countries in question were cut off?

CASE FOR DISCUSSION

The Great American Nursing Shortage

Jose Pineda, a doctor in the Philippines, went back to school—to be a nurse. At age 41, Pineda gave up his private practice in 2003 and moved to the United States. "I am not planning for myself anymore," said Pineda. "I am planning for my kids." Pineda makes $50,000 a year as a nurse at St. Mary Medical Center in Long Beach, California—four times what his physician's salary was in the Philippines. Thousands are making the career switch from doctor in the Philippines to nurse in the United States.

Nurses are in such short supply in the United States that hospitals are looking abroad to fill the gap—offering record salaries and signing bonuses. To satisfy the need for more nurses, the U.S. federal government promises priority immigration status. In the Philippines, economic and political uncertainty have many professionals planning to leave.

In this country, Pineda doesn't deliver babies or cure patients. He works in the telemetry ward at St. Mary's, monitoring seriously ill patients. Dr. Alex Leung is one of the few people at St. Mary's who knows his history. "When I talk to Jose, I talk to him like he's a doctor," Leung said. "I tell him, 'Don't call me doctor.' Because he knows more than I do."

One study surveyed 113 nursing students in 2003. Only 6 percent considered nursing an interesting career, and 59 percent said it was degrading to become a nurse. More than three-fourths said money had driven their decisions. "We feel a lot of shame," said 29-year-old Alberto del Pilar, who works the night shift at Western Medical Center in Anaheim, California for $26.22 an hour. "I never imagined myself changing someone's diapers," he said. "It is a real adjustment draining the urine from the urine bags, scratching their backs. Lots of patients like to be scratched."

"Which am I going to choose: to be an RN in America or a surgeon in my own country?" del Pilar asked his father, an engineer. He said, "Son, the opportunity is in America, not here in the Philippines."

Del Pilar plans to make another career switch—to being a doctor again. He spends most afternoons at Starbucks, keeping himself awake with double espressos while studying for the U.S. medical board exams in the hope of eventually practicing medicine in his new country. Many new arrivals come with the same dream, though nursing has proved so lucrative—and the path back to medicine so arduous—that few have time or resources to reinvest in medicine.

Some visas allow foreign physicians to enroll in U.S. medical residency programs, but there are many barriers to entering them. In addition, U.S. physicians have pushed to keep foreign doctors out of practice in America.

A recent federal study estimated that the United States will be 800,000 nurses short of its needs by 2020. Recruitment of nurses abroad has become big business, particularly in California, where nearly a fourth of nurses have received their training overseas. And a new state law mandates higher staffing levels, increasing the demand. Media ads in the Philippines promise high salaries, visa sponsorship, flights to Guam to take the U.S. nursing exams, and moving expenses. The process takes two years.

While paying as much as $10,000 per recruit, American hospitals have discovered that, once recruited, the doctors often save on training costs. For example, it typically takes three months to prepare a nurse for the operating room. "But if you get a surgeon training is shorter," said Manuel Atienza, a Philippine doctor who runs a nurse recruiting business in Las Vegas.

The nursing shortage in the United States may lead to a doctor shortage in the Philippines. The country produces too many nurses and has long been the biggest supplier of foreign-born nurses to the United States. This raises concerns that the country will eventually face a shortage of doctors, especially in rural areas. In the Philippines, it is precisely rural doctors who are most likely to turn to nursing in the United States. The supply of doctors countrywide is already low.

Source: Alan Zarembo, "Physician, Remake Thyself," *Los Angeles Times*, January 10, 2004.

QUESTIONS

1. Analyze the U.S. nursing shortage in terms of supply and demand. Has the demand curve shifted? If so, why? Has the supply curve shifted? If so, why? Do you think market forces will eventually eliminate the shortage? Why or why not?

2. From the point of view of a hospital, one effect of the "prospective payment" system is to raise the opportunity cost of using doctors' labor to provide health care, since the hospital can no longer be certain of reimbursement for unlimited doctors' fees. Why would this cause an increase in demand for nurses' labor? Does the example suggest that doctors' and nurses' labor are substitutes or complements in the production of health care?
3. Jose Pineda says that he quit medicine in the Philippines because of the prospect of higher pay as a nurse in the United States. Would the nursing shortage make hospitals more likely to improve nurses' working conditions? How will the influx of nurses from abroad affect the treatment of existing nurses in the United States? Explain your answer in terms of the theory presented in this chapter.
4. How is the situation in U.S. nursing related to the outsourcing issue in the lead-off case for this chapter? Why might customer service jobs leave the United States, while nursing jobs have remained?

END NOTES

1. Human-capital theory implies that workers with more education tend to be paid more than workers with less education because the knowledge they acquire makes them more productive on the job. This theory has been challenged by some economists, who think that the primary function of education is to help employers screen job candidates for certain desirable traits, such as intelligence and self-discipline, that are not themselves acquired through education.

CHAPTER 14

Public Policy and Labor Markets: Unions, Discrimination, and Equal Pay

After reading this chapter, you will understand:

1. How labor unions have evolved over time in the United States
2. The main provisions of U.S. labor law
3. How wage rates are determined in unionized markets
4. What unions do in addition to bargaining over wages and benefits
5. How labor markets are affected by discrimination
6. The nature of the controversy over equal pay for men and women

Before reading this chapter, make sure you know the meaning of:

1. Monopsony
2. Human capital
3. Efficiency wage theory
4. Inframarginal rent
5. Transaction costs
6. Opportunism
7. Asymmetric information
8. Median voter model

OUR EARLIER DISCUSSION of labor markets took a fairly abstract approach to the relations between workers and employers. As is the case with other sectors of the economy, however, models of supply and demand do not give a complete picture of labor markets. This chapter adds detail to our understanding of these important markets by discussing several public policy issues.

LABOR UNIONS AND PUBLIC POLICY

Craft union

A union of skilled workers who all practice the same trade.

Unions had their start in the United States toward the end of the eighteenth century. The earliest labor groups, called **craft unions**, were organizations of skilled workers who worked at the same trade. Their shared interests made it relatively easy for them to work together in union activities and gave their organizations some degree of monopoly power in dealings with employers.

However, most of the early local craft unions were short-lived and faced legal as well as economic problems. It was not until 1842 that the courts recognized unions as legal. Even after that date, the courts were often unfriendly. Moreover, few of the early local unions were strong enough to survive the frequent business downturns of that period.

The First Successful Unions

Unionism did not take root on a wide scale until after the Civil War. At that time the first successful national organization appeared—the Noble Order of the Knights of Labor. The Knights reached their peak membership of more than 700,000 workers in 1886.

Many local unions of skilled craft workers were affiliated with the Knights of Labor, but the Knights were much more than an association of craft unions. They welcomed anyone who worked for a living, including farmers, farm workers, and unskilled laborers. The Knights wanted to be more than just a labor union. They wanted to become the American Labor Party and along with specific workers concerns, they wanted to become a political force for reform.

Americans have been, traditionally uneasy and suspicious of unions and after 1886, the Knights of Labor lost ground to the American Federation of Labor (AFL, and if you refer to this as the Arena Football League, you will fail this course.), which had been founded in 1881. The AFL's founders included independent craft unions and some local craft unions affiliated with the Knights that felt that the bargaining power of skilled craft workers would be wasted in efforts to win benefits for unskilled workers.

The AFL found strong leadership under Samuel Gompers, its president for all but one year from 1886 until his death in 1924. Gompers sought to avoid the mistakes that had led to the downfall of the Knights of Labor. Under his leadership, the AFL reached a membership of 2 million by 1904. The federation owed its success largely to three features of its organization and philosophy:

1. *Craft unionism.* The AFL's leaders thought that the dangers of economic depressions and employer opposition could be overcome only by relying on skilled workers who could not easily be replaced during strikes.
2. *Business unionism.* The AFL's member unions devoted almost all of their energies to pay and working conditions. The AFL had little concern for any other considerations which didn't directly affect the pay, security or working condi-

tions (safety) of its *membership*. Unlike many European labor unions, they did not seek the overthrow of private property or the establishment of socialism.

3. *A limited political role*. Again in contrast to European labor movements and the Knights of Labor, the AFL did not try to become a political movement or labor party. Gompers believed that political involvement would weaken the organization's ability to achieve economic goals.

Industrial union

A union of all the workers in an industry, including both skilled and unskilled workers in all trades.

Although the AFL dominated the union scene around the turn of the century, the principle of craft unionism was not accepted everywhere. In some places there were notable early successes in organizing **industrial unions**—unions that included workers of all crafts and skill levels within a given industry. Brewery workers were organized in 1886; the United Mine Workers union was organized in 1890. During the same years, however, industrial unionism suffered some major failures. Strikes by steel and railway workers were broken after clashes involving Pinkerton detectives, state troopers, and hired strikebreakers. A number of labor leaders were jailed.

Unions and Public Policy During the Great Depression

In the 1920s unionism waned. One reason was the renewed hostility of the courts. Beginning in 1908, the Sherman Antitrust Act was applied to restrict union activities, on the grounds that they were conspiracies to restrain trade. Employers were able to obtain *injunctions* (court orders) barring striking, picketing, and many other union activities.

During the Great Depression of the 1930s, the decline was reversed. With unemployment high and wages falling, public sympathy toward unions increased. This sympathy was reflected in two landmark pieces of legislation. The Norris–La Guardia Act of 1932 gave workers the right to strike and picket. It was followed in 1935 by the Wagner Act, (National Labor Relations Act) which for the first time put the government squarely on the side of unions.

The Wagner Act declared that "employees shall have the right to self-organization, to form, join, or assist labor organizations, to bargain collectively through representatives of their own choosing, and to engage in concerted activities, for the purpose of collective bargaining or other mutual aid or protection." The law created its own enforcement agency, a three-member National Labor Relations Board. This board was to oversee enforcement of the act, arrange for representative elections, and serve as judge and jury whenever the act was violated.

The Wagner Act also outlawed a specific list of "unfair employer labor practices." Employers could no longer use lockouts, intimidation, blacklists, or spying. They could no longer force employees to sign contracts that made nonmembership in a union a condition of employment. In some cases, employers were even barred from speaking against unions.

During the Depression the nation saw renewed efforts to organize mass-production industries where earlier attempts had failed. This led to serious conflicts within the

AFL, whose old-line craft unionists did not believe that stable unions could be formed in those industries. As a result of this dispute, an opposition group formed within the AFL; it was led by John L. Lewis of the United Mine Workers. In 1938 the group was expelled from the AFL and became the rival Congress of Industrial Organizations. The CIO scored some major successes during the 1930s, notably the unionization of the steel, rubber, automobile, electrical, meatpacking, and textile industries. By the end of 1938, its membership of 4 million exceeded the AFL's membership of 2.9 million.

The CIO's successes clearly showed that craft unionism was not the only workable recipe for labor organization. They also contributed to a rapid growth in total union membership—although the AFL also grew quickly during that period. By 1939 union membership had risen to 29 percent of nonagricultural employees—more than double the figure of just four years earlier. In 1945 union membership reached a peak; over one-third of nonagricultural workers were organized into unions.

World War II to Present

After World War II, unions faced more difficulties. The political and legislative climate began to turn against them. In 1947 a Republican Congress passed the Taft-Hartley Act, which moved the government back toward a neutral position on labor issues. It created a list of unfair union practices to go with the Wagner Act's list of unfair management practices. It also restricted the conditions under which unions could form a "closed shop," in which union membership was a condition of employment, and it allowed for emergency federal intervention in labor disputes.

Unionization drives in the South, which had been expected to yield millions of new members, were relatively unsuccessful. In 1955, in an effort to strengthen the labor movement, the AFL and the CIO merged. The decline in union membership has continued to the present day, however. Many factors have contributed to that decline. For one thing, blue-collar workers, traditionally the easiest to organize, now make up a much smaller percentage of the labor force than in the past. Women, who account for an increasing portion of the labor force, have never belonged to unions in proportion to their numbers. Moreover, unions have not successfully followed the shift of jobs from the industrial Northeast and Midwest to the Sunbelt states. Finally, some observers believe that younger workers do not consider unions important to their well-being. Many conditions that compelled people to seek the protection of unions have been eliminated by legislation. Safety concerns, discrimination and termination unrelated to job performance are now matters of law and no longer matter of contract. Despite some success in the organization of state and local government employees and agricultural workers, the prognosis for unionism is one of continued gradual decline.

By 2005, only about 12 percent of employed individuals were represented by unions. This circumstance brought about great strains within the AFL-CIO. In 2005, when the labor group had hoped to be celebrating the 50th anniversary of its formation, it instead underwent a breakup. Led by the huge Service Employees International Union and joined by the Teamsters and several others, unions accounting for about a third of all membership broke away from the AFL-CIO. The major issue cited by breakaway unions was a failure of the AFL-CIO to stem the steady decline in union membership. Whether the spit will energize or further weaken the labor movement remains to be seen.

ECONOMIC ANALYSIS OF UNIONS

Partly because of the varied roles unions perform for their members, economists have interpreted unions in various ways. On the one hand, unions can be seen as attempts to exercise monopoly power in order to raise members' wages. On the other, they can be regarded as the collective voice of workers bargaining for safety, democracy, and dignity in the workplace. This section looks at both aspects of unions.

Unions as Monopolistic Maximizers

One approach to understanding labor unions is to treat them as maximizing organizations that operate in much the same way as firms and households. This approach emphasizes the monopoly power that union members achieve by presenting employers with a united front. Consider, for example, the case of a union that was formed in a competitive market and now seeks higher wages through the threat of a strike.

Figure 14.1 shows a labor market in which the competitive equilibrium wage rate is $8 an hour and the equilibrium level of employment is 300,000 worker-hours per year (point E_1). Now suppose that the newly organized workers tell employers that they want $10 an hour or else they will go on strike. The strike threat is shown in the graph by a change in the shape of the supply curve. Initially the supply curve had the usual positively sloped shape. After the strike threat, employers face a supply curve that contains a kink. The horizontal left-hand branch of the kinked supply curve shows that if the employers do not pay at least $10 an hour, no workers will be available. Up to 400,000 worker-hours will be supplied at $10 an hour. To hire more labor than that, the employers will have to raise the wage above what the union is demanding.

Craft Union

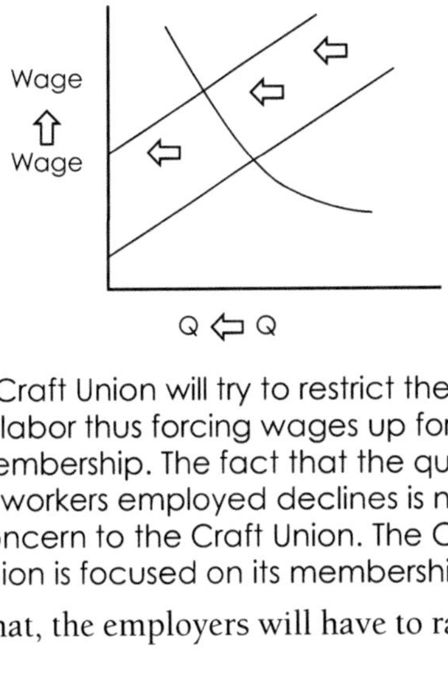

A Craft Union will try to restrict the supply of labor thus forcing wages up for its membership. The fact that the quantity of workers employed declines is not of concern to the Craft Union. The Craft Union is focused on its membership only.

If the employers accept the union's demand, they will react by shifting to a new equilibrium at point E_2, where the demand curve and the horizontal part of the new supply curve intersect. There they will hire 250,000 worker-hours per year at $10 an hour. The union will have succeeded in raising its members' wages, but only at the cost of reducing the amount of work available from 300,000 to 250,000 worker-hours per year.

FIGURE 14.1 EFFECT OF UNIONIZATION IN A COMPETITIVE LABOR MARKET

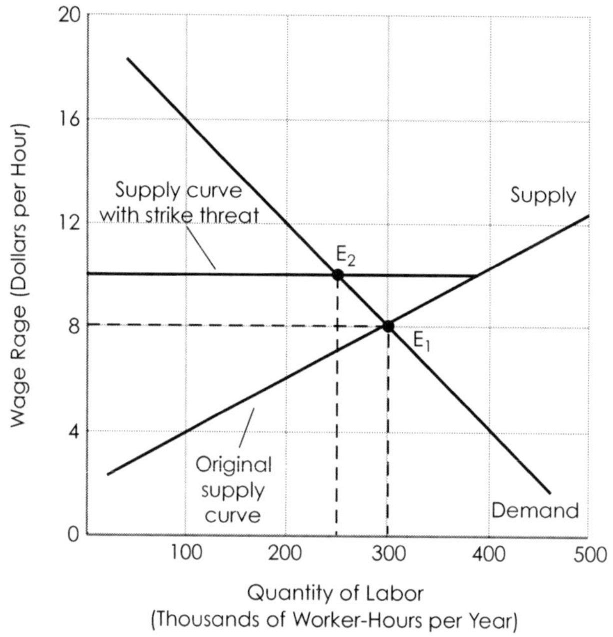

A union formed in a competitive labor market can use a strike threat to bargain for higher wages. Here the union threatens to strike unless the wage is raised from its competitive level of $8 an hour ($E_1$) to $10 an hour. At that point, the supply curve for labor becomes horizontal at $10 an hour up to 400,000 worker-hours per year. A new equilibrium is reached at E_2, where the new supply curve intersects the demand curve. The wage is higher than before, but the quantity of labor employed is smaller.

In this example the union can win a higher wage rate, but only at the expense of jobs for its members. This trade-off raises the question of what unions try to maximize. How far up the demand curve should they try to move in attempting to serve their members' interests? Over the years economists have proposed a number of answers, none of which apply to all cases. Several of those answers are illustrated in Figure 14.2.

MAXIMUM EMPLOYMENT One possibility is for a union to maximize the number of jobs open to its members. In Figure 14.2, this will require a wage of $8 an hour, as shown by the intersection of the supply and demand curves. At that wage, 300,000 worker-hours per year will be employed. At any higher wage, employers will be unwilling to use so much labor. At any lower wage, workers will not be available. However, $8 an hour is the same as the wage that would prevail in a competitive market without a union. Thus, an employment-maximizing union might represent workers politically or might provide social benefits, but it would not affect the wage rate.[1]

MAXIMUM WAGE BILL Another suggestion is that unions seek to maximize the *total wage bill*—that is, the product of the wage rate and the number of hours worked

FIGURE 14.2 MAXIMIZING MODELS OF UNION BEHAVIOR

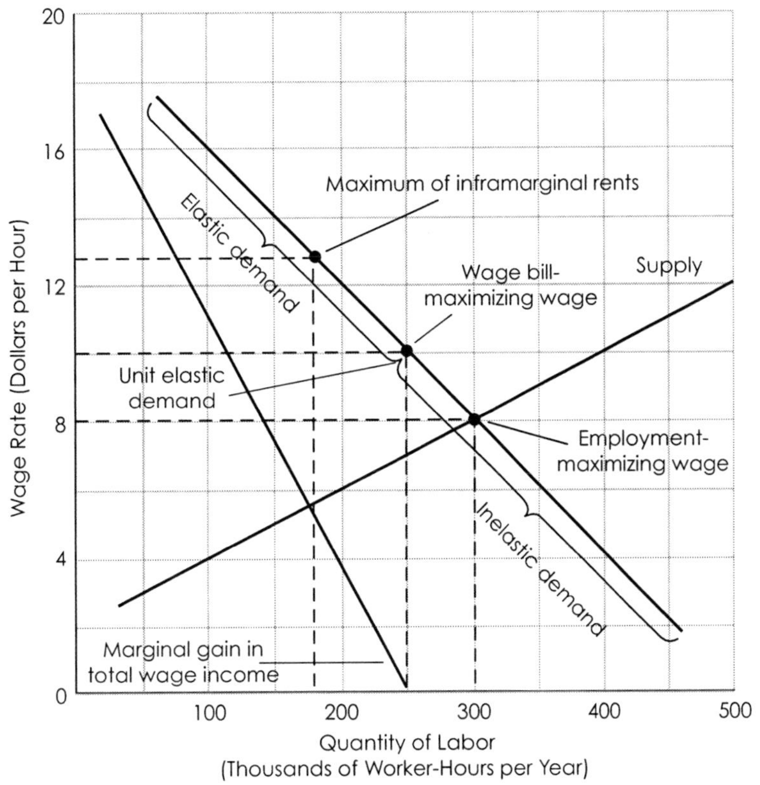

Unions in industries in which employers are price takers may choose various ways of dealing with the wage-job trade-off. If the union's goal is to maximize employment, it will not bargain for a wage higher than the competitive equilibrium. If the labor demand curve is inelastic at the competitive equilibrium point, the total income of union members can be increased by raising the wage to the point at which the demand curve becomes unit elastic. If unions take workers' opportunity costs into account, they may want to raise wages to the level that will maximize inframarginal rents.

per year. As Figure 14.2 shows, the wage bill is maximized at $10 an hour—the point at which the elasticity of labor demand is equal to 1. Keeping the wage at this level, however, creates an excess supply of labor. Workers will be willing to supply 400,000 hours per year, but only 250,000 will be required. The union can simply allow workers to compete for jobs on a first-come, first-served basis and not worry about who can get a job. Alternatively, it can try to divide up the available work among all the workers who want jobs in the industry. Each worker will be able to put in only a limited number of hours. Whatever route is taken, the union must be able to prevent nonunion workers from undercutting it by offering their services as strikebreakers.

MAXIMUM INFRAMARGINAL RENTS The positively sloped supply curve for workers in a given industry can be understood as reflecting the opportunity costs faced by different workers. Workers at the low end of the supply curve perceive opportunities in other industries as relatively unattractive, so they are willing to work in the given industry for a relatively low wage. Higher portions of the supply curve represent workers who perceive relatively more attractive opportunities elsewhere and, hence, need a greater inducement to enter the given industry.

The difference between the equilibrium wage and the minimum that a given worker would accept to work in this industry is that worker's *inframarginal rent*. For example, in Figure 14.2 worker 200,000 would be willing to work in the industry for \$6 per hour. If the equilibrium wage were \$8 per hour, that worker would receive an inframarginal rent of \$2 per hour.

Some economists have reasoned that rather than trying to maximize the total wage bill, unions should try to maximize inframarginal rents. To do this, they should permit employment to expand only to the point at which the marginal gain in total wage income for their members will begin to fall below the opportunity cost of supplying the marginal unit of labor. The marginal gain in total wage income for members can be represented by a line that is related to the labor demand curve in the same way that, in the product market, a firm's marginal revenue curve is related to the demand curve for its product. Such a line is drawn in Figure 14.2. The point at which this line intersects the labor supply curve (which represents the opportunity cost of supplying labor) is the point at which inframarginal rents are maximized.

Whether or not one accepts the idea that unions consciously maximize inframarginal rents, the notion of inframarginal rent is useful in understanding differences in people's attitudes toward their jobs and their unions. Some people do not feel strong attachments to their jobs. They work for a while and then switch to another employer or drop out of the labor force altogether. If they were let go from their current job, they would shrug and find another with no great sense of loss. These are the attitudes of workers earning small inframarginal rents.

On the other hand, some people identify strongly with a given job. They stay with a single employer for their entire careers. Losing those jobs would be disastrous for them. They would see little prospect of finding new jobs equally suited to their needs. These are the attitudes of workers earning high inframarginal rents. Workers with high inframarginal rents are often the ones who have the strongest attachment to unions.

Unions as Political Entities

Models of unions as maximizers treat labor organizations as though they were firms. In those models, unions are seen as single-mindedly pursuing some goal just as a firm pursues the goal of profits. However, the maximizing models have been criticized for glossing over a crucial difference between a labor union and a business firm: Union members have no common interest that unites them in the way that profits unite a firm's owners.

Consider a corporation that is trying to decide whether to increase output of its product. It compares marginal cost with marginal revenue. If marginal revenue exceeds marginal cost, increasing output will increase profit, and the added profit will be shared among all the owners—the partners in a partnership or the stockholders in a corporation. Thus, if the marginal cost–marginal revenue calculations are favorable, owners can be expected to agree unanimously to the increase in output; if the calculations are unfavorable, they will unanimously reject the increase.

The situation of a union bargaining for an increase in the wage rate is fundamentally different. Depending on circumstances, the increase in the wage rate may, as was shown earlier, increase the total wage bill, total inframarginal rents, or both, but the gain will not be shared among all union members. Instead, some will lose their jobs as the employer is forced up and to the left along the labor demand curve, while those who remain on the job will reap all the gains.

It follows that each worker's "maximizing" wage is different from every other's. Whether a given worker will favor a given wage increase will depend on whether he or she fears being laid off as a result. If, as is often the case, layoffs are made in reverse order of seniority, the more senior the worker, the higher the wage he or she favors.

THE MEDIAN WORKER MODEL Faced with the diversity of interests among union members, some labor economists have borrowed concepts from public choice theory to analyze union behavior. For example, Bruce E. Kaufman has suggested using a variant of the median voter model. If union leadership is responsive to the wishes of a majority of members, he says, the target wage rate will correspond to the interests of the *median worker*—the one in the middle of the seniority scale. The idea is that the median worker plus all more-senior workers form a majority voting bloc within the union. This bloc can, in principle, override the interests of less-senior workers, who are most threatened by layoffs.2

However, as Kaufman and others who take this approach recognize, the median worker model has some curious implications. Taken at face value, it suggests that 50 percent of the union plus one member would force through a wage increase that would get the rest of the membership laid off; the next year, half of those left would force through another such wage increase; and so on until only one worker remained on the payroll. The fact that this does not happen suggests that the median worker model by itself does not give a full explanation of union behavior.

INTERESTS OF UNION LEADERS In practice, other factors offset the tendency for unions to shrink to the vanishing point, as would happen in the pure form of the median worker model. One is the fact that unions are complex representative structures that are influenced by the interests of union leaders as well as those of the rank and file. Union leaders have an interest in keeping the union membership large to enhance their own power, income, and prestige. They may also be subject to pressures from community leaders, such as city council members and newspaper editors, to behave in a "responsible" manner. If so, union leaders will balance the interests of their members against those of local government officials, merchants, and others who do not want labor-management conflict to threaten the survival of the employer.

Whatever the specifics, the point remains that once unions are viewed as political entities, no simple maximizing model analogous to the profit-maximizing model of the firm can do justice to the process of collective bargaining. Rather, like governments, unions must be treated as instruments for reconciling the divergent interests of their members. And, as in the case of government, there can be no guarantee that the outcome will optimize or maximize any particular definition of those interests.

What Else Unions Do

To focus entirely on unions effects on wages would be misleading; unions do many other things besides bargain over wages. This has been true from the earliest days of unionism, when the Knights of Labor campaigned for worker education and self-improvement, to the present, when unions provide social activities, help members with personal and family problems, and serve as a channel for participation in national politics. Some of the things that unions do reach beyond the scope of economics. But even on the economic level, unions affect more than wages.

THE UNION VOICE IN THE WORKPLACE Most important, unions give workers a voice in how the workplace is run. They bargain with employers over health and safety conditions in the workplace. They help settle workers' grievances in matters ranging from job assignments to company policy to conflicts with supervisors. They bargain over issues of fairness, such as the role of seniority in layoffs and recalls. In many plants, unions and management also cooperate to elicit ideas from the work force that can lead to improvements in production processes and product design.

The role of unions within the firm reflects the more general role of firms in the market economy. Firms exist because they reduce the cost of organizing complex transactions, especially those in which the parties must make a long-term commitment of specialized resources. Through their internal governing structures, firms facilitate coordination, control tendencies toward opportunistic behavior, and adapt to changes in the business environment. Unions contribute to the accomplishment of these tasks. Consider the following points in particular:

1. Workers often make commitments of specialized resources, such as acquiring firm-specific job skills or moving to a location where few alternative jobs are available. Those commitments bind the firm and the workers to each other and make separations more costly for both sides. Unions can potentially reduce the transaction costs of managing such long-term relationships.
2. Both workers and managers face temptations to behave opportunistically. Supervisors and line managers are needed to prevent shirking by workers. At the same time, union shop stewards and grievance procedures are needed to prevent arbitrary behavior by supervisors, increases in workload beyond the agreed-upon level, and so on. Without a framework for resolving such prob-

lems, worker morale would drop and turnover would rise. Unions are one way of providing such a framework.

3. Circumstances may change unexpectedly for better or worse. If a firm prospers, workers will want to claim a share of the rewards. If it falters, workers may have to share hardships to ensure the firm's survival. New technologies may sharply change working conditions and require new skills. Collective bargaining often provides a way of making the necessary adjustments to change.

FIRMS WITHOUT UNIONS But, it is fair to ask, if unions are so helpful in facilitating coordination and cutting transaction costs, why has union membership been falling for nearly half a century? Three answers can be given.

First, some researchers think that U.S. unions have simply priced themselves out of the market. During the 1950s and 1960s, unions gained wage differentials some 20–25 percent above labor market rates for nonunionized workers. Economists David Blanchflower and Richard Freeman conclude that such differentials were "probably economically justified when the United States was the clear world economic leader," but that today, in a more competitive world economy, they have become "a major liability to the development of unionism in the country. They note that differentials over market rates earned by workers in other countries are significantly smaller, which may explain the fact that union membership has not declined elsewhere as it has in the United States.[3]

Second, although unions are sometimes partners with management in improving quality and raising productivity, there is a darker side to unions' voice in company affairs. Sometimes unions fight new technologies that they fear will eliminate jobs; they may try to prevent women, members of minority groups, and immigrants from gaining access to jobs that have traditionally been reserved for white males; they may stir up worker hostility to make themselves seem more needed; and they may battle competition by nonunion workers with threats and violence. These aspects of unionism reduce labor-management cooperation and economic efficiency.

Third, managers have discovered that harmonious and productive labor relations can be achieved without unions. In the earlier part of the century, workers were often treated as robots. Management attitudes of that period created a fertile climate for the growth of unions. Today, top nonunion firms often go out of their way to give workers a voice in company affairs. *Applying Economic Ideas 14.1* contrasts management practices then and now. The fact that some top nonunion firms are willing to pay high wages to a highly productive work force is consistent with efficiency wage theory as discussed in an earlier chapter.

MINORITIES AND WOMEN IN THE LABOR FORCE

As we have seen, workers have been attracted to unions not just by the hope of higher wages but also by the ideals of justice and equality in the workplace. However,

APPLYING ECONOMIC IDEAS 14.1
LABOR-MANAGEMENT RELATIONS

Bob Stinson remembers what labor-management relations were like in the automobile industry before the advent of unions.

"I started working at Fisher Body in 1917 and retired in 1962, with 45 and 8/10 years service," he says. "Until 1933, no unions, no rules: You were at the mercy of your foreman.

"I left the plants so many nights hostile. If I were a fella big and strong, I think I'd a picked a fight with the first fella I met on the corner. It was lousy. Degraded. You might call yourself a man if you was on the street, but as soon as you went through the door and punched your card, you was nothing more or less than a robot. Do this, go there, do that. You'd do it."

Today the "do this, go there, do that" style of management is out at top U.S. nonunion companies such as Black & Decker, Eli Lilly, Gillette, Grumman, IBM, and Polaroid. According to a study by Fred. K. Foulkes, these firms see the main advantage of operating in a nonunion environment as higher productivity, not lower wages. The higher productivity comes partly from lower employee turnover and less absenteeism, partly from greater worker loyalty, and partly from wider acceptance of new technology.

Foulkes found that managers of the companies he studies made special efforts to give workers a voice in company affairs and to improve the quality of work life. For example:

- Managers work hard to create a sense of equality. Executive status symbols, such as exclusive dining rooms, and country clubs, are avoided. In many firms, managers and workers park in the same parking lots and eat in the same cafeterias.
- Many firms do everything they can to avoid layoffs. Instead, they handle slack periods by reducing hours or producing goods to be stored for later sale. They respond to peak demands by employing part-time or recently retired workers rather than hiring workers who would have to be laid off when the peak had passed.
- The firms tend to promote from within. They post notices of job openings in their plants and offer training to workers who want to upgrade their skills.
- Many firms offer wages and fringe benefits that are competitive with those in unionized firms. (Exceptions can be found in such industries as steel, airlines, and trucking, where union wage scales are unusually high.) They also tend to pay blue-collar workers monthly salaries rather than hourly wages.
- Managers are good listeners and keep their office doors open. They are very careful about the handling of grievances and pay attention to workers' suggestions as well as complaints.

Should these practices be viewed as evidence that unions are not really necessary in a well-managed firm? Or should they be considered evidence that the threat of unionization causes nonunion firms to treat their workers better? You be the judge.

Sources: The Stinson quotes are from an interview in Studs Terkel, *Hard Times: An Oral History of the Great Depression* (New York: Pantheon Books, 1970), 129. The material on management practices today is based on Fred K. Foulkes, "How Top Nonunion Companies manage Employees," *Harvard Business Review* (September–October 1981): 90–96.

neither unions nor market forces have succeeded in eliminating inequality and perceived injustices.

Persistent differences in earnings between ethnic groups and between men and women are a particular focus of concern. On average, as of 2005, average weekly earnings of full-time black or African American workers were only about 78 percent of what white men earned.[4] Hispanic or Latino workers averaged only 71 percent of white workers, while Asian workers earned 112 percent of whites. Full time women workers earned, on average, about 81 percent as much as men. The gender gap was widest for whites (80 percent) and narrowest for hispanics (90 percent). The overall gender gap for the United States is about average for high-income countries, where it ranges from a low of about 61 percent in Japan to over 90 percent in Belgium. As Fig-

FIGURE 14.3 RATIO OF WOMEN'S TO MEN'S PAY IN THE UNITED STATES, 1955–2000

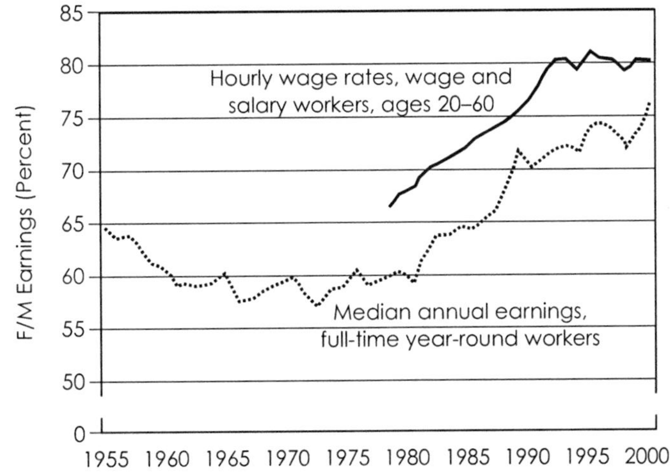

As this chart shows, although women in the United States earn less on average than men, the gap has narrowed over time. The gap is narrower for hourly wages than for annual earnings because women, on average, work fewer hours per year than men.

Source: June O'Neil, "The Gender Gap in Wages, Circa 2000," *American Economic Review*, Papers and Proceedings (May 2003) Figure 1.

ure 14.3 indicates, the gender gap in the United States has narrowed substantially in recent years.

In part, the wage gaps can be explained by the different human-capital endowments of men, women, and minorities. Among these are differences in years of formal education, years of job experience, amount of on-the-job training, and time spent out of the labor force after completion of schooling. Some of those differences reflect discrimination that takes place outside the labor market, and some may reflect cultural differences or differences in preferences. Such indexes of human capital are estimated to account for about half of the wage gap—the exact numbers vary from one group to another and from one study to another. The remaining half cannot be explained in terms of human capital or other easily observable economic factors. This section is concerned with this unexplained part of the wage gap, which is widely suspected to be a result of discrimination in labor markets, and with policies designed to correct the effects of discrimination.

Labor market discrimination

A situation in which employers are unwilling to hire members of a disfavored group at the same wage rate that they pay to equally productive members of a more favored group.

An Economic Model of Discrimination

Employers can be said to practice **labor market discrimination** against a group of workers if they are unwilling to hire members of that group at the same wage rate that they pay to equally productive members of a more favored group.

FIGURE 14.4 EFFECTS OF DISCRIMINATION ON WAGE RATES AND HOURS WORKED

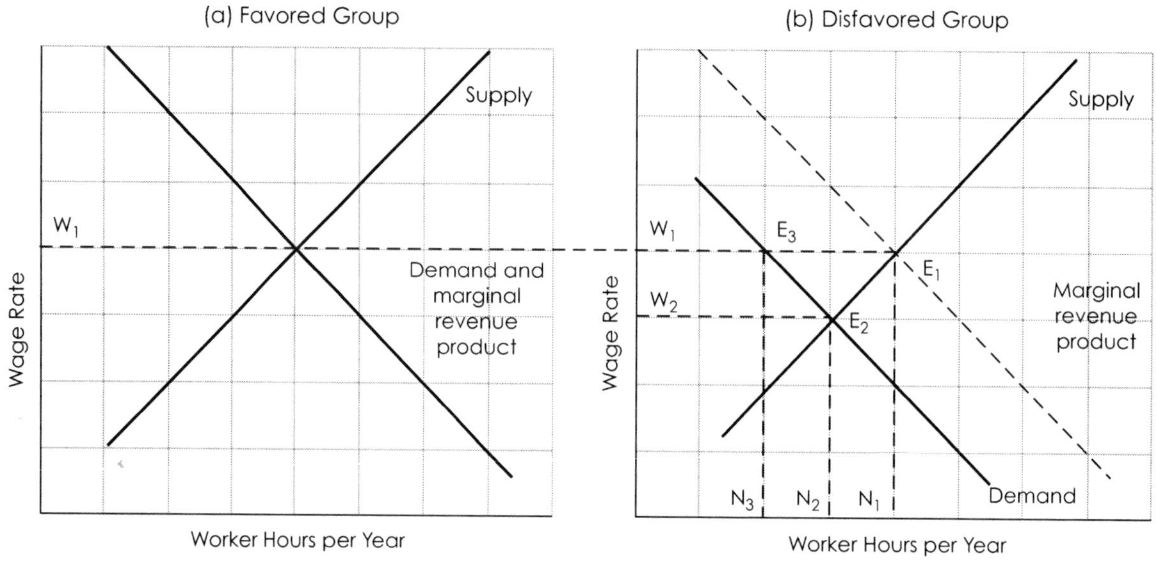

This figure shows the effect of discrimination in a labor market that can be divided into a group of workers who are favored by employers and a group of workers who are disfavored. The two groups are assumed to be equal in terms of productivity, but the demand curve for the disfavored group is shifted to the left of the corresponding marginal revenue product curve. If there are no equal-pay laws, the disfavored group's pay will fall to W_2, below the level of W_1 received by members of the favored group. If the law requires equal pay, both groups will receive wage W_1, but fewer members of the disfavored group will be employed. Many members of the disfavored group who would be willing to work in this occupation at wage W_1 will be forced into other, less attractive sectors of the job market or into unemployment. With or without the equal-pay law, then, discrimination is harmful to the disfavored group.

Figure 14.4 shows the effects of discrimination by employers. Part (a) shows the supply and demand curves for workers in the favored group. This demand curve, as usual, is the marginal revenue product curve. Part (b) shows the supply and demand curves for workers in the disfavored group. In this market the demand curve is shifted to the left relative to the marginal revenue product curve. This indicates that employers will hire members of the disfavored group only if they are more productive than members of the favored group or if they are equally productive but will work for less.

EQUILIBRIUM UNDER DISCRIMINATION Two types of equilibrium are possible under discrimination.

First, let us assume that there are no legal restrictions on discrimination. In this case, the wage rate for the disfavored group will fall to W_2 compared with a rate of W_1 for the favored group. Workers from the two groups will then work side by side, doing the same job, but will receive different pay. All members of the disfavored group who want to work at wage W_2 will be able to find jobs in this market.

In the second case, we assume that the law prohibits paying different wages to members of different groups for doing the same work. In this case, employers must pay wage W_1 to members of both the favored and the disfavored groups. As a result, they will employ only N_3 worker-hours per year from the disfavored group.

The effect of the equal-pay law on members of the disfavored group is mixed. On the one hand, members of that group who are employed in this market are paid more than they would be without the law. On the other hand, fewer workers from the disfavored group get jobs at wage W_1. Those who do not get jobs in this market either remain unemployed or are crowded into some other sector of the labor market, possibly one in which employers do not discriminate. However, whether employers in those markets discriminate or not, wages there will be pushed down by the increased supply of workers who are unable to find jobs in the market. In the end, then, discrimination lowers the average wage of members of the disfavored group even when the law requires equal pay for all workers doing a given job and when there are some markets in which employers do not discriminate.

COMPETITION AND DISCRIMINATION Now that we have examined the effects of discrimination on workers, we turn to the effect on employers. At first it might seem that employers gain from discrimination in that it pushes down the wages of members of disfavored groups. However, this is true only to the extent that employers are united in their desire to discriminate. Looking at the matter from the viewpoint of a single employer, there is an incentive not to discriminate.

Consider the case in which there is no equal-pay law. In that situation the wage rate for workers from the disfavored group is lower than that for workers from the favored group. Employers who set aside their prejudices and hire only workers from the disfavored group will have a cost advantage over employers who discriminate. This cost advantage potentially allows them to undercut their competitors' prices, either driving them out of the market or forcing them to change their hiring practices. In the long run, competition will tend to erode both the practice of discrimination and the pay gap.

All in all, the situation of discrimination in the labor market is somewhat like that of a cartel. Discriminating employers or cartel members can gain as long as they are united. But in practice each has an incentive to cheat on the system. Just as cartel members are pulled by the profit motive to undercut their fellow members, so are employers pulled by the profit motive to abandon established patterns of discrimination. *Applying Economic Ideas 14.2* looks at these forces in the South during the Jim Crow era. In that case competition and the profit motive undermined discrimination to such an extent that states passed laws fostering employer discrimination.

SOME QUALIFICATIONS Although competition is a force that tends to break down labor market discrimination, it does not necessarily eliminate discrimination in all cases. One possible case is that of employers that are monopsonists in the markets in which they hire labor. An employer that faces a positively sloped supply curve in

APPLYING ECONOMIC IDEAS 14.2

DISCRIMINATION AND THE LAW IN THE JIM CROW SOUTH

In the southern United States in the Jim Crow era (the 1890s through the early 1950s), there was no lack of discrimination against black workers. Especially in the early part of the period, the economy was dominated by white plantation owners who employed large numbers of blacks As a group, they had an interest in holding down the wages of black farmworkers, both to boost their own profits and to maintain the dominant position of the white race in social and political life.

There was one problem, however. The greed of many white employers overcame racial solidarity. Despite warnings in newspapers that "white men must stick together," the employers competed for black labor. Black workers often left their jobs for higher-paying ones, especially at harvest time, when labor was in short supply. In addition, labor recruiters from the North would appear in the South to entice black workers to come to work in the North's growing industries at wages that, while low by today's standards, were still better than those paid by the southern planters. Something had to be done to protect the traditional system of exploitation against erosion by market forces. The solution was a set of labor laws, which were passed in most southern states between 1890 and 1910, including the following:

- *Enticement laws*, which made it a crime for white employers to "entice" a worker who had a contract with another employer. The aim was to prevent competition for workers that might bid up wages.
- *Contract enforcement laws*, which made it a crime for a black worker to break a labor contract with a white employer in order to seek work elsewhere. The standard contract period was one year. The aim was to prevent competition at harvest time, when the demand for labor was strongest.
- *Vagrancy laws*, which made it a crime for any person who was able to work to "wander or stroll in idleness." The aim was to keep black workers in the labor force and to prevent them from spending time between jobs shopping around for the best wage offer.
- *Emigrant-agent laws*, which curbed the activities of labor recruiters from other states or even other counties. For example, a law passed by the city of Montgomery, Alabama, imposed a $100 fine or six months in jail on anyone who printed, published, wrote, delivered, posted, or distributed any advertisement that tried to persuade people to leave the city to seek work elsewhere.
- The *convict lease system*, which allowed black prisoners, including those who had been imprisoned for violating contract or vagrancy laws, to be leased to private employers. Being on the chain gang was worse than being a slave: Since the lease was short term, the employer, unlike a slave owner, did not even have an interest in preserving the worker's health.

In a study of the Jim Crow labor laws, economist Jennifer Roback finds that they were effective in keeping wages down and limiting migration. She concludes that without the laws, competition would have undermined racial exploitation of workers.

Source: Jennifer Roback, "Exploitation in the Jim Crow South: The Market or the Law?" *Regulation* (September–December 1984): 37–44. A longer version of the article appears in the *University of Chicago Law Review* (Fall 1984).

the labor market can be compared with a seller that faces a negatively sloped demand curve in the product market. It is profitable for a seller to practice price discrimination provided that the market can be divided into two or more segments with different price elasticities of demand. A higher price is then charged in the market in which the elasticity of demand is lower. In labor markets, a monopsonistic employer can discriminate if groups can be identified according to their elasticity of supply. The profit-maximizing strategy is to pay a lower wage to the groups with the least elastic supply. Those will be the groups that have the least attractive alternative employment opportunities—namely, women and minorities.

In other cases, competition may fail to eliminate discrimination because the discrimination originates with customers or fellow employees rather than with the employer. If customers do not want to be served by members of a minority group, they will take their business to employers who do not hire minority-group members. The discriminating employers may then be at a competitive advantage overall even if they have to pay somewhat higher wages, as the theory set forth earlier indicates that they will. On the other hand, workers from dominant groups may not want to work side by side with minority-group members. In that case, an employer who wants to hire a mixed labor force may have to pay higher wages to members of the dominant group than one who hires only members of the dominant group. Again, this could give the discriminating employer an advantage over the nondiscriminating employer, despite the considerations discussed earlier.

Finally, there are cases in which employers are shielded from market forces altogether. Government employers are an example. It is no accident that some of the major targets of the drive for equal pay for women have been city and state governments. In addition, some economists have argued that managers of large corporations do not always share their stockholders' interest in maximum profits. If the white male managers of such a corporation like to hire only other white males even when more highly qualified women or minority candidates are available, they may be able to get away with doing so, at least for a time, even if the firm's profits suffer as a result.

Discrimination and Asymmetrical Information

The preceding discussion assumes that someone *wants* to discriminate—that employers, fellow workers, or customers prefer not to deal on an equal basis with members of the other gender or other racial groups. It is possible, however, that discrimination can occur even when, other things being equal, all parties would prefer not to discriminate. This can happen when employers wrongly ascribe to an individual member of a certain group characteristics that may be statistically valid for the group as a whole, but are not true of that individual—a phenomenon sometimes termed *statistical discrimination.*

One commonly cited example concerns the tendency of women, on the average, to spend more time out of the labor force than men. It is not disputed that the number of years a person spends in the labor force has a positive effect on productivity and wages. Given these circumstances, suppose that I am an employer looking for entry-level workers to train for career positions, and that I am convinced that women and men who spend equal years with my firm will turn out to be equally productive in their jobs. I have just interviewed two young, unmarried candidates who are alike in all respects except that one is a woman. Which do I hire?

If I am a rational profit maximizer (and if I am constrained to offer the same wage to both candidates), I hire the man. I have no way of knowing how many years each candidate will remain in the job, but the statistical probability is that the man will stay longer. Suppose, though, that you are the woman who is passed over for the job. *You know* that you are career bound, that you, unlike many women, will not drop out of the labor force to raise children. *You know* that you will therefore be just as productive as the male candidate. You feel discriminated against, and you are right to feel that way.

The problem here is one of asymmetric information: I do not know as much about your future employment plans as you do, and I have no way of finding out. Can I ask? No. First of all, it is illegal for me to do so; even to ask about your family intentions is considered evidence of discrimination. Moreover, it would be pointless to ask. You might currently intend to stay with the job but later change your mind. Even if you intended to drop out of the labor force the minute you got married, there would be no reason for you to tell the truth. Asymmetric information and opportunism compound each other. In this case, they prevent me, the employer, from learning what I would like to know about you, the employee, in order to make a decision that is in all ways fair and efficient.

Now, the story just told contains some implicit assumptions that make it a worst-case scenario. In many cases there are other sources of information available to an employer who is not lazy or prejudiced. For example, if a job requires math skills, it would be ridiculous for an employer to exclude women on the basis of a belief that "women are not good at math." The generalization is not valid to begin with, and in any event, an employer who wrongly believed it to be true on average could determine an individual candidate's math skills by testing, looking at high school and college transcripts, and so on.

Also, the story assumes that employers cannot arrange contracts in a way that protects them against employees who leave their jobs before the employer reaps the full benefits of their on-the-job training. Seniority-based salary scales, bonus systems, and deferred compensation in the form of pensions and other devices can protect the employer against employees of either gender who leave for any reason.

Empirical studies suggest that the problem of asymmetric information does not always prevent employers from rewarding women and men equally when they are equal in terms of labor force attachment. One study showed, for example, that men who never marry and women who never marry have comparable labor force histories, whereas married women spend fewer than half as many years in the labor force as never-married women. Within the category of never-marrieds, women earn 99 percent as much as men, even though married women earn substantially less than married men. Another study focusing on college professors showed that never-married women actually did better in terms of salary and promotions than never-married men.[5]

Such studies suggest that labor markets—like markets for other goods and services—find ways of at least partially overcoming the problem of asymmetric information. Nevertheless, it is likely that at least some cases of perceived labor market discrimination are due to information asymmetry.

Federal Antidiscrimination Policies

Since the 1960s, the federal government has instituted a number of policies designed to combat discrimination in the labor market. The first of these was the Equal Pay Act of 1963. As explained earlier, however, mandating equal pay for members of different groups within the labor force is not enough by itself to protect disfavored groups against the effects of discrimination. In the face of employer discrimination, an equal-pay requirement alone may only reduce the number of workers hired from the disfavored group.

A more direct attack on employment discrimination was made by the Civil Rights Act of 1964. Title VII of that act outlaws discrimination of any kind based on race, color, religion, sex, or national origin. The law applies to firms with fifteen or more employees and also to labor unions. In the years since passage of the act, there has been much debate and litigation about what constitutes discrimination. The current interpretation is that any practice is suspect if it has a "disparate impact" on various groups. A practice with a disparate impact can be justified only if an employer proves that it is related to job performance. Thus, the requirement of a minimum height for employees holding a certain job could be challenged on the ground that it has a disparate effect on women. The requirement would be upheld if the employer could prove, say, that only a person over the minimum height could safely operate a certain piece of equipment.

A third important federal policy is Executive Order 11246, which was signed by President Johnson in 1965. This order sets antidiscrimination standards for all companies doing business with the federal government; it therefore covers most major firms. A key feature of the executive order is that major federal contractors must file *affirmative-action programs*. Under an affirmative-action program, a firm pledges to do more than simply not discriminate: it conducts a statistical analysis of its work force and takes concrete steps, through recruitment, training programs, and the like, to hire women and members of minority groups for jobs in which those groups are currently underrepresented. Federal law explicitly forbids the establishment of numerical quotas for hiring on the ground that they constitute discrimination against white males. However, affirmative-action measures are often criticized as constituting de facto quotas.

A number of empirical studies have attempted to determine the effectiveness of federal antidiscrimination policy. They have focused on reductions in the wage gaps among various groups before and after passage of the key civil rights acts. These studies have found federal policy to have had a modest, but measurable, favorable impact on the earnings of minority men. They appear to have had a strong effect in helping to close the wage gap between black and white women. Their effects on the earnings of white women have been negligible, however. In some cases affirmative action has caused white women to be displaced by minority-group members of both genders.[6]

The Comparable-Worth Controversy

In many respects, theory and policy issues having to do with discrimination by race and gender are similar, but there are some notable differences. One of the differences concerns segregation by occupation. Occupational segregation by gender is much stronger than segregation by race. For example, there are black and white truck drivers and black and white secretaries, but the truck drivers, whatever their race, tend to be men, whereas the secretaries tend to be women.

Duncan index of dissimilarity

For a set of occupations in which both men and women are employed, the percentage of men (or women) who would have to change occupations to equalize the numbers of men and women in each occupation.

MEASURING OCCUPATIONAL SEGREGATION A common measure of occupational segregation is the **Duncan index of dissimilarity**. This measures the percentage of either group alone that would have to change occupations to equalize the numbers of men and women in each occupation. The index is 100 if occupations are completely segregated and 0 if each group is equally represented in each occupation. For example, suppose that the labor force consists of 100 men and 100 women. Of the women, 75 are secretaries and 25 are truck drivers, while 25 of the men are secretaries and 75 are truck drivers. The Duncan index in this case would be 50. Occupational segregation could be eliminated if 50 of the male truck drivers (half of all male workers) became secretaries, or if 50 of the female secretaries (half of all female workers) became truck drivers.[7]

The Duncan index of gender segregation for the U.S. labor force was 57 in 1980. This implies that more than half of all men (or women) would have to change jobs to equalize representation by occupation. By contrast, the Duncan index for occupational segregation by race was 33 for men and just 28 for women. Moreover, occupational segregation by gender is changing less rapidly than segregation by race. Between 1960 and 1980 the index of occupational segregation by race fell by 17 points for men and by 28 points for women. Over the same period the index of gender dissimilarity fell by 14 points for blacks and by just 5 points for whites. The index of occupational segregation by gender is over 50 for all age groups; this is also true for all educational groups except people with graduate degrees, for whom it is 43.[8]

The occupational segregation of men and women would be of little consequence if the occupations dominated by women were paid as well as those dominated by men, but that is not the case. Instead, occupations dominated by women have significantly lower average pay levels than those dominated by men.

Occupational differences in pay contribute strongly to the gender gap in earnings. As we saw earlier, about half of that gap can be explained by differences in human capital. Nearly all of the remaining half can be explained by occupation. To put it in more concrete terms, male and female truck drivers with equal training and experience get paid about the same. So do male and female secretaries with equal training and experience. But the average pay of all truck drivers, most of whom are men, is higher than that of all secretaries, most of whom are women.

The policy implications of this situation are substantial. In the case of race, where there is relatively little occupational segregation, much progress toward equality can be made by ensuring that blacks and whites are placed on the same pay scales and have equal opportunities for promotion within their occupation. Those are the chief goals of the major civil rights legislation of the 1960s. In the case of gender, where there is much more occupational segregation, those measures will not by themselves equalize pay without either a change in the relative pay of various occupations or a major shift of genders among occupations.

ORIGINS OF OCCUPATIONAL SEGREGATION The source of occupational segregation by gender is one of the most controversial topics in labor market economics. There are two very different views on this matter.

According to one view, occupational segregation reflects choices made by women, choices that have both cultural and economic origins. Cultural factors might lead women into nurturing occupations such as teaching and nursing and men into more physical occupations such as construction or mining. For example, the idea of women as doctors and lawyers seemed strange to many people a generation ago, but today, 44 percent of medical school graduates and about half of law school graduates are women.) Economic choices leading women into certain occupations are said to reflect women's greater role in child care. That role causes women to favor occupations in which they can work in residential areas, arrange for flexible working hours, and move into and out of the labor force with relative ease. In return for these desired job characteristics, women are willing to accept lower pay.

According to the opposite view, occupational segregation reflects choices made by men. In this model, men choose first. They decide which occupations they would like, leaving the rest for women. Economist Barbara Bergman conjectures that the earmarking of jobs by sex has its origin in social systems that decree that women are and should be inferior in status to men. The result is that men feel uncomfortable when working side by side with women as equals, and even more so when working under the supervision of women. To avoid this discomfort, men confine women to a limited set of job categories.[9]

In both views, wages are set by supply and demand within each occupation, and it is supply and demand that determines the pay gap. The disagreement is over why the supply of women in certain occupations is as great as it is despite low pay. In the one view, women choose those occupations voluntarily because they have attractive nonwage characteristics. In the other view, men leave women no other place to go.

THE COMPARABLE-WORTH REMEDY The different views on the origins of occupational segregation by gender have very different policy implications. Those who see occupational segregation as a product of women's choices see no need for any remedy beyond those already on the books. Those measures prohibit paying different wages to men and women doing the same work and, through affirmative action, grant women access to nontraditional occupations. But those who see occupational segregation as male dominance of labor markets want more. They want equal pay for women now, without waiting for massive cultural and occupational shifts to occur.

No one claims that all occupations deserve exactly equal pay, because not all occupations are comparable. Some require more skills or education than others. Some are dirty and distasteful, others comfortable and pleasant. Some are boring, others exciting; some routine, others challenging. What the advocates of pay equity want is equal pay for work of *comparable worth*.

To measure the value of different occupations, such as those of secretary and truck driver, advocates of comparable worth propose the use of *job evaluation techniques* similar to those used by many large employers in setting internal pay scales. These techniques begin by identifying a number of traits that are relevant to the pay received by a worker, such as initiative, physical demand, and responsibility for equipment. Each job is assigned points for each trait, and total points are plugged into a formula that can be used to arrive at a pay recommendation. Such job evaluation techniques consistently identify traditionally female-dominated occupations as underpaid relative to traditionally male-dominated occupations.

Under a comparable-worth policy, job evaluations would be used to spotlight wage scales that, on the face of things, appear to be discriminatory. Not even the most enthusiastic advocates of comparable worth suggest rigid application of job evaluations as wage-setting formulas throughout the economy. Rather, they suggest that they be applied directly to wage setting in the public sector and indirectly as guidelines for wage setting in the private sector. Comparable-worth guidelines, like affirmative-action requirements, might be required for federal contractors and voluntary for other firms. Also, they might play a legally valid role in employee lawsuits, in conjunction with other indications of discrimination.

OBJECTIONS TO COMPARABLE WORTH Opponents of comparable worth see the concept not only as unnecessary (because they assume that current wage differences reflect voluntary choice) but as actively harmful, for several reasons.

First, they say, job evaluations fail to take supply and demand into account. Suppose that petroleum engineers and lawyers receive equal job evaluation points and hence are assigned equal pay. Then, during a boom in the oil industry, firms would have no way of bidding up wages to attract the extra engineers they need, and positions would go unfilled. And during a downturn in the industry, petroleum engineers would have to be laid off rather than be offered the option of continued employment at reduced pay.

Second, job evaluation techniques are inherently subjective. Different point scales and different evaluators produce different relative values for the same pair of jobs. Some scales use as few as four factors, some a dozen or more. Some evaluators might give a secretary more points for "responsibility for equipment" than a truck driver; others might give the secretary fewer points. For these reasons, private firms that now use such scales use them only as one factor among many in setting wages.

Finally, the critics point out that raising wages in traditionally female-dominated jobs would cause firms to cut back on employment in those occupations. Hospitals would use more automated monitoring equipment in order to economize on nurses. Insurance companies would substitute computers for clerical workers. The reduced employment opportunities would offset the wage gains for women in the affected occupations.

Advocates of comparable worth acknowledge that job evaluation techniques are imperfect. They agree that assigning every wage decision in the country to a federal bureaucracy would be a bad idea, and they deny that this is their intention. They claim that comparable-worth policies in other countries have had small if any employment effects. The debate over this issue is likely to continue for the foreseeable future.

SUMMARY

1. **How have labor unions evolved over time in the United States?** The earliest labor unions in the United States were *craft unions*—unions of skilled workers who practiced the same trade. The modern labor movement dates from 1881, when the American Federation of Labor, an association of craft unions, was founded. *Industrial* unions—which include all the workers in an industry regardless of their trade—were a later development. Union membership reached its peak in 1945 at about one-third of the labor force.

2. **What are the main provisions of U.S. labor law?** Before 1930 the courts were generally hostile to unions, limiting the goals they could pursue and the means they could employ. The Norris–La Guardia Act of 1932 was intended to place the government in a neutral position with respect to unions. Three years later the Wagner Act swung the power of government to the union side. This act created the National Labor Relations Board, set procedures under which workers could form unions, and limited the antiunion tactics that employers could use. The Taft-Hartley Act of 1947 limited the powers of unions somewhat and gave the government the power to intervene in strikes that threatened the national interest.

3. **How are wage rates determined in unionized markets?** In a competitive labor market, any increase in the wage brought about by unionization tends to reduce employment. Some models of unionization emphasize maximization of employment, the wage bill, or inframarginal rents. Other models view unions as political structures, applying concepts borrowed from public choice theory.

4. **What do unions do in addition to bargaining over wages and benefits?** Besides affecting wages, unions give workers a voice in how the workplace is run. In this regard, unions can be viewed as part of the mechanisms by which firms coordinate complex transactions under conditions of long-term commitment of specialized resources, opportunism, and change. Managers of top nonunion firms recognize that productivity is enhanced when workers are allowed a voice in company affairs.

5. **How are labor markets affected by discrimination?** A firm is said to practice *labor market discrimination* against a group of workers if it is unwilling to hire members of that group at the same wage rate that is paid to equally productive members of a more favored group. Discrimination by employers will reduce the wages of members of the disfavored group if there are no legal restrictions, and it will reduce employment of members of the disfavored group even if the law requires equal pay for equal work. Competition tends to erode discrimination by employers but not discrimination by customers or fellow workers. Where there is asymmetric information about

worker characteristics, discrimination can occur even though employers would prefer not to discriminate, other things being equal.

6. **What is the nature of the controversy over equal pay for men and women?** The degree of occupational segregation is much greater by gender than by race, and occupations that have traditionally been dominated by women are less well paid than those that have traditionally been dominated by men. To correct this situation, some have proposed that the equal-pay principle be extended so that workers performing jobs of comparable worth receive equal pay.

KEY TERMS

Craft union
Industrial union
Labor market discrimination
Duncan index of dissimilarity

PROBLEMS AND TOPICS FOR DISCUSSION

1. **Unions and monopsony.** Turn to Figure 10.9, which shows supply, demand, and marginal resource cost curves for a monopsonist. The equilibrium wage under monopsony is $6 per hour. Suppose now that the workers threaten to go on strike unless they are paid at least $8 per hour, and the employer is forced to accept this demand. What happens to the supply curve of labor, given the union's wage demand? What happens to the marginal resource cost curve? Compared with the initial equilibrium, what happens to the wage rate? To the number of workers? Is this an exception to the rule that a union can raise wages only if it is willing to accept a reduction in jobs? Is there a limit to how high this union can raise wages without sacrificing the jobs of members? If so, what is the limit?

2. **Unionization on campus.** Is the nonteaching staff of your university unionized? Is the teaching faculty unionized? Are any efforts under way to unionize either of these groups? Interview one member of the nonteaching staff and one member of the faculty to learn their attitudes toward unionization.

3. **Labor unions and cartels.** Review the section on cartels in Chapter 10. In what ways do unions resemble cartels? How do they differ from cartels? Do you think that public policy should treat unions and producer cartels differently? Discuss.

4. **Labor unions in the news.** Search the Internet for news about labor unions and collective bargaining. Have recent rounds of bargaining centered on issues of wages and benefits or on such matters as job security and productivity? Give examples.

5. **Discrimination at Hertz.** In 1981 two women who had worked as automobile rental agents at Hertz Corporation filed a suit saying that they had been discriminated against when they had applied repeatedly for jobs as station manager and had been passed over in favor of male candidates. Although most rental agents were women, few had ever been promoted to the position of station manager. Hertz's city manager in the city where the women worked had told them that a woman should not be given the job of station manager because she cannot go away for training and because, in the manager's view, "a woman's place is in the kitchen." The judge in the case decided in favor of the women. Do you think that the judge's decision was a proper one? Would it have been better to wait for competition to eliminate the discrimination? Or do you think there was no real discrimination? Discuss.

6. **The Duncan index of dissimilarity.** A company employs 200 men and 200 women as clerks and managers. Of the managers, 160 are men and 40 are women. Of the clerks, 40 are men and 160 are women. What is the Duncan index of occupational dissimilarity by gender for this firm?

CASE FOR DISCUSSION

Unions Struggle to Survive in Changing Labor Markets

Negotiations between 70,000 unionized grocery store employees and three major supermarket chains broke down in October 2003. Feeling pressure from nonunion, low-cost competitors, the supermarkets sought to cut costs by reducing wages and benefits. Albertsons, Ralphs, and Vons proposed a two-tiered wage system that would pay newly hired employees less and wanted to require all workers to share in health-insurance costs.

"I'm a single parent. I have two children," said a Ralphs employee, Oscar, who declined to give his last name. "I'm concerned about medical benefits. I'm concerned about our wages," he continued. "We're the real Ralphs, that's how I feel."

The United Food & Commercial Workers Union (UFCWU) voted to strike when it was unable to reach an agreement with the supermarkets. Workers set up picket lines that remained standing four months later.

According to Vons spokeswoman Sandra Calderon, the combination of higher health-care costs and falling pension-fund values make "this negotiation more difficult than negotiations in the past."

Despite union benefits falling to as low as $100 per week, and the loss of health-insurance coverage, the employees were determined to force a compromise with the supermarket chains.

"A lot of people are looking at us as an example," said Yvonne Gapasen, a 14-year employee of Vons supermarket. She said that other unions would lose bargaining power with their employers if the UFCWU strike was unsuccessful.

George Waylan, a retail management consultant, points out that grocery chains, especially those in California, are heavily unionized with a well-paid workforce.

Waylan said traditional supermarkets have "a very different way of doing business, offering lots of selection and lots of service." Vons, Ralphs, and Albertsons have to respond to the low-cost threat of retailers like Wal-Mart. "You have a competitor come in and sell essentially the same kind of merchandise for substantially less because their costs are less, then you have to do something to compete with that," he said.

Sources: Eric Anderson, "California Grocery Workers on Strike," *Morning Edition,* National Public Radio, October 13, 2003; Carrie Kahn, "Grocery Strike Talks Recommence," *All Things Considered,* National Public Radio, February 11, 2004.

QUESTIONS

1. Would you expect the market for supermarket employees to be approximately competitive or strongly monopsonistic? What difference would this make for the bargaining power of labor unions?
2. Review the discussion of efficiency wages in Chapter 13 and the case study of Sam's Club versus Costco. Do you think that cutting wages is the right response for Vons and others to make when faced with new competition from Wal-Mart? What other alternatives might be available?
3. Why do you think employers opted for a two-tier wage system with lower wages for new hires rather than pay cuts for all employees? Do you think the median worker model might be relevant to this decision? If the median worker model applied, how would this influence the likelihood of a strike over introduction of the two-tier system?

END NOTES

1. A possible exception is the situation in which the employer is a monopsonist. See the second item in "Problems and Topics for Discussion" at the end of the chapter.
2. Bruce E. Kaufman, *The Economics of Labor Markets and Labor Relations* (Hinsdale, IL: Dryden Press, 1986), 461–463.
3. David Blanchflower and Richard Freeman, "Going Different Ways: Unionism in the United States and Other Advanced OECD Countries," NBER Working Paper No. 3342, 1992.
4. Bureau of Labor Statistics, Current Population Survey, Second Quarter 2005, Table D-19.
5. These and other studies are discussed in Walter Williams, *Explaining the Economic Gender Gap* (Dallas: National Center for Policy Analysis, 1983).
6. For a brief summary of the empirical literature, see Kaufman, *Economics of Labor Markets*, 392–393.
7. Mathematically, the Duncan index is found by summing across occupations the absolute value of the differences between the percentages of the two groups employed in each occupation and dividing that sum by two. If M1 is the percentage of one group in occupation i and Ni is the percentage of the other group in occupation i, then the index, D, is found by the formula

$$\sum_i \frac{|M_i - N_i|}{2}$$

8. See Victor R. Fuchs, "Women's Quest for Equality," *Journal of Economic Perspectives* (Winter 1989), Table 1.
9. See Barbara Bergman, "Does the Marker for Women's Labor Need Fixing?" *Journal of Economic Perspectives* (Winter 1989): 43–60.

CHAPTER 15

Income Distribution and Poverty

After reading this chapter, you will understand:

1. How income distribution can be measured
2. How poverty differs from inequality and how it is measured
3. What are the effects of labor market policies intended to alleviate poverty
4. How transfer payments can be used to alleviate poverty and how design of transfer programs can be improved

Before reading this chapter, make sure you know the meaning of:

1. Income and substitution effects
2. Human capital
3. Public choice theory
4. Economics of discrimination

THIS CHAPTER EXAMINES the problems of income distribution and poverty. In one sense these subjects are an extension of the theory of resource markets. As we saw, workers and owners of capital and natural resources are rewarded according to the productivity of the factors of production they contribute. Entrepreneurs earn profits or losses according to their degree of success in finding and taking advantage of new opportunities. But not everyone starts from the same position when entering the labor market. People are born with different skills and talents. They grow up in different countries and different regions or school districts within a country. They control different amounts of capital and natural resources, and encounter different prejudices. These differences by themselves are enough to cause incomes to vary. As people go through life, the decisions they make, including those that affect their human capital, and the entrepreneurial risks they take cause incomes to vary still more. As a result, some earn little or nothing, while others earn millions of dollars a year.

In addition to what people earn in factor markets, taxes and government income transfers introduce further variations in the distribution of income. Some taxes and transfer payments are specifically designed to influence income equality. In the United States, the program known as Temporary Assistance for Needy Families (TANF) is a leading example. The tax systems of most countries are also designed to influence income distribution by taxing the poor comparatively less than the wealthy. In the United States however, the social security payroll tax falls disproportionately on the lower wage earners.

This chapter will take a comprehensive look at the sources of income inequality and poverty and at public policies that are intended to alleviate them.

MEASURING INEQUALITY AND POVERTY

Inequality in the United States and Around the World

Lorenz curve

A graph that represents the degree of income inequality in an economy.

Figure 15.1 provides a good place to begin a discussion of how inequality is measured. The diagram shows a **Lorenz curve**—a visual picture of income distribution. It is drawn as a square with the horizontal axis representing percentage of the population and the vertical axis percentage of income earned by those at or below each population percentile. Reading this particular Lorenz curve, we see that about 7 percent of all income is earned by the poorest 20 percent of the population, about 25 percent by the poorest 50 percent of the population and so on.

If income were distributed equally among all members of the population, the Lorenz curve would be a straight line, labeled as the line of perfect equality in the diagram. Twenty percent of the population would account for 20 percent of the income, 50 percent of the population for 50 percent of the income, and so on. The more unequal the distribution, the more the Lorenz curve sags below the line of equality. In a society where one person earned all the income and no one else had anything at all, the Lorenz curve would hug the axes, having a reverse-L shape.

Gini coefficient

A measure of inequality of income equal to zero under conditions of perfect equality and to one under perfect inequality.

Gini index

The Gini coefficient expressed as a percentage.

The fact that the Lorenz curve sags more and more as inequality increases provides a simple way to reduce the concept of inequality to a single number. The **Gini coefficient**, invented in 1912 by the Italian statistician Corrado Gini, is the ratio between the shaded area lying between the Lorenz curve and the line of equality to the whole triangle lying beneath the line of equality. If income is distributed perfectly equally, the Gini coefficient is zero. If one person has all the income, the Gini coefficient is 1. When the Gini coefficient is multiplied by 100 to convert it to a percentage, it is called **Gini index**.

Figure 15.2 provides data on income inequality in selected countries. As can be seen, inequality varies greatly around the world. Latin America and some African countries stand out as regions of the greatest inequality. The high-income countries of Europe and some high-income Asian countries are among the most equal. The United

FIGURE 15.1 A LORENZ CURVE FOR THE U.S. ECONOMY

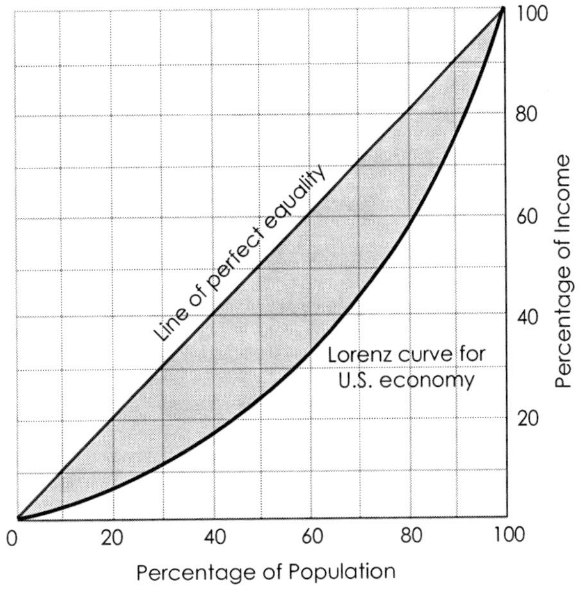

A Lorenz curve can be used to represent the degree of inequality in an economy. Such a diagram is drawn in a square, with the horizontal axis representing the percentage of the population and the vertical axis the percentage of all income earned by those at or below each population percentile. In an economy in which income was distributed equally, the poorest 20 percent of the population would earn 20 percent of all income, the poorest 40 percent would earn 40 percent of all income, and so on. In that case, the Lorenz curve would be a straight line from one corner of the box to the other. In the U.S. economy, where the poorest 20 percent of the population earns just 3.5 percent of all income and the richest 20 percent earns 50.1 percent, the Lorenz curve sags toward the lower right-hand corner of the box. The degree of inequality can be measured by the Gini coefficient—the ratio of the shaded area between the Lorenz curve and the line of perfect equality to the area of the whole triangle beneath the line of equality.

States is about in the middle with regard to income inequality as measured by the Gini index. A World Bank study estimates the Gini Index for the whole world, throwing together the poorest people in poor countries and the wealthiest people in the richest countries, as about 66—more unequal than the in-country distribution for the least equal individual countries.[1]

Trends in Earnings Inequality in the United States

Another way to summarize the information given by the Lorenz curve is to calculate the percentage of total income received by people in a given income range. Figure 15.3 uses the shares of the poorest 20 percent and the richest 5 percent to show how inequality of before-tax income has changed over time in the United States.

The figure shows that after reaching its historically most equal point from the mid-1950s to the late 1970s, U.S. income distribution has become steadily less equal

FIGURE 15.2 GINI COEFFICIENTS OF INCOME INEQUALITY FOR SELECTED COUNTRIES

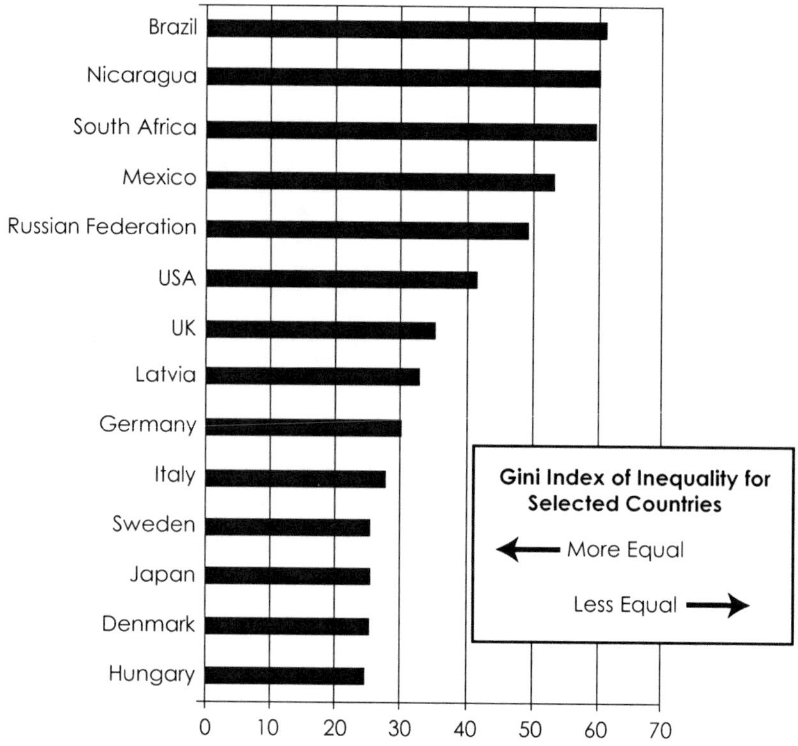

The Gini index is a measure of inequality that has a value of 0 under conditions of perfect equality and 100 under perfect inequality. As this figure indicates, the United States is near the middle of the range of world countries in terms of inequality. A world bank study estimates the Gini Index for the whole world, throwing together the poorest people in poor countries and the wealthiest people in the richest countries, as about 66—more unequal than the in-country distribution for the least equal individual countries.

Source: World Bank

since 1980. Despite what one might think from abundant political finger pointing, the trend has continued fairly steadily through changes in Democratic or Republican control of Congress and the White House during this period. The causes of the trend toward greater equality are not fully understood, but the best guess is that a number of factors are at work. The following are some of the most frequently mentioned:

TAXES Income tax rates have fallen substantially since the late 1970s, when the maximum rate was as high as 90 percent. "Tax cuts for the rich" are often mentioned as a source of increased inequality, but the claim must be treated with caution. For one thing, the trends shown in Figure 15.3 are for pre-tax income. Changing the share of

FIGURE 15.3 INCOME INEQUALITY TRENDS IN THE UNITED STATES, 1947–2001

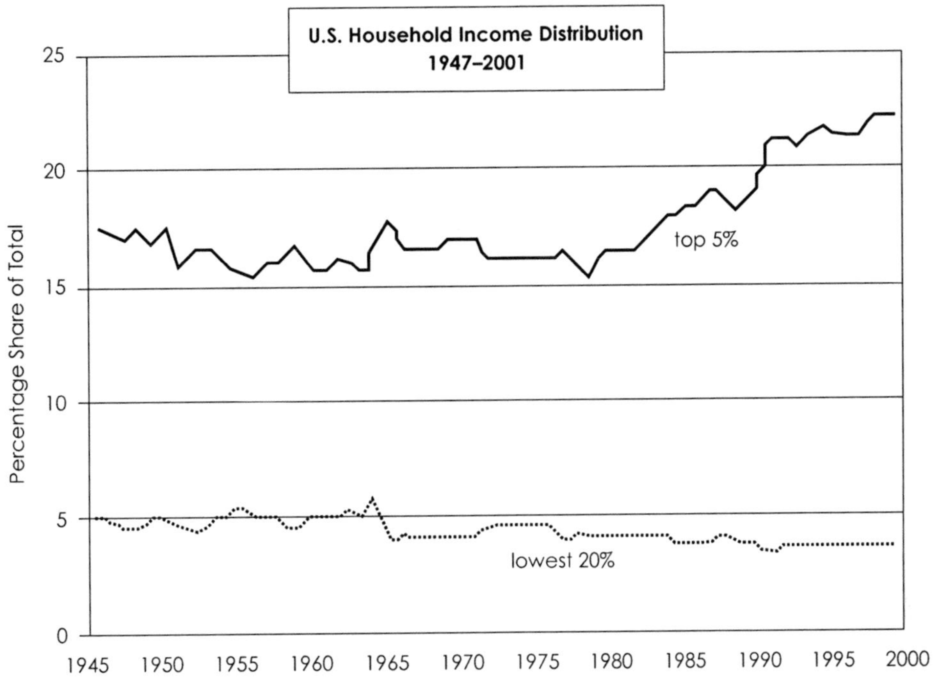

This figure shows the share of before-tax income received by the richest 5 percent and the poorest 20 percent of the U.S. population. The distribution of income reached its historically most equal values in the period between the mid-1950s and the late 1970s. Since 1980, the distribution of income has become steadily less equal. The trend toward greater inequality does not show any obvious correlation with changes in the political party dominating the White House or Congress.

Source: U.S. Bureau of the Census

total income that high earners take home after tax would not directly affect these data. Also, even after all tax cuts, the inequality of the income tax burden is still much greater than the inequality of income, in part because low-income families today pay very little or no income tax at all. According to IRS data, the top 1 percent of tax payers earned 16 percent of all adjusted gross income and paid 34 percent of income taxes. The top quarter of taxpayers earned 64 percent of income and paid 83 percent of taxes. The bottom half of taxpayers paid a tiny 3.5 percent of total income taxes.

These figures do not exclude the possibility that tax cuts indirectly contributed to increased inequality of pre-tax income. In part, cuts in taxes for high earners may have encouraged them to make greater efforts to earn more (supply side economic theory, or *trickle down* economics), although not many economists think this effect is large. Perhaps more likely, lower tax rates may have increased income *reported* by higher earners because tax cuts decreased incentives to participate in legal tax shelters and illegal tax avoidance.

CHANGES IN SOURCES OF INCOME From 1980 to 2004, wage and salary income decreased from 79 percent of all personal income to 68 percent, while interest and dividend income held a nearly unchanged 15 percent of personal income. Because wage and salary income is more equally distributed than investment income, its decline in relative importance contributed to an increase in overall inequality. A wise person has her money work for her; a foolish person works for his money. To have money work for you, *you must first have money!*

CHANGES IN RELATIVE WAGES OF SKILLED AND UNSKILLED WORKERS Some of the most dramatic changes in income inequality occurred within the category of wage and salary income. During the 1980s, there was a sharp increase in the earnings of college educated workers relative to those with a high-school education or less. (Again, here is the answer to the question: Why are YOU attending college?) This change continued, although at a slower rate, during the 1990s. Because college-educated workers already earned more than the less educated to begin with, this change added to overall inequality. Several explanations have been offered for this trend:

- *Skill-biased technological change.* One common explanation of the increased return to education is skill-biased technological change. Computerization of both manufacturing and services may have increased the demand for college educated workers more rapidly than they increased as a percentage of the labor force.
- *Immigration and trade.* Another possible explanation of the relative increase in pay of more educated workers lies in immigration and trade. If immigrants, including illegal immigrants, are less skilled than the average U.S.-born labor force, the relative supply of low-skill workers would have increased the relative supply at the same time the relative demand for low-skill workers was falling. If instead of "importing" workers, U.S.-based firms "exported jobs" by moving low-skill production processes abroad, the effect on relative demand and supply for low-skilled workers would have been much the same.
- *Decline of unionization.* Some observers believe that the decline of labor unions in the United States, a process that began earlier but continued during the 1980s and after, may also have contributed to inequality. The reason for thinking this is that unionized manufacturing jobs were traditionally among the best-paying alternatives for workers with a high-school education or less. In 1970, it was possible and perhaps, more likely for someone to get a union position at a steel mill, or an auto manufacturing plant which provided upper middle class wages and benefits. Today these opportunities are much less numerous. At one time, the largest employer in Baltimore was Bethlehem Steel. Now, the largest employer in Baltimore is Johns Hopkins Hospital and University. The General Motors plant at Broning Highway is now closed, though GM has opened a transmission plant in Whitemarsh.

The above explanations are not mutually exclusive. It is likely that each of them has played some role in the trend toward greater inequality of income in the United States over the past quarter century. Although many studies have been undertaken, there does not appear to be a firm consensus as to which of the causes is the most important.

What Is Your Economic Class?

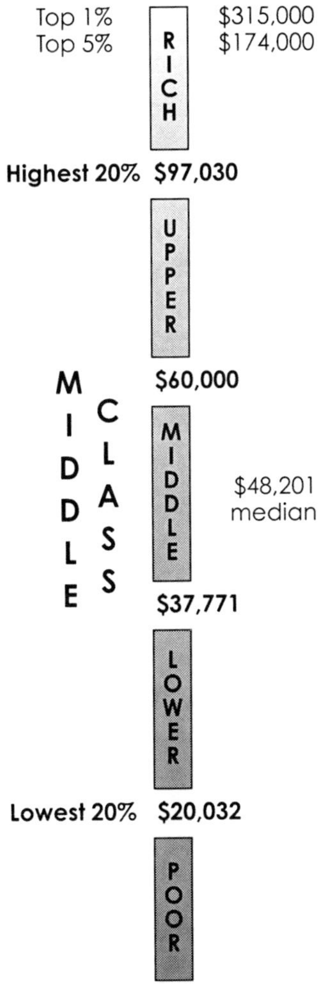

Using the U.S. Census Bureau findings, we can define the rich and the poor objectively based on income. If you define RICH as having an income greater than 80 percent of the population, then all you must do is determine where that UPPER 20 percent begins. And if you define the POOR as having an income less than 80 percent of the population, then you determine where the lower 20 percent ends.

Granted $97,030 may not feel rich in New York City, but the household earning that amount is earning more than the other 80 percent of the population, and so, they are in the upper income class or rich class. To be poor, your household income must be no more that $20,031, The 2006 median was just above $48,200 so the exact, smack-in-the-middle class is $48,000±. We Americans may not be as rich as we thought and there are not millions of millions of ultra rich sports stars in the country.

Many of student in this college, and even in this classroom, are living in a household that is in the top 20 percent or rich class. If two teachers are together, or a police officer and nurse, and filing a joint tax return and they earn $49,000 each, then they have made it into the TOP 20 percent or the RICH class. The smack middle is just $48,000±. So if you're a new teacher earning $33,000 married to a part time nurse's aid earning $15,000, then you are right in the middle class!

Measuring Poverty

Poverty and inequality are related concepts, but the relationship is not a simple one. Inequality is a statistical concept, whereas poverty is a sociological one. Poverty implies a lack of means to provide for basic material needs. At the same time, it tends to be associated not just with low earnings, but with loose attachment to the labor market, and not only with lack of means, but with dependence on others to meet basic needs. In short, it is possible to imagine a society in which income is not distributed completely equally, but yet no one is poor. At the same time, as is brought home by *Applying Economic Ideas 15.1,* we cannot only imagine, but actually observe, a country in which the lowest income families rank high on the global scale of income distribution, yet are poor in the sense in which the world is normally understood.

Since the 1960s, the U.S. government has followed an official definition of poverty based on a estimate of the income needed to provide a minimum standard of living. The definition starts from an economy food plan devised by the Department of Agriculture. The plan is supposed to provide a balanced diet at the lowest possible cost given prevailing market prices. By itself, a total income equal to the cost of the economy food plan is not enough to keep a family out of poverty. To take other needs into account, the government sets the poverty threshold—the dividing line between the poor and the nonpoor—at three times the cost of the economy food plan. In 2003 the low-income level was $18,660 for a family of four, about 30 percent of the median income for such families. Below that level, it is assumed that the pressure of a family's needs for shelter, clothing, and other necessities tends to become so great that the family will forgo the needed food to get other things.[2]

As shown in Figure 15.4, 12.5 percent of the U.S. population was officially considered poor as of 2003. Although the poverty rate tends to rise during recessions and fall during expansions, it has remained within a range of about 12 to 15 percent since the 1970s. The fact that the considerable rise in income inequality since 1980 has not resulted in a corresponding increase in poverty serves to underline the difference between the two concepts. The rise in income inequality has taken place against the background of a doubling of real gross domestic product in the past twenty-five years.

APPLYING ECONOMIC IDEAS 15.1

POVERTY IN THE UNITED STATES AND AROUND THE GLOBE

Poverty in the United States is undeniably a problem that merits serious attention by economists and policymakers. Nonetheless, to place things in perspective, it is worth keeping in mind that even low-income families in the United States are incomparably richer than the poor in many regions of the world.

The World Bank uses incomes of $1 or $2 per person per day as a measure of global poverty. Some 2.8 billion people, or 56% of the world population live on less than $2 per day, and 1.2 billion people, or 23 percent of the world's population, live on less than $1 per day. Sub-Saharan Africa is the poorest region of the world, where half of all people get by on $1 a day or less. In Ethiopia, four out of five people fall below this threshold. By comparison, an income of $2 per day, or $2,920 per year for a family of four, is just 16% of the U.S. government's official poverty threshold. In the United States, almost no one qualifies as poor by the World Bank's standards.

People in the United States and other high-income countries may have a hard time understanding what it means to live on less than $1 per day. Numbers alone fail to paint a clear picture. To help understand the nature of global poverty, try answering yes or no to the following questions:

1. *Yes/No: Do you own more than one change of underwear?*
2. *Yes/No: Do you own a pair of shoes?*
3. *Yes/No: Do you have access to transportation other than walking (e.g., car, bicycle, or public transportation system)?*
4. *Yes/No: Do you have more than one choice of food for your dinner tonight?*

If you answer "yes" to three or more of these questions, you are probably wealthier than 80 percent of the world's population.

FIGURE 15.4 OFFICIAL AND ALTERNATIVE MEASURES OF POVERTY IN THE UNITED STATES

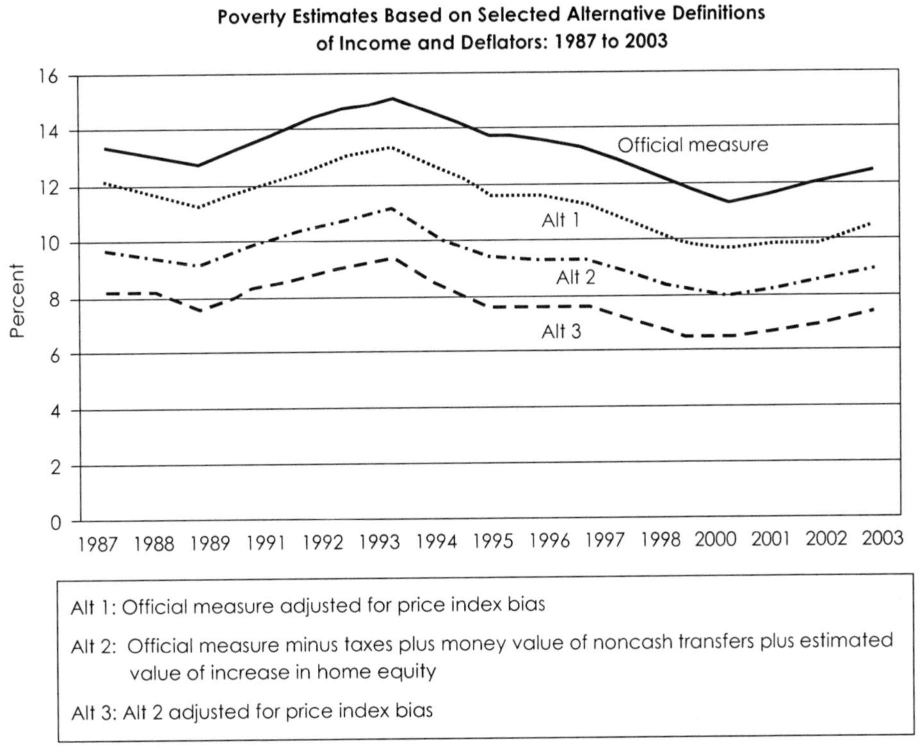

According to the official definition, about 12.5 percent of the U.S. population were poor as of 2003. This percentage has varied within a narrow range from about 12 percent to about 15 percent since the 1970s. Alternative definitions are shown that attempt to correct the official definition for nonmonetary sources of income and biases in the consumer price index.

Source: U.S. Bureau of the Census, Current Population Report P60-227, June 2005.

High earners have captured most of this increase. While the rich have gotten richer, not much has happened to the poor one way or the other, at least as measured by official statistics.

Almost since it was introduced, the official poverty definition has been subject to criticism. One set of criticisms stems from the way it defines income. The official definition includes income before taxes plus the value of cash transfers, such as TANF, unemployment compensation, and disability payments. In a sense, by including transfers intended to alleviate poverty, the official definition understates the magnitude of the underlying problem. A measure of *pre-transfer poverty* would be based on a family's income before receiving government aid. Such an adjustment would be substantial. In 1999, when the official poverty rate was 11.9 percent of the population, the Census Bureau estimated pre-transfer poverty to be 19.4 percent.

On the other hand, if the intention is to measure how many people remain poor *after* government programs have done their work, a different adjustment needs to be made. This would be to include the money value of noncash income. The most important sources of noncash income are noncash transfer payments like food stamps, medical benefits provided either by government or by private employers, and the increased equity value of homes owned by poor families. In addition, taxes should be subtracted from income. These adjustments would have lowered the poverty rate in 2003 from 12.5 percent to about 9 percent.

Finally, there are problems with the consumer price index used to adjust the poverty threshold from year to year. The official consumer price index (CPI) used to adjust the poverty rate is believed by many economists to overstate the rate of increase of the cost of living by something like .5 to 1.5 percentage points per year. This happens because the official CPI does not adequately reflect changes in qualities of good or the tendency of consumers to control their cost of living by substituting less expensive goods when relative prices change. Using a revised version of the CPI cuts nearly 2 additional percentage points from the official poverty measure. Three alternative definitions can be compared with the official one in Figure 15.4.

Although the different definitions give different absolute numbers of poor people, it is worth noting that changing the definition has very little effect on long-term trends. As the figure shows, the official and alternative definitions move up and down together over the business cycle.

Persistence of Poverty

A final important measurement issue concerns the persistence of poverty. The image that comes to mind when one thinks of a poor person is one without income, without assets, without skills, without a job, and without much hope for positive change in any of the above. Yet the official measure of low income captures many people whose income is only temporarily low. A person's income may be low because he or she is between two high-paid jobs. Construction workers, farmers, actors, writers, stock speculators, even professional poker players may experience good years and bad years, but still have adequate income on average. What we would like to know is how many people experience extended periods of poverty, and how many are poor only for short spells.

The data reported in Figure 15.5 attempt to address this question for the years 1993 and 1994. The years are representative in that they were neither years of unusually high nor low poverty, and in that the overall rate changed little from one year to the next. As the figure shows, many more people experienced short spells of low income than experienced persistent poverty. By the official measure, which asks whether a person's total annual income is below the poverty threshold, just under 13 percent of the population was poor in each year. Looking at periods shorter than a year, the figure shows that in any given month, more than 15 percent were poor in the sense that they had monthly income less than one-twelfth of the annual poverty

FIGURE 15.5 PERSISTENCE OF POVERTY IN THE UNITED STATES

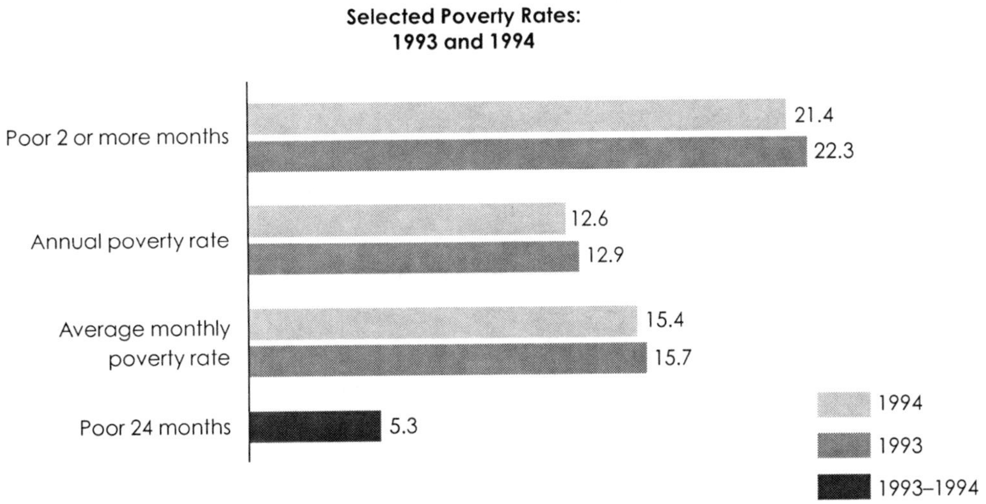

The data presented above come from a study that attempts to distinguish long-term, chronic poverty from short spells of low income. In 1993 and 1994, about 22 percent of the population had incomes below the poverty threshold in at least two months of a calendar year, yet just 5.3 percent of the population were poor for the entire 24-month period.

Source: Bureau of the Census, Current Population Report P70-63, July 1998.

threshold. Furthermore, more than 22 percent of the population had two or more low-income months in each year. However, when people were followed from the beginning of 1993 through the end of 1994, only 5.3 percent of the population were poor in every month of the two-year period. Is poverty a long-term trap or a revolving door? A little of both, it seems.

POLICIES TO FIGHT POVERTY

At one time, responsibility to support low-income individuals was thought to lie with families, local communities, and private charities. In some countries this remains true to this day. In the United States and other high-income countries, however, national governments have long made the alleviation of poverty a major focus of policy. In the mid-twentieth century, governments led by Labor or Social Democratic parties instituted comprehensive "welfare state" policies in may European countries. In the United States, the 1930s saw the advent of Social Security to combat poverty among the elderly. **Today, the elderly have lower poverty rates than those of the working-age population.** In the 1964, President Lyndon Johnson declared a "War on Poverty." By the end of that decade, poverty had declined to its present rate of 12 to 15 percent from rates higher than 20 percent in the 1950s. In the 1990s, a major legislative effort, led by the Republican Congress, resulted in extensive reform of antipoverty policy. This section briefly summarizes the main types of policy used to fight poverty in high-income countries.

Labor Market Policies

Without a doubt, *work* is the most effective of all antipoverty programs, at least in high-income countries. In the United States, the poverty rate for full-time workers is about a fifth of that for the population as a whole. Not surprisingly, then, governments have tried to combat poverty by improving wages and job prospects of people who might otherwise fall into poverty.

In the broadest sense, a whole range of public policies could be viewed in this light. For example, education fights poverty by improving labor market prospects. (Again, the answer to the question: Why are YOU taking courses at college?) In the United States, the poverty rate for people without a high-school diploma is nearly double the national average, while the poverty rate for college graduates is just *a third* of the average. Public health policies also combat poverty—the poverty rate for those who do not work is double that of people who do, and poor health is something that cuts many people off from the labor market. Important though such policies are, however, this section will focus on a narrower group of labor market policies that aim to ensure that those who do work will not fall into poverty.

MINIMUM WAGE POLICIES Although those who work are less likely to be poor than those who do not, it remains true that even in the United States, one of the world's highest income countries, 2.6 percent of full-time workers have incomes below the poverty threshold. But this also means that 97.4 percent of full time workers do not fall below the poverty threshold. This suggests that one way to raise the working poor to a more comfortable standard of living would be to legislate a minimum wage. The first federal minimum-wage law was passed in 1938 and required employers to pay $.25 per hour. Since then the federal minimum wage has been raised several times. (When Dr. Dougherty started his first job in 1970, the minimum wage was $1.45 per hour.) As of 2004, the minimum wage was $5.15 per hour. That is enough to raise a single full-time worker above the poverty threshold. However, it would require two minimum-wage workers to keep a family of four out of poverty, and even that might not be enough if work-related expenses were taken into account. Several states and a few cities mandate a wage above that rate. For instance, Washington has a state minimum wage of $7.16. As of January 2004, the city of San Francisco required an $8.50 per hour wage. With the election of 2006, the majority party in Congress was promised to raise the minimum wage to $7.20 per hour. In 2007, the Maryland legislature is proposing to raise the wage paid to employees who have contracts with the state to at least $10 per hour.

Unfortunately, minimum wage laws have unintended consequences that make many economists doubt their effectiveness as an antipoverty program. Although raising the minimum wage does make some low-skilled workers better off, *it reduces the quantity of such workers demanded.* (Recall the model of PRICE FLOORS. *Minimum wages are price floors.*) Each increase in the minimum wage therefore means that some people lose their jobs—restaurants remain open fewer hours, automated gates replace parking lot attendants, and so on. Think of the neighborhood baby sitter. If the County mandated that all babysitters be paid higher, living wage, say $10 per hour, then many younger parents would reduce their use of sitters and instead of going to dinner and/or a movie, find a substitute such as a NetFlix DVD. Moreover, as antipoverty policy, minimum wages are a bullet that often misses the target. On the one hand, something like half of all workers at the minimum-wage level come from households in the top half of the national income distribution. These workers include students working part time and living with their families whose financial goals are to pay for car insurance and nice prom outfits and limos, low-paid spouses in households in which both husband and wife work, and so on. *On the other hand, a minimum wage does little or nothing to help the great majority of poor families.* These rely only in small part on income from jobs, depending instead on pensions, disability payments, Temporary Aid to Needy Families (TANF- welfare), and other non-wage sources.

UNEMPLOYMENT COMPENSATION As discussed earlier, many people who are not chronically poor experience periods of poverty. One reason for such episodic poverty is unemployment. Unemployment compensation temporarily replaces the lost income of unemployed persons and keeps them out of poverty until they can find a new job.

Like minimum wages, however, unemployment compensation has unintended consequences. The principal such consequence is to lengthen the time workers take until they find a new job. Up to a point, this is not all bad. It takes time and careful search to match workers to the jobs for which they are best suited, and if people needed desperately to take the first thing that came along, the labor market might operate less smoothly. Still, excessively generous unemployment compensation leads to higher unemployment and, over all, a less productive economy. If a large percentage of the labor force is not working, then their production is lost to the economy and our collective standard of living is reduced.

Among high-income countries, there is somewhat of a divide between policies in the United States, paralleled to some degree by some other English-speaking countries, and the approach of continental European countries. The U.S. model emphasizes a time limit on unemployment payments. It tends to use payments high enough to keep the unemployed out of poverty without necessarily replacing the full income of their last jobs. And it tends to require those receiving unemployment benefits to participate actively in training and job-search programs, including placement in jobs that may pay less than those previously lost. The continental model tends to be more generous in terms of time limits, compensation levels, and retraining requirements. In recent years, unemployment rates in France, Germany, and some other continental European countries have risen above 10 percent, more than double the rates of the United States and the United Kingdom. This has brought about a movement to reform unemployment policies, although reform efforts are in their early stages and meeting much political resistance. It's not surprising that those out of work would resist attempts to make their time of unemployment more inconvenient or uncomfortable.

Another factor besides generous unemployment compensation leading to a more willingness of workers to endure longer periods of unemployment is the European universal health care coverage. In the United States, the cost of unemployment is not just a lose of wages but also a loss of medical insurance for many workers. So, in Europe, the pressure to get back to work is greatly reduced since the workers suffers little or no costs associated with a lack of health coverage. This lack of health coverage in the United States may have an incentive for workers to return to the work force quicker and maybe even at a lower wage. Again, the macro implications of this higher participation in labor is that there is more for us to consume and our standard of living is higher.

ANTIDISCRIMINATION AND JOB SECURITY POLICIES As discussed, the United States has a comprehensive range of policies to combat labor market discrimination against women and minority groups. Other high-income countries have similar policies. To the extent women and minority groups historically have higher poverty rates than white men, there is an antipoverty component to antidiscrimination policies. It is likely that these policies have contributed to the increase in earnings of women and minorities relative to white men. These gains have been a factor slowing the growth of income inequality for the population as a whole. As discussed, there are circumstances under which these programs, too, might have perverse unintended consequences, but they are considered so important for the sake of social justice that few people propose discarding them on the grounds that they undermine labor market efficiency.

In continental Europe, many countries have gone much further in protecting workers' job security than is the case in the United States. These policies tend to make it difficult for employers to dismiss workers. Often they also place strict limits on use of part-time workers (Germany has outlawed *part time* jobs.)and overtime work, with the intention of increasing the number of full-time jobs. France has one of the strictest policies, limiting almost all workers to a 35 hour work week, even making working more than 48 hours a week illegal. These policies, like generous unemployment schemes, are the subject of intense debate because of their perceived unintended consequences. Although they protect job security for employed persons, they make it more expensive for employers to create new jobs. Consequently, they contribute to high European unemployment rates. These policies are also targets of reform efforts. The recent street rioting in France was a reaction of the younger population to the proposal that employees under 25 years old could be laid off without the cumbersome process required for older employees. Because of the reaction, the government backed down and did not make changes in national labor law.

In sum, it is questionable whether labor market interventions are, on balance, an effective tool for combating inequality and poverty. In many respects they are more realistically seen as furthering the interests of middle-income workers who already have strong labor market attachment at the expense of marginal and entry level workers with low skills and weak labor market attachment.

Transfer Programs

The principal alternatives to policies intended to improve the labor market prospects of poor people are programs that give them cash or in-kind benefits. We refer to these as *transfer programs*. From 1935 to 1996, the best-known cash transfer program was Aid to Families with Dependent Children, now replaced by Temporary Assistance for Needy Families. The best-known in-kind transfer programs are food stamps and Medicaid. This section examines the intended and unintended consequences of such programs and reforms to U.S. transfer programs in the 1990s.

INCENTIVE EFFECTS OF TRANSFER PROGRAMS Transfer programs, like policies centered on the job market, have the intended consequence of raising the incomes of people who would otherwise be poor. Both types of programs also have unintended consequences. For transfer programs, the unintended consequences that have attracted the most attention are changes in work incentives. Figure 15.6 demonstrates the incentive effects of income transfer programs.

Suppose that the poverty threshold P for a certain family is determined to be $10,000. and suppose that the family's earned income is Y. We call the difference between P and Y the *poverty gap* for the family. One way to ensure that the family will not be poor would be to give them a cash grant equal to the poverty gap. For example, a family with no earned income would get a grant of $10,000; one with $3,000 of earned income would get $7,000; and families with earned income over $10,000 would get no grant.

Under such a program, the total disposable income for various families would follow the line PQRS. The program would be completely successful in terms of its intended effect of keeping the family out of poverty. Unfortunately, it would have a severe unintended effect on work incentives. The family would get no financial benefit whatsoever from earnings up to $10,000. Taking into account the effort of holding a job, not to mention job-related expenses like transportation, clothing, and child care, may families might prefer not to work even if they were offered a job paying somewhat more than $10,000.

Alternatively, payments to the family could be linked to earned income. A family with no income would still receive $10,000, but the amount would be reduced only

FIGURE 15.6 WORK INCENTIVES AND TRANSFER PROGRAMS

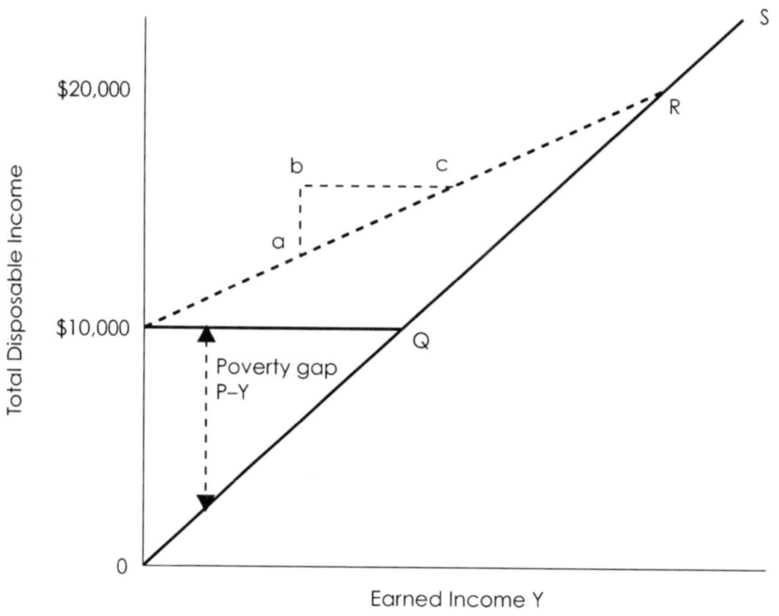

In this figure, the poverty threshold is P and earned income is Y. The poverty gap is the difference between P and Y. If a family is paid exactly what is needed to fill the poverty gap, its total disposable income follows the path PQRS as earned income increases. In that case work incentives are zero up to point Q. If the program is modified to include a benefit reduction rate of 50 percent (the ratio ab/bc), total disposable income follows the path PRS. Work incentives are increased but now some payments are made to families whose earned income is already above the poverty threshold.

Benefit reduction rate

The amount by which transfer benefits are reduced for each added dollar of earned income.

Net marginal tax rate

The sum of the benefit reduction rate and the rate of income tax.

by part of a dollar for each dollar of earned income—the **benefit reduction rate.** Graphically, the benefit reduction rate is represented by the ratio of line ab to line bc.

If the benefit reduction rate were 50 percent, the family's total disposable income would follow the path PRS in Figure 15.6. Compared with the program described in the previous paragraph, this would have the advantage of providing a substantial work incentive. However, reducing the benefit reduction rate has the further effect that some families now receive transfers even though their earned income is greater than the poverty threshold. For example, a family with $12,000 earned income, previously ineligible for assistance, would receive a grant of $4,000 under a program with a basic benefit equal to $10,000 and a benefit reduction rate of 50 percent. Whether such a program would cost less overall depends on how people respond to work incentives and how many families there are to begin with at various income levels.

The situation gets even more complex if earned income is subject to an income or payroll tax. If so, the amount by which total disposable income increases for each dollar earned depends on both the tax rate and the benefit reduction rate. The sum of the two is called the **net marginal tax rate.** Suppose, for example, that all earned income, starting at zero, is taxed at a 20 percent rate. If we add this tax to the previously described program, the result is a net marginal tax rate of 70 percent for income up to $20,000 and a net marginal tax rate of 20 percent above that level. There are some antidotal tales of people who are eligible for this program taking more and more time off in November and December as their income approaches the limit for benefits. As their benefits approach zero, the value of free time becomes greater than the value of marginal income that would be realized by working past the income limits.

Negative income tax

An antipoverty program under which low-income people receive grants from the government and high-income people pay taxes, subject to a net marginal tax rate of less than 100 percent for everyone.

WELFARE REFORMS OF THE 1990S In 1962, University of Chicago economist Milton Friedman proposed that all antipoverty programs be integrated with the income tax system. He called the scheme a **negative income tax**. Under this scheme, low-income families would receive payments from the government and higher income families would make payments to it, with the net marginal tax rate held low enough for everyone to provide adequate work incentive.

Friedman's proposal was made at a time when most welfare programs had very high net marginal tax rates, sometimes more than 100 percent. Such high rates occurred because the benefit reduction rates and tax rates of various programs are additive. For example, if a family received an AFDC grant with a benefit reduction rate of 67 percent, a food-stamp grant with a benefit reduction rate of 50 percent, and paid Social Security payroll taxes of 14 percent, its net marginal tax rate would be 131 percent. For each $100 earned, the family would end up $31 poorer in terms of total disposable income. *Applying Economic Ideas 15.2* provides details of an actual example of high net marginal tax rates during the 1980s.

Friedman's ideas helped focus the attention of economists and policy makers on the inefficiencies, not to say the injustices, of existing antipoverty programs. More and more, people came to perceive TANF, food stamps, and similar programs as "paying people to be poor." In response to these criticisms, many experiments in welfare reform took place during the 1970s and 1980s. Some of these were small-scale experiments with negative income taxes that aimed to measure the response of poor families to changes in benefit reduction rates. Others took the form of changes in the way antipoverty programs were implemented in different states. Many of these experiments showed promising results. In the 1990s, they culminated in major reforms of the welfare system at the national level. The reforms were promised by President Bill Clinton in the campaign of 1992 and enacted into law by the Republican Congress in 1996.

One major reform, enacted in 1993, was the expansion of a previously small federal program known as the Earned Income Tax Credit (EITC). Under the EITC, families with very low earned incomes receive a federal tax credit for each dollar earned. For example, as of 2000, a family with two children received a credit of $.40 for each dollar of earned income up to an income of $9,720. At that point, the tax credit reached a maximum of $3,888, and continued at that level up to an earned income of $12,690. After that point, the credit was reduced by approximately $.21 for each additional dollar of earned income until the credit fell to zero at an income of $31,152.

APPLYING ECONOMIC IDEAS 15.2

NEW MARGINAL TAX RATES FOR A LOS ANGELES FAMILY

Before the welfare reforms of the 1990s, poor families were often subject to an extremely high net marginal tax rate. The table provides a real-world example based on taxes and reductions in benefits for an inner-city family of four in Los Angeles in the 1980s. The column "monthly gross wages" includes wages paid plus employer and employee contributions to social security. The data on disposable income reflect all payroll and income taxes and assume that the family makes use of the maximum city, county, state, and federal welfare benefits to which it is entitled.

The net marginal tax rate is the sum of the marginal tax rates and benefit reduction rates to which the family was subject. The disincentive effects of benefit reductions and taxes reached a peak just above and below the poverty threshold, which was $833 a month for a family of four at the time. Note that as the family's gross wages increased from $700 a month to $1,200 a month, its disposable income would fall from $1,423 to $1,215. This reflects the loss of $385 in welfare benefits; the loss of $9 in food stamps; a reduction of $23 in the family's housing subsidy; an estimated reduction of $130 in the value of its medical benefits; an $8 increase in state income and disability insurance taxes; $68 in payroll taxes; and $85 in federal income taxes.

Source, Arthur Laffer, "The Tightening Grip of the Poverty Trap," Cato Institute Policy Analysis No. 41, August 30, 1984. Reprinted with permission.

Monthly Gross Wages (Dollars)	Monthly Family Disposable Income (Dollars)	Change in Disposable Income (Dollars)	Net Marginal Tax Rate (Percent)
0	1,261	NA	NA
100	1,304	43	57
200	1,341	37	63
300	1,366	25	75
400	1,391	25	75
500	1,419	28	72
600	1,429	10	90
700	1,423	–5	105
800	1,418	–5	105
900	1,420	2	98
1,000	1,432	12	89
1,100	1,253	–178	278
1,200	1,215	–39	139
1,300	1,217	2	98
1,400	1,296	39	61
1,500	1,294	38	62
1,600	1,330	37	63

The EITC operates on top of other existing federal taxes. For very low incomes, the EITC exceeds taxes due on earned income, so taxpayers receive a check from the government. For higher incomes, the EITC may be less than taxes due, but nevertheless, they reduce tax owed. The net marginal tax rate is the sum of the EITC rate and applicable rate of other income and payroll taxes.

The EITC is a variant on the negative income tax concept, but one that contains even more potent work incentives for the lowest-income workers than did Friedman's original proposal. The reason is that up to the maximum EITC threshold, payments actually rise rather than fall when earned income increases. Another way to put it is to say that the benefit reduction rate in this income tax range is not just low, but negative. One unintended consequence though it that if two working parents, if they marry, may have joint incomes above the $31,152. It could be to the benefit of this family NOT to MARRY and have both parents file tax returns as SINGLE.

The other major set of reforms was implemented in 1996 under the clumsy title Personal Responsibility and Work Opportunity Reconciliation Act (PRWORA). The PRWORA reforms are difficult to summarize because, although they establish certain federal guidelines, they are implemented at the state level. In practice, state programs vary greatly. Without examining all the variants, the main features of PRWORA were as follows:

- Aid to Families with Dependent Children (AFDC), previously the main welfare program, was replaced by Temporary Assistance for Needy Families (TANF).
- A complex set of training programs and work incentives was implemented. These included mandatory participation either in employment or training for most families, plus incentives like expanded child care grants for working parents.
- A time limit was established for TANF payments beyond which recipients were required to make the transition to self-sufficient employment.

The response to PRWORA was dramatic. In the late 1990s, welfare roles, measured as the number of families receiving AFDC or TANF, decreased sharply (Figure 15.7a), and labor force participation rates increased, especially for the key group, single women with children. As discussed earlier in the chapter, the 1990s did not bring a permanent reduction in the overall poverty rate for the United States. However, for single women with children, the poverty rate declined significantly, from over 35 percent in 1992 to under 25 percent by 2000.

A large amount of research has attempted to explain just why welfare roles fell and labor force participation increased in the late 1990s. All of it seems to agree that in combination, the EITC and PRWORA reforms made a helpful contribution to these trends. However, it remains difficult to determine exactly which parts of the reforms worked and how well. One reason is that the reforms took place against the background of a booming labor market that would have reduced welfare roles and increased employment even if there had been no reforms. Another reason is that many reforms were implemented at once. Furthermore, the reforms were implemented differently from state to state, a fact that sometimes helps researchers by providing contrasting state-level cases, and sometimes frustrates them by complicating the analysis of national trends.

FIGURE 15.7 EFFECTS OF WELFARE REFORM IN THE 1990S

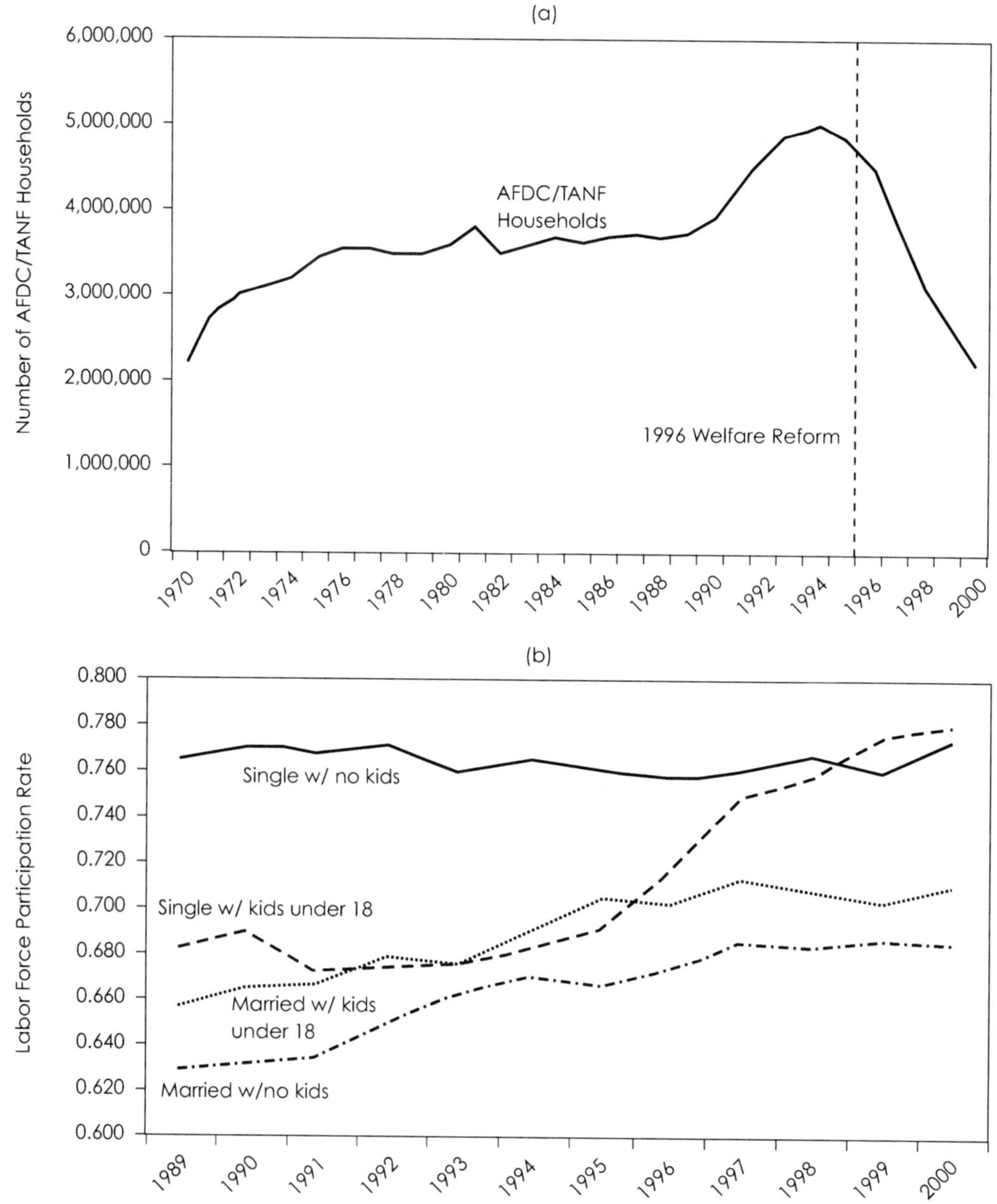

After passage of reforms in the 1990s, the number of families receiving AFDC or TANF fell sharply, and the labor force participation rate of women with children increased significantly.

Source: Rebecca M. Blanc, "Evaluating Welfare Reform in the United States," *Journal of Economic Literature*, Vol. XL, No. 2, December 2002, Figures 3 and 4.

Whatever the final outcome of the academic analysis, the U.S. reforms have attracted interest from many other countries. It remains safe to say that few people would prefer to return to the welfare system of the 1980s and before.

SUMMARY

1. **How can income inequality be measured?** Inequality is most often measured using the Gini coefficient or Gini index. The Gini coefficient is 0 under conditions of perfect equality and 1 under conditions of perfect inequality. The Gini index converts this to a percentage by multiplying by 100. The United States has a Gini index of about 40 for personal income before tax—about average for countries of the world. The income distribution in the United States reached its historically most equal point in the 1960s and 1970s. Since that time inequality has steadily increased.

2. **How does poverty differ from inequality, and how can it be measured?** Poverty implies a lack of ability to meet basic needs. In the United States, poverty is officially measured by a threshold equal to three times the cost of buying a minimum adequate diet for a family. Since the 1970s, the percentage of households in poverty in the United States has usually ranged from about 12 to 15 percent, with no strong trend one way or the other. On a global scale, poverty is often measured by a threshold of $1 or $2 per person per day. This is much lower than the U.S. poverty threshold.

3. **What are the effects of labor market policies intended to alleviate poverty?** One way to raise people out of poverty is to improve their prospects in the job market. Indirectly, policies supporting education and public health are helpful in this regard. Direct efforts to improve earnings and job security include minimum wages, unemployment compensation, and measures to discourage layoffs, part-time work, and overtime. All of these policies may improve the income of the employed but have the unintended consequence of raising the unemployment rate.

4. **How can transfer payments be used to alleviate poverty, and how can design of transfer programs be improved?** Transfer programs are intended to eliminate poverty by making up the gap between the poverty threshold and earned income. Their most troublesome unintended effect is to discourage work effort. Work incentives can be improved by keeping benefit reduction rates and net marginal tax rates low. The negative income tax is one proposal for maintaining work incentives. Welfare reforms in the United States in the 1980s incorporated some aspects of the negative income tax and also added direct incentives to participate in work or training.

KEY TERMS

Lorenz curve	Benefit reduction rate
Gini coefficient	Net marginal tax rate
Gini index	Negative income tax

PROBLEMS AND TOPICS FOR DISCUSSION

1. **Poverty versus inequality.** "It is a mistake to think of poverty in terms of absolute needs. The best way to measure poverty would simply be to consider the bottom fifth of the income distribution in each country to be 'poor' and the rest to be 'nonpoor.' Do you agree, disagree, or agree in part? Is this approach applicable to very rich countries? To very poor countries?

2. **Cash versus in-kind transfers.** What are the relative merits of cash and in-kind transfers? Review Chapter 5, paying particular attention to the concepts of marginal utility and consumer equilibrium. Suppose that program A gives a family a $1,000 cash benefit and program B gives it $1,000 worth of goods in kind, but in proportions that are not chosen by the family itself. Which program would be likely to give the family greater utility? *Bonus question:* If you read the appendix

to Chapter 5, illustrate these two programs for the case of an economy in which there are just two consumer goods: food and clothing.

3. **Social insurance.** Suppose that an effective negative income tax was in force and poverty, as defined by the Bureau of the Census, had been eliminated. Would you then be willing to see social-insurance programs such as social security and Medicare abolished? Why or why not?
4. **Transfer payments and the nonpoor.** Discussions of "waste" in poverty programs often focus on the fact that some benefits go to families whose incomes are above the poverty line. After reading this chapter, do you agree that it is wasteful to pay benefits to some nonpoor families? Would you favor a program that cut off all benefits when the poverty line was reached? In what ways might such a program itself be wasteful? Discuss.
5. **Fight Poverty—Get a Job.** A popular bumper sticker reads "Fight Poverty—Get a Job!" This slogan is presumably intended to do more than call attention to the fact that those who work are less likely to be poor. Rather, its purpose seems to be to evoke a set of normative judgments related to "deserving" versus "undeserving" poor, willingness to work versus opportunity as reasons for not working, and so on. What is your position on these issues? Discuss.

CASE FOR DISCUSSION

Two Steps Forward, One Step Back

The Sacramento City Council adopted a "living wage" ordinance that took effect on January 1, 2004. "This is a great day," said Chris Jones, chairman of the Sacramento chapter of the Association of Community Organizations for Reform Now. Jones added, however, that it is "just the beginning" of city efforts to improve pay for the region's low-wage workers.

The ordinance will increase wages to $9.00 an hour for private employees on city contracts, if the company provides health benefits. If the company does not provide benefits, the hourly wage will be $10.50 an hour. The living wage rises to $9.50 in 2005 and to $10 in 2006, with an additional $1.50 for companies that don't provide health coverage.

All that glitters is not gold, though. According to a city-funded report, when low-wage workers earn higher income, they no longer qualify for the same federal and state public assistance and social insurance benefits. For instance, a single parent with two children would receive $2,533.20 in annual food stamps if he/she earned minimum wage. With a living wage of $8.50/hr., that benefit falls to $1,273.20. Living-wage workers also receive less from the federal Earned Income Tax Credit and the state disability insurance fund, and pay more in federal and state taxes.

Even with reduced federal- and state-funded aid, the living wage does improve disposable income for prior minimum-wage workers. For households with two children, disposable annual income including transfer payments would rise by $1,553.65 with a $8.50/hr. living wage, and by roughly $2,700 with a $10.00/hr. living wage.

Who pays the bill? The cost of the living wage will be shared by city government, taxpayers, and employers. With higher wages, employers will not only pay more to their workers, but to social security taxes as well. Also, if the $9.00 living wage chases away potential contractors for the City of Sacramento, the remaining vendors may be able to bargain for more costly contracts to offset higher labor cost.

Source: Suzanne O'Keefe and Stephen Perez, "A Living Wage for Sacramento," CSUS Regional Development Initiative, September 2002; Andy Furillo, "City Living-Wage Plan Gets Final Approval," *Sacramento Bee*, December 10, 2003.

QUESTIONS

1. What do you think is the motivation for the additional $1.50 per hour to be paid to workers who do not receive health benefits? Which is better, health benefits or the extra money? How would you know? Would the answer be the same for all workers?
2. How does the living wage help to reduce poverty? Suppose a household with two children earns an additional $2,000 per year in annual gross income as a result of Sacramento's living wage. Will this household take home $2,000 in additional disposable income? Why or why not?
3. How does the living wage change the nature of public assistance in Sacramento? Who bears the cost of helping the poor now that the city has imposed the living wage? Who bore this cost before?

END NOTES

1. Research by the World Bank's Branco Milanovic summarized in Robert Wade, "Winners and Losers," *The Economist* (April 26, 2001).
2. The government's 3-to-1 ratio was based on a study done in 1961. More recent surveys suggest that poor families typically spend less than a quarter of their income on food. Thus, some have suggested that the poverty "multiplier" should be raised to 4 or even to 5.

GLOSSARY

Administrative assistance (AA) Top aide to a member of Congress who frequently acts on behalf of the legislator in dealing with staff, colleagues, constituents, and lobbyists.

Absolute advantage The ability of a country to produce a good at a lower cost, in terms of quantity of factor inputs, than the cost at which the good can be produced by its trading partners.

Access fee The part of a two-part pricing strategy paid for the right to become a customer.

Accounting profit Total revenue minus explicit costs.

Adverse selection The tendency of people facing the greatest risk of loss to be most likely to seek insurance.

Antitrust laws A set of laws, including the Sherman Act and the Clayton Act, that seek to control market structure and the competitive behavior of firms.

Arbitrage The activity of earning a profit by buying something at a low price in one market and reselling it at a higher price in another.

Benefit reduction rate The amount by which transfer benefits are reduced for each added dollar of earned income.

Barrier to entry Any circumstance that prevents a new firm in a market from competing on an equal footing with existing ones.

Bounded rationality The assumption that people intend to make choices that best serve their objectives, but have limited ability to acquire and process information.

Capita All means of production that are created by people, including tools, industrial equipment, and structures.

Capitalized value of a rent The present value of all future rents that a piece of land or other resource is expected to earn.

Cartel A group of producers that jointly maximize profits by fixing prices and limiting output.

Census income Cash income from all sources, including earned income and cash transfer payments.

Change in demand A change in the quantity of a good that buyers are willing and able to purchase that results from a change in some condition other than the price of that good; shown by a shift in the demand curve.

Change in quantity demanded A change in the quantity of a good that buyers are willing and able to purchase that results from a change in the good's price, other things being equal; shown by a movement from one point to another along a demand curve.

Change in quantity supplied A change in the quantity of a good that suppliers are willing and able to sell that results from a change in the good's price, other things being equal; shown by a movement along a supply curve.

Change in supply A change in the quantity of a good that suppliers are willing and able to sell that results from a change in some condition other than the good's price; shown by a shift in the supply curve.

Closed monopoly A monopoly that is protected by legal restrictions on competition.

Coase theorem The proposition that problems of externalities will be resolved efficiently through private exchange, regardless of the initial assignment of property rights, provided that there are no transaction costs.

Comparative advantage The ability to produce a good or service at a relatively lower opportunity cost than someone else.

Complementary goods A pair of goods for which an increase in the price of one results in a decrease in demand for the other.

Concentration ratio The percentage of all sales that is accounted for by the four or eight largest firms in a market.

Conditional forecast A prediction of future economic events in the form "If A, then B, other things being equal."

Conglomerate mergers Mergers of firms in unrelated markets.

Constant returns to scale A situation in which there are neither economies nor diseconomies of scale.

Constitutional choice A choice among various sets of rules for democratic government that is intended to produce desirable outcomes when applied to future situations whose details are not known.

Consumer equilibrium A state of affairs in which a consumer cannot increase the total utility gained from a given budget by spending less on one good and more on another.

Consumer surplus The difference between the maximum that a consumer would be willing to pay for a unit of a good and the amount that he or she actually pays.

Contestable market A market in which barriers to entry and exit are low.

Corporation A firm that takes the form of an independent legal entity with ownership divided into equal shares and each owner's liability limited to his/her investment in the firm.

Craft union A union of skilled workers who all practice the same trade.

Cross-elasticity of demand The ratio of the percentage change in the quantity of a good demanded to a given percentage change in the price of some other good, other things being equal.

Deadweight loss A loss of consumer or producer surplus that is not balanced by a gain to someone else.

Demand The willingness and ability of buyers to purchase goods.

Demand curve A graphical representation of the relationship between the price of a good and the quantity of that good that buyers demand.

Derived demand Demand for a productive input that stems from the demand for the product the input is used to produce.

Differential rent The rents earned by superior units of a resource in a situation in which units of a resource differ in productivity.

Discounting The procedure by which the present value of a sum that is payable in the future is calculated.

Diseconomies of scale A situation in which long-run average cost increases as output increases.

Distribution Who gets what and how much does each individual get.

Duncan index of dissimilarity For a set of occupations in which both men and women are employed, the percentage of men (or women) who would have to change occupations to equalize the numbers of men and women in each occupation.

Dutch auction An auction that begins with a high bid, which is lowered until a buyer is found.

Dynamic efficiency The ability of an economy to increase consumer satisfaction through innovation and technological change.

Econometrics The statistical analysis of empirical economic data.

Economic efficiency Means producing with a minimum of expense, effort, and waste.

Economic rent Any payment to a factor of production in excess of its opportunity cost.

Economics The social science that seeks to understand the choices people make in using scarce resources to meet their wants.

Economies of scale A situation in which long-run average cost decreases as output increases.

Efficiency in distribution A situation in which it is not possible, by redistributing existing supplies of goods, to satisfy one person's wants more fully without causing some other person's wants to be satisfied less fully.

Efficiency in production A situation in which it is not possible, given available knowledge and productive resources, to produce more of one good without forgoing the opportunity to produce some of another good.

Efficiency wage theory The theory that wages above the minimum necessary to attract qualified workers can raise productivity by enough to increase profit.

Elastic demand A situation in which quantity demanded changes by a larger percentage than price, so that total revenue increases as price decreases.

Elasticity A measure of the response of one variable to a change in another, stated as a ratio of the percentage change in one variable to the associated percentage change in another variable.

Empirical Based on experience or observation.

English auction An auction in which bidding starts low and proceeds until the good is sold to the highest bidder.

Entrepreneurship The tendency to assume RISK. The difference between management and entrepreneurship is the risk involved.

Equilibrium A condition in which buyers' and sellers' plans exactly mesh in the marketplace, so that the quantity supplied exactly equals the quantity demanded at a given price.

Excess burden of the tax The part of the economic burden of a tax that takes the form of consumer and producer surplus that is lost because the tax reduces the equilibrium quantity sold.

Excess quantity demanded (shortage) A condition in which the quantity of a good demanded at a given price exceeds the quantity supplied.

Excess quantity supplied (surplus) A condition in which the quantity of a good supplied at a given price exceeds the quantity demanded.

Expected value For a set of possible outcomes, the sum of the probability of each outcome multiplied by the value of that outcome.

Explicit costs Opportunity costs that take the form of explicit payments to suppliers of factors of production and intermediate goods.

Externalities The effects of producing or consuming a good whose impact on third parties other than buyers and sellers of the good is not reflected in the good's price.

Factors of production The basic inputs of labor, capital, and natural resources used in producing all goods and services.

Fixed costs The explicit and implicit opportunity costs associated with providing fixed inputs.

Fixed inputs Inputs that cannot be increased or decreased in a short time in order to increase or decrease output.

Full rationality The assumption that people make full use of all available information in calculating how best to meet their objectives.

Futures contract An agreement to exchange something at a specified date in the future at a price that is agreed upon now.

Giffen good An inferior good accounting for a large share of a consumer's budget that has a positively sloped demand curve because the income effect of a price change outweighs the substitution effect.

Gini coefficient A measure of inequality of income equal to zero under conditions of perfect equality and to one under perfect inequality.

Gini index The Gini coefficient expressed as a percentage.

Government failure A situation in which a government policy causes inefficient use of resources.

Heckscher-Ohlin theorem The proposition that countries tend to export goods that make intensive use of the factors of production that the country possesses in relative abundance.

Hedging An operation in which futures markets or options markets are used to offset one risk with another.

Herfindahl-Hirschmann index (HHI) An index of market concentration that is calculated by squaring the percentage market shares of all firms in an industry then summing the squared-values.

Hierarchy A way of achieving coordination in which individual actions are guided by instructions from a central authority.

High-power incentives Incentives that take the form of a claim to the residual profit resulting from a task, combined with bearing the risk of any loss.

Horizontal mergers Mergers of firms that compete in the same market.

Human capital Capital in the form of learned abilities that have been acquired through formal training or education or through on-the-job experience.

Import quotas A limit on the quantity of a good that can be imported over a given period.

Implicit costs Opportunity costs of using resources contributed by the firm's owners (or owned by the firm itself as a legal entity) that are not obtained in exchange for explicit payments.

Income effect The part of the change in quantity demanded of a good whose price has fallen that is caused by the increase in real income resulting from the price change.

Income elasticity of demand The ratio of the percentage change in the quantity of a good demanded to a given percentage change in consumer incomes, other things being equal.

Industrial union A union of all the workers in an industry, including both skilled and unskilled workers in all trades.

Inelastic demand A situation in which quantity demanded changes by a smaller percentage than price, so that total revenue decreases as price decreases.

Inferior good A good for which an increase in consumer incomes results in a decrease in demand.

Information asymmetry A situation in which some parties to a transaction possess relevant information that other parties do not possess.

Inframarginal rents The difference between the payment made to a unit of resource and the minimum required for that resource to be willingly supplied in a situation in which units of a resource differ in terms of the willingness with which they are supplied.

In-kind transfers Transfer payments in the form of goods or services, such as food, housing, or medical care, rather than cash.

Intrapreneurship Entrepreneurial activity carried out within a large business organization.

Inventory A stock of a finished good awaiting sale or use.

Investment The act of increasing the economy's stock of capital—that is, its supply of means of production made by people.

Labor The contributions to production made by people working with their minds and muscles.

Labor market discrimination A situation in which employers are unwilling to hire members of a disfavored group at the same wage rate that they pay to equally productive members of a more favored group.

Land Anything that can be used as a productive input in its natural state, such as farmland, building sites, forests, and mineral deposits. Or simply, an economic term for natural resources.

Law of demand The principle that an inverse relationship exists between the price of a good and the quantity of that good that buyers demand, other things being equal.

Law of diminishing returns The principle that as one variable input is increased while all others remain fixed, a point will be reached beyond which the marginal physical product of the variable input will begin to decrease.

Limit pricing A strategy in which the dominant firm in a market charges less than the short-run profit-maximizing price in order to limit the likelihood of entry by new competitors.

Loanable funds market A general term for the set of markets in which people borrow and lend, for whatever reason.

Lobbying Any method of communicating with elected officials to advocate a particular policy.

Logrolling The practice of trading votes among members of a legislative body.

Long run A time horizon that is long enough to permit changes in both fixed and variable inputs.

Lorenz curve A graph that represents the degree of inequality in an economy.

Low-power incentives Incentives that take such forms as promotion for work well done or reprimands for errors.

Macroeconomics The branch of economics that studies large-scale economic phenomena, particularly inflation, unemployment, and economic growth.

Marginal-average rule The rule that marginal cost must equal average cost when average cost is at its minimum.

Marginal cost The increase in cost required to raise the output of some good or service by one unit.

Marginal physical product The increase in output, expressed in physical units, produced by each added unit of one variable input, other things being equal.

Marginal productivity theory of distribution A theory of income distribution in which each input of production receives a payment equal to its marginal revenue product.

Marginal resource cost The amount by which a firm's total resource cost must increase for the firm to obtain an additional unit of that resource.

Marginal revenue The amount by which total revenue changes as a result of a one-unit increase in quantity sold.

Marginal revenue product The change in revenue that results from the sale of the output produced by one additional unit of an input.

Marginal utility The amount of added utility gained from a one-unit increase in consumption of a good, other things being equal.

Market People making decisions, without coercion, as to what they want to buy, own, or what they want to sell, produce.

Market concentration The degree to which a market is dominated by a few large firms.

Market failure A situation in which a market fails to coordinate choices in a way that achieves efficient use of resources.

Marketing The process of finding out what customers want and channeling a flow of goods and services to meet those wants.

Market performance The degree to which markets work efficiently in providing arrangements for mutually beneficial trade.

Market structure The key traits of a market, including the number and size of firms, the extent to which the products of various firms are different or similar, ease of entry and exit, and availability of information.

Median voter model A model showing that there is a tendency for decisions in a direct democracy to correspond to the interests of voters whose preferences lie near the middle of the community scale.

Microeconomics The branch of economics that studies the choices of individuals, including households, business firms, and government agencies.

Minimum efficient scale The output level at which economies of scale cease.

Model A synonym for theory; in economics, often applied to theories that are stated in graphical or mathematical form.

Monopolistic competition A market structure in which there are many small firms, a differentiated product, and easy entry and exit.

Monopoly A situation in which there is only a single seller of a good or service.

Monopsony A situation in which there is only a single buyer in a market; more generally, any situation in which a firm is a price searcher in a market in which it is a buyer.

Moral hazard Behavior that increases the risk of loss, yet is undertaken in the knowledge that losses will be covered by insurance.

Natural monopoly An industry in which long-run average cost is minimized when only one firm serves the market.

Natural resources Anything that can be used as a productive input in its natural state, such as farmland, building sites, forests, and mineral deposits.

Negative income tax An antipoverty program under which low-income people receive grants from the government and high-income people pay taxes, subject to a net marginal tax rate of less than 100 percent for everyone.

Net marginal tax rate The sum of the benefit reduction rate and the rate of income tax.

Normal good A good for which an increase in consumer incomes results in an increase in demand.

Normal profit (normal return on capital) The implicit opportunity cost of capital contributed by the firm's owners (equity capital).

Normal return on capital See Normal profit.

Normative economics The area of economics that is devoted to judgments about whether economic policies or conditions are good or bad.

Ockham's razor The principle that simpler theories are to be preferred to more complex ones when both are consistent with given observations.

Oligopolistic interdependence The need to pay close attention to the actions of rival firms in an oligopolistic market when making price or production decisions.

Oligopoly A market structure in which there are a few firms, at least some of which are large in relation to the size of the market.

Open monopoly A monopoly in which one firm is, at least for a time, the sole supplier of a product but has no special protection from competition.

Opportunism An attempt by one party to an agreement to seek an advantage at the expense of another party to the agreement.

Opportunity cost The cost of a good or service measured in terms of the forgone opportunity to pursue the best possible alternative activity with the same time or resources.

Options Contracts under which one party obtains the right (but not the obligation) to buy something at a specified date in the future at a price that is agreed upon now.

Partnership An association of two or more people who operate a business as co-owners under a voluntary legal agreement.

Perfect competition A market structure that is characterized by a large number of small firms, a homogeneous product, freedom of entry and exit, and equal access to information.

Perfectly elastic demand A situation in which the demand curve is a horizontal line.

Perfectly inelastic demand A situation in which the demand curve is a vertical line.

Political rent seeking (rent seeking) The process of seeking and defending economic rents through the political process.

Pollution abatement Reduction of the quantity of waste discharged into the environment.

Positive economics The area of economics that is concerned with facts and the relationships among them.

Present value The value today of a sum payable in the future. In mathematical terms, the present value of a sum Vp, payable t years in the future, discounted at r percent interest, would grow to the value Vt in t years; the present value formula is $Vp = Vt/(1 + r) t$.

Pretransfer poverty A measure of how many people would be poor on the basis of their private sources of income alone.

Price discrimination The practice of charging different prices for various units of a single product when the price differences are not justified by differences in cost.

Price elasticity of demand The ratio of the percentage change in the quantity of a good demanded to a given percentage change in its price, other things being equal.

Price elasticity of supply The ratio of the percentage change in the quantity of a good supplied to a given percentage change in its price, other things being equal.

Price fixing Any attempt by two or more firms to cooperate in setting prices.

Price leadership A situation in which price increases or decreases by a dominant firm in an oligopoly, known as the price leader, are matched by all or most of the other firms in the market.

Price searcher Any firm that faces a negatively sloped demand curve for its product.

Price taker A firm that sells its output at prices that are determined by forces beyond its control.

Principle of diminishing marginal utility The principle that the greater the consumption of some good, the smaller the increase in utility from a one-unit increase in consumption of that good.

Privatization The turning over of government functions to the private sector.

Producer surplus The difference between what producers receive for a unit of a good and the minimum they would be willing to accept.

Production possibility frontier A graph that shows possible combinations of goods that can be produced by an economy given available knowledge and factors of production.

Property rights Legal rules that establish what things a person may use or control, and the conditions under which such use or control may be exercised.

Protectionism Any policy that is intended to shield domestic industries from import competition.

Public assistance Programs under which transfers are made to people who meet some specified low-income standard.

Public choice theory The branch of economics that studies how people use the institutions of government in pursuit of their own interests.

Public goods Goods that (1) cannot be provided for one person without also being provided for others and (2) when provided for one person can be provided for others at zero additional sum.

Pure economic profit The sum that remains when both explicit and implicit costs are subtracted from total revenue.

Pure economic rent The income earned by any resource whose supply is perfectly inelastic with respect to its price.

Rate of return A firm's accounting profit expressed as a percentage of its net worth.

Rate of return on capital The marginal product of capital expressed as an annual percentage rate.

Rationality Acting purposefully to achieve an objective, given constraints on the opportunities that are available.

Rent seeking See Political rent seeking.

Reservation price The maximum price that a buyer is willing to pay for a good or the minimum price at which a seller is willing to offer it.

Revenue Price times quantity sold.

Revenue-equivalence theorem The proposition that under certain general circumstances English, Dutch, and sealed-bid auctions can be expected to produce approximately the same winning bid.

Risk aversion A preference for a certain outcome with a given value over a set of risky outcomes with the same expected value.

Risk neutrality Indifference between a certain outcome with a given value and a set of risky outcomes with the same expected value.

Risk pooling A technique in which the risk of loss is shared among many people so that the impact of a loss on any one of them is small.

Risk preference A preference for a set of risky outcomes with a given expected value over a certain outcome with the same expected value.

Scarcity Scarcity does not mean that we don't have enough. Rather, scarcity means that in order to get one more unit of something, we must give up something else.

Sealed-bid auction An auction in which all buyers submit bids at the same time, and the item is sold to the highest bidder (or bought from the lowest bidder)

Short run A time horizon within which output can be adjusted only by changing the amounts of variable inputs used while fixed inputs remain unchanged.

Simple monopoly A monopoly that offers its output at a single price that is uniform for all customers and allows all buyers to purchase as much or as little as they want at that price.

Social insurance Programs under which transfers are made available to everyone, regardless of income, upon the occurrence of a specified event such as retirement, unemployment, or disability.

Sole proprietorship A firm that is owned, and usually operated, by one person, who receives all the profits and is responsible for all the firm's liabilities.

Speculation Buying something at a low price in the hope of selling it later at a higher price.

Spontaneous order A way of achieving coordination in which individuals adjust their actions in response to cues from their immediate environment.

Spot price The price at which a good is offered for immediate sale.

Static efficiency The ability of an economy to get the greatest degree of consumer satisfaction from given amounts of resources and technology

Substitute goods A pair of goods for which an increase in the price of one causes an increase in demand for the other.

Substitution effect The part of the increase in quantity demanded of a good whose price has fallen that is caused by substitution of that good for others that are now relatively more costly.

Supply The willingness and ability of sellers to provide goods for sale in a market.

Supply curve A graphical representation of the relationship between the price of a good and the quantity of that good that sellers are willing to supply.

Sunk costs Once-and-for-all costs that, once incurred, cannot be recovered.

Tariff A tax on imported goods.

Tax incidence The distribution of the economic burden of a tax.

Theory A representation of the way in which facts are related to one another.

Time preference The tendency to prefer goods now over goods in the future, other things being equal.

Total physical product The total output of a firm, measured in physical units.

Transaction costs The costs, other than production costs, of carrying out a transaction.

Two-part pricing A pricing strategy in which people must pay for the right to become a buyer before choosing how much to buy at a given price.

Unit elastic demand A situation in which price and quantity demanded change by the same percentage, so that total revenue remains unchanged as price changes.

User charge The per-unit price offered in a two-part pricing strategy to qualified customers who have paid the access charge.

Utility The pleasure, satisfaction, or need fulfillment that people obtain from the consumption of goods and services.

Value of marginal product Marginal physical product times the product's per-unit price.

Variable costs The explicit and implicit costs of providing variable inputs.

Variable inputs Inputs that can be varied within a short time in order to increase or decrease output.

Vertical mergers Mergers of firms with a supplier-purchaser relationship.

Winner's curse The tendency for winners of an auction to pay more for a good or service than it is worth (or to offer to sell at a price below the cost of providing the good or service).

INDEX

N

O

P

R

S

Printed in the United States
209602BV00002B/1-34/P

9 781602 291027